# Experimental Psychology

SEVENTH EDITION

# Experimental Psychology

**Anne Myers**

**Christine H. Hansen**
*Oakland University*

**WADSWORTH**
CENGAGE Learning™

Australia • Brazil • Japan • Korea • Mexico • Singapore • Spain • United Kingdom • United States

**WADSWORTH**
CENGAGE Learning™

**Experimental Psychology, Seventh Edition, International Edition**
Anne Myers, Christine H. Hansen

Publisher/Executive Editor:
Linda Schreiber-Ganster

Acquisitions Editor: Timothy Matray

Assistant Editor: Phillip Hovanessian

Media Editor: Layren Keyes

Marketing Coordinator: Anna Andersen

Marketing Communications Manager:
Laura Localio

Content Project Management: PreMediaGlobal

Art Director: Pamela Galbreath

Production Technology Analyst:
Lori Jhonson

Print Buyer: Judy Inouye

Rights Acquisition Specialist: Roberta Broyer

Production Service: PreMediaGlobal

Cover Image: abstract watercolor background design
circle, © J.D.S.

Library of Congress Control Number: 2011921417

International Edition

ISBN-13: 978-0-495-81124-4

ISBN-10: 0-495-81124-6

**Cengage Learning International Offices**

**Asia**
www.cengageasia.com
tel: (65) 6410 1200

**Australia/New Zealand**
www.cengage.com.au
tel: (61) 3 9685 4111

**Brazil**
www.cengage.com.br
tel: (55) 11 3665 9900

**India**
www.cengage.co.in
tel: (91) 11 4364 1111

**Latin America**
www.cengage.com.mx
tel: (52) 55 1500 6000

**UK/Europe/Middle East/Africa**
www.cengage.co.uk
tel: (44) 0 1264 332 424

**Represented in Canada by Nelson Education, Ltd.**
www.nelson.com
tel: (416) 752 9100/(800) 668 0671

Cengage Learning is a leading provider of customized learning solutions with office locations around the globe, including Singapore, the United Kingdom, Australia, Mexico, Brazil, and Japan. Locate your local office at: **www.cengage.com/global**

For product information: **www.cengage.com/international**
Visit your local office: **www.cengage.com/global**
Visit our corporate website: **www.cengage.com**

Printed in the United States of America
2 3 4 5 6 7 15 14 13 12 11

# BRIEF CONTENTS

PREFACE   xvii

PART **1**   **Introduction**   **1**

**1**   **Experimental Psychology and the Scientific Method**   3

**2**   **Research Ethics**   35

**3**   **Alternatives to Experimentation**: Nonexperimental Designs   67

**4**   **Alternatives to Experimentation**: Surveys and Interviews   95

**5**   **Alternatives to Experimentation**: Correlational and Quasi-Experimental Designs   128

**6**   **Formulating the Hypothesis**   164

PART **2**   **Method**   **189**

**7**   **The Basics of Experimentation**   191

**8**   **Solving Problems**: Controlling Extraneous Variables   232

**9** Basic Between-Subjects Designs 261

**10** Between-Subjects Factorial Designs 290

**11** Within-Subjects Designs 315

**12** Within-Subjects Designs: Small *N* 345

PART **3** **Results: Coping with Data 371**

**13** Why We Need Statistics 373

**14** Analyzing Results 408

PART **4** **Discussion 455**

**15** Drawing Conclusions: The Search for the Elusive Bottom Line 457

**16** Writing the Research Report 483

APPENDIX **A** Computational Formulas 523

APPENDIX **B** Statistical Tables 536

APPENDIX **C** A Journal Article in Manuscript Form 545

APPENDIX **D** Answers to Selected Review and Study Questions and Critical Thinking Exercises 573

GLOSSARY 587

REFERENCES 595

INDEX 604

PHOTO CREDITS 612

# CONTENTS

PREFACE   xvii

PART **1**   **Introduction   1**

**1**   **Experimental Psychology and the Scientific Method   3**
The Need for Scientific Methodology   5
The Characteristics of Modern Science   11
The Objectives of Psychological Science   16
The Scientific Method: Tools of Psychological Science   18
Scientific Explanation in Psychological Science   22
From Pseudoscience to Psychological Science   26
The Organization of the Text   29
Summary   30
Key Terms   31
Review and Study Questions   32
Critical Thinking Exercise   33
Online Resources   33

**2**   **Research Ethics   35**
Research Ethics   36
The American Psychological Association Guidelines   42
Protecting the Welfare of Animal Subjects   48
Fraud in Science   58
Plagiarism   61
Ethical Reports   63

Summary   63
Key Terms   64
Review and Study Questions   65
Online Resources   65
Critical Thinking Exercise   66

**3  Alternatives to Experimentation**: Nonexperimental Designs   **67**
Describing Research Activities   69
Phenomenology   71
Case Studies   73
Field Studies   78
Archival Study   85
Qualitative Research   88
Summary   91
Key Terms   92
Review and Study Questions   93
Critical Thinking Exercise   94
Online Resources   94

**4  Alternatives to Experimentation**: Surveys and Interviews   **95**
Survey Research   96
Constructing Surveys   97
Measuring Responses   101
Important Considerations for Survey Items   105
Collecting Survey Data   110
Evaluating Surveys and Survey Data   116
Sampling   117
Probability Sampling   118
Nonprobability Sampling   121
Summary   124
Key Terms   125
Review and Study Questions   126
Critical Thinking Exercise   127
Online Resources   127

**5** **Alternatives to Experimentation**: Correlational and Quasi-Experimental Designs **128**

Correlational Designs   131
Causal Modeling   143
Quasi-Experimental Designs   147
Summary   160
Key Terms   161
Review and Study Questions   162
Critical Thinking Exercise   163
Online Resources   163

**6** **Formulating the Hypothesis**   **164**

The Characteristics of an Experimental Hypothesis   166
The Inductive Model   170
The Deductive Model   172
Combining Induction and Deduction   172
Building on Prior Research   173
Serendipity and the Windfall Hypothesis   174
Intuition   175
When All Else Fails   177
Searching the Research Literature   179
Summary   184
Key Terms   185
Review and Study Questions   186
Critical Thinking Exercise   187
Online Resources   187

P A R T **2** **Method**   **189**

**7** **The Basics of Experimentation**   **191**

Independent and Dependent Variables   193
Operational Definitions   201
Evaluating Operational Definitions   208
Planning the Method Section   225
Summary   227
Key Terms   229
Review and Study Questions   230

Critical Thinking Exercise  231
Online Resources  231

**8  Solving Problems**: Controlling Extraneous Variables  **232**
Physical Variables  233
Social Variables  237
Personality Variables  252
Context Variables  254
Summary  257
Key Terms  258
Review and Study Questions  259
Critical Thinking Exercise  259
Online Resources  260

**9  Basic Between-Subjects Designs**  **261**
Selecting and Recruiting Subjects  263
One Independent Variable: Two-Group Designs  267
Two Independent Groups  267
Two Matched Groups  277
Multiple Groups  282
Summary  286
Key Terms  287
Review and Study Questions  288
Critical Thinking Exercise  289
Online Resources  289

**10  Between-Subjects Factorial Designs**  **290**
More Than One Independent Variable  291
Laying Out a Factorial Design  296
A Research Example  300
Choosing a Between-Subjects Design  308
Summary  312
Key Terms  312
Review and Study Questions  313
Critical Thinking Exercise  314
Online Resources  314

**11 Within-Subjects Designs 315**

A Within-Subjects Experiment: Homophone
Priming of Proper Names 319

Within-Subjects Factorial Designs 320

Mixed Designs 321

Advantages of Within-Subjects Designs 323

Disadvantages of Within-Subjects Designs 325

Controlling Within-Subjects Designs 326

How Can You Choose a Design? 339

Summary 340

Key Terms 341

Review and Study Questions 342

Critical Thinking Exercise 343

Online Resources 344

**12 Within-Subjects Designs: Small *N* 345**

Small *N* Designs 346

*ABA* Designs 351

Multiple Baseline Design 357

Statistics and Variability in Small *N* Designs 360

Changing Criterion Designs 361

Discrete Trials Designs 362

When to Use Large *N* and Small *N* Designs 364

Summary 366

Key Terms 367

Review and Study Questions 368

Critical Thinking Exercise 368

Online Resources 369

**PART 3 Results: Coping with Data 371**

**13 Why We Need Statistics 373**

The Argument for Using Statistics 374

Weighing the Evidence 375

Statistical Inference: An Overview 376

Applying Statistical Inference: An Example 382

Going Beyond Testing the Null Hypothesis 389

The Odds of Finding Significance 391

Test Statistics 396
Organizing and Summarizing Data 397
Summary 403
Key Terms 405
Review and Study Questions 406
Critical Thinking Exercise 407
Online Resources 407

14 **Analyzing Results** 408
Which Test Do I Use? 409
Statistics for Two-Group Experiments 412
The Chi-Square Test 412
The *t* Test 417
Analyzing Multiple Groups and Factorial Experiments 428
Analysis of Variance 428
Sources of Variability 429
A One-Way Between-Subjects Analysis of Variance 431
One-Way Repeated Measures Analysis of Variance 438
Analyzing Data from a Between-Subjects Factorial Experiment 439
Two-Way Analysis of Variance 441
Repeated Measures and Mixed Factorial Designs 446
Summary 448
Key Terms 451
Review and Study Questions 452
Critical Thinking Exercise 454
Online Resources 454

PART **4** **Discussion** 455

15 **Drawing Conclusions**: The Search for the Elusive Bottom Line 457
Evaluating the Experiment from the Inside: Internal Validity 459
Taking a Broader Perspective: The Problem of External Validity 464
Handling a Nonsignificant Outcome 476
Summary 479
Key Terms 480

Review and Study Questions   481
Critical Thinking Exercise   482
Online Resources   482

**16**  **Writing the Research Report**   **483**
The Written Report: Purpose and Format   484
Major Sections   487
Looking at a Journal Article   496
Preparing Your Manuscript: Procedural Details   512
Making Revisions   516
Summary   519
Key Terms   520
Review and Study Questions   520
Critical Thinking Exercise   521
Online Resources   522

APPENDIX **A**  **Computational Formulas**   **523**

APPENDIX **B**  **Statistical Tables**   **536**

APPENDIX **C**  **A Journal Article in Manuscript Form**   **545**

APPENDIX **D**  **Answers to Selected Review and Study Questions and Critical Thinking Exercises**   **573**

GLOSSARY   587
REFERENCES   595
INDEX   604
PHOTO CREDITS   612

# PREFACE

## GOALS OF THE TEXT

*Experimental Psychology,* Seventh Edition, is an introduction to the basic principles of research in psychology. It explains the key principles of research design, clearly and within the context of concrete examples. It teaches students how to design and execute an experiment, analyze and interpret the results, and write a research report. Although the main focus is on experimentation, many alternative approaches are discussed as important complements to controlled laboratory experiments.

This text was designed to be as comprehensive as possible—without overwhelming the beginning researcher. The principles of experimentation and the skepticism of the scientific approach are concepts that are new to students and run counter to their commonsense notions about causal inference; for most psychology students, mastering experimental methods requires making a quantum leap from their original ideas about psychology as well as challenging them to learn an entirely new language. This text has been designed to address these issues and provide practical solutions to them. It was written with flexibility in mind for the instructor as well. Each chapter can stand on its own, and instructors can select text assignments to match individual course content.

## SPECIAL FEATURES OF THE TEXT

This text introduces the experimental process in a structured way that allows students to gain a thorough grasp of the scientific method. First, it is organized to carry students through the entire process of conducting an experiment. The major sections—Introduction, Method, Results, and Discussion—parallel the major sections of the research report in order to clarify the relationships among designing, conducting, and reporting the experiment. The *Publication Manual of the American Psychological Association,* Sixth Edition (2010), includes a number of changes and additions along with new requirements and recommendations. Throughout the text, we have included new material that incorporates these changes.

Second, we provide many practical aids. We discuss research ethics in detail, as well as specific techniques for developing a research hypothesis. In presenting research methods, we have stressed the integral relationship among the experimental hypothesis, the research design, and the statistical analysis. The process of selecting a design has been broken down into basic steps to provide structure for the student. A detailed chapter on report writing includes a sample journal article to illustrate the most current reporting conventions. (To assist students in producing an APA-style report, the manuscript version of this article is reproduced in Appendix C.) We explain the rationale behind all procedures to help students apply them. Important terms appear in color throughout the text and are listed and defined at the end of each chapter. Each chapter includes learning objectives, a summary, review and study questions, critical thinking exercises, and online resources. At the end of the book, a random number table (Appendix B), a glossary, references, and an index are included.

Third, we draw examples from many different research areas to emphasize the importance of sound research methodology throughout all subdisciplines of psychology. The examples, both classic and current, provide clear, concrete illustrations of the concepts under discussion. The eclectic choice of examples gives instructors the freedom to supplement the text with content-oriented readings in areas of their choice.

Statistical material is included to help students interpret research findings. The results section of the text provides students with a conceptual overview of the process of statistical inference, step-by-step instructions for selecting and carrying out many of the tests commonly used in simple experiments, and examples of SPSS output. Basic terms are reviewed, and statistical computations (Appendix A) and statistical tables (Appendix B) are provided so that all the required information is available in this single source.

We discuss the process of interpreting and describing statistical results in detail. The ability to analyze data using computer software programs has radically changed research design and statistics over the last decade or so, and the published research contains frequent examples of highly sophisticated statistical analyses and designs. Therefore, while we are aware that some of the research designs and statistics included in the text (e.g., partial correlations, causal modeling, factor analysis, ANCOVA, MANOVA) are advanced techniques not likely to be utilized by students in their initial projects, we made the decision to include them briefly because they are so frequently encountered in literature searches.

## ORGANIZATION OF THE SEVENTH EDITION

Those who used the text in the sixth edition will find that the overall plan and focus of the book have remained unchanged. Many interesting new examples have been included throughout. Some topics have been updated and expanded in response to reviewer and user feedback. A few topics have been added. In Part 1, "Introduction," Chapter 1 focuses on introducing the student to the need for scientific explanations of behavior and now includes more real-world examples of nonscientific inference. A very brief history of experimental psychology has been added. Chapter 2 presents extensive coverage of research ethics and includes broadened coverage of informed consent and consent forms (including a sample), as well as additional attention to plagiarism in the Internet age. Important knowledge gained from the Stanford prison study has been included per reviewer requests. Chapter 3 includes added coverage of nonexperimental designs, including expanded discussion of qualitative research methods. Chapter 4 presents techniques for survey and interview research and includes survey construction, data collection, and sampling issues with additional information geared toward Internet surveys. Chapter 5 on correlational and quasi-experimental designs includes expanded discussion of linear and multiple regression techniques, causal modeling, and quasi-experimental designs. Chapter 6 presents the basics of formulating a hypothesis. It now includes expanded coverage of meta-analysis and the use of computer databases for literature searches.

In Part 2, "Method," more information on reliability and validity has been included in Chapter 7, which teaches the basics of experimentation. Procedures for controlling extraneous variables, including many practical tips, are found in Chapter 8 along with expanded discussion of placebo effects. Chapters 9 and 10 focus on between-subjects designs: two-group designs, multiple-group designs, and factorials. Discussion of effect size estimates has been augmented in Chapter 9 along with added text on control and statistical considerations. Chapter 10 includes expanded coverage of interactions. Chapter 11 describes within-subjects and mixed designs and now includes more information about counterbalancing techniques, including techniques for constructing balanced Latin squares and block randomization of treatment conditions.

Chapter 12 focuses on small $N$ designs. It includes expanded discussion on the pros and cons of small $N$ and large $N$ designs, more variations of *ABA* and other small $N$ designs, including changing-criterion designs.

In Part 3, "Results: Coping with Data," many new examples have been added to the two chapters on statistics. Chapter 13 discusses hypothesis testing, statistical inference, probability, decision errors, measures of central tendency, and variance. Chapter 14 focuses on the selection and interpretation of statistics for all of the experimental designs covered in the text. We have augmented the discussion of statistical hypothesis testing, which now includes the controversy over null hypothesis testing ($p < .05$), the switch to the $p_{rep}$ statistic by APS's flagship journal, and added emphasis on computation of effect sizes and confidence intervals necessitated by the 2010 APA publication guidelines. The chapter also has been updated to reflect increasingly sophisticated ANOVA techniques and statistical analysis using SPSS or other computer statistics programs.

In Part 4, "Discussion," Chapter 15 includes even more practical information for students about interpreting findings and evaluating results from statistical tests. It also includes more discussion of the need to examine alternative explanations for findings. Chapter 16 features a very interesting sample article ("Effects of message framing and temporal context on college student drinking behavior") by Mary Gerend and Margaret Cullen, which is annotated in detail to help students write their own APA-style report. We think you will find the seventh edition even more comprehensive than before—but still user-friendly.

## ACKNOWLEDGMENTS

Many people contributed to the development of this textbook. We are especially grateful to Robert D. Nye, who served as an untiring sounding board in the early days. Howard Cohen, James Halpern, David Schiffman, Mark Sherman, and Jodi Solomon deserve special mention for reading portions of the original manuscript. Phyllis Freeman, Joanne Green, Zanvel Liff, Barbara Novick, David Morse, Robert Presbie, Richard Slaon, and Carol Vazquez also helped. Special thanks to Dave Carroll, Patrick Faircloth, Donna Lewandowski, Deanna Tepper, Andrea Kozak, Mark Hoheisel, Michelle Pelker, Garth Preuthun, Cynthia Shantz, Jo Ann Swaney, Cherese Williams, and Jane Youngs, who read and commented on previous editions from a student's and teaching assistant's point of view. And, finally, we are grateful to Haley Noble-Jack for helping us to find interesting new studies to write about in this edition.

Special thanks to all the students in research methods courses who read and commented on the previous edition, particularly those students from across the country who took the time and energy to write to us. We hope we have clarified any ambiguities and given you interesting new examples and cartoons. (We have also taken your advice and provided answers to selected end-of-chapter questions.) Thanks, also, to three methodological wizards— Bill Crano, Randy Hansen, and Larry Messé—as well as to Don Campbell and his colleagues, who have taught so many generations of students. We are also deeply indebted to the many researchers whose work inspired much of this text and to the many authors and publishers who permitted reproductions of portions of their works. They are cited throughout the text. Particular thanks to Robert A. Baron, Robert Rosenthal, and Phil Zimbardo whose work fills so many pages, and especially to the late Robert Zajonc, *cher ami*, for his imagination and good humor over the years. We are grateful to the literary executor of the late Sir Ronald A. Fisher, F.R.S., to Dr. Frank Yates, F.R.S., and to the Longman Group UK, Ltd. for permission to reprint portions of statistical tables used in Appendix B. And to Sidney Harris, immeasurable thanks for the new cartoons! They brought new smiles to our faces.

We gratefully acknowledge the contributions of those who reviewed the book in preparation for this edition. Their constructive suggestions improved the book greatly. And a special thank you to Dr. Emma Hampton—University of Texas—for explaining the genetics of calico cats and cloning, and to Dennis Shaffer—Ohio State University, Mansfield—for sending the photo of Lilly, the frisbee dog.

Finally, we would also like to thank the people at Cengage for their careful handling of the revision, particularly Tim Matray, Editor, and Phil Hovanessian, Assistant Editor. And an extra special thank you to Pam Galbreath, Art Director at Wadsworth/Cengage, for a spectacular cover design once again.

*Anne Myers*
*Christine Hansen*

# Experimental Psychology

# PART 1

# Introduction

1 Experimental Psychology and the Scientific Method

2 Research Ethics

3 Alternatives to Experimentation: Nonexperimental Designs

4 Alternatives to Experimentation: Surveys and Interviews

5 Alternatives to Experimentation: Correlational and Quasi-Experimental Designs

6 Formulating the Hypothesis

# Experimental Psychology and the Scientific Method

**The Need for Scientific Methodology**
Nonscientific Sources of Data
Nonscientific Inference

**The Characteristics of Modern Science**
The Scientific Mentality
Gathering Empirical Data
Seeking General Principles
Good Thinking
Self-Correction
Publicizing Results
Replication

**The Objectives of Psychological Science**

**The Scientific Method: Tools of Psychological Science**
Observation
Measurement
Experimentation

**Scientific Explanation in Psychological Science**
Identifying Antecedent Conditions
Comparing Treatment Conditions
The Psychology Experiment
Establishing Cause and Effect
Necessary versus Sufficient Conditions

**From Pseudoscience to Psychological Science**

**The Organization of the Text**

SUMMARY
KEY TERMS
REVIEW AND STUDY QUESTIONS
CRITICAL THINKING EXERCISE
ONLINE RESOURCES

## CHAPTER OBJECTIVES

- Understand why we rely on scientific methods rather than common sense to explain behavior
- Learn the principles of the scientific method
- Learn the basic tools of psychological research
- Understand how "cause and effect" is established by experimentation

Psychology is the science of behavior. As psychologists, we take a scientific approach to understanding behavior, and our knowledge about psychological processes is based on scientific evidence accumulated through research. As scientists, we rely on scientific methods when we conduct psychological research, such as specifying the conditions under which we make our observations, observing in a systematic or orderly way, and accepting or rejecting alternative explanations of behaviors on the basis of what we observe. In short, research about the psychological processes underlying behavior is known as psychological science.

The word science comes from the Latin word *scientia*, which simply means knowledge. As the word is used today, however, it has two meanings— content and process. The content of science is what we know, such as the facts we learn in our psychology or chemistry courses. But science is also a process—that is, an activity that includes the systematic ways in which we go about gathering data, noting relationships, and offering explanations.

Explaining the process of psychological science is the principal aim of this text. In the chapters that follow, we will examine some of the basic tactics used in psychological research. We will study methodology, the scientific techniques used to collect and evaluate psychological data (the facts and figures gathered in research studies).

All areas of psychology rely on scientific research methods. Researchers investigating perception, for example, collect data in formal laboratory experiments designed to provide the most precise information. Psychologists interested in understanding attitudes and social behaviors sometimes gather data under controlled laboratory conditions; at other times, they conduct surveys in the community or observe and record people's behavior in natural settings. Psychologists studying human development might observe young children's reactions under different conditions in the laboratory or in real-world settings. Clinical psychologists may collect data by administering psychological tests or by observing personality functioning during sessions with patients. Whether the data come from laboratory experiments, real-world settings, or therapy sessions, all psychologists use scientific criteria to evaluate their data.

---

## THE NEED FOR SCIENTIFIC METHODOLOGY

In our daily lives, we all collect and use psychological data to understand the behavior of others and to guide our own behavior. When you notice that your roommate is in a bad mood, you don't ask for a favor. You dress up when you are going for a job interview because first impressions are important. You don't invite John and Evan to the same party because they don't like each other.

You can probably think of many more examples of situations in which you used psychological data to predict the behavior of others and to guide your own behavior. The kind of everyday, nonscientific data gathering that shapes our expectations and beliefs and directs our behavior toward others has been called commonsense psychology (Heider, 1958). Commonsense psychology seems to work well enough for us most of the time.

At other times, though, nonscientific data gathering can leave us up in the air. Suppose, for example, that your significant other has just announced that she has been accepted for a summer program at the Sorbonne in Paris. Should you be worried? Some of the nonscientific data you gather about absent partners is reassuring ("absence makes the heart grow fonder"), but some is not ("out of sight, out of mind"). Most of your data seems to support the former conclusion, so you see her off at the airport in good spirits. On the drive home, you remember all the stories you have heard about Paris nightlife and sexy Parisian men.... Without knowing which outcome is really more probable, you are likely to spend an anxious summer. An understanding of the characteristics and limitations of commonsense psychology might not help with dilemmas like this one, but it may help you become a better psychological scientist—if only because it clearly demonstrates the need for a more scientific approach to understanding and predicting behavior.

As commonsense psychologists, we find that our ability to gather data in a systematic and impartial way is constrained by two very important factors: the sources of psychological information and our inferential strategies. Commonsense beliefs about behavior are derived from data we collect from our own experience and what we have learned from others. The data we collect in our everyday lives have been generated from a very small sample of behaviors, and the conclusions we draw from them are subject to a number of inherent tendencies, or biases, that limit their accuracy and usefulness. Often, the sources of our commonsense beliefs about behavior can be unreliable, and the explanations and predictions that we derive from them are likely to be imperfect. Do birds of a feather flock together? Or do opposites attract? Our language is filled with these kinds of conflicting, commonsense adages, and commonsense psychology does not help us know which one to use to predict behavior in any single instance.

## Nonscientific Sources of Data

Very often, the data we gather as commonsense psychologists come from sources that seem credible and trustworthy—friends and relatives, people in authority, people we admire, reports from the media, books we have read, and so forth—but, actually, these sources are not always very good ones for obtaining valid information about behavior. Nevertheless, psychological information, particularly when it is offered by people we like, respect, or admire, is typically accepted without question. These beliefs tend to become stable because we rarely, if ever, test them. Once we believe we know something, we tend to overlook instances that might disconfirm our beliefs, and we seek, instead, confirmatory instances of behavior. This has been termed the *confirmation bias*. If you believe that the full moon brings out psychotic behavior (the word *lunacy* comes from the Latin word for "moon"), you will notice and remember instances when people acted abnormally while the moon was full, and you will ignore the many, many more instances in which no unusual behavior occurred.

It is also unlikely that anyone can completely avoid assimilating some myths, superstitions, and pop psychology explanations for behavior. Do you believe in the power of crystals? (Some people believe that wearing amethyst will increase their intuition and that clear quartz will build inner strength.) Do you ever read your horoscope? Do you knock on wood to avoid bad luck? Do you feel a bit anxious on Friday the 13th? Interestingly, only the latter superstition—fear of Friday the 13th—has produced any supportive scientific documentation (see Box 1.1).

Research has shown that we are more likely to believe information if it comes from certain kinds of individuals: People who are popular, attractive, high in status, seemingly expert, or who appear highly confident are more powerful sources of information than others are. But other people are not our sole source of data about psychological processes. We gather a lot of information about behavior from our own observations and interactions with others and the conclusions we draw from them. Children learn very early that their smiles and vocalizations are rewarded and that touching a lit candle or a hot stove can have very negative consequences. We learn to predict consequences and direct our behavior toward desired goals. Frequently, we use our beliefs and feelings about how things operate to explain behavior—our own as well as that of others.

Researchers have discovered that we are not always privy to our own decision-making processes (Nisbett & Wilson, 1977). North, Hargreaves, and McKendrick (1999) conducted an interesting experiment that demonstrates this inability. In their experiment, French or German music was played on alternate days from a supermarket display featuring two French and German wines of similar price and sweetness. As predicted, on days that

BOX **1.1**    **The Power of Negative Thinking**

Friday the 13th has a mythical history of being unlucky, and if Friday falls on the 13th of the month, the superstition often comes to mind (or someone reminds us!). Do you feel a moment of anxiety when you realize it's Friday the 13th? Have you ever wondered whether it is really unlucky? Apparently it is, but probably not because of any dark and powerful, unseen force that exerts its will upon us. A study conducted in West Sussex in Great Britain and reported in the *British Medical Journal* (Scanlon, Luben, Scanlon, & Singleton, 1993) found that Friday the 13th did appear to be an unlucky day for drivers. When researchers compared each Friday the 13th with each Friday the 6th since 1989, looking at the number of emergency room visits from automobile accidents, more accident victims (as many as 52% more) were treated on Friday the 13th even though fewer cars were driven that day. According to the researchers, the higher accident rate for Friday the 13th was probably caused by increased trepidation about the date: Anxiety caused reduced attention to driving, and more accidents occurred. Whether their

reason is the correct one or not, it makes sense to be extra cautious if you are driving that day because other drivers might be more anxious and accident-prone than usual.

Jay Silverman Productions/The Image Bank/Getty Images

FIGURE **1.1** Oh no—it's Friday the 13th!

French music was being played, the French wine outsold the German wine; whereas German wine outsold French wine on days that German music was played (both by margins of about 3:1). Clearly, the music had an influence on purchases. When queried about the reasons for their choices, however, only 1 out of 44 people mentioned the music. Even when asked specifically whether they felt the music might have influenced their choice, only 6 out of 44 said that it might have.

We are often unaware of factors that influence our attitudes and behavior. For example, when we uncritically accept information from an attractive source, we are unlikely to be aware of what actually persuaded us. If someone were to ask us, we would probably believe that the information must have been extremely persuasive. We would be unlikely to realize that we were really persuaded because the person who communicated the information was highly attractive.

We frequently use data from our own experiences to come up with commonsense assumptions about cause and effect—but, if we were to rely only on commonsense psychology, we would frequently be wrong. The inferential strategies we use when we process data are sometimes too simple to be completely accurate. Let's look at a few areas in which the commonsense psychologist is likely to make errors.

MPI/Getty Images

FIGURE **1.2** An expert source like Einstein would be highly persuasive.

### Nonscientific Inference

One of the first and most important kinds of data we collect about others comes in the form of traits we assign to them. All commonsense psychologists are trait theorists—at least when it comes to explaining the behavior of others. When we understand other people's behavior, there is a strong bias to overlook situational data in favor of data that substantiate trait explanations (Gilbert, 1995; Ross & Nisbett, 1991). When we notice that Stacy is sporting another new designer outfit, we conclude that she is vain about her appearance and spends money frivolously.

We tend to miss or ignore important information about the situation (for instance, that Stacy's mother designs for the manufacturer and gets Stacy's clothes for almost nothing). Our ability to make accurate predictions about someone's traits increases with the length of acquaintanceship. We are generally more accurate when we know someone well than when we judge a stranger (Colvin & Funder, 1991). But, not always (see Box 1.2).

Perceiving others by their traits can be useful for predicting their behavior, but it can also lead to overestimations of the likelihood that they will act in trait-consistent ways across a wide variety of different situations. The research literature suggests that people may overestimate this kind of cross-situational behavioral consistency by as much as a factor of 10. And, apparently, this bias is hard to overcome, even with training. In one amusing study (Kunda & Nisbett, 1986), it was discovered that a group of trained research psychologists was not much better at estimating the actual predictive power of traits than were people in general—even when the psychologists were

BOX **1.2**    **The Accuracy of Nonverbal Behavior**

Even though people tend to be more accurate about the traits of others they know well, perceivers can be remarkably accurate about the personality of strangers when they are able to observe even thin slices of nonverbal behavior (Ambady & Rosenthal, 1993). Ambady and Rosenthal (1993; experiment 1) demonstrated this in a very interesting way by asking female judges to evaluate 13 university professors on the basis of three 10-second, silent video clips that showed each professor at the beginning, middle, and end of a class session. The judges could watch the facial expressions and other nonverbal behaviors, but they could not hear anything. Each judge evaluated the professors on 15 personal characteristics (accepting, active, anxious, attentive, competent,

confident, dominant, empathic, enthusiastic, honest, likable, optimistic, professional, supportive, and warm). Results indicated that the favorability of the judges' trait ratings was strongly predictive of the professors' actual class evaluations at the end of the semester.

Professors who were given the highest evaluations by the students in their classes were those who had been given the most positive evaluations by the judges. Based on these very thin slices of nonverbal behavior, the female judges were surprisingly accurate in predicting which professors would be judged most positively by their students at the end of the term.

Comstock/Jupiter Images

FIGURE **1.3** How would you evaluate this professor?

reminded of the bias by the presence of a very well-known personality researcher. For decades, psychologists have debated whether traits or situations are better predictors of behavior. In fact, there is evidence that both sides of the debate are probably correct some of the time—traits might be more useful for predicting how someone will behave over the long term, whereas situations might be better predictors of momentary behaviors (Fleeson, 2004).

The process of stereotyping illustrates a related problem of nonscientific inference. Once we know that Carol is a librarian, we automatically assume that she is probably also serious because that characteristic is part of a librarian stereotype (Hamilton & Rose, 1980). And, similar to what can happen to individuals who believe the full moon myth, stereotypic expectations can lead us to seek confirmatory instances of behavior: "See! She is so serious, she always has her nose in a book." (Of course she does! It's her job!)

Additional problems in prediction occur because people are not very good at using data to estimate the true probabilities of events. The well-known "gambler's fallacy" is a good example of this problem (see Figure 1.4). When we see that a certain slot machine has not paid off in a long time, we tend to believe that it is overdue for a payoff. In reality, it makes no difference whether the machine has recently paid off or not (unless the machine is rigged).

Phil Schermeister/Documentary Value/CORBIS

FIGURE **1.4** Do you believe the gambler's fallacy?

Each spin is entirely random and independent, so your odds of a jackpot this time are identical to your odds on any other try.[1]

Finally, compounding our inferential shortcomings is a phenomenon known as the *overconfidence bias*. Our predictions, guesses, and explanations tend to feel much more correct than they actually are, and the more data we have available (accurate or not), the more confidence we have in our judgments about behavior (Dunning, Griffin, Milojkovic, & Ross, 1990).

These and many other inferential biases exist in human information processing. They are believed to be the brain's way of coping with an immense volume of information. They are shortcuts, and most of the time, they allow us to function well enough, but they are not always accurate. In 2002, Princeton psychologist Daniel Kahneman won the Nobel Prize for his work with Amos Tversky on biases in human judgments (Kahneman & Tversky, 2000). If we want to be able to rely on our conclusions and use them as general principles to predict behavior across many settings and conditions, we need to proceed more systematically and objectively—in other words, scientifically. The steps scientists take to gather and verify information, answer questions, explain relationships, and communicate this information to others are known as the scientific method. We will now turn to several important characteristics of the scientific method.

## THE CHARACTERISTICS OF MODERN SCIENCE

### The Scientific Mentality

The psychologist's goal of prediction rests on a simple, but important, assumption: Behavior must follow a natural order; therefore, it can be predicted. This elementary assumption lies at the heart of what Alfred North Whitehead (1861–1947) called the "scientific mentality." Whitehead was a philosopher of science who traced the development of science in his now classic book *Science and the Modern World* (1925). He postulated that faith in an organized universe is essential to science. If no inherent order existed, there would be no point in looking for one and no need to develop methods for doing so. Research psychologists share the belief that there are specifiable (although not necessarily simple or obvious) causes for the way people behave and that these causes can be discovered through research. This belief is called *determinism*.

### Gathering Empirical Data

Whitehead traced the beginnings of modern science to the works of the Greek philosopher, Aristotle (384–322 BC). Like contemporary scientists,

---

[1] Calculating the true odds is easy if you know the number of wheels and the number of items on each wheel. If the machine has three wheels, and each wheel has five fruits, your chances of getting three cherries (or three of any fruit) for a payoff are $1/5 \times 1/5 \times 1/5 = 1/125$, or 0.8%, and the probability is identical for any single play.

Aristotle assumed that order exists in the universe, and he set about describing that order in a systematic way by collecting empirical data—that is, data that are observable or experienced. Aristotle advocated systematic observation and careful classification of naturally occurring events. From his own systematic observations, Aristotle argued that heavy objects fall faster than light objects because their "natural" place is down. Another important characteristic of empirical data, however, is that they can be verified or disproved through investigation. Later investigation of falling objects by Galileo (1564–1642) led to the inescapable conclusion that if we set up the proper testing conditions (in this case testing objects in a vacuum), light objects will fall just as fast as heavy ones. Thus, gathering empirical data in a systematic and orderly way, as Aristotle did, is preferable to commonsense data collection, but it still cannot guarantee that the correct conclusions will be reached.

### Seeking General Principles

Modern scientists go beyond cataloging observations to proposing general principles—laws or theories—that will explain them. We could observe endless pieces of data, adding to the content of science, but our observations would be of limited use without general principles to structure them. When these principles have the generality to apply to all situations, they are called laws. For example, astronomer Tycho Brahe (1546–1601) painstakingly gathered observations of the stars for nearly a lifetime. But Johannes Kepler (1571–1630) made these observations useful by explaining them through a system of equations now known as Kepler's laws.

Typically, we do not have enough information to state a general law, but we advance understanding by devising and testing an interim explanation, commonly called a theory. Theories pull together, or unify, diverse sets of scientific facts into an organizing scheme, such as a general principle or set of rules, that can be used to predict new examples of behavior. Testing predictions stemming from a theory has been the cornerstone of psychological science.[2] Constructing a testable prediction (called a *hypothesis*) is described in detail in Chapter 6.

Theories can explain many, but not all, instances of a situation or behavior—the more a theory can explain, the better it is. Sir Karl Popper (1902–1994), a modern philosopher of science, wrote that science progresses only through progressively better theories (Popper, 1963). Old theories are replaced by new theories with greater explanatory power. Laws are seldom determined outside the physical sciences, so the behavioral sciences like psychology largely progress by developing better and better theories.

---

[2]Not all researchers accept this notion completely. Some have argued for abandoning this hypothetico-deductive method in favor of other models. Among those voting for other models have been radical behaviorists, qualitative researchers, and parapsychology researchers. For a review, see Kimble (1989).

Theories also guide the course of future observations:

> We must remember that what we observe is very much determined by what theory suggests should be observed; and we must remember also that the way in which observation will be reported and interpreted is a function of the theory that is in the observer's mind (Schlegel, 1972, p. 11).

Theory-based expectancies can cause us to pay more attention to behavioral information that is predicted by the theory and to overlook nonpredicted behaviors. The next characteristic of the scientific method, good thinking, is essential to offset a predisposition to find only what we are seeking.

## Good Thinking

A central feature of the scientific method is good thinking. Our approach to the collection and interpretation of data should be systematic, objective, and rational. The scientist avoids letting private beliefs or expectations influence observations or conclusions. Good thinking includes being open to new ideas even when they contradict our prior beliefs or attitudes. Good thinking also follows the rules of logic. Conclusions will follow from the data, whether they are in agreement with our predictions or not.

Another important aspect of good thinking is the principle of parsimony, sometimes called Occam's razor. William of Occam was a 14th-century philosopher who cautioned us to stick to a basic premise: Entities should not be multiplied without necessity. What Occam had in mind was simplicity, precision, and clarity of thought. We must avoid making unnecessary assumptions to support an argument or explanation. When two explanations are equally defensible, the simplest explanation is preferred until it is ruled out by conflicting data. Crandall (1988) applied the idea of parsimony in an interesting way while investigating the causes of bulimia, an eating disorder typified by alternating periods of unrestrained binge eating followed by vomiting. Since the late 1960s or early 1970s, the incidence of bulimia in women has risen dramatically (Rosensweig & Spruill, 1986). It is estimated that between 4 and 15% of college women have the disorder (bulimia rarely affects men). Crandall designed his experiment to show that a social contagion explanation was more parsimonious than three existing explanations for binge eating: social norms, psychological disorders, and epidemiological risk factors. The study involved college women from two different popular and sought-after sororities. All participants were active members living in one of the sorority houses.

The participants responded anonymously to a set of questions about their social networks, their self-perceptions, and their attitudes about bulimia. Questionnaires were filled out in the fall and again in the spring. The results of the study showed that even though the two sororities differed greatly in their group norms for binge eating, over the academic year the eating behavior of women in both sororities became more like the behavior of their own friends. Comparisons of all four explanations showed that the social contagion explanation was the most parsimonious and accounted for the results better than any of the others.

### Self-Correction

Modern scientists accept the uncertainty of their own conclusions. The content of science changes as we acquire new scientific information, and old information is reevaluated in light of new facts. Changes in scientific explanations and theories are an extremely important part of scientific progress. Experience favors a "weight-of-evidence" approach: The more evidence that accumulates to support a particular explanation or theory, the more confidence we have that the theory is correct. According to Popper, old explanations often give way simply because the weight of supporting evidence tips the scales in favor of a different scientific explanation.

For example, for more than 30 years, the link between media violence and aggressive behavior was explained by social learning theory. This theory asserted that people would perform the same kinds of aggressive behaviors they had observed in films or on television by learning to imitate the aggressive behavior of the media models. At present, cognitive priming theory is more commonly used to explain these effects. The newer theory posits that observing violence triggers cognitive representations of aggressive behavior stored in memory in our own cognitive schemas. Cognitive priming theory has largely replaced social learning theory because it can explain more varied behaviors, such as people's tendencies to perform similar as well as identical behaviors after being exposed to them on TV, in films, or in music (Berkowitz & Rogers, 1986).

### Publicizing Results

Because of its dynamic nature, modern science has become a highly public activity. Scientists meet frequently through professional and special interest groups and attend professional conferences to exchange information about their current work.[3] The number of scientific papers published each year in

---

[3] The two largest professional organizations sponsoring the exchange of information about psychology are the American Psychological Association (APA) and the Association for Psychological Science (APS). APA is the oldest and largest organization, founded in 1892. The interests of APA members span all disciplines within psychology, and APA fosters the interests of psychologists engaged in both research and therapy (http://www.apa.org). In 1988, APS was formed to focus exclusively on psychological research and psychological science (http://www.psychologicalscience.org)

"IT'S UNIFIED AND IT'S A THEORY, BUT IT'S NOT THE UNIFIED THEORY WE'VE ALL BEEN LOOKING FOR."

scientific journals is growing, and new journals are constantly being added in specialized disciplines. This continuous exchange of information is vital to the scientific process. It would do little good for scientists to work in isolation. The opportunity to incorporate the most recent findings of others would be missed, and there would be a lot of wasted effort as researchers duplicated failures as well as successes.

## Replication

Replication is another important part of the scientific approach. We should be able to repeat our procedures and get the same results again if we have gathered data objectively and if we have followed good thinking. Findings that are obtainable by only one researcher have very limited scientific value. For example, people sometimes report dreams that seem to predict the future. A woman dreams of a stranger and meets him the following day; a man dreams of a car accident and then hears of a friend's fatal crash. Have these people seen into the future through their dreams? We cannot provide a scientific answer to that question. It is impossible to re-create the original conditions that led to these events, so we cannot replicate these experiences. It is also difficult to evaluate them objectively because the dreamer is the only observer of the dream.

In contrast, a researcher predicts that children will hit a doll after they have seen an adult hitting a small child on television. The prediction is confirmed. In this instance, we can apply scientific criteria to the researcher's findings. We can replicate the findings by setting up the same or similar conditions and observing whether or not the outcome is the same. Replication of research findings by others can be important; we have a great deal more confidence that we have explained something if the predicted effects are repeatable by other researchers.

Generally, replication is more common in the physical than in the behavioral sciences. For example, in 1989 investigators in Utah reported that they had created nuclear fusion in the laboratory without heat (a monumental scientific discovery). The report led to worldwide attempts to replicate their experiment in other laboratories, but, to date, other researchers have not substantiated the claim for cold fusion. As in other sciences, published replications of psychological research are more common when the reported findings either have important implications or when reported results directly contradict current conventional wisdom.

## THE OBJECTIVES OF PSYCHOLOGICAL SCIENCE

In this textbook, you will be introduced to many scientific research methods that can be used to acquire knowledge about psychological phenomena. As we shall see in later chapters, each research method makes a somewhat different contribution to our understanding, but all research methods contribute to one or more objectives of psychological science. There are four major objectives of research conducted in psychology: description, prediction, explanation, and control.

The first objective, *description*, is the initial step toward understanding any phenomenon, whether it is the path of the stars in the heavens or the complexities of human and animal behaviors. When we define *description* in psychological science, we are referring to a systematic and unbiased account of the observed characteristics of behaviors. Good descriptions allow us greater knowledge of behaviors because they provide us with information about what the behavior will be like. A description of grief, for example, will allow us to understand that people who are grieving are very likely to be sad and depressed and, even, perhaps, to be crying. There are many different methods of descriptive research; some are more systematic and objective, others are less.

Examples of descriptive research designs include case studies and field studies. In a case study, an outside observer records the behaviors or experiences, or both, of a single individual. Case studies are common in clinical, organizational, and forensic psychology and are used to make inferences about the origins of psychological disorders, developmental processes, and the influence of life events. Field studies are observational studies of groups of people (or animals) in real-life settings. Here, observers are able to gather descriptive data about many kinds of social and cultural experiences, including child development, organizational structure and function, and social customs. These and other descriptive research methods will be introduced in Chapter 3. Surveys and interviews are frequently used to gather descriptive information, such as attitudes and opinions, and these will be covered in Chapter 4.

*Prediction*, the second objective, refers to the capacity for knowing in advance when certain behaviors would be expected to occur—to be able to predict them ahead of time—because we have identified other conditions with which the behaviors are linked or associated. We know that the death of a grandparent, for example, is associated with grief, and we can predict that a person will feel grief if a grandparent has died recently. Thus, prediction is useful for psychologists, both researchers and clinicians.

A number of research designs, called correlational and quasi-experimental designs, are commonly used to predict behavior. In correlational designs, researchers look for a statistical relationship between different events, behaviors, or experiences. For example, there is a statistical link between adult obesity and type 2 diabetes. This relationship allows physicians and insurance companies to make predictions about an individual's risk of getting diabetes based on their weight. In some quasi-experimental designs, researchers look for systematic differences among groups of people and use the results to make predictions. For instance, the research finding that fans of different types of popular music have different personality characteristics can be used to make predictions about people based on their music preferences, even though we cannot be certain why these differences exist. These designs are discussed in Chapter 5.

*Explanation*, the third objective, goes a step further. When we have explained a behavior, we also understand what causes it to occur. Explanation includes knowledge of the conditions that reliably reproduce the occurrence of a behavior. To explain a behavior, we have to use an experimental research design in which we systematically manipulate aspects of the setting with the intention of producing the specific behavior. At the same time, we control for other factors that might also influence this behavior during the experiment. Only the results of true experiments allow us to make inferences about cause and effect, but, as we will learn shortly, it is not always feasible, or even desirable, to conduct an experiment. Many times, a nonexperimental or quasi-experimental research method is the preferred (or only) option. Coverage of experimental designs will begin in Chapter 7.

*Control*, the fourth objective, refers to the application of what has been learned about behavior. Once a behavior has been explained through experimentation, it may be possible to use that knowledge to effect change or improve behavior. Control is rarely the intent of experimentation, but some research is conducted with the intent of producing behavioral change along with increasing knowledge. For example, a clinical researcher might conduct an experiment to test whether cognitive-behavioral therapy ameliorates grief to a greater extent than another type of therapy (or no therapy at all). An organizational psychologist might compare the effects of flexible hours versus working 9-to-5 on employee morale. In these types of experiments, the intention of the researcher is really two-fold: testing the effects of specified conditions on behavior and changing behavior (i.e., control).

Research that is designed to solve real-world problems (like helping patients to deal with grief or improving employee morale) is known as applied research. In contrast, research designed to test theories or to explain psychological phenomena in humans and animals is called basic research. It is often many years before results of basic research are translated into practical applications, but there is growing interest in bringing the two together. An entire issue of one prestigious APA journal, *Developmental Psychology*, was devoted to bringing basic research on child violence together with public policy aimed at reducing it. In that issue, Pettit and Dodge (2003) explained that despite a great deal of attention paid to the issue of childhood violence, neither clinical practice nor public policy has had a significant long-term impact on reducing the violence. They argued that "a need exists for developmental psychology to have an impact on the formulation, implementation, and evaluation of science-based prevention and intervention programs and public policies" (p. 187).

Over the last few years, the need to bring the results of psychological research to bear upon issues in the public interest has become a major focus of both APA and APS. Both organizations routinely send out press releases describing important new research findings. Such outreach attempts seem to be successfully spreading information about the results of psychological science. For example, APS's public affairs office recently sent out a press release describing findings from an article showing that playing video games can actually improve vision by 20% (Green & Bavalier, 2007). The research was described in over 100 newspapers and magazines, and the story was picked up by television stations nationwide, exposing an estimated 100 million people to the study's results. Both APA and APS are firmly committed to bringing psychology out of the laboratory so that people can use it.

## THE SCIENTIFIC METHOD: TOOLS OF PSYCHOLOGICAL SCIENCE

By now, you are familiar with the scientific approach to research: We gather information objectively and systematically, and we base our conclusions on the evidence we obtain—not on our preconceived notions. Let us now begin to look at the three main tools of the scientific method: observation, measurement, and experimentation. These are also the basic tools of the psychological scientist. The research example described in Box 1.3 is a good illustration of observation, measurement, and experimentation.

### Observation

The first tool, observation, is the systematic noting and recording of events. Only events that are observable can be studied scientifically. At this point, it

## BOX **1.3**   An Experimental Example: What's in the Air?

Warm, dry, seasonal winds, like the sirocco in the southern Mediterranean or the Santa Ana winds in California, have been blamed for everything from insomnia to homicide, and some research evidence seems to support this. These winds increase air temperature, reduce humidity, and alter the atmosphere's electron balance, splitting atoms into positively and negatively charged particles, called ions. During these seasonal winds, there is a slightly higher concentration of positive ions in the air, and a small amount of research evidence suggests that positive ions can produce negative mood shifts. Could negative ions have the opposite effect, making people feel better? Robert A. Baron and his colleagues (Baron, Russell, & Arms, 1985) tested this prediction in an interesting laboratory experiment. (The actual experiment was more complex than this, and we will return to it again in later chapters.)

To set up the conditions for testing, the researchers used a machine that generates negative ions (as some electronic air cleaners do) to change the air in a laboratory room so that the concentration of negative ions was low (normal ambient), moderate, or high. In each session, a male undergraduate was led to believe that he was involved in an experiment about learning. His task during the session involved training another undergraduate to reduce his heart rate with biofeedback. The "learner" was actually a trained confederate of the researchers, and his performance was completely scripted in advance. Sessions were set up so that half of the volunteers were intentionally angered by nasty comments from the "learner" during the session; the other half were not. Each volunteer's mood was measured at the end of the session.

The results were not quite what Baron and his colleagues had predicted.

Instead of inducing more positive moods in everyone, higher concentrations of negative ions seemed to increase the strength of whatever mood the volunteers reported—good or bad. At the end of the session, nonangered volunteers who had been exposed to higher levels of negative ions reported that they felt less angry, less depressed, and less fatigued than did the nonangered volunteers exposed to normal levels. In contrast, the angered volunteers ended up feeling more angry if they had been exposed to higher levels of negative ions than if they had been exposed to normal levels. One explanation is that negative ions may be physiologically arousing, and arousal may increase the strength of whatever emotions people are feeling.

Courtesy of Robert Baron

FIGURE **1.5** Robert A. Baron.

might seem as though we are restricting what we can study in psychology to a very narrow range of events. Many behaviors are observable (smoking, smiling, talking), but what about internal processes such as feeling, thinking, or problem solving? How can we explore those areas? The key is how we apply the scientific method. It is perfectly legitimate to study events that take place inside a person, such as thinking and feeling—if we can develop observable signs of these events.

The key to studying internal processes is defining them as events that can be observed: the time it takes a person to solve a problem, a person's answers to a mood questionnaire, the amplitude of someone's electrodermal responses. (Finding a suitable definition is one of the problems we will discuss in Chapter 7.) In the experiment described in Box 1.3, Baron and his colleagues needed to observe people's moods. Moods, however, cannot be observed directly in any reliable manner. It is not possible to judge a person's mood reliably just by looking; instead, researchers like Baron typically ask people to report on their own moods by using questionnaires or other instruments.

Within the scientific framework, observations also must be made systematically—once the researcher has devised a system for observing, the same system must be applied consistently to each observation. For example, the same mood questionnaire would be given to each person in the study. Of equal importance, observations must be made objectively; another objective observer must be able to obtain the same record of these events. And, clearly, we must avoid distorting data by allowing our expectations to alter our records. Baron and his colleagues recorded their subjects' exact responses to the questionnaires, even though the responses did not quite match what the researchers had predicted.

## Measurement

Measurement is the assignment of numerical values to objects or events or their characteristics according to conventional rules. When we do research, we assign numbers to different sizes, quantities, or qualities of the events under observation.[4] We are all familiar with such conventional physical dimensions as length, width, and height. Rather than relying on global impressions ("It was really large"), we use standardized units, agreed-upon conventions that define such measures as the minute, the meter, and the ounce.

Standards are not always as clear-cut for dimensions of human behavior. We can use standardized intelligence tests and a variety of standardized personality measures, but our standards are often determined by the context of a particular study. We often want to describe the behaviors of individuals in a situation we have created (How much did they talk with strangers in a stressful situation?). Other times, we want to measure individuals' reactions to the situation (How depressed did they feel after a stressful situation?).

---

[4] When numbers are assigned to represent different features of an observation, the research is known as *quantitative* research. There are some occasions in which researchers choose to record observations in a *qualitative* way—that is, to describe their observations using words instead of numbers. Qualitative designs are less common in psychology, although they are fairly common in other fields that study behavior, such as sociology, education, and ethology. Qualitative approaches are discussed further in Chapter 3, when we learn about nonexperimental research methods.

Or we may want to quantify their evaluations of an object or another person (In a stressful situation, is a stranger judged more favorably on dimensions such as attractiveness and intelligence?). When Baron and his colleagues measured each volunteer's mood, they designed their mood questionnaire using numbered scales to represent progressively higher levels of anger, depression, and so forth.

As in Baron's experiment, we are typically interested in comparing the behavior of research participants (also called subjects) who have been exposed to different sets of conditions. Our measurements must be consistent across each set of conditions. If measurement is inconsistent, we cannot compare our measured observations directly (it's like comparing oranges and apples). The same unit of measurement needs to be used each time we measure our observations; we would not use ounces one day and teaspoons the next. And, to be consistent, we need to use the same instruments and procedures each time the event is observed. In Baron's investigation, for example, the questionnaires, as well as the way they were administered, were identical in each session. Because we most often use statistics to evaluate research findings, we need numbers, or scores, to represent different levels or amounts of the behavior of interest.

### Experimentation

Experimentation is a process undertaken to test a hypothesis that particular behavioral events will occur reliably in certain, specifiable situations. When we experiment, we systematically manipulate aspects of a setting to verify our predictions about observable behavior under specific conditions. Experimentation is not always possible. To do an experiment, our predictions must be testable. Three minimum requirements must be met: First, we must have procedures for manipulating the setting. Second, the predicted outcome must be observable. Third, we must be able to measure the outcome. Suppose we have predictions about the observable effects on humans traveling to Mars. Our predictions are not testable because we do not yet have the technology for humans to make the journey. Some hypotheses that cannot be tested now, however, may become testable in the future. Baron's prediction was testable because he could manipulate the setting to create the conditions he wanted to investigate, and he could observe and measure the outcome.

Experimentation must also be objective. Ideally, we do not bias our results by setting up situations in which our predictions will automatically be confirmed. We do not stack the deck in our favor by giving subjects subtle cues to respond in the desired way. (We will have more to say about this in Chapter 8.) Nor do we prevent them from responding in the nonpredicted direction.

At times experimentation might be possible, but it cannot be carried out for ethical reasons. For example, we would not test the effects of smoking on fetal development in pregnant women by asking a group of nonsmoking women to smoke during their pregnancies. We would not peep through windows to study people's sexual behaviors. We would not change students' exam grades to learn about how people respond to success and failure. In a moral society, there are many experiments that should never be conducted because it would be unethical to do so. (We will explain ethical guidelines in the next chapter.) This is not to say that these things cannot be studied by psychologists; it simply means we must study them in ethical ways. Sometimes this is done by using nonexperimental methods or by designing experiments that pose less risk to subjects.

# SCIENTIFIC EXPLANATION IN PSYCHOLOGICAL SCIENCE

## Identifying Antecedent Conditions

In a scientific context, explanation means specifying the antecedent conditions of an event or behavior. Antecedent conditions, or antecedents, are the circumstances that come before the event or behavior that we want to explain. In Baron's experiment, for example, different concentrations of negative ions were the specified antecedent conditions, and mood was the behavior explained by these conditions. If we can identify all the antecedents of a behavior, we can explain that behavior in the following way: When XYZ is the set of antecedent conditions, the outcome is a particular behavior. If the XYZ set of antecedents occurs again, we expect the same outcome.

## Comparing Treatment Conditions

In psychology, it would be virtually impossible to identify all the antecedents that affect the behavior of research participants at a particular time. But although we cannot identify all the antecedent conditions, we can focus on particular antecedents that we believe have an effect on behavior. In the psychology experiment, we create specific sets of antecedent conditions that we call treatments. We compare different treatment conditions so that we can test our explanations of behaviors systematically and scientifically. Keep in mind that the word *treatment*, as used in experimentation, does not necessarily mean that we must actively do something to "treat" each subject (although it can mean this). Rather, it means that we are treating subjects differently when we expose them to different sets of antecedents. We expose them to different antecedent conditions and then measure their behavior to ascertain whether different treatments produce predictably different outcomes. Sometimes, as Baron and his colleagues did, we test our explanations of behavior by creating treatment conditions in which some people are exposed to one set of antecedent conditions (e.g., a high concentration of negative ions) and others are exposed to a different set of antecedents (e.g., a low concentration of negative ions). Then, we compare the effects of these different antecedents on a particular behavior (mood). When we are able to specify the antecedents, or treatment conditions, that lead to a behavior, we have essentially explained that behavior.

## The Psychology Experiment

A psychology experiment is a controlled procedure in which at least two different treatment conditions are applied to subjects. The subjects' behaviors are then measured and compared to test a hypothesis about the effects of those treatments on behavior. Note that we must have at least two different treatments so that we can compare behavior under varied conditions and observe the way behavior changes as the treatment conditions change.

Note also that the procedures in the psychology experiment are carefully *controlled* so that we can be sure we are measuring what we intend to measure. For this reason, characteristics of subjects receiving different treatments are also controlled by special techniques like *random assignment of subjects* to different treatment conditions (Chapter 8). By assigning subjects to receive different treatments using random assignment techniques, we avoid the possibility that subjects in one condition may be systematically different from subjects in another even before the treatments are presented. We want to ensure that people who receive one kind of treatment are *equivalent* (as similar as possible) to subjects receiving a different treatment. If subjects who received one treatment had different characteristics than subjects who received another treatment, we would have no way of knowing whether we were measuring behavioral differences produced by differences in the antecedent conditions we had created or whether we were just measuring behavioral differences that already existed in our subjects. An experimental design in which subjects receive only one kind of treatment is called a *between-subjects design*; this design is the focus of Chapters 9 and 10.

Another way in which systematic differences in subjects might be ruled out is to present all treatments to each subject and measure the effect of each treatment after it is presented. Then, we could ascertain whether different treatments produced different effects. This experimental design is called a *within-subjects design* and is the focus of Chapter 11. At this point, you may be asking, "Why don't we always use a within-subjects design? Wouldn't that be the best way of being certain that subjects getting different treatments were not systematically different from each other?" Perhaps—but it is frequently impossible to give subjects more than one treatment condition of an experiment without creating new problems. Often the effect of one treatment will carry over to the next treatment condition, influencing subjects' behavior in the later treatment condition. Imagine you wanted to conduct an experiment to see whether reaction time was faster to identify photos of famous people who were smiling than photos in which they were frowning. You can't really show both kinds of photos to the same person, because once subjects have seen one photo of the person, the second should be easier to identify regardless of the expression on the famous person's face. Very often, a within-subjects design is simply not feasible for one reason or another, so random assignment to treatment conditions has become one of the cornerstones of most experimentation.

When you were a child, did anyone ever ask you: "Which falls faster, a feather or a rock?" If so, you probably said, "a rock" (as did Aristotle). And of course, you would have been right if the test were made under uncontrolled conditions. Rocks do fall faster than feathers, unless we control the effects of air currents and air resistance by measuring how fast they fall in a vacuum. As Galileo discovered, the acceleration caused by gravity is really the same for all objects.[5]

---

[5] Even if the rock and the feather fell at the same speed, however, the rock would hurt more if it fell on your toe because of its greater mass.

Successful experimentation relies heavily on the principle of *control*. For experimentation to produce valid conclusions, all explanations except the one(s) being tested should be clearly ruled out. Other factors that could be producing the effect we want to explain are carefully controlled. We can achieve the greatest degree of control with experiments that are run in the laboratory where the psychologist can shield subjects from factors that could influence behavior and lead to incorrect conclusions. Some critics have argued, however, that laboratory situations can be artificial and unrealistic and that laboratory results might not be applicable to everyday life. After all, not many rocks fall to earth in a vacuum. We sometimes sacrifice a certain amount of realism and generalizability to gain precision, but control is critical to experimentation.

In experimentation, explaining an event or behavior requires careful control of as many other possible explanations as possible. Control is most often achieved by (1) random assignment of subjects to different treatment conditions (or sometimes by using a within-subjects design), (2) presenting a treatment condition in an identical manner to all subjects, and (3) keeping the environment, the procedures, and the measuring instruments constant for all subjects in the experiment so that the treatment conditions are the only things that are allowed to change. In this way can we be reasonably certain that changes in the treatments are the cause of observed differences in behavior. The principle of control will be an important part of discussions throughout the remainder of the text.

### Establishing Cause and Effect

The greatest value of the psychology experiment is that, within the experiment, we can infer a cause-and-effect relationship between the antecedent conditions and the subjects' behaviors. If the XYZ set of antecedents always leads to a particular behavior, whereas other treatments do not, we can infer that XYZ *causes* the behavior. For example, with all other factors constant, Baron and his colleagues demonstrated that high concentrations of negative ions caused changes in moods. We will discover that many different research methods can be used to study behavior, but only a true experiment allows us to make causal statements. In Chapter 13, however, we will discover that our inferences about cause-and-effect relationships are stated in the form of probabilities—never certainties.

The type of cause-and-effect relationship we establish through experiments is called a *temporal* relationship, because a time difference occurs in the relationship. The treatment conditions come before the behavior, or, stated somewhat differently, the cause precedes the effect. We look for differences in behavior after subjects are exposed to the treatment—not before. If you got differences before the treatments, you would need to look for another cause! We expose subjects to different levels of negative ions, for example, and then we see how they feel. Temporal relationships are built into our experiments. For example, we give subjects various instructions, then we see how they behave. Or, we show children various cartoons, then we observe their play.

Other kinds of relationships can suggest cause and effect, but they are less convincing to the scientist because other potential causal explanations are never completely ruled out. Let's look at examples of two other types of relationships that people use: spatial and logical. A very large and rambunctious Newfoundland dog and a very tiny, but affectionate, Himalayan cat reside with one of the authors. The cat is much more fond of the dog than he is of her. When the dog runs out of patience, he will chase her around the house. One day, the author heard a crash from the living room and ran to see what happened. A prized figurine was in pieces on the floor next to the coffee table, and the cat was sitting on the edge of the table looking down interestedly at the pieces—the cat and the broken figurine had a spatial relationship. Naturally, the author scolded the cat. But was the cat the real culprit? (If so, why was the dog slinking away with his tail between his legs?) Using spatial relationships to infer cause and effect can be compelling—but not always correct.

Sometimes we use logical relationships to establish cause and effect. On another occasion, the same author discovered a small hole in the wall above the sofa. She identified the dog, rather than the cat, as the culprit because of a logical relationship. At about 4:30 every afternoon, the dog sprints at full speed around the house, carrying as many of his prized, wolf-sized, plastic bones as he can fit into his mouth. Running across the sofa is part of this ritual. Most of the time, he runs the course with great agility, but he has been known to run into walls, furniture, or people who happen to be in his way. Logically, then, although other causes might be possible, he seemed the most likely perpetrator.

As we search for cause-and-effect relationships through our research, we generally look for temporal relationships. Of course, the simple fact that one event precedes another is not sufficient, alone, to establish a causal relationship. The Scottish philosopher David Hume (1711–1776) argued that we can never establish causality from temporal relationships. Hume's objections were based on the argument that just because one event precedes another, it does not necessarily mean that the first causes the second. For example, on December 18, 1995, the Dow Jones Industrial Average dropped dramatically (along with other world markets). This event was preceded by an unusual astronomical event, the Sun passing very close to the position of Jupiter. Even so, few people would be willing to believe that stock prices are determined by the position of remote celestial bodies. Many other factors could have had an impact on the economy. The advantage of the experiment in bringing us closer to establishing cause-and-effect relationships is that in the experiment, we control for factors other than those we are testing.

### Necessary versus Sufficient Conditions

As we seek cause-and-effect relationships in science and psychology, we try to identify the conditions under which events will occur. We distinguish between *necessary* and *sufficient* conditions. Cutting down on carbohydrates might be a sufficient condition to produce weight loss. But is it a necessary condition? No. We also could lose weight by increasing our activity level or cutting calories; thus, reducing carbohydrates is not a necessary condition. In contrast, a snowmobile will not run without fuel. Therefore, fuel is a necessary condition for running a snowmobile.

The cause-and-effect relationships established through scientific research commonly involve identifying sufficient conditions. For example, a number of psychological studies have shown that being in a good mood increases our willingness to help others (Isen, 1987). But many other factors (characteristics of the person needing help, the number of other potential helpers, and so on) can also determine whether we will help or not (Latané & Darley, 1970). Being in a good mood is not a necessary condition to increase helpfulness—but it is sufficient.

When we seek causes, we rarely seek conditions that are both necessary and sufficient. To do so would involve a search for the first or primary cause—Cause with a capital C! Given the complexity of our universe, we would make slow progress in our search for order if we refused to settle for anything less than causes that were both necessary and sufficient. Researchers who study helpfulness would probably still be trying to trace the Cause of altruistic behavior—right down to the molecular chain that produces the biochemical changes associated with helping. How that chain got there, the Cause's Cause, would lengthen their search even further. The scientific approach to causality is more practical, relying on sufficient causes as explanations for events.

## FROM PSEUDOSCIENCE TO PSYCHOLOGICAL SCIENCE

Psychology as an experimental science did not emerge until the late 1800s. Wilhelm Wundt (1832–1926), is generally credited with being the first experimental psychologist, and the birth of psychological science is usually dated from the opening of his laboratory in Leipzig, Germany, in 1879. There Wundt employed the tools of the scientific method (observation, measurement, and experimentation) to study human sensory experience. He made great gains in the precise measurement of sensory phenomena by using scientific instruments to calculate how long it took individuals to complete different kinds of sensory and perceptual tasks. As Wundt's fame quickly grew, students from all over the world came to Leipzig to work in his laboratory. One of his first laboratory students was the American psychologist G. Stanley Hall. Hall went on to open the first psychology laboratory in the United States in 1883 at Johns Hopkins University.

As in Europe, early academic psychology in the United States found its home in departments of philosophy under the rubric of *mental philosophy*. Mental philosophy included the study of consciousness and mental processes and was based on the premise that the human mind begins as a blank slate, gaining knowledge of the world through sensory experiences. Mental philosophers were primarily engaged in the study of the five senses through introspection and observation of their own mental processes and observing those

Sidney Harris

FIGURE **1.6**

of others. (Reporting our own thoughts and feelings is called *phenomenology* and will be discussed in Chapter 3.) Mental philosophers were not practitioners of the scientific method and were not much bothered by the fact that the human mind was both the observer and the thing being observed (Haven, 1862).

Despite their methodological and philosophical differences, the mental philosophers and the experimental psychologists found a common adversary in the "pop psychology" of the time. Pseudoscientific practices were very popular during the 1800s, particularly phrenology, physiognomy, mesmerism, and spiritualism (Benjamin, 2007). (The term pseudoscience—*pseudo* is Greek for "false"—characterizes any field of study that gives the appearance of being scientific but has no true scientific basis and has not been confirmed using the scientific method. Box 1.4 takes a brief look at these four pseudoscientific practices.) The popularity of these pseudosciences had largely waned by the early 1900s, but pseudoscientific psychology is still very much alive and well today in the guise of astrology, palmistry, fortune telling, and numerology, all of which claim to be able to assess your personality (and predict your

## BOX **1.4** Pseudoscientific Remedies: Phrenology, Physiognomy, Mesmerism, and Spiritualism

The practice of *phrenology* involved assessing traits and dispositions by measuring the size and location of bumps on the skull. Individual traits, called "faculties," were believed to reside in specific areas in the brain. Overuse of faculties was believed to result in corresponding bumps on the skull, whereas underuse produced cavities or dents. Phrenology clients were counseled to develop underused positive faculties (like benevolence) and to curb overused negative faculties (like destructiveness).

*Physiognomy* involved using facial features, particularly the appearance of the eyes, nose, chin, and forehead, to evaluate traits, mental capacity, and skills. An arch in the upper part of the nose, for example, was believed to indicate fear and voluptuousness. Kindness was indicated in the uppermost part of the middle forehead. Unfortunately, physiognomy also promoted racial stereotypes and, for a time, even influenced criminal profiling and employee selection.

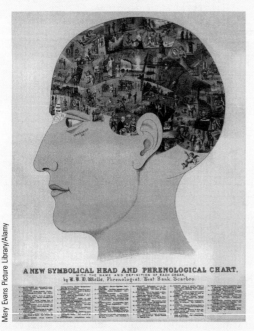

FIGURE **1.7** Phrenology map.

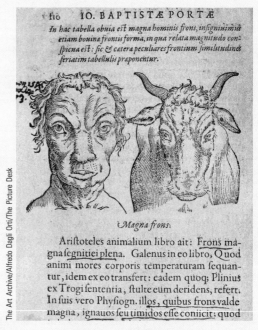

FIGURE **1.8** Physiognomy map.

future). It's quite easy to look around and see many contemporary examples of pseudoscientific psychotherapies (*Hint*: They are not taught in accredited psychology graduate programs.) Past life regression, reparenting, rebirthing, primal scream and other catharsis therapies, neurolinguistic reprogramming, eye movement desensitization therapy, inner child therapy, and alien abduction therapy are some examples of contemporary pseudopsychologies, all claiming to effect dramatic and speedy cures—but without the least bit of scientific evidence.

The pseudoscience of *mesmerism* was invented by an Austrian physician, Franz Mesmer (1734–1815). Mesmer believed that fluids in the body ebbed and flowed by magnetic principles and that both physical and mental illness could be cured by realigning these fluids using magnets, electrodes, or his hands passed across the patient's body. Mesmer later opened a lucrative clinical practice in Paris and produced a few spectacular "cures." In 1784, King Louis XVI appointed a commission (led by Benjamin Franklin) to investigate Mesmer's claims. The commission found no evidence for magnetic forces in body fluids, but mesmerism continued and spread to the United States in the 1830's. In hindsight, it appears that Mesmer and his trainees were most likely inducing a hypnotic state and planting suggestions in the minds of hypnotized patients—and sometimes they worked.

*Spiritualism* involved purported contact with ghosts and spirits of the dead. Acting as mediums, spiritualists held séances in which they claimed to speak with people who had died and provided psychological advice to the relatives of the departed who paid for these services. Even though spiritualism depended on a belief in an afterlife, it was strongly opposed by organized religions. Spiritualism was particularly strong just after the Civil War, when many lives were lost, and enjoyed a brief popularity in 1917–1918 following an influenza epidemic and World War I.

Adapted from: Benjamin, L. T., Jr. (2007) A brief history of modern psychology. Malden, MA: Blackwell Publishing.

Apic/Getty Images

FIGURE **1.9** Franz Mesmer with a patient.

Stock Montage Inc./Alamy Limited

FIGURE **1.10** A séance.

## THE ORGANIZATION OF THE TEXT

As part of your course, you may be required to design and conduct a research project. Writing a research report of your findings may also be a required part of the course. You will find that this text is divided into four major parts: Introduction, Method, Results, and Discussion. These parts parallel both the process of conducting an experiment and the corresponding sections of a research report. Part One, "Introduction," gives an overall orientation to the field of research methods, much as a literature review gives an overall picture of the state of research in a particular content area. Research ethics are covered first. Later chapters focus on descriptive and predictive research designs and prepare you to understand experimentation. This section of the book ends with a chapter on formulating a testable hypothesis. In short, Part One will provide you with all the information you need to begin thinking about an experiment in a particular area and will provide you with report-writing tips along the way.

Part Two, "Method," includes all the basic procedures used in conducting simple experiments, selecting subjects, and collecting data in a scientific way. Part Three, "Results: Coping with Data," reviews the common statistical procedures used to analyze data. Examples are included to help you understand how these procedures are used and what they mean. Computational formulas and statistical tables can be found in Appendices A and B. Part Four, "Discussion," looks at the major issues involved in drawing conclusions from data and communicating the findings. We examine problems of generalizing from a laboratory experiment to the real world. The final chapter on report writing includes information on how each section of a research report is organized and written following the style of APA's most recent *Publication Manual* (6th edition). Appendix C shows what your finished report should look like. Answers to selected Critical Thinking Exercises and Review and Study Questions can be found in Appendix D. Before we begin learning about the research process, though, it is important to understand the ethical principles that apply to all research in psychology—and this is the topic of Chapter 2.

## SUMMARY

Our knowledge of psychological processes is based on scientific evidence accumulated through research, and, as scientists, we rely on *scientific methodology* when we conduct psychological research. The alternative, *commonsense psychology*, is nonscientific and subject to many kinds of errors. Psychological science shares the key features of all modern *science*: an emphasis on gathering observable, objective data and the search for general *laws* or *theories* to organize and explain the relationships among isolated bits of *data*.

The scientific approach requires *good thinking*, thinking that is objective, organized, and rational. Our explanations of behavior should be *parsimonious*—that is, as simple as possible. Scientists constantly engage in self-correction, challenging their findings through tests of new hypotheses. The results of science are communicated through journals and professional meetings, stimulating *replication*. It should be possible for us or others to repeat our procedures and obtain the same findings again.

Psychological science has four major objectives: description, prediction, explanation, and control. The various research methods make different contributions to these objectives. These methods are used in both *applied* and *basic research*. The scientific approach requires observation, measurement, and experimentation. *Observation* is the systematic noting and recording of events. We can only make a scientific study of events that are observable. To make a scientific study of internal processes like feeling and thinking, we must be able to define those events in terms of observable signs. *Measurement* is quantifying an event or behavior according to generally accepted rules. We try to measure in standardized units so that our measurements will be meaningful. We keep our measurements consistent. *Experimentation* is a process undertaken to demonstrate that already observed events will occur consistently under a particular set of conditions. To conduct an experiment, the hypothesis must be *testable*; procedures must be available to test it, and it must be ethical to do so. Objectivity is essential in all phases of the scientific process; we cannot allow our personal feelings or expectations to influence the data we record.

A scientific explanation specifies the *antecedent conditions* of an event or behavior. If we can specify all the circumstances that come before a behavior, we say that we have explained that behavior, and we can expect the same outcome when the same set of antecedents occurs again. In the *psychology experiment*, we create specific sets of antecedents called *treatments*. The psychology experiment is a controlled procedure in which at least two different treatment conditions are applied to research participants, or *subjects*. The subjects' behaviors are then measured and compared so that we can test a hypothesis about the effects of those treatments on behavior. We may also infer a *cause-and-effect relationship* between the antecedent treatment conditions and the subjects' behaviors; we may say that the particular treatment causes the behavior.

Psychological science was born in 1879, when Wilhelm Wundt opened the first psychology laboratory in Germany. He applied the tools of the scientific method to the study of human sensory phenomena. G. Stanley Hall opened the first experimental psychology laboratory in the United States after training with Wundt. In America, psychology joined the discipline of mental philosophy. At that time, several *pseudoscientific* therapies (phrenology, physiognomy, spiritualism, and mesmerism) were very popular with the public—in the same way that people find "pop psychology" compelling today (even though there is no scientific evidence that these pseudopsychologies work).

As psychological scientists, we begin the experimental process with a review of the research literature to suggest a hypothesis about behavior. Next, we design a procedure to test that hypothesis in a systematic way. We use statistical procedures to analyze our observations and to decide whether or not the data support the hypothesis. We then reevaluate our procedures and write a research report of the findings.

## KEY TERMS

Antecedent conditions All circumstances that occur or exist before the event or behavior to be explained; also called *antecedents*.

Applied research Research that is designed to solve real-world problems.

Basic research Research designed to test theories or to explain psychological phenomena.

Cause-and-effect relationship The relation between a particular behavior and a set of antecedents that always precedes it—whereas other antecedents do not—so that the set is inferred to *cause* the behavior.

Commonsense psychology Everyday, nonscientific collection of psychological data used to understand the social world and guide our behavior.

Data Facts and figures gathered from observations in research. (*Data* is the plural form of the Latin word *datum*, so to be correct we say that data *are* gathered rather than that data *is* gathered.)

Empirical data Data that are observable or experienced; capable of being verified or disproved through investigation.

Experimentation The process undertaken to demonstrate that particular behavioral events will occur reliably in certain specifiable conditions; a principal tool of the scientific method.

Good thinking Organized and rational thought, characterized by open-mindedness, objectivity, and parsimony; a principal tool of the scientific method.

Laws General scientific principles that explain our universe and predict events.

Measurement The systematic estimation of the quantity, size, or quality of an observable event; a principal tool of the scientific method.

Methodology The scientific techniques used to collect and evaluate psychological data.

Observation The systematic noting and recording of events; a principal tool of the scientific method.

Parsimony An aspect of good thinking, stating that the simplest explanation is preferred until ruled out by conflicting evidence; also known as Occam's razor.

Pseudoscience A field of study that gives the appearance of being scientific but has no true scientific basis and has not been confirmed using the tools of the scientific method: observation, measurement, and experimentation.

Psychology experiment A controlled procedure in which at least two different treatment conditions are applied to subjects whose behaviors are then measured and compared to test a hypothesis about the effects of the treatments on behavior.

Replication The process of repeating research procedures to verify that the outcome will be the same as before; a principal tool of the scientific method.

Science The systematic gathering of data to provide descriptions of events taking place under specific conditions, enabling researchers to explain, predict, and control events.

Scientific method Steps scientists take to gather and verify information, answer questions, explain relationships, and communicate findings.

Subject The scientific term for an individual who participates in research.

Testable Capable of being tested; typically used in reference to a hypothesis. Three requirements must be met to have a testable hypothesis: procedures for manipulating the setting must exist, and the predicted outcome must be observable and measurable.

Theory A set of general principles that attempts to explain and predict behavior or other phenomena.

Treatment A specific set of antecedent conditions created by the experimenter and presented to subjects to test its effect on behavior.

## REVIEW AND STUDY QUESTIONS

1. Why do we need scientific methods?
2. How can commonsense psychology reduce objectivity when we gather data?
3. Give an example of how you used commonsense psychology in the past week.
4. What are the characteristics of modern science?
5. What do we mean by objectivity? How does objectivity influence observation, measurement, and experimentation?
6. Suppose that a researcher believed that firstborn children have higher IQs than their later-born sisters and brothers because the mother's ova are younger when

firstborns are conceived. This hypothesis would not be testable. Explain why not.

7. How does a psychology experiment demonstrate a cause-and-effect relationship between antecedent conditions and behavior?

8. What do we mean by treatment conditions in an experiment? Why must there be at least two?

9. For each of the following examples, state at least one of the basic tools of psychological science (observation, measurement, experimentation) that have been violated, and explain the correct procedure:

   a. Deanna wanted to do an experiment on gas mileage to see whether the name brands give better mileage. She filled her tank with Fuel-Up one week and with a well-known brand the following week. At the end of that time, she thought things over and said, "Well, I didn't notice much difference between the brands. I filled the car with Fuel-Up on a Tuesday and needed gas again the following Tuesday. It was the same story with the big-name brand, so they must be about the same."

   b. Mike has been telling all his friends that his 3-year-old daughter, Allie, can read. One evening, Mike invites some of his friends over for coffee and offers to give a demonstration of his daughter's remarkable skill. Allie then appears to read a small storybook that Mike keeps on the coffee table. One of the friends is not convinced and asks the little girl to read a page from a different but equally simple storybook. Allie remains silent.

   c. Mike explains Allie's behavior by saying, "She's just shy with strangers."

   d. An author advocates the use of large doses of vitamin C to prolong life. In an interview, he says he has tried this treatment only on himself.

   e. A researcher wanted to compare the effects of a funny cartoon versus a violent cartoon on viewers' moods. She measured mood by observing the body language of her subjects. She couldn't find any systematic differences in mood for the two treatments.

10. Explain why astrology is a pseudoscience rather than a true science.

11. Name and describe each of the four main sections of the experimental report.

## CRITICAL THINKING EXERCISE

*The myth:* When we are angry, it helps to vent our feelings by taking our anger out on inanimate objects, like punching bags or pillows.

*The scientific findings:* Venting our anger by physical aggression actually makes us feel more angry (Bushman, Baumeister, & Stack, 1999).

*Problem 1:* Discuss reasons why the myth may have become a part of our culture.

*Problem 2:* Reality-based talk shows, like the *Jerry Springer Show*, often erupt in violent behavior when angry guests confront each other. Use the scientific findings to predict what effect being on the show might have on these guests at a later time.

## ONLINE RESOURCES

The publisher of your textbook (Wadsworth, part of Cengage Learning) provides online workshops and other resources in the areas of research methods and statistics. You can view the information on the website or download it as a Microsoft Word document:

http://www.wadsworth.com/psycholog_d/templates/student_resources/workshops/workshops.html

A great dictionary for information about all kinds of new-age treatments, activities, and pseudopsychologies—everything from *abracadabra* to *zombies*—is located at:

http://skepdic.com

For an interesting look at an educational organization that takes a scientific look at paranormal phenomena, go to the following site:

http://www.randi.org/

## CHAPTER 2

# Research Ethics

**Research Ethics**
The Evolution of Ethics in Research

**The American Psychological Association Guidelines**
Deception and Full Disclosure
Anonymity and Confidentiality

**Protecting the Welfare of Animal Subjects**
The Animal Rights Movement

**Fraud in Science**

**Plagiarism**

**Ethical Reports**

SUMMARY
KEY TERMS
REVIEW AND STUDY QUESTIONS
ONLINE RESOURCES
CRITICAL THINKING EXERCISE

## CHAPTER OBJECTIVES

- Understand the roles of IRBs and the APA Guidelines in the ethical conduct of research using human participants

- Learn the meaning of animal welfare and how it is protected

- Learn the meaning of animal rights and the views of animal rights activists

- Understand scientific fraud and how to avoid plagiarism

- Become skilled at ethical considerations of research reports

In Chapter 1, we discussed the general concept of objective, data-based science. Science deals with facts, with truth seeking, and with understanding our universe. Science is commonly thought of as amoral; from a scientific point of view, facts discovered through science are neither moral nor immoral—they just happen to exist. As scientists, it is our responsibility to report our findings truthfully (whether we like them or not). Thus, science *per se* does not include values.

As researchers, however, we clearly do bring our own values, ethics, morals, and sense of right and wrong to the work we do. We have to deal with the important ethical and moral questions that arise: Is it right to uncover ways to increase obedience to authority? Is it prudent to investigate techniques that could be used to brainwash people? Do we have the right to perform any experiment imaginable just for the sake of new knowledge? In this chapter, we will focus on the last question. We will discuss the ethics of the researcher's relationship with human and nonhuman subjects and the researcher's responsibilities in every experiment.

---

## RESEARCH ETHICS

The researcher's foremost concern in recruiting and using subjects is treating them ethically and responsibly. Whether we work with animals or humans, we must consider their safety and welfare. Responsible psychological research is not an attempt to satisfy idle curiosity about other people's innermost thoughts and experiences. Rather, responsible research is aimed at advancing our understanding of feelings, thoughts, and behaviors in ways that will ultimately benefit humanity. The well-being of the individual research participant is no less important than the search for knowledge: Research that is harmful to participants is undesirable even though it may increase wisdom. For instance, early experience is an important aspect of child development—but we would not raise children in isolation just to assess the effects of deprivation. There is no way we can justify such a study, no matter how important the knowledge is that we might gain.

A researcher is also legally responsible for what happens to research participants. He or she is liable for any harm to subjects, even if it occurs unintentionally. This means that a researcher might be sued for damages if an experiment hurts someone, whether the injury is physical or psychological, intentional or accidental. To protect the subjects of psychological research, the federal government has formulated legal and ethical guidelines. From a legal standpoint, human participants are protected by a federal law (Title 45, Section 46.106[b]). This law requires each institution that accepts research funding from the Department of Health and Human Services to set up a review committee, called an institutional review board, or IRB, to evaluate proposed studies before they are conducted. Universities and hospitals engaging in research will almost always have an IRB, but many other types of institutions do not. For example, the law does not generally require private organizations, private clinics, or K–12 public school systems to set up an IRB to oversee their research activities.

If you are using this book for a university course, the likelihood is very high that your institution has an IRB and requires IRB approval of studies before they are undertaken; however, some two- and four-year colleges that do not receive federal research dollars do not currently have one, and this can pose serious problems for researchers, because many research journals require that the studies they publish have received IRB approval to assure that the safety of research participants is protected. A number of noninstitutional, "commercial IRBs" also exist across the country, but they are costly and are used mostly to oversee and approve clinical trials sponsored by drug companies or other for-profit industries.

Both laypeople and researchers serve on these committees to guarantee that the views of the general community, as well as those of scientists, are taken into consideration. The primary duty of a review board is to ensure that the safety of research participants is adequately protected (see Box 2.1). The IRB's first task is to decide whether the proposed study puts the subjects at risk. A subject at risk is one who is more likely to be harmed in some way by participating in the research. The IRB must determine whether any risks to the individual are outweighed by potential benefits or the importance of the knowledge to be gained. This is called a risk/benefit analysis. An understanding of research design is critical to such an analysis, and at least some members of a review board must be skilled in research methods. As we will see in the following chapters, there are important differences in the kinds of conclusions that can be drawn from different research designs, and research that is improperly designed has few benefits. Psychologist Robert Rosenthal (1994) has given three important reasons why poorly designed research can be unethical:

1. Students', teachers', and administrators' time will be taken from potentially more beneficial educational experiences.

2. Poorly designed research can lead to unwarranted and inaccurate conclusions that may be damaging to the society that directly or indirectly pays for the research.

3. Allocating time and money to poor-quality science will keep those finite resources from better-quality science.

Another very important task of an IRB is to safeguard the rights of individuals by making certain that each subject at risk gives informed consent to participate. Informed consent means that the subject agrees to participate after having been fully informed about the nature of the study. Several aspects of informed consent are particularly relevant to psychological research. First, individuals must give their consent freely, without the use of force, duress, or coercion. Second, they must be free to drop out of the experiment at any time. Third, researchers must give subjects a full explanation of the procedures to be followed and offer to answer any questions about them. Fourth, researchers must make clear the potential risks and benefits of the experiment. If there is any possibility of pain or injury, researchers must explain this in advance so that subjects know what they are getting into before they agree to participate. Fifth, researchers must provide assurances that all data will remain private and confidential. Finally, according to federal guidelines (45CFR 46.115), subjects may not be asked to release the researchers (or study sponsors, institutions, or other agents) from liability or to waive their legal rights in the case of injury.

Consent should be obtained in writing, and subjects should receive a copy to keep. Whenever the subject is a minor or is cognitively impaired, researchers need to obtain consent from a parent or legal guardian. In these cases, subjects should still be given as much explanation as they can understand and be

---

BOX **2.1**     **A Terrifying Research Experience**

Consider this example of research conducted before the establishment of IRBs and formal ethical guidelines for psychological research. Campbell, Sanderson, and Laverty (1964) established classical conditioning in a single trial using a traumatic event. Classical conditioning, first studied in Pavlov's laboratory, involves the pairing of an initially neutral conditioned stimulus (CS) with an unconditioned stimulus (UCS) that always leads to a specific unconditioned (unlearned) response (UCR). After repeated pairings, the originally neutral conditioned stimulus will lead to a response that resembles the unconditioned response. This response is known as the conditioned response (CR) because its occurrence depends on the success of the conditioning procedure.

Campbell, Sanderson, and Laverty used a drug, succinylcholine chloride dihydrate (Scoline), to induce temporary paralysis and cessation of breathing in their subjects. Although the paralysis and inability to breathe were not painful, according to subjects' reports, the experience was "horrific"; "all the subjects in the standard series thought they were dying" (p. 631). Not surprisingly, the effect of the drug (UCS) led to an intense emotional reaction (UCR). The drug was paired with a tone (CS). Subjects became conditioned to the tone in just one trial. After a single pairing of the tone with the drug, the tone alone was sufficient to produce emotional upset (CR) in most subjects. The emotional reaction persisted (that is, failed to extinguish) and actually increased with repeated presentations of the tone. Would you have wanted to be in this study? Do you think the researchers could have demonstrated classical conditioning in another way?

allowed to refuse to participate, even though the parent or guardian has given permission. The *assent* or agreement of minor children ages 7 and above is usually a requirement of their participation. To the extent possible, assent is also obtained from cognitively impaired subjects, both adults (e.g., adults with Alzheimer's) and children (e.g., children with autism or learning disabilities).

Consent forms need to be written in clear, understandable language at the appropriate reading level for participants. Merely allowing your subjects to read and sign the consent form, however, may not be enough to guarantee that they fully comprehend what they have signed. An interesting experiment by Mann (1994) demonstrated that most subjects retain little information from the consent forms they have signed. Fewer than half of Mann's subjects understood the procedures or what would happen to them in the case of injury. And even though it was explicitly stated in the consent form that subjects were not signing away any of their legal rights, the simple act of signing a consent form made most subjects believe that they had given up their rights to sue. Therefore, to ensure that informed consent is really being obtained, researchers need to verbally reinforce information that is important for subjects. Box 2.2 shows an example of the kind of informed consent form typically used in psychological experiments.

The consent form provides subjects with information relevant to their participation in the experiment: the nature of the experiment, an overview of the procedures that will occur, how long it will take, the potential risks and benefits, and what they will be required to do. The specific hypothesis of the experiment, however, is typically not disclosed on the form. If subjects are made aware of the researcher's expectations, their reactions during the experiment may be unintentionally or intentionally altered by this information. (We will talk about this and other demand characteristics in Chapter 8.) The purpose of informed consent is

---

**BOX 2.2**    **Sample Consent Form for Participation of Undergraduates in Psychological Research**
Informed Consent for Participation in a Research Project

Project title:
Name of investigator:
How to contact the investigator:
You are being asked to volunteer for a research study to investigate [provide details about the nature of the research, a brief description of specific procedures of the study, length of time for participation, and potential risks and benefits].

Your participation in this study is voluntary. If you agree to participate, you are free to withdraw from the study at any point without penalty. All information you provide in this study will be anonymous. Your name will not be linked to your information in any way; instead code numbers will be used. Adequate safeguards will be used to maintain the privacy and confidentiality of all information you provide. When the results of the study are reported, only group results will be described, not individual results.

The experimenter will answer any questions you have about the study before you agree to participate. You will be given a copy of this form to keep. For questions you may have after the study, please contact the investigator listed above. For questions about your rights as a research participant, please contact [include contact information for your institution's IRB]. If you agree to participate in this study, please sign and date the form below in the spaces provided.

_____    _____
(participant's signature)         (date)

to give subjects enough information about the experiment so that they can make an informed decision about whether or not they want to participate.

## The Evolution of Ethics in Research

Scientific research using human subjects has produced many social and intellectual benefits, but it has also generated important ethical questions. After World War II, ethics came to the forefront after the discoveries of brutal experiments conducted on Jewish concentration camp prisoners by about 200 Nazi doctors. According to information provided by the Simon Wiesenthal Center, more than 7,000 prisoners were forced to be subjects in cruel experiments that "broke all the rules and norms of medical research."[1] During international trials that followed the war (the Nuremberg War Crimes Trials), a code of ethical standards for scientific research was created. This Nuremberg Code of 1947 formed the basis of today's ethical standards. In 1974, the National Commission for the Protection of Human Subjects of Biomedical and Behavioral Research was created as part of the U.S. National Research Act. In 1979, the U.S. Department of Health, Education, and Welfare issued the Belmont Report, a statement of government policy on research involving human subjects. The Belmont Report contains three basic ethical principles—respect for persons, beneficence, and justice.

The first, *respect for persons*, maintains that every human being is an autonomous person with the right to make his or her own decisions about research. Respect for persons also provides extra protections for vulnerable populations (those who are economically or educationally disadvantaged, prisoners, or pregnant women) and individuals with diminished capacity (children or cognitively impaired persons) while respecting their self-determination to the greatest extent possible. The notion of informed consent comes from the principle of respect for persons.

The second principle, *beneficence*, refers to an obligation to minimize risk of harm and maximize possible benefits to individuals. Thus, beneficence forms the basis for the risk/benefit analysis at the core of IRB approval. Beneficence, however, refers to society as well as to individuals. At times, the potential for risk to human subjects must be weighed against possible benefits the research could provide for society. The principle of beneficence also refers to each researcher's responsibility to estimate potential risks as truthfully and accurately as possible before proposing any research. See Box 2.3 for a classic example of this principle in action.

*Justice*, the final principle, refers to fairness in both the burdens and benefits of research. Before the mid-20th century, most research was conducted on patients in hospital wards, while the benefits gained went largely to the wealthy. This is an example of injustice. Another example is the Tuskegee syphilis study, which used poor, rural black men to study the effects of syphilis when it remains untreated. The infected men never received treatment even though penicillin had been discovered as a cure for the disease. This was unjust because the

---

[1] Retrieved from http://motlc.wiesenthal.com/index.html on June 20, 2007.

BOX **2.3**　　**When Beneficence Goes Awry**

One famous study, the Stanford prison experiment (Haney & Zimbardo, 1973), is often used to illustrate the importance of the principle of *beneficence*— minimizing harm and maximizing benefits. You may recall learning about this experiment in your introductory psychology course. The volunteer subjects were healthy, normal young men who were randomly assigned to play the role of either a prisoner or a guard in a mock prison constructed in the basement of the Stanford University psychology building. Even though the prison study was approved by the university's IRB, the researchers ended it ahead of time because the treatment of the prisoner subjects by the guards became more and more abusive as the guards and prisoners increasingly began to live out their roles. In this instance, the true power of putting people in this kind of situation, even when they were simply playing a role, was not foreseen in advance, either by the researchers or by the IRB.

The researchers predicted that putting people in positions of complete authority would cause the guards to act aggressively toward their helpless prisoners, but the extent to which the prisoners were mistreated, degraded, and humiliated was not anticipated. Zimbardo (2004) put it this way:

> In 1971, I designed a dramatic experiment that would extend over a two-week period to provide our research participants with sufficient time for them to become fully engaged in their experimentally assigned roles of either guards or prisoners. Having participants live in that setting day and night, if prisoners, or work there for long 8-hour shifts, if guards, would also allow sufficient time for situational norms to develop and patterns of social interaction to emerge, change and become crystallized. The second feature of this study was to ensure that all research participants would initially be as normal as possible, healthy physically and mentally, and without any history of being involved in drugs or crime or violence....
>
> Pacifist young men were behaving sadistically in their role of guards, inflicting humiliation and pain and suffering on other young men if they had the inferior human status of prisoner. Some guards even reported they were enjoying doing

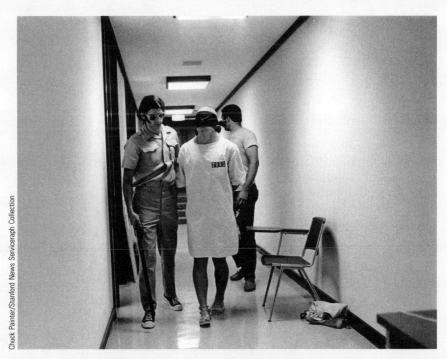

FIGURE **2.1** A photo taken during the experiment.

Chuck Painter/Stanford News Serviceraph Collection

BOX **2.3**    (continued)

so. Others, who had been intelligent, healthy college students were behaving pathologically, many having "emotional breakdowns," as in stress disorders, so extreme that five of them had to be terminated within that first week. Their fellow prisoners who adapted better to the situation were those who mindlessly followed orders, became blindly obedient to authority, who allowed the guards to dehumanize and degrade them ever more with each passing day and night....

I terminated the experiment not only because of the escalating level of violence and degradation by the guards against the prisoners that was apparent when viewing the video tapes of their interactions, but also because I was made aware of the personal transformation that I was undergoing personally ... I had become a Prison Superintendent, the second role I played in addition to that of Principal Investigator. I began to talk, walk and act like a rigid institutional authority figure more concerned about the security of "my prison" than the needs of the young men entrusted to my care as a psychological researcher. In a sense, I consider that the most profound measure of the power of this situation was the extent to which it transformed me.

Finally, we had extended debriefing sessions of guards and prisoners at the end of the study, and

for periodic checkups over many years. Fortunately, there were no negative lasting consequences of this powerful experience.... (pp. 38–40)

It has been argued that the study produced benefits by increasing our knowledge of the power of extreme situations to produce evil behavior, but the lesson from this study has not been universally learned. Even worse abuses were produced in real life in the Abu Ghraib prison in Iraq. At Abu Ghraib, Arab prisoners were videotaped being stripped and humiliated, and worse, by U.S. military guards, who, like the guards in the Stanford prison experiment, believed that they were acting appropriately. According to Zimbardo, who provided expert testimony at the trials resulting from the abuses at Abu Ghraib,

the same social psychological processes—deindividualization, anonymity of place, dehumanization, role-playing and social modeling, moral disengagement and group conformity—that acted in the Stanford Prison Experiment were at play at Abu Ghraib. (Dittmann, 2004, p. 3)

Excerpted from: Zimbardo, P. G., (2004). A situationist perspective on the psychology of evil: Understanding how good people are transformed into perpetrators. In A. Miller (Ed.), *The social psychology of good and evil: Understanding our capacity for kindness and cruelty.* New York: Guilford.

disease clearly affected people other than poor, black men, but these men were the only individuals subjected to this cruel and unethical test (see Figure 2.2).

The principle of justice requires that researchers select their samples of subjects with an eye toward fairness, to ensure that some people are not being selected simply because they are disadvantaged, readily available, or easily manipulated. Justice means that research subjects should come from the groups most likely to reap the benefits.

## THE AMERICAN PSYCHOLOGICAL ASSOCIATION GUIDELINES

Although the law contains specific provisions for the way research is to be conducted, questions may still arise in actual situations. For this reason, the American Psychological Association (APA) publishes its own set of ethical standards (2002).[2]

---

[2] The current (2002) guidelines are the third revision of the original APA guidelines published in 1971. The first APA committee on ethics was set up in 1952, but the society did not begin wide discussions for a formal code until 1966.

FIGURE **2.2** A subject in the Tuskegee syphilis study.
Department of Health Education and Welfare. Public Health Service. Health Services and Mental
Health Administration. Center for Disease Control. Venereal Disease Branch (1970–1973)/National
Archives

The code applies to psychologists and students who assume the role of psychologists by engaging in research or practice. Psychologists conducting research are responsible for maintaining ethical standards in all research conducted by them or by others they supervise. When submitting an article for publication in journals published by either APA or APS, researchers are required to stipulate that these ethical standards have been followed. The APA standards include the same general requirements for ensuring subjects' welfare as those that are set forth in civil law.

Whenever a question arises about the ethics of an experiment or procedure, the researcher should seek advice from an IRB or from colleagues and employ all possible safeguards for the research participants. The standards also require IRB approval of each study before it is performed.[3] Keep in mind that even after procedures have been approved, the individual researcher has the final responsibility for following the guidelines and carrying out the study in an ethical way. Obtaining informed consent is considered especially important.

Fully informed consent is required from all participants who are at risk because of the nature of the research. In some cases, participants are considered to be at minimal risk. The law defines minimal risk as "risk that is no

---

[3] Check with your instructor to clarify the procedures that apply in your institution. In some cases, research that is conducted as part of classroom activities does not require IRB approval, but you must always obtain approval for an experiment from your instructor or review board before you begin.

greater in probability and severity than that ordinarily encountered in daily life or during the performance of routine physical or psychological examinations or tests" (Title 45, Section 46.102[g]). Basically, this means that the research does not alter the participants' odds of being harmed. For example, a study of what proportion of the population uses soap and water to wash their hands in a public restroom would be considered minimal risk research; the participants are engaging in a public activity in a public place. Whether or not their behavior is recorded as part of a study is unlikely to affect them in any way. There is a small chance they could be injured during the study (for example, by falling on a slippery floor), but the research does not increase the chances of this happening. Even in minimal risk studies, the researcher has the responsibility of identifying any potential risks and minimizing them before conducting the research.

Observations of public behavior, anonymous questionnaires, and certain kinds of archival research (discussed in Chapters 3 and 4) fall into the minimal risk category. Informed consent is not always mandatory in minimal risk research. As a safeguard, however, it is usually desirable to obtain informed consent whenever possible, and many institutions require written documentation of informed consent as a matter of course in *all* research using human subjects. Personal health information and medical records are now protected under the Health Insurance Portability and Accountability Act (HIPAA, 2003; 45 CFR Parts 160 and 164), and data from medical records may not be used for research purposes without written authorization from potential research participants. The APA standards for informed consent are reprinted in Box 2.4. The responsibilities of both subject and experimenter must be

---

## BOX 2.4    APA Standard 3.11: Informed Consent to Research*

a. When obtaining informed consent as required in Standard 3.10, Informed Consent, psychologists inform participants about (1) the purpose of the research, expected duration, and procedures; (2) their right to decline to participate and to withdraw from the research once participation has begun; (3) the foreseeable consequences of declining or withdrawing; (4) reasonably foreseeable factors that may be expected to influence their willingness to participate such as potential risks, discomfort, or adverse effects; (5) any prospective research benefits; (6) limits of confidentiality; (7) incentives for participation; and (8) whom to contact for questions about the research and research participants rights. They provide opportunity for the prospective participants to ask questions and receive answers.

b. Psychologists conducting intervention research involving the use of experimental treatments

clarify to participants at the outset of the research (1) the experimental nature of the treatment; (2) the services that will or will not be available to the control group(s) if appropriate; (3) the means by which assignment to treatment and control groups will be made; (4) available treatment alternatives if an individual does not wish to participate in the research or wishes to withdraw once a study has begun; and (5) compensation for or monetary costs of participating including, if appropriate, whether reimbursement from the participant or a third-party payer will be sought.

*From "Ethical Principles of Psychologists and Code of Conduct," 2002, *American Psychologist, 57*(12), 1060–1073. Copyright ©2002 American Psychological Association. Reprinted with permission.

agreed upon in advance, and the experimenter must honor all commitments made to subjects. Commitments include promises to pay subjects, to give them credit in courses, to maintain confidentiality, and to share the results of the study with them.

## Deception and Full Disclosure

The relationship between researcher and participants should be as open and honest as possible. In some psychological studies, however, the true purpose of the study is disguised. Sieber and her colleagues (Sieber, Iannuzzo, & Rodriguez, 1995) evaluated the contents of all 1969, 1978, 1986, and 1992 issues of *Journal of Personality & Social Psychology*, looking for use of deception. According to this research, the percentage of deception in 1969 was 66%; in 1978, it was 47%; in 1986, it dropped to 32%; and in 1992, it increased again to 47%. Remember the negative ion study (Baron, Russell, & Arms, 1985) described in the first chapter? Besides merely testing the effects of different levels of ionization on subjects' moods, the researchers wanted to know if different levels of negative ions also would affect aggressive behavior—as the seasonal winds are believed to do. To test this hypothesis in the kind of controlled laboratory conditions necessary to manipulate ion levels, they needed to use deception to create a situation where aggressiveness could occur and where they could measure it systematically. Parts of their experimental procedures were based on the famous laboratory studies of obedience conducted in the 1960s and 1970s by Stanley Milgram (1963, 1974). To review the Milgram experiments and the controversy surrounding Milgram's use of deception, you can explore the online resources at the end of this chapter.

To create a situation in which aggressiveness could occur, Baron, Russell, and Arms enlisted the help of a *confederate* (in this case, a student accomplice). When one of the male subjects showed up for a session, the confederate was already there, posing as another subject. The experimenter explained that the experiment involved learning to decrease heart rate using biofeedback. One subject was to be the "teacher," the other the "learner." They drew slips of paper to select roles—but the drawing was rigged, and the subject was always the teacher. During the "training session," the learner made mistakes. Every time he made a mistake, the teacher was supposed to punish him by pushing a button on a machine that (supposedly) sent an unpleasant, but not dangerous, burst of heat to a cuff on the learner's wrist. The 10 buttons on the machine were labeled from very low to very intense, and the teacher was told to select any level he wanted. During the course of the session, the teacher had 20 opportunities to punish (i.e., display aggression toward) the learner. Of course, no real heat was ever delivered in this experiment, even though subjects believed that they were punishing the learner. The intensity levels selected by each subject, however, were recorded. (In addition, you will recall, this confederate angered half the subjects. Before the "learning" trials began, he provoked the real subject through a series of scripted nasty comments. These, of course, were part of the deception, too.) The entire ruse was thoroughly explained to each subject at the end of the session.

How do research subjects feel about being deceived in this way? A number of studies have been conducted to determine the answer to this question.

In a review of these studies, Christensen (1988) reports that most research subjects are apparently not bothered by deception. This review of the literature, which attempted to document the impact of deception on research participants, found that research participants do not perceive that they are harmed and do not seem to mind being misled. Soliday and Stanton reached similar conclusions in a more recent experiment (1995). Christensen (1988) also reports that evidence suggests that deception experiments are actually perceived by subjects to be more enjoyable and more beneficial than nondeception experiments, and, apparently, research professionals are much more bothered by deception than subjects are. The consensus among researchers seems to be that the use of deception is most often justified by the knowledge that is gained (Suls & Rosnow, 1988). Many important psychological problems cannot be studied without the use of deception, and it may be argued, as Christensen has, that failing to study important problems is even less justifiable. The standards covering the use of deception are shown in Box 2.5.

Sometimes a small omission, or outright deception, is necessary to make an appropriate test of the experimental hypothesis. How can this be reconciled with the principles of informed consent? The answer is that the deception must not influence a subject's decision to take part in the research—any deception that is used must be such that subjects would not refuse to participate if they knew what was really happening. For instance, it would not be ethical to recruit subjects for a learning experiment without telling them that we intend to punish their incorrect responses by exposing them to the sound of scratching nails on a blackboard. Because many subjects might decline to participate in such a study, our deception would be unethical. In contrast, as far as we know, Baron and colleagues' subjects would probably have consented to participate in the experiment even if they knew that they were not really punishing the "learner's" errors. Furthermore, the researchers adhered to the principle of full disclosure by completely debriefing subjects at the end of the experiment—that is, explaining the true nature and purpose of the study.

---

### BOX 2.5    APA Standard 8.07: Deception in Research*

a. Psychologists do not conduct a study involving deception unless they have determined that the use of deceptive techniques is justified by the study's significant prospective scientific, educational, or applied value and that effective nondeceptive alternative procedures are not feasible.

b. Psychologists do not deceive prospective participants about research that is reasonably expected to cause physical pain or severe emotional distress.

c. Psychologists explain any deception that is an integral feature of the design and conduct of an experiment to participants as early as is feasible, preferably at the conclusion of their participation, but no later than the conclusion of the data collection, and permit participants to withdraw their data.

*From "Ethical Principles of Psychologists and Code of Conduct," 2002, *American Psychologist*, 57(12), 1060–1073. Copyright ©2002 American Psychological Association. Reprinted with permission.

Even if subjects are debriefed, will the explanation completely undo the effects of deception? Perhaps not. Bramel's (1963) study of projection is an example of an experiment in which debriefing might have been insufficient. Bramel was interested in studying attributive projection, which is the process of projecting our own traits onto another person. The traits projected are traits the person is consciously aware of having, making this phenomenon different from the classical projection that Freud described. (In classical projection, the traits projected are those the person is *not* consciously aware of possessing.) To ensure that subjects were aware of possessing a trait they might project, Bramel employed a procedural deception. Male subjects were shown photographs of men in various stages of nudity. Subjects were given false feedback about their degree of sexual arousal to the pictures, which led them to believe they possessed homosexual tendencies. Bramel then tested the subjects for projection of sexual arousal onto others. He asked them to estimate how aroused other men would be when they saw the pictures. Bramel found that subjects projected sexual arousal onto men who were similar to themselves (other male students) but not onto men who were unlike themselves (criminals).

Of course, Bramel debriefed all his subjects at the end of the experiment. He told them the feedback had been false and that there was really no indication that they had become sexually aroused by the pictures—because this was never even measured. But was the explanation sufficient? It is possible that for subjects who had doubts about their sexual identity—remember, this study was published in 1963—the bogus feedback probably aroused considerable anxiety and discomfort. It is also possible that subjects may have doubted Bramel's final full disclosure. If he admitted deceiving them about the feedback, perhaps he was also deceiving them about their real responses. At the very least, subjects may have felt somewhat foolish at having been duped by the experimenter. Whether the effects of deception can ever be fully reversed by debriefing remains a serious ethical question. Regardless of any later explanation, the subjects' anxiety and discomfort during the experiment were real. Once done, these experiences cannot be undone.

We cannot always reverse our experimental effects, so it makes sense to avoid using procedures that are potentially harmful, painful, or upsetting to subjects whenever possible. In addition to their dubious ethical standing, such procedures often add little to our understanding of behavioral processes. For instance, we already know that high anxiety has debilitating effects on many behaviors. What would it add to our understanding of the thinking process to find that subjects learn nursery rhymes or solve riddles less efficiently after they are made extremely afraid by a noxious laboratory procedure?

Some kinds of important research will have unavoidably negative consequences for subjects (because negative consequences are precisely the effect being investigated). In cases like this, special steps need to be taken to remove any harmful effects. Experiments on the effects of violent pornography are a good example. When subjects, typically male undergraduates, are exposed to high levels of violent pornography in psychology experiments, they become more accepting of the "rape myth" than nonexposed men are (Donnerstein, Linz, & Penrod, 1987). Subjects exposed to the pornography are more likely to report callous attitudes toward women, as reflected in such statements as "Women really want to be raped." They are also more likely to say that they would consider raping a woman if they knew they would not be caught. Unfortunately, once established, these attitudes do not seem to disappear quickly on their own. Researchers discovered that a simple debriefing at the end of the experiment was not enough to erase the negative effects. Instead, extensive postexperimental debriefings that detail the unreality of the themes and images in violent pornography are necessary to remove the harmful beliefs created by the films. Misra (1992) found that including education about the persistence of false beliefs in a debriefing can also help subjects to modify erroneous beliefs.

### Anonymity and Confidentiality

Maintaining anonymity and confidentiality is another important consideration for researchers. It is our responsibility to protect the privacy of research participants. Whenever possible, data should be collected anonymously and identified by code numbers or fictitious names. In actual practice, we do not need to identify subjects by name—most psychological research uses aggregated or group data and reports statistical results as average scores for each treatment group. Also, data must be stored in a secure place, kept confidential, and used only for purposes explained to the subject. Subjects' reactions in experiments do not become items of gossip to be shared with friends. When shared with colleagues, data must also be treated with discretion and subjects' identities protected. Other identifying details are also disguised if there is a chance that a subject will be recognizable. Achieving the goals of anonymity and confidentiality are a serious challenge for researchers using the Internet to conduct research online (see Box 2.6).

## PROTECTING THE WELFARE OF ANIMAL SUBJECTS

The principles governing informed consent, debriefing, anonymity, and confidentiality are clearly important aspects of ethical research involving human participants. Other standards protect animal welfare—the humane care and treatment of animals. The care and treatment of animals in research is regulated by the Animal Welfare Act of 1966, which deals with general standards for animal care. Congress amended the act (*Federal Register*, February 15, 1991) to include new regulations that address the psychological well-being of higher animals. It requires, for example, that researchers enrich the environment of nonhuman primates by including means for engaging in species-typical activities. Enrichment includes such things as perches, swings, mirrors, objects that can be manipulated, foraging or task-oriented feeding methods, and interaction with human caregivers (see Figure 2.3). Primates and other animals known to live in social groups in nature must be provided with opportunities to socialize, either by being housed with other compatible

BOX **2.6**   **Ethical Problems in Online Research**

The spread of online research will change the way psychologists conduct research in the future. The Internet provides an inexpensive natural laboratory that allows researchers to collect vast amounts of data with very little involvement from experimenters. As an example, Nosek, Banaji, and Greenwald (2002) collected more than 2 1/2 million responses in tests of attitudes. In addition to economic savings and easy access to experimental subjects, psychologists can study interesting phenomena that only exist online or are difficult to study in more traditional locations. Clearly, Internet research is the direction of the future, but ethicists have serious concerns about protecting the anonymity and confidentiality of subjects of online research.

Anonymity can be easily protected in online surveys by simply not collecting identifying data. When studying online behaviors, however, it is more difficult to ensure that responses cannot be retrieved by hackers. Entries in online diaries or an online forum can be traced back to the individual by using Internet search engines. Even pseudonyms are not a guarantee of privacy, as posters can easily give away their identity by using part of their name in the pseudonym or by posting text that identifies them (Bassett & O'Riordan, 2002). "Sniffing" programs can locate data that is in transit, and hackers can gain access to data stored on a networked computer. The precautions that researchers need to implement are in direct proportion to the sensitivity of the data being collected, but whenever possible, identifying information should be retained separately from responses, or data should be encrypted.

Another ethical problem arises when considering informed consent. IRBs can waive written documentation of informed consent for certain kinds of minimal risk research, but that does not mean that informed consent should not be obtained before collecting data from online subjects. Instead of a written consent form, subjects can be given the same consent information that they would get in other kinds of research settings, and to ensure that they have seen the information, they should be able to click a button to accept and agree to participate. Debriefing subjects can be another ethical problem area. Debriefing materials can be posted on a website or researchers can create a "leave the study" button or pop-up that comes up when subjects leave the study. Ethically, however, unless researchers can guarantee that subjects will be appropriately debriefed, deception experiments probably should not be conducted online.

Creating appropriate safeguards like those discussed earlier for obtaining consent and protecting anonymity and confidentiality will probably provide enough protection for low-risk research on adult subjects. Research that places adults at a greater risk, however, or research using children or vulnerable populations may not be appropriate for the Internet.

Adapted from Kraut, R., Olson, J., Banaji, M., Bruckman, A., Cohen, J., & Couper, M. (2004). Psychological research online: Report of board of scientific affairs' advisory group on the conduct of research on the Internet. *American Psychologist*, *59*(2), 105–117.

members of their species or having other opportunities for social interaction with them. In the case of dogs, for example, another species that forms social bonds, the act requires that they be housed with other compatible dogs or, if that isn't practical, then they must receive positive physical contact (e.g., petting) from humans every day as well as opportunities to exercise and play.

As is the case with research using human subjects, institutions engaged in animal research must have a review board, called an institutional animal care and use committee (IACUC), to evaluate animal research before it can be conducted. As in the case of IRBs, the committee must be comprised of scientists and laypersons, but, in addition, IACUCs must also include a veterinarian with expertise in animal laboratory science. Federal regulations stipulate that before animal experimentation can be approved, all possible alternatives to

Mitsuaki Iwago/Minden Pictures/Getty Images

FIGURE **2.3** A close relationship can develop between researchers and their nonhuman subjects.

the use of animals must be carefully considered. The IACUC must determine that the researchers have appropriately researched alternatives and have provided written documentation that no other alternatives are feasible.

Several professional organizations around the country encourage ongoing monitoring of care of laboratory animals through self-policing by members of the scientific community. The American Association for Laboratory Animal Science (AALAS), for example, publishes detailed training manuals that include information on adequate housing, sanitation, and nutrition for all animals used in research. The American Association for Accreditation of Laboratory Animal Care (AAALAC) also promotes uniform standards. AAALAC uses the National Academy of Science's (1996) *Guide for the Care and Use of Laboratory Animals* as its principal set of guidelines. That publication provides specific standards for cage sizes, food and bedding, waste disposal, ventilation, drugs and anesthesia, and many other aspects of animal care. The guide also addresses issues of training, safety, and sanitation for the benefit of animal handlers working in the labs. APA's Committee on Animal Research and Ethics (CARE) has been influential in establishing national guidelines for animal welfare and includes standards for animal care among its ethical principles (see Box 2.7).

As with human participants, our concern about animal welfare includes avoiding any unnecessary pain or risk. Research involving any potentially painful procedure such as surgery, drug use, or shock must be closely supervised by a researcher specially trained in the procedures and monitored by

BOX **2.7**    **APA Standard 8.09: Humane Care and Use of Animals in Research***

a. Psychologists acquire, care for, use, and dispose of animals in compliance with current federal, state, and local laws and regulations, and with professional standards.

b. Psychologists trained in research methods and experienced in the care of laboratory animals supervise all procedures involving animals and are responsible for ensuring appropriate consideration of their comfort, health, and humane treatment.

c. Psychologists ensure that all individuals under their supervision who are using animals have received instruction in research methods and in the care, maintenance, and handling of the species being used, to the extent appropriate to their role.

d. Psychologists make reasonable efforts to minimize the discomfort, infection, illness, and pain of animal subjects.

e. Psychologists use a procedure subjecting animals to pain, stress, or privation only when an alternative procedure is unavailable and the goal is justified by its prospective scientific, educational, or applied value.

f. Psychologists perform surgical procedures under appropriate anesthesia and follow techniques to avoid infection and minimize pain during and after surgery.

g. When it is appropriate that the animal's life be terminated, psychologists proceed rapidly, with an effort to minimize pain, and in accordance with accepted procedures.

*From "Ethical Principles of Psychologists and Code of Conduct," 2002, *American Psychologist, 57*(12), 1060–1073. Copyright ©2002 American Psychological Association. Reprinted with permission.

the research facility's veterinarian. Despite the existence of legal and ethical guidelines, some critics have argued that animals have been abused in some psychological studies—a violation of ethical principles. In his book *Animal Liberation* (1975), Peter Singer chronicled numerous cases of animal abuse. Many of the examples dealt with studies involving electric shock or food deprivation. (However, an even greater portion of the book dealt with the treatment of animals being raised for food or used to test consumer products.) Let's look at one of Singer's examples.

This case comes from the work of Joseph V. Brady (1958). For several years, Brady studied the emotional behavior of rhesus monkeys. The monkeys were kept in restraining chairs that allowed them to move their heads and limbs but not their bodies (see Figure 2.4). They were placed in the chairs so that they could be trained through various conditioning procedures involving electric shock. The experimental setup, according to Brady, seemed to be highly stressful for the animals. Many of them died during the preliminary study. Autopsies showed that many of the dead subjects had developed ulcers, which are unusual in laboratory animals. Restraint alone was not the explanation; some animals had been kept in the restraining chairs for 6 months, received no shock, and did not develop ulcers. Therefore, in subsequent work Brady explored the effect of the conditioning procedures. He trained two monkeys, designating one an executive and one a control. Both monkeys were given brief shocks on the feet. However, the executive monkey could prevent shock by pressing a lever. Unless the executive acted appropriately, it (and its partner, the control monkey) would be shocked on the feet once every 20 seconds.

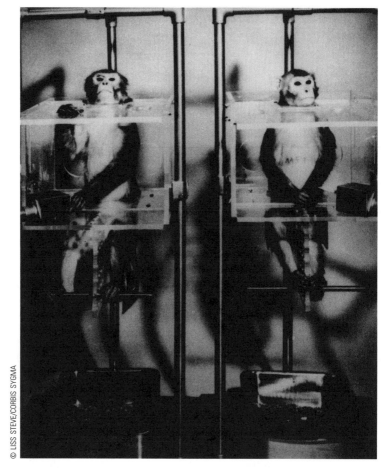

© LISS STEVE/CORBIS SYGMA

FIGURE **2.4** Rhesus monkeys being kept in restraining chairs.

The monkeys were exposed to alternating 6-hour periods of shock avoidance and rest (no shock). This procedure continued for 23 days, after which the executive monkey collapsed and was sacrificed. Subsequent experiments were conducted with different pairs of monkeys and with different time intervals.

There are several ethical objections to this line of research. First, the use of the restraining chairs alone is probably extremely distressing to the animals. (Bear in mind that some animals spent 6 months in these chairs.) Second, the use of electric shock concerns many critics of animal research. Brady's original article (1958) does not include the specific level of shock used in the experiment. We are told that the shocks were brief, but most of us try to avoid electric shock of any magnitude, no matter how brief. Monkeys apparently share this preference because they quickly learn to work to avoid shock. Third, ethical objections also can be raised because the study was poorly designed. Brady's findings were of diminished benefit because of

TABLE **2.1**

Accusations of animal abuses by psychologists and the percentage of articles in which such treatments and/or results were reported

| Allegation | Percentage of Articles in Which Reported |
|---|---|
| "Animals are given intense repeated electric shocks which they cannot escape, until they lose the ability to even scream in pain any longer." | 0.0% |
| "They are deprived of food and water to suffer and die slowly from hunger and thirst." | 0.0% |
| "They are put in total isolation chambers until they are driven insane, or even die, from despair and terror." | 0.0% |
| "They are subjected to crushing forces which smash their bones and rupture their internal organs." | 0.0% |
| "Their limbs are mutilated or amputated to produce behavioral changes." | 0.0% |
| "They are the victims of extreme pain and stress, inflicted upon them out of idle curiosity, in nightmarish experiments designed to make healthy animals psychotic." | 0.0% |

Note: Adapted from "How Radical Animal Activists Try to Mislead Humane People," by D. C. Coile and N. E. Miller, *American Psychologist*, 1984, 39, 700–701.

a bias in the way the executive and control monkeys were selected in the experiment. (We will return to this issue in Chapter 9.) Thus, in this case, Singer's criticisms were probably justified—although, in fairness, it should be pointed out that Brady's work predates the ethical guidelines that currently apply to research psychologists.

Psychologists Coile and Miller (1984) conducted a study to evaluate allegations of animal abuse. They reviewed all 608 articles reporting animal research that appeared in the major psychology journals between 1979 and 1983. Table 2.1 summarizes a portion of their findings. Overall, the psychology research literature for this 5-year period simply does not support the claims of extreme critics like Singer. Although shock and food deprivation were used in some studies, the manipulations were by no means as extreme as reported by the critics of animal research. In fact, not a single one of the specific extreme allegations was supported by the literature. Shock was used in 10% of the studies; inescapable shocks stronger than 0.001 ampere[4] were used in 3.9% of all the studies and in just 0.2% of the studies involving monkeys, dogs, or cats. The

---

[4] "A strength that most experimenters can easily endure on their fingers" (Coile & Miller, 1984, p. 700).

longest period of food or water deprivation reported was 48 hours. Less than 1% of the deprivation studies left animals without food or water for more than 24 hours; most used 24 hours of deprivation, which corresponds to feeding once a day as recommended for many house pets.

Nor were any studies done out of idle curiosity, as critics had alleged. As Coile and Miller (1984) noted,

> Experiments involving inescapable shock ... were aimed at understanding mechanisms believed likely to be involved in human depression, a condition that often causes its victims such intense suffering that they are driven to suicide. For young adults, suicide is the third leading cause of death. (p. 700)

Abuses do occur occasionally, but they are by no means encouraged or condoned by most psychological researchers.

## The Animal Rights Movement

The basic premise of the APA guidelines for animal research is that animal research is acceptable to further the understanding of behavioral principles and to promote the welfare of humans.[5] Even so, the position that the best interests of humans should automatically take precedence over the rights of animals is hotly debated (Shapiro, 1997). Some of the most vocal critics of animal research have been advocates of the concept of animal rights—the idea that all sensate species, particularly those that feel pain, are of equal value and have equal rights.

The essence of this debate was highlighted on October 26, 1984, when the heart of a healthy baboon was transplanted into a dying newborn baby. Do humans have the right to take the life of another animal to prolong the life of a human being? Most of us, consciously or not, make the decision that we do have that right. We decide yes every time we eat a steak or a drumstick (Regan, 1983). We also decide yes every time we open a can or a bag of pet food (Herzog, 1991). (See Box 2.8 for an interesting ethical dilemma regarding pets.) Although we might not want to give up our pets or become vegetarians, we may still question whether animals suffer needlessly. Singer made a strong case for this point of view. Other writers have shared his opinion:

> Many research projects are pointless, gratuitously repetitive, fatally flawed, or concerned with the obvious or the trivial. If animal suffering is of any significance whatsoever, its infliction can only be justified for clearly defined goals. But many experiments are ill-conceived or actually unconceived in that no hypothesis has been formulated before conducting the experiment. One or a very few repetitions of an experiment may be needed to confirm the results, but some experiments are repeated time and again with no epistemological[6] justification. (Miller & Williams, 1983, p. 326)

---

[5] Keehn (1977) noted that many animal studies benefit animals too. Animal research has resulted in vaccines for serious animal diseases such as rabies and feline leukemia, and animal behavior research has provided ways to help save endangered species (Miller, 1984).

[6] *Epistemological* refers to the gathering of knowledge.

BOX **2.8**   **Cloning Nine Lives (plus One)**

For $50,000, you can buy a clone of your cat, claims Genetic Savings & Clone, based in California. Cc (for carbon copy), their first cloned cat, was born in 2001. Cc does not look exactly like its DNA donor, Rainbow, a female calico (with gray, tan, orange, and white fur). Cc's fur is gray-striped and white. Cc is also slimmer and has a more playful and curious temperament, but the two cats have identical DNA.* According to Genetic Savings & Clone, five pet owners have already signed up to clone their pet cats. Eventually, the price of cat cloning is expected to drop to about $10,000. Genetic Savings & Clone believes that cloning pets is ethical. Stephanie Shain of the

Humane Society disagrees. She states that it is "irresponsible to duplicate an animal when we are euthanizing happy, healthy animals because there aren't homes for them." What do you think?

*The genetics of cat colors, particularly calicos, is complicated. For example, Rainbow's orange color was not expressed in Cc because orange is the result of a sex-linked gene with a random variation (sometimes it shows up; sometimes it doesn't). Interestingly, cat colors are also influenced by environmental factors such as womb position and nutrition.

Adapted from "Cloning Nine Lives + One by Karen Breslau, appearing in *Newsweek*, May 3, 2004, p. 11.

Texas A&M University/Getty Images

FIGURE **2.5** Cc and her surrogate mother, Rainbow.

In June 1990, 24,000 people attended the "March for Animals" rally in Washington, D.C. In a survey of 574 activists attending the rally, Plous (1991) found that approximately 85% of them would like to see a total ban on the use of animals for research; the comparison figure from a sample of 54 nonactivists (people who just happened to be walking by the protest) was only 17%. Sixty-one percent of the activists surveyed also said they favored laboratory break-ins, whereas only 14% in the nonactivist sample favored them. Most people see some benefits in animal research. (See Box 2.9 for a report on one recent break-in.)

There is no doubt that humans have benefited greatly from animal research. Miller (1985) has pointed out that psychological experiments with

| BOX **2.9** | Activists Target Psychology Labs* |

On April 5, 1999, animal rights activists representing the Animal Liberation Front vandalized the animal research laboratory at the University of Minnesota, destroying equipment and stealing research data. They also took more than 100 research animals and released them in a nearby field. The damage was estimated at more than $2 million. Vandalism of animal research laboratories has been a federal offense since 1992, but this was not the first time Minnesota had been a target of animal activists. During a previous protest, activists chained themselves together inside the office of a psychologist who conducted research on primates. Once, a Minnesota student hoping to force a dialogue with university officials, hung for several hours from a rope connected to the roof of a building.

In addition to monetary damages, the vandalism destroyed many months of researchers' work. For example, the research of one doctoral student who had been investigating learning and memory was completely destroyed. She had spent months training 27 pigeons who were stolen.

Fourteen of her pigeons were eventually recovered, but it was not known whether they could ever be used in the research again.

Releasing laboratory animals used to captivity into the wild usually means certain death. Some of the released animals were found by the side of the road, but a number of released rats had already died. As a result of the animal deaths, the Minnesota Senate passed a law making it a crime punishable by up to a year in jail plus civil damages for a person or organization to claim responsibility for the unauthorized release of animals. The FBI considers the Animal Liberation Front a terrorist organization. Currently, there is legislation pending in the U.S. Congress to increase penalties for damage and destruction to animal research laboratories. In Los Angeles, two animal rights activists were recently arraigned and charged with ten felonies, including stalking and threats to burn down the house of one UCLA psychiatrist who conducts animal research. In another 2009 incident, California activists claimed credit for firebombing the car of a UCLA professor who uses an animal model for schizophrenia. One California animal rights activist, Daniel Andreas San Diego, was recently added to the FBI's *Most Wanted Terrorists* list (Grant, 2009). It is estimated that the costs of damage by eco and animal terrorists has already exceeded $100 million (Trull, 2006). The loss of research data that could lead to cures for medical and psychological disease cannot be estimated.

*Adapted from "Destructive Lab Attack Sends a Wake-up Call," by B.Azar, *APA Monitor Online*, July/August, 1999, *30*(7), p. 16. Copyright © 1999 by the American Psychological Association. Adapted with permission.

animals have led to treatments of many psychological problems (such as depression, obsessive-compulsive disorder, enuresis [bedwetting], and anorexia nervosa). CARE reports that animal research has contributed significantly to knowledge about drug abuse and physical dependence as well as the development of new drugs for psychological disorders such as anxiety, schizophrenia, and depression (APA, 2007). Studying animals has also advanced our knowledge of human behavior in the areas of perception, conditioning, learning, memory, and stress (Domjan & Purdy, 1995).

An outstanding example of the benefits to human beings that can result from animal research can be found in the career of behavioral neuroscientist Edward Taub. Taub has recently received prestigious honors from both APA and APS for his research program investigating ways to reinstate human limb movements after stroke-induced paralysis (Taub & Morris, 2001). Taub began his research program using an animal model in which a monkey's sensory connections between the brain and a single limb were surgically detached

(Taub, 1977), immobilizing the limb. Monkeys whose limbs had been immobilized would not use the "bad" limb. When Taub restrained the monkey from using its "good" limb, however, the monkey eventually began using the paralyzed limb again, growing new sensory connections. This research on animals has led to therapeutic techniques for dramatically restoring the use of limbs that have been paralyzed by stroke in human beings. A policy statement by AALAS (October 26, 1984) presents the case for continued experimentation using animals this way:

> The use of experimental animals has been shown to be essential to the development of an understanding of many biochemical, behavioral, physiological, and disease processes. Many of the factors that affect both animal and human life can only be studied in intact animal systems by systematically manipulating specific research variables. Given an incomplete knowledge of biological systems, it is inconceivable that animal experimentation can be replaced, in the foreseeable future, by mechanical models or other incomplete biological systems.

The charges of animal rights activists, although exaggerated and overly dramatic at times, do heighten our awareness of the issues. And discussion of the issues has affected the amount of animal research that is conducted: Fewer animals are being used in research each year (Rowan & Andrutis, 1990). Many different species of animals have been used in psychology research, but only about 7–8% of psychology research involves the use of animals. About 90% of the animal research involves rodents and birds (especially rats, mice, or pigeons); about 5% includes monkeys or other nonhuman primates. The use of dogs or cats is extremely uncommon (APA, 2007). In the past, animal activists have focused largely on animals used in research—not on animal agriculture (animals used for food). In 1990, Nicoll and Russell evaluated several thousand pages of animal rights literature. They found that approximately two-thirds of the pages conveying concern about treatment of animals mentioned animals used in research and teaching—not animals used for food—even though only about 0.3% of all the animals used were part of animal research.

Interestingly, there seems to be a shift in the priorities of animal rights activists. In Plous's survey of activists attending the 1990 animal rights rally, 54% of the activists were most concerned about animals used in research. Only 24% reported that animal agriculture was their major concern. When Plous conducted a later survey of activists attending a 1996 "March for the Animals" rally (Plous, 1998), the percentage of people whose major concern was animal research had dropped to 38%. The percentage most concerned with animals used for food had doubled—from 24% to 48%. In addition, Plous found that there seem to be two subgroups of activists: one group that is younger and mostly concerned with animal agriculture (who do avoid animal products and leather) and an older subgroup that is mostly concerned with animal research. Despite these differences, the percentages of 1996 activists who would ban animal research completely remained high, 90% (compared with 86% in 1990).

Plous has also conducted surveys of psychologists and psychology majors to study their attitudes toward animal research (Plous, 1996a,

1996b). Not surprisingly, both groups overwhelmingly showed support for animal research and felt that it was both justified and necessary—as long as it did not cause pain or death to the animals. Respondents expressed significantly less support for painful or terminal experiments, particularly if they are conducted with higher animals such as primates, cats, and dogs. There also appeared to be an age trend among the psychologists; younger psychologists showed less support for animal research than older psychologists did. Generally, those who support animal research in psychology say they do so because it benefits human health and well-being and is well regulated; those who oppose it most frequently express beliefs that animal research is needless, cruel, and done without the animal's consent (Saucier & Cain, 2006).

As long as animal experimentation continues, researchers have an obligation to behave responsibly. The situations causing the grievances of the past cannot be undone, but the picture for the future of animal welfare is extremely hopeful. Before 1987, the E in APA's CARE stood for "experimentation." It now stands for "ethics." The challenge to contemporary researchers is to ensure that each human or animal subject contributes something worthwhile to scientific knowledge. In the chapters that follow, we will return to ethical questions about human and animal subjects in our examples of actual research projects.

## FRAUD IN SCIENCE

So far, we have discussed the ethical concerns of researchers designing experiments involving human or animal subjects. Reporting on research is a necessary part of the scientific process. It is also an ethical matter. We report our procedures and findings honestly and accurately. When we think of fraud in science, we typically think about researchers publishing false data. Data falsification is a breach of the ethical principle stated succinctly in APA standard 8.10a: "Psychologists do not fabricate data." In addition to reliance on individual ethics, several important safeguards are built into the public process of scientific reporting that help to keep fraud in check.

First, with only a few exceptions, research articles submitted for publication are reviewed by the editor of the periodical and by several experts in the field before they can be accepted for publication. (Because of limited journal space, only about 15% to 20% of all articles submitted for publication in psychological journals ever make it into print.) This procedure, called *peer review*, is an important part of the reporting process. The reviewers' task is to assess the merit of a submission; reviewers go over each submission with a fine-tooth comb, looking for problems and suggesting improvements. If there is something strange about the findings, expert reviewers are likely to discover it. Reviewers make recommendations about publication to the editor of the journal, who makes the final decision. The reviewers and the editor, then, are a first line of defense against data falsification.

Replication is the second line of defense. Researchers often attempt to replicate the published findings of others, particularly if those findings are surprising, novel, or important. If data have been falsified, it is unlikely that the experiment will be successfully replicated. Third, the competitive nature of academic psychology works against fraud (even though it may also be the major cause!). Tenure and promotion within academic departments of psychology are partly based on research productivity. You have probably heard the saying "Publish or perish." There is strong pressure on researchers to publish, and the pressure is probably strongest on those whose work has resulted in a series of failures. Fabricating some impressive data might seem very tempting when keeping one's job depends on publishing the results of a successful experiment. However, competition among colleagues for limited research resources can be a strong deterrent to fraud. As state funding for universities declines and federal funding sources become increasingly scarce, the competition stiffens; as resources become more limited, other researchers in the same area will be on the alert for fraud. Despite these safeguards, fraud does occur from time to time.

In one recent case, a promising young social psychology researcher, Karen Ruggiero, from the University of Texas at Austin, was found guilty of scientific misconduct for falsifying data in several experiments while she was an assistant professor at Harvard from 1996 to 2000. Her research on discrimination had been partially funded by money from the National Institutes of Health, and the published studies were used in applications for other federal grants. One of her former students, a coauthor on the publications, became suspicious and notified the university when Dr. Ruggiero was unwilling to turn over her notes on the project. During the scientific misconduct investigation, Dr. Ruggiero admitted that she had fabricated data in three experiments and resigned her position at the University of Texas. As a result, a promising academic career is probably over.

One of the most spectacular cases involved the famous English psychologist Sir Cyril Burt, who was awarded APA's prestigious Thorndike Award for distinguished service to educational psychology shortly before he died in 1971 (Green, 1992). Burt had achieved fame for his published studies on the inheritability of IQ in identical and fraternal twins who had been raised apart (Burt, 1966, 1972).

The data Burt published showed that the IQ scores of identical twins (twins with exactly the same genes) who were raised apart were almost identical, even though the twins had been exposed to very different life experiences. In contrast, the IQ scores of fraternal twins (twins with only a fraction of the same genes) raised apart could differ greatly. This was very important research in its time. Eventually, other researchers noticed that some of the statistical values Burt had reported in different articles were exactly the same, even though he had reported using different numbers of twins. Statistically speaking, this is a highly improbable, if not impossible, event. It is widely believed that Burt falsified his results, although his defenders argue that he was merely "sloppy" about reporting his data (which he had actually stopped collecting in 1939). They make the point that if Burt had intended fraud, "he would have done a better job of it" (Green, 1992, p. 330).

Sometimes data falsification can have important real-world implications, as it did in studies of the treatment of childhood hyperactivity with stimulant

Sidney Harris

"THAT'S IT? THAT'S PEER REVIEW?"

drugs. In the 1980s, a psychologist named Stephen Breuning admitted fabricating data showing that stimulants such as Ritalin and Dexedrine could dramatically reduce hyperactivity. He received a large federal grant from the National Institute for Mental Health (NIMH) on the basis of false data. One of his colleagues suspected that Breuning had falsified data and reported these suspicions to NIMH. After a 3-year scientific misconduct investigation conducted by NIMH, Breuning admitted in a plea bargain that he had falsified data on two occasions; in return, NIMH dropped perjury charges (Byrne, 1988).

Breuning's case, among others, has resulted in national discussions about the definition of scientific misconduct used by the two major granting agencies, NIMH and the National Science Foundation (NSF). The current definitions are vague and subjective; for example, NSF describes misconduct as "fabrication, falsification, plagiarism, or other serious deviation from accepted practices in proposing, carrying out, or reporting results from activities funded by NSF" (NSF [45CFR Part 689.1 (a)(1)]). Whatever definition is used, the consequences of scientific misconduct can be severe indeed for a researcher, ranging from suspension or firing by the university to a prison term if convicted in court. Universities can be penalized as well; they can be forced to return monies and can be excluded from future funding. In Breuning's case, his university was required to return more than $135,000 in funds to NIMH, and Breuning no longer has a research career. In almost all cases, funding from federal grants like Breuning's is actually given to universities, rather than to individual researchers. The university controls and monitors all spending. As funding becomes even scarcer, more frequent investigations and tighter controls are expected.

## PLAGIARISM

Let us turn to what is probably a more common kind of fraud, plagiarism. We must be careful in the way we draw on the work of others in our presentations. To plagiarize means to represent someone else's ideas, words, or written work as your own. Plagiarism is a serious breach of ethics and can result in legal action. It is not only "borrowing" facts and figures from someone else; plagiarism includes using someone else's ideas without giving proper credit. A well-known author was sued by a former professor who claimed the ideas in the author's best-selling book came directly from the professor's lectures. The professor won his suit and now receives a share of the author's royalties.

Unfortunately, plagiarism is rising among university students. Students are making increasing use of the Web to obtain source materials and even complete papers on almost any topic imaginable. In one recent survey, only 27% of college students believed that it was plagiarism to cut and paste other people's work into their own papers (Thompson, 2006). Thompson (2006) estimated that about 6% of the essays turned in by her recent freshman students had been plagiarized; and the percentage is likely to be much higher in classes requiring lengthy term papers and literature reviews. In another study (McCabe, 2003), half of the students who filled out a survey reported that they did not consider it plagiarism to cut and paste someone else's work into their own papers without citing the sources. And students are not the only ones plagiarizing from the Web. For example, the president of Hamilton College, Eugene Tobin, resigned in 2002 after it was discovered that he had plagiarized a speech from a book review available on Amazon.com (Lewin, 2002).

What is being done to halt this trend? Many professors who give writing assignments can now use web-based tools to detect plagiarism, but it is up to universities to include clear-cut guidelines on what constitutes plagiarism and to invoke penalties for students who have plagiarized the work of others. Most universities now consider student plagiarism to be a form of academic misconduct, and penalties are severe, ranging from a failing grade in the course to permanent expulsion from the university. And the consequences to students can indeed be severe. One of the authors recently had a plagiarism case that resulted in the student being given a failing grade in her final course before graduation. The case was particularly sad, because the B+ student had planned on completing graduate studies at the same university. Cutting and pasting the work of others into your paper or purchasing a ready-made term paper may be tempting at times, but it simply is not worth the risk now that plagiarism has also become very much easier to detect.

Although some forms of plagiarism are intentional, others occur through simple oversights. It would be a rather large oversight to forget to give authors credit when their words are cut and pasted into a new paper, but what about paraphrasing their work—using their ideas but changing the words around? Paraphrasing without giving credit is representing someone else's idea as your own; it is also plagiarism. Even if you believe that the information you wish to use is "common knowledge," if you have read it in someone else's book, give the author credit. If you have done a thorough review of the literature, your research report should contain many citations.[7] If you do this, the reader will know that you have read the important research in your topic area. Throughout this book, you will find figures, passages, and photographs used with the written permission of the original authors, artists, and publishers. Unfortunately, it is easy to plagiarize without even being aware of it. We read many things, jot down notes, and later forget where we got the information. If we use that information elsewhere, we may inadvertently forget or be unable to name the source. In preparing a research report, you should follow several guidelines to avoid the possibility of plagiarism (these guidelines also apply to works that are unpublished or not yet published and to sources in the media or on the Internet). Hints for avoiding plagiarizing are shown in Table 2.2.

TABLE **2.2**
## Tips to avoid plagiarism

1. Take complete notes, which include a complete citation of the source: author's name, title of article, journal name, volume number, issue number, year of publication, and page numbers. For books, include the author's name, the title of the book, the year, the names of the editors (if it is an edited volume), and the publisher's name, city, and state.
2. Within your report, identify the source of any ideas, words, or information that are not your own.
3. Identify any direct quotes by quotation marks at the beginning and end of the quotes and indicate where you got the quotes. Include the page number where you found the quote.
4. Be careful with paraphrasing (restating someone else's words). There is a great temptation to lift whole phrases or catchy words from another source. Use your own words instead or use quotes. Again, be sure to give credit to your source.
5. Include a complete list of references at the end of the report. In psychology, references are written in APA style, and the style is somewhat different for each type of source (see Chapter 16).
6. If in doubt about whether a citation is necessary, cite the source anyway. You will do no harm by being especially cautious. (And, citing many sources will inform the reader that you have read more of the important articles in your research area.)

© Cengage Learning

---

[7] The citation given for Regan's (1983) idea that eating meat and poultry is a decision that goes against the best interests of animals is a good example of this. Everyone has probably heard this argument (and so have we), but we came upon Regan's published article while reviewing the literature on ethics and cite this source because it gave us the idea to write about it.

## ETHICAL REPORTS

*Ethical Principles of Psychologists and Code of Conduct* provides further guidance concerning ethics and research reports. Section 8.12(a) states, "Psychologists take responsibility and credit, including authorship credit, only for work they have actually performed or to which they have substantially contributed" (APA, 2002). This means that your thesis advisor and department chair are not automatically listed as authors on your publication just because of their institutional role or status. To be given authorship credit, they need to have made an important contribution to the research. Using the same logic, students are not automatically listed as authors on publications of professors or research supervisors unless they have made a major contribution to the research or writing. Instead, smaller contributions, such as handing out questionnaires or entering data into the computer, are recognized in acknowledgments or footnotes included in the research report.

Finally, researchers do not take credit for the same research more than once. Data that have been previously published cannot be published again as if they were original data. However, it is ethical to republish parts of previously published reports or even entire reports as long as the initial publication is properly credited. A common example of duplicate publication occurs when a number of previously published journal articles on a similar topic show up again as chapters in an edited volume. When this occurs, you will see an acknowledgment of the original journal publication printed after the title and author.

## SUMMARY

A well-planned experiment includes careful treatment of the subjects who participate. Today, federal law regulates many aspects of psychological research. A research institution must, for example, have an *institutional review board (IRB)* to approve each study using human participants. The IRB's main tasks are to ensure the safety of human subjects and to conduct a *risk/benefit analysis*, and many of the law's provisions are reflected in the ethical guidelines of the American Psychological Association. Most important is obtaining the *informed consent* of all those who will be participants in an experiment, particularly if the study places them *at risk*. This consent must be given freely, without force or coercion. The person must also understand that he or she is free to drop out of the experiment at any time. In addition, subjects must be given as much information about the experiment as possible so that they can make reasonable decisions about whether to participate or not. Many institutions require that informed consent be obtained even if the research is considered *minimal risk*.

Sometimes a researcher may need to disguise the true purpose of the study to ensure that subjects will behave naturally and spontaneously. In experiments that require some deception, subjects must be *debriefed*. Because debriefing subjects does not guarantee that we can undo any upset we have caused them, researchers try to avoid the use of deception unless it is the only feasible way to test a hypothesis. Whenever possible, data should be collected anonymously and identified only by code numbers. Once collected, data are kept confidential; they may not be used for any purpose not explained to the subject. When they are reported, data should be identified by code numbers or fictitious names to protect subjects' identities.

Ethical principles apply in research with animals, too. Institutions engaged in animal research must have a review board, called an *institutional animal care and use committee (IACUC)*, to evaluate experiments before they are conducted. Researchers have a responsibility to promote *animal welfare* whenever they use animal subjects. Animals must receive adequate physical and social care to stay healthy and comfortable. If drugs, surgery, or any potentially painful procedures are involved, a researcher who is specially trained in the field (as well as a veterinarian) must closely supervise the animals. Despite allegations by critics of animal research, there is little evidence to support accusations of widespread abuse in psychological research.

Some animal research critics advocate *animal rights*, the position that all species are equally valued and have equal rights, and the animal rights movement has generated debate about the value of animal research. Most people, however, see a need for animal experimentation because of its benefits for human welfare.

*Fraud* in science is typically thought of as falsifying or fabricating data; clearly, fraud is unethical. The peer review process, replication, and scrutiny by colleagues help hold fraud in check. *Plagiarism*, representing someone else's work as your own, is a serious breach of ethics and is considered a type of fraud. Plagiarism by cutting and pasting information from the Internet has become widespread. Plagiarized work, however, can be detected using Internet tools. Penalties for plagiarism can be severe, so researchers must be careful to give proper credit (through citations) to others who contributed words or ideas to their work. In ethical reports, claiming authorship of a publication always necessitates an important contribution to the research. Previously published data may only be republished when the original publication is properly acknowledged.

## KEY TERMS

Animal rights The concept that all sensate species that feel pain are of equal value and have rights.

Animal welfare The humane care and treatment of animals.

At risk The likelihood of a subject being harmed in some way because of the nature of the research.

Debriefing The principle of full disclosure at the end of an experiment; that is, explaining to the subject the nature and purpose of the study.

Fraud The unethical practice of falsifying or fabricating data; plagiarism is also a form of fraud.

Informed consent A subject's voluntary agreement to participate in a research project after the nature and purpose of the study have been explained.

Institutional animal care and use committee (IACUC) An institutional committee that reviews proposed research to safeguard the welfare of animal subjects.

Institutional review board (IRB) An institutional committee that reviews proposed research to safeguard the safety and rights of human participants.

Minimal risk The subject's odds of being harmed are not increased by the research.

Plagiarism The representation of someone else's ideas, words, or written work as one's own; a serious breach of ethics that can result in legal action.

Risk/benefit analysis A determination, made by an IRB, that any risks to the individual are outweighed by potential benefits or the importance of the knowledge to be gained.

## REVIEW AND STUDY QUESTIONS

1. Explain why IRBs are necessary and what their major functions are.

2. What is informed consent? How is it related to *respect for persons* in the Belmont Report?

3. When is it appropriate to use deception? When is it not appropriate? How can the negative effects of deception be eliminated?

4. At the end of the semester, all students in a general psychology course are told they will not receive credit for the course unless they take part in the instructor's research project. Students who refuse to participate are given "Incompletes" and do not get credit for the course. How has the ethical principle of informed consent been violated?

5. An experimenter studying the effects of stress gave subjects a series of maze problems to solve. The subjects were led to believe that the problems were all quite easy. In fact, several had no solution. Some of the subjects were visibly upset by their inability to solve the problems. At the end of the study, the experimenter did not explain the procedures. What ethical principles apply in this case? What should the experimenter have done?

6. In a questionnaire study of sexual attitudes, a student experimenter finds that Pat, a friend's spouse, has responded yes to the question "Have you ever had an extramarital affair?"

The student is sure that the friend is unaware of Pat's behavior. The student decides to show Pat's answers to the friend. What ethical principles have been violated? How could this situation have been avoided?

7. What ethical principles apply when we propose and conduct research with animals?

8. What is the difference between animal welfare and animal rights?

9. To study the effect of a new drug to reduce depression, researchers must sacrifice animal subjects and dissect their brains. Discuss the ethical pros and cons of this line of research.

10. What is fraud? Describe the external pressures that can produce fraud. Describe the safeguards that keep it in check. What are the possible penalties for scientific misconduct?

11. Lee had put off doing a lab report until the end of the term. He was badly pressed for time. His roommate said, "No problem. I took that course last year. You can use my report. Just put your name on it." Lee decides it is all right to use the paper because he has the author's consent. Is that ethical? Why or why not?

## CRITICAL THINKING EXERCISE

*The myth:* Opposites attract.

*The scientific findings:* We are much more likely to be attracted to someone who shares our attitudes, values, and preferences; in other words, someone who is similar to ourselves (Sprecher & Duck, 1994).

*The problem:*   Suppose a researcher conducted an experiment to test this. In one condition of the experiment, she used confederates who were instructed to agree with everything an opposite-sex subject said while they were getting acquainted. At the end of the experiment, she measured how strongly the subject was attracted to the confederate.

The researcher could not tell subjects that they would be lied to before the experiment, but she did explain the deception at the end. What ethical arguments could the researcher use to justify this experiment?

## ONLINE RESOURCES

The Code of Federal Regulations (CFR) for protection of human subjects in research can be found at www.gpoaccess.gov/cfr/

You can find the APA guidelines, *Ethical Principles of Psychologists and Code of Conduct* (2002), online: www.apa.org/ethics/code2002.html

Animal use and care guidelines, *Guidelines for Ethical Conduct in the Care and Use of Animals*, can be found at www.apa.org/science/anguide.html

The CARE homepage can be found at www.apa.org/Science/resethicsCARE.html

Find out about the activities of People for the Ethical Treatment of Animals (PETA): www.peta.org

## CHAPTER 3

# Alternatives to Experimentation: Nonexperimental Designs

**Describing Research Activities**

**Phenomenology**

**Case Studies**

**Field Studies**
Naturalistic Observation Studies
Participant-Observer Studies

**Archival Study**

**Qualitative Research**

SUMMARY
KEY TERMS
REVIEW AND STUDY QUESTIONS
CRITICAL THINKING EXERCISE
ONLINE RESOURCES

## CHAPTER OBJECTIVES

- Learn about techniques for studying behavior that do not manipulate antecedent conditions

- Understand the concept of phenomenology and how it is employed in empirical phenomenology

- Learn how to conduct new research using data already collected by other researchers

- Learn about the techniques employed in observational research

- Familiarize yourself with the basics of qualitative research

In the traditional psychology experiment, we create specific sets of antecedent conditions, or treatments, to test a hypothesis about behavior. To use the experimental approach, the researcher must be able to set up these conditions for any individual who ends up as a subject in the experiment. Many times, this requirement cannot (or, sometimes, should not) be met. For example, we might want to study existing characteristics of participants (such as gender, intelligence, or occupation) to see how they influence behavior. Because we cannot create the antecedent conditions in these situations, we need to gather data in other ways. Sometimes the conditions a researcher wants to study (such as pregnancy, smoking, or homelessness) cannot be created for ethical reasons. Other times, researchers want to study behavior as it occurs naturally—not to construct treatment conditions for study.

Nonexperimental approaches are used in situations in which an experiment is not practical or desirable. They are also used whenever testing a hypothesis in an existing real-life situation is necessary or important. Nonexperimental methods are used to study behaviors in natural settings (children playing, chimps parenting, or life in a gang) to explore unique or rare occurrences (a case of multiple personality, a presidential election) or to sample personal information (attitudes, opinions, preferences). Because each of these nonexperimental approaches can provide useful data, either from single individuals or from large groups of people, it is important to understand how they are applied in psychological research.

As we discussed in Chapter 1, the primary purpose of an experiment is to establish a causal relationship between a specified set of antecedent conditions (treatments) and the subsequently observed behavior. The degree to which a research design allows us to make causal statements is called internal validity. Research is high in internal validity if we can demonstrate with certainty that the changes in behavior observed across treatment conditions were actually caused by differences in treatments. Researchers like to use laboratory experiments in part because they are potentially high in internal validity. We say "potentially" because experiments can fall short of this goal in a variety of ways, which will be discussed in later chapters. And, experiments are frequently criticized—in the media, by students, by laypersons, and by seasoned professionals—for being artificial and unrealistic, and to some extent this criticism may be justified.

True experiments often appear to lack external validity—that is, generalizability or applicability to people and situations outside the research setting. When observations can be generalized to other settings and other people, they are high in external validity. Nonexperimental designs are often preferred because they may have greater external validity; their generalizability to the real world may be more apparent. There is, however, some trade-off. What we gain in external validity we might lose in internal validity. A study that is fetchingly realistic might bring us no closer to the "truth" than one that seems painfully contrived. Fortunately, there are many different research tools available in the psychological scientist's toolbox.

## DESCRIBING RESEARCH ACTIVITIES

All approaches to research can be described along two major dimensions: (1) the degree of manipulation of antecedent conditions and (2) the degree of imposition of units (Willems, 1969). The degree of manipulation of antecedents theoretically varies from low to high, from letting things happen as they will to setting up carefully controlled conditions. For example, a study[1] of children's nutrition could involve simply tracking behavior along with subjects' normal diets (low manipulation of antecedents), or at the other extreme, we could place subjects on fixed diets where all meals are provided (high manipulation of antecedents). Selecting a high degree of manipulation has its

---

[1] As the term is commonly used in reference to methodology, research produced by any of the numerous research methods is called a *study*. Only true experiments are accurately called *experiments*.

pros and cons: We could then vary meals in predetermined ways and evaluate subsequent changes in behavior, but we would be imposing on subjects artificial conditions that might have little meaning in real life. Experiments are typically high in degree of manipulation; nonexperiments are usually low.

The degree of imposition of units is an equally important dimension. This term refers to the extent to which the researcher constrains, or limits, the responses a subject may contribute to the data. In a study of teenagers, for example, we might simply observe a group of teenagers and record whatever they say or do (low imposition of units). With such a plan, we would be imposing relatively little constraint on the teens' responses. Instead, suppose that we were interested only in a single behavior, such as the amount of time they listen to hip-hop music. We might then limit our subjects' responses to the answer to the question "How much time do you spend listening to hip-hop each day?" Our study would then score high on the dimension of imposed units. As you will see in later chapters, most experiments limit subjects' inputs to a narrow range of responses, placing such experiments high on the scale of imposed units. Nonexperimental designs, as you will discover in this chapter and Chapters 4 and 5, can vary from low to high in imposition of units.

Antecedent conditions and imposed units change independently, and we can represent the various research approaches visually as shown in Figure 3.1. As the figure illustrates, a range of possible research approaches exists. Laboratory experiments, which tend to fall in the high-high range, represent only one approach. As we discuss nonexperimental designs, we will refer to this figure again.

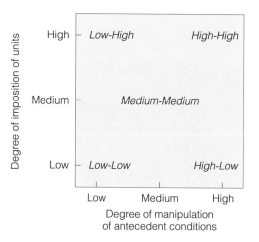

FIGURE **3.1** A space for describing research activities.

From "Planning a Rationale for Naturalistic Research," by E. P. Willems. In E. P. Willems and H. L. Raush (Eds.), 1969, *Naturalistic Viewpoints in Psychological Research.* Copyright ©1969 Holt, Rinehart and Winston. Reprinted by permission.

Let us now discuss five common nonexperimental approaches used by psychologists: (1) phenomenology, (2) case studies, (3) field studies, (4) archival studies, and (5) qualitative studies. Together, these approaches form an important source of data on human as well as animal behavior. They permit us to gather information and gain understanding when experimentation is not desirable or possible.

## PHENOMENOLOGY

So far, we have discussed the scientific method as observing and recording events that are assumed to be external to the observer. An important supplement to the scientific method is the phenomenological approach. Phenomenology is the description of an individual's immediate experience. Rather than looking at behaviors and events that are external to us, we begin with personal experience as a source of data.

As a research approach, phenomenology falls near the low-low end on our graph of research activities (Figure 3.1). Antecedents are not manipulated, and data may consist of any immediate experience; no constraints are imposed. Much early work in psychology, particularly that of the mental philosophers discussed in Chapter 1, was based on the phenomenological approach. Boring (1950) cites Purkinje as a good example of the phenomenologically based researcher. Johannes Purkinje (1787–1869) was interested in the physiology of vision, and he noticed that colors seemed to change as twilight deepened; reds appeared black, but blues retained their hue. This observation (now called the Purkinje effect) eventually led to our understanding of spectral sensitivity to colors of different wavelengths. Have you ever noticed that most automobile instruments are illuminated by red lights at night? They seem to have less negative impact on our night vision. This is just one example of the practical uses that have resulted from Purkinje's early work in phenomenology.

William James, arguably the world's most famous early psychologist (Figure 3.2), also used the phenomenological approach. In his 1200-page work *Principles of Psychology* (republished in 1950; originally published in 1890), James dealt with basic psychological issues, including habits, emotions, consciousness, and the stream of thoughts. James approached most ideas from the phenomenological perspective of his own experiences. One of his most appealing passages deals with his own difficulty in getting up in the morning. He pointed out that our resistance to getting up inhibits our movement. While we concentrate on the pleasure of warm sheets and the dread of a cold floor, we are paralyzed. Said James, "If I may generalize from my own experience, we more often than not get up without any struggle or decision at all. We suddenly find that we have got up" (p. 524). Therefore, if we don't resist, we ought to be able to get out of bed without very much effort.

The phenomenological approach precludes experimental manipulation. Comparison of behaviors under different treatment conditions is not required. When using this approach, we simply attend to our own experience. As Boring explained,

National Library of Medicine

FIGURE **3.2** William James (1842–1910), a famous early phenomenologist.

> Since phenomenology deals with immediate experience, its conclusions are instantaneous. They emerge at once and need not wait upon the results of calculations derived from measurements. Nor does a phenomenologist use statistics, since a frequency does not occur at an instant and cannot be immediately observed. (1950, p. 602)

When we describe our own experiences as James did, however, we cannot be sure that the process we are observing in ourselves is not altered in some way by our attention to it. And, when the observer is also the person whose process is observed, we may not be able to achieve the degree of accuracy and objectivity through phenomenology that we might achieve through other methods. Nor are descriptions of private experiences observable in public; it will be difficult for others to replicate our experiences and apply scientific criteria to our findings. Without replication, it cannot be known if others would have the same experiences. If Purkinje had been color-blind, his experience at sundown would have been very different from that of most people.

Phenomenology cannot be used to understand the causes of behavior. Like other nonexperimental designs, phenomenology describes, but cannot explain, behavior. Purkinje could not be certain that his experience of altered color was caused by an external change (a change in the amount of light) that would affect all observers in a similar manner. Had he not been a scientist, he might have explained his experience in terms of a demon that had taken possession of his sense organs. In the absence of further evidence, one explanation would have been as good as the other.

Phenomenology may lead us into areas of discovery that might otherwise go unnoticed. This can be a useful source of information that may lead us to formulate hypotheses (we will return to this issue in Chapter 6), but experimentation is still required to determine which antecedent conditions produce the behavior or experience. These days, phenomenology is seldom, if ever, used as a research method on its own; instead, elements of phenomenology are most often combined with other research methods. Experimentation, for example, often relies on phenomenological, or self-report, data to study the effects of various experimental manipulations. Recall that in the experiment by Baron and his colleagues (1985) cited in Chapter 1, subjects reported on their own moods. Phenomenology is also a frequent component of qualitative research, which we will describe later in the chapter. Our next method, the case study, makes extensive use of self-reports.

## CASE STUDIES

Like phenomenology, the case study method involves no manipulation of antecedent conditions. The case study is a descriptive record of a single individual's experiences, or behaviors, or both, kept by an outside observer. Such a record may be produced by systematically recording experiences and behaviors as they have occurred over time. Clinical psychology, in particular, has relied heavily on case studies. The case study method is also employed extensively in forensic psychology and organizational psychology. Frequently, as in the clinical case, we may work from a record made after the fact; the patient or other knowledgeable source provides information concerning events in the patient's life and the patient's reactions and behaviors.

Generally, there are few restrictions on the type of data to be included in a case study. Thus, many case studies would be expected to fall in the low-low portion of Figure 3.1. Even though many case studies will gather data without constraint, some case studies will severely restrict the kind of information collected, placing these in the low-high section of our graphic scheme. The exact procedures used to produce a particular case study will depend on the purpose of the study. Kazdin (2003) has argued that case studies serve five major purposes:

1. They are a source of inferences, hypotheses, and theories.
2. They are a source for developing therapy techniques.
3. They allow the study of rare phenomena.
4. They provide exceptions, or counterinstances, to accepted ideas, theories, or practices.
5. They have persuasive and motivational value.

Let us look at each point in turn. First, we may use a case study to make inferences about the impact of life events, the origin of disorders, or developmental processes (see Box 3.1). For example, this approach provided the first systematic data on the development of children's motor, cognitive, and linguistic abilities. By making extensive records of the behaviors of individual children, early researchers like Velten (1943) and Piaget (1954) arrived at descriptions of normal developmental sequences. Modern researchers have used neuropsychological case studies of brain-damaged individuals to identify brain areas related to specific abilities; for example, the right basal ganglia appears to be involved in mental rotation of objects (Harris, Harris, & Caine, 2002). Psychodynamic development has been inferred from case studies. Freud's case study of Little Hans (Freud, 1933) is an example of how an individual case may suggest a developmental process. Hans was afraid of horses. Freud's analysis of Hans's conversations with his father and the dreams he reported suggested that the fear of horses was a symbol for Hans's fear of his father and anxiety about castration. Such case studies led to Freud's formulation of the theory of the Oedipus complex.

The case study provides information about the impact of significant events in a person's life. We may evaluate whether changes occurred in the individual's adjustment following such critical events as loss of a job or birth of a child. Knowledge about these events may lead to a better understanding of the psychodynamics of experience. For example, the fact that an early loss, like the death of a parent or sibling, is associated with depression in later life is indicated by many case studies (e.g., Jacobson, 1971; Jones, Ghannam, Nigg, & Dyer, 1993).

Second, as we understand the impact of such events more fully, we may be able to devise more appropriate treatment techniques, as well as preventive measures. The "talking cure" in psychotherapy, for instance, began as a result of treatment of hysterical symptoms in Anna O., one of Freud's early cases (Breuer & Freud, 1957). Mary Cover Jones's case study of a 3-year old boy named Peter, who was afraid of rabbits (Jones, 1924), formed the basis of today's behavioral therapy techniques. More recently, case studies have been used to evaluate techniques of psychotherapy for depression (Honos-Webb, Stiles, & Greenberg, 2003; Jones et al., 1993).

---

## BOX 3.1  Case Study: An Example of the Role of Traumatic Experiences in the Development of Obsessive-Compulsive Disorder

Miss M, a 24-year-old single woman, was referred with a history of a serious sexual assault whilst on holiday abroad. Immediately after the traumatic event, she felt "quite dirty," and spent a long time washing herself and everything she had with her at the time. After her return home, she continued to feel dirty and said that she could not stop or resist the urge to wash repeatedly. She washed both her person and her clothes and other things in her flat; she would spend hours doing this. She also suffered many symptoms of PTSD [Post Traumatic Stress Disorder], including flashback experiences, numbing, nightmares, poor sleep, and hypervigilance. She had in fact had full-blown PTSD for some time after the attack, for which she had received some professional counseling. By the time she was seen by us, the main complaint was OCD [Obsessive-Compulsive Disorder], and she had a clear diagnosis of the disorder. She had obsessional thoughts about being dirty and unclean ("I am dirty," "I am filthy," "everything is unclean," etc.), which were linked to the washing compulsions. Miss M agreed that her washing was excessive and irrational, yet, despite her attempts to resist the compulsive urges, she continued to engage in these rituals. It was this problem that she specifically sought help for.

Third, the case study is a perfect forum for investigating unique cases or rare problems. Some variants of paraphilia (cross-dressing and sexual masochism, for instance) are very rarely diagnosed in clinical settings; here, case studies can be useful sources of information. One interesting recent case involved the influences of testosterone therapy on a female-to-male transgendered individual (Pennebaker, Groom, Loew, & Dabbs, 2004), a relatively rare occurrence. The researchers compared the subject's diary entries over a 2-year period looking for differences in writing style during the cycle between injections of testosterone (which occurred about every 20 days). The individual would have the highest testosterone levels in the days immediately following injection, then levels would gradually decrease until the next injection. The researchers found that there were measurable changes in the style of the individual's written language during the 20-day cycles. The diary entries were much more likely to mention social interactions and the individual's connections with others at times when testosterone was low. Mentions of social connections were much less frequent at times during the cycle when testosterone was high. Some previous research has indicated that increased testosterone can produce more anger, dominance, or aggression (in natural males), but there was no evidence for an increase of these behaviors when testosterone levels were highest in this transgendered individual.

Fourth, case studies can provide evidence that casts doubt on theories or generally accepted practices. For example, the psychoanalytic notion that it could be harmful to treat overt symptoms of dysfunction without treating their base causes was negated as counterinstances accumulated. Simply treating outward symptoms with behavioral therapy techniques is often very effective.

Fifth, case studies are sometimes a dramatic way to illustrate abstract concepts. Seeing can be believing; hence, advertisers frequently use case studies (highly selective ones to be sure) to sell products. Because they are so compelling, however, case studies can excite interest and bring about new research.

Furthermore, the case study is used in clinical work to evaluate an individual's overall level of psychological functioning. In this type of evaluative case study, we compare our case against some hypothetical standard of "normal" behavior. Based on this comparison, we may suspect some form of psychopathology. We may then compare our case against other cases to assess the degree of similarity or difference. This is the process underlying psychological diagnosis. The development of standard diagnostic criteria for categories of mental disorders appearing in the *Diagnostic and Statistical Manual of Mental Disorders,* revised fourth edition (2000; abbreviated as DSM-IV-TR), reflects groupings of many different patients' case histories. Clinicians have noted similarities among patients that permit their problems to be classified into groups. The records of persons previously diagnosed with "antisocial personality disorder," for example, have certain important similarities (see Box 3.2).

The deviant case analysis is an extension of the evaluative case study discussed earlier. Here cases of deviant and normal individuals are compared for significant differences. These differences may have important implications for

## BOX **3.2** Antisocial Personality Disorder

It is estimated that about 3% of adult American men and 1% of adult American women could be diagnosed with antisocial personality disorder (APD). Formerly, these individuals were called "psychopaths" or "sociopaths." Diagnosis requires that the individual meet several criteria.

The diagnostic criteria were determined by the clinical judgments of experts in psychiatry and psychology and evolved from many, many case studies. The terms *psychopath* or *sociopath* bring convicted serial killers like Ted Bundy or Jeffrey Dahmer to mind. However, psychologists Davison and Neale (1986) described an important fact about people with APD: They can be found anywhere. "Business executives, politicians, and physicians, plumbers, salespeople, carpenters, and bartenders— they are to be found in all walks of life. Prostitutes, pimps, confidence men, murderers, and drug dealers are by no means the only sociopaths" (p. 233).

Some individuals with aspects of antisocial personality disorder are quite a bit more successful at managing not to break the law than others are. What all these people have in common are personal histories that reflect similar kinds of behaviors and life events. Antisocial personality always begins in childhood or adolescence with occasions of truancy, aggression, vandalism, stealing, lying, physical cruelty, or other antisocial behaviors. Before the age of 18, such individuals are diagnosed as having a "conduct disorder." Their behavior rarely goes

unnoticed; they often find themselves in trouble with the authorities.

After age 18, a diagnosis of antisocial personality disorder is made if individuals fulfill specific behavioral criteria associated with the disorder. Individuals with the disorder carry the pattern of childhood antisocial behavior into adulthood, where they are seen to engage in repeated instances of behaviors that are assaultive, destructive, irresponsible, or illegal. In addition, these individuals do not suffer from (true) remorse for their actions. From collections of case studies, several predisposing childhood factors have also been identified: inconsistent parental discipline, substance abuse, attention deficits, and hyperactivity, for example; sociopathy is also more likely if one or both parents had the disorder.

DSM-IV-TR is the standard for diagnosing mental disorders, but not all experts agree with the diagnostic criteria. For example, many psychologists believe that sociopaths are also characterized by a great deal of charm that can make them exceptionally charismatic. Underneath it all, though, they feel little or nothing for others (Cleckley, 1976). Part of the problem with compiling information from case studies on individuals diagnosed with APD is that generally the individuals available for study are the extreme cases—typically, incarcerated criminals or psychiatric patients. One can argue, as have Davison and Neale, that the database for APD probably lacks valuable information about the most successful sociopaths.

the etiology, or origin, of the psychopathology in question. Mednick and his colleagues have used this procedure to study the etiology of schizophrenia (Mednick, 1969; Mednick, Schulsinger, & Venables, 1981). They found, for example, that the autonomic systems of normal and schizophrenic children function differently. Someday it may be possible to use this difference to predict which children will become schizophrenic. Deviant case analysis has also been used infrequently to study nonclinical issues such as social trends (Kendall & Wolf, 1949) and morale during adulthood (Estes & Wilensky, 1978).

The case study is a useful source of information; however, this approach has several limitations. First, working with only one or perhaps a few subjects, we cannot be sure the people we are evaluating are representative of the general population; we would obtain a very distorted picture of language development if we studied one exceptional child. Second, if we are not able to observe an individual directly all the time, we cannot be sure that we are

aware of all the relevant aspects of that person's life. Third, subjects or others providing data for case studies might neglect to mention important information, either because they believe it is irrelevant or because they find it embarrassing.

An even more severe problem is that case studies frequently rely on retrospective data. Retrospective data are data collected in the present that are based on recollections of past events. Information collected long after the fact is apt to be inaccurate for several reasons. People often cannot accurately remember all that happened at a particular point in time. We also know that human memories become altered or "reconstructed" over time by the cognitive system. In addition, retrospective data can also be easily biased by the situation in which the data are collected. The mood of the data provider, for example, will affect recollections; we tend to recall more positive events when we are in a good mood and more negative events when we are in a bad mood.[2]

Also, aspects of the situation can trigger particular kinds of recollections. Something that seems as innocuous as a reproduction of da Vinci's *Mona Lisa* on a therapist's wall might bring to mind past experiences with enigmatic,

---

[2] If you are a believer in Freud's concept of repression, you would be tempted to say that the most important (i.e., most traumatic) events in a person's life might not be recalled because they have been repressed.

dark-haired women that otherwise would not have been recalled at all. Even unintended hints from a therapist or researcher that certain kinds of data are more interesting than others can bias the kind of information that is brought to mind. For these reasons, reliance on retrospective data is a shortcoming. Records made at the time of an event are always much preferred. The use of retrospective data is not limited to case studies but frequently occurs in this research method. Finally, because we have not created the antecedent conditions in case studies, we cannot make cause-and-effect statements about the behaviors we observe. For example, we cannot say that the early loss of a parent causes later depression; we can merely say that there seems to be a relationship between the two occurrences. It is just as plausible that some related factor, such as moving or changing schools because of a parent's death, might explain later depression.

# FIELD STUDIES

Field studies are nonexperimental approaches used in the field or in real-life settings. Researchers doing field studies often combine various types of data gathering to capitalize on the richness and range of behavior found outside the laboratory. Antecedent conditions are not manipulated in field studies, but the degree of constraint on responses varies considerably from study to study. Depending on the measurements used, field studies can fall anywhere along the continuum of low-low to low-high in our graphic scheme (in Figure 3.1). Field studies include observational studies by ethologists, many studies of child development, market research, and studies of organizations. Let us look next at some different types of field studies.

## Naturalistic Observation Studies

Naturalistic observation is the technique of observing behaviors as they occur spontaneously in natural settings. It is a descriptive method: Like phenomenology and the case study method, naturalistic observation involves no manipulation of antecedent conditions. Subjects' responses are free to vary. Because the researcher imposes very few constraints, naturalistic observation would be considered low-low in Figure 3.1. The naturalistic observation approach has been used extensively in animal behavior research, called *ethology*, to study behavior in the wild as well as in captivity. Recent naturalistic observations have been made of such interesting phenomena as web-building strategies of black widow spiders (Salomon, 2007), stereotypic pacing behaviors of circus tigers (Krawczel, Friend, & Windom, 2005), and the use of navigational cues by migrating birds (Bingman & Able, 2002).

Perhaps the most well-known naturalistic observations were those recorded by Dian Fossey, who studied the family life and social bonds of rare mountain gorillas living in the Virunga Volcano mountains of central Africa. The striking pictures of the dominant male silverback, as he interacts with infant gorillas and their mothers, are impossible to forget (see Figure 3.3). Fossey's book *Gorillas in the Mist* brought world attention to the plight of the mountain gorilla and allowed her to open a gorilla sanctuary in Rwanda in 1978. In 1985, Dr. Fossey was found murdered in her cabin in Africa.

Elliot Hurwitt/iStockphoto.com

FIGURE **3.3** A silverback mountain gorilla

The mystery of her death has never been solved. The 1988 movie *Gorillas in the Mist* tells the story of Fossey's life in Africa. Today, primate psychologists and others continue her work in Rwanda to save the mountain gorilla from extinction and to stop illegal, but lucrative, trafficking in baby gorillas.

When they conduct naturalistic observations, researchers attempt to remain inconspicuous (for example, staying out of sight or blending in with the environment) so that the behaviors they observe are not altered by the presence of an observer. Whether the subjects of the observations are animal or human, every attempt is made to keep the setting as natural as possible so that the naturally occurring events will not be altered in any way. This element creates special challenges. In a typical laboratory experiment, the researcher has only a small set of behaviors to record. In contrast, researchers who conduct naturalistic observations must contend with a vast array of responses, often including unanticipated, unconventional responses. Deciding who and when to observe and what to record and analyze draws heavily on both the researcher's judgment and observational skills.

The use of naturalistic observation is often essential and even preferable to experimentation. Psychological phenomena are rarely simple; a researcher can fail to take all the important antecedent conditions of a behavior into account. The researcher using naturalistic observation accepts the larger challenge of dealing with data as they occur in real-life settings. Imposing a great deal of constraint on subjects' responses is not always desirable, either. Allowing subjects to behave as they usually would provides a much richer picture of the complex, multiple relationships among behaviors, and results from these studies may have more external validity, or generalizability, than laboratory demonstrations.

In an interesting example of naturalistic observation, Wheeler (1988) spent a year observing Chinese residents of Hong Kong and noted many interesting differences between these Chinese and typical Americans. For example, he observed that during construction of the new headquarters of the Hong Kong and Shanghai Bank (one of the most expensive buildings in the world), traditional *feng shui* (wind and water) experts had to be consulted all along the way. These experts ensured, for instance, that the building was not constructed "on the back of the dragon." Without the guidance of these experts in safely situating the building, people would not have used the bank.

Frequently, a naturalistic observation is designed to answer specific questions. Yepez (1994), for example, wanted to investigate whether teachers of English as a Second Language courses gave equal amounts of attention to their male and female students. With permission of the teachers (but without explaining her hypothesis beforehand), Yepez observed and recorded the number of classroom interactions between four different teachers and their pupils.

Each teacher was observed six times. Years of past research have shown that gender inequities are often found in the classroom. Male students tend to be given more attention by teachers. Surprisingly, in Yepez's observation, she found that only one of the four teachers seemed to give more attention to the men than to the women.

Yepez recorded behaviors in the classes using a special coding system, called INTERSECT, developed for scoring various kinds of teacher-student interactions (Sadker & Sadker, 1982). It allowed her to collect and evaluate data in a more objective, systematic, and structured manner. Many such coding systems have been developed for observational research in a wide variety of situations. Most of these systems allow observations to be quantified and permit statistical analyses. When she used INTERSECT, Yepez was engaging in the technique of systematic observation. In systematic observation, the researcher uses a prearranged strategy for recording observations in which each observation is recorded using specific rules or guidelines so that observations are more objective. An important feature of coding systems is that they would give the same results to different researchers. For example, INTERSECT provides guidelines for scoring four kinds of responses teachers are likely to use when interacting with students: positive reinforcement, acceptance, remediation, and criticism. Each type has been carefully defined in a scoring manual, and many examples for coding behaviors are provided (Sadker & Sadker, 1982).

Coding systems such as INTERSECT do not manipulate antecedent conditions or alter the naturally occurring behavior of subjects, but they clearly limit the types of responses that will be recorded, bringing these studies into the low-high portion of Figure 3.1. Observers need to learn and practice the coding system thoroughly before they can actually use the system in a research setting, and the results should be reproducible by different trained observers.[3] In Yepez's study, for instance, she and an assistant coded practice

---

[3] The degree to which different observers code behaviors in the same way is called *interrater reliability*. The degree of interrater reliability can be calculated. We usually like to see 80 or 90% agreement, or greater (see Chapter 7).

responses until they consistently generated identical coding results. The use of coding systems in which scoring categories are carefully defined also allows researchers to compare results across different studies that used the same coding system.

Occasionally, naturalistic observation is carried out in the laboratory. A researcher might recruit mother-infant pairs to the laboratory, for example, to study their interactions. One observational technique that has been used extensively by developmental psychologists is called the *strange situation* (Ainsworth, Blehar, Waters, & Wall, 1978). This method is used to assess the quality of attachments that very young children (usually between the ages of 1 and 2) have forged with their parents or other caregivers. The strange situation has eight parts designed to mimic activities that occur in real-world settings:

1. The experimenter introduces the parent and baby to the playroom and leaves.
2. The parent sits while the baby plays.
3. A stranger enters, sits, and talks to the parent.
4. The parent leaves, the stranger offers comfort if the baby is upset.
5. The parent returns, greets the baby, and offers comfort if the baby is upset. The stranger leaves.
6. The parent leaves the room.
7. The stranger enters and offers comfort.
8. The parent returns, greets the baby, offers comfort if necessary, and tries to interest the baby in toys (Shaffer, 2002, p. 397).

Commonly, the entire strange situation is inconspicuously videotaped and coded later by trained coders. In a recent study using this technique with year-old infants (Harrison & Ungerer, 2002), the researchers found that mothers who were more committed to working outside the home and who had returned to work earlier after the birth of the child had more securely attached infants. These infants demonstrated a strong bond with their mother and the ability to use her as a secure base from which to explore the environment (Shaffer, 2002, p. 397).

At times it is necessary to compare laboratory findings with behavior in natural settings to confirm the usefulness of the laboratory setting for a particular research topic. Because some behaviors may be distorted by bringing them into the laboratory setting, such behaviors are best observed where they occur naturally. Naturalistic observation provides a wealth of descriptive information, but this research method does not lend itself to testing causal antecedents of behavior or determining cause and effect. We would not know, for example, why the infants of mothers who were more committed to work appeared to be more securely attached than infants of other mothers. Nor would we know why one teacher in Yepez's study treated male students somewhat differently than female students.

A further limitation of observation in a natural setting is that we are dealing with specific samples of time that may or may not contain the behaviors we want to observe. If we bring our study into the laboratory as Harrison and

Ungerer (2002) did, we may be able to create conditions more likely to elicit the behavior of interest within a very circumscribed time and space. But when we do this, we must be aware of the possibility that behaviors in the laboratory setting might not be the same as they are in the real world. We might find, for example, that behaviors become very different when the subjects know they are being watched. This effect, the tendency of subjects to alter their behavior or responses when they are aware of an observer's presence, is known as reactivity. We may even find that subjects try to guess the purpose of the study so that they can either confirm the researcher's expectations or sabotage the results. (We will discuss these issues further in later chapters.)

Observers should remain as unobtrusive (inconspicuous) as possible when they conduct naturalistic observations. Researchers can make themselves less obtrusive by hiding behind a duck blind, by observing from behind a one-way mirror, or by blending in with the social surroundings so that they are not noticed. Many times, behavioral indicators can be observed without the subject's knowledge; such indicators are called unobtrusive measures. The amount of wear and tear on your textbook, for example, could be used to measure how much time you spend studying. The number of candy bar wrappers in your garbage could indicate your penchant for sweets. Your physical distance from another person could indicate how much attraction you feel toward that person. See Box 3.3 for an interesting example of unobtrusive measures.

Frequently, researchers make inferences about behavior from unobtrusive examination of aspects of the environment. For example, a researcher could study the traffic pattern in a supermarket by assessing the frequency of replacement of floor tiles in each aisle (or even the wear and tear on tiles in different parts of the store). The subjects—shoppers—would never know their behaviors were being measured. Unobtrusive measures are often preferred over conspicuous measurement techniques (*obtrusive measures*) because unobtrusive measures overcome the potential for reactivity. (Do you know people who would skip certain aisles at the supermarket, like the junk food or candy aisle, if they knew a researcher was watching?)

### Participant-Observer Studies

One special kind of field study is the participant-observer study. Here the researcher actually becomes part of the group being studied. Sometimes this is the only method that can be used to study a group—particularly if the group would not reasonably be expected to cooperate voluntarily with a research investigation. In some cases, group members are not told that they are part of a study. Once their presence is known, researchers run the risk that subjects' behavior may change merely because an observer is present. In some groups, disclosure might lead to being ousted (or perhaps worse). Participant-observer studies usually do not include systematic observation or measurement techniques. Instead, the data gathered tend to be qualitative (the researcher's impressions are merely described). Participant-observers are typically trying to gather as much information and detail as they can. Where would this kind of study fall in Figure 3.1?

BOX **3.3**    **Mailing Lost Letters**

In addition to voting for president of the United States, voters in the November 7, 2000 general election in the state of Alabama received ballots that included another important issue: Should the state remove Section 102 of the Alabama State Constitution (a "yes" vote) or should the section remain a part of the constitution (a "no" vote)? Section 102 had originated during the era of segregation and prohibited interracial marriage between Whites and Blacks (even though the ban was not enforced). At the time of the election, Alabama was the only state in the country to have this racist ban in its constitution.

Bridges, Keeton, and Clark (2002) took advantage of this naturally occurring event to attempt to predict voting patterns in an unobtrusive way using the "lost letter technique" (Milgram, Mann, & Harter, 1965). Two weeks before the election, Bridges and his colleagues addressed stamped letters to one of three fictional organizations: AL Voters in Favor of Legalizing Interracial Marriage, AL Voters Opposed to Legalizing Interracial Marriage, or (a control condition) AL Voters for Marriage Over Same-Sex Unions. They distributed 621 of these "lost letters" all around Mobile, Alabama, and less-populated adjacent counties. They left the letters in store aisles, phone booths, ATMs, and on frequently used sidewalks. Then, they waited to see how many envelopes of each type would be mailed by people who found them. Inside the envelopes were identical letters indicating that the organization would get a $250 contribution if they would drop by and pick it up.

The rationale behind the unobtrusive measure was that finders would be more likely to mail envelopes to organizations with which they agreed than to organizations with which they disagreed. Ninety-five letters were actually mailed back. Of these, 32 were addressed to AL Voters in Favor of Legalizing Interracial Marriage, 28 to AL Voters Opposed to Legalizing Interracial Marriage, and 35 to the control condition. The researchers then compared percentages of letters returned to the two fictitious interracial marriage organizations to percentages of "yes" and "no" votes in the actual election to see how well the letters predicted the real vote. As election polls had predicted, the ban against interracial marriage was overturned in the actual election (approximately 60.5% "yes" to 39.5% "no"). The percentages of letters returned totaled 53.33% "yes" and 46.67% "no." When the percentages of returned letters were compared with the percentages from the actual vote (using a chi-square "goodness-of-fit" statistic), there was no significant difference between them. Therefore, the authors concluded that their (unobtrusive) lost letter technique worked very well to predict voting patterns.

Eric Schrader/www.phutu.com

FIGURE **3.4** Could this dropped letter be part of an experiment?

As you might imagine, some very useful information can be gathered using this method. Recent participant-observer studies have centered on such topics as ethnic identity in an urban high school, homelessness, self-actualization in a spiritual community, supernatural beliefs of practicing Wiccans, reentry of long-term mental patients into the community, and urban crack addicts (see Box 3.4 for an interesting example of a participant-observer study). Each of these issues would be difficult to study in more typical ways. But the participant-observer needs to remain aware of the strong possibility that the mere presence of an observer can alter subjects' behaviors in unknown ways. And sometimes observers in these studies find it difficult to remain objective and unbiased. Often, particularly if friendships form, it is hard to remain an objective scientist.

---

## BOX **3.4**  Bodybuilders and Drug Use—A Participant-Observer Study

A very interesting participant-observer study was reported by Augé and Augé (1999). The researchers investigated drug use in professional bodybuilders (men and women who made their living competing as bodybuilders). Like other professional sports, professional bodybuilding can be a very lucrative occupation; prizes up to $100,000 are awarded in some competitions. Until this study was undertaken, drug use among bodybuilders was a topic about which very little reliable information had been gathered.

Over a year-long period, one of the authors participated as a member of the bodybuilding community, asking questions and engaging in conversations to elicit information about the types and quantities of drugs used by professional bodybuilders. Some bodybuilders refused to discuss drug use at all, but most were very open about it when conversing with other bodybuilders, discussing different drugs and their uses, availability, cost, and training cycles. During the year in which the study was conducted, not a single subject reported any drug-free periods. Interestingly, the participant-observer researcher also noted that the bodybuilders either exhibited resistance or provided false information to people considered "outsiders," but the researcher's repeated questioning of his subjects elicited consistent answers from them over a period of several months. All participants were debriefed at the end of the study and agreed that their anonymous data could be included in the study.

Maximum drug use was reported for anabolic steroids for muscle growth, but other drugs were taken when preparing for a competition and still others for treating side effects of the former drugs. Drug use was very high among this sample of professional bodybuilders (higher than previously reported for any type of professional athlete). The bodybuilders seemed to believe that the drugs were necessary to win competitions, and the drugs were readily available, but expensive, sometimes costing as much as $5,000 a month.

David Madison/Stone/Getty Images

FIGURE **3.5**

It has probably occurred to you that field studies can occasion special ethical concerns, and participant-observer studies are particularly problematic. Therefore, a great deal of thought needs to go into observational research before it is conducted. Is your observation going to make an important contribution to psychological knowledge? Are you invading the privacy of others? Is it ethical not to tell people they are being studied? Is it ethical to pretend to be a real group member? Keep in mind the ethical guidelines from Chapter 2. If you were a subject in your own study, how would you feel about it? When it comes to observational research, opinions from an IRB can be especially valuable for weighing these issues objectively. If the behaviors being observed are performed in a public place where individuals would not expect privacy, IRBs usually consider it ethical to conduct an observational study (e.g., observing dorm residents in the cafeteria). In contrast, when people expect that their behaviors are private (e.g., observing dorm residents in their dorm rooms), an IRB might require that participant-observers disclose their status as a researcher to the group they are studying and obtain informed consent from group members. Even though this procedure may be more ethical than deceiving participants about the researcher's real status, it greatly increases the potential for reactivity in participants' behaviors.

As with the other approaches we have discussed so far in this chapter, naturalistic observation studies do not involve direct manipulation of conditions: Behaviors are observed and recorded as they occur in the natural setting, and subjects may be interviewed in the "wild," where the contaminating effects of a laboratory setting are absent. It is a useful way of gathering many types of data, particularly when the researcher is studying behaviors that are not socially sanctioned or desirable, which we might not see in the laboratory. Note that a field study is not to be confused with a field experiment. A field experiment is a true experiment (the antecedent conditions are actually manipulated by the researcher) that is conducted outside the laboratory. To illustrate the difference, a clever example of a field experiment is described in Box 3.5.

## ARCHIVAL STUDY

An archival study is a descriptive research method in which already existing records are reexamined for a new purpose. Many opportunities for field research can be found in data that have been collected for other purposes and stored in data archives. Vast amounts of data are collected by government and private agencies, hospitals, businesses, schools, institutes, and so on. Information about such things as crime and death rates, education levels, salaries, housing patterns, and disease rates are accessible to researchers. There are also archives housing data from scientific research surveys, some using very large national samples.

In addition to demographic information, some of these surveys include information collected about people's attitudes. This information can be used to analyze societal trends or to gather information about population subgroups. A university librarian is a good place to begin if you want to use archival data. There may be a charge to use the data, but it can be well worth

BOX **3.5**   A Field Experiment in Chicago

Cunningham (1989) provides an example of a field experiment conducted in seven suburban Chicago-area bars. Cunningham trained several college students to approach opposite-sex bar patrons at random, delivering one of several different kinds of conversation-starters ("lines"). The positivity of each patron's response to the line was surreptitiously measured.

Cunningham discovered that women were much more sensitive to the kind of line an opposite-sex person delivered than were men. Women responded more positively to lines that were either self-disclosing or ordinary, like a simple "Hi," than they did to a flippantly delivered line such as "You remind me of someone I used to date" or "Bet I can outdrink you." Men, however, did not appear to care which kind of conversational gambit a woman used; they responded equally positively to all three.

It is sometimes possible to achieve high degrees of both external and internal validity, as Cunningham did, by conducting actual experiments in the field. We will return to field experiments in later chapters about experimental approaches.

Tim Pannell/Corbis Edge/CORBIS

FIGURE **3.6** Could some of these happy-looking people actually be subjects in a field experiment?

the investment. You can also conduct archival research on popular culture at low cost by using other kinds of existing materials (films, newspapers, and magazines, for instance).

In an interesting use of archival data, Bowman (1992) studied some controversial issues about African American men—namely, documented discouragement over barriers to employment and problems with family roles—from a positive perspective. His study looked at factors related to facilitative, adaptive coping mechanisms in a sample of 372 African American men who were responsible husbands and fathers. To gather data, he accessed a national data bank archived at the University of Michigan. Data were originally collected in 1979–1980 by face-to-face interviews with 2,107 African Americans residing in different parts of the United States. Bowman found that kinship bonds and religious beliefs were stronger in men who were happy in their family roles, and he suggested that family closeness and religion might help to mediate family role difficulties. Because this was not an experiment, causal inferences cannot be supported; however, valuable information for further study on these important issues was gained (without the great expense of finding the kind of subjects he wanted and traveling all across the country to interview them) by accessing and reanalyzing information from existing data archives in a creative new way.

## QUALITATIVE RESEARCH

You will recall that we touched on qualitative research in Chapter 1 when we compared quantitative and qualitative kinds of measurement. Qualitative research relies on words rather than numbers for the data being collected; it focuses on self-reports, personal narratives, and expression of ideas, memories, feelings, and thoughts. Even though it is fair to say that most psychologists conducting research today strongly favor the quantitative approach (and most of this text will focus on quantitative methods), without an understanding of qualitative methods, one cannot really appreciate the breadth of research methodology used by contemporary psychological scientists. In addition, qualitative research appears to be on the rise within psychology (Rennie, Watson, & Monteiro, 2002). Some psychologists are even going so far as to argue that qualitative research, which some call the big-Q, is a candidate for a *paradigm shift* within psychology (O'Neill, 2002; Rennie et al., 2002). A paradigm is the set of attitudes, values, beliefs, methods, and procedures that are generally accepted within a particular discipline at a certain point in time (Kuhn, 1970). As we described in detail in Chapter 1, hypothesis testing, experimentation, and quantitative data analysis constitute the accepted paradigm within contemporary psychology; however, a number of psychologists have eschewed the accepted paradigm in favor of the richness of the qualitative approach.

Qualitative research is used to study phenomena that are contextual, meaning they cannot be understood without the context in which they appear. These phenomena deserve to be studied within a rich background or unique environment. Let's look at the example of religious faith and belief in a divine being. Religiousness has been studied, quantitatively, for many years.

There are very good standard tests that can be used to measure strength of religious faith as a useful measurement in quantitative research. Typically, this kind of research looks at relationships between religiousness and other personality or health variables. Contrada and colleagues (2004), for example, conducted a quantitative study to investigate the impact of religiousness on outcomes of cardiac surgery. Among other results, they found that, on the average, more religious individuals tended to have shorter hospital stays after surgery—a very interesting finding.

A qualitative researcher, however, would not be contented with statistical averages or statistical relationships between scores on scales of religiousness and the number of days a patient stays in the hospital. A qualitative

"I KNOW THIS IS ALL NONSENSE, BUT THAT'S THE PARADIGM I'M STUCK WITH."

researcher might want, instead, to know about the fuller experience of people's religiousness and faith in the context of impending surgery to fully describe the experience and understand the meaning of the experience for individuals. Instead of using statistics to evaluate the relationship between religiousness and recovery after surgery, the qualitative researcher would use words to extract meaningful common themes and would support them with actual narratives from the study participants. See Box 3.6 for an example of how qualitative methods can sometimes enhance quantitative research.

BOX **3.6**    **Pinkerton Investigators Surveil Individuals Driving with a Suspended License**

Losing your driver's license for driving while intoxicated (DWI) is believed to be a deterrent to future DWIs. But how effective is it for keeping alcohol abusers off the road? McCartt, Geary, and Nissen (2002) reported the results of a two-part study designed to answer that question for the National Highway Traffic Safety Administration. Two geographic sites were selected for study: Milwaukee, Wisconsin (57 offenders), and Bergen Country, New Jersey (36 offenders). Only persons who were not allowed to drive at any time were studied.[*] In both locations, driver's license suspension is automatic after conviction of DWI. To conduct this study, licensed, bonded Pinkerton investigators were hired to observe each person unobtrusively at two different times during the last month of the suspension period—one weekday morning between 6:00 and 10:00 a.m. and one weekend evening (Friday or Saturday) between 6:00 and 10:00 p.m. The observation dates were determined randomly. Compliance with the sanction was far from uniform. In the Milwaukee sample, 88.2 % of the sample drove illegally during one or more of the observation periods. In the New Jersey sample, about 36.4% drove illegally at least once.

To find out why compliance differed so dramatically, McCartt and her colleagues used a qualitative research design in the second part of the study. Participants from both sites were invited to participate in a *focus group*. A focus group is a type of group interview; it is an organized discussion session with a small group of people, usually led by a trained *facilitator*. (You can read more about focus groups in Chapter 4.) Focus group conversations are typically tape-recorded so that researchers can study them in depth. After several focus groups, the researchers concluded that the major cause of differences in compliance across the two locations was that the severity of the laws differed greatly in the two states. New Jersey levies much more severe penalties for DWI than Wisconsin does. Financial penalties in New Jersey, for example, were greater because of an automatic state-imposed insurance surcharge of $1,000 per year for 3 years. Greater fear of detection and higher penalties for driving while suspended in New Jersey also appeared to play a role. From results obtained from the focus groups, the researchers concluded that a combination of strong sanctions and strong enforcement is likely to increase compliance with license suspension sanctions.

[*]Milwaukee allows some drivers to apply for a conditional license to drive to and from their place of work; New Jersey does not.

Adapted from McCartt, A. T., Geary, L. L., & Nissen, W. J. (2002a August). Observational study of the extent of driving while suspended for alcohol-impaired driving. DOT HS 809 491. Washington, DC: National Highway Traffic Safety Administration,.

Hutchings Stock Photography/CORBIS

FIGURE **3.7**

Earlier in the chapter, we mentioned that phenomenology was often used as part of other research techniques. This is clearly the case in qualitative research. Over the past two decades, the use of phenomenology has increased significantly as qualitatively oriented psychologists (as well as researchers in other social and health sciences) conduct research based largely on phenomenology (Hein & Austin, 2001). Contemporary phenomenology, also called empirical phenomenology, might rely on the researcher's own experiences or on experiential data provided by other sources. Empirical phenomenology relies on one or more of the following sources of data:

1. The researcher's self-reflection on experiences relevant to the phenomenon of interest
2. Participants' oral or written descriptions of their experiences of the phenomenon
3. Accounts of the phenomenon obtained from literature, poetry, visual art, television, theatre, and previous phenomenological (and other) research (Hein & Austin, 2001, p. 3)

Buchbinder and Eisikovits (2002) conducted a remarkable qualitative study of female victims of domestic violence in Israel. They did not use their own experiences as data; instead, they gathered oral descriptions of the experiences of 20 women who had been victims of spousal abuse. The researchers asked each of the women to describe their experiences growing up in their family of origin as well as their experiences living in their current (violent) family circumstances. Each woman took part in two 1-hour interviews; the interviews were tape-recorded and later transcribed. When the researchers examined the transcriptions, they found that a common theme—a feeling of shame—appeared to emerge from each woman's experiences. Empirical phenomenology relies on participants' actual words, and in the published report, the researchers provided a number of verbatim narratives to support their conclusions; here is one example:

> In fact, why doesn't a woman complain? She is ashamed to go to the police. This shame is one of the reasons that she doesn't complain, and when I complained I was not ashamed anymore. I prefer to be a divorcee than beaten. (p. 359)

When using the technique of empirical phenomenology, researchers go an additional step beyond collecting and evaluating experiential data. They also validate their conclusions by asking the study participants to verify them and to offer corrections, if needed. For instance, after evaluating the transcribed data, Buchbinder and Eisikovits returned to each woman in the study to allow her to confirm the study's conclusions and to offer changes and clarifications. The methods used in empirical phenomenology characterize the qualitative approach to research very well.

You may be wondering at this point about the validity of inferences (such as the theme of shame described earlier) derived from qualitative research. Clearly, there are many sources of potential bias in qualitative studies. As we learned in the earlier discussion of field research, there is a chance that interpretation of the data might be influenced by the researcher's own viewpoint. Or, the presence of a researcher could influence the way subjects respond.

And, there is always a concern about the accuracy of self-reports as well as the use of retrospective data. In fact, each of these potential sources of bias is a concern when we conduct experimental research too! However, because qualitative research does not control for many of the potential sources of bias that are carefully controlled in experiments, the potential for mistakes and erroneous conclusions may be greater.

Internal and external validity are issues of concern in qualitative as well as quantitative research (Johnson, 1997). In the study by Buchbinder and Eisikovits (2002), for example, the researchers would need to address these types of validity in their research report. To assess internal validity, we could ask the question, "Is it possible that something else besides shame is an important feature that stops women from reporting their abuse? Is fear important too?" To evaluate external validity, we could ask, "Would we expect to get the same data from non-Israeli women who were victims of spousal abuse?" Probably not. We would expect important differences among abused women in different cultures. Finally, qualitative researchers consider the reproducibility of their conclusions. A very important measure of the goodness of a qualitative study is its replicability. How likely is it that another researcher would obtain the same results with a similar sample? If the study is a good one, others should be able to replicate it.

## SUMMARY

Research activities may be described along two dimensions: degree of manipulation of antecedent conditions and degree of constraint on subjects' responses. Laboratory experiments tend to fall at the high end of both dimensions, representing only a small portion of the possible research options. Nonexperimental designs tend to be low on the first dimension but vary from low to high on the second. This chapter covers five major nonexperimental approaches to data collection: phenomenology, case studies, field studies, archival studies, and qualitative research. These approaches may be higher in *external validity* than are laboratory experiments, but they are probably lower in *internal validity*.

*Phenomenology* is the description of one's own immediate experience. Rather than looking out at behaviors in the world, the phenomenological approach requires us to begin with our own experience as a source of data. Phenomenological data are limited in three major respects: Because we do not compare subjects under different conditions, we cannot make cause-and-effect statements about our experience. We have no way of knowing whether attending to our experience alters it; it may not be completely accurate or objective. Our experiences might or might not be generalizable to others.

The *case study* is used to study individuals. It is a descriptive record made by an outside observer of an individual's experiences, behaviors, or both. Case studies are a useful source of ideas; they can lead to therapy techniques; they allow the study of rare phenomena; they demonstrate counterinstances; they can lead to more research. The record may be made systematically over a period of time or after the fact, using *retrospective data*, as is often the case in clinical practice. This approach enables us to study a variety of life events we could not study experimentally. In a variation of the case study, the *deviant case analysis,* researchers compare case studies of individuals with psychopathologies to those of normal individuals, looking for potentially important differences between them.

*Field studies* are studies done in real-life settings. These studies allow us to explore behavior that we probably would not see in the laboratory, but they cannot be used to make inferences about cause-and-effect relationships. Field studies include a variety of techniques for collecting data. *Naturalistic observation,* the technique of observing events as they occur in their natural settings, is a common component of field research. Naturalistic observation is quite common in animal research (ethology), but this method can be used to study human behavior as well. During naturalistic observation, the observer remains *unobtrusive* so that the behaviors being observed are not altered by the presence of an intruder. This approach reduces subjects' *reactivity* and allows study of behaviors that would be distorted or absent in the laboratory. When the researcher wants to answer specific questions during naturalistic observations, *systematic observation* techniques can be used. In another field technique, the *participant-observer study,* the researcher may interact with subjects as well as observe them to obtain information; this method is infrequently used and can present special ethical challenges. In an *archival study,* researchers can reexamine data that have already been collected.

*Qualitative research* relies on words rather than numbers for the data being collected. Instead of numbers, it uses self-reports, personal narratives, and expression of ideas, memories, feelings, and thoughts. Qualitative research is used to study phenomena that are contextual, meaning they cannot be understood without the context in which they appear. These are phenomena that qualitative researchers choose to study within a rich background or unique environment. Many qualitative studies use methods of *empirical phenomenology* to gather data. Empirical phenomenology relies on the researcher's own experiences or experiential data provided by others. There are many sources of potential bias in qualitative research, and the most important measure of the goodness of a qualitative study lies in reproducibility—others should be able to replicate it with similar results.

## KEY TERMS

Archival study A descriptive method in which already existing records are reexamined for a new purpose.

Case study The descriptive record of an individual's experiences, behaviors, or both kept by an outside observer.

Deviant case analysis A form of case study in which deviant individuals are compared with those

who are not to identify the significant differences between them.

Empirical phenomenology Contemporary phenomenology that relies on the researcher's own experiences, experiential data provided by study participants, or other available sources such as literature or popular media; a qualitative approach.

External validity How well the findings of an experiment generalize or apply to people and settings that were not tested directly.

Field study A nonexperimental research method used in the field or in a real-life setting, typically employing a variety of techniques, including naturalistic observation and unobtrusive measures or survey tools, such as questionnaires and interviews.

Focus group A type of group interview; it is an organized discussion session with a small group of people, usually led by a trained facilitator.

Internal validity The certainty that the changes in behavior observed across treatment conditions were actually caused by differences in treatments.

Naturalistic observation A descriptive, nonexperimental method of observing behaviors as they occur spontaneously in natural settings.

Paradigm The set of attitudes, values, beliefs, methods, and procedures that are generally accepted within a particular discipline at a certain point in time.

Participant-observer study A special kind of field observation in which the researcher actually becomes part of the group being studied.

Phenomenology A nonexperimental method of gathering data by attending to and describing one's own immediate experience.

Qualitative research Research that relies on words rather than numbers for the data being collected; it focuses on self-reports, personal narratives, and expression of ideas, memories, feelings, and thoughts.

Reactivity The tendency of subjects to alter their behavior or responses when they are aware of the presence of an observer.

Retrospective data Data collected in the present based on recollections of past events; apt to be inaccurate because of faulty memory, bias, mood, and situation.

Systematic observation A system for recording observations; each observation is recorded using specific rules or guidelines, so observations are more objective.

Unobtrusive measure A procedure used to assess subjects' behaviors without their knowledge; used to obtain more objective data.

## REVIEW AND STUDY QUESTIONS

1. Describe each of these nonexperimental approaches and give an example of how each might be used:
   a. Phenomenology
   b. Case study
   c. Field study
   d. Qualitative research

2. What is meant by external validity? Why are nonexperimental studies often higher in external validity than true experiments?

3. What is meant by internal validity? Why are nonexperimental studies often lower in internal validity?

4. What is retrospective data? Why is the use of retrospective data considered a shortcoming in scientific research?

5. Why are unobtrusive measures preferred?

6. Devise an unobtrusive measure to establish each of the following:
   a. Which professor at the university is the most popular?
   b. What are the most popular library books?
   c. Do people prefer to sit on the left or the right side of the theater when they go to the movies?
   d. How will people vote on the next school tax?

7. For each of the research topics listed here, indicate the type of nonexperimental approach that would be most useful and explain why. (You may find more than one approach potentially useful for some topics.)
   a. Pushing ahead in line

b. Daydreaming

c. Locating the most popular painting in an art gallery

d. Studiousness in college students

e. Determining whether a particular patient has improved with psychotherapy

8. For each of your answers to question 7, explain whether an experiment would generate more useful information than the nonexperimental method you selected. Would it be possible to set up experiments to explore all these problems? If not, why not?

9. What is the current paradigm in psychological science? What is meant by a paradigm shift?

10. Design a qualitative study to explore sibling rivalry. Use a method from empirical phenomenology as your data-gathering technique.

## CRITICAL THINKING EXERCISE

*The myth:* Clothes make the man (and woman).

*The scientific findings:* Clothes can have an important influence on how we are perceived by others. More formal attire (such as a business suit) seems to increase ratings on personality traits such as intelligence, credibility, and trustworthiness; but informal attire (like jeans) leads to higher ratings on approachability (Butler & Roesel, 1991).

*The problem:* Imagine that you conducted a participant-observer study to see if people wearing blue jeans were approached more often by strangers than were people wearing business suits. One day you dressed in jeans and stood on a corner in town and counted the number of people who smiled at you or spoke to you. The next day you dressed in a suit and stood at the same corner for the same length of time and, again, counted the number of people who smiled or made contact. You found that 21 people smiled or spoke to you when you wore jeans, but only 12 people did when you wore a suit. Clearly, clothes made a big difference. Or did they? Evaluate the internal validity of your study: How certain are you that the effect was produced by the clothes you wore and nothing else? Evaluate the external validity: Would you expect the same results with different researchers or in different settings?

## ONLINE RESOURCES

For a demonstration of the Purkinje effect, try http://www.yorku.ca/eye/purkinje.htm.

To learn about the kinds of information collected in case studies, try http://www.psychology.about.com/od/psychologywriting/a/casestudy.htm.

To participate in a virtual field study, try this website: http://www.colorado.edu/geography/extra/geogweb/bouldercreek/index.html.

For more about mountain gorillas go to: www.gorillafund.org

## CHAPTER 4

# Alternatives to Experimentation: Surveys and Interviews

**Survey Research**

**Constructing Surveys**

**Measuring Responses**
Selecting Levels of Measurement

**Important Considerations for Survey Items**
Response Styles

**Collecting Survey Data**
Self-Administered Questionnaires
Mail Surveys
Computer and Internet Surveys
Telephone Surveys
Interviews
Focus Groups

**Evaluating Surveys and Survey Data**

**Sampling**

**Probability Sampling**
Simple Random Sampling
Systematic Random Sampling
Stratified Random Sampling
Cluster Sampling

**Nonprobability Sampling**
Quota Sampling
Convenience Sampling
Purposive Sampling
Snowball Sampling
Reporting Samples

SUMMARY
KEY TERMS
REVIEW AND STUDY QUESTIONS
CRITICAL THINKING EXERCISE
ONLINE RESOURCES

## CHAPTER OBJECTIVES

- Learn about more nonexperimental techniques for studying behavior: survey and interview research

- Learn the factors involved in designing questionnaires and devising good questions

- Using standardized tests

- Learn how to administer questionnaires and conduct interviews

- Learn how focus groups work

- Learn the pros and cons of different sampling techniques

---

## SURVEY RESEARCH

We are all familiar with surveys because we are exposed to them all the time: telephone surveys, election polls, television ratings, and customer satisfaction surveys. Survey research is a useful way of obtaining information about people's opinions, attitudes, preferences, and behaviors simply by asking. Surveys allow us to gather data about experiences, feelings, thoughts, and motives that are hard to observe directly. Surveys can be particularly useful for collecting data on sensitive topics because they can be given anonymously, making it more likely that subjects will answer truthfully. Survey data can be useful for making inferences about behavior, although they do not allow us to test hypotheses about causal relationships directly. They are used in conjunction with many kinds of research designs in the field and in the laboratory (we will see many applications of surveys throughout the text). In addition, the principles of writing good survey questions are directly applicable to any research that measures cognition or behavior by asking questions.

Surveys allow us to gather large amounts of data efficiently. Although surveys are low in the manipulation of antecedents (see Figure 3.1 from the previous chapter), they can range from low to high in the imposition of units. When we ask subjects to answer the questions we pose to them, sometimes we allow only a small number of response alternatives (e.g., answering yes or no, circling one number on a 4-point scale). At other times, we allow subjects to answer in any way they wish.

Written questionnaires and face-to-face interviews are the two most common survey techniques in psychology research. Questionnaires can be handed out or sent through the mail; sometimes, surveys are conducted by computer in the laboratory or via the Internet. Interviews can be conducted face-to-face or over the telephone. When interviews are conducted in person, a single individual might be interviewed, or a group of individuals might answer questions posed to them as part of a focus group. The generalizability of survey and interview results is determined largely by the procedures we use to select our subjects, so we will go into detail about alternative sampling procedures later in the chapter. See Box 4.1 for a discussion of ethical considerations in survey research.

## CONSTRUCTING SURVEYS

The major problem with constructing surveys is that everyone thinks they already know how to do it! Some of the worst surveys we have ever seen have been constructed by college professors (outside of psychology, of course). Constructing a good survey is much more than a matter of sitting down for an hour and writing out a bunch of questions. Unless you understand the important components of survey construction, you are likely to construct a survey that will not provide any meaningful information at all. Actually, poor surveys frequently do more harm than good. Constructing a good survey is a research project all by itself, with steps that need to be followed to ensure that valid information is gathered and that the questions are really asking what the researcher intended to ask.

Experts in survey construction agree that the first step of any survey is to map out your research objectives, making them as specific as possible. Let's say your objective is to measure the attitudes of other psychology students toward animal research in psychology (you may recall surveys of just this type from the ethics chapter). To simply say you want to measure attitudes toward animal research in psychology is much too general for a research objective. You need to specify each aspect of animal research that you want to evaluate. Here is a possible list: animal rights, animal welfare, benefits to humanity, pain and suffering, humane treatment, euthanasia, different species, animals used for class demonstrations, etc. Once you have a list of the specific aspects of your topic that you want to measure, you can write one or more questions to evaluate each aspect. To get ideas for your objectives, you may want to look up research done by others on your topic.[1] Looking at surveys that other researchers have conducted should give you lots of ideas about the important elements of your topic, and you might even consider contacting the authors to ask permission to adapt their questions for your study (Suskie, 1992). Finally, put your objectives in writing so you can refer to them as you construct your questionnaire.

Once you have established your objectives, the next step is to design the survey items. The first step is to decide how you are going to address the imposition of units. Do you want to let your subjects give long, free responses to your questions or do you want to restrict their responses to a limited number of alternatives. Many surveys include an assortment of both types of questions. *Closed questions* (also called *structured questions*) take the form "Do you smoke?," "Should there be a ban on nuclear power plants?," and "On a scale from 1 to 10, how much do you like classical music?" Closed questions must be answered by one of a limited number of alternatives.

---

[1] Information on how to conduct a *literature search* is provided in Chapter 6.

BOX **4.1**    **Ethical Considerations in Survey Research**

Conducting surveys is generally thought of as low-risk research, but there are times when special care is necessary to protect survey respondents from potential harm. The potential for ethical problems needs to be just as carefully considered in survey research as in any other kind of psychological research. The two areas most likely to cause ethical concerns are breaches of confidentiality and stress brought about by answering sensitive questions.

Suppose you designed and conducted a survey about a sensitive topic, such as sexual orientation, drug use, HIV status, or depression. As part of your survey, people are asked to report their own status— What is their sexual orientation? What kinds of illegal drugs do they take? Are they HIV-positive? How depressed are they? Asking respondents about their own status is a common procedure in surveys, because attitudes are often different for people who engage in nonnormative behaviors or suffer from a disease or disorder when compared with people who do not. Making the survey anonymous is the most common protection, but even anonymous responses can sometimes be traced back to individuals through consent forms* or through other identifying information on the survey that singles out certain

people. Confidentiality may also be breached in surveys that appear anonymous but really are not. These are generally studies in which survey data are combined with other information about respondents. For example, a researcher may wish to compare attitudes about drug use in good and poor students. To do this, there needs to be a way of identifying survey results so that they can be matched up with a student's GPA. Special care needs to be taken to ensure that confidentiality is maintained and that any links between subjects and their data are kept in a secure location and disposed of carefully (e.g., shredded rather than thrown in the waste basket) as soon as the data are matched up. When sensitive information is gathered, breaches of confidentiality can result in severe social, psychological, and economic harm to individuals should their survey responses become known.

The second area of concern is potential reactions to answering survey questions themselves. Asking questions about traumatic or even sensitive issues can dredge up unpleasant thoughts and memories that can cause stress reactions in respondents. Recall that the APA ethical guidelines (from Chapter 2) communicate to researchers that they are responsible

*Open-ended questions* (also called *open questions*) solicit information about opinions and feelings by asking the question in such a way that the person must respond with more than a yes, no, or 1–10 rating. Examples of open questions are "Why do you prefer taking the train to flying?," "What are your feelings about animal rights?," and "What made you decide to come for treatment now?"

By asking a combination of questions, the researcher can gather a great deal of useful information. Open-ended questions can often be used to clarify or expand answers to closed questions. Let's look at an example. In a questionnaire or interview designed to study attitudes of preteens toward cartoon violence, you might begin by asking a closed question: "On the average, how much time do you spend watching Saturday morning cartoons?" You could allow the children to respond to one of the following options:

"An hour or less"

"Between one and two hours"

"Between two and four hours"

"More than four hours"

for removing any negative effects of their research to the extent possible. When informed consent is obtained in survey research on sensitive topics, potential respondents need to be cautioned about the possibility that answering some questions might be stressful. In cases in which individuals are surveyed about traumatic or extremely sensitive events or topics, the researcher might need to provide information about counseling or therapy services that are available to the respondent. In one example of the potential risks of answering questions about traumatic events, researchers who conducted a telephone survey after the terrorist attacks on September 11, 2001 (Galea et al., 2005) reported the incidence of people who were distressed by taking a telephone survey about the event. Of the 5,774 New York City residents interviewed, 12.9% of the respondents said that the survey questions were upsetting. Only 57 people (about 1%) remained distressed at the end of the interview, and 19 people (about 0.3%) requested a counselor. Ten people who were too upset to complete the survey also requested counseling help.

AP Photo/Jim Collins/FILE

*In some survey research, such as surveys of people with HIV or drug addiction, the potential for risk to participants if confidentiality is breached is deemed serious enough that written informed consent may be waived by the IRB. Informed consent is obtained verbally, but written records are not kept.

This could be followed up with one or more open-ended questions:

"Why do you like to watch cartoons?"

"What do you think about characters who hit each other?"

"What kinds of things might cause you to hit someone?"

However, unless you are simply going to describe people's responses verbatim, you will need to quantify the answers to open-ended questions in some way.

Answers to closed questions are much simpler to quantify than open questions are. For example, you could simply report the number (or percentage) of children who gave each of the four possible responses to the closed question about cartoon viewing time. To quantify answers to open questions, however, a system must be designed to evaluate and categorize the content of each answer. This process, called content analysis, is similar to coding behaviors using systematic observational techniques. In a content analysis, responses are assigned to categories that are created from the data according to objective rules or guidelines.

Suppose that the children's responses to the open question "What kinds of things might cause you to hit someone?" appeared to fall into six categories: (1) Someone looked at me funny, (2) Someone said something to me that I didn't like, (3) Someone wouldn't give me what I wanted, (4) Someone took something away from me, (5) Someone hit me first, and (6) Other responses. You could evaluate each response and code it into the proper category; then you could report the frequency of each kind of response, or you could submit the data to statistical analysis. You can probably think of other categorization schemes that could be constructed for the children's responses: low, moderate, or strong provocation; physical or nonphysical provocation; the number of provocations mentioned by each child; and so forth. Any of these schemes could form the basis of your content analysis. Software programs are available, such as *QSR Nud*ist 4*, which can greatly assist researchers in extracting categories and common themes from open-ended responses.

Constructing questions properly can take a great deal of skill. Here are some tips for getting started: Keep items simple, and keep people involved. Many problems come about because subjects do not understand the meaning of a certain question. Maybe you used words they did not understand. Maybe you used a double negative. Perhaps your question was ambiguous. Perhaps your sentences were too complex and included several ideas at once. Ambiguous or incomprehensible questions cannot generate useful data.

Think about the following question: "Have you ever considered the idea of abortion?" This question is ambiguous because you could judge it to mean "Have you (personally) ever considered having an abortion?" or "Have you ever thought about the concept of abortion?" Some subjects are likely to take the meaning of the question one way, whereas others will interpret it differently. The data you gather would be meaningless, because you would not know which question your subjects were answering. Use language that is easy to comprehend, but if you cannot avoid a term that you know many people won't understand, make sure you define it in the question. The word *antisocial* can fall into this category, because many people do not know what it really means. (Recall antisocial personality disorder from Chapter 3?) Nonpsychologists frequently think that it means "unsociable." You can see that any data you collected on a question using this term would not really be interpretable.

What is wrong with the following question: "Do you like strawberries and cream"? You might like strawberries but not cream (or vice versa), so you could not really answer this question as it is posed. Questions like this are called *double-barreled* (or *compound*), meaning they ask for responses about two (or more) different ideas in the same question, and should be avoided. A somewhat different problem is found in the following questionnaire item that asks about employment status and student status (Patten, 1998, p. 12):

**Occupational Status:**

- ❑ Full-time employment
- ❑ Full-time student
- ❑ Part-time student
- ❑ Unemployed
- ❑ Retired

How would individuals answer this question if they were retired but also attended college part-time? Should they mark two choices? What if someone attends school part-time and also works part-time? Obviously, this is a very poor survey item. It needs to be broken into two questions—one asking about employment status (full-time, part-time, unemployed, retired) and another asking about student status (full-time, part-time, not a student). Consider one more item. What is the problem here?

**What kind of exercise activity do you engage in most often?**

- ❏ Play a sport
- ❏ Power walk or jog
- ❏ Step aerobics or stair-stepper
- ❏ Weight or strength training
- ❏ Walk or treadmill

What if your favorite type of exercise, Pilates, is not listed in the question? Response choices need to be *exhaustive,* meaning they need to contain all possible options. If you are unsure, it is best to add a response category labeled "Other _____" and let respondents write in their answer if it is not provided among the response choices. Only use this latter option, however, if you do not expect people to use it very often, because it is difficult to interpret or analyze an option that could contain a large number of different answers (Patten, 1998). If your question would require more than six or seven response options, it is probably better to ask for the information in an open-ended response format, such as "What is your occupation? _____" (Suskie, 1992).

## MEASURING RESPONSES

Creating open-ended questions is usually just a matter of writing a simply worded question that requires subjects to answer in narrative form, rather than selecting from a choice of responses, and examples of open-ended questions were presented earlier. When we are creating closed questions for our survey, however, we can use a number of different formats. The type of format will largely determine the kinds of statistical analyses we can conduct on the data later, as different types of formats comprise different levels of measurement. The level of measurement is the kind of scale used to measure a response. Different statistical tests are required for different levels of measurement. There are four levels of measurement: nominal, ordinal, interval, and ratio. We will return to levels of measurement throughout the text because they also come into play whenever we design a strategy for measuring behavior in a study or experiment—they are not simply a feature of surveys.

The simplest level of measurement is called a nominal scale, which classifies response items into two or more distinct categories on the basis of some common feature. A nominal scale groups items together into categories that can be named (the term *nominal* comes from the Latin word for "name"). But it does not quantify the items in any way. Classifying subjects' answers to a true-false test uses the nominal level of measurement. For each item, subjects can circle "true" or "false" but not both. Nominal scaling is sometimes called

The New Yorker Collection 1982. Koren/www.cartoonbank.com

FIGURE **4.1** An example of nominal scaling.

the lowest level of measurement because it provides no information about magnitude. For some kinds of responses, however, it is the only type of scale that can be used. Political affiliation is a commonly used nominal measurement. You may be a Democrat, Republican, Independent, Green Party, or Other. There is no difference in magnitude among these categories; you are not more or less affiliated if you belong to one party rather than another. Nominal scales place responses into categories but do not provide the researcher with any information about differences in magnitude between the items.

The next level of measurement is called an ordinal scale, which is a rank ordering of response items. The magnitude of each value is measured in the form of ranks. Pre-election polls sometimes ask people to rank order a number of presidential candidates. Rankings of candidates are examples of ordinal scales. The candidate most often ranked number one is more popular than the candidate most often ranked number two, and so forth. Here, an ordinal scale gives us some idea about the relative popularity of the candidates, but it does not tell us precisely how popular any particular candidate is. To quantify the magnitude of differences between survey responses, we must turn to higher levels of measurement.

An interval scale measures magnitude or quantitative size using measures with equal intervals between the values. However, an interval scale has no true zero point. The Fahrenheit and centigrade temperature scales are interval scales. Although both have zero points, neither has an absolute zero. Neither 0° F nor 0° C represent true zero points (the true absence of any measurable temperature): Temperatures below zero are possible on both scales. For that reason, we cannot say 40° is twice as hot as 20°. But because the intervals between values (between degrees) are equal, we can say that the difference between 40° and 20° is the same as the difference between 20° and 0°.

Common number scales (like 1–4 or 0–100) that you have seen used in surveys are considered interval scales. The interval between any two numbers is equal, but even if a zero is listed as one of the options, it is not a true zero point. Some statisticians question whether number scales like this truly meet the criteria for an interval scale, but the value of the information that can be obtained from them and their common acceptance among psychologists argue strongly for using them. Some common methods of constructing interval scale questions are described in Box 4.2.

The highest level of measurement is called a ratio scale, which has equal intervals between all values and a true zero point. Measurements of physical properties, such as height and weight, are characteristics whose quantity or magnitude can be measured using ratio scales. Time (measured in seconds, minutes, or hours) is another common ratio-scaled item. The values of a ratio scale are expressed by numbers such as 3 feet, 18 kilograms, or 24 hours. Clearly, the intervals between scale values (feet, kilograms, hours) are equal. Measures of feet, kilograms, and hours also have a true zero point—values of 0 feet, 0 kilograms, and 0 hours represent the true absence of height, weight, or time. These attributes enable us to express relationships between values on these scales as ratios: We can say that 24 hours are twice as long as 12 hours.

As we move from lower to higher scales of measurement, we gain more precise information about the magnitude of variables or their quantitative size. Ordinal scales provide more information than nominal scales. Knowing that each of three candidates came in first, second, or third (ordinal scale) in an election, for example, is more informative than just knowing that each of three candidates won or lost (nominal scale), but neither provides as much information about the differences between candidates as knowing the percentage of people who actually voted for each one (ratio scale).

## Selecting Levels of Measurement

Survey responses can be measured by using one of the four types of scales. At times it is possible to measure a response by more than one of these scales (as in the candidate example in the previous paragraph). The best type of scale to use will depend on two things: the nature of the variable you are studying and how much measurement precision you desire. The level of measurement needs to fit the variable being measured. Sometimes a nominal scale is sufficient.

If we were interested in a respondent's marital status, for example, knowing whether someone is married, separated, divorced, widowed, or never married (nominal data) might be all the information that we need. A different kind of study might require knowing how many years subjects have been married (ratio data).

Often, psychological variables lend themselves to different levels of measurement because they represent a continuous dimension. Traits, attitudes, and preferences can be viewed as continuous dimensions, and each individual could fall at any point along each dimension. The trait of sociability, for example, can be conceptualized as a continuous dimension that ranges from very unsociable to very sociable—each person falls somewhere on that dimension. Attitudes can range from strongly negative to strongly positive, and

| BOX **4.2** | **Scaling Techniques: Interval Scales of Measurement** |

If we wanted to discover people's attitudes about scientific research, how could we go about measuring them? Well, we could just ask them an open-ended question, "What do you think about scientific research," and let them answer in their own words. But, as we discussed in Chapter 3, we would have to analyze the content of each response and come up with a system for assigning each one a numerical value. For example, imagine that one person answered, "Well, it's okay, I suppose," and another said, "I don't have a real strong opinion about that." Do these people have the same or a different opinion? Is one more favorable than the other? If so, how much more favorable?

Because it is much more convenient, psychologists who solicit attitudes standardize both the questions asked and the answers available to the respondents. Scaling is an example of this practice.

There are many different scaling techniques, but we are going to focus on the two most common: semantic-differential and Likert scales.

The semantic differential was devised by Osgood, Suci, and Tannenbaum (1957). If we were to use their semantic-differential technique for measuring people's attitudes toward scientific research, we would ask respondents to indicate their attitude by evaluating it on a number of dimensions. Each dimension would consist of two adjectives separated by a scale, usually consisting of 7 points. The adjectives on each scale are antonyms (having opposite meanings), so the semantic differential is composed of bipolar adjective scales. We position our adjectives so that about half of the positive adjectives from each adjective pair are on the left, and half are on the right. Our semantic differential might look like the following example:

### Scientific Research

| Positive | ____ | ____ | ____ | ____ | ____ | ____ | ____ | Negative |
| Worthless | ____ | ____ | ____ | ____ | ____ | ____ | ____ | Valuable |
| Wise | ____ | ____ | ____ | ____ | ____ | ____ | ____ | Foolish |
| Unethical | ____ | ____ | ____ | ____ | ____ | ____ | ____ | Ethical |
| Helpful | ____ | ____ | ____ | ____ | ____ | ____ | ____ | Destructive |

We would ask our subjects to indicate their attitude toward scientific research by placing a check mark on each scale. To quantify each person's attitude, we could score each scale from 1 (most negative) to 7 (most positive) and then sum the

person's score across all the scales. This means that when the negative adjective is on the left, the score you assign to the check mark would go from 1 (for checking the space furthest to the left—the most negative rating) to 7 (for the space furthest to the

preferences from very weak to very strong. Multiple scales are possible for these dimensions. Attitudes toward issues like animal experimentation, for example, could be measured using a nominal scale ("for" or "against") or an interval scale ("On a scale of 1 to 10, how strongly do you favor using animals in psychological research?").

Researchers generally use the following rule for selecting a level of measurement: When different levels of measurement will "fit" equally well, choose the highest level possible because it provides more information about a response. Also, keep in mind that various levels of measurement are analyzed with different statistical techniques, and the statistical tests we can use

right—the most positive rating). In contrast, when the positive adjective is on the left, the score would be reversed. You would assign a score of 7 to a check mark in the leftmost space, and a 1 to a check mark in the rightmost space.

The Likert scaling procedure (Likert, 1932) takes a different approach.

If we were to use this technique to measure attitudes toward scientific research, we would present people with some positively worded statements and some negatively worded statements about scientific research. We would arrange the possible responses to each statement in a multiple-choice format.

Most often, researchers give respondents five answer options: "strongly disagree," "disagree," "undecided" (or "neutral"), "agree," and "strongly agree." With this technique, we could ask people to indicate the degree of their agreement or disagreement with each of the following statements:

Scientific research has produced many advances that have significantly enhanced the quality of human life.

_____ strongly disagree

_____ disagree

_____ neutral

_____ agree

_____ strongly agree

Scientific research has frequently produced confusing results, based on statistics that are biased in the direction of the researcher's beliefs.

_____ strongly disagree

_____ disagree

_____ neutral

_____ agree

_____ strongly agree

We would quantify each person's attitude by scoring each question and then summing their scores across all the questions. We want higher numbers to indicate more positive attitudes, so we would have to make strong agreement with a positively worded statement (for example, the first question above) worth 5 points. We also would make strong disagreement with a negatively worded statement (for example, the second question above) worth 5 points. Strong disagreement with a positively worded statement or strong agreement with a negatively worded statement would each be worth 1 point.

A slightly different, Likert-type technique is commonly employed to assess individuals' evaluations of people, ideas, or things. If you were asked to rate the value of scientific research on a scale from 0 to 10 (0 is your least positive rating and 10 your most positive), a researcher would be measuring your answer using a common Likert-type scale. This type of rating scale can also be used to measure the strength of either the positive or negative attitudes an individual holds toward scientific research, as in the following example:

How do you feel about scientific research? (Circle a number on the scale below.)

| Strongly Against | Somewhat Against | Neutral | Somewhat For | Strongly For |
|---|---|---|---|---|
| −2 | −1 | 0 | +1 | +2 |

for interval or ratio data are more *powerful* than those for nominal and ordinal data. Thus, ratio and interval scales tend to be preferred by researchers over ordinal and nominal measurements.

## IMPORTANT CONSIDERATIONS FOR SURVEY ITEMS

Get subjects involved right away by asking interesting questions. Begin your survey with questions that people will not mind answering. The initial questions are very important because most refusals by subjects occur at the introduction of the survey or during the first few questions. According to Czaja and Blair (1996), in addition to being the start of data collection, the first question should have these characteristics:

1. Relevant to the central topic
2. Easy to answer
3. Interesting
4. Answerable by most respondents
5. Closed format

All these characteristics make it easier to get respondents started. The first few questions should be ones that (1) subjects do not have to think about a great deal (so, no open-ended questions), (2) subjects are able to answer without saying "I don't know," and (3) subjects will think are relevant to the topic of the survey. In a survey about crime, for example, you would not want to ask people their race right at the beginning because people will wonder what their race (or age, income, and so forth) has to do with attitudes about crime. The likely result is that you will lose some participants.

If you are collecting demographic information (people's vital statistics), consider placing those questions at the end of the questionnaire. People will be more likely to answer demographic items if they have already invested their time and energy in answering the survey questions up to this point. Keep in mind that people may be especially sensitive about some kinds of demographic information, such as information about income, race or ethnicity, and age. (Other kinds, such as a person's Social Security number, may be illegal to collect.) Many individuals consider being asked about their vital statistics to be an invasion of privacy. If knowing this information is not absolutely necessary, do not collect it. If it is, create the questions with care and sensitivity. When you need to know someone's income level to estimate their socioeconomic status, for example, you should use income ranges. People are probably more likely to respond to a range than to put down their exact income. Whenever possible, utilize commonly used response options. Here is a common question to solicit age (Patten, 1998, p. 25)[2]:

**What is your age?**

❏   18–24
❏   25–44
❏   45–64
❏   65 years and over

Make sure your questions are not *value laden*. Do not word your questions in ways that would make a positive (or negative) response seem embarrassing or undesirable. Consider how different the following two questions

---

[2] Alternatively, some survey experts ask for the year of birth instead of creating response categories, believing that people are more likely to be truthful about their year of birth than their age if asked directly.

sound, even though both were designed to measure attitudes toward abortion:

> *Version 1:* Do you believe doctors should be allowed to kill unborn babies during the first trimester of pregnancy?

> *Version 2:* Do you believe doctors should be allowed to terminate a pregnancy during the first trimester?

A person unopposed to abortion would find it much more difficult to answer yes to the first question simply because of the way it is worded. Be sure to keep the ethical guidelines in mind when you write survey questions.

## Response Styles

Sometimes subjects' own personal characteristics can inadvertently alter the way they answer questions, and this creates a special problem whenever we gather survey data. Response styles are tendencies to respond to questions or test items in specific ways, regardless of the content (Cronbach, 1950; Rorer, 1965). For example, people differ in response styles, such as willingness to answer, position preferences, and yea-saying and nay-saying. Research has also shown that response styles tend to differ across countries, nationalities, and languages (Harzing, 2006). These response styles need to be considered and, if possible, controlled for when you design survey questions.

First, be aware that people differ in their willingness to answer questions they are unsure about. Willingness to answer comes into play whenever questions require specific knowledge about facts or issues. When unsure, some people will leave questions blank; others will take a guess. An unwillingness to answer is often a problem in survey research. Subjects might omit answers to key questions, making both scoring and interpretation difficult. Some researchers attempt to control for this factor by explicitly telling subjects to guess if they are not sure of the answer to a question. Or you might tell subjects that there are no right or wrong answers to the questions (if that is true); sometimes that helps. Other researchers say nothing—and hope for the best. There is no hard-and-fast rule; each researcher must think this through and decide how best to handle it.

If your questions are multiple-choice, response styles can influence the selection of answers. When in doubt about the right answer on a multiple-choice exam, perhaps you always answer c. This is an example of a position preference.[3] Because of position preferences, sophisticated test builders vary the arrangement of correct answers throughout a test. Most surveys are not tests with right or wrong answers, but you need to keep position preference in mind anyway as you design your questions. In a multiple-choice survey gathering data about attitudes toward abortion, for instance, do not always put "prochoice" responses as option c.

---

[3] Even rats learning to run mazes are known to show position preferences. For example, if a food reward always requires a right turn into a white corridor, animals with a preference for turning right will have an advantage. Researchers control for this effect by varying the position of the white corridor so that the animal must sometimes go left, sometimes right.

A third kind of response style shows up in answers to statements like those in Table 4.1. Would you say that each is true or false for you? The items are similar to ones you might find on the Minnesota Multiphasic Personality Inventory-2 (MMPI-2), a test made up of a long series of items of this type. The way you answer the items on the test can tell a psychologist various things about you—for instance, whether you are anxious or depressed. At first glance, the way people answer such questions seems straightforward; a person who feels happy ought to answer "True" to the first item. We would expect subjects to respond to the manifest content of the questions, the plain meaning of the words that actually appear on the page. When we give a questionnaire or other paper-and-pencil test, we are usually interested in the manifest content of the items. "Have you ever visited another country?" means just that; the manifest content of the item is simply foreign travel. Most people would answer based on their actual travel histories. However, researchers have noticed that some interesting things can happen when subjects fill out questionnaires—especially when the questionnaires ask about feelings or attitudes. Some subjects seem to respond to questions in a consistent way: They will answer "Yes" or "True" to most items, or they will say "No" or "False" to most items. Some subjects are yea-sayers; others are nay-sayers. Yea-sayers are apt to agree with a question regardless of its manifest content (this is also called *response acquiescence*). Nay-sayers tend to disagree no matter what they are asked (also known as *response deviation*).

How can we avoid this problem? One way is by designing questions that force the subject to think more about the answer (Warwick & Lininger, 1975). For instance, think about the difference between these two items:

*Item 1:* Do you agree or disagree that the cost of living has gone up in the last year?

*Item 2:* In your opinion have prices gone up, gone down, or stayed about the same the past year, or don't you know?

When we phrase questions to have simple yes/no or agree/disagree answers, we make it easy for subjects to respond based on response style. By building some specific content into the options as in *item 2*, we encourage subjects to give more thought to each choice.

If we must use yes/no questions, we can still take some precautions. Table 4.2 shows two versions of the Unfounded Optimism Inventory. The "optimistic"

TABLE **4.1**

## Possible items on a personality scale

1. I feel happy most of the time.
2. I enjoy being with other people.
3. I dislike paying attention to details.
4. When I can, I avoid noisy places.
5. Sometimes I feel frightened for no apparent reason.

© Cengage Learning

TABLE **4.2**

## The Unfounded Optimism Inventory

| Version A: No Control for Response Style | | | Version B: Controlling for Response Style* | | |
|---|---|---|---|---|---|
| 1. I know that everything will be all right. | <u>Yes</u> | NO | 1. I know that everything will be all right. | <u>Yes</u> | NO |
| 2. I can pick the fastest line at the bank. | <u>Yes</u> | NO | 2. I always stand in the slowest line at the bank. | YES | <u>No</u> |
| 3. I often smile at nothing. | <u>Yes</u> | NO | 3. I rarely smile, even when provoked. | YES | <u>No</u> |
| 4. If I lose money, I expect it to be returned. | <u>Yes</u> | NO | 4. If I lose money, I expect it to be returned. | <u>Yes</u> | NO |

*The yes/no responses are also counterbalanced to control for order effects.

© Cengage Learning

choice is underlined for each item. All the items in version A are written so that the optimistic response is a yes response. Subjects who are yea-sayers would score high on unfounded optimism—even if they happen to be somewhat pessimistic. Now look at version B. To get a high unfounded optimism score, a subject would have to give both yes and no answers. Using version B would give more valid answers; subjects who turned up high on unfounded optimism are probably not pessimistic yea-sayers.

Once the questions have been designed, they need to be pretested before actual data collection can begin. Before pretesting with actual subjects, read each question out loud to yourself. If it doesn't sound easy to understand, it probably isn't. Rewrite it. Then, go on to pretest with subjects. The simplest way is to ask several people to read and respond to each question. Then, go over each question, individually, with each volunteer, asking them to comment on how easy or difficult it was to answer the question. Solicit any problems or difficulties that made a question hard to answer. Modify any questions that seemed difficult for the volunteers, and pretest the new questions until you are satisfied that they are reasonably easy for most people to answer. Better to catch the problem now than when you are trying to interpret the results later.[4]

Pretesting can also catch context effects; sometimes the position of a question—where it falls within the question order—can influence how the question is interpreted. Context effects are particularly likely when two questions are related. Sometimes it helps to separate related items by *buffer items*—questions unrelated to either of the related questions

---

[4] This was a lesson one of the authors learned the hard way. She used *antisocial* as a question response and found out later that the item was not interpretable because most respondents thought the word meant *unsociable*. If she had pretested the questionnaire, this problem would have been discovered very quickly.

(Wanke & Schwarz, 1997). Imagine that you want subjects to rate Britney Spears on the following semantic differential item:

Nice __ __ __ __ __ Nasty

Now, imagine that the nice/nasty item fell here in your questionnaire:

Not Sexy __ __ __ __ __ Sexy
Nice __ __ __ __ __ Nasty

In the context of the not sexy/sexy item, the nice/nasty item is more likely to be interpreted in a sexual way than it would if it fell here:

Kind __ __ __ __ __ Cruel
Nice __ __ __ __ __ Nasty

In this latter case, the nice/nasty item would probably be interpreted in some other way, perhaps by how caring or considerate an individual she was perceived to be. Context effects are too complex for us to be able to predict them. Furthermore, they rely on information in memory, so they are expected to be somewhat different for each individual. We probably cannot stop context effects altogether, but we need to be aware that they exist.[5]

## COLLECTING SURVEY DATA

Collecting survey data can take many forms: written questionnaires, mail surveys, telephone surveys, Internet surveys, interviews, and focus groups. There are pros and cons for each method. We will explore each method, briefly, in the sections that follow.

### Self-Administered Questionnaires

If you are using a written questionnaire, be sure the instructions are simple and clear. If you are handing out your questionnaire in person, consider the possibility of reactivity. Recall from the last chapter that reactivity is the tendency of subjects to alter their responses if they are aware of the presence of an observer. If possible, let subjects fill out the questionnaire in private. Collect questionnaire data anonymously. Do not ask subjects to identify themselves on their questionnaires. If subjects know they can be identified, there is a much greater chance that their responses will be affected by the social desirability response set (see Box 4.3). Weigh the pros and cons of group sessions. Even though it is a lot easier to collect data from many people at once, subjects may not take your survey as seriously in a group setting. Also consider whether sensitive questions would cause more embarrassment in group sessions. And unless the group consists of complete strangers, you are likely

---

[5] For an excellent, advanced discussion of context effects, see Wanke, M., & Schwarz, N. (1997). Reducing question order effects: The operation of buffer items. In Lyberg, L., et al. (Eds.), *Survey Measurement and Process Quality*. New York: Wiley.

## BOX **4.3**   The Social Desirability Response Set

Remember the various response styles (willingness to answer, position preference, yea-saying and nay-saying) discussed in an earlier section of the chapter? Response styles can reduce the validity of responses if subjects are not responding to the *manifest content*, the plain meaning, of our questions in the way we intend. A different problem occurs when subjects ignore manifest content and, instead, answer questions based on latent content, the "hidden" meaning behind the question. People frequently shape their responses to latent content with a particular goal in mind. That goal can be a response set—a picture we want to create of ourselves. An excellent example of a response set is behavior during a job interview. Unless we don't want the job, we answer the interviewer's questions with the goal of appearing qualified and hardworking. Few prospective applicants would say they want to work as little as possible (even though many people probably fantasize about winning the lottery and never working again!). Instead, most applicants try to put their best foot forward.

In psychological research, we frequently worry that subjects will respond based on what they believe their answers say about them. For example, a study by Louie and Obermiller (2000) demonstrated that subjects may be unwilling to tell researchers the real reasons for their behavior in experiments when the reasons seem socially undesirable. Crowne and Marlowe (1964) developed a 33-item true-false questionnaire, which is used widely to test whether subjects have the response set called "social desirability." To look good on many of the items, subjects would have to lie. Table 4.3 lists a few of the items designed to measure social desirability. For example, few of us would find it easy to get along with "loud-mouthed, obnoxious people," although it is socially desirable, or nice, to be able to get along with everyone. People who respond "True" to this item are most likely distorting the truth.

What can we do about response sets? A person with a response set will answer based on the latent content of questions. Some subjects may try to give the most socially desirable response; others might try to give a deviant response. To counteract a response set, we can develop alternative questions that have the same latent content. For example, which statement in each pair best describes your attitudes toward pets?

> Everyone should have a pet.
>
> I think pets are a waste of time.
>
> or
>
> Pets are fun but not everyone wants the responsibility.
>
> Pets make good companions.

You can see how the implications of the choices differ. In the first pair, one answer seems to be more socially desirable than the other. Some people would feel pressured to pick the first choice so that they would appear to be animal lovers. In the second pair, the choices are about equally acceptable. People can show that they like animals by selecting either item. They can also express the feeling that pets can be a nuisance without worrying about being stigmatized in some way by the response. The second set of alternatives is more likely to lead to valid data.

### TABLE **4.3**
### Selected items from the Marlowe-Crowne Social Desirability Scale*

Listed below are a number of statements concerning personal attitudes and traits. Read each item and decide whether the statement is true or false as it pertains to you personally.

- Before voting I thoroughly investigate the qualifications of all the candidates. (T)
- I never hesitate to go out of my way to help someone in trouble. (T)
- I sometimes think when people have a misfortune they only got what they deserved. (F)
- I don't find it particularly difficult to get along with loud-mouthed, obnoxious people. (T)
- I have never intensely disliked anyone. (T)
- I sometimes feel resentful when I don't get my way. (F)

*The responses shown are socially desirable ones. From *The Approval Motive*, by D. P. Crowne and D. Marlowe. Copyright ©1964 John Wiley & Sons, Inc. Reprinted with permission.

to find that your subjects spend as much time talking to each other as they do filling out your questionnaire.

## Mail Surveys

If you are sending a questionnaire in the mail, be sure to include a polite and professional cover letter (and include a stamped, self-addressed envelope). Make sure your questionnaire and return procedures protect subjects' anonymity. Unless you have contacted people in advance about your survey, and they have agreed to fill it out, do not expect that everyone will fill out and return your questionnaire. Typical response rates for mailed surveys are somewhere between 45% and 75% (Czaja & Blair, 1996).

If you have the resources, including a small gift can increase the return rate (Fowler, 1993). Including a monetary incentive can be especially effective in mail surveys; as little as a dollar can significantly increase response rates. Cash incentives have been found to be more effective, in general, than other kinds of gifts or prizes (Ryu, Couper, & Marans, 2006) but can be an expensive practice when large numbers of respondents are needed. One incentive technique that can be successful and cost-effective is to hold a drawing for a prize (maybe a bookstore or coffee shop gift certificate or movie tickets). Always keep track of the number of people who do not return the questionnaires; you will need to report it. Consider a second mailing to people who did not return the first survey; this can add an additional 50% to the number of surveys returned from your first mailing (Suskie, 1992). Always keep mail surveys as short as possible and include a convincing cover letter.

If the nonreturn rate is high, interpreting your results can be difficult indeed. Suppose you designed a questionnaire to gather data about drug use and only 40% of the subjects returned it. Suppose, also, that 99% of the returned questionnaires were from people who reported they had never smoked marijuana (one or two said they had smoked, but never inhaled). Would it be reasonable to conclude that 99% of people had never smoked pot? Probably not. On sensitive issues, some subjects just won't answer, particularly if their answer would indicate they had engaged in socially undesirable, deviant, or illegal activities. Any time that nonreturn rates are high, be aware that the people who returned the questionnaire may be different in some way from those who did not. You will need to be extremely cautious here in drawing conclusions.

## Computer and Internet Surveys

If you have some programming knowledge and access to laboratory computers, you might consider building a computer-based survey in a psychology laboratory. As an alternative, online companies such as SurveyMonkey.com and SurveyGizmo.com will allow you to create and manage online surveys relatively inexpensively (and usually offer free trial programs). Your subjects can complete the survey on the computer, and you may even be able to have the computer score it for you and put the data in a file for later statistical analysis. Some SPSS statistical packages, for example, have such a program.

If you have Internet programming skills, you might consider adding your survey to the many Web-based surveys already posted. As long as subjects are given a measure of privacy to make their responses and data are collected anonymously, there may be less concern with a social desirability response set than there would be with either telephone interviews or face-to-face interviews (Beckenbach, 1995). And, not having an experimenter present can reduce the potential for coercion to participate (Nosek, Banaji, & Greenwald, 2002)—in Internet surveys, people really are free to participate or not and to stop any time they wish. If your survey is posted on the Web, you still need to provide participants with the same kinds of informed consent information you would provide if they came to your laboratory, and you are responsible for safeguarding the confidentiality of their data to the greatest extent possible. The use of deception is unlikely to be ethical because participants might choose to leave the study before they have been debriefed.

The quality of data obtained using these methods has not yet been thoroughly evaluated, and for now we consider these methods to be extensions of the written versions of questionnaires. Internet surveys, however, present some unique opportunities and some unique problems. For example, your samples may be much more diverse than those you could obtain when subjects must visit the lab to participate, and you may be able to get large samples very quickly, especially if you advertise your Web survey. However, you cannot see your subjects, so there is no way to determine whether respondents are adults or children (or male or female, etc.). Also, the possibility that some individuals may take your survey multiple times is real—especially if it is in a topic area they consider important or particularly interesting. One study found that in an Internet survey of sex practices, approximately 11% of responses were invalid because respondents took the survey more than once (Konstan et al., 2005). One individual, in fact, took the survey 65 times!

## Telephone Surveys

At the present time, telephone surveys are the most widely used method for conducting survey research (Czaja & Blair, 1996). More than 95% of households in the United States now have telephones. In the past, researchers used phone books to locate volunteers. This meant that people with unlisted numbers were not called. The problem that was created was similar to the problem of nonrespondents in a mail survey—the people who listed their phone numbers might be different in some ways than people whose numbers were unlisted.[6] This makes it difficult to draw conclusions or to generalize the results of surveys. Now, many large-scale telephone surveys use a technique called *random digit dialing*. Computers can aid survey researchers by generating random telephone numbers and even dialing them.

---

[6] The popularity of cell phones adds to the potential for biased samples when the phone book is used because cell phones are not listed. Random digit dialing overcomes this problem, but calling cell phones creates ethical (and perhaps legal) problems because the cell phone customer is often paying for usage, including unsolicited incoming calls. It is not currently illegal to make unsolicited calls to cell phones, but it is illegal to use automatic dialing systems or to leave prerecorded messages on cell phones.

Currently, the response rates for telephone surveys usually fall between 60% and 90% when survey takers keep trying to reach someone at a randomly dialed telephone number. New technology, though, is making the future success of telephone surveys uncertain. With the advent of caller ID, for example, fewer and fewer people are answering their phones when they suspect that the caller is conducting a survey. And each year more people who are contacted are refusing to participate in telephone surveys. In 1979, refusal rates were less than 20%; in 2003, they reached almost 30% (Curtin, Presser, & Singer, 2005), and the trend is growing. In an attempt to increase response rates, some survey researchers have begun to send out advance mailings describing the survey and its purposes before contact is attempted. It appears that advance mailings do increase response rates and are even more effective when monetary incentives are included in the mailing (Hembroff et al., 2005).

There are some special considerations for telephone surveys: you need interviewers who are able to establish rapport quickly with strangers and maintain a consistent interview style; and the survey items and response formats need to be kept simple. Have you ever tried to answer a phone survey question that had so many response options that you forgot them all by the end of the question? We have. The use of interviewers can have advantages over mailed surveys. When the interviewers are well trained, they can be expected to obtain high-quality answers, particularly if the questions are non-threatening. In contrast, however, interviewers might not get completely forthright answers about extremely sensitive topics because respondents might be more concerned about social desirability than they would be if they were answering a mailed survey. It is not usually possible to use open-ended questions in telephone surveys, but it is an easy method for respondents—the interviewers do most of the work. Interestingly, research suggests that male telephone interviewers generally may be more effective than female interviewers, either because they are perceived to be more authoritative or because they are more persistent in trying to persuade people to take the survey after someone has refused the first time (Hansen, 2007).

## Interviews

One of the best ways to gather high-quality survey data is to conduct face-to-face interviews, but in terms of time and money, this is the most expensive method for collecting survey data. Interviewers must be thoroughly trained in interviewing skills and techniques. In face-to-face interviews, researchers have found that female interviewers tend to be more successful than male interviewers in gaining cooperation (Pickery & Loosveldt, 2002). Here, we focus on face-to-face interviewing as a technique for collecting survey data, but psychologists and researchers conduct many different kinds of interviews. A clinical psychologist, for example, might conduct a diagnostic interview; an organizational psychologist might conduct a job or personnel interview. Qualitative researchers often conduct in-depth interviews exploring people's experiences, attitudes, or opinions. One difference between interviews to gather survey data and more in-depth interviewing is in the form of the questions that are asked. Survey interviews are frequently made up completely or mostly of closed questions, whereas in-depth interviews are generally made up of open-ended questions.

Even though different types of interviews require somewhat different skills and techniques, there are some common principles that bring about successful interviews. These include techniques such as establishing *rapport* (i.e., winning the interviewee's trust), avoiding judgmental statements, and knowing how to keep the interview flowing (Kaplan & Saccuzzo, 2005).

Before data collection begins, the interviewer will need to spend time winning the subject's confidence and establishing trust. Face-to-face interviews take, on average, more than twice as long as conducting the same survey over the telephone. Remember that even subtle changes in the interviewer's behavior or tone of voice can influence subjects' responses. Your questions must be asked the same way each time. To achieve the necessary interviewer consistency requires a lot of practice. You will also need to decide whether your interview will be structured, unstructured, or a little of both. In a *structured interview,* the same questions are asked in precisely the same way each time—deviations from this structure are not permitted. Structured interviews provide more usable, quantifiable data. *Unstructured interviews* are more free-flowing; the interviewer is free to explore interesting issues as they come up, but the information may not be usable for a content analysis or statistics

The interviewer's appearance and demeanor can affect the ways subjects will respond. Individual characteristics, such as physical appearance, race, accent, and socioeconomic status, may influence the responses obtained by an interviewer. Most interview experts suggest that the best results will be obtained when the interviewer matches the respondent as closely as possible in these characteristics (Crano & Brewer, 2002). Crano and Brewer (2002) also suggest that other personal characteristics of the interviewer, such as enthusiasm for the research, professionalism, friendliness, and interest in the respondent, are all important factors for obtaining good survey data.

## Focus Groups

Another face-to-face technique used less often for collecting data about a particular topic is the focus group method. Chapter 3 contained an example of a study that used focus groups to clarify data from an observational study (Box 3.6). Focus groups (as depicted in Figure 4.2) are usually small groups of people with similar characteristics (e.g., all women, all young Black men, all university students, all working-class people, and so forth) who are brought together by an interviewer, called a *facilitator,* who guides the group in a discussion of specific issues (Czaja & Blair, 1996). Usually, the facilitator wants the group to answer a set of open-ended questions, but the discussion is not usually limited to just those questions. The discussion can easily move beyond the facilitator's questions to other topics. Unless the facilitator is very skilled at leading group discussions, it is difficult to guarantee that a focus group will yield useful data for for content analysis or statistics. Qualitative researchers often employ focus groups as a method of data collection.

David Hoffman/Alamy

FIGURE **4.2** A focus group in progress.

One area in which focus groups have been very successful is pretesting survey questions and procedures. Czaja and Blair (1996) discuss a nationwide telephone survey of physicians that one of them conducted. In pretests, the response rates were very poor (less than 50%), even after 15 callbacks. To improve response rates, the researcher conducted two focus groups with physicians who were similar to those being surveyed. From the focus groups, the researcher learned that physicians wanted to be able to choose either a telephone or a mail survey. When this strategy was used, response rates rose about 40% from the pretest level.

## EVALUATING SURVEYS AND SURVEY DATA

The "goodness" of the survey itself is typically evaluated in two areas: reliability and validity. Reliability is the extent to which the survey is consistent and repeatable. There are different kinds of reliability, and a survey that is reliable will have the following three qualities: responses to similar questions in the survey should be consistent; the survey should generate very similar responses across different survey-givers; and the survey should generate very similar responses if it is given to the same person more than once. The concept of reliability is an important aspect of every research method that measures human responses, and we will return to it throughout this book. Reliability is covered in more detail in Chapter 7.

When we are talking about surveys, validity usually refers to the extent to which a survey actually measures the intended topic. There are several different questions about validity: Does the survey measure what you want it to measure? Does performance on the survey predict actual behavior? Does it give the same results as other surveys designed to measure similar topics? Do the individual survey items fairly capture all the important aspects of the topic? Pretesting the questionnaire helps ensure that survey-takers are answering the questions in the way you intended, increasing its validity. If your questionnaire contains sensitive items that might trigger a social desirability response set, you might choose to include a few items from Crowne and Marlowe's (1964) scale to assess respondents' tendencies to alter their responses to make them more socially desirable. Alternatively, you might include a bogus or nonsense question, such as whether or not the respondent belongs to a fictitious group, to try to identify untruthfulness (Suskie, 1992).

Unless you are heavily into test validation or you expect to publish or present the results of your survey, it is unlikely that you will need (or have time) to evaluate the reliability and validity of your survey. One of the nice features of using standardized tests or surveys commonly used by other researchers is that their reliability and validity have been extensively evaluated. Like reliability, validity is an important aspect of all methods of assessing behavior and cognition and will be discussed in greater detail in Chapter 7.

# SAMPLING

Regardless of how you conduct your survey, one of the most critical issues is sampling, deciding who the subjects will be and then selecting them. Selecting subjects is an important part of any research regardless of its design, and it is a particularly critical issue in survey research. Ideally, when we conduct research, we would include all the members of the population we want to study. The population consists of all people, animals, or objects that have at least one characteristic in common—for example, all undergraduates form one population, all nursing home residents form another, all jelly beans form still another. It is almost never possible to study the entire population; instead, we rely on samples.

A sample of subjects is a group that is a subset of the population of interest. Data collected from samples can be used to draw inferences about a population without examining all its members. In this way, pollsters like Gallup are able to make predictions about the outcome of important elections. Different samples, though, may produce very different data. How accurately we can generalize our findings from a given sample to a population depends on its representativeness, or how closely the sample mirrors the larger population—more precisely, how closely the sample responses we observe and measure reflect those we would obtain if we could sample the entire population. In survey research, as in all psychological research whether conducted in the lab or in the field, our ability to generalize findings to people outside of the sample tested (an important component of external validity) is directly related to how well our sample represents the larger population. We would be very wrong about the percentage of votes going to a candidate if we based our predictions on a preelection sample that included only Republicans! There are two general sampling approaches: probability sampling and nonprobability sampling.

# PROBABILITY SAMPLING

Probability refers to the study of the likelihood of events. What are your chances of rolling a 7 with a pair of dice? What are your chances of winning the lottery today? What are your chances of being selected for a survey sample? Probability is a quantitative discipline; to study probabilities, we must be able to count events and possible outcomes. From a theoretical standpoint, some form of probability sampling is the preferred means of selecting subjects for research.

Probability sampling involves selecting subjects in such a way that the odds of their being in the study are known or can be calculated. We begin by defining the population we want to study. For example, our target population might be all women born in 1975 and now living in Seattle, Washington. (It would take time, but we could count them and establish each woman's odds of being in the sample.) A second condition for probability sampling is that the researcher must use an unbiased method for selecting subjects, such as flipping a coin, drawing a number out of a hat, or using a table of random numbers (see Box 4.4). This process is called random selection, meaning that any member of the population has an equal opportunity to be selected. Random selection is also a common assumption of the statistical tests used most often to analyze data. Now let us look at four types of probability samples—simple random sample, systematic random sample, stratified random sample, and cluster sample.

## Simple Random Sampling

The most basic form of probability sampling is the simple random sample, in which a portion of the whole population is selected in an unbiased way. Huff described the basic procedure in these colorful terms:

> If you have a barrel of beans, some red and some white, there is only one way to find out exactly how many of each color you have: Count 'em. However, you can find out approximately how many are red in much easier fashion by pulling out a handful of beans and counting just those, figuring that the proportion will be the same all through the barrel. (1954, p. 13)

Through random sampling, we can find out what the population is like without studying everyone. To obtain a simple random sample, all members of the population being studied must have an equal chance of being selected. If there are 1 million people in the population, the chance of any particular person being selected should equal one in a million. Even then, using random selection procedures does not guarantee that our sample will be truly representative of the whole population. Suppose someone put all the white beans into Huff's barrel first. If he took his sample from the top, he might conclude incorrectly that the barrel contained only red beans. Random sampling yields only an estimate of what is *likely* to be true.

## Systematic Random Sampling

An elegant variation of random sampling occurs in systematic random sampling. In cases where all members of a population are known and can be

## BOX **4.4**   Using the Random Number Table for Random Selection

Suppose we want to collect data on beliefs about the relationship between regular exercise and "quality of life" among older persons. The population we are interested in studying is people over age 75. Clearly, we cannot study the entire population; what we want is a random, representative sample. In practice, we often find that even this goal cannot be achieved. We may, for example, only have access to the residents of one nursing home. Thus, the "population" available for study is already a select group. Although we would ultimately like to make statements about the general population of older people, our sample must be taken from this smaller group.

Suppose there are 32 residents over age 75, but we only want to interview 20 subjects. Assuming that all the residents are willing to be interviewed, how do we decide which 20 will take part? We could simply ask everyone over 75 to report to the interview room and allow the first 20 arrivals to be in the study. But some residents may arrive later than others for a variety of reasons. Those who are new to the home might not know their way around the grounds and might take more time to find the correct room. General health could be a factor. Individuals who do not feel well might not want to walk to the interview room. Furthermore, there could be significant personality differences between those who get up early and those who sleep late. Thus, a sample of subjects based on arrival time might not be representative of the group as a whole; it would be biased to include a disproportionate number of healthy early risers who know their way around the building.

We can get a fairly good random sample of the nursing home residents if we write all the prospective subjects' names on small pieces of paper, put them into a hat, mix well, and draw them out one by one

until we have as many as we need. The hat method is usually adequate, but it is not foolproof: A small variation in the size of the papers may bias the selection. The papers might not be mixed enough, so you draw out only names beginning with the letters M through Z or only the last numbers you wrote. A better procedure might be to use the random number table (see Appendix B), a table of numbers generated by a computer so that every number to be used has an equal chance of being selected for each position in the table. Unlike the hat method, the computer-generated table is totally unbiased.

How do we use the random number table? We begin by assigning code numbers to all members of our subject pool. At the nursing home, we might simply number the subjects in the order they appear on an alphabetical list. If there are 32 people available, we assign them numbers 1 through 32. If we need only 20 subjects, we go through the random number table in an orderly manner (such as by reading vertically down each successive column of numbers) to find the first 20 numbers between 1 and 32 that appear in the table. Look at Appendix B, Table B1.

Beginning at the top of the first column and reading down, we find the numbers 03, 16, and 12. All are between 1 and 32. So subjects 3, 16, and 12 will be in our sample. (The numbers 97 and 55 also appear in the first column, but since they are greater than 32, we ignore them.) We continue going through the table systematically until we have a total of 20 subjects. This group of 20 is a random sample of the 32 people available for the experiment. The starting point for each study should be decided in a blind manner. For instance, you might close your eyes and put your finger on a part of the table. You would begin your selection there.

listed in an unbiased way, a researcher may select every *n*th person from the population. The *n* is determined by the size of the population and the desired sample size. For example, suppose an alphabetic list of the population of sophomore psychology majors at your university totals 5,000 students, and you would like a sample of 250 people for your survey. Just divide 5,000 by 250 (the answer here is 20) and that number is your *n*; from the list of sophomores, you would select every 20th person. If the list order is truly unbiased, your sample will be as well.

TABLE **4.4**
Types of Probability Sampling

| |
| --- |
| Simple random sampling |
| Systematic random sampling |
| Stratified random sampling |
| Cluster sampling |

## Stratified Random Sampling

When the population is known to contain distinct subgroups, researchers often prefer another variation of probability sampling known as stratified random sampling. A stratified random sample is obtained by randomly sampling from people in each subgroup in the same proportions as they exist in the population. Here is an example. A particular factory is made up of 10% managers and 90% production workers. If you wanted to measure employee morale in this plant, it would be desirable to use stratified random sampling. Managers and production workers might not have the same feelings about the company. If you wanted a stratified sample of 100 employees, you could randomly select 10 managers (10%) and 90 production-line workers (90%). Then your sample would reflect the makeup of the entire staff. If you had decided to use a simple random sample, instead, it could result in a sample that included only production-line workers. By using stratified random sampling to include management, you ensure that their views are fairly represented in the data.

A researcher conducting a survey of urban attitudes might use stratified random sampling to mirror ethnic differences. A market researcher might use it to represent various age and income groups more accurately. There are two advantages to stratified sampling: First, the subsets are sampled separately so that important minorities or subgroups are represented in the total. Second, different procedures can be used with different subgroups to maximize the usefulness of the data. This strategy is desirable when the various subgroups are likely to respond differently.[7]

## Cluster Sampling

When the population of interest is very large, it is often too costly or impractical to randomly select subjects one by one. In such cases, researchers may use another form of probability sampling called cluster sampling. Instead of

[7] When conducting surveys, researchers need to be particularly sensitive to cultural differences among subgroups in the population. Will questions be equally understandable and have the same meaning for all subgroups? Are there language problems or other barriers to communication that need to be overcome? Cross-cultural researchers have emphasized that unless researchers are very familiar with each subgroup, their survey items may not be assessing what they intend (Lonner, 1990). For more information on this topic, you might find the following reference helpful: Matsumoto, D., & Juang, L. (2008). *Culture and Psychology* (4th ed.). Belmont, CA: Wadsworth/Cengage.

sampling individuals from the whole population or from subgroups, researchers sample entire clusters, or naturally occurring groups, that exist within the population. As with all forms of probability sampling, participants are randomly selected, but whole groups of people are selected rather than individuals. Suppose you wanted to survey attitudes about the education system in Connecticut. It would be very expensive and time-consuming to randomly sample all 3.5 million people. Instead, you could randomly select clusters that already exist, such as zip code areas, school districts, cities, or counties. If you selected five counties at random, then everyone in those five counties could be surveyed, or you could survey randomly chosen individuals within each cluster.

The main advantage of cluster sampling is that the researcher can sample data efficiently from relatively few locations. A potential disadvantage of this approach is that subjects within clusters may resemble one another. The people in one county, for instance, might be quite similar in economic status, education, ethnicity, and even age. For that reason, it is desirable to sample many clusters and to obtain as large a sample as possible.

Some form of probability sampling is generally preferred for research purposes because it increases the external validity of the study. Probability samples are more representative of the population, so research conclusions have greater generalizability. There are, however, other ways of selecting samples, which fall under the heading of nonprobability samples.

## NONPROBABILITY SAMPLING

It is sometimes impossible to use the kinds of procedures we have just described, despite their advantages. Even though random selection of subjects is accepted as a cornerstone of good survey research, in reality many surveys are based on nonprobability samples. As the name implies, in nonprobability sampling, the subjects are not chosen at random. Let us look at four common examples of nonprobability samples—quota, convenience, purposive, and snowball sampling.

### Quota Sampling

In quota sampling, researchers select samples through predetermined quotas that are intended to reflect the makeup of the population. Samples can reflect

TABLE **4.5**

### Types of Nonprobability Sampling

| |
|---|
| Quota sampling |
| Convenience sampling |
| Purposive sampling |
| Snowball sampling |

the proportions of important subgroups, but the individuals are not selected at random. For example, a newspaper might want to document campus attitudes toward nuclear arms. A reporter is sent to a university with instructions to interview 40 students, half male, half female, because the student body is roughly half men, half women. There are no constraints on how the reporter selects people to interview as long as the quota is filled. Because the selection is not random, the resulting sample might or might not be a good representation of the college community.

The reporter, for example, could arrive early in the morning and approach students gathered around the vending machines in the student union building. There are many sources of potential bias in this approach—students who have late classes are missing; those who have money for the vending machines might be overrepresented; the reporter might want to approach only those who appear most friendly and cooperative. Such samples have human interest value and are sometimes used in public opinion polls, but quota sampling lacks the rigor required in scientific research and is low in external validity.

## Convenience Sampling

Convenience sampling is obtained by using any groups who happen to be available—for example, a church choir, a psychology class, a bowling league, or a supermarket checkout line. This is considered a weak form of sampling because the researcher exercises no control over the representativeness of the sample. Despite this drawback, convenience sampling (also called *accidental sampling*) is probably done more often than any other kind. It is convenient, it is certainly less expensive than sampling the whole population at random, and it is usually faster. Researchers who rely on convenience samples, however, must be cautious in the conclusions they draw from their data. Convenience samples greatly limit any study's external validity. Whatever qualities distinguish choir members, classmates, or bowlers from the rest of the population can also lead to atypical research findings. It might not be valid to generalize observations beyond the group studied.

## Purposive Sampling

When nonrandom samples are selected because the individuals reflect a specific purpose of the study, the selection is called purposive sampling. Imagine that the purpose of a study was to measure the success of a new training program for employees in two departments (sales and human resources) within a large company. Because the purpose is to compare these departments, you might select the employees of those departments as your purposive sample.

There is nothing wrong with comparing these two departments, but, as with other forms of nonprobability sampling, researchers must be extremely careful about generalizing the results obtained using a purposive sample to any other members of the population.

## Snowball Sampling

In snowball sampling, another form of nonprobability sampling, a researcher locates one or a few people who fit the sample criterion and asks these people to locate or lead them to additional individuals. Snowball sampling is used predominantely for sampling very small, uncommon, or unique populations at times when researchers do not know who the population members are or how to contact them. Suppose you wanted to survey a sample of animal rights activists. After locating one activist who agrees to be part of the research, you might ask this individual to help you find other activists and then ask them to help find others, and so on. Clearly, a snowball sample may not be representative of the whole population. If your activist was a fellow classmate, for instance, your sample might overrepresent highly educated activists or younger activists. We always have our best chance of obtaining a sample that is representative of the whole population through random selection.

## Reporting Samples

The way a sample is chosen influences what can be concluded from the results. A research report must explain the type of sample used and how subjects were recruited so that the results can be interpreted properly. After all, in many circumstances college students might respond differently than do nursing home residents, and results obtained from one convenience sample might not be generalizable to everyone. So we need to tell the reader exactly how the sample was obtained. This includes identifying the specific population sampled (for example, college students), as well as giving an exact description of where and how subjects were obtained. For example, you could say, "The subjects were 60 undergraduates, 30 men and 30 women, at the University of Oregon who responded to an ad in the college newspaper." Include gender, age, and other important demographic characteristics (education level, racial and ethnic heritage, socioeconomic status, etc.) if they could be important in interpreting the results.

Any details that might have influenced the type of subject participating in the study need to be included. If subjects were paid for participating or students' participation fulfilled a course requirement, readers should be told that, too. Any limitations on who could participate should also be noted. In the nursing home example from Box 4.4, we might say,

> The participants were 20 (6 male and 14 female) randomly selected residents of the Valley Nursing Home in Elmtown, Ohio. To participate, subjects needed to be at least 75 years old and in good health. The average age was 77.3 years; the ages ranged from 75.2 years to 83.4 years.

Note that this statement immediately tells readers that, although we are discussing attitudes about the values of exercise in healthy older persons, our participants were drawn at random from a very small pool. It also tells readers that we studied both men and women who fell within a particular age range. Occasionally, some participants who are selected are not included in the report: They dropped out, their data were discarded because they could not follow the instructions, and so on. These facts should also be reported. This may seem like a lot of information to report, but details about your sample are a critical component of all research, and they are of major importance in survey research. These details give the reader the information necessary to evaluate the generalizability of the results or to compare the results of different studies. The details are also necessary for replication. In the next chapter, we will learn about other nonexperimental designs—correlational and quasi-experimental designs—that provide additional techniques for describing relationships among behaviors and for investigating individual differences in attitudes, behavior, and personality.

## SUMMARY

*Survey research* (questionnaires and interviews) is a frequent component of field studies, and surveys can be part of many research designs. Surveys can contain closed or open-ended questions, or a combination of both. Quantifying open-ended questions requires *content analysis.* Response formats for closed questions can be designed from one of four levels of measurement: *nominal, ordinal, interval,* or *ratio scales.* Often, psychological variables lend themselves to multiple levels of measurement because they represent a *continuous dimension;* in this case, researchers often prefer the highest level of measurement possible.

Subjects do not always respond to the *manifest content* (the plain meaning) of survey questions. When constructing surveys, the researcher also needs to consider *response styles,* such as *willingness to answer, position preference,* and *yea-saying* or *nay-saying.* At times, subjects will respond to the *latent content* (hidden meaning) of survey items because of *response sets,* such as social desirability.

Survey data may be collected in several different ways. Self-administered questionnaires may be handed out to subjects or completed on desktop computers or via the Internet. Mail surveys are a popular and cost-effective approach. Telephone surveys have become a popular data collection method, especially when assisted by computers in random digit dialing. Face-to-face interviews are more time-consuming and require trained interviewers but can result in high-quality data. The goodness of surveys is reflected in *reliability* and *validity.*

*Sampling* procedures are important for all types of research and are particularly important for *survey research.* Our ability to generalize research findings depends on the *representativeness* of our *sample of subjects* to the *population* we are studying. *Random selection* of subjects is a cornerstone of good survey research. Some form of *probability sampling* (*simple random sampling, systematic random sampling, stratified random sampling,* or *cluster sampling*) is preferred, but *nonprobability samples,* such as *convenience samples, quota samples, purposive samples,* and *snowball samples,* are more frequently used.

# KEY TERMS

**Cluster sampling** A form of probability sampling in which a researcher samples entire clusters, or naturally occurring groups, that exist within the population.

**Content analysis** A system for quantifying responses to open-ended questions by categorizing them according to objective rules or guidelines.

**Context effects** Effects produced by the position of a question; where it falls within the question order can influence how the question is interpreted.

**Continuous dimension** The concept that traits, attitudes, and preferences can be viewed as a continuous dimension, and each individual can fall at any point along each dimension; for example, sociability can be viewed as a continuous dimension ranging from very unsociable to very sociable.

**Convenience sampling** A convenience sample is obtained by using any groups who happen to be convenient; considered a weak form of sampling because the researcher exercises no control over the representativeness of the sample (also called *accidental sampling*).

**Interval scale** The measurement of magnitude, or quantitative size, having equal intervals between values but no true zero point.

**Latent content** The "hidden meaning" behind a question.

**Level of measurement** The type of scale of measurement—ratio, interval, ordinal, or nominal—used to measure a variable.

**Manifest content** The plain meaning of the words or questions that actually appear on the page.

**Nay-sayers** People who are apt to disagree with a question regardless of its manifest content.

**Nominal scale** The simplest level of measurement; classifies items into two or more distinct categories on the basis of some common feature.

**Nonprobability sampling** Sampling procedures in which subjects are not chosen at random; two common examples are quota and convenience samples.

**Ordinal scale** A measure of magnitude in which each value is measured in the form of ranks.

**Population** All people, animals, or objects that have at least one characteristic in common.

**Position preference** When in doubt about answers to multiple-choice questions, some people always select a response in a certain position, such as answer *c*.

**Probability sampling** Selecting samples in such a way that the odds of any subject being selected for the study are known or can be calculated.

**Purposive sampling** The selection of nonrandom samples that reflect a specific purpose of the study.

**Quota sampling** Selecting samples through predetermined quotas that are intended to reflect the makeup of the population; they can reflect the proportions of important population subgroups, but the particular individuals are not selected at random.

**Random number table** A table of numbers generated by a computer so that every number has an equal chance of being selected for each position in the table.

**Random selection** An unbiased method for selecting subjects in such a way that each member of the population has an equal opportunity to be selected, and the outcome cannot be predicted ahead of time by any known law.

**Ratio scale** A measure of magnitude having equal intervals between values and having an absolute zero point.

**Reliability** The extent to which a survey is consistent and repeatable.

**Representativeness** The extent to which the sample responses we observe and measure reflect those we would obtain if we could sample the entire population.

**Response set** A tendency to answer questions based on their latent content with the goal of creating a certain impression of ourselves.

**Response style** Tendency for subjects to respond to questions or test items in a specific way, regardless of the content.

Sample of subjects A selected subset of the population of interest.

Sampling Deciding who the subjects will be and selecting them.

Simple random sampling The most basic form of probability sampling whereby a portion of the whole population is selected in an unbiased way.

Snowball sampling A form of nonprobability sampling in which a researcher locates one or a few people who fit the sample criterion and asks these people to locate or lead the researcher to additional individuals who fit the criterion.

Stratified random sampling A form of probability sample obtained by randomly sampling from people in each important population subgroup in the same proportion as they exist in the population.

Survey research A useful way of obtaining data about people's opinions, attitudes, preferences, and experiences that are hard to observe directly; data may be obtained using questionnaires or interviews.

Systematic random sampling A variation of random sampling in which a researcher selects every $n$th person from the population.

Validity The extent to which a survey actually measures the intended topic and not something else.

Willingness to answer The differences among people in their style of responding to questions they are unsure about; some people will leave these questions blank, whereas others will take a guess.

Yea-sayers People who are apt to agree with a question regardless of its manifest content.

## REVIEW AND STUDY QUESTIONS

1. Pick a survey topic and list seven objectives for a possible survey.

2. Evaluate the pros and cons of open-ended and closed questions.

3. How are open-ended questions quantified? Give an example of an open-ended question and how you might quantify the responses. How else might you do it?

4. Imagine that you are writing survey questions for the topic you chose for item 1. Select one objective and design four questions to explore it: one using a nominal scale, one using an ordinal scale, one using an interval scale, and one using a ratio scale.

5. When designing survey questions, how would you control for each of the following response styles?
   a. Willingness to answer
   b. Position preference
   c. Yea- or nay-saying

6. What is wrong with this question? "Do you think it is acceptable to kill animals with painful procedures and use them to advance scientific knowledge to benefit human beings?" Rewrite the item to fix the problem.

7. What type of measurement scale is being used in each of these instances?
   a. A researcher measures the brand of car purchased by subjects who heard one of three advertising campaigns.
   b. A counselor compares the frequency of divorces in couples that had marriage counseling and those who did not.
   c. A seamstress estimates how much fabric will be needed to make a coat.
   d. Three racks of sweaters are labeled "small," "medium," and "large."
   e. On a scale from 0 to 10 (0 = not at all; 10 = extremely), how hungry are you right now?

8. You have designed a survey for nurses, and you have mailed it to 500 nurses across the country. It has now been several weeks since you mailed out the surveys, but so far only 20% of the nurses have filled out and

returned the survey. What are three things you could do to increase the response rate?

9. What are the pros and cons of telephone surveys and face-to-face interviews?

10. What is the difference between reliability and validity?

11. Explain the difference between probability sampling and nonprobability sampling and describe the different forms of each.

12. Discuss the logic behind random selection and why it is important in research.

13. Evaluate each of the following as a technique for obtaining a random sample of subjects.
    a. An experimenter obtains subjects by asking every third driver stopping at the stoplight on the corner of Hollywood and Vine streets in Los Angeles to be in an experiment.
    b. A researcher places an ad in a local paper asking for volunteers for a psychology experiment.
    c. An experimenter calls every fourth number in the phone book and asks for volunteers for a research project.
    d. A wealthy graduate student posts signs on the university bulletin boards offering $8 per hour for participating in a 2-hour perception experiment.

14. Using Table B1, the random number table in Appendix B of this book, select a random sample of 10 subjects from a subject pool of 20.

## CRITICAL THINKING EXERCISE

*Questionnaires on the Internet:* Find and participate in a survey on the World Wide Web. (Several hundred of them are listed on http://psych.hanover.edu/Research/exponnet.html and http://www.socialpsychology.org/expts.htm) Then, think critically about the sample of subjects for this survey: What kind of a sample is being used? What sampling problems occur with Internet surveys that would not occur with in-person or mail surveys?

## ONLINE RESOURCES

For ideas on writing demographic questions, see www.census.gov.

For additional information about content analysis, try this website:
http://writing.colostate.edu/guides/research/content/pop2a.cfm

For an in-depth look at real-world survey sampling procedures and problems, go to:
http://aapor.org/

A free program that you can use for creating random samples can be accessed at the following website:
http://www.randomizer.org/.

Try the Wadsworth research methods workshop on surveys:
http://www.wadsworth.com/psychology_d/templates/student_resources/workshops/workshops.html.

## CHAPTER 5

# Alternatives to Experimentation: Correlational and Quasi-Experimental Designs

**Correlational Designs**
Correlation
Linear Regression Analysis
Multiple Correlation and Multiple
   Regression

**Causal Modeling**
Path Analysis
Cross-Lagged Panel Design

**Quasi-Experimental Designs**
Ex Post Facto Studies
Nonequivalent Groups Design

Longitudinal Design
Cross-Sectional Studies
Pretest/Posttest Design

SUMMARY
KEY TERMS
REVIEW AND STUDY QUESTIONS
CRITICAL THINKING EXERCISE
ONLINE RESOURCES

## CHAPTER OBJECTIVES

- Learn more techniques that do not manipulate antecedent conditions: correlations, other correlational-based methods, and quasi-experimental designs

- Learn how causal models can be constructed from correlation-based designs

- Understand how the results of these nonexperimental techniques may (and may not) be interpreted

In this chapter, we continue our discussion of nonexperimental designs. We will focus on two important categories of nonexperimental research methods: correlational designs and quasi-experimental designs. Correlational designs are used to establish relationships among preexisting behaviors and can be used to predict one set of behaviors from others (such as predicting your college grades from scores on your entrance exams). Correlational designs can show relationships between sets of antecedent conditions and behavioral effects (the relationship between smoking and lung cancer in humans, for instance), but, as you will see, the antecedents are preexisting. They are neither manipulated nor controlled by the researcher. Advanced correlational methods, however, such as path analysis and cross-lagged panel designs, can be used to propose cause-and-effect relationships by developing causal models. As with all nonexperimental methods, however, it is much more difficult to establish cause-and-effect relationships conclusively using correlational techniques.

Another nonexperimental approach that is widely used by researchers when they cannot manipulate or control antecedent conditions is a quasi-experimental design. The prefix *quasi* comes from Latin and means "seeming like." Quasi-experiments often seem like real experiments, but they lack one or more of the essential elements, such as manipulation of antecedents or random assignment to treatment conditions. Instead of assigning subjects to different treatment conditions at random as we do in a true experiment, subjects are selected for the different conditions of the study on the basis of preexisting characteristics. For example, quasi-experiments can be used to compare behavioral differences associated with different types of subjects (e.g., normal or schizophrenic children), naturally occurring situations (e.g., being raised in a one- or two-parent home), or a wide range of common or unusual events (e.g., the birth of a sibling or surviving a hurricane) that cannot be manipulated by an experimenter. In cases such as these, the experimenter wants to study a set of preexisting antecedent conditions. Subjects are selected and placed into groups on the basis of the characteristic or circumstance that the experimenter wants to investigate; thus, the "treatments" are either selected life events or preexisting characteristics of individuals.

Manipulating antecedent conditions is frequently not an option for researchers. Many of the behaviors of interest to psychologists are preexisting conditions. A behavior such as childhood schizophrenia certainly falls into the category of behaviors that may never lend themselves to true experimentation. We might never be able to fully explain behavioral disorders such as schizophrenia, but quasi-experimentation can increase our understanding of its environmental, biological, cognitive, and genetic attributes, as well as its symptoms and manifestations. Quasi-experimentation often allows the researcher more systematic control over the situation than do the nonexperimental designs from Chapter 3 (phenomenology, naturalistic observation, etc.) and can be used in a wide variety of research settings—both in the field and in the laboratory.

Experimenters also use quasi-experimental designs whenever subjects cannot be assigned at random to receive different experimental manipulations or treatments. Suppose, for example, that a researcher wanted to compare the effects of fluorescent and incandescent lighting on worker productivity in two manufacturing companies. The researcher could manipulate the lighting conditions, installing fluorescents in Company A and incandescent bulbs in Company B, but because subjects are already working for one of the companies, they would already be preassigned to receive a particular treatment. The researcher could not randomly assign workers to the different treatment conditions of the experiment. If the researcher found that productivity differed in the two lighting conditions, it would be difficult to establish with certainty that the lighting treatments were the true cause—the workers themselves may have differed, or other working conditions influencing productivity might have differed dramatically in the two manufacturing plants. (The inability to establish cause with certainty in research is called *confounding* and is discussed in detail in Chapter 7.) Quasi-experiments can seem to have all the trappings of a true experiment, but unless other antecedents that can influence productivity are carefully controlled, the experiment will not be high in internal validity.

Recall from Chapter 3 that internal validity is our ability to establish a causal relationship between a specified set of antecedent conditions (called *treatments*) and the subsequent observed behavior. Research is high in internal validity if we can conclude with a high degree of confidence that the specified set of antecedents—and not something else, such as differences in the subjects or the environment—caused the observed differences in behavior among the various groups of subjects in the experiment. Using quasi-experiments, the researcher can explore consistent differences between preexisting groups of people or compare treatments in nonrandom groups of subjects, but the cause of behavioral differences cannot be established with confidence. As a group, correlational designs and quasi-experiments tend to be higher in external validity, or generalizability, than are laboratory experiments, but external validity must be assessed on a case-by-case basis.

Returning to the two-dimensional scheme we used in Chapter 3 (Figure 3.1), we could say that correlations are low in the manipulation of antecedents. As our examples have shown, quasi-experiments will vary in the degree of manipulation of antecedents, but without random assignment, they are not considered high. Both correlational and quasi-experimental designs, however, tend to be high in the imposition of units. They restrict, or limit, the responses subjects can contribute to the data being collected. In both types of designs, researchers are typically interested in obtaining only specific kinds of information from each subject. Both methods rely on statistical data analyses, which allow the significance, or importance, of results to be evaluated objectively. Some of these designs use correlational analyses; others use inferential statistics (like the *t* tests and analysis of variance covered in Chapter 14). Some designs (like path analysis), use sophisticated correlational techniques to create causal models, although each has limited internal validity. Let us begin with correlational designs.

---

## CORRELATIONAL DESIGNS

Frequently, we want to go beyond describing our observations to provide a statistical summary of what we have seen. We can describe the data of nonexperimental studies in a great many ways. One approach, correlation, is so common in nonexperimental studies that it is discussed as a research method in its own right. Correlation can be used with both laboratory and field data.

## Correlation

You already know that some questions cannot be answered experimentally for practical and ethical reasons. Questions such as "What are the long-term effects of TV violence on aggressiveness?" fall into this category. To find the answer experimentally, it would be necessary for researchers to manipulate children's exposure to TV violence for many years while controlling for other potential influences on aggressiveness—clearly an impossible (and unethical) task. Instead, you might consider conducting a correlational study.

A correlational study is one that is designed to determine the correlation, or degree of relationship, between two traits, behaviors, or events. When two things are correlated, changes in one are associated with changes in another. Researchers often use correlational studies to explore behaviors that are not yet well understood. By measuring many behaviors and seeing which go together, we begin to see possible explanations for behaviors. With the widespread availability of computers, researchers can measure and analyze the relationships among countless numbers of variables in a single study. (Incidentally, a *variable* is any observable behavior, characteristic, or event that can vary or have different values.) Although this shotgun approach is not always the most elegant research strategy, it may have *heuristic* value, aiding us in the discovery of important influences on behavior. Correlational data may serve as the basis for new experimental hypotheses, as we shall see in Chapter 6.

In a correlational study, selected traits or behaviors of interest are measured first. Numbers (i.e., scores) are recorded that represent the measured variables. Next, the degree of relationship, or correlation, between the numbers is determined through statistical procedures. Correlation, however, is really a statistical technique for summarizing data that could be used in studies falling in any portion of our graphic scheme. In the correlational study, the researcher measures events without attempting to alter the antecedent conditions in any way; the researcher is simply asking how well the measures go together. Correlational studies thus fall in the low-high portion of Figure 3.1. Once the correlation is known, it can be used to make predictions. If we know a person's score on one measure, we can make a better prediction of that person's score on another measure that is highly related to it. The higher the correlation, the more accurate our prediction will be.

Suppose a researcher wonders whether there is a relationship between television viewing and the size of people's vocabularies. The researcher could gather data to determine whether such a relationship exists by first devising an objective measure of vocabulary. For instance, the researcher might ask subjects to go through a dictionary and check off all the words that are familiar. The researcher would also carefully measure daily television viewing time. The degree of relationship, or correlation, between the two measures would then be evaluated through statistical procedures. Relationships between pairs of scores from each subject are known as simple correlations. The Pearson

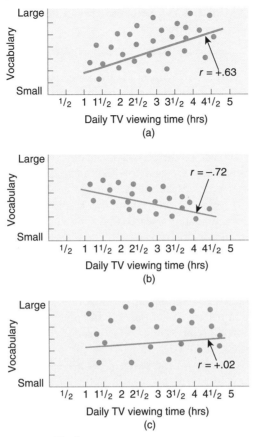

FIGURE **5.1** Some hypothetical relationships between size of vocabulary and length of daily TV viewing: (a) a positive (direct) relationship; (b) a negative (inverse) relationship; (c) no strong relationship.
© Cengage Learning

Product Moment Correlation Coefficient ($r$) is the most commonly used procedure for calculating simple correlations; you will see the Pearson $r$ reported in most correlational studies.[1] When $r$ is computed, three general outcomes are possible: a positive relationship, a negative relationship, or no relationship. These are illustrated in Figure 5.1.

*Because of the way the statistic is computed, the values of a correlation coefficient can only range between −1.00 and +1.00.* The sign (plus or minus) tells us the positive or negative direction of the relationship; the absolute value of $r$ (the unsigned value) tells us the strength of the relationship.

---

[1] The Pearson $r$ is used when interval or ratio scale data are collected. Other correlation coefficients are computed when the data from both measurements are ordinal (Spearman's $r_S$), nominal (phi or $\phi$), or one of the two is nominal (point biserial correlation, or $r_{pb}$).

Correlation coefficients can be depicted on a number line going from $-1.00$ to $+1.00$, like the one below:

$$-1.00 \text{——————} -.50 \text{——————} 0 \text{——————} +.50 \text{——————} +1.00$$

We always carry correlation coefficients out to two decimal places. The computational formula can be found in Appendix A-1.

You will notice that a collection of dots is shown in each section of Figure 5.1. These dots illustrate what researchers call scatterplots (also known as *scattergraphs* or *scattergrams*), visual representations of the scores belonging to each subject in the study. Each dot stands for one subject, and each subject has two scores—one for TV viewing time and one for vocabulary. One score is used to place the dot along the $X$ (horizontal) axis. The second score is used to place the dot along the $Y$ (vertical) axis. Scatterplots are often the researcher's first step toward analyzing correlational data. As you can see, the arrangement of dots gives a rough indication of both the direction and strength of the relationship that has been measured. Figure 5.1 depicts three possible correlational outcomes for the TV viewing and vocabulary study. In Figure 5.1a, the scatterplot shows that as viewing increased, vocabulary also increased (a positive relationship). In Figure 5.1b, as viewing increased, vocabulary declined (a negative relationship). In Figure 5.1c, the dots form no particular pattern (no strong relationship). This is reflected in the value of the computed $r$, which is quite small $(+.02)$.

The lines drawn on the scatterplots are called regression lines, or *lines of best fit*. They illustrate the mathematical equation that best describes the linear relationship between the two measured scores. The direction of the line corresponds to the direction of the relationship. As you can see in Figure 5.1, the position of the line changes as the correlation changes.

When the computed value of $r$ is positive, there is a positive correlation between vocabulary and TV viewing time; the more a person watches television, the larger his or her vocabulary. This is also called a direct relationship. The absolute (unsigned) value of $r$ tells us how strong the relationship is. If $r = +1.00$, we have a perfect positive correlation, and we can predict the value of one measure with complete accuracy if we know a subject's score on the other measure. Positive values of $r$ that are less than $+1.00$ (for example, $+.52$) tell us there is a direct relationship between our two measures, but we cannot predict the value of one from the other with complete accuracy because the relationship between them is imperfect.

A second possibility is a negative correlation between vocabulary and TV viewing time (that is, $r$ is negative). This would mean that the more a person watches television, the smaller his or her vocabulary would be. This is also called an inverse relationship. One of the most difficult concepts to grasp about correlations is that *the direction of the relationship (positive or negative) does not affect our ability to predict scores.* We could predict vocabulary just as well from a negative correlation as from a positive one, provided that the strength of the relationships was the same. You will recall that the strength of the relationship is indexed by the absolute (or unsigned) value of $r$. A correlation of $r = -.34$ actually represents a stronger relationship than does $r = +.16$. The sign merely tells us whether the relationship is direct or inverse; the absolute value tells us how strong it is. As the absolute value gets larger, we can make more and more accurate predictions of a person's score on one measure when we know the person's score on the other.

A third possibility is no relationship between vocabulary and TV viewing time ($r$ is near zero). In that event, our prediction may be no more accurate than any random guess, and we would not learn anything about a person's vocabulary through knowledge of his or her television habits.

The use of scatterplots for correlational data can help in other ways. Correlation coefficients can be strongly affected by several features of the data: a nonlinear trend, range truncation, and outliers. Statistical formulas for simple correlations use a General Linear Model, which assumes that the direction of the relationship between X and Y generally remains the same. It does not change direction. The plotted values of X and Y can appear to be rising (as in Figure 5.1a) or falling (as in Figure 5.1b), or there is no apparent linear trend at all (as in Figure 5.1c). But the linear trend in the scatterplot may not reverse direction. Relationships between some psychological variables, such as the relationship between test anxiety and test performance, do not fit a linear model such as this one; instead, their relationship appears curvilinear (like an inverted U) when graphed on a scatterplot. A curvilinear relationship between test anxiety and test performance is illustrated in Figure 5.2. Notice that the relationship between anxiety and performance rises for a while, peaks, and then begins to fall. Curvilinear data patterns (or other patterns in which the relationship changes direction) cannot be adequately captured by simple correlations; the $r$s would be very small (or even zero) because the data do not have a simple, straight-line relationship.

Correlation coefficients are also affected by *range truncation*, an artificial restriction of the range of values of X or Y. For example, we would expect a strong positive correlation between age and shoe sizes in children between the ages of 4 and 16. As children get older, their shoe size increases. Imagine that

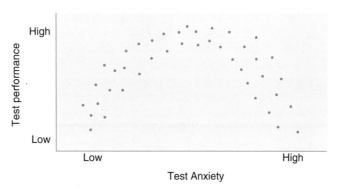

FIGURE **5.2** A curvilinear relationship between test anxiety and test performance.
© Cengage Learning

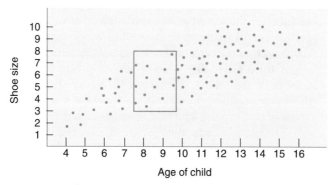

FIGURE **5.3** The correlation between children's ages and shoe sizes.
© Cengage Learning

we conducted this study in a large sample of children and found $r = +.67$; as we predicted, we found a strong positive relationship between age and shoe size. These hypothetical data are plotted in Figure 5.3. The strong positive trend is easy to spot; the pattern of data looks very much like Figure 5.1a. Now, imagine that we wanted to know, instead, what the correlation would be for a smaller age range of these children—just the 8- and 9-year- old children. In Figure 5.3, we have put a box around the data that would fit this narrower age range. Do you still see a strong positive trend? No. The area in the box now looks much like the very weak correlation shown in Figure 5.1c. By restricting the age range, the positive trend becomes very weak. If we computed the correlation coefficient for this truncated range, we would be likely to get a correlation coefficient close to zero.

Have you ever wondered why standardized achievement tests are not better predictors of grades? Part of the answer appears to lie in range truncation. For example, the correlation between grades in graduate school and individuals' Graduate Record Exam (GRE) scores is not very high ($rs = .22$ to .33; House & Johnson, 1998). Testing experts argue that one reason for this is that the ranges of both types of scores are truncated. First, graduate schools tend to admit only the top GRE scorers, resulting in an artificially narrow range of scores. Second, graduate school grades tend to be mostly A's and B's—a narrow range indeed. If we plotted data from such restricted ranges, the scatterplot would appear to show only a weak positive trend.

Another problem that can affect correlation coefficients is the presence of *outliers* (extreme scores). Imagine that you wanted to correlate the amount of time adolescents spent listening to pop music with their grades in high school. Figure 5.4 depicts hypothetical data collected in such a study. This scatterplot shows that for many adolescents, grades seem to decrease as listening time increases (a negative correlation), but this is not always the case, is it? A number of subjects do not fit this pattern at all. Their scores are very different from those of most subjects; these scores are outliers. The presence of outliers can dramatically reduce the size of the correlation coefficient because it disturbs the general linear trend of the data.

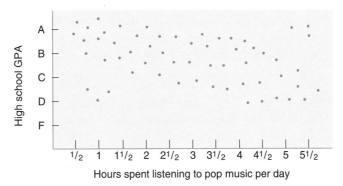

FIGURE **5.4** The correlation between high school grades and time per day spent listening to pop music.
© Cengage Learning

Because they are so useful and are relatively easy to conduct, researchers in every branch of psychology conduct correlational studies. They have become indispensable in many areas that cannot be investigated using experimental approaches. For example, the link between smoking and many serious health problems was revealed from correlational studies. Correlational data, though, have one serious drawback. When we are dealing with correlational data, we cannot make causal inferences: *Correlation does not imply causation.* In other words, even though a relationship exists between two measures, we cannot say that one causes the other, even when such a statement appears reasonable.

Even a perfect correlation (+1.00 or −1.00), if it were obtainable, does not indicate a causal relationship. The fact that two measures are strongly related does not mean that one is responsible for the occurrence of the other. For example, Bowman's archival study of African American men from Chapter 3 produced high positive correlations between family closeness and satisfaction with family roles (and also between religiousness and satisfaction with family roles), but it did not prove that family closeness (or religious beliefs) caused greater satisfaction.

Chaplin, Phillips, Brown, Clanton, and Stein (2000) conducted an interesting correlational study of the relationship between the firmness of a man's or woman's handshake and the positivity of first impressions. Even though the two variables were strongly correlated ($r = .56$)[2], the researchers explained that other personality variables, such as extraversion, could have caused both firm handshakes and more positive impressions. During the last hundred years, there has probably been a positive correlation between the number of automobiles and the number of airplanes in the world. But it would be illogical to say that automobiles cause airplanes or vice versa.

Another look at the earlier example of studying the effects of TV violence on aggressiveness illustrates the limitations of trying to explain the cause of behavior from correlational studies. It would not be difficult to correlate

---

[2] By mathematical convention, we drop the plus sign when a correlation coefficient is positive.

the amount of time a person spends watching television violence with some measure of trait aggressiveness (indeed, similar studies have been done many times since the advent of television). Let us imagine that we actually carried out this study and found that exposure to TV violence and aggressiveness were strongly related. Can we say that violent TV causes aggressiveness? No. No matter how reasonable this hypothesis sounds, we have not established that TV violence causes aggression. Why not? *Because the causal direction between two variables cannot be determined by simple correlations.* We cannot be certain which behavior is the cause and which is the effect—nor, as you will see, can we be certain that there is a causal relationship at all between the measured behaviors. Along with our hypothesis that aggression is caused by exposure to TV violence, there are three alternative possibilities whenever two behaviors are strongly correlated.

First, innate aggressiveness might determine a preference for violent TV—not the other way around. More aggressive people could simply gravitate toward more violent programs. A second alternative is also plausible. It is possible that innate aggressiveness results in more exposure to TV violence, but at the same time the more exposure a person has, the more aggressive he or she becomes. The behaviors could affect each other. This is known as *bidirectional causation.*

Finally, some third agent may actually be causing the two behaviors to appear to be related. (Could this explain the automobile/airplane relationship?) This is known as the *third variable problem.* It is also plausible that a preference for violent TV and a tendency toward aggressiveness both result from an unknown or unmeasured variable, such as underactive autonomic nervous system functioning. Violence produces negative arousal in many individuals, and so does aggressiveness, but some people might be less adversely affected than others. Less arousable individuals might be able to both watch more violent TV and behave more aggressively. All in all, there are always four possible causal directions for any strong correlation between two variables. A summary is provided in Box 5.1.

---

## BOX **5.1**   Summary Table for the Four Possible Causal Directions for Any Simple Correlation

Let $X$ equal the amount of violent television a child watches. Let $Y$ equal the child's aggressiveness. Assume that the correlation between $X$ and $Y$ is strong ($r = +.60$). There are four possible causal directions:

1. $X \longrightarrow Y$

Watching more violent television causes a child to have higher levels of aggressiveness.

2. $Y \longrightarrow X$

Higher levels of aggressiveness cause a child to watch more violent television.

3. $X \longleftrightarrow Y$

Higher levels of aggressiveness cause a child to watch more violent television, and, at the same time, watching more violent television causes a child to have higher levels of aggressiveness.

4.
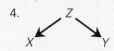

An unmeasured third variable ($Z$), low autonomic arousal, causes a child to watch more violent TV and causes a child to have higher levels of aggressiveness.

Once we have calculated $r$, it is useful to compute the coefficient of determination $(r^2)$. The coefficient of determination estimates the amount of variability in scores on one variable that can be explained by the other variable—an estimate of the strength of the relationship between them. For example, in the handshake study Chaplin and colleagues (2000) conducted, firmness of handshake and positivity of first impressions were correlated $r = .56$. If we square the value of $r$, the coefficient of determination, $r^2, = .31$. From this, we can say that about 31% of all the fluctuation in subjects' positivity scores can be accounted for by the firmness of the handshake. When we think about all the influences that can produce variability in scores, 31% is a substantial proportion. In fact, Cohen (1988) has argued that $r^2 \geq .25$ can be considered a strong association between two variables.

## Linear Regression Analysis

You will recall from our discussion of simple correlations that correlations can be used for prediction. When two behaviors are strongly related, the researcher can estimate a score on one of the measured behaviors from a score on the other. This technique is called linear regression analysis. If we knew, for example, that time spent watching TV and scores on a vocabulary test were correlated, we could substitute someone's viewing time into the equation for the regression line; solving the regression equation would give us an estimate of what that person's performance should be on the vocabulary test. The stronger the correlation, the better the prediction, in general.

The regression equation (as you learned in the previous section) is a formula for a straight line that best describes the relationship between the two variables. It is an equation for a straight line that has both a slope (the direction of the line) and an intercept (the value on the Y, or vertical, axis when $X = 0$). To predict someone's score on one variable (a vocabulary test) when we know only their score on the other variable (TV viewing time), we would need to know the value of $r$ and be able to calculate subjects' average scores (called *means*) on both variables and the standard deviations for both sets of scores. (Computing a mean score $[\overline{X}, \overline{Y}]$ and standard deviation $[s]$ is explained in Chapter 13.) TV viewing time is designated as variable $X$; vocabulary scores are designated as variable $Y$. The new score we are trying to predict is labeled $Y'$ ($Y$ prime). Let's try an example:

Assume that in adult subjects, TV viewing time and vocabulary scores are strongly correlated, and the correlation is negative: $r = -.64$. The mean for TV viewing time is 20 hours, and the standard deviation is 4. The mean score for the vocabulary test is 70, and the standard deviation is 5. We want to calculate an estimated score on the vocabulary test for an adult who watches 24 hours of TV.

Here is the computational formula:

$$Y' = \overline{Y} + r\left(\frac{S_Y}{S_X}\right)(X - \overline{X})$$

Substituting our values in the formula:

$$Y' = 70 + (-.64)\left(\frac{5}{4}\right)(24 - 20)$$
$$Y' = 70 + (-.64)(1.25)(4)$$
$$Y' = 66.8$$

If you understand the concept of negative correlation, you should be able to figure out why the score we predicted for this person (66.8) is lower than the average (70).

## Multiple Correlation and Multiple Regression

Sometimes we want to know whether a measured behavior can be predicted by a number of other measured behaviors (as in Box 5.2), rather than a single

---

BOX **5.2**  **Factor Analysis**

A common correlational procedure that is used when individuals are measured on a large number of items is called *factor analysis*. Factor analysis allows us to see the degree of relationship among many traits or behaviors at the same time. Such complicated statistical procedures have become common now that computers are available for statistical data analysis. When measurements of many behaviors are taken, those measurements that are most strongly intercorrelated are grouped together by the analysis as factors. Factor analysis is commonly used in personality research. Over the years, researchers have measured hundreds of trait dimensions (warm/cold, shy/sociable, dominant/submissive), but factor analysis routinely groups them into only a few basic factors (Cattell, 1946), such as sociability, agreeableness, conscientiousness, emotionality, and culture. Many researchers now believe that a few basic factors underlie all human personality structure.

Factor analysis can identify the important dimensions underlying a large number of responses. Using factor analysis, Conway and Rubin (1991), for example, ascertained that six different dimensions (i.e., factors) seemed to underlie people's motivation for watching TV. In one part of a larger study, they asked subjects to respond to a questionnaire containing 27 motivational statements that had been synthesized from the results of past research on why people like to watch television.

Results of the factor analysis are shown in Figure 5.5. Numbers reported in the factor analysis represent *factor loadings*. Factor loadings are statistical estimates of how well an item correlates with each of the factors (they can range from −1.00 to +1.00, like other correlational statistics). The factor analysis determines the factors and sorts items according to their groupings in the different factors, allowing the researcher to identify items belonging in each factor. We have boxed the items in each factor to make them easy to see at a glance. Notice that the items with high factor loadings (these researchers selected a cutoff of .60) are grouped together, showing that subjects' scores on these items are all strongly interrelated. The factor analysis also sorts the factors in order of importance: Factor 1 is the most important because it can account for more variation in all of the subjects' scores. (We will return to statistical variation in Chapter 13.)

Another important use of factor analysis is *data reduction*. For example, when researchers create a new questionnaire, or scale, to measure attitudes or personality, they often begin by testing many more items than they will eventually use in their scale. Factor analysis can help to determine which items seem to be measuring similar qualities, allowing researchers to drop some items that are less important or redundant (Kerlinger & Lee, 2000).

*(continued)*

| I watch television . . . | Viewing Motive Factors | | | | | |
|---|---|---|---|---|---|---|
| | Pass Time | Enter-tainment | Infor-mation | Escape | Relax-ation | Status Enhancement |
| **Factor 1: Pass Time** | | | | | | |
| Passes the time away, especially when I'm bored. | .75 | .21 | .07 | .13 | .11 | .04 |
| When I have nothing better to do. | .73 | −.02 | −.03 | .18 | −.02 | −.11 |
| Something to occupy my time. | .70 | .27 | .06 | .15 | .14 | .16 |
| No one else to talk to or be with. | .70 | .00 | .07 | .06 | .27 | .12 |
| Just because it's on. | .69 | −.06 | .00 | .24 | −.07 | −.02 |
| **Factor 2: Entertainment** | | | | | | |
| It's enjoyable. | .00 | .79 | .15 | .06 | .17 | .01 |
| It entertains me. | .10 | .70 | .11 | −.07 | .21 | −.09 |
| Just like to watch. | .27 | .69 | .07 | .23 | −.05 | .00 |
| It amuses me. | .03 | .69 | .10 | .14 | .19 | .28 |
| **Factor 3: Information** | | | | | | |
| Learn how to do things. | .01 | .19 | .78 | .06 | .01 | .02 |
| Learn what might happen to me. | .01 | .05 | .72 | .24 | −.02 | .15 |
| Know others have the same problems. | .17 | .02 | .72 | .08 | .16 | .17 |
| Learn about myself and others. | −.12 | .12 | .69 | .01 | .12 | .09 |
| **Factor 4: Escape** | | | | | | |
| Get away from what I'm doing. | .33 | .03 | .06 | .68 | .26 | .03 |
| Get away from the rest of the family and others. | .35 | .02 | .07 | .64 | .12 | .28 |
| Something to do when friends come over. | .24 | .19 | .07 | .60 | .00 | .24 |
| **Factor 5: Relaxation** | | | | | | |
| It relaxes me. | .13 | .16 | .08 | −.06 | .75 | .15 |
| It allows me to unwind. | .12 | .34 | .13 | .18 | .70 | −.03 |
| **Factor 6: Status Enhancement** | | | | | | |
| Feel more important than really am. | .19 | .15 | .21 | .25 | .02 | .70 |
| Impress people. | .14 | .01 | .33 | .27 | .06 | .68 |

FIGURE **5.5** Viewing motives: primary factor loadings.

Adapted from "Psychological Predictors of Television Viewing Motivation," by J. C. Conway & A. M. Rubin, 1991, *Communication Research, 18*(4), 443–463. Copyright ©1991 Sage Publications, Inc. Adapted with permission of Sage Publications, Inc.

predictor. We can use a statistic known as multiple correlation, represented by $R$, to test the relationship of several predictor variables ($X_1$, $X_2$, $X_3$ ...) with a criterion variable ($Y$). Conceptually, $R$ is quite similar to $r$, but $R$ allows us to use information provided by two or more measured behaviors to predict another measured behavior when we have that information available. For example, let us say that we took three measurements (age, amount of television viewing, and vocabulary) for a large sample of children, whose ages ranged from a few days old to 10 years old. We would like to know how well we could predict vocabulary (the criterion variable, $Y$) from the combination of scores for television viewing time ($X_1$) and age ($X_2$). We might find that a large multiple correlation was obtained ($R = .61$), showing that TV viewing and age together correlated .61 with vocabulary. This is not too surprising, really, because infants do not watch TV or know any words, but as children get older they watch more TV and also learn more words. As we did when we computed $r^2$, we can also compute $R^2$ (here, .61 × .61 = .3721, or about 37%) to estimate the amount of variability in vocabulary scores that can be accounted for by viewing time and age considered together.

But this multiple correlation would tend to put a damper on the earlier hypothesis that watching TV increases vocabulary, wouldn't it? More likely, both television time and vocabulary are age-related changes. The multiple correlation does not explain why the three measures are related, but it suggests the hypothesis that age is an important "third variable" that could be explored in subsequent research.

We could actually test this prediction by computing another statistic, a partial correlation. This analysis allows the statistical influence of one measured variable to be held constant while computing the correlation between the other two—the *partial* correlation. If age is an important third variable that is largely responsible for both increased television viewing and increased vocabulary, statistically controlling for the contribution of age should greatly decrease the correlation between television viewing time and vocabulary. Imagine that when we computed the partial correlation, the correlation between TV viewing and vocabulary dropped to .06 (not statistically significant). Although it would not be conclusive proof, this outcome would certainly add evidence to our case that age was the important third variable.

When more than two related behaviors are correlated, a multiple regression analysis can be used to predict the score on one behavior from scores on the others. Multiple regression analyses are very common in the literature. We could use multiple regression analysis, for example, to predict vocabulary scores from TV viewing time and age. Logically, we might imagine that age would be more important in predicting children's vocabulary than viewing time; if so, the regression equation would weight age more heavily than viewing time. Regression equations determine the weight of each predictor, and we could simply report these weights (called *beta weights*) in a research report. Or we could use the weights in a path analysis, one advanced correlational method, to construct possible causal sequences for the related behaviors. Let us proceed to designs that use correlational techniques to create causal models from sets of related behaviors.

# CAUSAL MODELING

As computer statistics programs become widely available, more sophisticated research designs based on advanced correlational techniques have become increasingly frequent in the literature. One inherent drawback of all correlational designs, of course, is the problem of the direction of cause and effect, discussed earlier. For example, we know that time spent watching violence on television is positively correlated with aggressiveness levels, but simple correlational designs do not provide information about the direction of the cause-and-effect sequence, if it exists. Even if experimentation is not possible, we would like to be able to design and conduct research that allows us to speculate about whether watching TV violence causes aggressiveness, or whether more aggressive people just naturally gravitate toward programs containing more violent content. Researchers have tools for causal modeling in correlation-based designs, such as path analysis and cross-lagged panel designs.

## Path Analysis

Path analysis is an important correlation-based research method that can be used when subjects are measured on several related behaviors. In path analysis, the researcher creates models of possible causal sequences. For example, Serbin and her colleagues (Serbin, Zelkowitz, Doyle, Gold, & Wheaton, 1990) were interested in trying to explain differences between boys' and girls' academic performance in elementary school. Through path analysis, they confirmed that the best models to predict school performance differed for boys and girls. Socioeconomic and parental education factors were important for predicting success in all the children. Beyond these factors, girls' performance in the lower grades seemed to be better accounted for by social responsiveness and willingness to follow directions. Boys' academic performance, however, was better predicted by their level of visual/spatial skills.

Clearly, path analysis is another descriptive method, but it generates important information for prediction and can generate experimental hypotheses. Path analysis is limited, however, in an important way. The models can only be constructed using the behaviors that have been measured. If a researcher omits an important behavior, it will be missing in the model, too.

Path analysis uses beta weights to construct path models, outlining possible causal sequences for the related behaviors. Computers can easily compare many multiple regression equations testing different paths, looking for the best model. Finally, the selected model can be further tested for "goodness of fit" to the actual data. Path models can be very complex. When there are many interrelated characteristics and behaviors to be considered, each path may have many steps. Some models include multiple paths to the same predicted "effect." It is not difficult to find path analyses in the literature that include multiple sets of interweaving paths linking as many as a dozen or more predictors (e.g., Pedersen, Plomin, Nesselroade, & McClearn, 1992).

Figure 5.6 shows a simpler path model, constructed by Batson, Chang, Orr, and Rowland (2002). These psychologists investigated the effect of empathy on the amount of help someone was willing to give to stigmatized groups of people. Past research has demonstrated that feelings of empathy

FIGURE **5.6** Path model predicting helping from the empathy manipulation, self-reported empathy, and attitudes toward the stigmatized group.
Adapted from Batson, et al. (2002). From Schwartz, Lerman, Miller, Daly, and Masny (1995).

(sympathy, compassion, etc.) are related to more positive attitudes toward people with social stigmas, including people with AIDS, homeless people, drug addicts, and criminals, but these researchers wanted to know whether greater levels of empathy would also translate into a higher likelihood of actually helping people in these groups.

Subjects in their study listened to an interview (actually fictitious) with a 22-year-old, male drug addict from a neighboring town who was serving 7 years in prison for possession and sale of heroin. In the interview, the young man talked about how he became addicted to heroin and described how he started to steal and then to deal heroin in order to support his habit. He also described what his life was like in prison. At one point, the interviewer asked the young man about his plans when he was released from prison:

> I think I need to get out of the area. Think maybe I'll head down to Texas and see if I can't make a better start on my life. Try to find a second chance; try to make something of myself and my life (pause). Of course I know it's going to be tough. Now I've got two labels—junkie and ex-con. It's like they expect you to just mess up again and be right back where they think you belong. I really want to make it, to have a life. Staying clean will be tough, but I've got to do it (p. 1660).

Empathy was induced by instructing subjects to try to imagine how the young man felt and how what happened to him had affected his life. After listening to the interview, subjects reported how they felt while they were listening. Then, they were given an additional task—to choose how they would like to allocate a limited amount of university funds ($20,000) among several community outreach programs (also fictitious). As predicted, the more empathy the subjects felt for the young man, the more money they chose to allocate to a program for drug addiction counseling within the community. Batson et al. tested several possible paths to helping, but the best-fitting path analysis model is depicted in Figure 5.6. Beta weights are indicated above each arrow linking one variable to the next. The model indicates that the empathy manipulation affected levels of empathy, which, in turn, affected attitudes toward drug addicts, which then produced helping behavior.

Researchers who use a path analysis approach are always very careful not to frame their models in terms of causal statements. Can you figure out why? We hope you reasoned that the internal validity of a path analysis is low because it is based on correlational data. The direction from cause to effect cannot be established with certainty, and third variables can never be ruled out completely. Nevertheless, causal models can be extremely useful for generating hypotheses for future research and for predicting potential causal sequences in instances where experimentation is not feasible.[3]

## Cross-Lagged Panel Design

Another method used to create causal models is called a cross-lagged panel. This design uses relationships measured over time to suggest the causal path. In a cross-lagged panel design, subjects are measured at two separate points in time on the same pair of related behaviors or characteristics (the time "lag" can be quite a few years). Then the scores from these measurements are correlated in a particular way, and the pattern of correlations is used to infer the causal path. The most famous cross-lagged panel study was done by Eron, Huesmann, Lefkowitz, and Walder (1972). Their study looked at the correlation between a preference for violent TV and aggressiveness in kids as they grew to young adulthood. The researchers measured aggressiveness levels and preferences for violent TV among a large group of youngsters. Subjects were assessed once in the third grade and again 10 years later. The results of the cross-lagged panel indicated that it was more likely that TV violence caused aggressiveness than the other way around. Interestingly, a newer cross-lagged panel study investigating the same variables with a different sample was recently reported by Huesmann, Moise-Titus, Podolski, and Eron (2003). The new study showed similar patterns of correlations across a time lag of about 15 years, indicating, once again, that the most likely direction of cause and effect was from early television violence viewing to later aggressive behavior.

Let us explore the logic of this design. Figure 5.7 shows the pattern of correlational results from a hypothetical cross-lagged panel study of two related behaviors—TV viewing time and vocabulary scores. Imagine that we made observations of 70 boys and girls at two different times, at ages 3 and 8. At each observation, we measured the TV viewing time and vocabulary of each subject. Then we computed six $r$ values, one for each of the six possible paths between them. Let's assume that values below $r = .20$ are not high enough to indicate a significant, strong relationship (for those of you who have not had a first course in statistics, the idea of statistical significance can wait until later chapters).

In a cross-lagged panel design, the correlations along the two diagonals (see Figure 5.7) are the most important for determining the probable causal path because they represent effects across the time lag. On the one hand, if vocabulary size is the cause of TV viewing, we would expect that vocabulary size at age 3 and the amount of time spent watching TV at age 8 should be strongly correlated. Are they? No. The $r$ value is only .07. On the other hand, if time spent watching TV at age 3 determined vocabulary size at age 8, there should be a strong relationship between them. And there is. The $r$ value is $-.59$, a highly significant correlation.

In a cross-lagged panel, we are looking for the largest diagonal correlation to indicate the causal direction. In our hypothetical example, then, we would

---

[3] A more complex, advanced form of path analysis, called *structural equation modeling* (SEM), is becoming increasingly popular among researchers. For an introduction to SEM, go to: http://assets.cambridge.org/97805217/81336/sample/9780521781336ws.pdf.

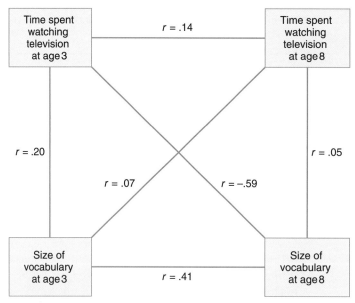

FIGURE **5.7** Results of a hypothetical cross-lagged panel design.
© Cengage Learning

infer that the most likely path from cause to effect is the one from viewing time to vocabulary size. Note, however, that in this example the correlation is negative. We would have to say that watching a lot of TV appears to decrease—not increase—the size of a child's vocabulary (cf. Ennemoser & Schneider, 2007).

But we also need to examine the rest of the panel. Does it all make sense? What else can it tell us? For example, notice the moderate correlation between viewing time and vocabulary size at age 3 ($r = .20$). It is positive, indicating that for the 3-year-olds, more time watching TV is related to a *larger* vocabulary. If watching television is related to a larger vocabulary at age 3, why is the correlation close to zero ($r = .05$) when the children are age 8? (Perhaps influences on vocabulary change with age. Or, perhaps the initial relationship was really produced by something else—a third variable, such as curiosity?). Also notice that our panel shows a strong positive correlation between vocabulary size at age 3 and vocabulary size at age 8 ($r = .41$). How might you interpret that? (Perhaps verbal skills are relatively stable.)

You can see that carefully exploring the relationships in a cross-lagged panel design can lead to many new ideas and new questions. Keep in mind that a cross-lagged panel design can only suggest the possible direction of a cause-and-effect relationship between two behaviors. Evidence from this design is never conclusive. For instance, bidirectional causation and the third variable problem cannot be ruled out. A summary of uses of the different correlation-based designs is provided in Table 5.1.

Let us move on from causal models to quasi-experimental designs, which are sometimes used to measure changes over time.

TABLE **5.1**

Summary of correlation and correlation-based research designs

| Type | Purpose |
|---|---|
| Correlation | Determines degree of relationship between two variables. |
| Multiple correlation | Determines degree of relationship between three or more variables. |
| Linear regression analysis | Uses regression equation to predict scores on one variable from scores on a second correlated variable. |
| Multiple regression analysis | Uses regression equation to predict scores on one variable from scores on sets of other variables. |
| Factor analysis | Determines subsets of correlated variables within a larger set of variables. |
| Path analysis | Uses beta weights from multiple regression analysis to generate possible direction of cause and effect from correlated variables. |
| Cross-lagged panel | Measures the same pair of variables at two different points in time; looks at patterns of correlations across time for possible direction of cause and effect. |

© Cengage Learning

## QUASI-EXPERIMENTAL DESIGNS

Quasi-experimental designs can seem like a real experiment, but they lack one or more of its essential elements, such as manipulation of antecedents or random assignment to treatment conditions. Quasi-experiments can be used to explore the effects of different treatments on preexisting groups of subjects or to investigate the same kinds of naturally occurring events, characteristics, and behaviors that we measure in correlational studies. But quasi-experiments and correlations have somewhat different goals: In correlational studies, we are looking for relationships or associations between variables, whereas in quasi-experiments, we are comparing different groups of subjects looking for differences between them, or we are looking for changes over time in the same group of subjects.

Researchers who want to compare people exposed to a naturally occurring event with a comparison group (usually unexposed people) often use a quasi-experiment, also called a *natural experiment* (Shadish, Cook, & Campbell, 2001). For example, Ganzel and her colleagues (Ganzel, Casey, Glover, Voss, & Temple, 2007) investigated emotional reactivity after the traumatic World Trade Center bombing in New York City on September 11, 2001. They found that even after 3 years had passed, people who had been within 1.5 miles of the buildings when they collapsed were more reactive when exposed to pictures of fearful faces than were people who were at least 200 miles away at the time of the terrorist attacks. In another example, Mellman and his colleagues (Mellman, David, Kulick-Bell, Hebding, & Nolan, 1995) conducted a natural experiment to compare sleep disorders in people who had survived Hurricane Andrew and people who had not been exposed to the hurricane. Not surprisingly, there was a much greater prevalence of sleep disorders in the hurricane survivors.

In the simplest quasi-experiments, we form *quasi-treatment groups* based on the particular event, characteristic, or behavior whose influence we want to investigate. Our statistical analyses are based on aggregated data from each group. For example, we could use a quasi-experimental design to look at gender differences in school-age children's sleep patterns. By monitoring the sleep of boys and girls, we might discover that, on the average, girls sleep more and move about less when they are sleeping than boys do (Sadeh, Raviv, & Gruber, 2000). But, can we say for sure that children's sleep patterns are caused by their gender? Does merely being born male or female determine the quantity and quality of children's sleep? Probably not. There are many other influences, such as daytime activity, levels of stress, and hormones associated with different stages of pubertal development that help to determine sleep patterns. (This is the same problem we encountered with correlation.) The point to remember is that when we conduct quasi-experiments, we can never know for certain what causes the effects we observe—so, relative to true experiments, we say these designs are low in internal validity.

In some quasi-experiments, subjects are exposed to different treatments (as they are in true experiments), but in quasi-experiments the experimenter cannot exert control over who receives which treatment because random assignment is not possible. An important difference between experiments and quasi-experiments is the amount of control the researcher has over the subjects who receive treatments. In an experiment, the researcher randomly assigns subjects to receive different treatments so that the only conditions that will systematically influence behavior are the treatments being tested. Without random assignment, other individual differences between members of different treatment groups could produce misleading effects on behavior. In the remainder of the chapter, we will take a closer look at several kinds of quasi-experimental designs.

## Ex Post Facto Studies

Often, researchers are interested in the effects of traits, behaviors, or naturally occurring events that cannot or should not be manipulated by a researcher. In those cases, the researcher may choose to do an ex post facto study—that is, a study in which the researcher systematically examines the effects of subject characteristics (often called subject variables) but without actually manipulating them. The researcher forms treatment groups by selecting subjects on the basis of differences that already exist.

Ex post facto means "after the fact." In effect, the researcher capitalizes on changes in the antecedent conditions that occurred before the study. The result is a study that looks a great deal like an experiment, with the important exception that the antecedent conditions have not been manipulated by the experimenter. The experimenter also has no direct control over who belongs

Sidney Harris

"IF WE DIDN'T DO SO WELL IN THE EASY
BOX, THEY WOULDN'T HAVE GIVEN US THIS
COMPLICATED BOX."

to each of the treatment groups of the study. These studies generally fall in the low-high portion of Figure 3.1 from Chapter 3.

Preexisting differences define membership in different treatment groups in the study: Hannah's father died last year, so Hannah is placed in a group of subjects who have experienced the loss of a parent. Subjects come into an ex post facto study with attributes that already differ from one subject to another. The differences are used as the basis for separating them into groups (for example, extroverts, introverts), and the researcher then looks for differences in behavior that are related to group membership. Age and gender are two commonly researched subject variables.

The ex post facto approach has some special advantages. Like the correlational study, it deals with things as they occur. There is no manipulation of the conditions that interest the researcher. However, the ex post facto study allows a researcher to zero in on those occurrences in a more systematic way; instead of studying the whole range of people along a particular dimension (e.g., from extremely introverted to extremely extroverted); the focus can be on a carefully chosen subset. Very often, the ex post facto researcher studies the extremes, the subjects who rank highest and lowest on the dimension of interest. This focus increases the likelihood that the researcher will be able to see the effects of changes along that dimension more clearly. Ex post facto studies are also generally done with many of the same rigorous control procedures used in experiments. The researcher makes a prediction in advance and attempts to test it in the most objective way.

Systematically forming groups based on differences in preexisting characteristics is a critical feature of an ex post facto study, but it also prevents such a study from being classified as a true experiment. In a true experiment, there should be no systematic differences between people in different treatment conditions. As we will see in Chapter 9, guarding against these kinds of systematic differences is an important benchmark of true experiments. Experimenters typically use *random assignment of subjects* to create treatment groups in which any preexisting differences in people are distributed evenly across all the treatment groups. In an ex post facto study, those preexisting differences become the "manipulation," and measuring the effects they produce is the objective of the research.

Franklin, Janoff-Bulman, and Roberts (1990) were interested in studying the potential effects of divorce on attitudes and beliefs of children. Using an ex post facto design, they assessed whether college-age children of divorced parents held different beliefs about themselves and other people than did college students who came from intact families. Franklin and colleagues were interested in measuring these subjects' beliefs about the world in general, about people in general, about their own self-worth, and about interpersonal relationships. Interestingly, the researchers found no differences between the two groups of college students on any of the first three kinds of beliefs. Both groups reported similar beliefs about the world, others, and themselves. Differences were found, though, on beliefs about relationships—especially on issues related to love and marriage. As a group, the students from divorced families reported more accepting attitudes toward divorce and more pessimistic beliefs about their own success in a marriage. Students with divorced parents believed that they were less likely to have a long and successful marriage than did the students whose parents had stayed together. And a subsequent ex post facto study by Story, Lawrence, Karney, and Bradbury (2004) found that women whose parents had divorced were more likely to report marital dissatisfaction and divorce within the first 4 years of their own marriages than women from intact families. Using an ex post facto design, Franklin and her colleagues were able to demonstrate that a life event, the divorce of parents, does not seem to have global, negative effects on children's belief systems. Instead, divorce seemed to influence only a narrow range of beliefs, those related to the possibility of divorce in their own future.

A strong word of caution: As with correlations, the results of ex post facto studies can be easily misinterpreted (see Box 5.3). Because the kinds of effects Franklin et al. (1990) found greatly resembled the event used to classify subjects into groups, it would be tempting to make a causal inference—to say that divorce alters beliefs about marriage and divorce. However, because the researchers did not create the group differences but instead relied on a naturally occurring event, there is no way to be certain that the effects were actually produced by the ex post facto variable and not by something else. It is always possible that something other than divorce was the actual cause: Perhaps the parents who eventually divorced held similar pessimistic attitudes about marriage. The parents' negative expectations might have caused both the divorce and their children's pessimistic attitudes about marriage. You may have noticed that this is the same problem that we encountered with correlational studies—that nemesis of nonexperimental designs, the third variable. All ex post facto studies are low in internal validity because there is always the possibility that other differences between the groups of subjects were the true cause of the effects. Because of this, we cannot explain behavior from an ex post facto study. We can, however, learn a great deal of useful information.

In addition to studying personal attributes (such as gender, age, or handedness) and life events (such as divorce or the loss of a parent), researchers often use ex post facto studies to learn more about the behavioral ramifications of individual differences in psychological functioning and personality processes. As you can probably guess, we cannot study mental illness or personality in a strictly experimental manner. How would we go about manipulating antisocial personality disorder, Type A behavior, or agoraphobia to create the tendency we want to study? If we could devise procedures that would accomplish that goal, would we really want to use them?

The ex post facto approach enables us to explore many dimensions that we could not or would not choose to study experimentally. For that reason, it is a very useful source of information.

For example, using an ex post facto design, researchers discovered that a person's coping style when faced with a negative experience could be important in the treatment of cancer patients (Ward, Leventhal, & Love, 1988). The investigators studied cancer patients who had been identified as either repressors or nonrepressors. Repressors are individuals who minimize negative emotional experiences. (You may remember the theory of repression from studying Sigmund Freud.) A repressive or nonrepressive coping style can be reliably identified by a personality questionnaire. Using interviews and questionnaires to measure the patients' symptom-related behavior, the researchers found important differences between the two kinds of people. Repressors were much less likely than nonrepressors to report awareness of either cancer treatment side effects or symptoms of their illness. Even though these differences cannot be explained, the information may be very important for the prevention and treatment of cancer. As the researchers noted, repressors may be less likely to notice cancer symptoms and seek early treatment. Once the disease is diagnosed, however, repressors may actually cope better with cancer treatment.

Despite its limitations, the ex post facto approach is an extremely useful technique that allows us to demonstrate that certain predictable relationships exist. We can establish, for instance, that gender, or personality traits, or life events, or mental disorders are associated with particular patterns of behavior. In some respects, ex post facto studies are more useful than certain kinds of experiments, because the information they provide helps us understand the kinds of complex behaviors that occur in real life. These studies have greater external validity because they focus on naturally occurring events. Even

## BOX 5.3    Are Big Cars Safer Than Small Cars?

For people who do not understand research designs, interpreting the results of an ex post facto study presents a serious challenge. All too frequently, results of these studies are misinterpreted in media reports. Here is one of our favorites (even though the models change slightly from year to year, the interpretation reported in newspapers, in magazines, and on TV news does not!). The headline typically reads something like this:

DRIVERS BUY SMALL CARS EVEN THOUGH THEY CAN BE DEADLY*

The article begins with statements like this one:*

> Americans are buying more small cars to cut fuel costs, and that might kill them. As a group, occupants of small cars are more likely to die in crashes than those in bigger, heavier vehicles are, according to data from the government, the insurance industry and the National Academy of Sciences....

MORE DRIVERS DIE IN SMALL CARS

### Driver Deaths per Million Vehicles

| | |
|---|---|
| All small cars | 108 |
| Midsize cars | 70 |
| Large cars | 67 |
| SUVs | 55 |

The top three, safest, 2007 vehicles were the Acura RDX SUV, the Acura RL sedan, and the Audi 4. The most dangerous were the Chevrolet Cobalt, the Ford Focus, and the Mazda 3.** Let's look at the conclusion that small cars are more dangerous than larger cars a little more carefully. This conclusion is based on an ex post facto design. Groups were selected based on car size, and the average death rates for cars in each group were compared.

Do you believe that they have proven their case that large cars are safer than small cars? Do you think that the size of the car is the only reason that drivers of, let's say, Acura RL sedans have many fewer deaths per thousand than drivers of small cars like the Ford Focus? (Small, inexpensive cars are usually at the bottom in terms of safety along with some sports cars, such as the Nissan 350Z, which has death rates about double those of the average sports car.) Do you think the higher death rates in the smaller cars are really attributable to their smaller size?

What else might be going on here? *What about the kinds of people who typically drive these different cars?* According to Russ Rader, communications director for the Insurance Institute for Highway Safety, "the 350Z tends to be driven by younger, less-experienced or riskier drivers, and stands out for having high death rates, through no particular fault of the car."***

How are Acura RL (along with Acura RDX and Audi 4) drivers and Ford Focus (along with Chevrolet Cobalt and Mazda3) drivers likely to differ? (age, gender,

though we cannot draw conclusions about cause and effect, ex post facto studies provide more realistic data that can be applied in practical ways. Often, researchers will include subject variables in their experiments to see whether their treatments produce different effects on different kinds of subjects (see Box 5.4).

## Nonequivalent Groups Design

A nonequivalent groups design is one in which the researcher compares the effects of different treatment conditions on preexisting groups of participants. The researcher cannot exert control over who gets each treatment because random assignment is not possible. Recall the example of a nonequivalent groups design, which tested lighting in two different companies, that was used earlier in the chapter. Suppose the researcher had installed fluorescent

Karan Kapoor/Stone/Getty Images

FIGURE **5.8** Could this be one reason why small cars can be unsafe?

wealth ... other factors?) There are probably many differences between the owners of cars in the large and small categories. These differences are likely to play a very important role in the difference in death rates. Large, expensive cars will have more built-in safety features than small, inexpensive cars, and these safety features do play a role in death rates, but they are clearly not the only cause of statistics such as these, are they?

*From "People Buy Small Cars Even Though They Can Be Deadly," by James R. Healey, *USA Today*, August 19, 2007.
**Data from Forbes.com, retrieved September 29, 2007.
***Forbesauto.com, retrieved September 29, 2007.

lighting in Company A and incandescent lighting in Company B. After workers had used the lights for 3 months, productivity was measured, and the researcher found that workers with incandescent lighting were more productive. How confident could we be that the lighting actually produced the difference in productivity? Not as confident as we would like to be, because there are any number of other potential causes. For instance, the workers in Company B might be more productive even without the incandescent lights (or Company A's workers might be less productive). In this example, other conditions within the two companies also might have altered the productivity of subjects in one or both groups (a bonus from Company B, threats of a layoff in Company A, and so forth). In true experiments, other outside influences are carefully controlled, so the only systematic effect on behavior results from the treatments—not from anything else.

## BOX **5.4**    Negative Ions and Type A Behavior

Remember the study by Baron, Russell, and Arms (1985) from Chapters 1 and 2? These researchers found that a high concentration of negative ions increased the intensity of people's good and bad moods. Negative mood shifts were reported by subjects who had been intentionally angered by a confederate; positive mood shifts were reported by nonangered subjects. Besides testing the effects of different concentrations of negative ions, this study also included a subject variable. The researchers used subjects who were Type A and Type B personalities (Jenkins, Zyzanski, & Rosenman, 1979) to see whether ionization would have different effects on these two types of people. Type A people have characteristically high levels of irritability, a sense of time urgency, and strong reactions to stressors; Type B people are low in all three traits.

Part of the subjects' (supposed) task in this experiment was to punish all of the "learners'" errors with a painful burst of heat to the wrist. Each time they delivered the heat punishment, the subjects selected how intense it would be (the 10 buttons on

the machine were labeled from "very low" to "very intense"). The intensities chosen by subjects represented a measure of aggressive behavior toward the "learners." Interestingly, even though the negative ions affected the moods of both Type As and Type Bs in similar ways, the negative ions affected the aggressiveness of the two types of subjects differently. For Type B subjects, ion levels produced no effect at all on the intensity of the bursts. But for Type A subjects, there was a dramatic effect—both moderate and high levels of negative ions significantly enhanced the aggressiveness of the Type A subjects.

The intensity of the bursts used to punish the "learners'" errors got much higher, particularly if they had been angered. Even though this design does not allow the researchers to state with certainty that the differences in effects produced by ionization were caused by the subjects' Type A or Type B personality, the results are clearly useful for predicting different kinds of behaviors for Type As and Type Bs!

In the lighting study as presented so far, internal validity would be low. There are methods, however, that can be used to increase the internal validity of this design, but they require a great deal of thought before any treatments are implemented. The researcher needs to consider whether other influences might affect results, and, if so, what these influences might be. Even though they cannot be controlled, the potential effects of some influences can be made less plausible if thought out and addressed beforehand. For example, if the researcher conducting the study at Companies A and B was concerned that workers in the two companies differed in their ordinary levels of productivity (or motivation, etc.), it would be a good idea to measure productivity levels in the two companies before the study to rule out prior productivity levels as a plausible alternative explanation for the results.[4] When using this design, it is a good idea to measure subjects on any attributes that strongly threaten internal validity. This way, you might be able to demonstrate

---

[4] It is also possible to evaluate the effects of plausible alternatives by using covariate statistical analyses. The logic is very similar to that of partial correlations. If, for example, prior productivity levels of workers were responsible (or somewhat responsible) for the lighting results, you could use individuals' normal productivity levels as a covariate in statistical analyses, essentially removing its influence (Kerlinger & Lee, 2000). If the results disappear when productivity is used as a covariate, it is highly likely that normal productivity was influencing the results. If the results remain strong, normal productivity was probably not an important factor.

statistically that the nonrandom groups did not differ in any important way. If you can demonstrate that your groups were "equivalent" on other plausible alternative causes for the results, you will have greatly improved the study's internal validity, and your study will more closely approximate a true experiment (Shadish et al., 2001).

## Longitudinal Design

Psychologists also use quasi-experiments to measure the behaviors of the same subjects at different points in time and look to see how things have changed. Here the specific question is often the influence of time on behaviors, rather than how different behaviors are related, as we saw in the cross-lagged panel design. These long-term studies employ longitudinal designs. Longitudinal designs are used in all areas of psychology, but they are particularly important for psychologists studying human (and animal) growth and development.

Stewart, Mobley, Van Tuyl, and Salvador (1987) conducted an interesting longitudinal study to assess behavioral changes in firstborn children after the birth of a second child. They observed and interviewed 41 middle-class families at five different times: 1 month before the birth of the second child, and at 1, 4, 8, and 12 months after the birth. One of the behaviors the researchers were interested in was regression.

Regression, in psychoanalytic theory, is a way of escaping the reality of a stressful situation by reverting to more childlike patterns of behavior. More cognitively oriented developmentalists see it as a child's falling back to an earlier cognitive stage as a way of learning to cope with new, and more complex, situations. Previous work had suggested that after the birth of a sibling, firstborns sometimes showed more independent, "grown-up" behavior (in language, feeding, toileting, etc.); other times, they seemed to regress or become more infantile. Stewart and his colleagues found some evidence for regressive behavior in the firstborns, particularly when they were measured 1 month after the birth. Interestingly, though, there were more regressive behaviors if the firstborn and the new baby were the same sex! One explanation is that the behaviors they were seeing might be imitation, not regression. Firstborns might have been imitating behaviors of the new baby as a way of trying to direct maternal attention away from the newborn toward themselves; imitating a same-sex sibling might be more natural than imitating an opposite-sex sibling. (Incidentally, the imitation strategy seemed to have been abandoned by the 12-month interview.)

Longitudinal studies can take place over periods of months, years, or even decades. Clearly, long-term longitudinal studies are relatively difficult to conduct because the same sample must be tracked for a long time, even as participants (and researchers) age, move away, or become deceased. In one interesting longitudinal study of children from divorced families, Wallerstein and Lewis (2004) were able to track a sample of children from divorced families for 25 years. At the 25-year follow-up, the men and women in the sample were 28–43 years old. Interviews with these adults showed that (similar to findings from the ex post facto studies described earlier) feelings of inadequacy that they had experienced in the areas of love, intimacy, and commitment appeared to translate into their adult behavior; they showed a greater tendency toward short-term intimate relationships than a comparison group of similar individuals whose parents had remained married—fewer of the children from divorced families had ever married or become parents themselves than in the comparison group. Their numbers were also lower than the national averages.

## Cross-Sectional Studies

Longitudinal design studies are time-consuming and hard to conduct. Retaining subjects over a long period of time can be very difficult. Often researchers use another method that approximates results from a longitudinal design. Instead of tracking the same group over a long span of time, subjects who are already at different stages are compared at a single point in time using a cross-sectional study. For example, instead of following the same group of subjects for more than a year, Stewart and colleagues (1987) could have observed groups of families who were already at each of the five different stages: The researchers might have observed one group of families expecting a second child in a month, another group whose second child was a month old, another group whose child was four months old, and so on. Then they could have compared the amount of "regressive" behavior among firstborns in the five different groups to see whether it differed.

There are trade-offs to consider when choosing between the two designs. On the one hand, the longitudinal design study takes much longer to complete. On the other hand, a cross-sectional study will require more subjects; the more groups to be compared, the more subjects needed. The statistical tests needed to analyze effects across different groups are typically less powerful than those used to verify the same kind of effects within one group of subjects. And using different groups of subjects runs the risk that people in these groups might differ in other characteristics that could influence the behaviors you want to investigate. (In this respect, a cross-sectional design is similar to an ex post facto design.) In a longitudinal design, the same people are observed each time. Important information about changes across the life span can be gained from both longitudinal and cross-sectional designs, but neither can be used to infer cause and effect—potentially, many influences could have produced the changes in behavior. Clearly, antecedents are not manipulated in either type of study; however, imposition of units is generally high.

## Pretest/Posttest Design

Sometimes we want to assess whether the occurrence of an event increases or decreases the existing level of a person's behavior. Does aversion therapy reduce the number of self-abusive behaviors? Do attitudes toward a product become more positive after a new TV commercial airs? Does the president's approval rating go up after the State of the Union Address? We can measure people's level of behavior before and after the event and compare these levels using a pretest/posttest design. This design may be used to assess the effects of naturally occurring events (like approval ratings before and after a presidential speech) when a true experiment is not possible. Or, the pretest/ posttest design can be used in the laboratory to measure the effect of a treatment presented to subjects by researchers, but the design has a number of problems that reduce its internal validity.

Let's look at an example. Suppose a school counselor wanted to assess the effectiveness of a preparation course for college admissions tests that she had developed for college-bound students. Sixty students have signed up to take the course from her. Optimally, she would like to be able to give the training to only half these students so she could compare admissions test scores of students who received the training with scores of those who did not. But she feels it might be unethical to deny training to some students who want it. She considers using another group of students who did not sign up as a comparison group, but she decides against it because she is worried that the two groups of students might have very different characteristics.[5] So, she decides to use a pretest/posttest design instead.

The first day of the course, she gives all 60 students in the course a pretest—a practice SAT—to establish a baseline score for each student. She is hopeful that at the end of the 6-week preparation course, students will get higher scores than they did the first time around. At the end of the course, she tests them again. She finds that, on the average, their scores improved by 20 points. Should she keep the training program? This is an internal validity question. Using this design, how confident can she be that her training program caused the improvement? Not as confident as she would like to be.

In a pretest/posttest design, particularly if the study extends beyond a single, brief research session, there are simply too many other things that can influence improvement. Improvement might be influenced by factors external to the research, such as incidental (or intentional) learning outside of the research session. In addition, in a pretest/posttest design, the possibility of *practice effects* (also called *pretest sensitization*) cannot be ruled out. Anastasi (1958), for example, has shown that people do better the second time they take an intelligence test—even without any special training in between! Simple familiarity with a test can improve performance. Test takers may be less anxious the second time around. They also may have learned new information (in their other classes, reading the paper, or watching TV) that improves their scores. Or they may think about their answers on the pretest, and this can influence how they answer the second time around. And without a group that receives no training to control for other things that may occur with the

---

[5] Actually, this kind of comparison group option has been used when researchers cannot randomly assign subjects to treatment or comparison groups for practical or ethical reasons. Threats to internal validity present in the pretest/posttest design can be partially controlled by comparing subjects who received treatment with another group of subjects who did not. Subjects in the comparison group receive no treatment, but they are measured (pretest and posttest) according to the same time schedule as the treatment group. Threats to internal validity are lessened by this procedure, but they cannot be completely ruled out because the comparison group is taken from another population and is unlikely to be equivalent to the treatment group. This design is called a *nonequivalent control group design*.

passage of time, it is clear that a pretest/posttest design lacks internal validity. Even so, it has been widely used in situations, particularly outside the laboratory, where a comparison group is impossible or unethical.

A pretest/posttest design has often been used to test the effects of foreseeable real-world events, such as attitude changes after a series of public service announcements airs on television or ticket sales before and after renovations are made to a concert hall. When there is a long time between the pretest and the posttest, the researcher needs to be particularly aware that the event being assessed might not be the only cause of differences before and after the event. Any number of other uncontrolled, outside influences also could be affecting the results. A pretest/posttest study of this kind can be extremely low in internal validity.

Sometimes, a pretest/posttest design is used in circumstances where the time between the pretest and the posttest is short, as in a single laboratory session. A researcher who wants to test the benefits of subliminal self-help tapes designed to increase self-esteem could use a pretest/posttest design. He might test 30 subjects, one at a time. Using a standard test, he could measure self-esteem when subjects first arrive at the laboratory. Subjects could listen to the 45-minute tape, and the researcher could measure self-esteem again. If all other potential influences had been carefully controlled during the sessions, we would be somewhat more confident that an increase in self-esteem after the treatment was really attributable to the tape, rather than other outside influences. However, we still could not be certain that the rise in self-esteem was not brought about by practice with the test,[6] because people also seem to get better scores on personality and adjustment tests with practice (Windle, 1954).

Sometimes this design is used along with one or more comparison groups that attempt to control for these internal validity issues (see Box 5.5 for an example). If subjects can be randomly assigned to different groups by the experimenter, some of these problems can be attenuated by adding comparison or control groups. (We will cover control groups in Chapter 8.) But to achieve maximum control over outside influences, you would need a number of comparison groups: (1) a *nonequivalent control group*—a group that took both the pretest and posttest but was not exposed to the "treatment," (2) a group that received the treatment and took only the posttest, and (3) a posttest-only group. When all four groups are included in the design, it is called a *Solomon 4-group design* (Campbell & Stanley, 1966). But, it should be pointed out that when a researcher has this much flexibility, it is usually better to do without the pretest and select, instead, one of the experimental designs covered in the following chapters.

---

[6] Actually, this explanation is quite plausible. Greenwald, Spangenbert, Pratkanis, and Eskenazi (1991) used a more complex pretest/posttest design to test subliminal self-help tapes. After replicating the study on three different samples, they concluded that the tapes had no effect on self-esteem. With or without the tapes, posttest self-esteem scores were somewhat higher than pretest scores.

BOX **5.5**   **Dogs Improve Behavior of Prisoners**

From the results of a wide variety of studies done during the last quarter of a century, there is no doubt that companion dogs can have a tremendous, positive impact on our health and well-being. Companion dogs can also positively impact the way we are viewed by others, increasing perceptions of our friendliness and likeability. Fournier, Geller, and Fortney (2007) conducted an interesting pretest/posttest study to evaluate the impact of dogs on the behavior of incarcerated prisoners. They recruited volunteers for a human-animal interaction program, PenPals, from a minimum security prison oriented toward drug abuse treatment. The program volunteers were men with either a history of substance abuse or charges related to drugs or alcohol. To control for the influence of outside factors that can reduce the internal validity of the design, they also included a comparison group of volunteers who were waiting to get into the PenPals program. Each program participant trained a shelter dog in basic obedience for 8 to10 weeks; during that time the dog lived with the prisoner. After the program, the dogs were adopted by members of the local community.

Both PenPal and comparison group participants were pretested on a number of behaviors, including their social and emotional communication skills, the number of recent prison infractions, and the level of treatment they had achieved in the drug therapy

program (prisoners' behaviors were verified by prison staff). At the end of the PenPals program, the behaviors were measured again (the posttest). Several interesting findings emerged: the number of infractions declined for the PenPals group, whereas they increased for the waiting-list group; social sensitivity increased for the PenPals group but decreased for the waiting-list group; and the therapy treatment level increased significantly more for the PenPals group than for the waiting-list group (see Figure 5.9). You can see from the figure that both groups started at the same average level of treatment, and while both groups improved to a higher level during the time of the program, the PenPals group improved quite a bit more. Interacting with a companion dog apparently improved prisoner behavior and social skills and facilitated their drug therapy treatment.

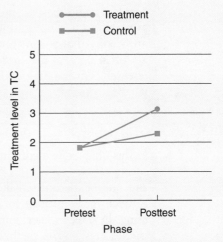

FIGURE **5.9** Treatment level in the therapeutic community as a function of intervention group and phase (pretest or posttest)
From Fournier et al., 2007.

Despite their limitations, quasi-experimental approaches are clearly very important adjuncts to experimentation. A summary of the different quasi-experimental designs is provided in Table 5.2. Quasi-experimental designs can be extremely useful for showing relationships and for predicting

TABLE **5.2**
Summary of quasi-experimental research designs

| Type | Purpose |
|------|---------|
| Quasi-experiment | Investigates differences in preexisting groups of subjects; group differences on some variable may be explored or different treatments given to preexisting groups may be compared. |
| Ex post facto | Explores characteristics, behaviors, or effects of naturally occurring events in preexisting groups of subjects. |
| Nonequivalent groups | Compares the effects of different treatment conditions on preexisting groups of subjects. |
| Longitudinal | Investigates changes across time by measuring behavior of same group of subjects at different points in time. |
| Cross-sectional | Investigates changes across time by comparing groups of subjects already at different stages at a single point in time. |
| Pretest/posttest | Explores the effects of an event (or treatment) by comparing behavior before and after the event (or treatment). |

© Cengage Learning

behavioral differences among people. At times, they are the only approaches available to us. In addition, the quasi-experimental approaches may lack the artificiality that is sometimes criticized in experimental research. Finally, they are often used as the sources of experimental hypotheses that lead to further research. Formulating a research hypothesis just happens to be the topic of our next chapter.

## SUMMARY

In this chapter, we continued our discussion of nonexperimental designs, focusing on two categories of nonexperimental research methods: correlational and quasi-experimental designs. Because antecedents are not manipulated, it is much more difficult to establish cause-and-effect relationships conclusively using these techniques, but they can be high in external validity. *Correlational studies* may be run in the laboratory or in the field. A correlational study is done to determine the *correlation*, or degree of relationship, between two traits, behaviors, or events.

First, the variables of interest are measured; then the degree of relationship between them is established through statistical procedures. The relationship between a pair of variables is called a *simple correlation (r)*. When statistics find two variables to be related, the relationship between them may be a *positive correlation* or a *negative correlation*; this relationship is evident when data are graphed in a *scatterplot*. The magnitude of the relationship can be estimated by the *coefficient of determination (r²)*. But we cannot infer cause and effect from a correlation. When two measures are strongly correlated, however, we can use the *regression line* to predict the value of one if we know the value of the other using *linear regression analysis*. Hypotheses about third-variable causation can sometimes be tested using *partial correlation*. Interrelationships among three or more variables can be investigated using a *multiple correlation*, and *multiple regression analysis* can be used for predicting one variable from other related variables.

Researchers can use sophisticated correlational methods to create *causal models* using a *cross-lagged panel design* or *path analysis*. Causal models can suggest cause-and-effect relationships, but they cannot establish these relationships conclusively because other potential influences and causal directions cannot be entirely ruled out.

As the prefix *quasi-* implies, *quasi-experimental designs* "seem like" experiments, but they are not. Quasi-experimental designs are used when subjects cannot be randomly assigned to receive different treatments. Quasi-experiments also can be used to explore the effects of different experimental manipulations on preexisting groups of subjects or to investigate the same kinds of naturally occurring events, characteristics, and behaviors that we measure in correlational studies. Researchers often use an *ex post facto study* to examine the effects of subject characteristics (often called *subject variables*) systematically without actually manipulating them. Here the researcher forms groups on the basis of differences that already exist between subjects and measures behavioral differences between the groups. In a *nonequivalent groups design*, the researcher tests the effects of a treatment on preexisting groups of subjects.

Some quasi-experiments look for changes or differences over time. In a *longitudinal design*, a researcher follows the same group of subjects and takes measurements at different points in time. *Cross-sectional studies* select groups of subjects who are already at different stages and compare them at a single point in time. A *pretest/posttest design* can be used to assess whether the occurrence of an event alters behavior, but the design is low in internal validity. Pretest sensitivity and the possibility that outside influences could affect results are particular problems.

Correlational and quasi-experimental designs can be used to show relationships and predict behavior. They can result in research hypotheses that can be tested in future research.

## KEY TERMS

Causal modeling Creating and testing models that may suggest cause-and-effect relationships among behaviors.

Coefficient of determination ($r^2$) In a correlational study, an estimate of the amount of variability in scores on one variable that can be explained by the other variable.

Correlation The degree of relationship between two traits, behaviors, or events, represented by *r*.

Correlational study A study designed to determine the correlation between two traits, behaviors, or events.

Cross-lagged panel design A method in which the same set of behaviors or characteristics are measured at two separate points in time (often years apart); six different correlations are computed, and the pattern of correlations is used to infer the causal direction.

Cross-sectional study A method in which different groups of subjects who are at different stages are measured at a single point in time; a method that looks for time-related changes.

Ex post facto study A study in which a researcher systematically examines the effects of pre-existing subject characteristics (often called subject variables) by forming groups based on these naturally occurring differences between subjects.

Linear regression analysis A correlation-based method for estimating a score on one measured behavior from a score on the other when two behaviors are strongly related.

Longitudinal design A method in which the same group of subjects is followed and measured at different points in time; a method that looks for changes across time.

Multiple correlation Statistical intercorrelations among three or more behaviors, represented by $R$.

Multiple regression analysis A correlation-based technique (from multiple correlation) that uses a regression equation to predict the score on one behavior from scores on the other related behaviors.

Negative correlation The relationship existing between two variables such that an increase in one is associated with a decrease in the other; also called an *inverse relationship*.

Nonequivalent groups design A design in which the researcher compares the effects of different treatment conditions on preexisting groups of participants.

Partial correlation An analysis that allows the statistical influence of one measured variable to be held constant while computing the correlation between the other two measured variables.

Path analysis An important correlation-based method in which subjects are measured on several related behaviors; the researcher creates (and tests) models of possible causal sequences using sophisticated correlational techniques.

Positive correlation The relationship between two measures such that an increase in the value of one is associated with an increase in the value of the other; also called a *direct relationship*.

Pretest/posttest design A research design used to assess whether the occurrence of an event alters behavior; scores from measurements made before and after the event (called the *pretest* and *posttest*) are compared.

Quasi-experimental designs Often seem like (as the prefix *quasi-* implies) real experiments, but they lack one or more of its essential elements, such as manipulation of antecedents and random assignment to treatment conditions.

Regression line The line of best fit; represents the equation that best describes the mathematical relationship between two variables measured in a correlational study.

Scatterplot A graph of data from a correlational study, created by plotting pairs of scores from each subject; the value of one variable is plotted on the $X$ (horizontal) axis and the other variable on the $Y$ (vertical) axis.

Simple correlations Relationships between pairs of scores from each subject.

Subject variable The characteristics of the subjects in an experiment or quasi-experiment that cannot be manipulated by the researcher; sometimes used to select subjects into groups.

## REVIEW AND STUDY QUESTIONS

1. What is a correlation? When can it be used?

2. Leilani just computed the Pearson Product Moment Correlation Coefficient for two sets of data. She got $r = 2.30$. Leilani is thrilled, marveling at what a large relationship she found. What can she conclude from her findings?

3. A college administrator has located a new aptitude test that is correlated with academic achievement ($r = -.54$). The admissions committee of the college now uses a screening test also correlated with academic achievement, but the correlation is $r = $

+.45. Which test would be a better choice if the admissions committee is interested in predicting how well prospective students would do at the school? Explain your answer.

4. A researcher found that variable $X$ and variable $Y$ are very strongly correlated. She claimed that variable $X$ causes variable $Y$ to occur. Why can't this statement be made?

5. How are beta weights used to construct paths in a path analysis?

6. What does a cross-lagged panel design attempt to do? What cannot be ruled out as an alternative to any cause-and-effect model found with a cross-lagged panel design?

7. Define the term *quasi-experiment* and discuss the pros and cons of quasi-experimentation.

8. Explain the pros and cons of longitudinal versus cross-sectional studies.

9. Claire conducted an ex post facto study comparing attitudes of a group of rap music fans and a group of classical music buffs. She found that the rap fans had more sexist attitudes about women than the other group did. She claimed that rap music causes people to become sexist. Explain why she cannot say

that from the results of her study. How can her results be stated accurately?

10. What four groups are needed in the Solomon 4-group design?

11. Design a correlation-based study or a quasi-experiment to test each of the following:
    a. Hot weather is associated with higher rates of violence in the streets.
    b. Rap music causes people to become more sexist (rather than the other way around).
    c. Childhood schizophrenia can be predicted from cognitive deficits, genetic predisposition, and autonomic arousal in childhood.
    d. Older people exercise less than middle-aged people.
    e. A college education increases people's SAT scores.

12. For each study you designed for question 11, list all the reasons you can think of that explain why your study would be low in internal validity.

## CRITICAL THINKING EXERCISE

*The myth:* More men than women are left-handed.

*The scientific findings:* It's true. Approximately 12.6% of male Americans are left-handed, but only 9.9% of female Americans are (Gilbert & Wysocki, 1992).

*The problem:* There are age differences in handedness. Among young people age 10 to 20, the figures are higher: 14% for boys, and 12% for girls. Why do you think the percentages are different? Design a quasi-experimental study to investigate your hypothesis.

## ONLINE RESOURCES

For an excellent look at scatterplots, go to this site: http://www.statcan.gc.ca/edu/power-pouvoir/ch9/scatter-nuages/5214827-eng.htm

Investigate the correlation between money and happiness at www.sciencemag.org/cgi/content/abstract/312/5782/1908

## CHAPTER 6

# Formulating the Hypothesis

**The Characteristics of an
Experimental Hypothesis**
Synthetic Statements
Testable Statements
Falsifiable Statements
Parsimonious Statements
Fruitful Statements

**The Inductive Model**

**The Deductive Model**

**Combining Induction
and Deduction**

**Building on Prior Research**

**Serendipity and the Windfall
Hypothesis**

**Intuition**

**When All Else Fails**

**Searching the Research Literature**
Getting Started
Writing the Report
Finding the Articles You Need

SUMMARY
KEY TERMS
REVIEW AND STUDY QUESTIONS
CRITICAL THINKING EXERCISE
ONLINE RESOURCES

## CHAPTER OBJECTIVES

- Learn the differences between nonexperimental and experimental hypotheses
- Understand the components of a good experimental hypothesis
- Explore where hypotheses come from
- Learn how to conduct a literature search

The term *hypothesis* has appeared a number of times in the preceding chapters. Most psychological research is designed to test hypotheses. We will look first at the differences between experimental and nonexperimental hypotheses and then turn our attention to hypotheses for experimental designs—the major focus of this chapter. We will look at the characteristics of the experimental hypothesis and discuss several ways of arriving at hypotheses suitable for experimental study: induction, deduction, building on prior research, serendipity, and intuition. Then we will see how the hypothesis forms the basis of a research report, beginning with the Introduction section.

The hypothesis represents the end of the long process of thinking about a research idea. The hypothesis is the thesis, or main idea, of an experiment. It is a statement about a predicted relationship between at least two variables. Some nonscientific synonyms are *speculation, guess,* or *hunch.* The statement of a research hypothesis is designed to fit the type of research design that has been selected. You know from Chapter 5 that some nonexperimental designs are used to demonstrate relationships between sets of behaviors, but they may not be used to infer a cause-and-effect relationship between them. For this reason, a nonexperimental hypothesis is a statement of your predictions of how events, traits, or behaviors might be related—not a statement about cause and effect. In a true experiment, the hypothesis predicts the effects of specific antecedent conditions on some behavior that is to be measured.

Some nonexperimental designs, particularly those that do not restrict subjects' responses, do not typically include a hypothesis. Phenomenology, case studies, naturalistic observation, qualitative studies, and surveys of attitudes or opinions, for example, are primarily intended to explore and describe behaviors as they occur naturally. And it would be difficult to make guesses about behaviors or events that might or might not occur.

TABLE **6.1**

Examples of nonexperimental hypotheses

| Type of Design | Hypothesis |
|---|---|
| Correlational | The amount of TV viewing will be directly related to vocabulary size. |
| Ex post facto | Repressors will report fewer treatment-related side effects than will nonrepressors. |
| Non-equivalent groups | Incandescent lighting (in Company A) will produce better performance than fluorescent lighting (in Company B).* |
| Longitudinal | Firstborn children will show imitative behaviors after the birth of a sibling. |
| Cross-sectional | Firstborns with a 4-month-old sibling will show more imitative behavior than firstborns with a 1-month-old sibling. |

*Hypotheses for quasi-experiments might appear to predict a cause-and-effect relationship, but the results must be interpreted cautiously in the context of other possible differences between treatment groups.

© Cengage Learning

Other nonexperimental designs, such as correlational and quasi-experimental studies, generally include hypotheses about predicted relationships between variables. Nonexperimental hypotheses are straightforward predictions of the relationships the researcher expects to find between variables. See Table 6.1 for examples.

## THE CHARACTERISTICS OF AN EXPERIMENTAL HYPOTHESIS

Every experiment has at least one hypothesis. Complicated experimental designs that compare several treatments at the same time may test various hypotheses simultaneously. Each experimental hypothesis is a tentative explanation of an event or behavior. It is a statement that explains the effects of specified antecedent conditions on a measured behavior. By the time you are ready to formulate your hypothesis, you have already thought a great deal about a behavior. You may have discarded several improbable explanations of it and are ready to propose one explanation that seems plausible.

Suppose you began to make a list of all the conditions that could affect a behavior. Say the behavior is the speed at which you are reading this book. Some factors that affect your reading speed include the authors' writing style, your typical reading speed, and the size and clarity of the typeface. Your pace might also be affected by the amount of noise outside, the amount of light in the room, and whether or not you have eaten lunch. Perhaps it is even affected by the number of people who are now singing in Tibet or the number of fish in the sea. An enormous number of factors might affect your behavior at any given time. Before doing an experiment to determine which factors are critical to your reading speed, you would want to narrow down the possibilities.

Things far removed from one another are not likely to be causally related. Thus, we would not consider the fish population as a likely explanation for reading speed. Similarly, we would not spend much time on singing in Tibet. However, factors such as writing style, your normal reading speed, typeface, or lighting probably do determine your speed. If you have not had lunch, images of food could certainly reduce your speed.

This process of whittling away at the number of possible factors affecting your reading speed is the key to formulating a hypothesis. Now that we have selected a small, finite number of possibilities, we are ready to propose an explanation for your reading speed. We are ready to state a hypothesis. To be scientific, each hypothesis should meet certain basic criteria. As you will see, the criteria have very little to do with personal beliefs or attitudes. Believing that something is true or interesting is not enough to make it a useful hypothesis. Hypotheses must be synthetic statements that are testable, falsifiable, parsimonious, and (we hope) fruitful.

## Synthetic Statements

Synthetic statements are those that can be either true or false. Psychologists have borrowed the terminology from the field of logic. Each experimental hypothesis must be a synthetic statement so that there can be some chance it is true and some chance it is false. "Hungry students read slowly" is a synthetic statement that can be supported or contradicted. An experiment designed to test the statement will yield information we can use to decide between the two possibilities.

Nonsynthetic statements should be avoided at all costs. These fall into two categories: analytic or contradictory. An analytic statement is one that is always true; for example, "I am pregnant or I am not pregnant." Even the most well-constructed experiment could not disprove that statement because the statement itself can explain all possible outcomes. Sometimes we inadvertently generate analytic statements by failing to state our predictions adequately. For example, the prediction "The weight of dieters will fluctuate" is essentially an analytic statement because it is sufficiently vague to be true for everyone. Everyone's weight fluctuates a bit, whether dieting or not. When stating a hypothesis, we want to be concise enough to be proven wrong. Similarly, we want to avoid making contradictory statements—that is, statements with elements that oppose each other—because contradictory statements are always false. "I have a brother and I do not have a brother" is an example of a contradictory statement. Because analytic statements are always true and contradictory statements are always false, we do not need to conduct experiments to test them: We already know what the outcome will be.

To ensure that a hypothesis is a synthetic statement, we must evaluate its form. A hypothesis meets the definition of a synthetic statement when it can be stated in what is known as the "If ... then" form. This form is another way of expressing the potential relationship between the antecedents and the behaviors to be measured: "If you look at an appealing photograph, then your pupils will dilate" is such a hypothesis. It expresses a potential relationship between a particular antecedent condition (looking at an appealing photograph) and a behavior (pupil dilation). The statement can be true or false.

## Testable Statements

An experimental hypothesis must also be testable—that is, the means for manipulating antecedent conditions and measuring the resulting behavior must exist. Many interesting hypotheses are currently of no scientific use because they do not meet this criterion. For example, have you ever wondered whether your dog dreams? Dogs can certainly make movements and sounds in their sleep that resemble the way they behave when they are awake and engaging in familiar activities—if its legs move and it barks just like it does when it chases the cat, maybe it's dreaming about chasing the cat. And some people hypothesize that dogs dream because they exhibit behaviors that correspond to behaviors associated with dream reports in humans—rapid eye movements, muscle twitches, even occasional vocalizations. Suppose we propose a research hypothesis in the "If ... then" form: "If dogs display muscle twitches and vocalizations during sleep, then they must be dreaming." We now have a hypothesis in proper form. But how do we proceed to test it? We could manipulate any number of antecedents to encourage sleep. We might start with a simple comparison of dogs fed warm food versus those fed room-temperature food. Some might sleep more than others, and some might bark and twitch more than others while asleep. But how will we know if they are dreaming? We can ask them, of course, although we cannot expect any useful answers. The difficulty here is that we have an interesting but, alas, untestable hypothesis. The means for observing and recording the behavior of interest—namely, dreaming in dogs—does not currently exist.

Still, untestable hypotheses are not necessarily useless. Scientists who speculated on what it would be like to walk on the moon probably generated quite a few untestable hypotheses at the beginning of the space program. But there is always the hope that new technology will open new areas of discovery. Someday, perhaps, dreams will be projected on television screens. We will then know not only whether dogs dream but also—if they do—what they are dreaming about. In the meantime, if you are reading this book as part of a course assignment, it will be to your advantage to work with hypotheses you can test.

## Falsifiable Statements

Statements of research hypotheses must be falsifiable (disprovable) by the research findings. Hypotheses need to be worded so that failures to find the predicted effect must be considered evidence that the hypothesis is indeed false. Consider the following (purely illustrative) "If ... then" statement: "If you read this book carefully enough, then you will be able to design a good experiment." Suppose you carefully read the book, spending hours on each chapter, and after you finish, we ask you to design an experiment. You come up with an experiment, but your design is not very good. Given the wording

RORSCHACH MULTIPLE-CHOICE TEST

1.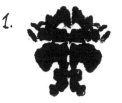

2.

3. PATRIOTISM

a.

b.

c.

a. JEALOUSY
b. ANGER
c. ESPRESSO
   MACHINE

a. NOSTALGIA FOR
   THE SIXTIES
b. TIGHT SHOES
c. NOSTALGIA FOR
   THE SEVENTIES

of the statement (it contains the qualifier "enough"), would we be willing to accept this evidence that our book did not teach experimental methods very well? More likely, we would be tempted to say that you simply did not read it carefully enough. As the hypothesis was worded, it simply is not falsifiable because any failures to produce the predicted effect can be explained away by the researcher.

## Parsimonious Statements

A research hypothesis should also be parsimonious. You will recall from Chapter 1 that parsimony means that the simplest explanation is preferred. Thus, a simple hypothesis is preferred over one that requires many supporting assumptions. The hypothesis "If you look at an appealing photograph, then your pupils will dilate" would be preferred over "If you look at an appealing photograph, then your pupils will dilate if it is a warm Saturday in June."

## Fruitful Statements

Ideally, a hypothesis is also fruitful; that is, it leads to new studies. It is often difficult to know in advance which hypotheses will be the most fruitful. There is some indication that a hypothesis is fruitful when we can think of new studies that will become important if the hypothesis is supported. An example of a fruitful hypothesis is Watson and Rayner's 1920 study of classical conditioning. These researchers hypothesized that fear of otherwise neutral objects could be acquired through learning. Their hypothesis might be stated in the

"If ... then" form as follows: "If a child, Albert, is repeatedly exposed to a loud, cry-inducing noise in the presence of a harmless furry animal, then Albert will begin to cry at the sight of the animal alone." This hypothesis and its confirmation led to a multitude of studies on classical conditioning in human subjects that continue today.

We have considered what may seem like an overwhelming number of criteria for a good hypothesis. The good hypothesis is a synthetic statement of the "If ... then" form. It is testable, falsifiable, parsimonious, and fruitful. With so many criteria and so many areas of research, how does an experimenter ever arrive at a hypothesis? According to Bertrand Russell, "As a rule, the framing of hypotheses is the most difficult part of scientific work, and the part where great ability is indispensable. So far, no method has been found which would make it possible to invent hypotheses by rule" (1945, p. 545).

Even so, a number of general approaches can describe the way in which hypotheses are most often formed. Although there are no rules that can be used to generate hypotheses, an understanding of these approaches will help you to think about the psychological issues you might like to study experimentally.

## THE INDUCTIVE MODEL

The inductive model of formulating a hypothesis, the process of reasoning from specific cases to more general principles, is often used in science and mathematics. By examining individual instances, we may be able to construct an overall explanatory scheme to describe them. Has something like this ever happened to you at a party? A stranger comes over to you and says, "You must be a Libra. I can tell by your beautiful clothes, your meticulous grooming, and the birthstone ring you're wearing." The stranger has tried a somewhat overworked conversation starter—but it illustrates the basics of inductive thinking. He or she has taken certain specific facts about you (what you are wearing and how you look) and used them to reach a more general conclusion about you—your birth sign. A person familiar with astrology may take certain specific facts about you and arrive at a hypothesis about your birth sign through induction.

Research hypotheses often come from the use of inductive reasoning. While standing in line at the dorm cafeteria, you may have noticed many instances of athletes (who tend to wear clothes advertising their sport) cutting to the front of the food line. You also notice that no one seems to challenge their behavior. You come up with your own explanation for this: Being identified as an athlete allows a person privileges not available to nonathletes. This is a hypothesis that came about through induction. You observed several specific instances of behavior and used these instances to form a general principle to explain the behavior. You may be able to come up with an interesting idea for testing it experimentally.

B. F. Skinner was a convincing advocate for inductive research in psychology. Skinner (see Figure 6.1) extensively studied operant conditioning in rats and pigeons. In operant conditioning, the organism is reinforced or

Courtesy of the B. F. Skinner Foundation

FIGURE **6.1** B. F. Skinner (1904–1990).

rewarded when it produces a particular response, such as bar pressing, which has been selected by the experimenter for reinforcement.

Skinner studied many variations of the basic operant procedures, keeping careful records of what happened to behavior under various conditions. He tried giving reinforcement on some but not all occasions when the animal emitted the required response. He tried new reinforcement contingencies based solely on the number of responses emitted (one pellet of food for each three bar presses) or on the elapsed time (one pellet of food per minute for one or more bar presses). He tried withholding reinforcement after the response was well established. From the results of numerous experiments, Skinner developed the concepts of partial reinforcement and extinction, along with reliable descriptions of the way intermittent reinforcement alters behavior (Ferster & Skinner, 1957). Concepts essential to understanding the learning process grew out of Skinner's inductive approach.

Induction is the basic tool of theory building. A *theory* is a set of general principles that can be used to explain and predict behavior. Through induction, researchers construct theories by taking bits of empirical data and forming general explanatory schemes to accommodate those facts. Although we might not put much faith in it, the 12 astrological signs represent a theory of behavior. Some scientific theories have been constructed on the work of a single researcher, such as Skinner. Other times, theories come about by assimilating the research of many experimenters into general explanatory principles. For instance, the theory of the mere exposure effect came about as a result of reviewing the published results of many past experiments that seemed to zero in on the same conclusion: The more we are exposed to something, the more we like it (Zajonc, 1966). Over the years, Zajonc and his students have refined the theory through experimentation, and its success can be seen by how often the theory is still used as the basis of advertising and political campaigns.

## THE DEDUCTIVE MODEL

The deductive model of formulating a hypothesis is the reverse of the inductive model. Deduction is the process of reasoning from general principles to make predictions about specific instances. The deductive model is most useful when we have a well-developed theory with clearly stated basic premises. Then it is possible to deduce predictions about what should happen in new situations in which the theory would apply. Testing such predictions provides a test of the value of the theory.

An excellent example of the deductive method in psychology is research that stemmed from predictions generated by equity theory (Walster, Walster, & Berscheid, 1978). These psychologists were not the first to consider equity (or perceived fairness) an important determinant of behavior in human relationships. Philosophers such as Aristotle also believed it was important. But Walster, Walster, and Berscheid provided a comprehensive and useful theory of equity in interpersonal situations. They proposed that the behavior of individuals could be predicted by three simple propositions:

1. Individuals will try to optimize their outcomes (outcomes = rewards minus costs).
2. When individuals believe they are in an inequitable relationship, they will feel distress in direct proportion to the perceived degree of inequity.
3. The more distress they feel, the harder they will work to restore equity.

For the past three decades, equity theory has been used by researchers to predict behavior. It has successfully predicted outcomes in a great number of interpersonal circumstances; victimization, helping, employment, and love are only a few. Apparently, whether we feel overbenefited or underbenefited in a relationship, we will do what we can to restore a sense of fairness. For example, Ingersoll-Dayton, Neal, Ha, and Hammer (2003) used equity theory to explain the ways in which siblings redressed perceived inequities in the care of older parents. They either attempted to persuade their siblings to make caregiving activities more equitable or they cognitively restructured their feelings of inequity (e.g., a brother who provides minimal caregiving support would tell himself that "it's a gender thing; mom just calls on her more").

## COMBINING INDUCTION AND DEDUCTION

We have looked at induction and deduction as two separate approaches to formulating a hypothesis. In practice, these approaches are not so neatly separated. As you might imagine, theorists like Walster, Walster, and Berscheid did not formulate equity theory without some reference to specific cases. They formulated the theory on the basis of their own and others' observations. Actually, the list of references used for the book describing their theory included more than 500 such observations, which were used as evidence for the theory. Thus their propositions were formed initially through induction from specific cases. Later tests of the propositions were based on predictions derived through deduction.

Both induction and deduction are important in research, and both are useful in formulating hypotheses for study. Through induction, we devise general principles and theories that can be used to organize, explain, and predict behavior until more satisfactory principles are found. Through deduction we rigorously test the implications of those theories.

## BUILDING ON PRIOR RESEARCH

So far we have discussed global approaches that can be applied to a variety of research topics. Now we will look at how the researcher narrows down the field of possibilities enough to formulate a single hypothesis. The most useful way of finding hypotheses is by working from research that has already been done. Sometimes, nonexperimental studies can suggest cause–and–effect explanations that can be translated into experimental hypotheses. One very important example is the research on cigarette smoking and cancer. In ex post facto studies, smokers had higher rates of lung cancer than nonsmokers did. This finding suggested the hypothesis that smoking causes cancer. Stated in the "If … then" form: "If people smoke, then they will get cancer."

Experimenters test the hypothesis under controlled conditions. Because of ethical issues, the subjects in these experiments are animals rather than humans: If smoking really does cause cancer, scientists would not want to expose human subjects to smoking. The experiments begin with the creation of different antecedent conditions—groups of rats are exposed to varying amounts of cigarette smoke. If rats that "smoke" develop higher rates of cancer than rats that do not, the conclusion is that smoking causes cancer. Again, the systematic manipulation of the antecedent conditions permits us to make cause-and-effect inferences that cannot be made on the basis of nonexperimental data alone.

Prior experimental research is an excellent source of hypotheses. If you do not already have a specific hypothesis in mind, you will find the experimental literature useful in focusing your thinking on important issues. As you read more and more studies in a topic area, you may begin to see points that other researchers have missed or new applications for previously tested hypotheses. These may form the basis for new experiments.

For instance, if you are interested in equity theory, reading what others have done can trigger ideas for new applications of the theory—perhaps feelings about the fairness of course grades would predict how many hours students are willing to put into a course. Other times, past research will suggest additional variables that could mediate an effect demonstrated in an experiment—perhaps children's aggressiveness toward a doll after watching an aggressive adult model is mediated by how much the child likes the adult model. From time to time, you will encounter published experiments with conflicting outcomes. You may come up with an idea about why inconsistent findings were produced, and your idea might generate a testable hypothesis (McGuire, 1997). By reading prior studies, you will also see the kinds of problems others have had in researching a topic. This will help you to anticipate difficulties you might not have thought of alone.

A thorough search of the literature available on your topic is important in designing a good experiment and essential to writing an effective report, as we will see at the end of this chapter. Regardless of where an experimental hypothesis originates, reviewing the literature is still a necessary component of report writing. An important goal of report writing is to integrate your findings into existing facts. A good literature review will also help you avoid duplicating someone else's work when a replication is not what you had in mind.

## SERENDIPITY AND THE WINDFALL HYPOTHESIS

All the approaches we have looked at so far are purposeful; the experimenter is usually looking for a new hypothesis on which to base an experiment. However, at times a discovery has been made where none was intended; such discoveries may be attributed to serendipity. The word comes from the 18th-century tale "The Three Princes of Serendip" by Horace Walpole, which describes the adventures of three princes who found many valuable things they were not seeking. Serendipity is the knack of finding things that are not being sought. Discoveries through serendipity have been made in the physical sciences as well as in psychology.

An element of serendipity appeared in the work of Ivan Pavlov (1927), a Russian physiologist whose main interest was the digestive glands (Figure 6.2). His studies involved feeding dogs and observing the changes that occurred in

National Library of Medicine

FIGURE **6.2** Ivan Pavlov (1849–1936).

their stomach secretions. Through his work Pavlov became interested in salivation. He asked such questions as, "If I feed the dog, how long will it be before the dog begins to salivate?" The questions seemed straightforward enough until Pavlov began to notice some distracting things. As the dogs became familiar with the bread Pavlov fed them, they began to salivate even before they were actually fed. Seeing the food seemed to produce salivation. Indeed, in a short while the dogs began to salivate as soon as he entered the room. Pavlov found these observations so interesting that he began to study the "psychic secretions" that he hypothesized were the result of the dogs' mental activity. His unplanned observations pulled him in a most unexpected direction. What Pavlov observed was the phenomenon of classical conditioning. Initially, salivation was elicited only by eating the food, but, after repeated pairings, the sight of the food as well as the sight of Pavlov elicited salivation. Pavlov won the Nobel Prize for his work on digestion, but he also made an unplanned contribution to the psychological study of learning.

Are such happy accidents really achievements? Didn't animal trainers and many parents know about conditioning already? Couldn't anyone have made the same contribution as Pavlov, if not with salivation, then with some other response? The answer is probably "No." What distinguishes a scientist like Pavlov is that he was able to distinguish between a commonplace incident and something of great importance. Another person might have abandoned the salivation research as hopeless. Pavlov continued his research, performing many new experiments and offering unique interpretations of his findings.

Serendipity can be useful in generating new hypotheses only when we are open to new possibilities. The good scientist takes note of all potentially relevant observations and analyzes and evaluates them: Are they interpretable? Do they explain something that was previously unexplained? Do they suggest a new way of looking at a problem? Serendipity is not just a matter of luck; it is also a matter of knowing enough to use an opportunity.

## INTUITION

Intuition, another approach we will examine here, is not discussed in most experimental psychology texts. Psychology is a science, and as such it should be governed by formal, logical rules. But using intuition is not necessarily unscientific; rather, the inferences drawn from intuition can sometimes violate scientific criteria.

Intuition may be defined as knowing without reasoning. As such, it is probably closest to phenomenology. We acquire phenomenological knowledge simply by attending to our own experience. We have a hunch about what might happen in a particular situation, so we set up an experiment to test it. Intuition guides what we choose to study. Of course, our experiments are still conducted in the context of prior research. We review the experimental literature to avoid carrying out experiments that are pointless given what is already known. For example, we may believe intuitively that dogs can see colors like people can, but a review of the prior work on perception shows

"PERHAPS, DR. PAVLOV, HE COULD BE TAUGHT TO SEAL ENVELOPES."

that they cannot.[1] Knowing this, we would not begin a new series of tests to check whether dogs can see all of the same colors that people can.

When is intuition likely to be most helpful? According to Herbert Simon (1967), a psychologist and computer scientist who won the Nobel Prize, intuition is most accurate if it comes from experts. He believes that good hunches are really an unconscious result of our own expertise in an area. The more we know about a topic, the better our intuitive hypotheses are likely to be (Halpern, 1989).

We must be careful to remain within the bounds of science when we use our intuition. By intuition, we may have a tentative explanation for behavior or events. But such an explanation is truly tentative. It cannot be accepted as valid until it has been translated into a hypothesis and subjected to empirical tests. Also keep in mind the discussion from Chapter 1 about the kinds of cognitive and judgment errors people tend to make—intuition should not destroy objectivity. Even though we believe intuitively that something is true, we must be prepared to change our thinking if the experimental evidence does not confirm our belief. Unless we find flaws in the experiment that would

---

[1] Dogs are able to discriminate brightness, but dogs do not have very good color vision. Apparently, dogs can see in only two hues: one in the violet and blue-violet range (all probably seeming blue) and the other in the greenish-yellow, yellow, and red range (all probably seeming yellow). They can, however, distinguish shades of gray better than humans can, which means they can see better in dim light.

account for why our expectations were not confirmed, the observable data take precedence over intuition. Box 6.1 contains an example of some results that don't match what our intuition tells us.

## WHEN ALL ELSE FAILS

If you are reading this text as part of a course requirement, you may be required to design an experiment of your own. You realize by now that you must have a hypothesis. Perhaps you also realize that our discussion of how

---

### BOX **6.1**    Counterstereotypic Performance

The effects of stereotyping have been studied more by psychologists than by researchers in any other discipline. A widely held stereotype—held by both men and women—is that women, in general, possess less ability in math and related areas than men. Is this really true, or can women's poorer performance be explained by other factors, such as a self-fulfilling prophecy? Stereotype researchers Spencer, Steele, and Quinn (1999) conducted an interesting experiment to find out. They hypothesized that women would perform more poorly than men on a math test only if test-takers believed that women generally performed more poorly on this test than men did. The research sample consisted of male and female college students (who had received grades of B or better in calculus). Before taking the math test, all subjects were provided with the following information:

> As you may know, there has been some contro-versy about whether there are gender differences in math ability. Previous research has sometimes shown gender differences and sometimes shown no gender differences. Yet little of this research has been carried out with women and men who are very good in math. You were selected for this experiment because of your strong background in mathematics. (p. 12)

Next, subjects were provided with one of two types of additional information: (1) the test has been shown to produce gender differences or (2) the test has been shown *not* to produce gender differences. Then, all subjects completed the math test. Figure 6.3 shows what happened.

When subjects had been told that the test produced gender differences, the stereotype was upheld: Women indeed performed much more poorly

than men did. When subjects had been told that the test did not produce gender differences, men and women performed equally well. Identical results were found in two other experiments reported in the multiple-experiment article.

The authors clearly demonstrated that a stereotype threat to one's ability is sufficient to severely debilitate performance. In another experiment, Steele and Aronson (1995) found identical effects on African Americans faced with a difficult verbal test. When told that Blacks perform more poorly on the verbal test than Whites, that's exactly what happened. In contrast, when subjects were told that Blacks and Whites perform equally well—they did.

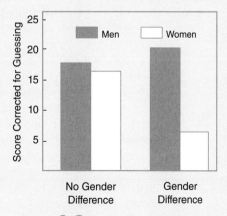

**FIGURE 6.3**

From "Stereotype Threat and Women's Math Performance," by S. J. Spencer, C. M. Steele and D. M. Quinn, *Journal of Experimental Social Psychology*, 1999, 35, 4–28. Copyright © 1999, with permission from Elsevier.

others derive hypotheses has not been particularly helpful. As Russell said, there are no rules that can be used to generate hypotheses. If you feel completely lost, here are some suggestions that have helped other students.

One method is to pick a psychology journal from your library's shelves and just read through an issue. Chances are good that you will find an article that piques your interest in a topic area. You are *least* likely to come up with a hypothesis by trying to think about everything you know about psychology. Instead, begin by focusing on one or two broad areas that interest you.[2]

Perhaps you like learning and memory. If so, that is the place to start. Once you select some broad areas of interest, reread the sections on these areas in an introductory psychology text. You may now be able to narrow the number of possible topics even further. Perhaps you are most interested in the work on learning lists of words. Now locate the latest research that has been done in this area. You might have to do quite a bit of reading before you can derive a hypothesis of your own. Try to focus your reading on the approaches we have discussed. Do you find any specific instances that suggest general principles? Is there a study that sets out a theory leading to deductions that are testable? Were there nonexperimental studies that can be redone as experiments to test cause-and-effect inferences? You might hit upon something by accident, or you might develop a hunch about what could happen in a slightly new experimental setting.

Here is another suggestion: Try observation. Some very good hypotheses come from observing how people behave in public places. In graduate school, an early class assignment of one of the authors was to go to a public place and observe people until a testable experimental hypothesis was found. It worked because forming hypotheses about the kinds of antecedent conditions that affect people's behavior comes naturally—we do it all the time. These hypotheses are called *causal attributions* (Kelley, 1971). We search for a cause to which we can attribute someone's behavior. Has the following ever happened to you? You are driving behind a slow automobile on a one-lane road, and it seems to you that the driver speeds up whenever it is legal to pass and slows down in the no-passing areas. You can form a hypothesis about this behavior (and you probably will). You may decide that the cause of the slowing down is internal (dispositional)—the person is a bad driver or, worse, a real blockhead. Or you could decide that the cause is external (situational)—the no-passing lanes are always on hills, and some cars have trouble maintaining their speed on hills. Either causal attribution could be turned into a research hypothesis.

Finally, if all else fails, turn your attention to a real-world problem and try to figure out what causes it. An added benefit of this approach is that once the cause can be determined, a solution often suggests itself. Social and health psychologist Angela Bryan set her sights on finding a way to increase condom use among undergraduate women. During a postdoctoral fellowship funded by the National Science Foundation, she first identified factors

---

[2] "A first principle not formally recognized by scientific methodologists—when you run onto something interesting, drop everything else and study it!" (B. F. Skinner)

associated with unprotected sex in this population (e.g., reduced perceptions of control over sexual encounters) and then went on to design an intervention to change this perception and increase the use of condoms. Her important applied research program earned the prestigious Award for Distinguished Scientific Early Career Contributions to Psychology in 2006 from the American Psychological Association. You can read about the intervention she designed in Bryan, Aiken, and West (1996). Attempting to discover causes of littering, vandalism, cheating, or shoplifting might be examples of some other real-world problems to explore.

Set realistic goals for yourself. Work from hypotheses that can be tested in the time frame you have available. You will probably need all the time you can get, which means that it is not a good idea to wait until the last minute to begin thinking about a hypothesis—or to begin searching the literature, the topic of the next section.

# SEARCHING THE RESEARCH LITERATURE

## Getting Started

Once you have decided on a hypothesis, you will want to become familiar with other published studies in your topic area. Conducting a thorough literature search is an important part of conducting research, and it is necessary for writing a research report. Thousands of research articles are published each year in psychological journals, periodicals that publish individual research reports and integrative research reviews (up-to-date summaries of what is known about a specific topic).

If your literature search is thorough, you are likely to locate work done to test your hypothesis or one that is closely related. Published research reports on your topic can also help you develop good ideas for procedures to use in your own experiment, and reports are full of tips for measuring your observations. Once you have found a good journal article on your topic, you might be able to find other related publications in the article's reference section.

Conducting a literature search is bound to seem daunting at first because there are simply so many sources available. Besides journal articles, entire books may have been written on the topic that interests you. Be on the look-out for edited volumes that contain chapters written by experts in your topic area; they can be a particularly good place to start because they summarize the most important recent work. (You may find a few useful references in psychology textbooks, too.) Research reviews, whether they come from journals or books, give you an overview of a topic area, and they are an invaluable source of references as well. If an experiment is summarized that seems like it might be relevant to your experiment, you can use the reference to look up and read the original research report.

Another particularly good source of information is a meta-analysis conducted on your topic, which can be found in either journals or edited volumes. Meta-analysis is a statistical reviewing procedure that uses data from many similar studies to summarize research findings about individual topics. A meta-analysis has the added benefit of quantifying past findings—it uses special statistical procedures to measure how strong the cause-and-effect relationship between the antecedent conditions and measured behaviors appears to be. And because they are statistically derived, conclusions from a meta-analysis can be more objective than review articles (for an interesting example, see Box 6.2).

---

BOX **6.2**    **The Effects of Media Violence on Youth**

In December, 2003, a distinguished group of media researchers from universities around the country published an important article on the effects of media violence in *Psychological Science in the Public Interest,* a journal of the Association for Psychological Science.* They examined five decades of experimental and nonexperimental research investigating the effects of violence in television, films, music, music videos, and video games. They examined cross-sectional studies, cross-lag panel studies, longitudinal studies, and true experiments. Beyond examining the studies and reporting on the effects found in each type of study, the authors also reviewed numerous meta-analyses that have been done on the topic of media violence and aggression.

In addition, they used statistics to assess how strong the effects were (like a meta-analysis of meta-analyses). They found that all forms of media violence produced significant amounts of aggressiveness and violence in children, adolescents, and adults and that the effects are "real, causal, and significant" (p. 82). They also concluded that no one completely escapes the effects of media violence, but its effects appear strongest on individuals with a history of aggression or violence, and males tend to be affected more than females are. The article also describes theoretical explanations for media effects, offering many exciting, testable hypotheses.

One of the ways the media industry responded to years of claims that media violence is harmful was to implement rating systems. But, are they working? Another meta-analysis, recently published by Bushman and Cantor (2003) can answer that question.** The authors examined all previously published ratings studies, evaluating the overall effect of ratings across all of the studies. The results were interesting, but only somewhat encouraging. For children under the age of 8, violence ratings do have a

deterrent effect, but the effect reverses once children reach age 11. From about 11 to 22, violence ratings have the opposite effect—they actually attract viewers, particularly boys and young men. Although weaker, the effect reverses again in people over age 36—here it has a deterrent effect once again.

Like the first meta-analysis, this one generates lots of hypotheses for future research. One that comes to mind immediately: Are parents' attitudes responsible for the deterrent effect on the younger children? If yes, how might that work? Modeling? Keeping the younger kids away from violent movies? You've heard the phrase "That's an empirical question"—that simply means that we won't know the answer until someone tests the hypothesis.

FIGURE **6.4**

---

*Anderson, C. A., Berkowitz, L., Donnerstein, E., Huesmann, L. R., Johnson, J. D., Linz, D., Malamuth, N. M., & Wartella, E. (2003). The influence of media violence on youth. *Psychological Science in the Public Interest, 4*(2), 81–110.
**Bushman, B. J., & Cantor, J. (2003). Media ratings for violence and sex: Implications for policymakers and parents. *American Psychologist, 58*(2), 130–141.

In general, it is best to skip popular books written by nonresearchers, essays, and sources from popular media, such as popular magazines and newspapers. Although they can be a source of interesting hypotheses, these are not considered reliable or scientific sources of information (remember the safety report about car size?). Finally, you will need to use extreme caution when "googling" the Internet for information on your topic. Blogs, personal websites, and wikis (like Wikipedia) are not considered reliable sources. Avoid them. Published journal articles and scholarly books should comprise most of your sources.

## Writing the Report

Published research reports from psychological journals will form the bulk of the reading you are expected to do as background for writing a research report. The Introduction section of a research report consists of a selective review of relevant, recent research. Only if your topic has a long history (like Pavlov's classical conditioning) would you include early articles. We say the review is selective because the writer selects only the articles that are *directly related to the research hypothesis*—not everything that has ever been done on the topic. The specific studies cited in the Introduction should provide empirical background for your experiment and guide the reader toward your research hypothesis. (Specific tips on writing can be found in Chapter 16.)

Another goal of a research report is to integrate your experiment into the existing body of knowledge: to show how the results of your research advance knowledge, increase generalizability of known effects, or contradict past findings. To do this, you may need to refer to specific past work in the Discussion section of your research report as well. (You can read more on this in Chapters 15 and 16.) The implications of your findings—what the results mean—also go in this section. If your findings are inconsistent with past results reported by other researchers, you will need to explain that here as well by contrasting your study with theirs.

## Finding the Articles You Need

Fortunately, many library and Web-based aids can help you find the journal articles you need. The primary resource for psychologists is PsycINFO, an online database published by the American Psychological Association. Abstracts (summaries) of published research are the primary source for locating the articles you will need from psychological journals. Each week, APA adds new abstracts of research that has been published on your topic in more than 2,400 journals worldwide. In PsycINFO, you will also find summaries of English-language books, book chapters, and dissertations.

Almost all university libraries now have online computer literature search systems, such as PsycINFO, available for students. Many of the articles can be immediately downloaded via online databases such as PsycARTICLES and Psychology: SAGE Full Text; others will need to be retrieved through library copy services or interlibrary loans. Most libraries in research universities will e-mail requested articles directly to your e-mailbox. Temporary, low-cost home subscriptions to PsycINFO and PsycARTICLES are also available through APA (www.apa.org/psycinfo/), which allow you to search for relevant abstracts and to download full-text articles from about 60 APA journals and complete chapters from a number of APA-published books. Even though abstracts from journal articles, books, and book chapters are now relatively easy to retrieve, you still have to select the abstracts that seem most relevant, locate the journal articles or books, and read them.

Using PsycINFO makes finding articles on your topic very simple. For example, it allows you to use several keywords at once to narrow down your topic precisely so that abstracts only peripherally related to your topic are skipped. Start with the most recent abstracts. Remember that journal articles contain lists of references that can be used to go farther back into a problem if necessary. You will probably find that the most difficult part of using PsycINFO (or other online retrieval databases) is determining the correct keywords to use for the search. APA's *Thesaurus of Psychological Index Terms,* available on PsycINFO, is the best guide to keyword terminology. PsycINFO also allows a search by author as you identify key people in your area of interest.

Figure 6.5 shows how we searched PsycINFO online for information about the negative ion study by Baron, Russell, and Arms (1985) cited in Chapters 1, 2, 3, and 5. The first search was by authors; the second by keywords. Using several names or words narrows down the number of potential articles from hundreds or, in some cases, thousands to the single article we want in only a few steps. The citation and abstract information actually retrieved by PsycINFO is shown in Figure 6.6.

Once you have found abstracts of promising articles, you can copy them from journals owned by your library, download the articles (if they are available), or arrange to have them sent through an interlibrary loan or copy service. Unless your university library is very large (and heavily endowed), do not expect it to have all the journals you want in either print or electronic format. Even though many articles are now available online through electronic journals, your library may not subscribe to these electronic journal packages. Thanks to OpenURL technology, some university libraries provide links from PsycINFO to full-text articles available from other database vendors.

Another good source of journal articles (after you have identified key people) is the *Social Sciences Citation Index* located in print in your university library or online through the Web of Science. Here you will find each author's publications listed and, after each publication, a list of other authors who have used those publications in their research reports. Generally, these newer reports are articles about research on a closely related topic. The sources listed here are the major ones for psychology; however, many more abstract retrieval services are available, such as Academic OneFile, ERIC (education research), Education Abstracts from Wilson Select, OneFile, MEDLINE (biomedical and biobehavioral research); and Lexis-Nexis. Ask your reference librarian what is available at your library.

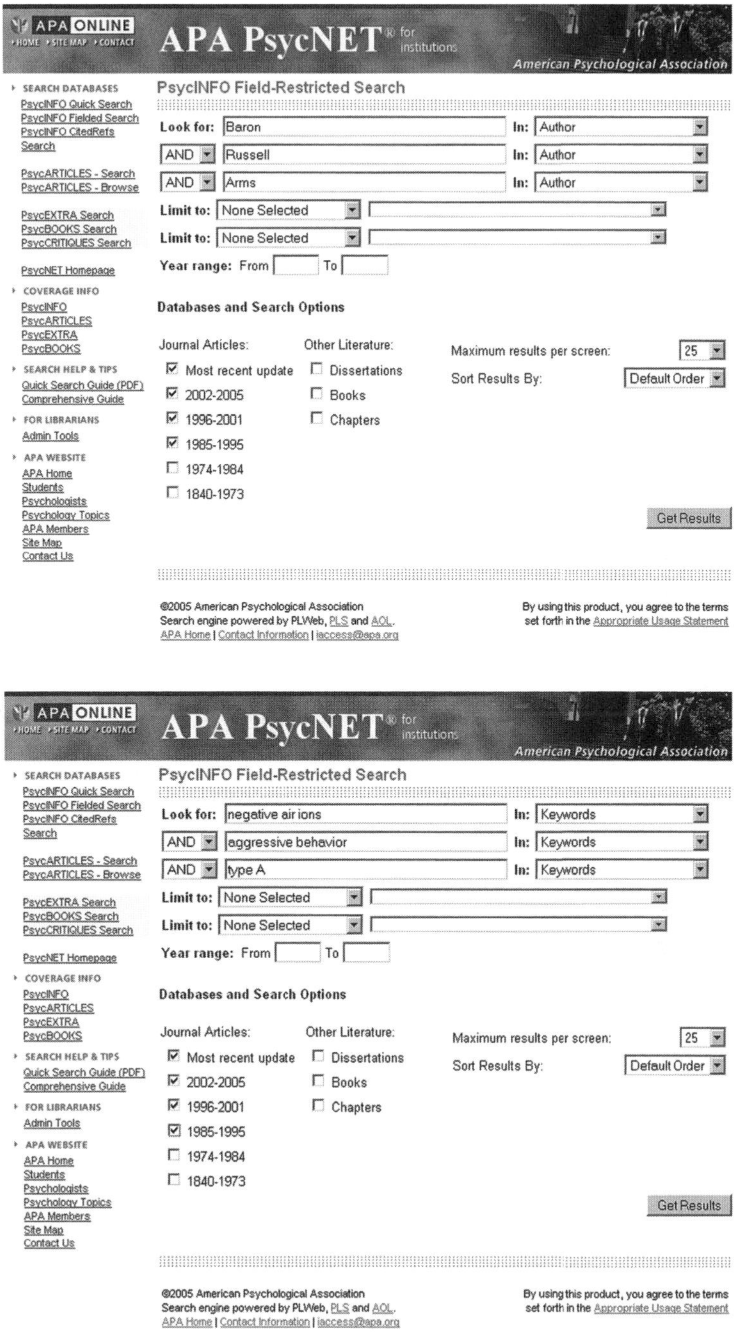

FIGURE **6.5** PsycINFO searches for Baron, Russell, and Arms (1985) by authors (panel a) and by keywords (panel b).

Courtesy of the American Psychological Association This material is reprinted with permission of the American Psychological Association publisher of the PsycINFO Database  and may not be reproduced without prior permission.

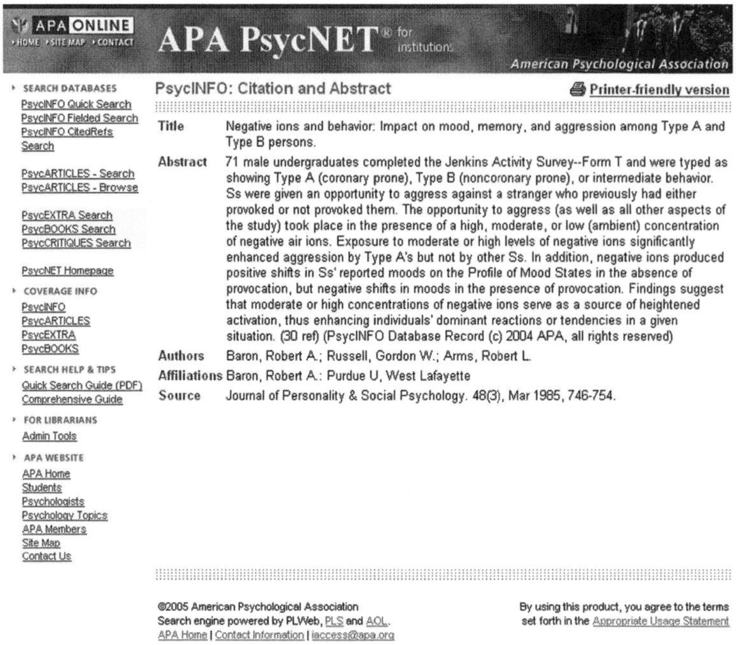

APA ONLINE
›HOME ›SITE MAP ›CONTACT
APA PsycNET® for institutions
American Psychological Association

› SEARCH DATABASES
PsycINFO Quick Search
PsycINFO Fielded Search
PsycINFO CitedRefs Search
PsycARTICLES - Search
PsycARTICLES - Browse
PsycEXTRA Search
PsycBOOKS Search
PsycCRITIQUES Search
PsycNET Homepage
› COVERAGE INFO
PsycINFO
PsycARTICLES
PsycEXTRA
PsycBOOKS
› SEARCH HELP & TIPS
Quick Search Guide (PDF)
Comprehensive Guide
› FOR LIBRARIANS
Admin Tools
› APA WEBSITE
APA Home
Students
Psychologists
Psychology Topics
APA Members
Site Map
Contact Us

PsycINFO: Citation and Abstract — Printer-friendly version

| | |
|---|---|
| Title | Negative ions and behavior: Impact on mood, memory, and aggression among Type A and Type B persons. |
| Abstract | 71 male undergraduates completed the Jenkins Activity Survey--Form T and were typed as showing Type A (coronary prone), Type B (noncoronary prone), or intermediate behavior. Ss were given an opportunity to aggress against a stranger who previously had either provoked or not provoked them. The opportunity to aggress (as well as all other aspects of the study) took place in the presence of a high, moderate, or low (ambient) concentration of negative air ions. Exposure to moderate or high levels of negative ions significantly enhanced aggression by Type A's but not by other Ss. In addition, negative ions produced positive shifts in Ss' reported moods on the Profile of Mood States in the absence of provocation, but negative shifts in moods in the presence of provocation. Findings suggest that moderate or high concentrations of negative ions serve as a source of heightened activation, thus enhancing individuals' dominant reactions or tendencies in a given situation. (30 ref) (PsycINFO Database Record (c) 2004 APA, all rights reserved) |
| Authors | Baron, Robert A.; Russell, Gordon W.; Arms, Robert L. |
| Affiliations | Baron, Robert A.: Purdue U, West Lafayette |
| Source | Journal of Personality & Social Psychology. 48(3), Mar 1985, 746-754. |

©2005 American Psychological Association
Search engine powered by PLWeb, PLS and AOL.
APA Home | Contact Information | iaccess@apa.org

By using this product, you agree to the terms set forth in the Appropriate Usage Statement

FIGURE 6.6 Citation and abstract information about Baron, Russell, and Arms (1985) retrieved from PsycINFO.

Courtesy of the American Psychological Association This material is reprinted with permission of the American Psychological Association publisher of the PsycINFO Database and may not be reproduced without prior permission.

## SUMMARY

Most psychological research is designed to test a hypothesis. The *hypothesis*, a tentative explanation of behavior, is the thesis or main idea of the research. The hypothesis for nonexperimental research designs is called a *nonexperimental hypothesis;* it is a statement of your predictions about the association between the variables under study. For true experiments, the *experimental hypothesis* predicts the effects of specified antecedents on behavior. An experimental hypothesis has several characteristics.

First, it must be a *synthetic statement,* one that can be demonstrated to be either true or false. It cannot be an *analytic statement* (one that is always true) or a *contradictory statement* (one that is always false). A hypothesis meets the definition of a synthetic statement if it can be stated in the "If ... then" form. Second, the experimental hypothesis must be *testable:* The means for manipulating the antecedent conditions and measuring the resulting behavior must exist. The hypothesis must be disprovable or *falsifiable.* The hypothesis must also be *parsimonious;* the simplest hypothesis is preferred until it is ruled out by conflicting evidence. Ideally, the hypothesis is also *fruitful* and will lead to new research.

Hypotheses can be found through induction, deduction, prior research, serendipity, intuition, and more. *Induction* is the process of reasoning from specific cases to more general principles. *Deduction* is the process of reasoning from general principles to predictions about specific instances. In practice, induction and deduction are often used together. Through induction we may devise general principles, or theories, that may be used to organize, explain, and predict behavior until more satisfactory principles are found. Through deduction, we may rigorously test the implications of a theory. Regardless of which method we use, we are generally building on prior research. Sometimes nonexperimental studies may suggest experiments to test cause-and-effect relationships. Other times, reading published experiments can suggest hypotheses that can be tested experimentally. Hypotheses occasionally grow out of *serendipity,* the knack of finding things that are not being sought. Researchers occasionally make unexpected observations that lead them in surprising directions. *Intuition* may also lead to testable hypotheses, particularly in areas in which we are very familiar or expert. Hypotheses can also arise out of systematic searches through the research in specific areas of interest. Finally, hypotheses can come from everyday observation of behaviors and real-world problems.

The first step in designing research and writing a research report is to conduct a thorough literature search. Abstracts (summaries) are the primary source for locating the articles you will need from *psychological journals.* Computer searches of the abstracts are available through PsycINFO. *Meta-analyses* conducted on your topic are a particularly useful type of research article. The articles you select provide the basis for the *Introduction* section of the report and can also be used in the *Discussion* section to integrate your experiment into the existing body of literature on your topic.

## KEY TERMS

Analytic statement A statement that is always true.

Contradictory statement A statement that is always false.

Deductive model The process of reasoning from general principles to specific instances; most useful for testing the principles of a theory.

Discussion Concluding section of the research report, used to integrate the experimental findings into the existing body of knowledge, showing how the current research advances knowledge, increases generalizability of known effects, or contradicts past findings.

Experimental hypothesis A statement that is a tentative explanation of an event or behavior; it predicts the effects of specified antecedent conditions on a measured behavior.

Falsifiable statement A statement that is worded so that it is falsifiable, or disprovable, by experimental results.

Fruitful statement A statement that leads to new studies.

Hypothesis The thesis, or main idea, of an experiment or study consisting of a statement that predicts the relationship between at least two variables.

Inductive model The process of reasoning from specific cases to more general principles to form a hypothesis.

**Introduction** Beginning section of a research report that guides the reader toward your research hypothesis; includes a selective review of relevant, recent research.

**Intuition** The development of ideas from hunches; knowing directly without reasoning from objective data.

**Meta-analysis** A statistical reviewing procedure that uses data from many similar studies to summarize and quantify research findings about individual topics.

**Nonexperimental hypothesis** A statement of predictions of how events, traits, or behaviors might be related, but not a statement about cause and effect.

**Parsimonious statement** A statement that is simple and does not require many supporting assumptions.

**Psychological journal** A periodical that publishes individual research reports and integrative research reviews, which are up-to-date summaries of what is known about a specific topic.

**Serendipity** The knack of finding things that are not being sought.

**Synthetic statement** A statement that can be either true or false, a condition necessary to form an experimental hypothesis.

**Testable statement** A statement that can be tested because the means exist for manipulating antecedent conditions and for measuring the resulting behavior.

## REVIEW AND STUDY QUESTIONS

1. What is a hypothesis? What is the difference between a nonexperimental hypothesis and an experimental hypothesis?

2. What are the characteristics of a good hypothesis?

3. Which of the following are synthetic statements? Why?
   a. If I am cold, then it is December.
   b. Out of sight, out of mind.
   c. Virtue is its own reward.
   d. A statement that is always true is never true.

4. Explain the differences between induction and deduction. Describe the way they are used together to create theories and generate hypotheses.

5. Is a discovery made through serendipity just a matter of luck? Explain your answer.

6. a. What is the role of intuition in research?
   b. Is intuition scientific?
   c. Why are our hunches often correct?

7. Before you set up an experiment, you should conduct a review of the research literature. What is the purpose of this review?

8. Dr. G. has just completed a study that shows a correlation between the amount of time children watch television and their attention spans. Assume the correlation was $r = -.34$. State an experimental hypothesis based on this finding and devise a simple procedure for testing it.

9. Mary is lost: She just cannot think of a hypothesis. Give her some advice about how to proceed.

10. Select one of the research areas listed below. Review some of the prior work in that area and formulate a new experimental hypothesis based on your review.
    a. Paired-associates learning
    b. The influence of a mental set on problem solving
    c. Solving anagrams (scrambled words)
    d. Bystander apathy
    e. The mere exposure effect

11. Sit in a public place and observe people for an hour. Write down all the hypotheses that come to mind to explain their behaviors.

## CRITICAL THINKING EXERCISE

*The myth:* Animals have emotions the same as humans do.

*The scientific findings:* Most often false. For example, infant rats emit a distress cry when separated from their mothers, just like human infants do. For baby rats, however, the cry appears to result from physiological changes due to decreased cardiac rate (produced by extreme cold or induced by the drug clonidine)—not psychological distress as in human infants (Blumberg, Sokoloff, Kirby, & Kent, 2000).

*The problem:* Find the authors' hypothesis in the Introduction of the article published in the January 2000 volume of *Psychological Science.* Discuss the hypothesis relative to the idea of parsimony.

## ONLINE RESOURCES

Find interesting videos on psychology at:
http://www.psychexchange.co.uk/videos/view/20774

For additional ways to generate hypotheses, try the following:
http://faculty.vassar.edu/jamorrow/mcguire.html

# PART 2

# Method

**7** The Basics of Experimentation

**8** Solving Problems: Controlling Extraneous Variables

**9** Basic Between-Subjects Designs

**10** Between-Subjects Factorial Designs

**11** Within-Subjects Designs

**12** Within-Subjects Designs: Small $N$

## CHAPTER 7

# The Basics of Experimentation

**Independent and Dependent Variables**
Some Research Examples
Identifying Variables

**Operational Definitions**
Defining the Independent Variable:
   Experimental Operational Definitions
Defining the Dependent Variable: Measured
   Operational Definitions
Defining Constructs Operationally
Defining Nonconstruct Variables
Defining Scales of Measurement

**Evaluating Operational Definitions**
Reliability
Validity
Evaluating the Experiment: Internal Validity
Extraneous Variables and Confounding
Classic Threats to Internal Validity

**Planning the Method Section**

SUMMARY
KEY TERMS
REVIEW AND STUDY QUESTIONS
CRITICAL THINKING EXERCISE
ONLINE RESOURCES

## CHAPTER OBJECTIVES

- Learn the two types of variables that are the focus of an experiment
- Understand how variables are defined in an experiment
- Understand the importance of reliability and validity
- Learn about problems caused by extraneous variables and confounding

Once you have formulated a hypothesis, the next step is to design a procedure to test it. As you saw in Chapters 3, 4, and 5, there are many useful nonexperimental approaches to research. Each demands special skills, and each could form the basis of an entire textbook. The remainder of this book, however, deals primarily with experimentation. Much of the research currently done in the field of psychology is experimental. Moreover, an understanding of the principles of experimentation strengthens any researcher's potential for success.

When it is feasible, psychologists prefer experiments to other research methods because a properly conducted experiment allows us to draw causal inferences about behavior. When an experiment is well conducted, it is high in internal validity. To review briefly, the psychology experiment has these main features: We first manipulate the antecedent conditions to create at least two different treatment conditions. At least two treatments are required so that we can make statements about the impact of different sets of antecedents; if we used only one treatment, there would be no way to evaluate what happens to behaviors as the conditions change. We expose subjects to different treatment conditions so that we can measure the effects of those conditions on behavior. We record the responses or behaviors of subjects under various conditions and then compare them using statistics. We can then assess whether our predictions are confirmed.

When conducted skillfully, an experiment allows us to make cause-and-effect statements about behavior. If behavior changes as the antecedent conditions change, we can say that the differences in antecedent conditions caused the changes in behavior. However, a causal inference is justified only when a carefully controlled test of our predictions has been made, and a researcher must consider several influences that can threaten an experiment's internal validity. The chapters in this section of the text deal with the basic methods and problems involved in planning a good experiment.

In this chapter, you will begin to see how researchers move from the general idea expressed in a hypothesis to the specific actions required to carry out an experiment. For the purposes of scientific research, the experimenter must clearly define what is being studied, and how, so that the research can be evaluated as well as replicated. By the end of this chapter, you will be familiar with the basic components of experiments: the independent variable, the dependent variable, operational definitions, and control. We will examine these concepts in the context of specific experiments. We will also discuss some issues involved in evaluating definitions and experiments—reliability, validity, and confounding—and look at some classic threats to internal validity. The concepts presented in this chapter are fundamentals of experimental design that we will return to throughout the remainder of the book.

---

## INDEPENDENT AND DEPENDENT VARIABLES

In the simplest experiments, an experimental hypothesis states a potential relationship between two variables: If *A* occurs, then we expect *B* to follow. In an experiment, variables are measurable elements that can vary or take on different values along some dimension. To be more precise, the experimental hypothesis expresses a potential relationship between two kinds of variables, the independent and the dependent variable. We will begin with some formal definitions of these terms and then look at some concrete examples from actual research.

An experiment's independent variable (IV) is the dimension that the experimenter intentionally manipulates; it is the antecedent the experimenter chooses to vary.[1] This variable is "independent" in the sense that its values are created by the experimenter and are not affected by anything else that happens in the experiment. Independent variables are sometimes aspects of the physical environment that can be brought under the experimenter's direct control. Lighting (bright or dim) and noise levels (loud or soft) are some examples of environmental variables. Aspects of a given task, such as difficulty (easy, hard) and meaningfulness (nonsense syllables versus real words) may also become independent variables. Sometimes, experimenters manipulate experimental conditions so that subjects experience different

---

[1] The simplest experiments will have a single independent variable and a single dependent variable. We will see in Chapter 10, however, that experiments can have more than one independent variable. In Chapter 15, we will talk about experiments with more than one dependent variable.

psychological states: anxious versus nonanxious, happy versus sad, succeeding versus failing—psychological states can be independent variables. Or experimenters may use different sets of instructions as independent variables, such as instructing subjects to pay attention to the red circles or to the blue squares. Other times, experimenters will compare the efficacy of different types of psychological interventions on problem behaviors; the type of intervention can be an independent variable. The list of potential independent variables is endless.

To meet the definition of an experiment, at least two different treatment conditions are required; thus, an IV must be given at least two possible values in every experiment. The researcher decides which values of the IV to use. These values are called the levels of the independent variable in the experiment. The researcher varies the levels of the IV by creating different treatment conditions within the experiment. Each treatment condition represents one level of the IV. If the IV is to have two levels, there must be two different treatment conditions; if three values of the IV are to be used, there must be three different treatment conditions, and so on. Be careful not to confuse the levels of the IV with the IV itself. For example, suppose a professor gives tests on either blue or yellow paper to see if the color of the paper influences the scores. Blue and yellow represent two levels of the one IV, color. We could add other levels such as pink, green, and orange. We would still have only one IV—color.

In an ex post facto study (discussed in Chapter 5), the researcher can explore the way behavior changes as a function of changes in variables outside the researcher's control. These are typically subject variables, characteristics of the subjects themselves (age, personality characteristics, gender, and so on) that cannot be manipulated experimentally. It is common for researchers to refer to these quasi-experimental variables as independent variables too. Although the researcher does not manipulate them, quasi-experimental variables are often independent in the sense that the researcher selects the particular values that will be included in the study. For instance, in their study of cancer patients' reactions to chemotherapy, Ward, Leventhal, and Love (1988) selected patients who showed repressor or nonrepressor coping styles.

In ex post facto and other quasi-experimental studies, researchers often behave as if they were doing true experiments; they have treatments and measured observations (Cook & Campbell, 1979). However, in these kinds of studies, the independent variable is not manipulated the way it is when we study something under our direct control, such as a drug dose or the brightness of a light. In quasi-experiments, the researcher selects rather than creates the levels of the IV by assigning subjects to treatment groups on the basis of a subject variable. In an ex post facto study, individuals in various treatment groups are supposed to differ on a subject variable because the subject variable is the one we are testing.

In a true experiment, we test the effects of a manipulated independent variable—not the effects of different kinds of subjects. Therefore, in a true experiment, we have to make certain that our treatment groups do not consist of people who are different on preexisting characteristics. To guard against systematic differences in people in our treatment groups, we randomly assign subjects to receive different treatments (see Chapter 9). If we simultaneously varied both a subject variable and a manipulated independent variable, there would be no way of knowing whether effects we observed were caused by differences between subjects or by the IV. For example, if we gave introverts their exams on blue paper and extroverts their exams on yellow paper, we would not know whether differences in their exam grades were caused by the color of the paper or by personality differences. Or, if we studied worker productivity by placing incandescent lights in one company and fluorescent lights in another, we could not be sure that the differences in productivity were caused by the lighting and not by preexisting differences in the two groups of subjects. This problem is known as *confounding,* and we will return to it later in the chapter.

"THEN, AS YOU CAN SEE, WE GIVE THEM SOME MULTIPLE CHOICE TESTS."

How will we know whether changes in the levels of the IV have altered behavior? We measure another variable, called the dependent variable, to determine whether the independent variable had an effect. The dependent variable (DV) is the particular behavior we expect to change because of our experimental treatment; it is the outcome we are trying to explain. Sometimes it helps to think of it this way: In an experiment, we are testing effects of the IV on the DV. Because we manipulate the IV and measure its effects on the DV, dependent variables are sometimes called *dependent measures*.

If the hypothesis is correct, different values of the independent variable should produce changes in the dependent variable. The dependent variable is dependent in the sense that its values are assumed to depend on the values of the independent variable: As the IV changes value (as we look at behavior under different treatment conditions), we expect to see corresponding changes in the value of the DV. See Table 7.1 for other terms used to describe the independent and dependent variables in an experiment.

Selecting appropriate independent and dependent variables is an important part of designing every experiment. If we expect to understand the causes of behavior, we need to focus on the relevant antecedent variables. Remember, if we can specify the antecedents that lead to a particular behavior, we have explained that behavior from a scientific viewpoint.

We also need to assess accurately the impact of our treatment conditions. In an experiment, we cannot rely solely on our overall impression about whether the independent variable has some effect. We need more precision: We need an objective measure of the effect of the independent variable. We do not want the evaluation of the experiment's outcome to depend on our subjective judgment, which might be somewhat biased. In addition, our findings will have more widely understood meaning if they are presented in terms of an observable dimension that can be measured again and again. By clearly defining the way we are measuring the effect of the independent variable, we make it easier for others to replicate our research. Let us turn now to some specific examples of independent and dependent variables in the research literature.

TABLE **7.1**

## Other terms used to describe IVs and DVs

Independent variables are also referred to as:

> *treatments*
> *manipulations*
> *interventions*
> *conditions*

Dependent variables are also referred to as:

> *measures*
> *effects*
> *outcomes*
> *results*

© Cengage Learning

## Some Research Examples

### *Schachter*

Consider this hypothesis, tested in a classic experiment by Schachter (1959): If people are anxious, then they will want to affiliate, or be, with others. Put another way, misery loves company. The hypothesis states a potential relationship between two variables—anxiety and affiliation. To test the hypothesis, Schachter (see Figure 7.1) conducted the following experiment: Subjects were brought into a room with an experimenter who was wearing horn-rimmed glasses and a white laboratory coat. The experimenter introduced himself as Dr. Gregor Zilstein of the Departments of Neurology and Psychiatry. He explained that this was an experiment on the effects of electric shock. The subjects were split into two groups. One group was shown some elaborate electrical equipment and led to expect painful shocks: "These shocks will hurt, they will be painful. As you can guess, if, in research of this sort, we're to learn anything at all that will really help humanity, it is necessary that our shocks be intense" (p. 13). The other group received instructions leading them to believe they would feel no pain: "Do not let the word 'shock' trouble you; I am sure that you will enjoy the experiment … I assure you that what you feel will not in any way be painful. It will resemble more a tickle or a tingle than anything unpleasant" (p. 13).

Thus, both groups were told that they would receive electric shock, but one group expected pain, whereas the other did not. The group that expected

FIGURE **7.1** Stanley Schachter (1922–1997).

pain was anticipated to be more anxious than the group that did not. The experimenter then explained that there would be a delay while the experiment was being set up and asked the subjects to indicate on a questionnaire whether they preferred to wait for the next part of the experiment alone, with other subjects, or had no preference. Based on the hypothesis, those subjects who were more anxious would be more likely to want to wait with others. This was the end of the experiment. The real purpose of the study was then explained, and no one ever actually received electric shock.

In his hypothesis, Schachter stated a potential relationship between two variables, anxiety and affiliation: If subjects are anxious, then they will want to affiliate with others. The hypothesis expresses the relationship between the independent and the dependent variables. The independent variable in any experiment is the antecedent condition (the treatment) deliberately manipulated by the experimenter. Its values are represented by the various treatment conditions of the experiment. Schachter created two levels of anxiety (high and low) by using different sets of instructions. He manipulated anxiety by giving subjects varying instructions, leading them to believe that they either would or would not be exposed to painful shock; anxiety was the independent variable in this experiment. The variable was independent in the sense that its values were set by Schachter; it was not affected by anything else that occurred in the experiment.

In Schachter's experiment, the dependent variable was affiliation. The dependent variable is the variable measured to determine whether the independent variable had the expected effect on behavior. Affiliation was dependent in the sense that its values were assumed to depend on the values of the independent variable. According to the hypothesis, anxious subjects will be less likely to want to wait alone. If anxiety has no effect on affiliation, all subjects, anxious or not, will be equally willing to wait alone. But, in fact, Schachter's experiment supported his hypothesis; he found that the subjects who expected painful shocks were less likely to want to wait alone.

### Hess

Let us look at another classic research example of testing the effects of an independent variable on a dependent variable. Hess (1975) tested the following hypothesis: Large pupils make people more attractive. Throughout history, there has been popular support for this notion. Women once used belladonna to make themselves more beautiful; one of the drug's effects is dilation (widening) of the pupils. Candlelight dinners seem to flatter everyone, and aside from masking minor imperfections, dim light also causes pupils to dilate.

To test his hypothesis, Hess asked male subjects to rate four photographs of two women. The photographs were retouched so that each woman had small pupils in one photograph and large pupils in another. (Examples resembling Hess's photographs are shown in Figure 7.2.) Subjects were asked to select which woman in a series of pairs of these photographs appeared to be more friendly, charming, and so on.

The independent variable in this experiment was pupil size. Hess deliberately varied the size of the pupils so he could test the effects of pupil size on attractiveness. The two treatment conditions were two different values, or levels,

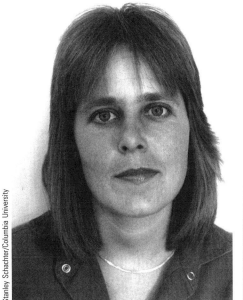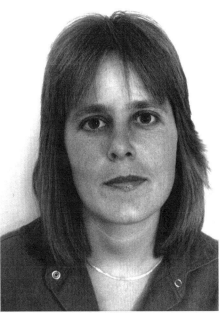

Stanley Schachter/Columbia University

FIGURE **7.2** Photographs of a woman retouched so that she has small pupils in one photograph and large pupils in the other.

of the independent variable, pupil size. The dependent variable, of course, was attractiveness. If the hypothesis is correct, measures of attractiveness should depend on size of pupils. And in fact Hess found that his male subjects were more likely to attribute the attractive traits to the women with large pupils. Later, Niedenthal and Cantor (1986) replicated Hess's findings on both male and female subjects using photos of men as well as women. These researchers also showed that similar attractiveness effects on impressions were produced by photos of both men and women whose pupil sizes were enlarged artificially.

### Identifying Variables

You will have little difficulty identifying the independent and dependent variables in an experiment if you take the time to think about what the experimenter did. Ask yourself the following questions: What did the experimenter manipulate? Is this the independent variable? What was used to assess the effect of the independent variable? Is this the dependent variable? Suppose we are designing an experiment to test our own hypothesis. How will we identify the independent and dependent variables? When you are working with your own hypothesis, you must ask the same types of questions you ask about an experiment that has already been done: What will you manipulate or vary to test the hypothesis? (This is your independent variable.) What behavior are you trying to explain; what will you measure to find out whether your independent variable had an effect? (This is your dependent variable.) Keep in mind that if you do not need to manipulate the antecedent conditions by creating different treatment conditions (if you will simply measure behaviors as they occur), you do not have an experimental hypothesis.

Suppose this is your hypothesis: People learn words faster when the words are written horizontally than when they are written vertically. You have come to this hypothesis through your review of research on the effects of practice. Because your English-speaking subjects customarily see words printed horizontally, you suspect that words oriented vertically might seem more unfamiliar and thus be harder to learn. What are the independent and dependent variables in this hypothesis?

First, what will be manipulated? To test the hypothesis, you must manipulate the way the words are oriented when you present them. You must present some words vertically and some horizontally. The independent variable is *word orientation.* You could run the experiment with two treatment conditions, horizontal orientation and vertical orientation.

---

A N I M A L (horizontal condition)

or

A
N
I
M
A
L
(vertical condition)

---

Note again the distinction between the IV and its levels. The IV is the general dimension that is manipulated—in this case, word orientation. There are a great number of possible word orientations along the many diagonal lines that could be drawn between horizontal and vertical. We could use only these two levels of the independent variable, word orientation, or we could use more levels (e.g., horizontal, vertical, diagonal) as in the embedded word puzzle below, which presents two words at each of these three levels.

What will you measure to evaluate the effect of word orientation? According to the hypothesis, the orientation of the words will affect the rate of learning. So, rate of learning is the dependent variable. If the hypothesis is correct, subjects will learn words faster if they are presented horizontally. You are predicting that the rate of learning depends on the way the words are presented.

The independent variable in one experiment may function as the dependent variable in another. Whether a particular variable is an independent variable, a dependent variable, or neither depends on the hypothesis being tested. In Schachter's experiment, the independent variable was anxiety, and the dependent variable was affiliation. Schachter found that subjects who were anxious wanted to wait for the next part of the experiment with others.

Based on Schachter's findings, we might suggest a new hypothesis. Perhaps people want to be with others when they are anxious because being with others causes them to become less anxious. How would we go about testing this hypothesis? We might assign subjects to one of two conditions. In one condition, subjects are asked to spend 20 minutes waiting alone in a room. In another condition, they are asked to spend 20 minutes waiting in a room with another person. At the end of the waiting period, the subjects' anxiety levels are measured. If the hypothesis is correct, subjects who wait alone should be more anxious than subjects who wait with another person. The independent variable in this experiment is affiliation. We manipulate affiliation by assigning subjects to wait either alone or with others. The dependent variable is anxiety. According to the hypothesis, anxiety depends on whether subjects wait alone or with another person. In Schachter's original experiment, anxiety was the IV and affiliation was the DV. As you can see, we changed the status of these variables when we modified the hypothesis.

## OPERATIONAL DEFINITIONS

So far, we have talked about independent variables primarily in everyday language. We all have a conceptual notion of what we mean by "brightness" or "rate of learning," for example. However, because one criterion of science is replicability, it is not enough to have only conceptual definitions. Earlier we talked about color as an IV and blue and yellow as treatment levels. For scientific purposes, we would have to be much more precise in our designation of these colors. There are many shades and hues of blue and yellow (one source—Judd and Kelly, 1965—identified 7,500 different colors). In our experiment, we would have to specify which blue we are using by giving a standardized definition. Psychologists use the Munsell color chart, developed by Albert Henry Munsell in 1905, that describes colors by hue, saturation, and lightness.

Similarly, what one person means by "anxiety" may actually be quite different from what another person means. And so, in addition to giving conceptual, everyday labels to our variables, we also need to specify what they mean in the context of each experiment. The definition of each variable may change from one experiment to another. When we run an experiment, we naturally want to be sure that others will understand what we have done. Many concepts have more than one meaning, and those meanings are often vague. If we study variables without defining them exactly, the meaning of our findings will be unclear. As scientists, we also want to be sure that our procedures are stated clearly enough to enable other researchers to replicate our findings.

Thus, each IV and each DV has two definitions—one conceptual definition that is used in everyday language and one operational definition that is used in carrying out the experiment. An operational definition specifies the precise meaning of a variable within an experiment: It defines a variable in terms of observable operations, procedures, and measurements. It is called an operational definition because it clearly describes the operations involved in manipulating or measuring the variables in an experiment. Operational definitions are statements of operating procedures, sets of instructions that tell others how to carry out an experiment. These statements are essential because many variables of interest to psychologists cannot be observed directly, and operational definitions describe variables in terms of observable reality. We include operational definitions in written reports of experiments so that other researchers will understand exactly what was done and will be able to replicate it.

Operational definitions are quite different from ordinary dictionary definitions. A dictionary may define anxiety as "a state of concern or painful uneasiness about a future or uncertain event" or learning as "acquiring skill or knowledge." Although both definitions might be adequate for everyday use, neither will do in the context of an experiment because they do not tell us how to produce different levels or values of the variables. They do not give us procedures we could follow to make people feel anxious or nonanxious or to produce more or less learning. Similarly, they contain no information on how to measure or quantify the variables. How would we determine who has more anxiety or more learning? Operational definitions provide both of those types of information.

## Defining the Independent Variable: Experimental Operational Definitions

We can distinguish between two kinds of operational definitions, experimental and measured. Experimental operational definitions explain the precise meaning of the independent variables; these definitions describe exactly what was done to create the various treatment conditions of the experiment. An experimental operational definition includes all the steps that were followed to set up each value of the independent variable. Schachter gave experimental operational definitions of high and low anxiety. The high-anxiety condition was defined by the electronic equipment set up in the room, the ominous behavior of Dr. Zilstein, and the explicit statement that the subjects should expect painful shocks. The low-anxiety condition was defined by the absence of equipment, Dr. Zilstein's more relaxed manner, and the explicit statement that the shocks would not be painful. If we were to replicate Schachter's experiment, we would be able to follow all these procedures in setting up each of the two treatment conditions. Note that if Schachter had merely said, "I set up a high-anxiety condition and a low-anxiety condition," we would not know how to go about repeating his experiment. We would also have difficulty interpreting his findings because we would have no way of judging just how "anxiety-producing" his conditions may have been.

If we were constructing an experiment to test our hypothesis about the learning of words presented horizontally or vertically, we would need to specify the precise nature of the experimental procedures and stimuli. For others to evaluate our procedures and replicate our work, we would need to provide a detailed description of how we set up our treatments: the procedure used to present the words, the size of the words, the type of printing, the level of illumination in the room, the distance and location of words in the subject's visual field, and the duration of word presentation.

In the case of nonexperimental studies in which no treatment conditions are present, the experimental operational definition is somewhat different. In ex post facto studies, for example, it is essentially the procedure used to select subjects who fit the required levels of the independent variable. In the Ward, Leventhal, and Love (1988) study described earlier, the researchers selected subjects on the basis of a written test of repressive coping style. The operational definition included a description of the test and the cutoff scores used to place people into repressor or nonrepressor groups. In quasi-experimental designs in which the researcher compares the effects of different treatment conditions on preexisting groups of participants (nonequivalent groups design), the different treatment conditions would be experimentally

operationally defined just like the independent variable in a true experiment. Whether the IV is manipulated or selected, we need precise experimental operational definitions.

## Defining the Dependent Variable: Measured Operational Definitions

Dependent variables are defined by measured operational definitions, which describe what we do to measure the variables. Measured operational definitions of the dependent variable describe exactly what procedures we follow to assess the impact of different treatment conditions. These definitions include exact descriptions of the specific behaviors or responses recorded and explain how those responses are scored. If we are using scores on a standardized test to measure our dependent variable, we identify the test by name: "scores on the *Culture Fair Intelligence Test*," not simply "scores on an intelligence test." If our dependent measure is not standardized, we describe it in enough detail to allow other researchers to repeat our procedures. In Schachter's experiment, the dependent variable, affiliation, was given a measured operational definition. Schachter scored the desire to affiliate by having subjects check off their preferences on a questionnaire. The questionnaire is described in detail in his report. Again, it would be easy to replicate his procedures for measuring affiliation: We would simply administer the same questionnaire in the same way.

## Defining Constructs Operationally

The need for operational definitions becomes easily apparent when we zero in on variables, such as anxiety, that are actually hypothetical constructs, or concepts, which are unseen processes postulated to explain behavior. Many psychological variables are hypothetical constructs, that is, constructs that cannot be observed directly. We infer their existence from behaviors that we can observe: An ordinarily good student panics and does poorly on an important exam. An actor has stage fright and forgets his lines. From these observations, we infer the existence of "anxiety." We could say that "anxiety" is a peculiar feeling of queasiness that inhibits behavior. Unfortunately, that definition also neatly fits the time one of the authors ate raw clams. She was not anxious, but she was definitely queasy, and she has not eaten clams since. Furthermore, what we mean by "anxiety" may be quite different if we are talking about a person's experience before taking a test compared with waiting in line for a roller coaster ride. Just labeling the variable "anxiety" would be much too vague without a precise operational definition.

Researchers often formulate different definitions for the same construct variable when it is used in different experiments. Schachter's experiment illustrated one kind of experimental operational definition for anxiety. In effect, Schachter said that "high anxiety" is the feeling experienced in a particular kind of situation—namely, one in which the person expects pain. In the low-anxiety condition, the subjects saw no equipment and did not expect pain. By definition, the feeling they experienced in this setting is "low anxiety." You may or may not agree with Schachter's decision to define anxiety in this way, but you do know what definitions apply in this particular experiment.

Operational definitions for constructs like anxiety are also important for another reason: Effects produced on behavior may differ from one operational definition to another. When anxiety is defined in another way, its effects on the desire to affiliate might be very different. Another research example shows that this is indeed the case. Sarnoff and Zimbardo (1961) conducted a study in which anxiety was operationally defined in a very different way. Undergraduate men were told that they would be participating in a study of sensory stimulation of the skin around the mouth. Subjects in a "high-anxiety" condition were told that the procedure would require them to suck for 2 minutes on various objects while physiological sensations around the mouth were being measured. An experimenter showed them several different objects they would be sucking on: things like baby bottles, oversized nipples, and pacifiers. They were also shown vivid slides of a man demonstrating the sucking procedure on each of the objects.

You may have guessed by now that Sarnoff and Zimbardo were trying to create a different sort of high anxiety than that manipulated by Schachter! In a "low-anxiety" condition, a similar procedure was used; but subjects were told instead that they would be placing objects (whistles, kazoos, and the like) in their mouths for 10 seconds while their skin sensations were recorded. To make the waiting period seem natural, all subjects were told that they would need to wait in another room while their preexperimental (baseline) physiology was recorded. As in the Schachter experiment, they were given the option of waiting alone or with others. Do you think the high-anxiety men in this experiment wanted to wait with others or alone? Not surprisingly, men exposed to the high-anxiety condition showed much less desire to affiliate than did men in the low-anxiety condition—a reversal of what Schachter had found. You can see from this amusing example how important an experimental operational definition is for defining construct variables.

Similarly, we need a measured operational definition when a construct variable like anxiety is a dependent variable. There are many possible measured operational definitions of anxiety, too. One such definition might be "a heartbeat in excess of 100 beats per minute following 5 minutes rest on a sofa." This definition could be used to explain what we mean by "anxiety" in a particular experiment. Notice that the components of the definition are observable dimensions; we can readily determine a person's pulse. We would expect to get good agreement on whether or not a person is "anxious" according to this definition.

We can also define anxiety by a score on a written test like the Taylor Manifest Anxiety Scale, or TMAS (Taylor, 1953). This test includes a variety of items that are assumed to index different degrees of anxiety, such as the frequency of nightmares, fear of spiders, worries about work, and so on. In using the test, we assume that people who express many of these concerns are more anxious than those who express few of them. We use predetermined cutoff scores to determine who is anxious and who is not. Again, we have an objective, observable set of measures (the subjects' responses to a fixed set of test items) to define anxiety. To say that anxiety is "feeling queasy" is not acceptable. We cannot observe queasiness directly, nor can we be sure that subjects will know what we mean if we simply ask them whether they are "anxious."

Learning is also a construct. Like anxiety, it cannot be observed directly; it must be operationally defined by objective criteria. We can define learning in terms of performance on a written test, a maze, or a bicycle. We can count the number of correct responses or errors. We can also use the time taken to complete a task as an index of learning. In an experiment to test our word-orientation hypothesis, we can define learning as the number of words that subjects are able to remember and write down or as their scores on a written recognition test that we devise. Although the operational definitions vary, they all specify learning in observable terms. We cannot measure learning directly, but we can infer its occurrence from these objective measures—and we can state our procedures clearly enough to permit other researchers to measure learning in the same way.

## Defining Nonconstruct Variables

It is easy to see why operational definitions are required when we are dealing with constructs. Something that cannot be seen must be defined by observable dimensions before we can deal with it scientifically. However, operational definitions are equally important when we are working with variables that can be observed more directly. Suppose we want to test the effects of lighting on newborn babies. We might want to compare crying among babies in light rooms versus crying in dark rooms, as did Irwin and Weiss in 1934. The comparison seems straightforward enough, but before it can be made, we must operationally define what we mean by "light" versus "dark" rooms. Is a "light" room as bright as a sunny day? Is a "dark" room completely shielded from any source of light, or one in which the shades are drawn? To make a legitimate comparison, we must define what we mean by "light" and "dark" as objectively as possible, ideally by the use of a photometer or light meter.

The dependent variable, "crying," must also be defined. It must be done in such a way that independent observers would reliably agree on its occurrence. Do intermittent sounds constitute "crying," or must the sound be sustained for a given time period? Is a whimper also a cry or must the sound reach a certain level of intensity (some decibel level)? All these decisions must be made before the experiment is conducted. Otherwise, the results might not mean anything to anyone except the experimenter.

## Defining Scales of Measurement

In setting up experiments and formulating operational definitions, researchers also consider the available scales of measurement for each variable. You might have noticed that in our examples of independent variables, some of the levels we specified were simply comparative labels (bright or dim illumination, large versus small typeface). However, we could have indicated precise quantitative measurements, such as 50 versus 100 luxes (standard units of illumination) and 10-point versus 14-point typeface.

Many variables can be measured in more than one way. The measurement alternatives differ in the degree of information they provide. Setting treatment levels at 5 versus 10 milligrams of a drug, for example, is more precise than dividing subjects simply on the relative basis of low versus high doses. Stating the level of room illumination in luxes allows other researchers to evaluate and replicate an experiment more thoroughly than knowing only that a room was bright or dim.

Dependent variables can also be measured in more than one way, and the amount of information provided will depend on how the variable is measured. The two experiments that tested the effects of "anxiety" on affiliation used the same dependent variable (desire to affiliate), but the way affiliation was measured differed somewhat. In the Schachter (1959) experiment, subjects simply stated whether they wanted to wait with others, alone, or had no preference (a nominal scale). But Sarnoff and Zimbardo (1961) had subjects rate the intensity of their preference on a scale from 0 (very weak preference) to 100 (very strong preference). The second type of measurement provides the researcher with additional information and uses a different level of measurement (an interval scale).

Recall from Chapter 4 that the level of measurement is the kind of scale used to measure a variable (see Table 7.2). When we have a choice between different levels of measurement, researchers generally choose the highest level possible because it provides more information about a variable. In addition, the statistical tests we can use for interval or ratio data are more *powerful* than those for nominal and ordinal data, making ratio and interval scales preferred by researchers.

TABLE **7.2**

## Levels of measurement

| | |
|---|---|
| Nominal | The simplest level; classifies items into two or more distinct categories that can be named (e.g., men or women; yes or no; low, moderate, or high anxiety). |
| Ordinal | The next level; the magnitude of each value is measured in the form of ranks (e.g., first, second, or third place; most preferred to least preferred). |
| Interval | Higher level; measures magnitude or quantitative size using measures with equal intervals between the values (e.g., a semantic differential scale, a Likert scale, a number scale from 1 to 7). |
| Ratio | Highest level; measures magnitude or quantitative size using measures with equal intervals between all values and a true zero point (e.g., height, weight, inches). |

# EVALUATING OPERATIONAL DEFINITIONS

The same variable can have many definitions, so how can we know which definition is best? This question has no hard-and-fast answers. As with many other aspects of experimentation, what works well in one experiment may simply not be appropriate in another. Our definition must be objective and precise so that others can evaluate and replicate the procedures. There are more general criteria as well, which can be grouped under the general headings of reliability and validity.

## Reliability

Reliability means consistency and dependability. Good operational definitions are reliable: If we apply them in more than one experiment, they ought to work in similar ways each time. Suppose we have specified all the operations that must be performed to create two treatment conditions, "hungry" and "not hungry." If our operational definition is reliable, every time we apply the definition (each time we create these two conditions), we should obtain similar consequences. Subjects in the "hungry" condition should consistently show signs of hunger—increased activity, food-seeking behavior, or a verbal report of hunger if our subjects are people. If our "hungry" subjects show signs of hunger only occasionally, our operational definition is not reliable. If the procedures we have specified to define the various levels of the independent variable work haphazardly, better definitions are needed.

Measured operational definitions should also be reliable. If we took several sets of measurements according to our operational definition of the dependent variable, we should get the same results each time. When possible, we select measuring instruments, such as standardized tests, that have been shown to be reliable. When we are not using standardized measures, we make sure our measurement procedures are clearly and simply defined. The more accurate they are, the more likely they are to be reliable. Some of the procedures for checking the reliability of measurement techniques are interrater reliability, test-retest reliability, and interitem reliability.

### Interrater Reliability

One way to assess reliability of measurement procedures is to have different observers take measurements of the same responses; the agreement between their measurements is called interrater reliability. Typically, this method is used in a content analysis (described in Chapter 4) when raters must score the qualitative content of subjects' responses. For example, several raters might score all subjects' essays for "assertiveness." When two or more raters score each response, scores given by different raters can be statistically compared. Reliability coefficients (similar to correlations) can be computed that range from 0.0 (only chance levels of agreement) to 1.0 (perfect agreement). If there is little agreement between them, the chances are good that the measuring procedure is not reliable. Other types of measurement reliability also can be evaluated using statistical techniques.

### Test-Retest Reliability

Reliability of measures can also be checked by comparing scores of people who have been measured twice with the same instrument. They take the test once, then they take it again (after a reasonable interval). This is called test-retest reliability. Reliable measures should produce very similar scores each time the person is measured. If people consistently get about the same scores on a personality test, the test is considered reliable. A coefficient of test-retest reliability can be calculated. Standardized intelligence tests, like the Wechsler Adult Intelligence Scale, Third Edition (WAIS-III), have been shown to have excellent test-retest reliability coefficients; people's scores do not change very much from one testing session to another. The test-retest reliability coefficient for overall IQ scores on the WAIS-III is .95—very high indeed.

### Interitem Reliability

A third way of checking the reliability of measurement procedures is to assess interitem reliability. Interitem reliability is the extent to which different parts of a questionnaire, test, or other instruments designed to assess the same variable attain consistent results. Scores on different items designed to measure the same construct should be highly correlated.

There are two major approaches to evaluating interitem reliability. Both approaches measure the *internal consistency* of the test items. An evaluation of internal consistency is most often used when a researcher has created a multiple-item questionnaire to measure a single construct variable like intelligence, need for achievement, or anxiety. The individual items on a standardized test of anxiety, such as the TMAS (Taylor, 1953), will show a high degree of internal consistency if they are reliably measuring the same variable.

The first method of assessing interitem reliability, called *split-half reliability,* involves splitting the test into two halves at random and computing a coefficient of reliability between the scores obtained on the two halves. The two halves of the test should correlate strongly if the items are measuring the same variable. The second approach evaluates the internal consistency of the entire set of items using statistical tests such as Cronbach's $\alpha$. Cronbach's $\alpha$ is the most widely used method for evaluating interitem reliability because it considers the correlation of each test item with every other item; it is like measuring split-half reliability for all possible ways a test could be split up into halves.

## Validity

A second important problem in formulating definitions is stating definitions that are valid. Validity in experiments refers to the principle of actually studying the variables that we intend to study. How valid were Schachter's and Sarnoff and Zimbardo's experimental operational definitions of anxiety? Did they really manipulate anxiety in their subjects as they claimed? If the answer to this last question is yes, then we can say their definitions were valid. We can formulate precise, objective definitions that might even be reliable, but if they are not valid, we have not accomplished the goals of our experiment. Often, several procedures can be used to manipulate the same variable, like "anxiety." But which is the most valid? Which represents what we want to call "anxiety"?

One approach to the problem is a comparison of the consequences of the various procedures. If they all produce "anxiety," they should all lead to the same observable signs of anxiety: heart rate acceleration, sweaty palms, self-reported anxiety, and so on. Researchers make these kinds of comparisons to develop the best procedures. Comparing all the available procedures is not always feasible, particularly during a single experiment. However, it is clear that we need to evaluate the validity of our experimental manipulations. In some experiments, it is necessary to provide evidence for the validity of the experimental manipulation.

For example, suppose we conducted an experiment in which we created two different levels of anxiety in subjects (as Schachter did). How can we be certain that we had created high anxiety in one group of subjects and low anxiety in another? To provide evidence that our procedures actually created two different levels of anxiety, we would need to find a way to assess subjects' anxiety levels after they had received one of the procedures. Providing evidence for the validity of an experimental procedure is called a manipulation check. (We will return to this important topic in Chapter 15; see Box 7-1 for a research example.) Evidence for validity can be established in several ways, including through face, content, predictive, concurrent, and construct validity.

### Face Validity

Validity of operational definitions is least likely to be a problem with variables that can be manipulated and measured fairly directly. For instance, in studying the effects of pupil size, it is reasonably easy to know whether we are using a valid experimental operational definition of pupil size. We simply use a standard measuring device—for instance, a ruler—to define the treatment conditions. Defining pupil size by the marks on a ruler has face validity. The procedure is self-evident; we do not need to convince people that a ruler measures width. Face validity, however, is considered the least stringent type of validity because it does not provide any real evidence (Kaplan & Saccuzzo, 2005).

Similar issues arise in evaluating definitions of the dependent variable. The validity of a measured operational definition centers on the question of whether we measured what we intended to measure. As with experimental definitions, there should be some consensus that our procedures yield information about the variable we had in mind when we started the experiment. But because many psychological variables require indirect measures, the validity of a measured definition might not be self-evident—but it might still be a good measure. Response time is considered a valid measure of attitude importance (judgments about important attitude objects are made more quickly), even though the connection between time and attitude strength is not readily apparent (Fazio, 1990). Three other kinds of validity are of greater importance as we develop measures: content validity, predictive

BOX **7.1**    A Manipulation Check on the Validity of Cohesiveness in
Minimal Groups

Research about group behavior has shown that
people tend to be positively biased toward their own
ingroups and negatively biased toward outgroups. For
example, when allocating resources, people will
generally give their own group more resources than
they will give another group that they do not belong
to. In the laboratory, researchers have found that it is
possible to create this ingroup-outgroup bias by
simply assigning people to be part of a group for
purposes of an experiment. To create these *minimal
groups*, they sometimes use procedures that seem to
have validity, but really do not.

A study by Petersen, Dietz, and Frey (2004) used
an "aesthetic preference test" to create the illusion
that subjects had been assigned to 3-person groups
based on their preferences for art by either Klee or
Kandinsky. Actually, their group assignment was
completely random. The researchers predicted that
the ingroup-outgroup bias would be more pronounced
when subjects perceived their group to be cohesive
than when they did not. They manipulated 3 levels of
cohesiveness for different groups: (1) individual
condition—subjects were strangers before the
experiment and never interacted with other members
of their groups during the session; (2) ad hoc
condition—subjects were strangers but interacted
and made decisions as a group during the session; or
(3) cohesive condition—subjects were already friends
before the session and interacted and made decisions
as a group during the session.

To check the validity of the cohesiveness
manipulation, the researchers asked each subject in
the group conditions to fill out a questionnaire
describing their feelings about their group, the group
atmosphere, and how much they would like to
interact with their group members in the future.
Statistical analyses of the responses to the
manipulation check showed that Petersen, Dietz, and
Frey had successfully created groups that differed in
cohesiveness.

Each of the subjects was paid about 5 dollars to
participate in a study of group decision-making, and,
during the experiment, individuals were allowed to
distribute a small, "leftover" pot of money. They

could not allocate the money to themselves or
members of their own 3-person group, but they
could allocate it to members of other Klee or
Kandinsky groups. Consistent with past research
findings, Klee group subjects allocated more money
to members of other Klee groups and less to
members of other Kandinsky groups; Kandinsky
group members did just the opposite. And, as
predicted, the extent of the ingroup-outgroup bias
was related to perceived group cohesiveness. The
more cohesive subjects felt their group was, the
more money they allocated to members of similar
groups, and the less they allocated to members of
dissimilar groups.

(a) Klee Painting

(b) Kandinsky Painting

Adapted from Petersen, L-E., Dietz, J., & Frey, D. (2004). The
effects of intragroup interaction and cohesion on intergroup bias.
*Group Processes & Intergroup Relations*, 7(2), 107–118.

validity, and concurrent validity. Measures that appear to have face validity do not necessarily meet these criteria.

### Content Validity

Content validity depends on whether we are taking a fair sample of the variable we intend to measure. When we evaluate content validity, we are asking: Does the content of our measure fairly reflect the content of the quality we are measuring? Are all aspects of the content represented appropriately? For example, an instrument to measure depression in college students would have poor content validity if it measured only psychological disturbances and failed to include questions about behavioral disturbances. In addition to fairly measuring the content of the variable we are studying, high content validity means that the measuring instrument is not evaluating other qualities (such as reading level or general verbal skills) that we do not intend to measure. This problem can easily occur when the measuring instrument is written using language that is difficult for people to understand.

The questions students might raise about an exam are often questions of content validity. An exam is supposed to measure what students have learned. However, students sometimes feel an exam includes only questions about the things they did not study! Whether a particular measure has content validity is often a matter of judgment. Teachers and students sometimes disagree on whether particular tests or particular questions are fair representations of the course material. For experimental purposes, however, we try to obtain some consensus on the content validity of our measures.

Suppose you have devised a questionnaire to measure racial attitudes. You have a series of questions about whether people would live in integrated neighborhoods, whether they would help a person of another race who was in trouble, and so on. You could simply administer the questionnaire, but you would have a better idea of whether your questionnaire had content validity if you obtained ratings of the items from objective judges with expertise in the area of racial attitudes. Each judge would be asked to rate each item for its measurement of racial attitudes. You would then have the opportunity to include items that are most representative of that variable, according to the raters' judgments. If the raters do not agree on the items, you will have to rework the questionnaire.

The degree of content validity we can achieve depends on the variable we want to measure. The more specific the variable, the easier it will be. For example, it would be relatively easy to define weight gain in a way that would have high content validity, but adequately measuring psychological variables such as emotions, attitudes, and personality traits poses more difficult problems. And sometimes it is difficult to attain high content validity because the circumstances you want to measure are very infrequent. Researchers studying the content validity of tests used to assess combat readiness in the military, for example, find it difficult to achieve a high level of content validity because most tests are simulations conducted in peacetime (Vineberg & Joyner, 1983).

### Predictive Validity

We can also ask whether our measures of the dependent variable have predictive validity. Do our procedures yield information that enables us to predict future behavior or performance? They should, if we are measuring what we intend to measure. Schachter (1959) defined the desire to affiliate in terms of subjects' responses to a questionnaire. You will recall that they were asked to indicate whether they preferred to wait alone, with others, or had no preference.

This definition has face validity. It seems to have something to do with people's desire to be together. It seems to have content validity, too; part of the desire to affiliate is a wish to be with other people. When we raise the question of predictive validity, however, we are asking this: Can we use people's responses to this questionnaire to predict how they will actually behave? If people have the desire to affiliate, it is reasonable to predict that they will stay near others when they have the opportunity. In Schachter's study, we could evaluate the predictive validity of the affiliation measure by changing the procedures slightly. Instead of telling subjects that the experiment was over after they completed the questionnaire, we could take them all into a large waiting room. If the affiliation measure has predictive validity, the subjects who said they wanted to wait with others will seat themselves closer together and perhaps talk to each other more than would subjects who preferred to wait alone. If we do not observe these overt signs of the desire to affiliate, we might have to conclude that the written measure does not have predictive validity: It does not predict what people will do.

### Concurrent Validity

Another type of validity to consider is called concurrent validity. Like predictive validity, concurrent validity compares scores on the measuring instrument with an outside criterion, but concurrent validity is comparative, rather than predictive. Concurrent validity is evaluated by comparing scores on the measuring instrument with another known standard for the variable being studied.

The idea of concurrent validity reflects whether scores on the measuring device correlate with scores obtained from another method of measuring the same concept. If the measuring instrument has high concurrent validity, both sets of scores should be highly correlated. For example, to evaluate the concurrent validity of an instrument designed to measure anxiety, we could compare people's scores on our anxiety test with their ratings from clinical evaluations of anxiety. People judged by a clinician to be highly anxious should score very high on our test; people who are judged to be nonanxious should score very low on our test.

### Construct Validity

The fifth, and perhaps most important, aspect of validity is construct validity. Somewhat different from the other forms of validity we have discussed, construct validity deals with the transition from theory to research application. We start with a general idea of the qualities that characterize the construct we want to test; then we seek to find ways of putting our idea to an empirical test. The issue of construct validity arises when we ask: "Have I succeeded in creating a measuring device that measures the construct I want to test? Are my operational definitions tapping only the construct I want to test?" The specific modern methods for evaluating construct validity are largely statistical and highly theoretical.

Basically, researchers ask whether the data make sense in the context of the overall theoretical framework in which they operate. One way of doing this is to see whether the data follow expected patterns in relation to other concepts. Suppose we want to study intelligence. Depending on our hypothesis, intelligence could be either a quasi-independent or dependent variable. If intelligence were the IV, we might separate subjects into groups on the basis of high or low intelligence test scores. Or if intelligence were the DV, we might introduce some environmental change (for example, better nutrition) and observe its impact on subsequent IQ scores. In either case, we would want to be sure that our intelligence test truly measures only "intelligence" and we have not inadvertently measured another construct.

From a scientific standpoint, we are faced with a construct validity question. Does the test we use actually measure the hypothetical construct we call "intelligence"? Perhaps the test measures something else, such as cultural experiences or motivation. There is extensive research literature dealing with such issues, and testing experts have tried to create tests that minimize the influence of these other factors. The Raven Progressive Matrices Test, a non-verbal test of intelligence, is one example of a test that is considered relatively culture fair. Figure 7.3 illustrates the type of item found on such a test.

As a student, you are unlikely to be heavily involved in construct validation. The experts who have created standardized tests have already addressed the problem for you. Your task would be to select the most appropriate test on the basis of the research literature. In constructing tests, experts work with many sources of data as they assess validity. Computer applications have made much of this work feasible. For instance, to the extent that an intelligence test measures intelligence, test scores ought to show certain predictable relationships with other related variables, such as school achievement and reading level. Test results should also correlate highly with scores on other intelligence tests (this is called *convergent validity*). A valid intelligence test should also be able to appropriately classify groups of people with known high and low levels of intelligence. The test should have no trouble discriminating between members of Mensa (a society admitting only high-IQ individuals) and individuals with mental retardation. Finally, the test should

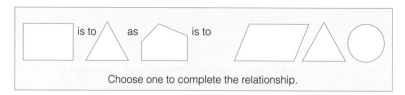

Choose one to complete the relationship.

FIGURE **7.3** Example of item found on a *culture-fair* intelligence test.
© Cengage Learning

not correlate highly with scores measuring other constructs. A valid intelligence test, for example, should not be strongly correlated with results on tests measuring socioeconomic status or self-esteem (this is called *discriminant validity*). Thus, the validation process focuses on how well the test scores fit in an overall theoretical network of understanding how the concept works in human functioning.

Clearly, researchers cannot always use tests that have already been standardized; therefore, they sometimes have to solve their own validation problems. How they go about establishing construct validity is illustrated in an article by Allinson and Hayes (1996). These researchers assessed the construct validity of the Cognitive Style Index (CSI), an instrument that was intended to measure consistent individual differences in organizing and processing information (i.e., an *analytical* versus an *intuitive* style). Allinson and Hayes conducted several tests to empirically confirm an intuition-analysis dimension of cognitive style that is measurable by the CSI. Sample items from the 38-item true/false questionnaire include the following:

1. Formal plans are more of a hindrance than a help in my work. (intuitive)
2. I am most effective when my work involves a clear sequence of tasks to be performed. (analytical)
3. My philosophy is that it is better to be safe than risk being sorry. (analytical)
4. I am inclined to scan through reports rather than read them in detail. (intuitive)

As in the previous example of intelligence testing, Allinson and Hayes looked for predictable relationships between CSI scores and other variables. They were able to do that through sophisticated statistical procedures. First, through factor analysis they determined that the 38-item scale was, as predicted, assessing a single construct. Then they evaluated the relationships between CSI scores and several other variables, such as standardized test scores, on a large number of personality, learning style, critical thinking, and workplace style items. As expected, scores on the CSI were significantly correlated with scores on the predicted dimensions of the standardized tests. For example, they found that analytical individuals appeared to prefer a work setting which is quiet, clearly structured, private, and well organized; intuitives, in contrast, preferred a setting that is activity-oriented, flexible, offers opportunity for relationships, and is open to change—just what you would expect from the construct.[2]

### Evaluating the Experiment: Internal Validity

So far, we have focused on the notion of validity in connection with operating procedures. We want to develop procedures that define our variables in valid ways. However, a more global evaluation of validity is also required: Is the whole experiment valid? We can talk about two kinds of validity when

---

[2] In the same article, Allinson and Hayes (1996) also assessed two types of reliability (internal consistency and test-retest) and concurrent validity.

we look at the experiment as a whole: internal validity and external validity. Internal validity is the degree to which a researcher is able to state a causal relationship between antecedent conditions and the subsequent observed behavior. In upcoming chapters, we will talk more about external validity, how well the findings of the experiment generalize or apply to situations that were not tested directly (for example, real life). But before we can think about the external validity of an experiment, we must first evaluate its internal validity.

When we set up an experiment, we plan procedures to measure the effects of various treatment levels. The goal of an experiment is to assess the impact of the independent variable. We can ask whether we have achieved that goal in the context of the experiment: An experiment is internally valid if we can be sure that the changes in behavior observed across the treatment conditions of the experiment were actually caused by the independent variable (Campbell, 1957). If other explanations are possible, the experiment is not internally valid—we cannot identify the impact of the independent variable with certainty. And, logically, we cannot make any correct decisions about how well the findings of an experiment would generalize if the experiment is not, first and foremost, internally valid. *Internal validity is one of the most important concepts in experimentation.*

In the following sections, we will look at three important concepts that are tied to the problem of internal validity: extraneous variables, confounding, and threats to internal validity. These important factors affect our ability to understand and interpret the effects of our treatment conditions.

## Extraneous Variables and Confounding

From an experiment, we can draw a causal inference about the relationship between the independent and dependent variables. If the value of the dependent variable changes *significantly* as the independent variable changes, we can say that the independent variable caused changes in the dependent variable.[3] But this inference is justified only when the experiment is well controlled. Many things other than the independent and dependent variables may be changing throughout an experiment—time of day, the experimenter's level of fatigue, the particular subjects who are being tested. Such variables are called extraneous variables; they are factors that are not the focus of the experiment but can influence the findings. They are neither intentionally manipulated independent variables nor dependent variables measured as indexes of the effect of the independent variable. They can include differences among subjects, equipment failures, inconsistent instructions—in short, anything that varies within the experiment. Extraneous variables can affect results: Experimental subjects may be tired if they are in an experiment at the end of the day; equipment breakdowns can change the results produced

---

[3] *Significance* is a statistical term we will return to many times. In an experiment, there is always some probability that observed events were produced by chance, rather than by our treatment. A significant effect is one in which statistics have determined that the odds of the observed effect occurring by chance are quite small (usually less than 5%).

by an independent variable during a treatment session; differences in the way instructions are presented can alter subjects' responses.

In a well-controlled experiment, we attempt to recognize the potential for extraneous variables and use procedures to control them. Realistically, though, even the most well-controlled experiment will be influenced from time to time by extraneous variables that cannot be controlled in advance. As long as these influences are infrequent, random events, they do not necessarily invalidate an experiment. However, random influences from extraneous variables do introduce errors into the scores obtained from subjects, so it is important to control them as carefully as possible. These influences will obscure the effects we are really interested in and make it more difficult to detect significant treatment effects.

The real gremlin that wreaks havoc on an experiment is an extraneous variable that changes in a *systematic* way along with the independent variable. In a well-controlled experiment, the variation in the independent variable must be the only systematic variation that occurs across treatment conditions. Whenever different levels of an extraneous variable are linked to different treatment conditions, an experiment cannot be internally valid. If uncontrolled extraneous variables are allowed to change along with the independent variable, we might not be able to tell whether changes in the dependent variable were caused by changes in the independent variable or by extraneous variables that also changed value across conditions.

When the value of an extraneous variable changes systematically across different conditions of an experiment, we have a situation known as confounding. Identifying potential confounding variables is one of the most important activities in research. When there is confounding, experimental results cannot be interpreted with certainty, and causal relationships between the independent and dependent variables cannot be inferred. In effect, confounding sabotages the experiment because the effects we see can be explained equally well by changes in the extraneous variable or in the independent variable. Our experiment is not internally valid. In subsequent chapters, we will study some of the basic techniques used to avoid confounding. Our goal is always to set up an experiment in such a way that the independent variable is the only variable (except for the dependent variable) that changes value across conditions. To draw causal inferences about the effects of the independent variable, we must be sure that no extraneous variables change along with the independent variable.

What's wrong with this experiment? Suppose a researcher was interested in the effects of age on communicator persuasiveness. She hypothesized that older communicators would be more persuasive than younger communicators—even if both presented the same arguments. She set up an experiment with two experimental groups. Subjects listened to either an 18-year-old man or a 35-year-old man presenting the same 3-minute argument in favor of gun control.

After listening to one of the communicators, subjects rated how persuaded they were by the argument they had just heard. As the researcher predicted, subjects who heard the older man speak were more persuaded.

Would she be justified in stating that a speaker's age influences persuasiveness? Did you identify this as a confounded experiment? Too many extraneous variables could have changed along with the independent variable (age): The older speaker may have seemed more attractive, better educated, more intelligent, or more self-confident (all these variables can influence our persuasiveness). Even though the researcher believed she was manipulating only the age of the speaker, several other extraneous variables also might have varied systematically along with the independent variable. We could not say with assurance that age—rather than one of the other variables—influenced persuasion. The experiment was low in internal validity. What might the researcher have done to control for these potential sources of confounding?

## Classic Threats to Internal Validity

Psychologist Donald Campbell (Campbell, 1957; Campbell & Stanley, 1966; Cook & Campbell, 1979) identified eight kinds of extraneous variables that can threaten the internal validity of experiments and quasi-experiments (see Box 7-2). Since that time, Campbell's listing of these potential sources of confounding has become required course material for successive classes of experimental psychology students; hence, they have become known as the *classic threats to internal validity.*

You will recognize some of these classic threats from the previous chapters covering nonexperimental and quasi-experimental designs. All quasi-experimental designs contain one or more classic threats to internal validity—in fact, that is the reason they are not true experiments; they are potentially confounded. As you are learning the classic threats, see if you can recognize which threats are inherent to each of the quasi-experimental designs from Chapter 5: longitudinal, cross-sectional, ex post facto, nonequivalent groups, and pretest/posttest designs.

Remember that a confound is an extraneous variable that varies systematically along with experimental conditions. An extraneous variable that pops up randomly across conditions is not a confound—it simply increases the amount of variability in the scores, making it more difficult to detect a significant treatment effect. Designs using different subjects in each treatment group can be confounded if an extraneous variable affects some experimental groups but not others with regularity. (These are called between-subjects designs, and we will proceed to them in Chapter 9.) Other designs in which the same subjects are measured multiple times can be confounded if an extraneous variable is present only in certain experimental conditions but not in others. (These are called within-subjects designs, and we will deal with them in Chapter 11.)

Whenever you design or evaluate experimental research, you must consider each of these eight classic threats to internal validity. In Chapter 9, we will begin learning about the various types of experimental designs. Controlling for extraneous variables that might confound experiments is one of the most important elements of research design. If one or more of these threats are present, the experiment will lack internal validity, and you can never be

## BOX **7.2**    Third Variables and Confounding

The problem of confounding was actually described earlier in the text when we discussed correlational and quasi-experimental designs in Chapter 5. In nonexperimental designs, confounding is known as the *third variable* problem. Recall that a major reason that results from all correlation-based and quasi-experimental designs cannot be used to infer a cause-and-effect relationship is the potential for third variable causation. It is always possible that an unmeasured extraneous variable—one that is not part of the study—is actually causing the effects we are observing in the study. Confounding by third variables can have important consequences on real-world behavior and can be a particularly important concern in the area of health psychology, which relies heavily on nonexperimental designs because many health-related behaviors cannot be manipulated either for practical or ethical reasons.

This problem was faced by researchers using an ex post facto design to study the effects of breast-feeding on the IQ of infants. Clearly, it would be impractical as well as unethical to randomly assign new mothers to either breast-feed or bottle-feed their infants. So, researchers needed to rely on comparing the IQs of infants who had been breast-fed with IQs of infants who were bottle-fed. When this comparison was made, infants who were breast-fed showed an average IQ that was 4 points higher than the average IQ of bottle-fed infants. These scientific results were reported in popular media as evidence that breast-feeding increased IQ.

Unfortunately, some early studies did not control for an important third variable: the mother's IQ. When researchers statistically controlled for the mother's IQ (Der, Batty, & Deary, 2006), the assumed benefit of breast-feeding disappeared. What they found was that women who breast-fed their infants had higher IQs, on average, than women who did not, and, given the known heritability component of IQ, it is more likely that the observed increase in infants' IQs in this group was probably linked to the higher IQs of their mothers and was not caused by breast-feeding. Additional studies by Der et al. (analyses of siblings and meta-analysis) supported this conclusion. Therefore, even though breast-feeding may have many benefits for both mothers and infants, it is not likely to increase an infant's IQ.

Karuka/www.Shutterstock.com

From Der, G., Batty, G. D., & Deary, I. D. (2006). Effect of breast feeding on intelligence in children: Prospective study, sibling pairs analysis, and meta-analysis. *British Medical Journal, 333*, 945.

sure that the effects produced on the dependent variable were really caused by the experimental manipulation.

### History

The first classic threat is called history, and it refers to the history of the experiment. Ask yourself whether any outside event or occurrence, rather than the independent variable, could have caused the experimental effects. (It need not be a great historical event, although it could be.) History is most often a problem when a whole group of individuals is tested together in the same experimental condition. Some outside event that occurred before their group testing session could influence responses of the entire group, and effects produced by the event could be mistaken for effects of the IV. History effects can be very problematic.

Suppose you were testing two different weight-loss programs in which subjects were exposed to your treatments during daily group meetings. You assessed the benefits of the program by measuring how much weight each person lost at the end of a 7-day program. After weighing subjects in both groups, you discover that individuals who received treatment *B* lost an average of 2 pounds that week, whereas the average for treatment *A* was 4 pounds. You want to make sure that the "history" of both groups before weighing was the same. Imagine the confound in your experiment if individuals in group *B* were weighed right after lunch, but the subjects in group *A* were weighed just before lunch. You would not know if the differences you observed were caused by your diet program or by the fact that one group had just eaten and the other had not.

### Maturation

The second classic threat, maturation, refers to any internal (physical or psychological) changes in subjects that might have affected scores on the dependent measure (not just "maturing" in the way we typically think of it, although it could be). The kinds of internal changes that we usually worry about in experimentation are things like boredom and fatigue that can occur during a single testing session. Boredom and fatigue are more likely in within-subjects designs that require lengthy testing sessions. You will learn that there are techniques for balancing out the order of treatments subjects receive (Chapter 11) so that whatever boredom or fatigue exists will be spread evenly across all the conditions of the experiment.

It should be obvious that maturation effects can also be a problem in studies that take months or even years to finish. For example, maturation must be considered in longitudinal studies, such as the one by Stewart, Mobley, Van Tuyl, and Salvador (1987) that observed firstborn children's behavior before and after the birth of a sibling. Young children can make cognitive and physical leaps during certain ages, so researchers need to consider that effects might be produced by these changes, rather than by the event being studied. For example, Stewart and colleagues found that the number of imitative behaviors at 1 month postpartum was positively correlated with the firstborn's age.

Another kind of maturation can occur even in brief experiments whenever university students are the subjects. Just as you are now more sophisticated about research than you were when you first opened your textbook, other students are gaining knowledge during the course of the semester, too. In psychology experiments, the subjects are often students taking a course in introductory psychology, and they might be much more sophisticated about correctly guessing your hypotheses later in the semester than they are in the beginning. You would not want to run treatment condition *A* in September and October and leave condition *B* for November and December!

### Testing

A testing threat refers to effects on the dependent variable produced by a previous administration of the same test or other measuring instrument (remember what we said about the pretest/posttest design?). It is not uncommon to measure subjects on a dependent variable (e.g., anxiety, depression, or extroversion) at the beginning of the experiment and then remeasure them using the same test after a treatment is given. Unfortunately, this procedure introduces a testing threat because individuals frequently perform differently the second time they are tested—even without any intervening experimental treatment. This is one reason that test-retest reliability (described earlier in the chapter) can be an important piece of information for a researcher. Low test-retest reliability can mean that the researcher can expect large differences in scores from one testing session to the next even without any experimental manipulation. Even the most reliable tests that psychologists use—standardized intelligence tests like the WAIS-III—do not have perfect test-retest reliability. Performance tends to improve somewhat with practice even without any special treatment.

### Instrumentation

Whenever some feature of the measuring instrument itself changes during the experiment, the researcher is faced with the possibility of an instrumentation threat to internal validity. The example most often used to illustrate this concept is the case of the rubber ruler. Imagine that your dependent measure was the length of a line drawn by subjects. To measure it, you use the only ruler you have—a rubber ruler. Unknown to you, it stretches a bit every time you use it. Each consecutive measurement is a little more inaccurate, and successive measurements tend to underestimate line length. If you measure lines drawn by subjects in one treatment condition before you measure lines drawn in a different condition, your measurements in one group will systematically underestimate line length to a greater extent than will your measurements in another group. Instrumentation threats are not always this obvious. For example, mechanical measuring instruments can break or become less accurate. Or a speedometer could falter at high speeds but not at low, underestimating how fast subjects are pedaling an exercise bike in your "high-motivation" condition.

Instrumentation is also a potential problem whenever human observers are used to record behavior, score questionnaires by hand, or perform content analyses. For example, the behavior of subjects in one condition can be inherently more interesting than in another, and observers might pay much less attention in a particular condition, making more errors in recording. Or raters doing a content analysis might find their judgments changing a little as the analysis goes on and they become more familiar with the procedure.

Instrumentation of a different sort can be a problem when you administer written instruments to subjects. Are all your questions equally easy to read in all conditions? Are the intervals you typed on all the scales really equal? When you ran out of questionnaires, were your new copies as good as the first set? Did you allow subjects in all conditions the same amount of space to write stories? Such seemingly small things can alter subjects' responses; if they vary systematically with your treatment conditions, your experiment is confounded by an instrumentation threat.

### Statistical Regression

The threat of statistical regression (also called *regression toward the mean*) can occur whenever subjects are assigned to conditions on the basis of extreme scores on a test. Statistically, extreme scores tend to have less test-retest reliability than do moderate scores (those closer to the mean, or average). If the same extreme scorers are retested, their scores are likely to be closer to the mean the second time around. Extreme high scores tend to go down a bit, and extreme low scores tend to rise somewhat; thus, scores at both extremes typically get closer to the mean even without any treatment at all. Statistical regression is illustrated here:

Time 1:

Extreme Low Scores_$X_1$_____Mean_____$Y_1$_Extreme High Scores

Time 2:

Extreme Low Scores____$X_2$_____Mean_____$Y_2$____Extreme High Scores

$X_1$ represents a person, X, with an extremely low score at the first testing (Time 1); $Y_1$ represents a different person, Y, with an extremely high score at the first testing (Time 1). The second time persons X and Y are tested (Time 2), their scores tend to get closer to the mean: The very low score tends to be a bit higher, and the very high score tends to be a bit lower (even without any intervening treatment).

Statistical regression can easily be mistaken for treatment effects. For example, suppose a psychologist selected a group of highly anxious subjects (such as $Y_1$ at Time 1) to test a new procedure to reduce anxiety. After the procedure, most of the highly anxious subjects were indeed less anxious (their anxiety scores were closer to people's average scores for this test). The researcher would like to conclude that the new procedure reduced subjects' anxiety; unfortunately, the results would look very similar if statistical regression were operating.

### Selection

Whenever the researcher does not assign subjects randomly to the different conditions of an experiment, a selection threat is present. In experimentation, we control for individual differences in each subject's characteristics by assigning subjects to different conditions of the experiment using randomization procedures. In this way, we attempt to balance differences among subjects across all the conditions of the experiment so that the subjects in one condition are not different from the subjects in another condition in any *systematic* way. Random assignment is an important feature of true experiments that will be discussed in detail in Chapter 9.

Always consider how members of the treatment groups were chosen. If nonrandom assignment procedures were used (or if random assignment failed to balance out differences among subjects), the subjects in one treatment condition may begin the experiment with different characteristics than those of the subjects in another condition. And there is always a chance that these characteristics—not your IV—might be the cause of observed effects on the DV. This would clearly be a problem in quasi-experimental research with nonequivalent groups. See Box 7-3 for an example of how a selection threat can generate erroneous conclusions that can have important real-world effects on people's behavior.

### Subject Mortality

Always consider the possibility that more subjects dropped out of one experimental condition than another. If so, subject mortality threatens internal validity. Dropout rates should always be stated in a research report so that the reader can be on the lookout for this threat. Whenever the attrition rate in a particular treatment condition is high, it should be a red flag: Something about the treatment could be making subjects drop out. Often it means that the treatment is frightening, painful, or distressing. If the dropout rate is very high, it can mean that the treatment is sufficiently obnoxious that typical subjects would choose to leave, and the ones who remain could be unusual in some respect. You need to ask yourself, "Why did so many subjects drop out?" (Maybe the experimental tasks were too repetitive or the weight-loss regimen was too difficult.) "And what does this tell me about the subjects who finished this condition of the experiment?" (They were probably more patient than most people or they were more motivated than most dieters.) Your answers are likely to uncover a confounding variable. Effects on the dependent measure might have been produced by this characteristic, not by the independent variable.

### Selection Interactions

The last threat is really a family of threats. A selection threat can combine with another threat to form a selection interaction. If subjects were not randomly assigned to groups (or if random assignment failed to balance out differences among subjects), any one of the other threats may have affected some experimental groups but not others. Selection can interact with history,

## BOX **7.3**   Selection Threats and Real-Life Parenting Decisions

The intervention research in child development has repeatedly produced a paradoxical conclusion: In correlational studies, parental assistance with children's homework has been associated with *lower* academic achievement. As a result, some psychologists have concluded in published reports that parents should not help their children with homework. They have speculated that helping with homework can hinder a child's development because it can promote dependency. This conclusion, however, has been contradicted by clinical outcome studies that consistently find improvement in homework quality and quantity when parents supervise their children's homework. So what is really going on?

An interesting review article by Larzelere, Kuhn, and Johnson (2004) provided a persuasive demonstration that the conclusion that parental assistance causes lowered achievement is probably false and most likely resulted from a selection threat

in past studies. Larzelere and his colleagues have explained that the apparent reductions in achievement might actually be a result of a bias in the samples of children who were studied. They explain it this way: "When children are doing poorly in school, parents tend to respond by supervising homework more closely. This may explain why most correlational studies have found parental assistance with homework to be associated with lower achievement" (p. 292). They argued that help with homework might be associated with lower achievement because the poorer students are getting the most help with their homework. And this conclusion was supported in a study conducted by Pomerantz and Eaton (2001). In their study, Pomerantz and Eaton used sophisticated statistical techniques to control for prior academic achievement. When achievement was controlled, parental assistance actually improved children's academic achievement.

© JLP/Deimos/CORBIS

FIGURE **7.4**

maturation, mortality, and so on to produce effects on the dependent variable. Suppose that your two groups of dieters were selected nonrandomly from among patrons of two different gyms—a selection threat—and, as a result, your dieters in condition *A* were much more body conscious than were those in condition *B*. And, since joining the experiment, many of the group *A* subjects had succumbed to those TV commercials showing what their bodies could look like after only a few minutes a day on an elliptical machine—many had bought one and were using it. The less body-conscious subjects in group *B* never even considered buying one (now the study has a history threat). Not surprisingly, subjects in the *A* group lost a lot more weight during the course of their program than the other subjects did. Could you say that treatment *A* was really better? Of course not. This experiment would not be internally valid. Here you would be faced with a selection-by-history threat: a history threat that combined with other characteristics of only one of your treatment groups to produce a serious confound.

You can see that it is difficult to control all the sources of possible confounding in an experiment. We must often compromise in setting up our experimental design by focusing on the extraneous variables most likely to affect the dependent variable we are measuring. For example, in a study of learning in the classroom, we would be more concerned about finding classes of comparable intelligence than about finding classes containing equal numbers of brown- and blue-eyed students. Just as we narrow the number of possible independent variables we want to explore, we narrow the number of extraneous variables we choose to control. The rule is this: Control as many variables as possible. If a variable can be held constant in an experiment, it makes sense to do so even when any impact of that variable on the results may be doubtful. In the next chapter, we will further explore the topic of controlling extraneous variables.

## PLANNING THE METHOD SECTION

The Method section of the research report is the place to describe what you did in your experiment (who, what, when, and how). It needs to be detailed enough that another researcher could read it and replicate what you did. Typically, the Method section is divided into labeled subsections such as *Participants, Materials,* and *Procedure*, but a great deal of flexibility in labeling is allowed to accommodate specific experiments. Chapter 16 gives more detailed information about style and content but an overview at this point will help you plan the report as you are planning your experiment.

First, you will need to describe your subjects (this first subsection is labeled *Participants* or *Subjects*). The information in Chapter 4 about reporting samples is relevant to describing experimental participants, but you probably will not need quite as much detail as survey researchers put in their reports. It is a good idea, however, to track the genders and ages of your subjects, as well as how many participated, because you are expected to report this minimal amount of information about them. Also report any participants who did not complete the study and the reasons they dropped out, if known.

BOX **7.4**    **The Apparatus Section**

In the Method section of some journal articles, you will find a subsection headed *Apparatus*. This subsection contains a description of specialized equipment used to conduct the experiment. The technology of stimulus generation and response recording has become more sophisticated across the field of psychology as personal computers have become widely available. These advances have been documented across the years in the *Apparatus* sections of journal articles. Today, participants in experiments are shown digitized visual images that have been generated or manipulated with computers running sophisticated software. Computer-controlled event recorders track complex human and animal behaviors and can measure micromomentary differences in response times.

Sometimes an *Apparatus* section is appropriate, sometimes not. Remember that the purpose of the *Method* section is to provide enough information about the experiment that it can be evaluated and reconducted by another researcher. An *Apparatus* section, then, is particularly appropriate in the description of an experiment that was conducted with unique or specialized equipment or equipment with capabilities that are important for the reader to know to evaluate or replicate the experiment.

Imagine that we had conducted an experiment in which people watched a videotape on a television set and we are now writing a report that we will submit to a scientific journal. Should our report include an *Apparatus* section? Maybe not. It probably would not be necessary to provide an extensive description of the videotape machine and the television set. If any VCR and television set would do, one or two sentences describing the important features of the equipment (such as the size of the television set and, of course, its location in relation to the subject) would probably be sufficient.

But imagine instead that we had conducted an experiment in which we showed people a series of visual images. We very carefully controlled the length of time each image was shown using shutters mounted on slide projectors, operated by a computer. In this case, we would probably want to include an *Apparatus* section in which we described all the equipment: the shutters, the slide projectors, the computer, and even the software used to operate the shutters. Many times, this turns out to be easier than it seems. For example, most researchers who would be interested in the experiment often know the equipment. We could give these researchers almost everything they needed to know by simply providing

If data from some subjects could not be included because they did not fill out their questionnaire completely, then you will need to report this as well.

Any other information that you feel might limit the generalizability of your results should also be included. For example, if the participants came from a highly selective university or from your church group, the subjects might have special characteristics that could affect the external validity of results from certain kinds of experiments. Ask yourself whether your results would generalize just as well to people with fewer academic skills or different religious values. If your sample included (or omitted) certain ethnic or racial groups, include this information, if appropriate. Report also how subjects were recruited and anything tangible they received in return for participation.

All items presented to subjects, such as films, questionnaires, stories, and so forth, need to be described in detail (except for standardized tests and measures, which are cited in the text so that readers can look them up). Describe these items in a subsection that is labeled appropriately—perhaps *Materials* for written items and *Stimuli* or *Interventions* for other types of variables. Also, you will need to describe any special or unusual equipment or software used in the study (this is explained in Box 7-4). If it is specialized equipment,

the name of the manufacturer and the model number of each item. We have explained how we presented the visual images to the people in our experiment. But we might also have to describe the equipment we used to obtain the measurements we took while the people in our experiment were watching the visual images.

Suppose we measured the electrical activity of each person's brain while each image was shown. To do this, we placed electrodes at specific sites on their heads, amplified the signal with a polygraph, and had our computer record the signal from the polygraph. (This technique is called electroencephalography— EEG for short—and it is a psychophysiological measure, which means that we are looking for evidence of a psychological process in a physiological event.) Our *Apparatus* section just got longer! We must now describe the electrodes, the polygraph, and the computer software we used to make our measurements.

When you write a report, you must decide what is appropriate. Just remember the rule that guides what is needed: You must provide enough information for another researcher to reasonably evaluate or replicate the experiment.

FIGURE **7.5** A psychophysiological study.

record the name, manufacturer, model number, and so on. If it was custom designed, you may need a diagram or photo. Finally, keep careful notes about everything you did in your experiment, including any verbal instructions given to subjects, because you will need to describe all of the procedures you used in your experimental sessions (this subsection is often labeled *Procedures*). Listing them in chronological order is often the simplest way to present your procedures.

## SUMMARY

In this chapter, we have examined several basic experimental concepts. The *independent variable* is the antecedent condition (the treatment) that is deliberately manipulated by the experimenter to assess its effect on behavior. We use different values, or *levels, of the independent variable* to determine how changes in the independent variable alter the value of the dependent variable, our index of behavior. The *dependent variable* is an indicator of change in behavior. Its values are assumed to depend on the values of the independent variable.

Both independent and dependent variables must be defined operationally. Psychological variables are frequently *hypothetical constructs*. An *operational definition* specifies the precise meaning of a variable within an experiment: It defines the variable in terms of observable operations, procedures, and measurements. *Experimental operational definitions* define exactly what was done to create the various treatment conditions of the experiment. *Measured operational definitions* specify the procedures used to measure the impact of the independent variable. The researcher must select the *level of measurement* of each dependent variable: nominal, ordinal, interval, or ratio. We generally use the highest level of measurement that is appropriate.

Operational definitions are developed according to criteria of *reliability* and *validity*. Reliable procedures have consistent and dependable outcomes. The consistency of dependent measures, for example, can be evaluated for *interrater, test-retest*, and *interitem reliability*. If our definitions are valid, we will be manipulating and measuring the variables we intend to study. Evidence needs to go beyond *face validity*. We can evaluate the *content validity, predictive validity,* and *concurrent validity* of our measuring instruments. Researchers are also concerned with *construct validity,* the fit between operations and theory.

An experiment is *internally valid* if we can be sure that the changes in behavior that occurred across treatment conditions were caused by the independent variable. Ideally, only the independent and dependent variables will change value in the different treatment conditions of the experiment. Sometimes we find that *extraneous variables,* variables that are neither independent nor dependent variables in the experiment, also change systematically across conditions. When extraneous variables change value from one treatment condition to another along with the independent variable, we have a situation known as *confounding*. When there is confounding, we cannot say for sure whether the changes we see in the dependent variable from one condition to another were caused by the changes in the values of the independent variable or by an extraneous variable that was also changing. Confounding threatens internal validity.

Campbell and his colleagues have identified eight classic threats to the internal validity of experiments and quasi-experiments: *history, maturation, testing, instrumentation, statistical regression, selection, subject mortality,* and the set of *selection interactions*.

Tips for planning the *Method* section of the research report include keeping careful notes about gender, age and other relevant demographic information, and the number of subjects who did not complete the experiment (and why). It will also be necessary to describe any equipment and written or other materials, as well as the procedures you used in the experiment.

## KEY TERMS

**Concurrent validity** The degree to which scores on the measuring instrument correlate with another known standard for measuring the variable being studied.

**Confounding** An error that occurs when the value of an extraneous variable changes systematically along with the independent variable in an experiment; an alternative explanation for the findings that threatens internal validity.

**Construct validity** The degree to which an operational definition accurately represents the construct it is intended to manipulate or measure.

**Content validity** The degree to which the content of a measure reflects the content of what is being measured.

**Dependent variable (DV)** The specific behavior that a researcher tries to explain in an experiment; the variable that is measured.

**Experimental operational definition** The explanation of the meaning of independent variables; defines *exactly* what was done to create the various treatment conditions of the experiment.

**Extraneous variable** A variable other than an independent or dependent variable; a variable that is not the focus of an experiment but can produce effects on the dependent variable if not controlled.

**Face validity** The degree to which a manipulation or measurement technique is self-evident.

**History threat** A threat to internal validity in which an outside event or occurrence might have produced effects on the dependent variable.

**Hypothetical construct** Concepts used to explain unseen processes, such as hunger, intelligence, or learning; postulated to explain observable behavior.

**Independent variable (IV)** The variable (antecedent condition) that the experimenter intentionally manipulates.

**Instrumentation threat** A threat to internal validity produced by changes in the measuring instrument itself.

**Interitem reliability** The degree to which different items measuring the same variable attain consistent results.

**Internal validity** The certainty that the changes in behavior observed across treatment conditions in the experiment were actually caused by the independent variable.

**Interrater reliability** The degree of agreement among different observers or raters.

**Level of measurement** The type of scale of measurement—either ratio, interval, ordinal, or nominal—used to measure a variable.

**Levels of the independent variable** The two or more values of the independent variable manipulated by the experimenter.

**Manipulation check** An assessment to determine whether the independent variable was manipulated successfully.

**Maturation threat** A threat to internal validity produced by internal (physical or psychological) changes in subjects.

**Measured operational definition** The description of *exactly* how a variable in an experiment is measured.

**Method** The section of a research report in which the subjects and experiment are described in enough detail that the experiment may be replicated by others; it is typically divided into subsections, such as *Participants*, *Apparatus* or *Materials*, and *Procedures*.

**Operational definition** The specification of the precise meaning of a variable within an experiment; defines a variable in terms of observable operations, procedures, and measurements.

**Predictive validity** The degree to which a measuring instrument yields information allowing prediction of actual behavior or performance.

**Reliability** The consistency and dependability of experimental procedures and measurements.

**Selection interactions** A family of threats to internal validity produced when a selection threat combines with one or more of the other threats to internal validity; when a selection threat is already present, other threats can affect some experimental groups but not others.

**Selection threat** A threat to internal validity that can occur when nonrandom procedures are used to assign subjects to conditions or when random assignment fails to balance out differences among subjects across the different conditions of the experiment.

**Statistical regression threat** A threat to internal validity that can occur when subjects are assigned to conditions on the basis of extreme scores on a test; upon retest, the scores of extreme scorers tend to regress toward the mean even without any treatment.

**Subject mortality threat** A threat to internal validity produced by differences in dropout rates across the conditions of the experiment.

**Testing threat** A threat to internal validity produced by a previous administration of the same test or other measure.

**Test-retest reliability** Consistency between an individual's scores on the same test taken at two or more different times.

**Validity** The soundness of an operational definition; in experiments, the principle of actually studying the variables intended to be manipulated or measured.

## REVIEW AND STUDY QUESTIONS

1. Define and give an example to illustrate each of the following terms:
   a. Independent variable
   b. Dependent variable
   c. Extraneous variable

2. Identify the independent variables and levels of the IV in each of the following hypotheses:
   a. Absence makes the heart grow fonder.
   b. It takes longer to recognize a person in a photograph seen upside down.
   c. People feel sadder in blue rooms than in pink rooms.
   d. Waiting with others reduces anxiety.

3. Identify the dependent variables in each hypothesis in question 2.

4. Formulate an experimental operational definition for each independent variable in question 2.

5. Formulate a measured operational definition for each dependent variable in question 2.

6. For each hypothesis in question 2, discuss three extraneous variables that might interfere with making a valid test of that hypothesis.

7. Define and give an example to illustrate each of these terms:
   a. Interrater reliability
   b. Test-retest reliability
   c. Interitem reliability
   d. Content validity
   e. Predictive validity
   f. Concurrent validity
   g. Construct validity

8. What is internal validity? Why is it important for an experiment to have internal validity?

9. Define each of the eight classic threats to internal validity and give an example of each.

10. List each classic threat to internal validity that is intrinsic to the following designs:
    a. Ex post facto study
    b. Longitudinal study
    c. Pretest/posttest study
    d. Nonequivalent groups

## CRITICAL THINKING EXERCISE

*The myth:* Laughter is the best medicine.

*The scientific findings:* Laughter can lower blood pressure, increase immune function, and reduce stress (Cousins, 1989).

*The problem:* Imagine that you have just read an article in the newspaper describing a scientific study in which researchers found that people who tend to laugh a lot may have lower blood pressure, stronger immune systems, and feel less stressed out. Evaluate the internal validity of this conclusion. (*Hint:* The findings came from an ex post facto study—not a true experiment.)

## ONLINE RESOURCES

Read more about Stanley Schachter at

www.columbia.edu/cu/pr/96_99/19150.html

Use Wadsworth's Research Methods Workshop to test yourself on reliability and validity and other important concepts from Chapter 7:

www.wadsworth.com/psychology_d/templates/ student_resources/workshops/workshops.html

## CHAPTER 8

# Solving Problems: Controlling Extraneous Variables

**Physical Variables**
Elimination and Constancy
Balancing

**Social Variables**
Demand Characteristics
Experimenter Bias

**Personality Variables**
Experimenters
Volunteer Subjects

**Context Variables**
When the Subjects Select the Experiment
When the Experimenter Selects the Subjects
Some Folklore About Subjects

SUMMARY
KEY TERMS
REVIEW AND STUDY QUESTIONS
CRITICAL THINKING EXERCISE
ONLINE RESOURCES

## CHAPTER OBJECTIVES

- Learn to control for aspects of the physical environment
- Understand demand characteristics and experimenter bias and how to control for their effects
- Learn how an experimenter's personality can influence experiments
- Learn how volunteers differ from nonvolunteers
- Understand how to control for special problems created by the experimental context

When we experiment, we want to create treatment conditions that will let us clearly see the effects of independent variables. We want our experiments to be internally valid; therefore, only the independent variable should change systematically from one condition to another. In the last chapter, you were introduced to extraneous variables and confounding and began to learn the importance of controlling for them. In this chapter, we will look closely at some techniques for handling other extraneous variables that can threaten an experiment's internal validity: physical, social, personality, and context variables. In some instances, these variables can also threaten an experiment's external validity by reducing the generalizability of the findings. Each poses special problems in an experiment. Many can be controlled by the same procedures, but some require special procedures. Let us begin by looking at the first type, physical variables.

## PHYSICAL VARIABLES

Poor Emily was trying to run a memory experiment that required a lot of concentration. On Thursday, her first day of testing, Emily recruited subjects in the library and tested them in a quiet reading room. The next day she came back to run the rest of the experiment. To her dismay, Emily found that the reading room closed early on Fridays. The only place she could test her subjects was the building's lobby. It was fairly quiet there, but people walked by now and then, laughing and talking about plans for the weekend. Emily cried, "What a dummy I am! These testing conditions will confound my experiment! Why did I run all of my subjects getting treatment *A* yesterday?"

The day of the week, the testing room, the noise, the distractions are all physical variables, aspects of the testing conditions that need to be controlled. Emily's experiment was in real trouble because she ran all subjects getting treatment *A* on a Thursday and all of those getting treatment *B* on a

Friday—and we all know that Fridays are different![1] The *A* group was tested under quiet conditions in one setting; the *B* group was tested in a different place with more noise and distractions. Clearly, there was confounding in Emily's experiment because the testing conditions changed along with the independent variable. She could have avoided her problems by using one of the three general techniques for controlling physical variables: elimination, constancy of conditions, and balancing. We cannot possibly identify all the extraneous variables that influence the outcome of a study—but we try to find as many as we can. By using control techniques, we increase the chances of an internally valid experiment.

## Elimination and Constancy

To make sure that an extraneous variable does not affect an experiment, sometimes we just take it out—we eliminate it. If noise might confound the results, we test in a quiet location. If we do not want interruptions, we hang a sign on the door saying, "Do not disturb. Experiment in progress." Ideally, we would like to eliminate all extraneous variables from an experiment, but this is easier said than done. Sometimes there is no quiet location. Factors such as the weather, the lighting, and the paint on the walls are simply there; we cannot eliminate them. Instead, we use the second control procedure—constancy of conditions.

Constancy of conditions simply means that we keep all aspects of the treatment conditions as nearly similar as possible. If we cannot eliminate an extraneous variable, we try to make sure that it stays the same in all treatment conditions. We cannot take the paint off the walls, but we can test all subjects in the same room. That way, we make sure that the pea-green walls offend all subjects equally in all conditions. The same goes for lighting, the comfort of the chairs, the mustiness of the drapes; all stay the same for all the subjects. We also try to keep the mechanics of the testing procedures the same. For instance, it is helpful to write out instructions to subjects before beginning the experiment. The written instructions are then read to subjects to guarantee that all subjects in each condition get exactly the same instructions. Audio- or videotaping the instructions might be even better. Exactly the same amount of time is allowed for each subject to complete each task—unless time is the independent or dependent variable.

Many physical variables such as time of testing, testing location, and mechanical procedures can be kept constant with a little effort. An experimenter may end up controlling some variables that would not have affected the results anyway, but it is better to use the controls than to have regrets later. If someone can punch holes in the results simply by pointing out that the *A* group had lunch but the *B* group did not, the experimenter will have a hard time making a strong case for the effects of the independent variable.

---

[1] Many of our colleagues try to avoid running any experiments on Fridays. We are not sure if it is because they are worried that subjects will be less motivated to participate, that fewer will actually show up, or whether they themselves are just looking forward to the weekend.

## Balancing

Sometimes neither elimination nor constancy can be used. Perhaps some variables cannot be eliminated. For example, we would like to test in a quiet room, but we do not have access to one. We would like to test all subjects together at the same time, but they cannot all come at once. What can we do in these situations? Confounding occurs when something in the experiment changes systematically along with the independent variable. If we cannot eliminate extraneous physical variables or keep them constant throughout an experiment, we can still make sure that they do not confound the results. The key to the problem is the way the variables change. If they change in a way that is systematically linked to the levels of the independent variable, we are in trouble because a confound is present. If we test subjects receiving treatment *A* in one room and subjects receiving treatment *B* in another, we have created an orderly, or systematic, change in many of the variables that make up the testing conditions. We will not be able to tell for sure whether the independent variable or something about the different testing rooms produced changes in the groups. The *A* group may do better if it is tested in the same sunny room in which the *B* group is tested. The key to controlling variables that cannot be eliminated or held constant is the third technique for physical variables—balancing.

We know that ideally we should not test subjects in two different rooms. But perhaps we have no choice; it is two rooms or nothing. We still want to be sure testing conditions do not change in a way that is related to the independent variable. We can do this through balancing, distributing the effects of an extraneous variable across the different treatment conditions of the experiment. One way that we might do this with room assignment is shown in Table 8.1.

TABLE **8.1**

Balancing the effects of the testing room across two treatment conditions
(*A* and *B*)

| Green Testing Room Subjects | Pink Testing Room Subjects |
|:---:|:---:|
| $A_1$ | $A_4$ |
| $A_2$ | $A_5$ |
| $A_3$ | $A_6$ |
| $B_1$ | $B_4$ |
| $B_2$ | $B_5$ |
| $B_3$ | $B_6$ |

Note: Half the subjects are assigned randomly to each testing room. Half the subjects in each room are then assigned randomly to *A*, half to *B*. (Procedures for random assignment are in the next chapter.)
© Cengage Learning

We begin by randomly assigning half the subjects to the first testing room. The other half will be tested in the second room. Next, we randomly assign half the subjects in each room to the treatment condition *A;* the remaining subjects will be in treatment condition *B.* Notice that we have not wiped out the differences between the two testing rooms; they are just as different as ever. However, the hope is that the effects of the rooms are the same, or balanced, for both treatment conditions. For every *A* subject tested in the green room, a *B* subject is also tested in that room; for every *A* subject tested in the pink room, a *B* subject is also tested there.

Emily could have salvaged her memory experiment by using balancing. Instead of testing all treatment *A* subjects on the first day, she should have randomly assigned each subject to either treatment *A* or treatment *B.* Then she would have tested, by chance, roughly half the *A* subjects and half the *B* subjects on Thursday. Roughly half the *A* subjects would have taken part in the quiet reading room along with roughly half the *B* subjects. On the second day, Emily would have continued assigning subjects to the two treatment conditions at random. She would then have tested about half the *A* subjects and half the *B* subjects in the noisy lobby. Notice that she still would have had subjects who were tested under two different testing conditions. But the effects of these conditions would have been about the same for the two treatments in the experiment, so the testing conditions would not have confounded the results of her experiment.

We can use balancing for many other variables as well. For example, if we cannot test all subjects at the same time of day, we can arrange things so that we test equal numbers of treatment *A* and treatment *B* subjects before and after lunch. Many physical variables will be balanced across conditions automatically as we assign our subjects to treatment conditions at random. Time of testing, weather conditions, and day of the week are typically controlled in this way. Usually, we do not even think about these sorts of extraneous variables. As long as there is no systematic change in an extraneous variable, things are fine. If we assign subjects to treatment conditions at random, we can be reasonably sure that we will not accidentally test all subjects receiving one treatment on a cool, comfortable day and all subjects receiving a different treatment on a hot, muggy day. We can, of course, easily improve control by using block randomization (see Chapter 9).

At this point, you may be wondering whether there is a limit on the number of extraneous variables that must be controlled. There may indeed be many possibilities, but you can set up a reasonably good experiment by taking these precautions: Eliminate extraneous variables whenever you can. Keep treatment conditions as similar as possible. Balance out the effects of other variables, such as the testing room, by making sure that the effects are distributed evenly across all treatment conditions. As always, be sure to assign individual subjects to treatment conditions at random. The experimental literature will also help you plan a strategy. If other experimenters have carefully controlled the size of the testing room, you will want to be more cautious with that variable than with some others, such as the day of the week. If you can avoid it, do not let extraneous variables change along with the independent variable. You can never rule out the possibility of confounding if you let that happen.

Keep in mind as you design experiments that there is often a trade-off between internal and external validity. The more extraneous variables we control, the more we increase internal validity, particularly when we control variables that could change along with the independent variable. In a well-constructed experiment, we are confident that the independent variable, not extraneous variables, caused the effects—the experiment is high in internal validity. At the same time, however, by controlling extraneous variables, we may be reducing external validity.

Suppose that in a weight-loss experiment, we had decided to test all of our A and B subjects before lunch. This procedure would be one way of eliminating the problem that subjects would weigh more after lunch. Unfortunately, by eliminating this extraneous variable, we have reduced the study's external validity; now there is no way of knowing that our effects would generalize to people who have eaten lunch because we have not tested any subjects who have eaten lunch. In this case, balancing (by testing equal numbers of people in both groups before and after lunch) would have been a better procedure than elimination. By using balancing, the study would have internal validity and greater external validity. A cautionary note: When you design your procedures, do not sacrifice internal validity for external validity because internal validity is more important. You cannot have external validity unless a study, first, has internal validity!

## SOCIAL VARIABLES

Besides controlling physical variables that might alter the outcome of the experiment, researchers are concerned about social variables, qualities of the relationships between subjects and experimenters that can influence results. Two principal social variables, demand characteristics and experimenter bias, can be controlled through single- and double-blind experiments.

### Demand Characteristics

Demand characteristics are aspects of the experimental situation that demand that people behave in a particular way. Have you ever noticed that people behave in a very peculiar way in elevators? Elevator passengers who are unacquainted rarely look at each other; instead, they stare at some point up on the walls in front of them or move their eyes across the ceiling—anywhere but toward the other passengers. You have probably found yourself avoiding eye contact with strangers on elevators, too. This is a good example of what we mean by demand characteristics.

What we do is often shaped by what we think is expected behavior in a particular situation. When you enter a classroom, even on the first day

"WHAT IT COMES DOWN TO IS YOU HAVE TO FIND OUT WHAT REACTION THEY'RE LOOKING FOR, AND YOU GIVE THEM THAT REACTION."

of the term, you probably walk in and take a seat. When the professor begins talking, you stop what you are doing and listen. You are fulfilling a role you learned in your earliest days at school. The cue of being in the classroom leads you to behave in a predictable way. The same applies for research subjects. They want to conform to what they think is the proper role of a subject. They might not even be consciously aware of the ways in which they alter their behavior when they come into an experiment. For example, subjects might assume a very active role. They might try to guess the hypothesis of the experiment and adjust their responses accordingly.

Suppose we want to run a perception experiment in which two lights move at the same speed but in different paths: circular or square. We are looking for a difference in the way subjects perceive the movement of these lights. Specifically, we expect subjects to perceive the light in the circular path as moving faster. We ask: "Did the light in the circular path move faster, slower, or about the same as the light in the square path?" If you were a

| BOX **8.1** | The "Good Subject" Phenomenon |

Martin Orne (1927–2000) is well known for his programmatic research on social variables in the experimental setting. According to Orne, the experimental setting creates a situation of extraordinary control over the behavior of research subjects. Certainly, subjects volunteer for experiments for any number of reasons (course requirements, extra credit, money, a hope that the psychologist can make them feel better, etc.), but over and above these reasons, Orne believed that college student subjects share with experimenters the belief that the experiment is important. And even though the experiment may require a lot of effort or even discomfort, they want to perform well for the experimenter—he called this the "good subject phenomenon."

Orne demonstrated this phenomenon in an amusing experiment (Orne, 1972). Subjects were given a task of adding up pairs of adjacent numbers on sheets filled with rows of random digits (just like the random number table in Appendix B). Each subject was given a stack of 2,000 sheets, clearly an impossible task. Subjects' watches were taken away, and they were told to keep working until the experimenter returned. Five and a half hours later, the experimenter finally gave up. Most subjects kept working until the experimenter eventually came back and told them to stop!

The surprised Orne tried to make the task even more frustrating (and completely meaningless) to see if that would reduce compliance. In the second experiment, subjects were given the same task and instructions, but after they completed each sheet, they were told to pick up a card that would tell them what to do next. Each card was identical; it instructed them to tear up the sheet they had just completed into a minimum of 32 pieces and to go on to the next sheet. Orne expected subjects to stop when they realized that each card said the same thing. But, according to Orne, subjects kept at the task for several hours. When he asked them why, they all came up with reasons that made the task seem meaningful (e.g., an endurance test). They were indeed "good subjects."

subject in this experiment, what would you think about this question? The experimenter has gone to a lot of trouble to set up these lights and recruit subjects. Suppose you really could not see any difference in the speed of the lights. But why would anyone go to the bother of showing you two lights that move at the same speed and then ask you whether one moved faster? You might begin to suspect that there really was some subtle difference in the speeds and somehow you did not notice it. But you want to be a good subject; you do not want to tell the experimenter that you were not paying attention or that you are not very good at judging speed. So you guess. You say, "Well, maybe the round one really was moving a little faster because it didn't make all those turns. So I'll say the round one was faster even though I'm not sure that's what I saw." Box 8.1 illustrates this problem further.

An experimenter generally wants participants to be as naive as possible. They should understand the nature and purpose of the experiment but not the exact hypothesis. The reason for this is simple. If subjects know what we expect to find, they might try to produce data that will support the hypothesis. On the surface, that might seem like a good thing. Wouldn't it be wonderful if experiments always confirmed their hypotheses? It would—if the experiments were valid. We want to be able to say that the independent variable caused a change in behavior. If behavior changes simply because subjects think the researcher wants an experiment to turn out in a particular way, the experiment has not measured what it was intended to measure.

Subjects often try to guess the hypothesis. This is a problem, especially in within-subjects experiments (to be covered in Chapter 11). In these experiments, participants take part in more than one treatment condition, so they usually have a better chance of guessing the hypothesis. Of course, participants sometimes guess incorrectly. They might think they are helping by responding in a particular way, but their help produces data that make it impossible to confirm the hypothesis. Occasionally, subjects will actually try to produce data that conflict with the hypothesis. They might guess the hypothesis, disagree with it, and set out to disprove it. Again, they might be wrong; they might actually wind up supporting the predictions. But either way, our problem is that their data are not worth much. We want to set up experiments in which we can test the effect of an independent variable, not the subjects' skill at guessing the experimental hypothesis.

Does this sort of thing really happen? Do subjects' experiences and answers change depending on what they think is supposed to happen in the experiment? Can the demand characteristics of an experiment lead to changes in subjects' behavior? What if subjects simply do what they think they are supposed to do? In an experiment that has now become classic, Orne and Scheibe (1964) devised a clever experiment to evaluate the effects of demand characteristics in research on sensory deprivation.

Traditionally, participants in sensory-deprivation experiments were isolated from sensory experiences of all kinds. They wore translucent goggles so that they could not see shapes clearly; they were typically restricted to lying on a soft bed; they wore coverings over their arms to minimize sensations from movement and touch. White noise (noise of all frequencies that sounds very much like static on a radio) was played to mask ordinary sounds. With these procedures, prolonged sensory deprivation led to emotional upset, disorientation, and even hallucinations. Orne and Scheibe followed a very different procedure. They placed their subjects alone in a room that hardly created any deprivation at all. The room was 6 x 7 x 8 feet in size and was furnished with a desk and two chairs. The subjects could easily hear sounds from the hallway and birds chirping outside. They did not wear goggles and so had their normal vision. There was water and a sandwich in case they got hungry. They were given a set of arithmetic problems to work on if they wanted something to do, and they could move around as much as they wanted to within the room.

The difference between the two groups in this study was the way the experiment was presented to each group. In the first treatment condition, subjects were interviewed by a man in a white medical coat. A tray of drugs and medical instruments, labeled "Emergency Tray," was in the room. Subjects were told that there was an alarm button in the "deprivation chamber." If they became upset, they were advised to press the alarm button. They were also told that a physician was present. Pulse and blood pressure readings were taken. Everything possible was done to create an atmosphere of seriousness and preparation for a possible crisis. Subjects were also read some instructions for reporting their experiences while in the chamber, including possible visual imagery, unusual feelings, and disorientation—the typical sensory-deprivation effects.

Subjects in the other treatment group were told that they were "control" subjects who were not receiving the experimental treatment. The experimenter wore regular business clothes. There was no emergency tray or alarm button. Subjects were told that if they wanted to leave the chamber, they could simply knock on the window. They were given the same general instructions to report their experiences, but everything was done to create a relaxed impression. When the blood pressure and pulse readings were made, the control subjects were told that the readings were being taken simply because they had been taken for the "experimental" subjects. (We will learn about creating true control and experimental conditions in the next chapter.)

If we compare the two procedures, we see that Orne and Scheibe manipulated demand characteristics in their experiment. All subjects were placed in the same "deprivation" setting, but the experimental subjects were given every reason to expect that something awful, or at least out of the ordinary, might happen to them. The "control" subjects were treated in a more casual way that probably communicated something like, "You'll be in this room for a while." What would you expect to happen in this experiment? Would subjects show the usual effects of sensory deprivation? If we look only at the physical layout of this experiment, we can see that there is little reason to expect anyone to become disoriented or show any other unusual symptoms in a short period of time. The subjects had full use of all their senses. Their movements were not restricted, they could eat, and they had a task to do if they got bored.

Orne and Scheibe's findings implicated demand characteristics as a cause of some of the prior sensory-deprivation findings: Subjects led to expect some strange experience showed significantly more signs of disturbance. Compared with the controls, the experimental subjects gave the "impression of almost being tortured" (1964, p. 11). All the subjects in Orne and Scheibe's experiment experienced the same "deprivation," but only the experimental group showed the usual effects of sensory deprivation. For the experimental group, the researchers had created the impression that something unusual would happen to them. The subjects' expectations were confirmed; they experienced a variety of changes that did not occur for the control subjects, who had a different set of expectations. The changes were varied and at times dramatic: "The buzzing of the fluorescent light is growing alternately louder and softer so that at times it sounds like a jackhammer"; "There are multicolored spots on the wall"; "The numbers on the number sheets are blurring and assuming various inkblot forms" (p. 10). Indeed, one subject hit the panic button and listed "disorganization of senses" as one of his reasons for stopping. These findings do not rule out the possibility that some genuine changes occur when subjects undergo an actual restriction of sensory experience. They do, however, illustrate the importance of demand characteristics in shaping the outcome of such studies.

### Controlling Demand Characteristics: Single-Blind Experiments

When we run experiments, we try not to give participants clues about what may happen to them when they are exposed to the independent variable. We do not want to influence the outcome of the experiment by having subjects know the hypothesis. A good way to control some effects of demand characteristics is through a single-blind experiment, an experiment in which subjects do not know which treatment they are getting.

When we do a single-blind experiment, we can disclose some but not all information about the experiment to subjects. We can disclose what is going to happen to them in the experiment; we can also keep them fully informed about the purpose of the study. But we keep them "blind" to one thing: We do not tell them what treatment condition they are in. This approach is very common in experiments with drugs. If we give a subject some substance, the subject might react based on what he or she *expects* the drug to do. For instance, suppose we want to test a new drug designed to reduce anxiety. If we give the drug to several anxious individuals, some of them will report that they feel better. But, did the medicine help? We don't know. To answer this question, we need to compare their behavior with that of a group of subjects who did not receive the drug. Researchers know that if you give a person any pill, the person is apt to say that the pill helped. We call this the placebo effect.

To control for the possibility of a placebo effect, researchers give one group of subjects a placebo—a pill, an injection, or other treatment that contains none of the actual medication. Subjects are not told whether they are receiving the actual drug or the placebo. Because subjects do not know what effects to expect, changes in their behavior are more likely to be caused by the independent variable.

Subjects, however, typically know they are getting *some* kind of treatment, and so we may rarely be able to measure the actual effects of a drug by itself. Instead, we see the effects of treatment plus placebo effects that are shaped by the subjects' expectations. We then compare those effects with the effects of the placebo alone. Accounting for placebo effects has become common in drug studies because the effects can be huge. For example, one meta-analytic study of clinical drug trials with 2,318 depressed patients (Kirsh & Saperstein, 1998) showed that about one-fourth of the reported reductions in depression symptoms were probably caused by actual effects of the antidepressive drugs, another fourth by the natural course of the illness, and over half of the reductions were probably caused by the placebo effect (see Figure 8.1).

In other kinds of experiments, we can get placebo effects too (see Box 8.2). Suppose we want to conduct a simple learning study; we want to see whether the brightness of a room influences how easily people learn. We will test half the subjects in a room with normal illumination (a 75-watt bulb), and we will test the other half under brighter-than-normal illumination (a 150-watt bulb). Both groups will be asked to memorize a list of 10 nonsense words—like

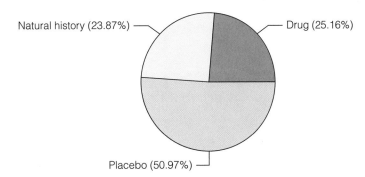

FIGURE **8.1** Drug effect, placebo effect, and natural history effect as proportions of the response to antidepressant medication
© Cengage Learning

*bragzap* and *crumdip*. The length of time it takes subjects to memorize all 10 words will be the dependent measure.

We want to conduct a single-blind study. Therefore, we might tell subjects: "We are investigating the effects of room lighting on learning. We are asking people to learn a list of 10 made-up words as quickly as possible. Different people will learn the list under different lighting conditions, and we will see whether lighting makes a difference." We have given subjects information about the purpose of the experiment and have told them what would happen to them during the experiment. Notice that we have not disclosed our expectations about their performance, and we have not told them which condition they are in.

But have we structured the situation so that these parameters are fairly simple to figure out? Probably we have. Subjects are quite likely to figure out our hypothesis—and behave accordingly. If they believe the light is normal or even a bit dim, they may take longer to learn the list simply because they expect it to take longer. If the light seems bright, they may learn the list more quickly because they expect the added light makes learning easier. This could confound the experiment because their expectation varies systematically with the independent variable—it would take them longer in the 75-watt condition than in the 150-watt condition, just as we predicted, but the difference might not be due to the light levels at all.

What alternatives do we have? We could give them less information. We could simply say that we are investigating the influence of different study environments on learning. This might keep them from guessing our true hypothesis or it might not. Perhaps some experimental subjects guess that we are testing quiet versus noisy spaces or different kinds of chairs or different colored walls. Whatever they guess, there is always the possibility that their guess will be confirmed by the way they behave. Whatever they guess might alter the time it would normally take to learn the list. Nevertheless, most researchers would agree that this situation is somewhat better than the first. Chances are that individual subjects would guess different things and behave in different ways, but their behavior would not change systematically along

BOX **8.2**    **Exercise and the Placebo Effect**

The U.S. Surgeon General has recommended that a healthy lifestyle should include at least 30 minutes a day of physical exercise (Centers for Disease Control and Prevention, CDC, 1996). In an ingenious experiment, Crum and Langer (2007) demonstrated

that the placebo effect can influence the health benefits of exercise.

The study volunteers were women working as room attendants in seven similar hotels who were recruited for a study to find ways to improve the health and happiness of women in a hotel workplace. The women ranged from 18 to 55 years of age, worked between 32 and 40 hours a week, and cleaned an average of 15 rooms a day. Most of the women in the sample were Hispanic; others were Caucasian, African American, or Asian. All the women working in a given hotel were randomly assigned to either the experimental or control group.

Women in both groups answered questions about their health-relevant behaviors (exercise, diet, smoking, drugs, alcohol, etc.), and measurements of their height, weight, waist-to-hip ratio, and blood pressure were taken. Subjects in both groups were told that the health information was needed to study improvements and that they would receive information about research on health and happiness. The experimental group was given additional information. These women were also informed about the health benefits of exercise and the caloric values of typical cleaning activities (e.g., vacuuming, changing linens, and cleaning bathrooms) were provided. It was also made clear to the women that their daily work activities exceeded the Surgeon General's recommendations for exercise. Women in both groups were reassessed on the behavioral and physiological measures after four weeks and debriefed.

with the independent variable. This situation would not be a confound, but it would certainly make the impact of the independent variable more difficult to detect. It would introduce large individual differences in responding, which is something we work hard to avoid when we can.

### Controlling Demand Characteristics: Cover Stories

There is another alternative for controlling the possibility that subjects may guess the experimental hypothesis—we could use a cover story. When we create an experimental situation, we want subjects to respond as normally as possible. At the very least, we do not want their expectations to alter their responses on the dependent measure. Sometimes the best control over demand characteristics is gained by using a cover story, which is a plausible but false

There were no changes in (1) the amount of work actually performed by the women or (2) reports of their health, diet, and lifestyle activities. But even though no real changes in activity had occurred, there were significant differences between the groups in both perceptions of their exercise activities and in the physiological indices. After four weeks, the experimental group reported that they engaged in significantly more exercise at work than the control group did, and their average weight dropped by 3 pounds (the average weight of the control group did not change). See Figures 8.2a and b.

The experimental group, but not the control group, also showed reductions in body mass index and percentage of body fat as well as a drop in systolic blood pressure. Because the two groups of women actually engaged in the same amount of exercise, the researchers interpreted the results as supporting the hypothesis that "increasing *perceived* exercise independently of actual exercise results in subsequent physiological improvements (p. 170)." In other words, simply thinking that you are exercising more can make you healthier!*

*At the end of the study, the control group subjects were provided with the same information given to the experimental group about the exercise value of their cleaning activities.

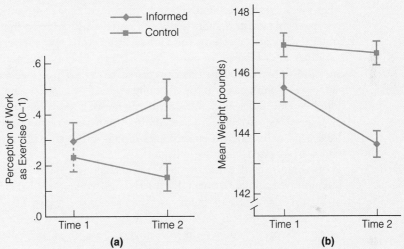

FIGURE **8.2** (a) Changes in self-reported exercise over time (b) Changes in average weight over time
© Cengage Learning

explanation for the procedures used in the study. It is told to disguise the actual research hypothesis so that subjects will not guess what it is.

Consider the following situation. Numerous studies have shown that the way you dress can impact the kind of impression you make on others. Professors who dress casually, for example, are typically judged by students as being more approachable but less knowledgeable than if they dress more formally. Similarly, students who dress casually tend to be judged by their teachers as less intelligent and lower in academic potential than if they dress more formally. This effect is usually explained as an example of how individuals apply stereotypes to form impressions. Hannover and Kuhnan (2002), however, explored an alternative hypothesis in an interesting way. They believed that the style of dress might actually influence how people feel about themselves and, therefore, change the way they behave toward others, resulting in people forming different impressions of them. To test this, they had college students rate themselves on a number of traits while dressed in one of two ways: casually (jeans and a sweatshirt) or more formally (a blazer and nice pants or skirt). But Hannover and Kuhnan were justifiably concerned that their subjects might guess the experimental hypothesis, so they created a clever cover story.

A few days before the experiment, subjects were informed that they would be participating in a study of eyewitness identification and that they would be part of a "police line-up." Thus, they needed to show up at the lab dressed similarly to a description of the ostensible criminal—half were told to dress casually; the other half were told to dress more formally. To maintain the cover story, each participant was told to stand in front of a one-way mirror and then to walk slowly back and forth so that the "eyewitnesses" in the other room could see them. Then, subjects were taken to another room where they participated in a supposedly unrelated trait study to help out a graduate student who was working on a dissertation. Here, they were asked to press computer keys labeled "me" or "not me" to describe themselves on 40 different traits. The traits had been pretested to reflect traits generally ascribed to people who were casually or formally dressed (e.g., easygoing, tolerant, emotional versus cultivated, accurate, restrained). As predicted, subjects' own style of dress strongly influenced their self-descriptions. Subjects who were dressed casually rated themselves as having more casual traits than did those who were dressed more formally.

Hannover and Kuhnan (2002) could simply have instructed subjects to dress either casually or formally for the experiment, told them the experimental hypothesis, and had them rate themselves on the traits once they arrived for their experimental session. But if the results had come out the way the researchers predicted, would you have been convinced? Probably not. What if the researchers did not disclose the hypothesis but simply instructed subjects to come to the lab dressed a certain way and rate themselves on the traits? Would you have been convinced if the data came out as predicted? No, because there is a strong chance that subjects might figure out such a simple hypothesis: "You told me to dress this way because you want me to rate myself a certain way, so I'll rate myself that way."

This is the type of situation in which a cover story must be developed. And we have to be clever because the cover story has to give the subjects an explanation for what we want them to do—dress formally or casually—without tipping them off to the hypothesis being tested. The cover story provided subjects with an explanation for dressing in a certain way that had nothing to do with the experimental hypothesis. Given this plausible explanation, subjects would not look for another explanation and would be unlikely to discover the real experimental hypothesis. Of course, Hannover and Kuhnan explained the real purpose of the style of dress to subjects at the end of the experimental session.

Why not always use a cover story such as one devised by Hannover and Kuhnan? Quite simply, cover stories involve deception. Deception is a departure from fully informed consent, and you will need to persuade your IRB that using deception is the only way to test your hypothesis. As we discovered in Chapter 2, researchers must increasingly be concerned about the rights of the participant as the departure from fully informed consent becomes more dramatic. For this reason, cover stories should be used sparingly. Remember that debriefing is required for all subjects in such experiments. If you believe your experiment can have internal validity without a cover story, do not use one.

## Experimenter Bias

Perhaps without realizing it, an experimenter can give subjects cues that tell them how the experimenter would like them to respond. Subjects will often comply with these subtle requests and give the data the experimenter is seeking. Imagine the experimenter running the earlier perception experiment. She asks, "Does the light in the circular path move faster, slower, or at the same speed as the light in the square path?" As she says "faster," she leans forward slightly, raises her eyebrows, and speaks a little louder. Most of her subjects say that the light in the circular path moved "faster." We call this sort of influence experimenter bias; the experimenter does something that creates confounding in the experiment. The experimenter could give a cue to respond in a particular way or might behave differently in different treatment conditions. Dr. R. might be warm and friendly in one treatment condition, but he might seem indifferent in the other condition. That is all right if the experimenter's demeanor is the independent variable. If it is not, it can confound the results. Subjects in the first treatment condition might feel more at ease and so perform better.

Sometimes, as in the case of Dr. R., the nature of the treatments can bring on experimenter bias. Dr. R. might have found the first treatment condition much more interesting than the second. If so, then Dr. R. probably found it much more fun to run sessions in which subjects received the first treatment, and his preference showed up as increased warmth toward subjects in this condition. But experimenter bias doesn't always work in this way.

Imagine that one of Dr. R.'s conditions was particularly noxious for subjects and Dr. R. knew it. Researchers do not enjoy putting subjects through unpleasant procedures. Every time Dr. R. knew that a subject would be undergoing the noxious procedure, he became somewhat anxious, and he transmitted this anxiety to subjects. As you can imagine, his behavior would be a particular problem if the dependent variable was anxiety. If Dr. R.'s hypothesis was that the noxious procedure would make subjects more anxious than the other procedure, his experiment would be confounded. Subjects in the noxious condition could have picked up the cue from Dr. R. that there was something to be anxious about, and so they were. Effects on subjects' anxiety might have had every bit as much to do with Dr. R.'s demeanor as with the independent variable.[2]

---

[2] This actually happened to one of the authors in the first experiment she ran in graduate school. The experiment was ruined, but it taught her a valuable lesson—one that both authors hope you will not learn through your own personal experience.

So far it seems that experimenter effects can be a problem only with human subjects, but experimenter effects can be just as important in animal studies as they are in human ones. After all, a rat will not notice a smile and then learn faster. Probably not, but experimenters might handle rats more and handle them more gently if they think the rats are special.

Experimenters might also treat subjects differently depending on what they expect from them. They might give more time to subjects who have gone through a particular treatment. This outcome is called the Rosenthal effect after the man who first reported it (Rosenthal, 1976). It is also called the *Pygmalion effect,* after the legend in which the sculptor Pygmalion fell in love with his own statue of the perfect woman. Box 8.3 summarizes some of Rosenthal's key findings. The Rosenthal effect can be another source of confounding in an experiment.

Experimenter bias occurs in other ways, too. Experimenters might also make errors in recording the data from the experiment. They might "misread" a scale or score an item incorrectly. Coincidentally, Rosenthal (1978) reported that researchers are more likely to make errors that favor the hypothesis. In a sample of 21 published studies, he found that about 1% of all observations made were probably wrong. Of those, two-thirds favored the experimenters' hypotheses. By chance, we would expect only about 50% of the errors to support the researchers' hypotheses.

### Controlling Experimenter Bias: Double-Blind Experiments

How can we eliminate experimenter effects from research? The first step, of course, is to be aware of them. We want to be sure we do not do anything that will contaminate the data. By following a set of written directions, timing all phases of the experiment, and being as consistent as possible, we can avoid some mistakes. We make our observations as objective as possible. We try to set up experiments to minimize the amount of personal contact between an experimenter and a subject so that unintentional bias does not happen. But sometimes we just cannot anticipate how bias can creep into an experiment.

Let us say we are doing a study of cartoons and children's art. We want to see whether children who have just watched a cartoon will draw more abstract pictures than will children who have just watched a filmed version of the same story. The cartoon group sees animated drawings of people; the film group sees real people acting out the same story. We show the children the cartoon or film, and then we ask them to draw pictures.

We have developed a way of scoring the children's drawings for abstractness. Our measure includes a number of specific dimensions, such as whether objects are colored in their true-to-life colors. We will score each child's picture on the abstractness scale. If our hypothesis is correct, the drawings of the children who saw the cartoon will be more abstract than the drawings of children who saw the film.

As we sit down to score the pictures, we notice different features in the drawings. We might also notice that we tend to score somewhat differently depending on which child drew the picture. Sometimes it is not clear how we

## BOX **8.3**   The Rosenthal Effect

Courtesy of Robert Rosenthal

**Robert Rosenthal**

In a variety of laboratory and nonlaboratory studies, researchers have documented the self-fulfilling prophecy: Expectations can alter the behavior of others, even animals (Rosenthal & Fode, 1963). As Rosenthal explained,

> Fode and I told a class of 12 students that one could produce a strain of intelligent rats by inbreeding them to increase their ability to run mazes quickly. To demonstrate, we gave each student five rats, which had to learn to run to the darker of two arms of a T-maze. We told half of our student-experimenters that they had the "maze-bright" intelligent rats; we told the rest that they had the stupid rats. Naturally, there was no real difference among any of the animals.
>
> But they certainly behaved differently in their performance. The rats believed to be bright improved daily in running the maze—they ran faster and more accurately—while the apparently dull animals did poorly. The "dumb" rats refused to budge from the starting point 29 percent of the time, while the "smart" rats were recalcitrant only 11 percent of the time.
>
> Then we asked our students to rate the rats and to describe their own attitudes toward them. Those who believed they were working with intelligent animals liked them better and found them more pleasant. Such students said they felt more relaxed with the animals; they treated them more gently and were more enthusiastic about the experiment than students who thought they had dull rats to work with. Curiously, the students with "bright" rats said they handled them more but talked to them less. One wonders what students with "dull" rats were saying to those poor creatures. (Rosenthal, 1976, p. 58)

Rosenthal and Jacobson (1966) found a similar effect in the classroom. They gave a nonverbal IQ test to children in 18 classrooms at the start of the school year. Next, randomly selected children in each class were labeled "intellectual bloomers." "We gave each teacher the names of these children, who, we explained, could be expected to show remarkable gains during the coming year on the basis of their test scores. In fact, the difference between these experimental children and the control group was solely in the teacher's mind" (Rosenthal, 1973, p. 248). Eight months later, they found greater gains in the IQ scores of the "bloomers" relative to the other children, and these gains persisted over the next two years. Based on this and many other studies, Rosenthal (1973) proposed a fourfold explanation for the phenomenon. People who have been led to expect good things from their students, children, clients, or what-have-you appear to

- Create a warmer socioemotional climate for their special students (climate)
- Give more feedback to these students about their performance (feedback)
- Teach more material, and more difficult material, to their special students (input)
- Give their special students more opportunities to respond and question (output) (p. 60).

From "The Pygmalion Effect Lives" by R. Rosenthal, in R.E. Schell (Ed.), 1973, *Readings in Developmental Psychology Today*, 2nd edition, pp. 247–252.

should score a particular item. LaTanya drew what appears to be a green orange. Oranges really are green before they get ripe, but they are usually orange in pictures. Should we score this picture as "abstract" or not? Scoring the dependent measures is no time to be making subjective judgments. We should have worked out these kinds of issues before running the experiment. But if these questions do arise in scoring, we might find ourselves deciding in favor of the more abstract rating if we knew we were scoring a picture drawn by a child who saw the cartoon. We might distort the scoring a little by being inconsistent; we would bias the data so that they would support our own hypothesis. In doing so, we have created an instrumentation threat to the internal validity of the experiment. It is easy to do this without even realizing it.

One of the best ways of controlling for experimenter bias is to run a double-blind experiment, one in which the subjects do not know which treatment they are receiving, and the experimenter does not know either. The value of the double-blind experiment is this: If the experimenter does not know which treatment the subject is getting, he or she cannot bias the responses in any systematic way. The subject is kept in the dark, too, so the effects of demand characteristics are controlled along with experimenter bias.

Wasson and colleagues (1984) followed this same basic procedure in a study of outpatient health care in elderly men. The researchers randomly assigned patients to a "continuous" or "discontinuous" condition. In the continuous condition, subjects saw the same health-care provider (physician, nurse practitioner, or physician's assistant) each time they visited the clinic. Subjects in the discontinuous condition were assigned for treatment in such a way that on each visit there was a 33% chance of seeing a different provider, and no provider could be seen more than three consecutive times.

Only 10% of the clinic patients participated in the study. They were not identified to the health-care providers, and changes in patient assignments were made gradually so that patients would not suspect the pattern of assignments. Although we can easily question whether patients caught on to the nature of the study, in principle, it was a double-blind experiment. The outcome was that patients in the continuous group had fewer hospital admissions, had shorter stays, and perceived that providers were more knowledgeable, competent, and interested in patient education.

Earlier in the chapter, we discussed the use of single-blind procedures in drug studies with a placebo condition. Single-blind procedures can control for demand characteristics in these studies by keeping subjects unaware of their condition, but single-blind procedures do not control for experimenter bias. Whenever the experimenter is aware of the drug condition of the subject, it is possible that measurement of the dependent variable can be biased by this knowledge. Therefore, whenever possible, the best procedure to use in these studies is the double-blind.

Berman and Taylor (1995) conducted an interesting double-blind study that investigated the effects of triazolam (Halcion), a hypnotic drug prescribed for transient or temporary insomnia, on increases in aggressive behavior in men. In their laboratory experiment, college men were given a capsule—either a placebo or triazolam. Neither the subject nor the experimenter knew whether the capsule contained the drug or not. After about an hour (giving the triazolam time to take effect for those who received it), each subject was seated in front of a task board that appeared to measure his reaction time, and a shock electrode was placed on his nondominant wrist. He was told that he would be competing with a subject in the adjoining room on a reaction-time task and that on each trial the slowest subject would be shocked by his faster opponent. In reality, there was no opponent! The experiment was programmed ahead of time so that the subject lost 50% of the time. It was also rigged so that the subject got increasingly severe shocks as the experiment progressed.[3] The dependent variable was the severity of shocks the subject gave the fictitious opponent when he supposedly "won" a trial. As expected, triazolam significantly increased the severity of the shocks that subjects delivered during the experiment. For both placebo and triazolam subjects, shock levels became higher as the "opponent" became more provocative, but the intensities differed dramatically. Men in the triazolam condition gave what they believed to be Level 10 (the highest level) shocks to their "opponent" about 26% of the time. Men who received a placebo only gave the highest level shock about 4% of the time.

In some experiments, the subjects always know what treatment condition they are getting. For instance, in our study of cartoons and children's art, each child would know whether he or she saw a cartoon or a film. The children would not know the exact hypothesis of the study. Still, we could not really say that they are "blind" to the treatment conditions. In these experiments, we might not be able to use a truly double- or even single-blind procedure. Even so, we can build in some controls for experimenter bias. We can try not to assign participants to their conditions until after we have finished interacting with them. We can make sure that the person who scores the subjects' responses does not know which treatment each subject received. We might have an independent rater score subjects' drawings. We do not tell the rater which subjects belonged to which group. If we are doing our own scoring, it is more difficult to remain naive. With some planning, however, we can skirt the most serious temptations. We standardize the testing and scoring procedures as much as possible. We try to be consistent in the way we handle the experiment from one subject to another. We avoid giving subjects extraneous clues as to how to behave.

When the researcher does know the subject's condition (which happens if there isn't an assistant available), researchers often find a way to standardize the instructions that need to be given to subjects. There are several good ways to do this: You can give subjects written instructions or you can have them listen to the instructions on tape. You can videotape the instructions for subjects or computerize the presentation. If you choose to read the instructions to subjects, avoid relying on memory. Remember, it is important that the words *and* your voice stay the same each time.

---

[3] Before the experiment, each participant was pretested to determine the shock level that he reported as "definitely unpleasant." During the experiment, subjects never received any shocks that strong.

As you design experiments, you will work very hard to control sources of confounding. If effects on the independent variable are produced by your behavior, the experiment does not have internal validity. Always keep in mind that you might be the biggest extraneous variable of all.

Double-check your procedures. As you think about your experiment, try to anticipate subjects' reactions. Put yourself in the subjects' place. How would you feel about answering your own questions? Would you be inclined to distort your answers because you would be too embarrassed to answer honestly? Would the experimental hypothesis be obvious to you? Think about your own behavior and the design of the experiment. Have you stacked the deck in any way? Do your instructions suggest the changes you expect to observe? Have you taken precautions to keep your own behavior as consistent as possible from one treatment condition to another? Are your instructions written down so that you will follow the same procedures each time? Are you prepared to introduce yourself and interact with all your subjects in the same way? It is always a good idea to make a dry run before you start testing subjects. You might even consider a pilot study (discussed in the next chapter) so that any bugs in the procedures can be worked out before you actually collect data for the experiment.

# PERSONALITY VARIABLES

## Experimenters

We saw in the last section that the behavior of the experimenter can be an important extraneous variable in an experiment. You learned that social variables, qualities of the relationships between subjects and experimenters, can influence results if they are not carefully controlled. The personal characteristics, or personality variables, that an experimenter brings to the experimental setting can be important, too. An experimenter who is warm and friendly can elicit very different responses from subjects than can one who is cold and aloof: Subjects sometimes learn better, talk more, get better scores on intelligence and adjustment tests, and are typically more compliant and eager to please when the experimenter acts in a friendly manner (Rosenthal, 1976).

Remember the response set called social desirability? Apparently, experimenters who score high on the social desirability scale (Crowne & Marlowe, 1964) are particularly good at being likeable experimenters; they are more enthusiastic, more friendly, and smile more at their subjects. Interestingly, experimenters who come across as likeable can alter the kinds of responses, as well as the number of responses, obtained from subjects. For instance, studies on interviewing styles have shown that a likeable interviewer will collect better data, more usable responses, and fewer "I don't know's" from respondents. But keep in mind that an experimenter who improves subjects' performance might attenuate an experiment's external validity; such high levels of performance might not be obtained in another setting. Conversely, an experimenter who appeared hostile, aggressive, or authoritarian (demanding obedience) would get less than optimal performance from research subjects (Rosenthal, 1976).

The research setting is a novel one for most subjects, and they are often a bit anxious. We want to establish rapport with subjects so that they will feel at ease, but (unless the experimenter's demeanor is the independent variable) we do not want to make subjects behave in an atypical way. So be pleasant, but remember that you can affect the outcome of your experiment.

It is extremely important to maintain consistency in your interactions with subjects. Remember that when you act more friendly (or hostile, or anxious, etc.) toward subjects from time to time, you are introducing another source of variability into the experiment. The more you vary your behavior, the more you are likely to produce variability in the responses of your subjects. The more variability in their responses, the harder it will be to detect the effect of the independent variable. Most important, however you act toward subjects, do it consistently across all the treatment conditions.[4] Do not allow your behavior to change systematically along with the conditions of the experiment. If your behavior is different in the experimental and control conditions, the experiment will not have internal validity because you are a potential history confound. With many personality variables, the influence is unpredictable and can interact with characteristics of particular subjects.

Some of the control techniques discussed earlier in the chapter will reduce the influence of personality variables. If possible, use multiple experimenters and make sure that each experimenter runs about the same number of people in each of the conditions of the experiment (in effect, balancing them across the experiment). Some researchers advocate including the experimenters as a factor in the data analysis (McGuigan, 1971). If you do not analyze for experimenter differences, you will never know for certain if they were a problem in your experiment or not. Chances are, your first experiment will have only a single experimenter—you—so you will need to take precautions to keep from influencing your subjects in unknown ways. The best control is to keep face-to-face contact to a minimum and always adhere strictly to the experimental procedures.

## Volunteer Subjects

Do we need to be concerned about the personality variables associated with characteristics of subjects in the same way that we are about personality variables associated with experimenters? Not exactly. As we will see in the next chapter, when we design experiments we use random assignment to balance out these kinds of individual differences in subjects across all conditions of an experiment. You already know that if subjects' characteristics vary systematically in the different conditions of an experiment, we have a selection threat to the experiment's internal validity. But as long as a sufficient number of subjects are randomly assigned to each treatment group, we can assume that extraneous subject variables are controlled.

---

[4] Be especially careful not to treat male and female subjects differently. Studies have found, for example, that male experimenters are apt to be more friendly toward their female subjects than toward their male subjects.

When we consider personality variables of experimental subjects, we are generally thinking about the characteristics shared by typical subjects. We want to know if the subjects tested in experiments are truly representative of the population. No one has stated the problem better than McNemar (1946) when he said, "The existing science of human behavior is largely the science of the behavior of sophomores" (p. 333). Reading journal articles, you will find that the majority of published experiments are conducted on college students taking introductory-level psychology courses because this is the most convenient source of samples for academic researchers. However, the sophomores who volunteer to be research subjects might not be entirely representative even of the general population of sophomores from which they come.

During the 1960s, it was popular to conduct studies looking at the kinds of personality variables that discriminated volunteers from nonvolunteers; Rosenthal and Rosnow (1969) conveniently summarize the effects. For example, results of personality tests have shown that volunteers are likely to be more sociable and score higher in social desirability (Crowne & Marlowe, 1964) than nonvolunteers. Volunteers tend to hold more liberal social and political attitudes and tend to be less authoritarian than nonvolunteers. Interestingly, people willing to volunteer for experiments also tend to score higher on intelligence tests, on the average, than do nonvolunteers. Whether these differences remain today is an empirical question, but if they do exist, they would suggest that experiments using university samples might have somewhat less external validity than researchers would wish. These differences would be expected to limit the generalizability of some kinds of experiments more than others.

## CONTEXT VARIABLES

The preceding sections have covered the most important extraneous variables and ways to control them. In this final section, we will look at another set of extraneous variables, context variables, that can influence the results of experiments. Context variables are those that come about from procedures created by the environment, or context, of the research setting. Context variables include subject recruitment, selection, and assignment procedures, as well as typical problems encountered in research on a university population. Most are easily controlled with some forethought. We will cover two basic kinds of context variables: those occurring when subjects select their own experiments and those produced when experimenters select their own subjects.

### When the Subjects Select the Experiment

When you run an experiment using human subjects, you may be allowed to recruit your subjects from a *subject pool* of psychology students. Most departments of psychology in major universities rely on students to serve as research subjects from time to time. (Perhaps you have already had the experience of serving as a subject in someone else's research.) At research universities, psychology students are typically required either to participate in a certain number of experiments or to fulfill a substitute requirement. Frequently, a list of experiments needing subjects is posted on a website or in a central location on campus. Sometimes students can sign up for a session on the spot, or other arrangements can be made. Students can often look over what is available, select one that seems interesting, and make an appointment to participate.

Usually, two factors are involved in the decision: Am I free at a time when subjects are needed? And what kind of experiment is it? Often, the only information that potential subjects are given is the name of the experiment. Sometimes these titles can bias your sample, reducing the external validity of your experiment. Suppose students have the following two choices: "The Memory Test Experiment" and "The Heavy Metal Music Experiment." Do you think students who volunteer for the two experiments might be somewhat different? Of course. To avoid getting a biased sample, researchers try to keep the names as neutral as possible, without sounding boring: "The Impression Formation Experiment," "The Close Relationships Experiment." Instead of "The Sexual Practices Survey," a questionnaire study could be called "Contemporary Judgments." A biased sample greatly reduces your ability to generalize your findings; the experiment will have less external validity.

The time for subjects to decide not to participate in your experiment, if that happens, is after the experiment has been explained to them at the beginning of the session. Always keep a record of subjects who drop out (and what condition of the experiment they were assigned to) for your research report, even though it is unlikely that your experiment will include conditions that are noxious enough to produce a subject mortality threat. Keep in mind that some subjects who volunteer probably will miss their sessions for a variety of reasons (Friday sessions are notorious for no-shows), so it is always a good idea to plan for about 10% more sessions that you actually need.

## When the Experimenter Selects the Subjects

You may be required to recruit your own subjects from the university population or from outside the university community. The information you learned about random selection procedures (Chapter 4) also applies here. If you do not select your subjects randomly, your sample will be biased, resulting in less generalizability. If you use a convenience sample, your results might not be generalizable beyond these subjects. There are some common pitfalls to avoid when selecting subjects.

It is always best to use people you do not know because the behavior of your friends in your experiment will differ from more typical subjects (Rosenthal, 1976). Once you have chosen a population (perhaps other university students), you cannot recruit only those people who smile and seem friendly and approachable. Control for this possible threat by constructing a procedure for randomly selecting the people you approach ahead of time, and stick to it. For instance, if you decide to ask every fifth person who walks by, you must adhere to this procedure even if person 5 is the president of the university or has six rings in each nostril. You must plan your procedures for acquiring subjects as carefully as you plan your experimental procedures, and you must keep your demeanor uniform throughout the selection process.

Assigning subjects to conditions can have similar pitfalls. If you conduct your experiment in the laboratory using volunteers from the subject pool, you probably will not be tempted very much to deviate from your procedure for determining random assignment to conditions. However, if your experiment is conducted in the field, you can expect to find some subjects a bit aggressive or intimidating. If you had your choice, you would probably prefer to give them the easier condition and send them on their way. Avoid this temptation. What would happen if all your "nice" subjects ended up in one experimental condition, while the "nasty" subjects all fell in the other? The actual effects would depend on what you were testing, but regardless of the experimental outcome, your experiment would be confounded by a selection threat. Again, the best way to control for this possibility is to design an assignment procedure, and stick with it.

## Some Folklore About Subjects

The conventional wisdom among academic researchers is to beware of data collected from the end-of-the-term subject pool: Students who sign up late in the term might be less motivated to participate than those who volunteer early. Rosenthal puts the problem this way: "In the folklore of psychologists, there is the notion that sometimes, perhaps more often than we would expect, subjects contacted early in an experiment behave differently from subjects contacted later" (1969, p. 190). He argues, though, that changes are just as likely to be caused by changes in the experimenter—namely, practice and fatigue effects. As you read your instructions over and over to subjects, you become more practiced, more accurate, and faster. During the experiment, you become more fatigued (i.e., less interested or bored). The first can be controlled, somewhat, if you become highly practiced before you run any subjects; the second is more difficult to counteract. Make sure that your random assignment procedure ensures that one condition is not finished up earlier than another, or you could become an instrumentation threat. Again, the best advice is to minimize face-to-face contact so that you will have less impact on how your subjects behave.

In previous chapters, we have covered some important techniques for running solid experiments. We have discussed control over extraneous variables that can threaten both internal and external validity. In the next chapters, we will learn the basic experimental designs: what they are, how they are used, and the control procedures needed to produce valid tests of hypotheses.

# SUMMARY

One of the major goals in setting up experiments is to avoid confounding by controlling extraneous variables. The independent variable should be the only thing that changes systematically across the conditions of the experiment. This principle is essential to all good experiments. Several control procedures can be used to handle extraneous *physical variables*—aspects of the testing conditions that need to be controlled, such as the nature of the testing room, the time of day, and the mechanics of running the experiment. The three general techniques for dealing with physical variables are *elimination, constancy of conditions,* and *balancing*.

Uncontrolled *social variables*—demand characteristics and experimenter bias—can threaten the internal validity of an experiment. *Demand characteristics* can create problems in experiments. Just being in an experiment can lead to changes in a subject's behavior that might have nothing to do with the experimental manipulation. Subjects might want to be "good" subjects; they might try to provide data that confirm the hypothesis. Their expectations about what will happen to them in the experiment can also shape their responses. A *placebo effect* can occur when subjects know which condition of an experiment they are participating in. One way of controlling demand characteristics is to run a *single-blind experiment.* Here the experimenter tells subjects everything about the experiment except which treatment they will receive. Because the subjects in a single-blind experiment do not know for sure which treatment condition they are in, they are less likely to provide data that are distorted to conform to their notion of what the researcher expects to find. Another way to reduce demand characteristics is to use a *cover story*, which disguises the real research hypothesis.

Another potential source of error is *experimenter bias.* Without realizing it, an experimenter can give subtle cues that tell subjects how they are expected to behave. If an experimenter smiles at subjects every time they give the predicted response, he or she might not be getting an accurate picture of the way the independent variable operates. Experimenter bias can also take the form of the *Rosenthal effect,* in which experimenters' expectations can influence their treatment of subjects. One way to control for experimenter bias is the *double-blind experiment,* in which neither the experimenter nor the subjects know which treatment the subjects are getting. This approach enables the experimenter to measure the dependent variable more objectively.

Characteristics of experimenters and volunteer subjects, called *personality variables,* can also affect the results of experiments. Experimenters who are warm and friendly, for example, tend to produce more and better-quality data from subjects than do experimenters who are hostile or authoritarian. We control for these variables by strictly adhering to our procedures and minimizing face-to-face contact with subjects. Levels of certain personality variables, like sociability and intelligence, tend to be higher in volunteer subjects than in nonvolunteers. This difference might decrease the external validity, or generalizability, of experiments using college student subjects.

Some extraneous variables, called *context variables,* are created by the experimental context or setting. If subjects are allowed to select their own experiments, the names of experiments can bias the sample when different kinds of subjects volunteer for different-sounding experiments, reducing generalizability further. When the experimenter selects the subjects, there are certain pitfalls to avoid, such as selecting subjects or assigning them to treatment conditions based on how friendly or unfriendly they seem. This bias, too, can reduce generalizability or, in extreme cases, can even confound the experiment. Experimenters also need to be aware of the possibility that they can show practice and fatigue effects over the course of running an entire experiment and take precautions to control for them.

## KEY TERMS

Balancing A technique used to control the impact of extraneous variables by distributing their effects equally across treatment conditions.

Constancy of conditions A control procedure used to avoid confounding; keeping all aspects of the treatment conditions identical except for the independent variable that is being manipulated.

Context variable Extraneous variable stemming from procedures created by the environment, or context, of the research setting.

Cover story A plausible but false explanation of the procedures in an experiment told to disguise the actual research hypothesis so that subjects will not guess what it is.

Demand characteristics The aspects of the experimental situation itself that demand or elicit particular behaviors; can lead to distorted data by compelling subjects to produce responses that conform to what subjects believe is expected of them in the experiment.

Double-blind experiment An experiment in which neither the experimenter nor the subjects know which treatment condition the subjects are in; used to control experimenter bias.

Elimination A technique to control extraneous variables by removing them from an experiment.

Experimenter bias Any behavior of the experimenter that can create confounding in an experiment.

Personality variables The personal characteristics that an experimenter or volunteer subject brings to the experimental setting.

Physical variables Aspects of the testing conditions that need to be controlled.

Placebo effect The result of giving subjects a pill, injection, or other treatment that actually contains none of the independent variable; the treatment elicits a change in subjects' behavior simply because subjects expect an effect to occur.

Rosenthal effect The phenomenon of experimenters treating subjects differently depending on what they expect from the subjects; also called the *Pygmalion effect.*

Single-blind experiment An experiment in which subjects are not told which of the treatment conditions they are in; a procedure used to control demand characteristics.

Social variables The qualities of the relationships between subjects and experimenters that can influence the results of an experiment.

## REVIEW AND STUDY QUESTIONS

1. What are physical variables in an experiment?

2. How is elimination used as a control procedure? Give two examples of variables that could be controlled by elimination.

3. What is constancy of conditions? Give two examples of variables that could be controlled through constancy of conditions.

4. What is balancing? Give two examples of variables that could be controlled by balancing.

5. You are doing a study at a local school. Because of the way things are scheduled, you can have one small testing room in the morning and another, much larger testing room in the afternoon. If you have two treatment conditions (*A* and *B*), how can you assign subjects to the testing rooms so that the type of room will not lead to confounding in your experiment?

6. What are demand characteristics? How do they affect our data? How can they be controlled?

7. A researcher says, "I want my experiment to be a success. I'm sure my hypothesis is correct, so I'll just give my subjects a couple of hints here and there. You know, maybe a wink now and then if they give a good answer. That way I'll really be able to show that my independent variable had an effect."

   a. How would you convince her that her plan is faulty?
   b. What is a double-blind experiment? Would you recommend that she use it? Why or why not?

8. Dr. L. is planning a large-scale learning experiment. He would like to have 100 rats in one treatment group and another 100 in the other group. Because he needs so many rats, he says, "Well, I can't test all these animals by myself. I'll ask Dr. P. to help me. He can run the animals in the one group while I test the animals in the other group."

   a. Knowing what you know about confounding, is Dr. L.'s solution a good one? What can happen if one experimenter tests all the subjects in one group while another tests all the subjects in another group?
   b. Given what you know about balancing procedures, work out a better plan for Dr. L.

9. When should a cover story be used? When shouldn't one be used? Discuss the ethical problem raised by the use of cover stories.

10. Why is it important that an experimenter behave in the same way toward all subjects in the experiment? What precautions can be taken to ensure that the experimenter does this?

11. In what ways are volunteer subjects different from nonvolunteers? What difference does it make?

12. Find out the names of several experiments that are being conducted in your department this term. Evaluate each name for its potential to bias the sample.

13. Think of two things an experimenter could do to safeguard against fatigue effects during the experiment.

## CRITICAL THINKING EXERCISE

*The myth:* Fridays are different.

*The scientific findings:* Many researchers believe it, but the true answer is unknown.

*The problem:* How could you design a simple test to answer this question about subjects? About researchers?

## ONLINE RESOURCES

Read about Robert Rosenthal's early experiences with experimenter bias at the following website:

http://www.psichi.org/pubs/articles/article_121.aspx

Read about the importance of double-blind procedures to the credibility of "The Afterlife Studies":

http://www.csicop.org/si/show/critique_of_schwartz_et_al.s_after-death_communication_studies/

Learn how "Facilitated Communication" of children with autism was debunked with single- and double-blind studies:

http://www.skeptic.com/eskeptic/06-05-25

## CHAPTER 9

# Basic Between-Subjects Designs

**Selecting and Recruiting Subjects**
Practical Limits
How Many Subjects?

**One Independent Variable: Two-Group Designs**

**Two Independent Groups**
Random Assignment
Experimental Group–Control Group
  Design
Two-Experimental-Groups Design
Forming Two Independent Groups
When to Use a Two-Independent-Groups
  Design

**Two Matched Groups**
Matching Before and After an Experiment
When to Use Two Matched Groups

**Multiple Groups**
Assigning Subjects
Choosing Treatments
Practical Limits

SUMMARY
KEY TERMS
REVIEW AND STUDY QUESTIONS
CRITICAL THINKING EXERCISE
ONLINE RESOURCES

## CHAPTER OBJECTIVES

- Learn how subjects are assigned to conditions of a between-subjects experiment and what random assignment accomplishes

- Learn the elements of simple two-group designs and how to control for confounding

- Learn how to conduct experiments with more than two groups

- Understand why one design is selected over another

To test an experimental hypothesis, a researcher must develop a basic plan or design for the experiment. The experimental design is the general structure of the experiment. It is like the floor plan of a building, which specifies how many rooms there are and how they are connected but says nothing about what is inside the rooms and how they are used. Just as a floor plan describes rooms that can serve many purposes, an experimental design can be used to answer many kinds of research questions. Experiments that test different hypotheses may have the same design. Or, alternatively, the same hypothesis can sometimes be approached through more than one design. The design is simply the general structure of the experiment, not its specific content; the design is made up of things such as the number of treatment conditions and whether the subjects in all conditions are the same or different individuals. The design used in an experiment is determined mainly by the nature of the hypothesis. However, prior research, the kind of information the researcher is seeking, and practical problems in running the experiment also influence choice of design.

Although there are an infinite variety of potential hypotheses, most research questions use a few basic designs. Three aspects of the experiment play the biggest part in determining the design: (1) the number of independent variables, (2) the number of treatment conditions needed to make a fair test of the experimental hypothesis, and (3) whether the same or different subjects are used in each of the treatment conditions. We will look at these aspects of basic research designs. In this chapter and the next, we will look at designs in which different subjects take part in each condition of the experiment. These are called between-subjects designs because we draw conclusions from between-subjects experiments by making comparisons between the behaviors of different groups of subjects. In Chapter 11, we look at within-subjects designs in which the same subjects take part in more than one treatment condition of the experiment. In those designs, we look for changes in behavior within the same group of subjects. But before we discuss the details of specific designs, let us look at the researcher's first important decisions—selecting and recruiting the sample of subjects.

---

## SELECTING AND RECRUITING SUBJECTS

In the context of designing survey research in Chapter 4, you learned about sampling procedures for selecting subjects. In experiments, as in surveys, we rely on samples to test hypotheses. How accurately we can generalize the results of experiments depends on the representativeness of our sample: *The more the sample resembles the whole population, the more likely it is that the behavior of the sample mirrors that of the population.* Some form of random sampling procedure is highly desirable because it greatly increases an experiment's external validity. Ideally, when we take a random sample, every individual in the population has an equal chance of being selected. In practice, this ideal is rarely achieved.

### Practical Limits

As you recruit subjects, you are likely to find that you have to use procedures that do not guarantee a random sample. You might have to recruit all your subjects from a single class or location, resulting in a convenience sample. Sometimes, you may have access to students who are part of a university "subject pool," usually students in introductory psychology or other behavioral science classes who are required to participate in a research experience as part of course requirements. Or, you may have to recruit people from around the campus or outside local business establishments. Students in our classes have found that the lobby of the college library and outside the bookstore or student union can sometimes be good places to find willing subjects. In desperation, students sometimes must resort to asking their friends, family, or co-workers to participate. This sample is likely to be very low in representativeness, because these individuals may share many of the same characteristics and attributes. Asking people you know is risky on several counts. First, it can result in personal conflicts between experimenters and subjects. Second, people you know might not be completely ignorant about the purpose of an experiment that you have been talking about for two weeks. They might also be sensitive to your subtle cues to behave in particular ways. These cues can influence how they respond in the experiment and can lead to erroneous data. And most important, they might feel obliged to participate, which raises ethical questions concerning free choice. But even when we have the time, energy, and resources to do extensive sampling, another difficulty remains. As we discovered in the last chapter, people who volunteer to participate in

"ABOUT THIS EXPERIMENT FOR GENERATING RANDOM NUMBERS — EACH TIME YOU DO IT, IT COMES OUT DIFFERENT."

research might be somewhat different from those who do not. Perhaps we would obtain very different data if we tested everyone regardless of personal choice. Without resorting to coercion, there is no way we can ever guarantee a truly random sample.

Most of the time, our samples must be drawn from subsets of the population, such as the residents of a nursing home in the example from Chapter 4. Our nursing home example, however, dealt with a situation in which we have more individuals available than are needed, but this is not always the case. People are often reluctant to participate in an experiment because they feel it will take too much time.[1] Also, people are often wary of psychological research. At times, individuals seem fearful that the experimenter will uncover very private information. This attitude stems partly from the popularization of Freud's ideas, especially the idea that every action contains an important hidden meaning known only to the trained psychologist. This makes it especially important that we follow ethical guidelines and keep subjects informed of what we are doing.

It can be difficult at times to obtain subjects, but there are some tried-and-true methods for encouraging prospective subjects to volunteer: Make your appeal interesting, nonthreatening, and meaningful. You can emphasize

---

[1] One of the authors recalls scouting for subjects to take part in a brief, on-the-spot perception experiment that lasted about a minute. Prospective subjects often provided elaborate explanations of why they had no time to participate. Their stories usually lasted longer than the actual experiment.

that participating in research can help others and point out that lots of people do it. Pay them if you can and give token gifts (a stick of gum would do) for taking time to hear you out. Some researchers have included a prize drawing for a tangible reward such as a gift certificate or theatre tickets at the conclusion of the research to encourage people to participate. Finally, always assess whether you should ask for volunteers publicly (show of hands) or privately (fill out a form). Try to put yourself in the other's place and ask what would make you most likely to say yes.

## How Many Subjects?

How many subjects are enough for an experiment? Ten? One hundred? There is no simple answer to this question. In later chapters, we will discuss experiments that require only one or two subjects and others that require many more. In between-subjects designs, we want to have more than one or two subjects in each treatment condition. Remember that we use samples of subjects to make inferences about the way the independent variable affects the population. Too small a sample can lead to erroneous results. For instance, if we wanted to know the height of the "average" American adult, we would want a large sample. Samples of two or three people would probably be inadequate even if they were randomly selected. We would hesitate to make statements about millions of people based on such a small sample. Similarly, in an experiment, we might hesitate to make great claims for our independent variable on the basis of a few subjects.

Of course, if everyone were exactly the same, if everyone behaved exactly the same way, we could use samples of one or two subjects with confidence. We would know that the experimental results reflect what we would find if we tested everyone in the population. But we also know that in reality, subjects are not all the same. Our independent variable could affect different subjects in different ways, and different subjects will probably get different scores on the dependent variable. The more responses can vary, the harder it is to get a sample that reflects what goes on in the population. *If individuals in the population are all very similar to one another on the dependent variable, small samples are adequate. When individuals are likely to be quite different, larger samples are needed.* If we take larger samples, we are more likely to obtain individuals who represent the full range of behaviors on the dependent variable—some people who score high, some who score low, and some who score in between. Thus, a larger sample is more likely to mirror the actual state of the population.

Typically, we get slightly different responses from different subjects in an experiment because of individual differences. Subjects' scores should also differ because of the treatment conditions. We expect the behavior of subjects under different treatment conditions to be noticeably different. We use statistical tests to make comparisons of subjects' behavior under different treatment conditions.

When we discuss test results (Part Three), you will see exactly how these procedures work. As we choose our samples, though, certain general characteristics of the statistical procedures shape our decisions. Most statistical procedures we will discuss in this text require computing averages of the results under different treatments. In effect, we ask whether, on the average, our independent variable had an effect. We evaluate the effect relative to the amount of variation we would expect to see among any samples measured on our dependent variable. We are not especially interested in the performance of individual subjects in the experiment; we know that individual scores will differ. The question is whether we see more of a difference if we look at responses obtained under different treatment conditions.

For many students taking this course, statistics were already covered in a previous course. You know already that we use statistical procedures to decide whether the differences we observe between responses under different treatment conditions are significant differences: Are they larger than the differences we would probably see between any groups that we measure on the dependent variable? Are they so unlikely to have happened accidentally that they are noteworthy and require a scientific explanation? From a statistical standpoint, an experiment has less power to detect effects with smaller samples (Cohen, 1988). It is much harder to show that differences between treatment groups are significant when we use a small number of subjects. This is especially true when individual responses are apt to vary a great deal from one subject to another under any circumstances. For that reason, we usually try to have a reasonably large number of subjects in each treatment group.

The number of subjects necessary to detect the effect of an experimental treatment depends, in part, on the size of the effect produced by the independent variable. Effect size is a statistical estimate of the size or magnitude of the treatment effect.[2] The larger the effect size, the fewer subjects needed to detect a treatment effect. If the effects of the independent variable are strong, we should be able to detect them with about 10 to 20 subjects per group. A moderate-sized effect should show up with about 20 to 30 subjects per group. Weaker effects may be detected in larger groups. Of course, these are only rough estimates. If you know in advance the approximate effect size for your independent variable, you can use *power charts* (available in most statistics textbooks) to estimate the minimum number of subjects needed for each treatment group. For example, Herz (1999) tested the effects of caffeine on mood and memory. She knew from past research that she could expect a large effect size from the dose of caffeine (5 mg/kg) she planned to use. From a power chart, she determined that testing 12 subjects in each group would give her a 70% chance of detecting an effect from caffeine. Increasing her sample size to 18 subjects in each group would have increased her chances to 80% (Cohen, 1992). (Formulas for calculating effect sizes are found in

---

[2] Effect size is important in research reports as an estimate of the magnitude of treatment effects found in an experiment after the data are analyzed statistically. Effect sizes can be calculated for results from several different kinds of statistics. We will discuss this further in Part Three. Reporting effect sizes in research reports is recommended in the current *Publication Manual of the American Psychological Association*.

Chapters 13 and 14.) As you have already learned, many other factors besides the number of subjects and the impact of the independent variable can influence the outcome; a larger sample is no guarantee that an experiment will turn out as you expect.

Practical considerations also affect the total number of subjects to be used. You might plan to have 50, but if you can only get 30, that may have to do. If the experiment requires lengthy individual testing sessions, it might not be feasible to run large numbers of subjects. You can use a review of prior research as a guide. If other researchers have had success with 20 subjects, that is probably a reasonable number. As a general rule, it is advisable to have at least 20 subjects in each treatment group; however, most researchers are more comfortable if there are 30 subjects in each group. Smaller numbers make it very difficult to detect an effect of the independent variable unless the effect is huge.

## ONE INDEPENDENT VARIABLE: TWO-GROUP DESIGNS

The simplest experiments are those in which there is only one independent variable. As you know, an experiment must have at least two treatment conditions: The independent variable is manipulated in such a way that at least two levels or treatment conditions are created. When only two treatment conditions are needed, the experimenter may choose to form two separate groups of subjects. This approach is known as the two-group design. There are two variations of the two-group design: One is the two-independent-groups design; the other is the two-matched-groups design. Both use two treatment conditions, but they differ dramatically in how the researcher decides which subjects will take part in each treatment condition.

## TWO INDEPENDENT GROUPS

In the two-independent-groups design, subjects are placed in each of two treatment conditions through random assignment. *In an experiment, subjects are always randomly assigned to treatment conditions.* Even if a researcher cannot use true random selection in deciding who the subjects of an experiment will be, he or she *always* uses random assignment to the treatment conditions. Even when it is not possible to select your subjects entirely at random, the two-independent-groups design can still be used as long as subjects are randomly assigned to each group.

### Random Assignment
Random assignment means that every subject has an equal chance of being placed in any of the treatment conditions. When we use an independent groups design, we use the same unbiased procedures for assigning subjects to groups that are used in random selection of subjects. Putting subject 3 in group *A* should not affect the chances that subject 4 will also be assigned to that group. In an independent groups design, the groups are

"independent" of each other. The makeup of one group has no effect on that of the other.[3]

If subjects are not randomly assigned to treatment groups, confounding can occur. We might inadvertently put all our witty subjects in group *A* and so distort the outcome of the experiment. Random assignment gives us a better chance of forming groups that are roughly the same on all the extraneous variables that might affect our dependent variable. Assigning subjects at random controls for the differences that exist between subjects before the experiment. In short, this method controls for subject variables. Our separate treatment groups will not consist of identical individuals, of course, but any potential differences will be spread out randomly across the conditions of the experiment. Thus, random assignment guards against the possibility that subjects' characteristics will vary systematically along with the independent variable. When there are two treatment conditions, as in the two-independent-groups design, assignment may be made by simply flipping a coin. When there are more than two conditions, we may use a random number table (discussed later in the chapter). These methods eliminate bias; they reduce the chances that our experiment will be confounded because treatment groups are already different when we start the experiment.

Remember that random selection and random assignment are two separate procedures. It is possible to select a random sample from the population but then assign the subjects to groups in a biased way. The reverse is also possible. We can start out with a nonrandom, biased sample of subjects and randomly assign those subjects to our different treatment groups. But the original sample is still biased and might not represent the population we are trying to study. Nonrandom selection affects the external validity of an experiment—that is, how well the findings can be applied to the population and other situations. Random assignment, however, is critical to internal validity. If subjects are not assigned at random, confounding can occur—a selection threat might be present. The experiment will not be internally valid because we will not be sure that the independent variable caused the differences observed across treatment conditions. It could be that the differences we see were created by the way we assigned the subjects to the groups.

Even though the researcher attempts to assign subjects at random, without objective aids the assignments might be biased in subtle ways. For instance, without being aware of it, the experimenter might put all the subjects he or she dislikes into condition *A* because it is the most tedious. The treatment groups would then be different even before the experiment begins. If the groups are already different at the start, it might look as though the experimental manipulation is having some effect, even if it is not. The opposite can also happen. Differences in the treatment groups can mask the effect

---

[3] Sometimes we may have to deviate from this ideal plan. For practical reasons, we may want to have equal numbers of subjects in all treatment groups. That may mean that we have to throw our last few subjects into one group to even up the numbers. We call this *random assignment with constraints*. The assignment is random except for our limitations on numbers per group, equal numbers of men and women per group, and so on.

of the independent variable. Either way, the experiment leads to false conclusions about the effects of the IV.

Randomization was important in a classic study by Kelley (1950). Kelley, who was interested in the effects of people's expectations on their impressions of others, carried out a two-independent-groups experiment. Introductory psychology students were given one of two written descriptions of a guest lecturer before he came to class. Half the students were told the visitor was a "warm" person; half were told he was "cold." Kelley was careful to hand out the descriptions of the lecturer at random. The guest came and led a 20-minute class discussion. After that, students were asked to report their impressions of him. Their ratings differed in ways that indicated that students who expected the lecturer to be warm reacted more favorably to him.

Why was it important to hand out the descriptions of the lecturer at random? What might have happened if, say, all the "warm" descriptions were given out first? For one thing, students who sit in different parts of the classroom might be different. If we gave out all the "warm" descriptions first, they might go to all the students who sit in the front of the class. Perhaps these students sit up front because they are more interested in the material or because they arrive earlier. In any case, their reactions to the class might be different from those of people who sit in the back. When it comes time to rate a guest speaker, these attitudes could alter the ratings as much as the descriptions that were given. Again, unless subjects are assigned randomly to different conditions of the experiment, differences among subjects can confound the results of the experiment.

In Box 9.1, we return to Brady's (1958) study of ulcers in monkeys. You will recall from Chapter 2 that this study raised several ethical concerns. It also raised methodological questions because the researcher failed to assign subjects at random to the two treatment conditions.

## Experimental Group–Control Group Design

To assess the impact of the independent variable, we must have at least two different treatment conditions so that we can compare the effect of different values of the independent variable. At times, one condition is an experimental condition and the other is a control condition. In the experimental condition, we apply a particular value of our independent variable to the subjects and measure the dependent variable. The subjects in an experimental condition are called an experimental group. The control condition is used to determine the value of the dependent variable without an experimental manipulation of the independent variable. The subjects in a control condition are called a control group. In the control condition, we carry out exactly the same procedures that are followed in the experimental condition, except for the experimental manipulation.

Sometimes the control condition is a "no-treatment" condition. We simply measure subjects' responses without trying to alter them in any way. A no-treatment control condition tells us how subjects ordinarily perform on the dependent measure. We can use this control condition as a point of comparison; we can see whether subjects' performance in the experimental

## BOX **9.1**    Ulcers in Executive Monkeys: A Confounding Variable

Brady's (1958) study of ulcers in executive monkeys has received a great deal of publicity over the years. Recall that the monkeys were divided into two groups. An executive group was given control of a button connected to an apparatus that produced electric shock. The executive's task was to prevent a painful electric shock by hitting the control button at least once every 20 seconds. Each nonexecutive was coupled (or yoked) with an executive. If the executive failed to hit the button in time, the nonexecutive would also receive a shock. The nonexecutives had no control over the shock; only the executives could prevent it.

The independent variable in Brady's experiment was control over the shock. The executives had control; the nonexecutives did not. The dependent variable was the development of gastrointestinal ulcers. Brady hypothesized that monkeys with the responsibility of remaining vigilant and preventing the shock would be more apt to develop ulcers. In other words, their "executive" responsibilities in the experiment would be stressful; they would develop ulcers just as a hard-driving human executive might. After the experimental phase of the experiment ended, Brady sacrificed the monkeys and studied their tissues for signs of ulcers. As predicted, the executives had many ulcers; the nonexecutives did not.

On the face of it, his experimental procedure appears sound. Brady devised a controlled task that would presumably be more stressful to one treatment group than the other. Executives and nonexecutives were coupled so that both received the same total number of shocks. The only difference was the degree of control the monkeys had over the shocks. Nevertheless, the study has been severely criticized because Brady's treatment groups were not formed using random assignment. Instead, Brady had used a pretest to determine which monkey in each pair could learn to avoid the shock more quickly, and this monkey was then made the executive.

Therefore, the study was not internally valid; the way the treatment groups were formed introduced a confounding variable. We cannot be sure that the requirements of the executive job produced ulcers. The executive monkeys might have been more sensitive to the shock, or they might have differed in other ways from the nonexecutives before the experiment began. They could, for example, have been more prone to ulcers under any circumstances. In fact, in another study using rats as subjects, Weiss (1972) demonstrated that lack of control over the shocks was apt to be more stressful than being in charge of things—if subjects were assigned to treatment conditions at random.

Science Source/Photo Researchers

condition was better, worse, or the same as that of subjects who were not exposed to any experimental manipulation. For instance, we could compare test performance of students who engaged in 15 minutes of aerobic exercise before the exam with the performance of students who did not exercise. Without the no-treatment group, we cannot say whether the experimental subjects did better or worse than usual.

Whenever researchers use a no-treatment control condition, however, they must be on the lookout for potential confounds. You always need to think about what the subjects in the control group are doing while subjects in the experimental group are being treated. Whenever possible, the behavior of the control group subjects should be "controlled" so that they are not inadvertently engaging in behaviors that would affect the results of the experiment. For instance, in the exercise experiment you would need to make sure that the subjects in the no-treatment control condition are not spending their 15 minutes studying for their exam while the other students are exercising! Even if aerobic exercise generally did improve test performance, higher test scores for the experimental subjects are likely to be obscured by improved performance from the control group as well—because the control group studied an extra 15 minutes.

This experiment is now confounded by a maturation threat to internal validity; the no-treatment control subjects have undergone internal cognitive changes (i.e., they increased their knowledge of the exam material) that the experimental group did not. Remember what we said in the beginning of this section: In the control condition, we carry out exactly the same procedures that are followed in the experimental condition, except for the experimental manipulation. Very often, control conditions involve carefully arranging conditions that control for what control group subjects are doing. In the exercise experiment, we might decide to create a situation in which the control group is engaged in a similar, but nonaerobic, activity that would not be expected to have any effect on how well subjects will perform on the upcoming test.

Vohs and Schooler (2008, experiment 1) faced this problem when they investigated whether inducing people to believe that their behavior was predetermined (i.e., a result of genetic and environmental factors) would encourage them to be more likely to cheat when the opportunity arose. To induce a belief in predetermination, the researchers randomly assigned half of their subjects to read a passage from *The Astonishing Hypothesis,* a book about human consciousness written by Francis Crick (one of the discoverers of the molecular structure of DNA). The passage asserts that the human belief that behavior results from *free will* is illusory and explains that the belief comes about because of the architecture of the brain itself. The other half of the subjects were assigned to a control condition in which they read a different passage from the book—a neutral passage that discussed consciousness but did not mention free will or predetermination at all. After they read their assigned passages, subjects were asked to solve 20 math problems on a computer (e.g., $1 + 8 + 18 - 12 + 19 - 7 + 17 - 2 + 8 - 4 = ?$). Subjects were told to work out the problems on their own, but the computer was programmed so that subjects could easily cheat by having the computer show them the correct answers. As predicted, subjects exposed to the predetermined behavior passage cheated significantly more than did subjects who read the neutral control passage.

Without the control condition, the experiment would have lacked internal validity because plausible alternative explanations for the increased cheating could not be ruled out. For example, it could be argued that completing any reading assignment beforehand might make it less likely that people will cheat. Or, perhaps reading a difficult passage makes completing math problems seem relatively easy, so cheating wasn't necessary to complete the task easily. By comparing the behavior of subjects in the experimental and control conditions, the researchers could be much more certain that the increased cheating occurred because of the specific information contained in the predetermination passage.

The type of control group you select will depend on what you want to show, but remember that the only difference between the experimental and control groups should be the treatment itself. In the last chapter, we discussed the placebo effect and how researchers control for it in drug experiments. The placebo group in a drug study is an excellent example of a true control group. In drug studies, both the experimental and placebo groups are treated identically: They follow identical procedures, they receive seemingly identical treatments, and they have the same expectations. The only difference is that the experimental group is receiving the actual drug, whereas the placebo group is not. The closer our control groups can approximate a placebo group, the less the chances of accidental confounding, and the more internal validity our experiment will have. Experiments using placebos, however, can sometimes present ethical problems (see Box 9.2).

## Two-Experimental-Groups Design

It may not always be possible or even desirable to use a treatment condition in which subjects are not exposed to some value of the independent variable. Control group experiments are most useful in the first stages of experimentation on a variable. But once it has been established that an IV produces some effect not ordinarily present, researchers will often use a two-experimental-groups design to gather more precise information. A two-experimental-groups design can be used to look at behavioral differences that occur when subjects are exposed to two different values or levels of the IV. For example, we could test whether a highly violent music video produces more aggressiveness than a music video with a low level of violence. Or we could investigate whether 15 minutes of aerobic exercise is better than 10 minutes. Or we could test whether reading a predetermination passage would produce more cheating than reading a passage about free will (see Vohs & Schooler, 2008, experiment 2).

A well-designed study using two experimental groups was carried out by Anderson and Dill (2000). They argued that playing violent video games would increase both aggressive thoughts and aggressive behavior. Male and female college student subjects were brought into the laboratory where they

BOX **9.2**   **Ethical Dilemmas in Human Research Using Control Groups**

Researchers use the guidelines provided by law and by the APA to guide their ethical decisions. In Chapter 2, we discussed some of the ethical decisions that must be made: whether to use deception, whether the information gained from an experiment justifies the risk of harm to participants, and so on. Sometimes researchers face another kind of ethical decision. In some experiments, the need for a control group actually creates an ethical dilemma.

Testing the efficacy of psychotherapeutic procedures and medical and drug treatments often requires a control group so that effects of the treatment can be compared with the absence of treatment. In drug-testing experiments, a special type of control group (called a placebo group) is used. The placebo group is the prototype of a good control group: a control condition in which subjects are treated exactly the same as subjects who are in the experimental group, except for the presence of the IV. Subjects in the experimental group get some dosage of a drug, but subjects in the placebo group get something that looks like a drug but is actually a placebo (a pill containing an inert substance or an injection of a saline solution). Physiological effects on both groups of subjects are measured and compared to see whether the drug produced the effects. At some time, however, the drug needs to be tested on people who have the medical problem the drug is designed to help. This need creates the ethical dilemma. When the placebo procedure is carried out on people who actually need the benefits expected from the medication, the

researcher—for the sake of scientific advancement—might in effect be denying treatment to people who need it. A common solution to this ethical dilemma is to compare a new drug with one that is currently being used. If the new drug performs as well or better, then positive results have been obtained.

A similar problem occurs in psychological research. Testing the efficacy of a psychotherapeutic treatment for mental disorders sometimes requires comparing its results against a group of people with the disorder who have received no treatment. The control group for a psychotherapy study is frequently a waiting-list control group—people who are waiting their turn for treatment. If the therapy proves beneficial, does the researcher then have the responsibility to treat the control group as well? It is sometimes argued that the control group would not normally be receiving treatment, so they are not being denied a benefit. But this is an ethical decision the researcher must make. More and more often, researchers are deciding in favor of offering treatment to control group subjects in experiments in which the treatment has been shown to be beneficial.

Dugas et al. (2003) were faced with this decision when they used a waiting-list control group in an experiment to test a cognitive-behavioral intervention to reduce Generalized Anxiety Disorder (GAD). Community volunteers diagnosed with GAD were randomly assigned to a program of 14 weeks of once-a-week group therapy that combined awareness training, reevaluation of beliefs about worry, and problem-solving strategies or to a waiting-list control group. Without a control group, there would have been no way of knowing whether individuals receiving the intervention were being helped by it. (Every 3 weeks during the original sessions, the diagnosing clinician called members of the waiting-list group to monitor their state.) As predicted, individuals receiving the cognitive-behavioral therapy had a significant reduction of symptoms, and the treatment gains were maintained over a 2-year follow-up period. At the conclusion of the 14-week experimental sessions, the group-therapy program was also offered to the individuals on the waiting list.

Jeanell Norvell/istockphoto.com

played one of two video games for 15 minutes: *Wolfenstein 3D* (extremely violent content) or *Myst* (a nonviolent adventure game). After playing one of the games, the subjects were instructed in a competitive reaction-time task in which the goal was to press a button faster than an unseen opponent. In the reaction-time task, they were told to administer a noise blast (between 55 and 100 decibels) every time their opponent lost. Subjects could choose the intensity and duration of the noise blasts. You may have already guessed that subjects were not really playing against a real opponent—instead, their wins and losses and their "opponent's" wins and losses were carefully controlled by a computer. Out of 25 trials, subjects won 13 and lost 12. After a loss, all subjects received the same random sequence of noise blasts. As predicted, subjects in the violent game condition administered significantly longer (but not more intense) blasts to their opponent than did subjects in the nonviolent game condition.

## Forming Two Independent Groups

Let us look a little more closely at the randomization procedures used to form two independent groups. In an experiment that has now become classic, Zajonc, Heingartner, and Herman (1969) tested the hypothesis that cockroaches would run faster through a simple maze when other roaches were present than when they had to run alone. The hypothesis is based on the principle of social facilitation in human beings: In the presence of an audience, the performance of some behaviors improves. If social facilitation operates for cockroaches as it does for people, the cockroaches should do better in some mazes when other roaches are present. We can test this hypothesis ourselves using two independent groups.[4] One group, the experimental group, runs through the maze in the presence of an audience. The control group runs with no one watching. The dependent variable is the average time it takes each group to run the maze. Just like human subjects, the cockroaches must be assigned at random to each condition.

We begin by assembling our cockroaches. As we take each roach out of its cage, we flip a coin to decide whether it goes into the experimental or the control group. By assigning subjects at random, we hope to create two groups that are roughly equivalent on important subject variables that could influence the outcome of the experiment. One such variable is the weight of each individual subject; heavy subjects might run more slowly than light ones under any circumstances. Weight, then, is a potential source of confounding in this experiment. Table 9.1 shows the hypothetical weights of our subjects assigned at random to the two treatment conditions.

As you can see, the weights of individual subjects differ. We would expect this because subjects differ from one another. If we look at each of the groups as a whole, however, we find that their average weights (represented by $\overline{X}$) are about the same. Even though individual roaches in each group weigh different amounts, the average weight of the groups is about

---

[4]Zajonc, Heingartner, and Herman's actual experiment had a more complicated design to include a test of the effect of drive level as well as the presence of an audience.

FIGURE **9.1** Robert Zajonc (1923–2008).

TABLE **9.1**

Cockroaches randomly assigned to treatment conditions: Hypothetical weights

| Experimental Group | | Control Group | |
|---|---|---|---|
| Subject Number | Hypothetical Weight (gm) | Subject Number | Hypothetical Weight (gm) |
| $S_1$ | 1.59 | $S_6$ | 3.52 |
| $S_2$ | 1.26 | $S_7$ | 1.57 |
| $S_3$ | 1.34 | $S_8$ | 2.31 |
| $S_4$ | 3.68 | $S_9$ | 1.31 |
| $S_5$ | 2.49 | $S_{10}$ | 1.18 |
| $N = 5$ | | $N = 5$ | |
| $\overline{X}_E = 2.072$ | | $\overline{X}_C = 1.978$ | |

Note: Randomization produced two groups of very similar average weight ($\overline{X}_E$ is about the same as $\overline{X}_C$).

© Cengage Learning

equal. If we chose to, we could evaluate whether the small difference between the groups is statistically significant. We would find that although the groups are not identical, the difference between them is not significant; that is, it is not enough to merit concern. We can accept the groups as equivalent enough for our purposes. Assigning our subjects to the groups at random, we created two groups that are equivalent on an important subject variable. We will not have confounding caused by weight in this experiment.

When we assign subjects at random, we expect to form groups that are roughly the same on any subject variables that could affect our dependent variable. This is important because we might not always be aware of every variable that should be controlled. Sometimes we are aware of variables but do not have the tools, the time, or the resources to measure them. Assigning subjects at random controls for differences we have not identified but that might somehow bias the study.

The more subjects we have available to assign to treatment conditions, the better the chances are that randomization will lead to equivalent groups of subjects. For example, if we have only two cockroaches available, one light and one heavy (like $S_2$ and $S_4$ in Table 9.1), there is no chance at all of forming similar groups. We will always have one heavy group and one light group. With 10 cockroaches (as in Table 9.1), our chances of attaining groups with similar weights is increased. As we add additional subjects, the odds are even better that random assignment will produce similar groups. This becomes particularly important when we consider humans. We expect people to differ on many characteristics that could potentially affect their responses on the dependent variable. The more subjects we have, the better our chances are of achieving groups that are equivalent on a number of different characteristics.

## When to Use a Two-Independent-Groups Design

How do we decide whether the two-independent-groups design is appropriate for an experiment? We begin by looking at the hypothesis. If there is only one independent variable, the two-independent-groups approach is a good choice if the hypothesis can be tested with two treatment conditions. In an experiment such as the one on cockroaches, two groups made sense. We simply wanted to see whether cockroaches would run faster with or without an audience. When we run the experiment, we carefully assign subjects to the treatment conditions at random.

When we use the two-independent-groups design, we assume that randomization is successful. We assume that when we start the experiment, the treatment groups are about the same on all the extraneous subject variables that might affect the outcome. Unfortunately, this is not always the way things turn out.

In our cockroach experiment, we assigned subjects to the treatment groups at random. As you saw in Table 9.1, the random assignment produced two groups of very similar average weight. But suppose we do the experiment again. We again take the cockroaches from their cages and flip a coin to decide which group to put them in. The hypothetical weights of these new groups are shown in Table 9.2. What is wrong? We assigned our subjects at random, but the control group looks much heavier than the experimental group. How can this be? Well, you know that random assignment means every subject has an equal chance of being assigned to either treatment

TABLE **9.2**

## Cockroaches randomly assigned to treatment conditions

| Experimental Group | | Control Group | |
|---|---|---|---|
| Subject Number | Hypothetical Weight (gm) | Subject Number | Hypothetical Weight (gm) |
| $S_{10}$ | 1.18 | $S_4$ | 3.68 |
| $S_2$ | 1.26 | $S_6$ | 3.52 |
| $S_3$ | 1.34 | $S_8$ | 2.31 |
| $S_9$ | 1.31 | $S_5$ | 2.49 |
| $S_7$ | 1.57 | $S_1$ | 1.59 |
| $N = 5$ | | $N = 5$ | |
| $\overline{X}_E = 1.332$ | | $\overline{X}_C = 2.718$ | |

Note: Randomization produced two groups of very different weights.

© Cengage Learning

condition. There is always a chance that treatment groups will end up being very different on some subject variables, and this is particularly true when we have a small number of subjects in each condition.[5]

In this instance our random assignment did not produce comparable groups. Just by chance, the control group turned out to be heavy compared with the experimental group. Because the dependent variable in this experiment is running speed, the difference in weight could contaminate the results. The way things turned out here, the weight of the two groups is a confounding variable. If there is a difference in the running speed of the two groups, we cannot be sure whether it is the result of the audience or the difference in weight. The difference in running speed can be explained equally well by either variable.

## TWO MATCHED GROUPS

Randomization does not guarantee that treatment groups will be comparable on all the relevant extraneous subject variables. Researchers therefore sometimes use another two-group procedure, the two-matched-groups design. In this design, there are also two groups of subjects, but the researcher assigns them to groups by matching or equating them on a characteristic that will

---

[5] You can test this principle, called *Bernoulli's law of large numbers,* by flipping a coin. The laws of chance predict equal odds (50/50) for heads or tails each time you flip; this means that half your flips should end up heads and half tails. But, if you flipped a coin only 4 times, it would not be unusual to get three heads and one tails or even four heads and zero tails. However, as you increase the number of coin flips, your chances of getting an equal number of heads and tails improve. If you flipped a coin 100 times, your chances of getting an equal number of heads and tails is much better than if you only flipped it 4 times. The same law applies to random assignment to treatment conditions: The likelihood that treatment groups will be equivalent on extraneous subject variables increases as the number of subjects increases.

probably affect the dependent variable. The researcher forms the groups in such a way that they are sure to be comparable on an extraneous variable that might otherwise produce confounding.

## Matching Before and After an Experiment

To form matched groups, subjects must be measured on the extraneous variable that will be used for the matching. Table 9.3 shows the way our cockroaches might be divided into two groups matched on weight. Once the roaches have been weighed, we separate them into pairs. The members of each pair are selected so that they have similar weights. For instance, the first pair is made up of subjects 2 and 10. Subject 2 weighs 1.26 grams; subject 10 weighs 1.18 grams. Although members of each pair are not exactly equal in weight, they are closer to each other than to any other cockroaches in the sample. When it is not possible to form pairs of subjects that are identical on the matching variable, the researcher must decide how much of a discrepancy will be tolerated. A difference of 0.8 grams might be acceptable, but a difference of 2 grams might not. We obviously want to make good enough matches to ensure that our groups are not significantly different on the matching variable. If there is no suitable match for an individual in the sample, that individual must be eliminated from the study.

After all the pairs have been formed, we randomly assign one member of each pair to a treatment condition; then, the remaining member is placed in the other condition. We can do this simply by flipping a coin. It is very important to put the members of each pair into the treatment conditions at random. If we do not, we could create a new source of confounding—exactly what we are trying to avoid.

TABLE **9.3**

### Cockroaches assigned to two groups matched on weight

| Pair | Experimental Group | | Control Group | |
| | Subject Number | Hypothetical Weight (gm) | Subject Number | Hypothetical Weight (gm) |
|---|---|---|---|---|
| a | $S_2$ | 1.26 | $S_{10}$ | 1.18 |
| b | $S_3$ | 1.34 | $S_9$ | 1.31 |
| c | $S_1$ | 1.59 | $S_7$ | 1.57 |
| d | $S_8$ | 2.31 | $S_5$ | 2.49 |
| e | $S_6$ | 3.52 | $S_4$ | 3.68 |
| $N = 5$ | | | $N = 5$ | |
| $\overline{X}_E = 2.004$ | | | $\overline{X}_C = 2.046$ | |

Note: The matched groups have very similar average weights ($\overline{X}_E$ is about the same as $\overline{X}_C$). Within each pair, the members are assigned to the treatment conditions at random. One member of each pair is randomly chosen to be in the control group; the other member is placed in the experimental group.

In our cockroach example, the matching is done before the experiment is run. In some experiments, it might not be feasible to do the matching beforehand. Suppose we need to match our subjects on intelligence. We might not be able to give an intelligence test, score it, match and assign subjects to groups, and run the actual experiment in a single block of time. We must know the test scores before we can do the matching, so we might need a separate testing session just to give the test. In these situations, we could proceed differently. We make the initial assignment to conditions at random and run the experiment with two randomly assigned groups of subjects that might or might not be comparable on our matching variable. Our subjects take part in the treatment conditions as usual. However, we also give them the intelligence test (that is, we measure them on the matching variable). When the experiment is over, we use the intelligence test scores to match the subjects across the two groups, discarding those subjects in each group who cannot be matched.

We can do this in three ways: We may use precision matching, in which we insist that the members of the matched pairs have identical scores. A more common procedure is range matching, in which we require that the members of a pair fall within a previously specified range of scores. The process of range matching subjects after the experiment is run is illustrated in Table 9.4. In the table, you can see that subjects are considered matched if their scores fall within 3 points of each other. The choice of range is arbitrary. The smaller the range, however, the more similar the subjects must be on the matching variable. If we set the range at 50 points on an intelligence test, we would obviously gain little through matching.

As you can see from the table, range matching after the experiment is run can create problems. Some subjects will have to be discarded if no match is available, and this could raise questions about the representativeness of the remaining subjects. Subjects who can or cannot be matched could differ in important ways that will affect their scores on the dependent variable. In using matching, it is therefore advisable to sample as many subjects as possible.

TABLE **9.4**

Matching subjects after the experiment: Pairing of scores on the matching variable, intelligence

| Experimental Group | | Control Group | |
|---|---|---|---|
| Subject Number | IQ | IQ | Subject Number |
| $S_1$ | 109 | 91 | $S_6$ |
| $S_2$ | 94 | 100 | $S_7$ |
| $S_3$ | 116 | 111 | $S_8$ |
| $S_4$ | 102 | 63 | $S_9$ |
| $S_5$ | 133 | 115 | $S_{10}$ |

Note: Connecting lines represent final pairs of subjects. Subjects 5 and 9 must be discarded because there are no suitable matches for them in the sample.

© Cengage Learning

Testing many subjects will minimize the chances that no match will exist within the sample. If we must discard subjects, the net result is that the total number available for analysis is smaller than we had planned. Having less data reduces the chance of detecting the effect of the independent variable. For this reason, matching before running the experiment is preferable to matching after it.

A third matching procedure, rank-ordered matching, is sometimes used. The subjects are simply rank ordered by their scores on the matching variable, and subjects with adjacent scores then become a matched pair. With rank-ordered matching, we do not specify an acceptable range between members of each pair. The benefit of rank-ordered matching is that unless you have to discard a subject because you have an uneven number of scores, all subjects are typically used. The downside is that there might be unacceptably large differences between members of a pair on the matching variable. This would certainly have been the case if we had used rank-ordered matching to form pairs from subjects in Table 9.4.

## When to Use Two Matched Groups

Whether to match at all is an important question. The advantages are clear: By matching on a variable that is likely to have a strong effect on the dependent variable, we can eliminate one possible source of confounding. We do not need to assume that our treatment groups are comparable on an important extraneous variable; we can make them comparable through matching.

In some cases, matching can also make the effects of the independent variable easier to detect even if random assignment has worked successfully and confounding is not a concern. Students who have already taken a statistics course will recall that when we match, we use statistical procedures that differ from those used with independent groups. (These procedures are covered in Part Three of the text.) It is important to know that statistics for matched groups allow us to make comparisons based on the differences between the members of each of our matched pairs of subjects. Because some effects of individual differences are controlled within each pair, the impact of the independent variable is clearer. We are able to compare the responses of rather similar subjects who were tested under different treatment conditions. Statistical procedures for independent groups, however, require that we combine, or "pool," all the data from each treatment group and make comparisons between group averages. This makes it somewhat harder to detect the effect of our independent variable: We are forced to look at treatment effects along with the effects of individual differences. If our independent variable has an effect, we are more likely to detect it in our data if we have used matching.[6]

Matching was used successfully in a recent study by Devlin (Devlin, 2005). She investigated the use of a training program designed for

[6] The appropriate statistical test for the two matched groups of cockroaches would be a *t* test for matched groups (also called a dependent groups or within-subjects *t* test). The same experiment conducted with two independent groups would be analyzed with an independent groups *t* test (also called a between-subjects *t* test). The *t* test for matched groups is a more powerful test and is more likely to result in significant differences between the groups (see Chapter 14).

teacher-paraprofessional teams to increase the ability of elementary school students with disabilities to function when mainstreamed into regular general education classes. From an initial pool of elementary students with disabilities ranging from mild to severe, Devlin was able to match 6 pairs of severely disabled students on (1) intellectual level and (2) major characteristics identified as holding the disabled children back from participating alongside nondisabled students in general education classes (such as communication issues or behavioral problems). Devlin selected these matching variables because they were highly correlated with interaction and engagement in regular classroom activities. The members of the matched pairs were randomly assigned to either the experimental group or a control group. At the end of the experiment, students whose teachers had received the special training program showed significantly more engagement in class activities and more interaction with their teachers than students in the control group. Without matching, it probably would have required a much larger sample of students and teacher-paraprofessional teams for the improvement to be detected.

Matching procedures are especially useful when we have very small numbers of subjects because there is a greater chance that randomization will produce groups that are dissimilar. This risk is not as great when we have large numbers of subjects available. As pointed out before, the larger the treatment groups, the better the chances are that randomization will lead to similar groups of subjects and the less need there may be for matching.

There are advantages in using the matched groups design, so why not always use it? By matching on a variable such as weight in the cockroach experiment, we can guarantee that our treatment groups will be similar on at least one extraneous variable that is likely to impact the dependent variable, speed. Unfortunately, there are also potential disadvantages to using this procedure. When we match, it is essential that we match on the basis of an extraneous variable that is *highly related to the dependent variable of the experiment.* In an experiment on weight loss, for example, it would make sense to begin by matching subjects on weight. Subjects who are already heavy might be more likely to lose weight during the experiment. It would not make sense to match subjects on weight in an experiment on how to teach spelling to 12-year-olds because it is difficult to see any clear connection between weight and spelling ability. It would be more appropriate to match on another variable, such as intelligence; intelligence does affect the ability to spell. We might want to match on intelligence to avoid getting two groups of subjects with different IQs who would learn spelling at different rates regardless of the teaching method.

Unfortunately, it is not always easy to know what variables are the best to use for matching. If we match on a variable that is strongly correlated with the dependent variable, then matching can increase the researcher's ability to detect changes. But if we match on a variable that is not strongly correlated with the dependent variable, it will be much more difficult to detect the effect of experimental manipulations. This is true because of the special statistical procedures used for data from matched groups (see Chapter 14). There is another potential problem when matching is used. Matching on one variable could accidentally result in larger differences in other extraneous variables that could dampen effects produced by the independent variable. To know whether to use two matched groups or two independent groups, it is necessary to search the research literature on your topic. If others have consistently used matching to control an important extraneous variable, you will probably want to match your subjects, too. Or, if your literature search uncovers a subject variable that is strongly related to your dependent variable, you might consider matching your subjects on that variable.

# MULTIPLE GROUPS

We have seen how we can test a variety of hypotheses by using two groups of subjects. We run subjects through two sets of treatment conditions so that we can see how their behaviors differ when the independent variable has different values. We can use two groups of subjects who are assigned to the treatment conditions at random or are matched on a relevant subject variable. Sometimes, however, it takes more than two treatment conditions to make a good test of a hypothesis: In an experiment to test the effectiveness of a new drug, we might need to test several different dosages. A simple comparison between the presence and absence of the drug would be too crude to assess its effects adequately because the amount of a drug makes a difference in how well it works.

In situations in which the amount or degree of the independent variable is important, we usually need a multiple-groups design—a design in which there are more than two groups of subjects and each group is run through a different treatment condition. One of the treatment conditions may be a control condition in which subjects receive the zero value of the independent variable. The most commonly used multiple-groups design is the multiple-independent-groups design in which the subjects are assigned to the different treatment conditions at random. It's also possible to use multiple groups and matched subjects. The basic procedures are the same as those used in the two-matched-groups design, except that there are more than two treatment conditions. The more treatment conditions there are, of course, the more difficult it will be to match subjects.

## Assigning Subjects

When there are only two treatment conditions, assigning subjects randomly to each condition is a simple matter. But how do we deal with the problem of assigning subjects to several treatment conditions in such a way that no bias results? One way would be to use a random number table (see Appendix B). Suppose we are set to run an experiment with three different treatment conditions and 30 subjects. We could first pick a starting point in the random number table in an unbiased way, for instance, by closing our eyes and pointing. Because there are three treatment conditions, we then read vertically (or horizontally—it does not matter) looking for the numbers 1, 2, and 3 in the table. Whatever order they appear in (2, 3, 1, 3, for example) would be the order in which we assign subjects to the three treatment conditions. The first volunteer would be assigned to treatment condition 2; the second volunteer would be assigned to treatment condition 3; the third to condition 1; and so on.

We could proceed this way until we have assigned all the available subjects to the three conditions of the experiment. (Box 9.3 shows another procedure, block randomization, that works very well for multiple-groups designs.)

Suppose we want to design an experiment to test the hypothesis that exercise improves exam performance. Everyday experience tells us that exam answers seem to come to us more easily when we are wide-awake and attentive, and exercise can be a way of increasing our attentiveness and concentration. We suspect that some amount of exercise is probably beneficial to performance—but how much? If 15 minutes is beneficial, perhaps 30 minutes or more might be even better. Because we are interested in the effects of different levels of the independent variable, we could test our hypothesis with three groups of subjects—one control group and two experimental groups.

---

## BOX **9.3** Block Randomization

Using the random number table works fairly well; however, because we have followed a random sequence, the number of subjects in each treatment group will not necessarily be the same. For 30 subjects, we might find 14 in condition 1, 9 in condition 2, and only 7 in condition 3. To obtain equal numbers of subjects in all treatment conditions, psychologists use a sophisticated procedure called block randomization.

Basically, the researcher begins the process of randomization on paper by creating treatment blocks. If there are three different treatment conditions in the experiment, each treatment block contains the three conditions listed in random order. As subjects sign up for the experiment, the researcher fills each successive treatment block. The more blocks she or he can fill, the more subjects there will be in each treatment condition.

Table 9.5 shows a block randomization design created to guarantee five subjects per condition for an experiment with three treatment conditions. Note that there are five blocks, A, B, C, D, and E, and each of the three conditions is represented once per block. The order of the treatments within each block comes from the random number table. To set up a block, pick a spot at random from the random number table. Look for the number 1, 2, or 3. Whichever occurs first is the first treatment in that block. Continue down the random number table until you find a different number between 1 and 3. This will be the second treatment in the block. Because each treatment can be used only once per block, the last number is the one we have not used yet.

Then create a second treatment block in exactly the same way. Repeat the process for each treatment block. Every additional block we can fill with subjects adds one subject to each treatment condition. Through block randomization, we thus create a scheme by which subjects can be assigned to conditions at random while still ensuring equal numbers across conditions.

Here we have described the process for an experiment with three conditions. However, the same procedures apply for any number of treatment conditions. Simply set up blocks in which each treatment occurs once in a random order. For an experiment with four conditions, each block must contain the four conditions in random order. A five-condition experiment would have five conditions per block, and so on. The total number of blocks determines the number of subjects in each treatment group. The more blocks you fill, the larger your treatment groups are.

### TABLE **9.5**

Example of block randomization in a three-condition experiment

| Block A | | Block B | | Block C | | Block D | | Block E | |
|---------|---|---------|---|---------|---|---------|---|---------|---|
| $S_1$ | 2 | $S_4$ | 2 | $S_7$ | 3 | $S_{10}$ | 1 | $S_{13}$ | 2 |
| $S_2$ | 1 | $S_5$ | 1 | $S_8$ | 2 | $S_{11}$ | 3 | $S_{14}$ | 1 |
| $S_3$ | 3 | $S_6$ | 3 | $S_9$ | 1 | $S_{12}$ | 2 | $S_{15}$ | 3 |

Note: Here we have five subjects per condition. To have more subjects per condition, successive blocks are filled as subjects ($S_n$) sign up for the experiment. The order of treatments within blocks is random.

© Cengage Learning

The experiment would be quite simple to conduct. Exercise is our independent variable and exam performance is our dependent variable. Exercise could be operationally defined as walking on a treadmill set to a speed of 2 mph. A speed of 2 mph is not a very strenuous pace for healthy individuals. The operational definition here is important. There might be differences between exercising on a treadmill and other forms of aerobic exercise that could be explored in the future. Our dependent variable, performance, can be operationally defined as the percent of correct answers on an exam.

The control group (C) does not exercise at all; the first experimental group ($E_1$) walks on the treadmill for 15 minutes; the second experimental group ($E_2$) walks for 30 minutes. Assume that the hypothesis is confirmed: The more subjects exercise, the better their exam performance. Our hypothetical results are illustrated in Figure 9.2, which reflects an average increase in performance as the amount of exercise increases.

We might be convinced that exercise enhances performance. But let us try just one more experiment. This time we will have four groups, one control and three experimental groups. The hypothetical outcome of this experiment is illustrated in Figure 9.3. Again, we see that moderate amounts of exercise appear to enhance productivity. However, something different seems to be happening to group $E_3$: It exercised the longest, but its performance is low relative to the other groups. Although the lower amounts of exercise seem to increase exam performance, the higher amount seems to inhibit it. These fictitious results resemble many actual research findings (see review by Anderson, 1990) in which physiological arousal and performance show an "inverted-U relationship." That is, if scores were graphed (as in Figure 9.3), they would result in a curve that resembles an inverted letter U. As we found in our hypothetical experiment, up to a certain point, increasing arousal stimulates better performance; after that point, increasing the arousal results in performance decrements.

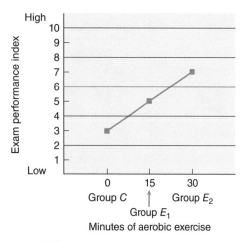

FIGURE **9.2** Exam performance as a function of the minutes of exercise performed (fictitious data from a three-group experiment).
© Cengage Learning

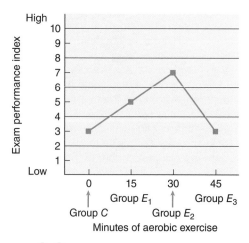

FIGURE **9.3** Exam performance as a function of the minutes of exercise performed (fictitious data from a four-group experiment).
© Cengage Learning

Because different values of the same independent variable can produce different effects, researchers often test more than two levels of an independent variable. By using more than two conditions, researchers can often get a better picture of how the independent variable operates. They need to test such variables across a wide range of values to get a complete understanding of how the variables work.

## Choosing Treatments

What if we decide that we need more than two treatment conditions? How do we know how many to use? Some variables have an infinite number of possible values; we could not test them all even if we wanted to. We might be able to create many different conditions, but using all of them might not make sense. Frequently, an experimenter will select treatment conditions that are proportional, such as drug doses of, say, 5, 10, and 15 milligrams or exercise periods of 15, 30, and 45 minutes. It is possible to do experiments with conditions that are not proportional, and sometimes that is the only possible way. Remember the illumination experiment that used 75- and 150-watt bulbs for the normal and bright conditions? If you wanted an intermediate illumination condition, you would have to choose 100 watts, because light bulbs only come in a limited selection of watts. Many researchers, however, prefer to be able to make statements about conditions that are proportional.

When you think about using a multiple-groups design, always think in terms of the hypothesis you are testing. The principal question you should ask is this: What will I gain by adding these extra conditions to the experiment? If two groups are all that are necessary to test our hypothesis, then it is more economical to use a two-group design, even though a multiple-groups design is possible. As a general rule: Select the simplest design that will make an adequate test of your hypothesis.

## Practical Limits

As you set up experiments, you will make decisions about which comparisons will provide the most appropriate test of the hypothesis. An experiment that includes several levels of the independent variable can often yield more information than one that includes only two groups. However, practical considerations also affect choice of design. The multiple-groups procedure assumes that treatment groups are formed by random assignment. Thus, there will be as many different treatment groups in the experiment as there are levels of the independent variable. If you have five levels of the independent variable, you will need five groups of subjects. It might be difficult to find enough subjects to make this design feasible. Running additional levels also takes more time, and the statistical procedures are more complicated than those used with the two-group design. Thus, it makes sense to think through all the advantages and disadvantages of the multiple-groups design before you begin your experiment. A review of the experimental literature in the topic area should guide you. If prior researchers have consistently used two-group designs to compare only opposite values of the independent variable, you might want to do the same. If others have used additional levels to gather information, however, this may be the most appropriate strategy.

Sometimes researchers conduct a pilot study to pretest selected levels of an independent variable before conducting the actual experiment. A pilot study is like a mini-experiment in which treatments are tested on a few subjects to see whether the levels seem to be appropriate or not. Pilot studies are also a good way to work out any bugs in the procedures of an experiment before the real experiment is underway. A pilot study allows you to make changes before you invest the time and resources in a large-scale experiment.

## SUMMARY

The design of an experiment is its general structure—the experimenter's plan for testing the hypothesis—not the experiment's specific content. The researcher decides on the *experimental design* mainly on the basis of three factors: (1) the number of independent variables in the hypothesis, (2) the number of treatment conditions needed to make a fair test of the hypothesis, and (3) whether the same or different subjects are used in each of the treatment conditions.

A basic assumption behind each experimental design is that subjects selected for the experiment are typical of the population they represent. The number of subjects needed in an experiment can depend on factors such as the amount of variability we would expect among subjects' scores and the *effect size* of the IV. After subjects have been selected for the experiment, *random assignment* is used to place them in different groups of the experiment. *Between-subjects designs* are those in which different subjects take part in each condition of the experiment; we draw conclusions by making comparisons between the behaviors of different groups of subjects. The simplest experimental design is the *two-group design*. We looked at two types of between-subjects designs with two treatment groups: two independent groups and two matched groups.

The *two-independent-groups design* is used when one independent variable must be tested at two treatment levels or values. Sometimes one of the treatment conditions is a *control condition* in which the subjects in the *control group* receive the zero value of the independent variable; a *placebo group* is the classic example of a good control group. When a control group is used, the second condition is an *experimental condition* in which the subjects are given some nonzero value of the independent variable. Other times, a *two-experimental-groups design* is used in which each *experimental group* receives a different (nonzero) value of the independent variable. The independent-groups design is based on the assumption that subjects are assigned at random; as long as a sufficient number of subjects is used, we assume that randomization was successful.

Sometimes, however, especially when the total number of subjects is small, we do not want to rely on randomization. Even with random assignment, treatment groups sometimes start out being different from each other in important ways. If treatment groups are different on a variable related to the dependent variable of the experiment, the result could be confounding. Instead of relying on randomization, we might want to use the *two-matched-groups design*, in which we select a variable that is highly related to the dependent variable and measure subjects on that variable. For a two-group experiment, we form pairs of subjects having similar scores on the matching variable and then randomly assign one member of each pair to one condition of the experiment. The remaining member of each pair is placed in the other treatment condition. One of three types of matching procedures can be used: *precision matching, range matching,* or *rank-ordered matching.* Matching is advantageous because we can guarantee that groups start out the same on variables that matter. If the matching variable is strongly related to the DV, matching can make treatment effects easier to detect statistically. However, there are also disadvantages: We do not always know what we should use as our matching variable. If the variable is not strongly related to the DV, matching can actually work against us—making it more difficult to see whether the independent variable had an effect.

At times, we might need more than two treatment conditions to test an experimental hypothesis. A *multiple-groups design* serves this purpose. In a *multiple-independent-groups design,* there are more than two levels of the independent variable and subjects are assigned to treatment conditions at random. *Block randomization* can be used to ensure that each condition has an equal number of subjects. With several treatment conditions, researchers can look at the effects of different values of the independent variable and see whether low, medium, and high values of a variable produce increasing changes in the dependent variable. Researchers can also detect more complex patterns. For instance, some variables might produce little change at low and middle values but a lot of change at extreme values. Although we can get additional information from a multiple-groups design, it is not always practical or necessary to do so. For some experimental hypotheses, a comparison of just two values of the independent variable is sufficient. Researchers sometimes conduct a *pilot study* to pretest selected levels of an independent variable.

## KEY TERMS

**Between-subjects design** A design in which different subjects take part in each condition of the experiment.

**Block randomization** A process of randomization that first creates treatment blocks containing one random order of the conditions in the experiment; subjects are then assigned to fill each successive treatment block.

**Control condition** A condition in which subjects receive a zero value of the independent variable.

**Control group** The subjects in a control condition.

**Effect size** A statistical estimate of the size or magnitude of the treatment effect(s).

**Experimental condition** A treatment condition in which the researcher applies a particular value of

an independent variable to subjects and then measures the dependent variable; in an experimental group–control group design, the group that receives some value of the independent variable.

**Experimental design** The general structure of an experiment (but not its specific content).

**Experimental group** The subjects in an experimental condition.

**Multiple-groups design** A between-subjects design with one independent variable, in which there are more than two treatment conditions.

**Multiple-independent-groups design** The most commonly used multiple-groups design in which the subjects are assigned to the different treatment conditions at random.

Pilot study A mini-experiment using only a few subjects to pretest selected levels of an independent variable before conducting the actual experiment.

Placebo group In drug testing, a control condition in which subjects are treated exactly the same as subjects who are in the experimental group, except for the presence of the actual drug; the prototype of a good control group.

Precision matching Creating pairs whose subjects have identical scores on the matching variable.

Random assignment The technique of assigning subjects to treatments so that each subject has an equal chance of being assigned to each treatment condition.

Range matching Creating pairs of subjects whose scores on the matching variable fall within a previously specified range of scores.

Rank-ordered matching Creating matched pairs by placing subjects in order of their scores on the matching variable; subjects with adjacent scores become pairs.

Two-experimental-groups design A design in which two groups of subjects are exposed to different levels of the independent variable.

Two-group design The simplest experimental design, used when only two treatment conditions are needed.

Two-independent-groups design An experimental design in which subjects are placed in each of two treatment conditions through random assignment.

Two-matched-groups design An experimental design with two treatment conditions and with subjects who are matched on a subject variable thought to be highly related to the dependent variable.

## REVIEW AND STUDY QUESTIONS

1. What do we mean when we say that the *experimental design* is like the floor plan of a building?

2. What guidelines are used to determine the number of subjects to use in an experiment?

3. In a between-subjects design, why is it important to assign subjects to each treatment condition at random?

4. A researcher wanted to test the effect that riding the subway has on mental health. She formed two groups of subjects, an experimental group and a control group. The experimental group rode the subway for 60 minutes every morning. The control group jogged for an equal period of time. At the end of one month, both groups were measured on a scale of adjustment and well-being. The control group was found to be better adjusted than the experimental group. Do you accept the conclusion that riding the subway damages mental health? Why or why not?

5. A skeptical student tells you that it's silly to bother with a control group. After all, you're really only interested in what the experimental group does. How would you convince the student otherwise?

6. If people stand closer together, they will communicate better. How would you test this hypothesis? How many treatment conditions would you need? Would it be possible to test this hypothesis with more than one design?

7. People who have known each other for a long time may communicate better than people who have known each other for a short time. Imagine you are carrying out the study suggested in question 6. All your subjects know each other, but for varying lengths of time. How can you make sure that the length of time that subjects have known each other will not be a confounding variable in your study?

8. Describe a two-matched-groups design. How is the matching done?

9. A watched pot never boils. What design can you use to test this notion? How many treatment conditions do you need?

10. A researcher would like to match subjects on weight for an experiment on weight control. The weights of each subject in the sample are shown in the table below.

| Subject Number | Weight | Subject Number | Weight |
|----------------|--------|----------------|--------|
| $S_1$ | 115 | $S_9$ | 122 |
| $S_2$ | 185 | $S_{10}$ | 160 |
| $S_3$ | 163 | $S_{11}$ | 159 |
| $S_4$ | 122 | $S_{12}$ | 154 |
| $S_5$ | 165 | $S_{13}$ | 143 |
| $S_6$ | 183 | $S_{14}$ | 143 |
| $S_7$ | 184 | $S_{15}$ | 138 |
| $S_8$ | 115 | $S_{16}$ | 137 |

Match them into pairs and form one experimental and one control group by using random assignment. Carry out the procedure using precision matching, range matching, and rank-ordered matching.

11. Referring back to question 10, how did the outcomes of precision, range, and rank-ordered matching differ? What are the pros and cons of using each procedure?

12. Explain the advantages of using a multiple-groups design rather than a two-group design.

## CRITICAL THINKING EXERCISE

*The myth:* No news is good news.

*The scientific findings:* Unknown, but possibly true.

*The problem:* Imagine that researchers conducted a two-group experiment to test the hypothesis that "no news is good news." While spending 20 minutes in a waiting room, subjects in one condition were given an interesting news story to read, whereas subjects in the other condition were not given anything to read. Later, subjects were asked to make judgments about human nature. The news group made more positive judgments than the no-news group. The researchers claimed that they had demonstrated that the maxim was false: Any news is better than no news. List two confounding variables and describe how each (rather than the IV) might explain the results.

## ONLINE RESOURCES

Generate your own random numbers at

www.randomizer.org/form.htm

Try the Research Methods Workshop on True Experiments at

http://www.wadsworth.com/psychology_d/templates/studentresources/workshops/workshops.html

CHAPTER **10**

# Between-Subjects Factorial Designs

**More Than One Independent Variable**
Looking for Main Effects
Looking for Interactions

**Laying Out a Factorial Design**
Describing the Design
Factor Labeling Methods

**A Research Example**
Understanding Effects from Factorial
    Designs

**Choosing a Between-Subjects Design**

SUMMARY
KEY TERMS
REVIEW AND STUDY QUESTIONS
CRITICAL THINKING EXERCISE
ONLINE RESOURCES

## CHAPTER OBJECTIVES

- Learn how to test more than one independent variable in the same experiment
- Learn about main effects and interactions between variables
- Learn how to diagram and label factorial experiments
- Understand how to interpret effects from factorial experiments

In the last chapter, we saw how a variety of hypotheses about a single independent variable can be tested by using two or more groups of subjects. We run different groups of subjects through two or more sets of treatment conditions so that we can see how their behaviors differ when the independent variable has different values. We can use groups of subjects who are simply assigned to the treatment conditions at random or we can match them first on a relevant subject variable and then randomly assign them to different treatment conditions. In this chapter, we will study another type of research design—the factorial design. Like two-group and multiple-groups designs, factorial experiments can be carried out using the between-subjects approach: Different groups of subjects participate in the different treatment conditions of the experiment. When we want to explore more than one independent variable in the same experiment, we use a factorial design.

---

## MORE THAN ONE INDEPENDENT VARIABLE

All the designs we have examined so far have tested only one independent variable. But in real life, variables rarely occur alone. It can often be more appropriate to look at more than one variable in the same experiment. Suppose we wanted to see whether talking to plants actually makes them grow better. Like any other hypothesis, this one would have to be tested in a rigorous, controlled fashion. We could set up a simple experiment in which talking is the independent variable. But we might also want to know whether music is beneficial to plants. We could run another experiment in which music is the independent variable. *This approach is very inefficient;* we might need twice as many plants and perhaps twice as much time to carry out two experiments rather than one. It also has another disadvantage: A relationship could exist between the effects of music and talking. Perhaps plants that get conversation do not need music, or maybe they prefer music to conversation. There is no way to look for these kinds of relationships if we study music and conversation separately. We need another kind of experimental design, one that enables us to look at the effects of more than one independent variable at a time. Experiments with multiple independent variables are efficient and provide more information than experiments with one independent variable, so they are the preferred design of most experimental psychologists.

Designs in which we study two or more independent variables at the same time are called factorial designs. The independent variables in these designs are called factors, and each factor will have two or more values or levels. The simplest factorial design has only two factors and is called a two-factor experiment. The results we get from a factorial experiment give us two kinds of information: They give us information about the effects of each independent variable in the experiment, called main effects. They also enable us to answer this question: How does the influence of one independent variable affect the influence of another in the experiment?

## Looking for Main Effects

A main effect is the action of a single independent variable in an experiment. When we measure a main effect, we are asking: How much did the change in this one independent variable change subjects' behavior? A main effect is simply a change in behavior associated with a change in the value of a single independent variable within the experiment.

When more than one independent variable exists, each one has a main effect. There are as many main effects as there are factors. These main effects, however, might or might not be important enough to be statistically significant. To tell if they are, we need to carry out the appropriate statistical tests, such as analysis of variance (ANOVA), which is described in Chapter 14. When we compute statistical tests for factorial experiments, we first evaluate the separate impact of each independent variable in the experiment. We test whether each main effect is statistically significant or not.

Our plant study, for example, would have two factors—talking and music. We would want to know about the main effects of both factors. A factorial experiment allows us to know if each factor alone produces a *significant* effect on behavior.

Factor 1: How much did changes in talking affect plant growth?

Factor 2: How much did changes in music affect plant growth?

We would conduct statistical tests to determine if one or both factors produced significant main effects. (Notice that this provides us with exactly the same information we would get if we ran two separate experiments on plant growth—one on the effects of talking and another on the effects of music.) In addition to determining the main effects for each factor, statistical tests conducted on factorial experiments also tell us whether the two factors operate independently or not.

## Looking for Interactions

A factorial design allows us to test for relationships between the effects of different independent variables. Earlier, we posed the hypothesis that plants that are spoken to might not need music. Alternatively, of course, plants that get both speech and music might show truly spectacular growth. These possibilities are examples of how effects produced by two factors might influence each other. When the effects of one factor depend on another factor, we have an interaction.

An interaction is present if the effect of one independent variable changes across the levels of another independent variable. For instance, we could suppose that music might be helpful to plants that have not been spoken to at all, but the same music might have no effect on plants that have been exposed to speech. The impact of one independent variable (music) might change at different levels of the other (no speech versus speech). In other words, there could be an interaction between these two variables. Figure 10.1 depicts this interaction.

Whenever an interaction is present in a two-factor experiment, we cannot get a complete picture of the results of the experiment without considering both factors because *the effects of one factor will change depending on the levels of the other.* This is an important point that is often missed by beginning researchers. The presence of an interaction between two factors also tells us that the main effects of one factor will be altered by the other factor; their effects will depend on which levels of both factors we are interpreting. An interaction tells us that there could be limits or exceptions to the main effects of one or more factors. Thus, we say that an interaction *qualifies* the main effects.

Let us look at a different example. A couple of drinks at a party can make you feel relaxed and happy. If you are upset or anxious, a sleeping pill might help you to sleep. Alone, a little alcohol or a sleeping pill might not be especially harmful. But, take the two together, and you could end up dead or in a coma. This is because these two substances interact.

Let's examine this further. Imagine that on an "increased drowsiness scale" ranging from 0 (no increase in drowsiness) to 10 (coma or death), a couple of alcoholic drinks—but no sleeping pill—increase drowsiness to an average of 4 on our imaginary scale. And imagine that taking a sleeping pill—but no alcohol—increases drowsiness to about 3 on our scale. What would you expect to happen if someone had a few drinks and a sleeping pill? If the two variables did not interact, we would simply add up the main effects of a couple of drinks (drowsiness = 4) and a sleeping pill (drowsiness = 3), and we would expect to

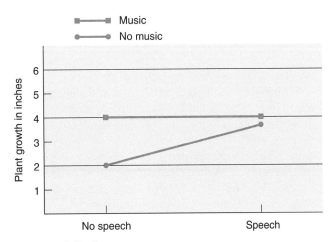

FIGURE **10.1** Hypothetical results of an experiment showing music ✕ speech interaction.

© Cengage Learning

TABLE **10.1**

Mean drowsiness in an experiment without an interaction

|  | Drinks | |
|---|---|---|
|  | No | Yes |
| Sleeping pill | | |
| No | 0 | 3 |
| Yes | 4 | 7 |

© Cengage Learning

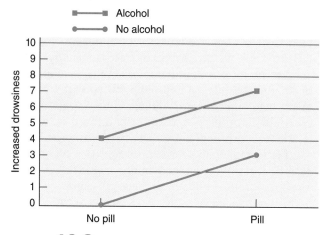

FIGURE **10.2** Hypothetical results testing the effects of alcohol and sleeping pills on drowsiness—without an interaction.

© Cengage Learning

see drowsiness increase to around 7 (see Table 10.1). These effects are graphed in Figure 10.2, which represents the results when the main effects of the two factors are independent and do not interact.

But, when the effects of alcohol and sleeping pills are interactive, as they are in real life, the effects are different. Instead, the effects of alcohol on drowsiness are altered, in this instance *increased,* by the other variable, a sleeping pill.[1] The two variables interact, and the effect that is produced is quite a bit stronger (9) than the combined effects of both variables alone (7); see Table 10.2. A drug interaction such as this is a classic example of an interaction: The effect of one drug changes at different levels of the other drug. These effects are graphed in Figure 10.3.

In a factorial experiment, the number of possible interactions depends on the number of independent variables in the experiment. When two independent

---

[1] Or, you could say that the effect of a sleeping pill is altered, in this instance increased, by the other variable, alcohol—both interpretations are correct.

TABLE **10.2**

Mean drowsiness in an experiment with an interaction

|  | Drinks | |
| --- | --- | --- |
|  | No | Yes |
| Sleeping pill |  |  |
| No | 0 | 3 |
| Yes | 4 | 9 |

© Cengage Learning

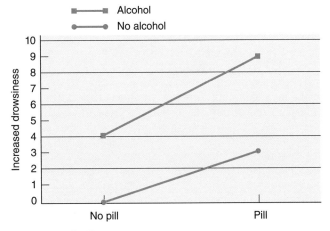

FIGURE **10.3** Hypothetical results testing the effects of alcohol and sleeping pills on drowsiness—with an interaction.

© Cengage Learning

variables are present, there is only one possible interaction.[2] The two independent variables may interact with each other. When there are more than two independent variables in a factorial experiment, the picture becomes more complex; we can get higher-order interactions that involve more than two variables at a time. In a three-factor experiment, it is possible to get an interaction among all three independent variables. The action of each factor could be influenced by the values of the other two. Driver experience, alcohol, and degree of darkness, for example, could interact in causing traffic accidents. In an experiment with three independent variables, it is also possible that any two factors, but not the third, could interact just as they might in a two-factor experiment.

As with main effects, we measure interactions quantitatively through statistical tests such as ANOVA—we evaluate their significance. It is possible to run an experiment and find that an interaction between variables is significant even though the main effects are not. We could also get significant main

---

[2] The picture is a bit more complicated when we have the same subjects in more than one treatment condition of the experiment.

effects with no significant interaction. It is also possible to have an interaction along with one or more significant main effects. All possible combinations of outcomes can occur. We will look at some of these possibilities more closely later in the chapter. Box 10.1 presents an actual research problem that can be approached through a factorial design.

## LAYING OUT A FACTORIAL DESIGN

We can use a factorial design to approach the research problem outlined in Box 10.1. We can study the effects of name type and name length in the same study. Type of name is one factor; length of name is another. We will

---

**BOX 10.1**    **What's in a Name: A Factorial Approach**

Does the length of your first name say something about you to others? Apparently it can. Mehrabian and Piercy (1993a) conducted an experiment to test whether people assign different kinds of personality characteristics to others based solely on their first name. In one experiment, the researchers had people rate the characteristics of people with various given names or nicknames. Based partly on previous findings from their own work and that of other researchers, they hypothesized that nicknames would receive more favorable judgments than given first names—at least on certain kinds of traits. The researchers predicted that nicknames would be rated more positively for characteristics like warmth, friendliness, and popularity. However, they predicted that given first names would be judged higher in traits related to intelligence and trustworthiness than nicknames would. Were they right? Yes. A person with a nickname like Liz, for example, would probably be rated as friendlier and more popular than a person with the given name Elizabeth, but Elizabeth would probably be rated more intelligent and trustworthy.

Mehrabian and Piercy noticed, however, that nicknames were usually shorter than given names. This led them to wonder whether name length, by itself, could have similar effects. In a second experiment (1993b), they used only given names—no nicknames—and asked subjects to infer the characteristics of people with each of 858 given names of various lengths. They predicted that shorter names would be associated with greater warmth and similar traits, but longer names would be judged higher in traits like intelligence and trustworthiness. In general, their hypotheses (particularly for male names) were supported.

What would happen if, instead of conducting two separate experiments, we combined both independent variables in a factorial experiment? We could call one factor "type of name," and compare two levels: given names and nicknames. The other factor could be "name length," and again we could use two levels: short or long. We would need to operationally define each of the variables and select valid names for each condition. Then we could use procedures similar to those of Mehrabian and Piercy and have subjects judge each kind of name on a number of traits.

What would we gain by a factorial experiment? It would be more efficient to do one rather than two separate experiments. We could still learn whether each factor, independently, produced main effects. In addition, however, we could learn whether the two independent variables interact when they are combined—information we cannot get if we do two separate experiments. Perhaps name length operates differently for given names than for nicknames.

Have you ever noticed that lots of longer nicknames end in the letters $y$, $ie$, or $i$ ("Timmy," "Jeri," "Terry," and "Susie," for instance)? Maybe nicknames that are diminutive forms of given names make people seem just as unintelligent as very short nicknames do. Perhaps the short nickname "Kim" and the longer "Kimmy" would be judged equally unintelligent—less intelligent than the given name "Kimberly." Maybe the nicknames "Jim," "Jimmy," and even "the Jimster" would be judged equally warm and friendly—more warm and friendly than the short given name "James." You can probably come up with other potential interactions between name type and name length that are just as plausible. The point to be made here is that unless a factorial experiment is conducted, interaction effects will not be discovered.

use only two levels (values) of each factor. It helps to look at our design graphically as we set it up. If you can translate your thinking about an experiment into a simple diagram, called a *design matrix,* you will find it easier to understand what you are testing, what kind of design you are using, and how many treatment conditions are required.[3] Figure 10.4 illustrates our two-factor experiment. Your diagram will be more complex if you are working with more than two factors or more than two levels of each factor.

We begin by diagramming the basic components of the design, the two factors (Figure 10.4, step 1). Notice that we label each factor with a number—type of name is factor 1, and length of name is factor 2. These numbers can be used later as a shorthand way of referring to the factors in the final report. We predicted that the type of name has an effect; given names and nicknames will be the two values we select for factor 1. We indicate "given name" and "nickname" in our diagram (Figure 10.4, step 2). We are also planning to use two levels of the length factor. Our question about the effect of name length at this point is simply whether length has any effect on judgments of traits. We can indicate the two levels of the length factor in the diagram simply by "short" and "long" (Figure 10.4, step 3); we can always explore more subtle differences in future studies. We now draw the four separate *cells* of the matrix that represent the four treatment conditions needed in the experiment (Figure 10.4, step 4). If we assign our subjects to the conditions at random, each cell also represents a different group of randomly assigned subjects. Some subjects will rate given names that are short; others will rate given names that are long, and so on. Using a design matrix to lay out a factorial design is a quick and easy way to create a visual image of your experimental design.

## Describing the Design

When we are describing the design of a factorial experiment in a report, however, we cannot use a design matrix. Instead, there are special techniques used to describe factorial designs in a way that corresponds to the statistical analyses that are needed to analyze them. Let's use the name experiment to illustrate these techniques.

The name experiment is a two-factor experiment because it has two independent variables, and each independent variable has two levels. This design can be written in shorthand form as a 2 × 2 (read as "two by two") factorial design. This shorthand notation tells us several things about the experiment it describes. First, the numbers tell us the number of factors involved. Here there are two numbers (2 and 2); each number refers to a different factor. Hence, this experiment has two factors. The numerical value of each number tells us how many levels each factor has. If we have a 2 × 2 design, we automatically know that each of the experiment's two factors has two levels. We also know that the experiment has four different conditions (the product of 2 × 2).

---

[3] You can use the design matrix later as you do the statistical tests. Values of the dependent variable—for instance, the average ratings for the traits "warm" and "intelligent"—can be recorded in the cells (see also Part Three). This provides a picture of the treatment effects in each condition, making interpretation easier.

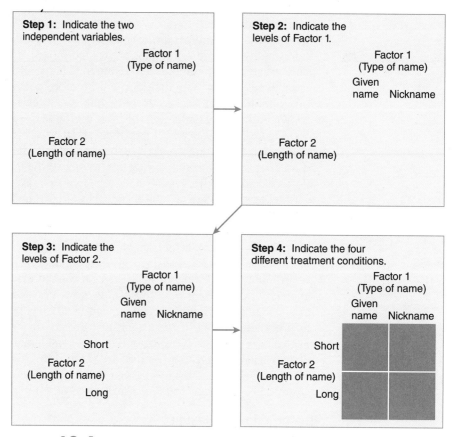

FIGURE **10.4** Diagramming a design matrix for the two-factor experiment described in Box 10.1.
© Cengage Learning

When factorial designs are described in research reports, the shorthand notation system is usually expanded to include the variable names. This system makes it easy to understand a complete research design at a glance. There are several ways to do this, and you will find examples of each of these methods in the research literature. For simplicity, we will illustrate how the 2 × 2 name experiment would be described using each different method, but the same methods can also be used to describe larger factorial designs.

## Factor Labeling Methods

The names of each factor are placed in parentheses following the numerical notations. The name of the factor represented by the first digit would be the first name you would list; the name of the second factor would be the second. Just like the numbers used in shorthand notation, the factor labels are separated by ×. Because different subjects have been assigned to each of the four treatment conditions, the experiment is a between-subjects factorial design. (Notice the differences in capitalization in the different methods; variable names are only capitalized if they are separated by ×.)

*Example 1:* 2 × 2 (Type of Name × Length of Name) between-subjects factorial design

*Example 2:* 2 (type of name) × 2 (length of name) between-subjects factorial design

These methods also can be expanded to include the factor levels. You can include the factor name (capitalized) and its levels (lowercase), separated by a colon, or you can simply use the levels (lowercase).

*Example 3:* 2 × 2 (Type of Name: given, nickname × Length of Name: short, long) between-subjects factorial design

*Example 4:* 2 (given name or nickname) × 2 (short or long name) between-subjects factorial design

Although our example involves only two factors, it is possible to design factorial experiments with any number of factors. The number of factors will determine how the design is characterized—an experiment involving three independent variables, for example, is called a three-factor experiment. The shorthand notation indicates additional information. If an experiment is referred to as a "2 × 3 × 2 factorial design," we immediately know several things about it. Three digits are mentioned (2, 3, and 2), so we know this experiment involves three factors. The numerical value of each digit tells us the number of levels of each of the factors. We know that the first factor has two levels, the second has three, and the third has two. We also know that this experiment has 12 separate conditions (the product of 2 × 3 × 2). Figure 10.5 presents a design matrix for a 2 × 3 × 2 experiment.

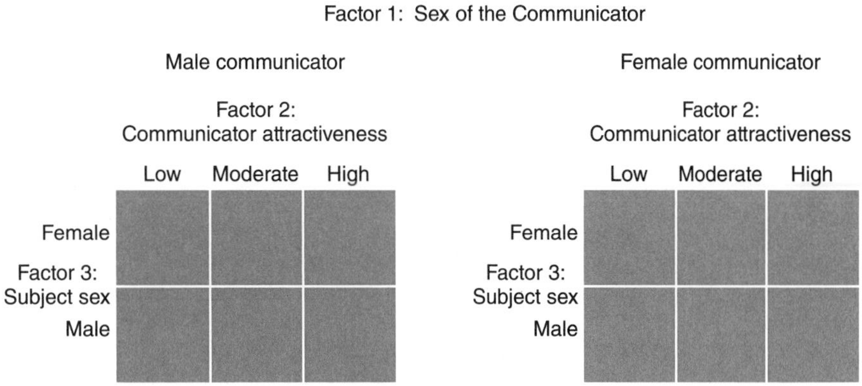

Factor 1: Sex of the Communicator

FIGURE **10.5** Diagram of a 2 × 3 × 2 factorial design. The diagram represents an experiment in which there are three independent variables: the sex of the person delivering a persuasive communication, the attractiveness of that communicator, and the sex of the subjects being exposed to the communication. The hypothesis of this experiment is as follows: Subjects will be more persuaded by a message delivered by a more attractive communicator, but only when the communicator is the opposite sex from the subject.
© Cengage Learning

## A RESEARCH EXAMPLE

Let us take a closer look at an experimental example of a 2 × 2 factorial experiment. This experiment produced one significant main effect along with a significant interaction. Pliner and Chaiken (1990) were interested in the relationship between gender and eating behavior. It is well known that, in our culture at least, young women show a greater concern with eating lightly and being slim than do men. Even though research has shown that young men do not really prefer slim over average-weight women, many American women seem obsessed with being thin. Anorexia and bulimia, potentially life-threatening eating disorders, can be an end product of this distorted view of the "ideal" female body image.

Pliner and Chaiken believe that thinness and light eating have come to be viewed as appropriate sex-role behaviors for women, making them appear more feminine than their heavy-eating counterparts. If this is the case, women should be especially prone to eat lightly in situations where they want to appear most feminine—when they are with an attractive person of the opposite sex! Young men, the authors argue, don't worry about how much they eat in front of others because it does not affect the kind of impression they will make.

The authors conducted an experiment that tested the following hypothesis: Women will eat less in the presence of an opposite-sex partner than in the presence of another of the same sex, but men's eating behavior will not be influenced by their partner's gender. Pliner and Chaiken predicted that two variables—subject sex and partner sex—would interact in their effects on eating behavior. Let us look at the variables in their experiment.

What must be manipulated to test the hypothesis? First, the behavior of women must be compared with that of men. The first independent variable is the sex of the subject. Notice that this factor is a subject variable. The "manipulation" is simply the selection process; subjects are automatically assigned to an experimental group based on their gender. Second, the sex of the subject's partner must be manipulated. The second independent variable is the gender of a second person with whom the subjects are paired: a partner of the same or opposite sex. Here the experimenters manipulate which type of partner subjects will get.

Individual subjects in the experiment were led to believe that they and a partner (actually a *confederate* who had been trained to play this role) were taking part in a study on the effects of hunger on task performance. They had been asked not to eat anything the day of the experiment so that they would be hungry when they arrived. Each subject was told that he or she and the partner had been assigned to the "full" condition of the experiment and would be asked to eat as much as it took for them to feel comfortably full while working on the experimental task. Crackers with various toppings were provided. Early in the session, the subject and partner were interviewed together by the experimenter. This interview was designed to give subjects the impression that their partner was single and socially attractive.[4]

---

[4] For simplicity, we are including only effects that occurred when subjects actually perceived their partner to be socially attractive.

The dependent variable in this experiment was eating behavior. The researchers measured eating by counting how many crackers each subject ate. To make sure that the partner's eating did not confound the experiment, the partner always ate 15 crackers (about 315 calories). The researchers' hypothesis would be supported if a significant interaction between the two factors was obtained: if women ate fewer crackers in the presence of an opposite-sex partner than with a same-sex partner, but men's eating did not differ. Before we explore an interaction between the factors, however, let us look at the main effects produced by each factor alone.

Remember that in a factorial experiment we always look at the effect of each independent variable separately as well as looking for an interaction. These main effects explore each factor by itself, ignoring the other. These are like the effects we would get if we had conducted two separate experiments—one testing the effect of subject sex on eating and one testing the effect of partner sex on eating.

Did the first factor, subject sex, produce any effects on eating? Yes. Statistical tests indicated that the experiment produced a significant main effect for this factor. (We will have more to say about statistical tests in Part Three.) If we just consider how many crackers men and women tended to eat in the experiment, we find that men ate more crackers on the average than women (about 13.5 versus 10.9). This is not too surprising; we expect men to eat more than women do.

Did the second factor, same- or opposite-sex partner, have any effect by itself on eating? No, the statistical tests confirmed that, in general, it did not make any difference whether the partner was the same or opposite sex. If we combine the data for all subjects in the experiment, we find that, on the average, people ate about the same amount of crackers whether their partners were the same sex or the opposite sex. There were a few more men than women in the experiment, which brought the average for the entire group up slightly, so the average number of crackers eaten in the presence of either type of partner was about 12.3.

Finally, we look at the interaction (see Figure 10.6). Recall that the interaction describes the effects of one factor (male versus female subjects) at different levels of the other (same-sex versus opposite-sex partners). The interaction asks whether men's or women's eating habits change with different kinds of partners. Was Pliner and Chaiken's hypothesis supported? Yes, statistical tests indicated that there was a significant interaction between subject sex and type of partner. Men ate about the same amount whether their partner was the same or the opposite sex. But, as expected, women varied their eating depending on the gender of their partner. If their partner was the same sex, they ate more than if their partner was the opposite sex.

Study Figure 10.6 until you can understand the three effects described earlier as they are depicted in the graph:

1. In general, men ate more crackers than women. If we averaged the male subjects' scores (the two points on the left side of the graph), the mean would be about 13.5 crackers for men. If we averaged the

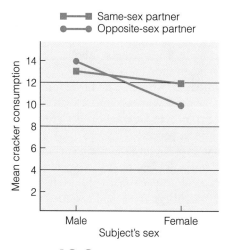

FIGURE **10.6** Cracker consumption by women and men in the presence of a same-sex or opposite-sex partner.
From results reported by Pliner and Chaiken (1990).

female subjects' scores (the two points on the right), the mean would be about 10.9 crackers for women. Statistical analysis indicated that the average number of crackers eaten by men was *significantly* higher than the average number of crackers eaten by women; thus, there was a significant main effect for the subject-sex factor in the experiment.

2. In general, the type of partner did not alter the number of crackers eaten. When we averaged the scores representing the two points for same-sex partners (using the points on the left and right ends of that line on the graph) and averaged the scores representing the two points for opposite-sex partners (using the endpoints of that line), the two means did not differ significantly. On the average, same-sex and opposite-sex partners ate approximately the same number of crackers (about 12.3), and the statistical analysis indicated that there was not a significant main effect for this factor in the experiment.

3. There was a significant interaction between the sex of the subject and the type of partner. *The two lines are not parallel, indicating that the effects on eating produced by the type of partner were not the same for men and women.* Eating behavior depended on both the gender of the subject and the type of partner. The left side of the graph tells you that men actually ate slightly more crackers with an opposite-sex partner than with a same-sex partner. Compare this with the right side of the graph. For women, the effects of the type of partner were entirely different; as the researchers predicted, women ate significantly less with an opposite-sex partner than they did with a same-sex partner.

## Understanding Effects from Factorial Designs

Pliner and Chaiken's (1990) study came out just as they predicted, but a variety of other patterns of results might have occurred. Many different patterns of results may be observed in a factorial experiment, and each requires a different interpretation. Figures 10.7 to 10.13 present additional possibilities for this

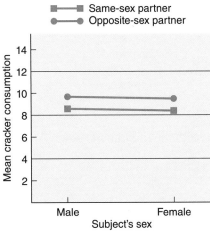

(a) No significant main effects or interaction

FIGURE **10.7** Hypothetical outcome—no significant main effect or interaction.
© Cengage Learning

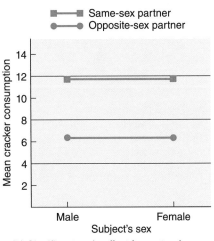

(b) Significant main effect for partner's sex

FIGURE **10.8** Hypothetical outcome—significant main effect for partner's sex.
© Cengage Learning

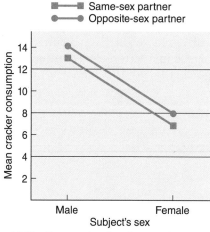

(c) Significant main effect for sex of subject

FIGURE **10.9** Hypothetical outcome—significant main effect for sex of subject.
© Cengage Learning

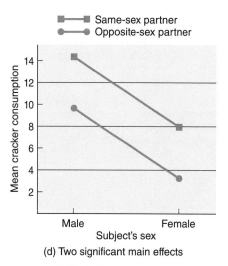

(d) Two significant main effects

FIGURE **10.10** Hypothetical outcome—two significant main effects.
© Cengage Learning

experiment to help you understand the difference between main effects and inter-actions. Keep in mind, though, that these figures do not represent actual data.

In Figure 10.7, the experimental data show no significant main effects or interactions. This is the way the data would look when graphed if the subject's sex had not influenced eating and if subjects ate about the same amount regardless of the type of partner they had. This would mean that the

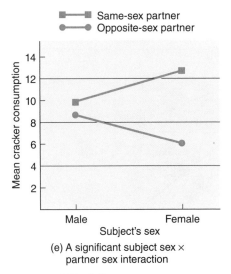

(e) A significant subject sex ×
partner sex interaction

FIGURE **10.11** Hypothetical outcome—significant subject sex × partner sex interaction.

© Cengage Learning

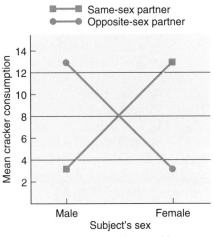

(f) A maximum significant subject
sex × partner sex interaction

FIGURE **10.12** Hypothetical outcome—maximum significant subject sex × partner sex interaction.

© Cengage Learning

experimenters' hypothesis was wrong or that the procedures used were inadequate to detect the effect.

Figure 10.8 illustrates the outcome if there were a significant main effect for type of partner, but the main effect for subject sex and the interaction were not significant. The figure depicts an outcome in which both male and female

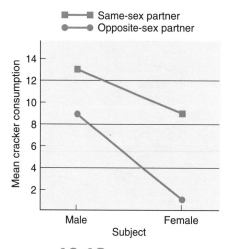

FIGURE **10.13** Hypothetical outcome—a significant subject sex main effect, a significant partner sex main effect, and a significant subject sex × partner sex interaction.
© Cengage Learning

subjects ate less in the presence of an opposite-sex partner. This finding was actually reported in an earlier experiment by Mori, Chaiken, and Pliner (1987).[5]

What would the graph look like if a significant main effect for type of partner indicated that both male and female subjects ate less in the presence of a same-sex partner than they did in the presence of an opposite-sex partner? The two lines would be reversed from those in Figure 10.8; the line for same-sex partners would be lower than the line for opposite-sex partners.

A significant main effect for sex of subject is illustrated in Figure 10.9. The graph would look like this if men ate more than women regardless of who their partners were. In this graph, neither the main effect for type of partner nor the interaction is significant. What would the graph look like if a main effect for sex of subject showed that women ate more than men did? The points on the left would be lower than the points on the right.

Figure 10.10 shows one possible outcome when there are two significant main effects in the data but no interaction. As shown in the figure, whether a subject is male or female affects how much they eat. However, whether the partner is the same or opposite sex also makes a difference. Men in all conditions eat more than women do, and everyone eats more with a same-sex partner than when they have an opposite-sex partner. Both independent variables exert an influence on eating, but they do not interact; the influence of one variable does not depend on the level of another.

[5] In a second experiment reported by Pliner and Chaiken (1990), both men and women ate less in the presence of an opposite-sex partner. The authors suggested that eating might be influenced by the kinds of personal and social motives that are important at the time. Wishing to appear cooperative or similar to their opposite-sex partner or wishing to have their behavior appear "socially desirable" might have reduced eating among men in the presence of women.

Figures 10.11 and 10.12 depict two examples of significant interactions in the absence of any significant main effects. The graphs of data that reflect an interaction always show a characteristic pattern: The lines are not parallel. Graphs showing an interaction can diverge (spread out, as in Figure 10.11), converge (come together), or intersect (as in Figure 10.12). Notice that the interaction depicted in Figure 10.12 is the maximum possible interaction. The effects of each factor completely reverse at each level of the other factor. We call this a *crossover interaction*.

Remember that an interaction can also occur along with any number of significant main effects. Figure 10.13 depicts two significant main effects and a significant interaction. In this figure, both the subject's sex and the partner's sex have effects on eating—and the two factors interact. Here both factors produce effects on eating, but the magnitude of the effects of one factor changes across the levels of the other factor. For example, this graph shows that, in general, women eat less than men do, and both eat less in the presence of an opposite-sex partner. And in addition, the interaction tells us that women's eating in front of an opposite-sex partner drops a great deal more than a man's eating does.

Measuring interactions is one of the key reasons for doing factorial research. By looking at two (or more) variables together, we can assess whether the effect of one variable depends on the level of another variable. When we have an interaction, knowing the value of just one independent variable will not necessarily enable us to predict the performance of subjects with any degree of accuracy. For instance, suppose the data came out like those displayed in the graph in Figure 10.11, which represents an outcome in which men ate the same amount regardless of type of partner but women varied their eating with different partners. Women ate a lot more with a same-sex partner than with an opposite-sex partner. Because there is an interaction, eating depends on both factors. If we want to predict accurately how many crackers would be eaten by any subject, we would need to know both the subject's sex and the type of partner.

This effect is even more apparent in the crossover interaction depicted in Figure 10.12. Here the effect of type of partner on eating is exactly opposite for male and female subjects. Clearly, to predict for any subject in the experiment, we would need to know whether the subject was male or female and what type of partner the subject had. Box 10.2 describes a research example of a crossover interaction.

From the interaction in Figure 10.13, we can also see that we do not have a complete picture of the effects of the independent variables unless we look at the effects of both factors together, because the effects differ in magnitude across the levels of both factors. Here, the type of partner influenced both men's and women's eating, but it affected women much more than it did men. In factorial experiments, main effects and interactions are quantified and evaluated through statistical tests. Chapter 14 contains additional information about these concepts and the procedures required to evaluate them.

## BOX **10.2**   An Interesting Crossover Interaction

In Chapter 6, we discussed an experiment that demonstrated the effect of a stereotype threat on women's mathematics performance. Apparently, men's math performance can be similarly affected by a relevant stereotype threat. In this experiment (Aronson et al., 1999), only White male subjects enrolled in a second-semester calculus course participated as subjects. The researchers first identified each subject's level of "math identification," the importance of math abilities to their self-concept, and formed two groups: subjects moderate or high in math identification (none of the subjects were truly low in math identification!). Before they took a math test, half of the subjects in each math identification group were reminded of the stereotype that Asians usually outperform Whites in mathematics and were told that the study was investigating these differences. The other subjects (the control group) were told only that the test measured math abilities. Analysis of test scores showed that the instructional sets produced a crossover interaction between level of math identification and stereotype threat (shown as a bar graph in Figure 10.14).

In this experiment, neither factor produced a significant main effect. Overall, average test scores were about the same when subjects were moderate in math identification (the mean of the white bars) or high in math identification (the mean of the blue bars). They also were about the same whether subjects received the stereotype threat (the average of the two bars on the left) or no threat (the average of the two bars on the right).

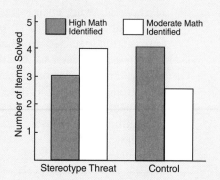

FIGURE **10.14** Depiction of crossover interaction between stereotype threat and math identification.
Adapted from Aronson et al., 1999.

Only the interaction was significant: In the control condition with no stereotype threat present, subjects high in math identification significantly outperformed subjects whose math identification was only moderate; whereas the effect completely reversed for the threat group. For men given the Asian stereotype threat, test scores were significantly lower for subjects with high math identification than for subjects with moderate math identification. These results suggest that stereotype threats can have a much more debilitating effect on people when the ability being measured is an important one than when people consider it less important.

## CHOOSING A BETWEEN-SUBJECTS DESIGN

As you begin planning your first experiments, you will probably experience the temptation of trying to do everything in one experiment. You might try to set up studies with as many as five or six different factors. But if you try to do too many things at once, you can lose sight of what you are trying to accomplish. A simple set of hypotheses that zeros in on the most important variables is better than a more elaborate set that includes everything from astrological signs to zest for life. Keep your first experiment simple. Focus on the variables that are critical. Once again, a review of the experimental literature will be a helpful guide. If other researchers have simply controlled time of day by testing all their subjects together, there is no need to vary time of day in your study so that you can include it as an independent variable—unless you have strong reasons for doing so. You will develop a better understanding of the experimental process by starting with simple designs and working up to more complex ones.

There are several practical reasons for keeping factorial designs simple. First, subjects are usually assigned to each of the treatment conditions at random. This means you will need as many groups of subjects as you have treatment conditions. It is not always easy to find enough subjects to ensure that each group has an adequate sample size. More treatment conditions also means more time to run the experiment and more time to do the statistical analysis. Moreover, the results of complicated designs can be virtually uninterpretable. It is very difficult to describe the interaction of three factors, let alone explain why it happened. A significant three-way interaction is rarely a predicted result, and four-way interactions are practically impossible to conceptualize and explain. There is not much point in collecting data that we cannot understand. It is just not practical to include unnecessary factors. The same logic applies to selecting how many levels of each factor to include. Both explanation and statistical analysis become more complicated as the design gets larger. Use your review of prior research in the area to help you decide what variables and what levels to include.

In a two-factor between-subjects design, there can be only three possible effects: a main effect for each factor and an interaction between the two factors (total = three possible effects). Whenever a factorial design expands beyond two factors, the number of possible main effects and interactions increases dramatically. Let's use $A$, $B$, and $C$ to represent three factors in an experiment. What kind of significant effects are possible? First, each factor can produce a significant main effect: a main effect for $A$, a main effect for $B$, and a main effect for $C$. Next, each pair of factors can interact: Interactions between $A$ and $C$, between $A$ and $C$, and between $B$ and $C$ are possible. Finally, all three factors can interact: an interaction among $A$, $B$, and $C$. If we add up the possible significant effects, the total equals 7. (In a four-factor design, the total equals 15.) Think about this as you design your experiment!

Recall the negative ion experiment conducted by Baron and colleagues (1985). In the full design, they had three independent variables: type of subject (type A, indeterminate, or type B); provocation condition (angered or not angered); and ion level (low, moderate, or high). In all, there were 18 different experimental conditions. The results on aggressiveness were very complex; 2 two-way interactions were obtained. The three-way interaction was almost statistically significant, too. The presence of 2 two-way interactions made interpretation of the experimental findings extremely difficult. A two-way interaction between the type of subject and the level of negative ions in the air is shown in Figure 10.15.

Statistics done to test for differences between each of the nine experimental conditions showed that increasing the level of negative ions only increased aggression in type A subjects. For type As, both moderate and high levels of

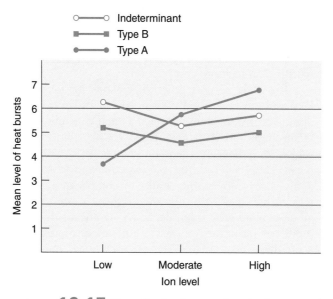

FIGURE **10.15** Hypothetical mean level of aggression as a function of ion level and type A–type B dimension.
© Cengage Learning

negative ions caused significantly stronger "heat bursts" to be directed toward the confederate than did low levels of negative ions. Notice in Figure 10.15 that the line for type As shows a distinct upward trend as the ion level is increased. The lines for indeterminate and type B subjects are relatively flat across all three ion levels, because increasing the level of negative ions did not produce any significant effects on their aggressive behavior toward the confederate.

So far, we have covered four different kinds of between-subjects designs. We looked at two-group designs that had either independent or matched groups. We also looked at multiple-groups designs and factorial designs. You might still feel a bit uneasy about trying to select the appropriate design for your own between-subjects experiment. To make things easier, you should always begin with some basic questions. Your design will be determined largely by the number of independent variables you have and by the number of treatment conditions needed to test your hypothesis. You should also use your literature review to get an idea of the kinds of designs others have used for similar problems. To help make your search more systematic, we summarize the basics of the decision-making process in Figure 10.16. Simply begin at the top and work down, answering the questions for your experiment.

In the next chapter, we will look at another important type of experimental strategy—within-subjects designs. In all the designs we have already covered, each subject participates in only one treatment condition and is measured on the dependent variable after the experimental manipulation has

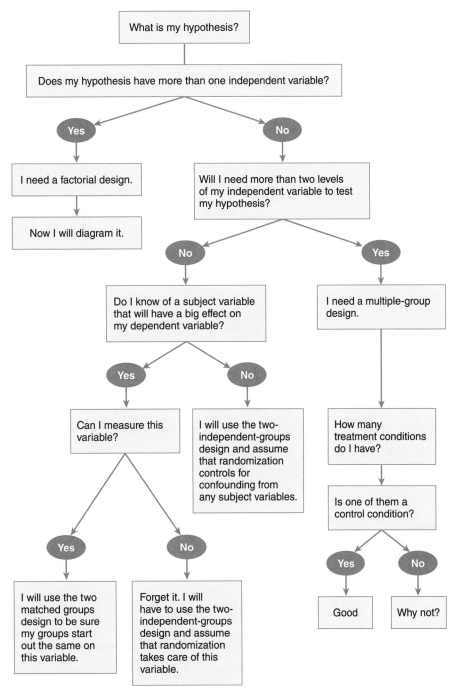

FIGURE **10.16** Questions to ask when designing a between-subjects experiment. (Start at the top and work down.)
© Cengage Learning

taken place. In a within-subjects experiment, subjects participate in more than one treatment condition of an experiment, and a measurement is taken after each treatment is given. Factorial experiments can also be conducted using a within-subjects design. In a within-subjects factorial design, subjects receive all conditions in the experiment instead of receiving only one.

## SUMMARY

A *factorial design* has two or more independent variables, which are called *factors*. The simplest factorial design is a *two-factor experiment*. Factorial designs testing two or more factors are more efficient than are separate experiments testing the same set of independent variables. By studying more than one factor at a time, we can measure *main effects*—the action of each independent variable in the experiment. We can also measure *interactions*—a change in the effect of one independent variable across the levels of another independent variable. Psychological variables are often complex, and only a factorial design can detect and measure interactions.

Factorial designs are described with *shorthand notation*. If we are told that an experiment has a $3 \times 2 \times 4$ design, we know it has three factors because three numbers are given. The numerical value of each number tells us how many levels each factor has. The first factor has three, the second has two, and the third has four. We also know there are 24 treatment conditions, the product of $3 \times 2 \times 4$. *Higher-order interactions* can be produced in experiments with more than two factors.

Statistics, such as ANOVA (Chapter 14), are used to assess the significance of each effect in a factorial experiment. All combinations of significant and nonsignificant main effects and interactions are possible. For example, Pliner and Chaiken's (1990) $2 \times 2$ factorial experiment on eating in the presence of same- or opposite-sex partners produced one significant main effect along with a significant interaction. However, there are a number of other possible outcomes.

There are practical limitations on using factorial designs: They often require many subjects. They can be time-consuming, and they require more complicated statistical procedures than do the other designs we have discussed. However, factorial designs also provide valuable information that other types of experiments cannot.

## KEY TERMS

Factor An independent variable in a factorial design.

Factorial design An experimental design in which more than one independent variable is manipulated.

Higher-order interaction An interaction effect involving more than two independent variables.

Interaction The effect of one independent variable changes across the levels of another independent variable; can only be detected in factorial designs.

Main effect The action of a single independent variable in an experiment; the change in the dependent variable produced by the various levels of a single factor.

Shorthand notation A system that uses numbers to describe the design of a factorial experiment.

Two-factor experiment The simplest factorial design, having two independent variables.

## REVIEW AND STUDY QUESTIONS

1. What is the difference between a factorial design and a multiple-groups design?

2. Explain what we mean by the terms *main effect* and *interaction*.

3. What are the advantages of running experiments with a factorial design?

4. After watching a group of nursery school children, we get the idea that some toys are more popular with children than others are. We would like to test the difference in time spent playing with toys that are used for building (for example, blocks) and toys that are not (for example, stuffed animals). Because there are many differences between boys and girls, we would also like to look at gender as an independent variable. What kind of design do we need?

5. Diagram the experiment suggested in question 4.

6. Describe the design in the diagram in question 5 using all four labeling methods.

7. A researcher decides to run an experiment to study the effects of two independent variables on learning. (1) She will vary background noise by playing or not playing a radio while subjects study a list of words. (2) She will vary the length of the list to be learned: Half the subjects will try to learn a short list; half will try to learn a long list in the same amount of time. The dependent variable is the percentage of words recalled. Take this hypothetical experiment and do the following:

   a. Describe this experiment using shorthand notation for factorial designs.

   b. Diagram the experiment using a design matrix.

   c. Identify three extraneous variables you think might affect the outcome of this study.

8. What features of an experimental hypothesis are important in selecting a design?

9. In a study of interpersonal closeness (Holland, Roeder, van Baaren, Brandt, & Hannover, 2004, experiment 2), researchers primed either independence or interdependence by asking male and female subjects to think about the differences (independence) or similarities (interdependence) between themselves and their family and close friends. Then they were asked to take a seat in a waiting area full of chairs where a jacket indicated the presence of another person. The dependent variable was the number of chairs between the subject's chair and the chair with the jacket. As predicted, subjects in the independent condition seated themselves farther away from the chair that appeared occupied than subjects in the interdependent condition did. In addition, men tended to sit further away from the jacket than women did.

   a. What is the design of this experiment? Describe it using shorthand notation. Diagram it.

   b. How many main effects were reported?

   c. Using a simple graph, illustrate the pattern of the overall results of this experiment.

10. A crossover interaction was depicted in a bar graph in Box 10.2. Change the bar graph to a line graph to depict this interaction.

## CRITICAL THINKING EXERCISE

*The myth:* The grass is always greener on the other side.

*The scientific findings:* In a sense, yes. Perceptually, greater distance does make the green *seem* greener (Pomerantz, 1983).

*The problem:* Design a 2 × 2 between-subjects factorial experiment to test the everyday meaning of the aphorism—rather than its literal meaning as tested by Pomerantz (1983). Use subjects high and low in optimism as one factor in the design. Diagram your experiment and graph the results predicted by the hypothesis that the grass on the other side will look greener, and it will look *particularly* green to optimists.

## ONLINE RESOURCES

Want to know more about the effects of negative ions? Try

www.negativeionsinformation.org

Interested in the origin and meaning of your first name? Try

www.zelo.com/firstnames/findresults.asp

## CHAPTER 11

# Within-Subjects Designs

**A Within-Subjects Experiment: Homophone Priming of Proper Names**

**Within-Subjects Factorial Designs**

**Mixed Designs**

**Advantages of Within-Subjects Designs**

**Disadvantages of Within-Subjects Designs**
Practical Limitations
Interference Between Conditions

**Controlling Within-Subjects Designs**
Controlling for Order Effects:
    Counterbalancing

Subject-by-Subject Counterbalancing
Across-Subjects Counterbalancing
Carryover Effects
Choosing Among Counterbalancing
    Procedures
Order as a Design Factor

**How Can You Choose a Design?**

SUMMARY
KEY TERMS
REVIEW AND STUDY QUESTIONS
CRITICAL THINKING EXERCISE
ONLINE RESOURCES

## CHAPTER OBJECTIVES

* Learn about designs in which subjects participate in more than one experimental condition

* Understand the pros and cons of within-subjects designs

* Learn how to control for problems specific to these designs

We have focused on four main types of designs so far: two independent groups, two matched groups, multiple groups, and factorial designs. All our examples of these designs had one underlying assumption—that the subjects in each of the treatment conditions were different, randomly assigned individuals. We assumed that each subject would be in only one treatment condition. These are called between-subjects designs. Conclusions are based on comparisons among different subjects (that is, among the different groups of the experiment). This approach can work well, but only in certain cases. Other experiments call for a different type of design, as the following example illustrates.

People seem to smile more when there is an audience to see the smile than when they are alone (Fridlund, 1989). Smiling seems to serve a social and communicative function; it can notify others when we are feeling happy or pleased. Psychologists still debate whether smiles serve mostly to communicate emotions or are automatic manifestations of an inner emotional state. (There is evidence for both sides.) If smiles function to communicate emotions to other people, the behavior of smiling to others would probably be a learned behavior, and researchers have wondered just how early it is learned. Jones and her colleagues have been investigating communicative smiles in infants. In one experiment, they found evidence for an audience effect in 18-month-old infants (Jones & Raag, 1989). The infants smiled more at their mothers when the mothers were attending to the infants than when they were not. When the mothers were not attending, the infants simply smiled at an available stranger who was paying attention to them.

However, 18-month-old infants are already well socialized in many respects and are beginning the word explosion period (a time of rapid vocabulary growth and development of an understanding of symbolic communications). Jones wondered if infants might begin the social control of

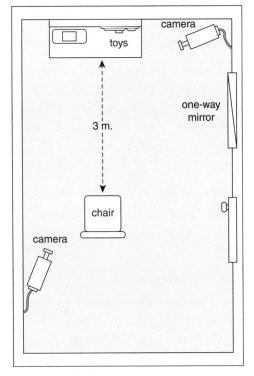

FIGURE **11.1** Experimental setting.

From "An Audience Effect in Smile Production on 10-month-old Infants," by S. S. Jones, K. Collins and H. W. Hong. *Psychological Science*, 1991, 2, 45–49. Reprinted by permission of Sage Publications.

facial expressions, including smiles, even earlier. She set up a laboratory testing situation in which she could observe 10-month-old infants and their mothers (Jones, Collins, & Hong, 1991). The setup of the testing room is shown in Figure 11.1. Each mother spent a minute describing and demonstrating several toys affixed to a pegboard stand, then left the baby next to the toys and sat down in the chair. Two 6-minute segments followed: In one, the mother paid attention to the baby playing; in the other, she read a magazine.[1] Using the two cameras in the room, the baby was videotaped and smiles were later scored and recorded by judges who viewed the tapes. Jones and her colleagues made the following prediction: If 10-month-old infants use their smiles to communicate, they should smile

---

[1] For half the mother-baby pairs, the attention segment came first; for the other half, the nonattention segment came first.

much more at their mothers if the mothers are paying attention to them than if they are not. Their hypothesis was strongly supported. The 20 babies smiled at their mothers almost 4 times as much when the mothers were attending than when they were not.

Suppose we used a between-subjects approach for this research. Each mother and baby would take part in only one of the two 6-minute segments—either attending or not attending—and we would compare the average number of smiles from the babies in each group. We would have a few problems if we tried to do this. First, 10-month-old infants vary significantly in the number of smiles they produce. Some only smiled once or twice; others smiled a lot. Such large differences exist in the amount of smiling in babies that a difference between the two groups might not be detectable with statistical tests. Whenever we expect responses from subjects to be extremely dissimilar, finding effects from an independent variable is like looking for a needle in a haystack. Second, we would probably need a much larger sample of mothers and babies if we had to divide them into two groups—and finding mothers with babies just the right age (who are also willing to volunteer for an experiment) can be extremely difficult.

For this kind of research, it is much better to use a within-subjects design—a design in which each subject serves in more than one condition of the experiment. By having the same subjects in both attention conditions, Jones and her colleagues improved their chances of detecting differences between the attention and nonattention conditions. From a statistical viewpoint, we refer to this as increasing the power of the experiment. Increased power means a greater chance of detecting a genuine effect of the independent variable. In a within-subjects design, subjects serve in more than one condition of the experiment and are measured on the dependent variable after each treatment; thus, the design is also known as a *repeated-measures design*.

Some hypotheses and research topics naturally require a within-subjects approach: Does a family's perception of itself change over the course of family therapy? Do you improve each time you take the same intelligence test? Do additional reviews of class notes yield better exam scores? Let us turn to another laboratory experiment in which a within-subjects approach was used.

---

# A WITHIN-SUBJECTS EXPERIMENT: HOMOPHONE PRIMING OF PROPER NAMES

We can set up a variety of within-subjects designs. The basic principles remain the same: Each subject takes part in more than one condition of the experiment. We make comparisons of the behavior of the same subjects under different conditions. If our independent variable is having an effect, we are often more likely to find it if we use a within-subjects design. In a between-subjects design, the effects of our independent variable can be masked by the differences between the groups on all sorts of extraneous variables. A comparison within each subject is more precise. If we see different behaviors under different treatment conditions, these differences are more likely to be linked to our experimental manipulation. Remember that the whole point of an experiment is to set up a situation in which the independent variable is the only thing that changes systematically across the conditions of the experiment. In a between-subjects design, we change the independent variable across conditions. However, we also use different subjects in the different conditions. We can usually assume that randomization controls for extraneous variables that might affect the dependent variable. But we have even better control with a within-subjects design because we use the same subjects over and over.

Burke, Locantore, Austin, and Chae (2004) used a within-subjects design to investigate the effects of priming using homophones (words that sound alike) on the ability of younger and older adults to recall a famous person's name. Researchers have documented that proper names, in general, can be more difficult to recall than other types of information about people (Young, Hay, & Ellis, 1985). We have all experienced this memory problem—someone's name is on the tip of our tongue, but we just can't quite retrieve it! Burke and her colleagues predicted that when people have just retrieved a homophone for a person's last name from memory (e.g., the word "pit" is a homophone for the last name of the actor Brad Pitt), retrieval of the person's name should be much easier and faster. To test this hypothesis, they needed to compare the effects of homophones and nonhomophones on retrieval of a target person's name. They also wanted to test a large number of proper names. Their procedure is illustrated by the sample stimuli shown in Figure 11.2.

All stimuli were presented by a computer, which also recorded subjects' responses and response times. In each set of 4 trials, subjects were presented with alternating "fill-in-the-blank" definitions and pictures of famous people: (trial 1) the definition of the homophone or unrelated word, (trial 2) a filler picture, (trial 3) a filler definition, and (trial 4) the target picture. If the researchers were correct, retrieving a homophone (trial 1) would facilitate retrieval of the name of the target person (trial 4). Using a within-subjects design allowed the researchers to get a more precise picture of how the priming and retrieval worked. They discovered, for example, that priming with homophones significantly speeded up naming times and reduced the tip-of-the-tongue problem.

Burke et al. (2004) made their data more precise by comparing responses of the same subjects under different conditions, which eliminated the error from differences between subjects. The responses of the same subjects are

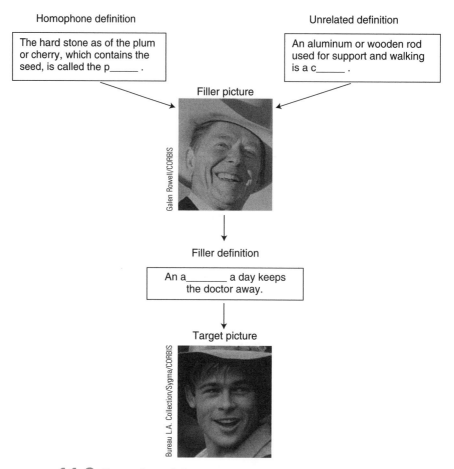

Homophone definition

The hard stone as of the plum or cherry, which contains the seed, is called the p_____ .

Unrelated definition

An aluminum or wooden rod used for support and walking is a c_____ .

Filler picture

Galen Rowell/CORBIS

Filler definition

An a_____ a day keeps the doctor away.

Target picture

Bureau L.A. Collection/Sygma/CORBIS

FIGURE **11.2** Illustration of the sequence of trials presenting definitions and pictures.

Adapted from Burke, D. M., Locantore, J. K., Austin, A. A., & Chase, B. (2004). Cherry pit primes Brad Pitt: Homophone priming effects on young and older adults' production of proper names. *Psychological Science*, 15(3), 164–170. Reprinted by permission of Sage Publications.

likely to be more consistent from one measurement to another. Therefore, if responses change across conditions, the changes are more likely to be caused by the independent variable. Because it controls for individual differences among subjects, the greater power of a within-subjects design also allowed the researchers to use fewer subjects.

## WITHIN-SUBJECTS FACTORIAL DESIGNS

So far we have talked about within-subjects designs that tested a single independent variable. However, these designs can also be set up as factorial designs. Suppose a researcher was interested in measuring how long it takes to identify different facial expressions. She might decide to show subjects slides of people displaying four different expressions—perhaps anger, fear, happiness, and sadness—and measure how quickly people can recognize each one. She could use a within-subjects design, showing each subject all four kinds of faces and timing how long it takes each subject to identify each expression. Past research suggests that for communicating emotions on their faces, women are generally better "senders" (Fridlund, Ekman, & Oster, 1987), so the researcher also wants to show subjects both male and female faces. In this case, she can use the sex of the person in the slide as an additional within-subjects factor, creating a within-subjects factorial design, a factorial design in which subjects receive all conditions in the experiment. This experiment would be a 4 × 2 within-subjects factorial design; each subject would take part in all eight conditions (4 × 2 = 8). Subjects would see and identify eight different faces: a man and a woman displaying each of the four expressions.[2] It is easy to see that a within-subjects factorial can require many fewer subjects than a between-subjects factorial design that is testing the same hypothesis.

## MIXED DESIGNS

We can also use a factorial design that combines one factor that is manipulated within subjects (such as the four types of expressions) with a between-subjects factor (often a subject variable, such as gender or age of the subjects) that cannot be manipulated by an experimenter. A design that combines within- and between-subjects variables in a single experiment is called a mixed design. For an example, let's return to the homophone experiment by Burke and her colleagues (2004). We all have trouble recalling a name from time to time, but older adults are particularly prone to name retrieval failures, and, in fact, they report failures to recall people's names as one of their most irritating and embarrassing memory problems (Maylor, 1990). In their homophone experiments, Burke and her colleagues used both younger ($\overline{X} = 19.05$ years) and older ($\overline{X} = 72.23$ years) adult subjects. They predicted that older subjects would benefit more from homophone priming than younger subjects would. Testing this hypothesis required a 2 (homophone or unrelated word) × 2 (younger or older subject) mixed factorial design. The type of word used in the definition was a within-subjects factor; the age group of the subject was a between-subjects factor. Statistical analysis of the mixed design (Burke et al., 2004, experiment 2) showed that homophone priming increased the naming speed for both groups of subjects, but it significantly improved name recall only for the older group.

Australian researchers Jones and Menzies (2000) used a mixed factorial design in an interesting experiment to explore differences between spider phobics and nonphobics. The between-subjects factor was spider phobia status, a

---

[2] As you will discover later in the chapter, the experimenter would also need to use a special control procedure, called *counterbalancing*; different subjects would see the eight faces in different orders to prevent confounding.

Tim Laman/National Geographic/Getty Images

FIGURE **11.3** A Huntsman spider.

subject variable. The phobic group was composed of subjects reporting the strongest levels of fear of harmless spiders. A group of control subjects reporting the lowest levels of fear were selected from the same student population. The within-subjects factor consisted of measuring subjects' estimates of the likelihood of being bitten in three successive treatment conditions: spider photo, real spider, and post-spider.

In the spider photo condition, subjects were taken to the testing room containing a large, but empty, glass cylinder with the top uncovered. Once inside the testing room, they were shown a photograph of the cylinder when it contained two large, but harmless, Huntsman spiders (see Figure 11.3). Huntsman spiders, found in Australia, are huge, gray-brown spiders with flat bodies, measuring as much as 15 centimeters (almost 6 inches) across the legs. Subjects were asked to imagine being in the room with the spiders in the uncovered cylinder. Along with other measurements, subjects reported their feelings about how likely it was that they would be bitten by a spider in that circumstance.

In the spider condition, subjects were exposed to the cylinder containing real spiders (the spiders were actually dead and had been pasted to the inside of the cylinder, but subjects thought they were alive). The dependent measures were taken again. Finally, in the third treatment condition, subjects were once again exposed to an empty cylinder and asked to give their ratings. The average ratings of the two phobia status groups are shown in Figure 11.4. As expected, in the presence of real spiders, the phobics gave much higher estimates of the chances of being bitten, but their estimates in the two conditions in which no real spider was present were also higher than estimates of controls. This finding is interesting because it contradicts the common wisdom about people with phobias—namely, that phobics can accurately evaluate the danger of phobic stimuli when the stimuli are not immediately present.

Mixed designs are very common in all areas of psychology. The statistical procedures for analyzing mixed designs are more complex than those for

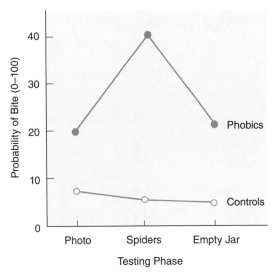

FIGURE **11.4** Mean probability of bite scores for phobics and controls.
Adapted from Jones, M. K., & Menzies, R. G. (2000).

within-subjects or between-subjects factorial designs; however, with computer statistical analysis programs so widely available, student experimenters frequently select mixed designs. See Box 11.1 for another example.

## ADVANTAGES OF WITHIN-SUBJECTS DESIGNS

In within-subjects experiments, we use the same subjects in different treatment conditions. This is a big help when we cannot get many subjects. If we have four treatment conditions and want 15 subjects in each condition, we would only need 15 subjects if we used a within-subjects design. Each of the 15 subjects would run through all four conditions. If we ran the same experiment between subjects, we would need 60 subjects, 15 in each condition. A within-subjects design can also save us time when we are actually running the experiment. If subjects must be trained, it is more efficient to train each subject for several conditions instead of for just one.

We usually have the best chance of detecting the effect of our independent variable if we compare the behavior of the same subjects under different conditions. The within-subjects design controls for extraneous subject variables, the ways in which subjects differ from one another. That way, if we see differences in behavior under different conditions, we know that they are not likely to be simply the differences that occur because the subjects in one group do not act like the subjects in another just because they are different individuals. From a statistical standpoint, we have a better chance of detecting the effect of our experimental manipulation if we use a within-subjects design. By using this type of design, we have increased the power of the experiment. The reasons parallel the reasons we discussed in connection with

## BOX 11.1   Creating False Memories in Children: A Mixed-Factorial Design

A large literature exists indicating that false memories for events that never happened can be created in research subjects—whether the subjects are adults or children—using a variety of techniques. In one fascinating experiment, Strange, Hayne, and Garry (2007) used a mixed factorial design to investigate the impact of photos on children's memories for events that had actually happened (true memories) and events that had never happened (false memories). In each of three interview sessions, 10-year-old children were shown a series of four photographs: three real photos provided by parents depicting events that occurred when the children were about 6 years old and one false photo (a photo of a hot air balloon). The four photos were the within-subjects factor.

The between-subjects factor was the nature of the hot air balloon photo. For half the children, the photo showed a group of unknown people in the balloon's basket (child-absent condition). For the other half, the photo had been doctored using Adobe Photoshop so that an image of the child along with some family members was inserted among other people in the basket (child-present condition). In reality, of course, none of the children had actually been in a hot air balloon.

While viewing each photograph, the children were asked to describe what they remembered about the events in each of the photos. Transcripts of the children's reports were coded by judges. The researchers found that almost all of the children reported memories for the events pictured in the real photos. More importantly, many of the children also reported memories of riding in the hot air balloon,

whether their picture appeared in the photo or not. False memories occurred significantly more often, however, when children had seen themselves in the photo (about 47%) than when they had not (about 18%). In addition, the children were just as confident about their false memories as they were about their true memories.

Charles Stirling/Alamy

the matched-groups procedures. In a sense, the within-subjects design is the most perfect form of matching we can have. The influence of subject variables across different treatment conditions is controlled because the same subjects take part in all the treatment conditions. Each subject serves as his or her own control for extraneous subject variables in the experiment.

In a within-subjects, or repeated-measures, design, the subject is measured after each treatment condition. Therefore, in a within-subjects experiment, we can also get an ongoing record of subjects' behavior over time. This gives us a more complete picture of the way the independent variable works in the experiment. We have both practical and methodological gains with this approach. A within-subjects design has so many advantages, why not always use it?

# DISADVANTAGES OF WITHIN-SUBJECTS DESIGNS

## Practical Limitations

There are several reasons why within-subjects designs do not always work. Sometimes such designs are just not practical. Within-subjects designs generally require each subject to spend more time in the experiment. For instance, the various conditions of an experiment might require the subjects to read and evaluate several stories. A researcher might need to schedule several hours of testing if this experiment is run with a within-subjects design; each subject must spend several hours reading and scoring several stories. The same experiment might be run with a group of subjects in only an hour using a between-subjects design; each individual subject would spend just one hour reading and evaluating one story.

If a procedure involves testing each subject individually, a great deal of time can be taken up by resetting equipment for each condition. That could lead to extra hours of testing per subject. In a perception experiment that requires calibrating several sensitive electronic instruments for each condition, the researcher and subjects are in for some tedious testing sessions. As an alternative, several subjects in a row could be tested in each condition, requiring fewer changes to the equipment.

Keep in mind that experiments can easily become tedious for subjects. Subjects who are expected to perform many tasks might get restless during the experiment and begin to make hasty judgments to hurry the process along—leading to inaccurate data. For the most part, these limitations are really just inconveniences. We can seek out subjects who are willing to invest a lot of time in a study. We can spend an additional 10, 20, or even 100 hours testing subjects if it is essential to the value of the experiment. Sometimes it is, and experimenters may spend hours or even days testing each subject. But more serious problems, linked to the independent variable, limit the within-subjects approach.

## Interference Between Conditions

Often each subject can be in only one condition of an experiment. Taking part in more than one condition would be either impossible or useless or would change the effect of later treatments. Imagine that we are doing a study on car-buying preferences. We hypothesize that the type of car individuals first learned to drive will influence their own purchasing choices later. For simplicity, let us say that people who learn to drive in small cars (compact or smaller) will be more likely to buy small cars than will people who learn to drive in full-sized cars. With the cooperation of a local driving school, we randomly assign half of the subjects to each treatment condition (small or full-sized car).

We suspect that car-buying preferences are influenced by a wide range of other factors, too—including financial status, parents' choice of car, advertising, and perhaps even unidentified genetic differences in personality that influence our choices. The numerous makes and models on the market attest to the diversity of tastes. People differ greatly in what they want in a car. Because so many subject variables are involved, perhaps a within-subjects design would be a better choice.

Actually, in this experiment our choice is simple: We cannot do a within-subjects experiment. Once people learn to drive in a small car, they can never learn to drive again in a full-sized car. Even if we put subjects through the same sets of lessons again, they would not respond to them in the same fashion because they are not novices anymore. The first training condition would interfere with all later attempts. If one treatment condition precludes another, as it does in this kind of experiment, a between-subjects design is required.

Sometimes it is possible to run all subjects through all treatments, but it does not make sense to do it. What if we want subjects to learn a list of words? In one condition, we tell the subjects to learn the words by forming mental pictures (images) of them. In the other condition, we ask subjects to repeat the words over and over. We want to use the same list in both conditions so that the difficulty of the list will not be a confounding variable. But once the subjects have practiced the list in one condition, they will recall it more easily in the next condition. The interference between different conditions of an experiment is usually the biggest drawback in using within-subjects designs. If the treatments clash so badly that we cannot give them to the same subjects, we will need to use a between-subjects design.

Whenever we consider a within-subjects design, we also need to consider the possibility that effects on the dependent variable might be influenced by the order in which we give the treatments. Subjects' responses might differ from one treatment to another just because of the position, or order, of the series of treatments. In a within-subjects experiment, an order effect is a potential confound. For instance, if we were asking people to watch a series of television commercials and rate how much they liked each one, the order in which we presented the commercials might affect ratings. The first commercial they saw might always get a higher rating than it deserves simply because it is novel. By the third or fourth one, ratings of any commercial might be lower than they should be because subjects have tuned out. Advertisers know about this kind of order effect and keep their fingers crossed that their commercials will be placed first in any long commercial break. In a within-subjects design, we use special counterbalancing procedures to offset interference and to control for potential order effects between conditions.

# CONTROLLING WITHIN-SUBJECTS DESIGNS

## Controlling for Order Effects: Counterbalancing

Suppose we want to do some market research on a new brand of cola. We know that people differ greatly in their preferences for foods and beverages, so we decide to use a within-subjects design. We would like to get people to compare their present brand of cola with our new brand. We will get ratings on how good our cola tastes compared with the old brands. That information will tell us whether we can expect the new product to compete with well-known brands. Our hypothesis is that our new cola will get better ratings than the old brands.

We recruit cola drinkers and bring them to our testing center. For 2 hours before the taste test, we keep them in a lounge in which they can relax and read magazines—but cannot eat or drink. Then we give each subject a glass of the new cola. After subjects have had time to drink it, we ask them to indicate on a rating scale how much they liked the taste. We want to compare subjects' ratings of the new cola with their ratings of their regular brand, so we introduce a second condition. We ask all subjects to drink a glass of their favorite cola. After they finish, we get them to rate their favorite drink on the rating scale. Now we have ratings of the two types of colas, new and old. We can compare the average ratings and see how our product competes.

Would it surprise you to learn that the average rating of our new brand was much higher than the average rating of the old brands? What is wrong with this experiment? The problem, of course, is that any cola might taste good after you have had nothing to drink for several hours.

In this experiment, we varied the brand of cola that people were asked to drink. There were two conditions, "new brand" and "old brand." Unfortunately, in addition to varying the brand of cola, we varied an important extraneous variable—order. We created confounding by always giving subjects the new cola first. Subjects might have rated the new brand higher because it really is delicious, but the ratings were probably distorted because subjects had not had anything to drink for a full 2 hours before they tasted the new product. In addition, the subjects might have given their old brand lower ratings because they had just had something else to drink and were no longer thirsty. In this experiment, we see that the order in which we presented the treatment conditions could have changed the subjects' responses. We have confounding caused by order effects.

Two other kinds of changes can occur when subjects are run in more than one condition. First, fatigue effects can cause performance to decline as the experiment goes on: Subjects get tired. As they solve more and more word problems, for instance, they could begin to make mistakes. They might also become bored or irritated by the experiment and merely go through the motions until it is over. Second, different factors may lead to improvement as the experiment proceeds—that is, to practice effects. As subjects become familiar with the experiment, they could relax and do a little better. They get better at using the apparatus, develop strategies for solving problems, or even catch on to the real purpose of the study.

All these changes, both positive and negative, are called progressive error: As the experiment progresses, results are distorted. The changes in subjects' responses are not caused by the independent variable; they are order effects produced when we run subjects through more than one treatment condition. Progressive error includes any changes in the subjects' responses that are caused by testing in multiple treatment conditions. It includes order effects, such as the effects of practice.

We control for any extraneous variable by making sure it affects all treatment conditions in the same way. We can do that by eliminating the variable completely, by holding it constant, or by balancing it out across treatment conditions. In a within-subjects experiment, we cannot eliminate order effects. Nor can we hold them constant, giving all subjects the treatments in the same order because we are trying to avoid just this kind of systematic effect. But we can balance them out—distribute them across the conditions—so that they affect all conditions equally.

Think about the cola experiment. We did a poor job of setting it up because we let the order of the colas stay the same for all subjects. Everyone tasted the new brand first. How could we redo the experiment so that progressive error would affect the results for both kinds of colas in the same way? We want to be sure that subjects' ratings reflect accurate taste judgments, not merely a difference between the first and second glass of cola. Suppose we modify our procedures a little. We run the first condition the same as before: Subjects do not eat or drink for 2 hours; then they drink a glass of the new brand of cola and give their ratings. But instead of having them drink the old brand immediately, we have them return to the lounge for another 2 hours. At the end of that time, we give them the old brand of cola and get the second set of ratings. Does this help? We avoid the problem of having subjects drink the new brand after 2 hours in the lounge and the old brand when they are not as thirsty. However, our data may still be contaminated by the order of the conditions. When the subjects drink the new brand, they have been in the lounge a total of 2 hours. When they drink the old brand, they have spent 4 hours in the lounge. By this time, they may be tired of hanging around. They may be getting hungry. They have also had practice filling out the rating scale, as well as time to think about what they said before.

"HE'S BEEN AT IT TOO LONG. NOW, WHEN THE BELL RINGS, DR. PAVLOV SALIVATES."

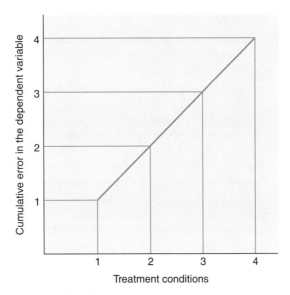

FIGURE **11.5** The impact of progressive error on responses in an experiment. The later trials (conditions) are affected more than the earlier ones.
© Cengage Learning

Let's look at how progressive error can accumulate during the course of an experiment in which subjects solve four successive word problems. Progressive error can be illustrated by the graph in Figure 11.5. You can see that progressive error is low in the early part of the experiment and increases gradually as the experiment continues. Here, the first treatment produces only 1 unit of error; the second treatment produces 2 units. Because error increases as the experiment progresses, the third treatment produces 3 units, and the fourth treatment produces 4 units. When we sum the progressive error from all four treatments, we find that during the course of the experiment we have accumulated 10 units of progressive error $(1 + 2 + 3 + 4 = 10)$.

Fortunately, researchers have worked out several procedures for controlling for order effects. These procedures are called counterbalancing, and they all have the same function: to distribute progressive error across the different treatment conditions of the experiment. By using these procedures, we can ensure that the order effects that alter results on one condition will be offset, or counterbalanced, by the order effects operating on other conditions.

## Subject-by-Subject Counterbalancing

We can control for progressive error in the cola experiment through one of two general approaches. First, we can control it by using subject-by-subject counterbalancing, a technique for controlling progressive error for each individual subject by presenting all treatment conditions more than once. The idea is to redistribute the effects of progressive error so that they will equal about the same amount in each condition that a subject completes. Two common techniques used to create subject-by-subject counterbalancing are reverse counterbalancing and block randomization.

### Reverse Counterbalancing

Let's see what happens to progressive error in the cola experiment if we present each treatment more than once. We give each subject two glasses of each cola instead of one, but we use reverse counterbalancing, a technique for controlling progressive error for each individual subject by presenting all treatment conditions twice, first in one order, then in the reverse order. We can call the new brand "condition *A*" and the old brand "condition *B*." We can equalize progressive error for these two conditions by presenting them in the order *ABBA*. Subjects now drink four glasses of cola instead of two, and we can use Figure 11.5 again to describe how the *ABBA* procedure works to balance out the effects of progressive error.

If we run the conditions in the *ABBA* order, we can add up the units of progressive error for each condition. Recall that for the first treatment (or trial), progressive error is equal to 1 unit; for the second trial, 2 units; for the third, 3 units; and for the fourth, 4 units. Because condition *A* is given in trials one and four, progressive error for condition *A* works out to be 5 units (1 + 4 = 5). For condition *B*, given in trials two and three, progressive error also equals 5 units (2 + 3 = 5). Of course, these numerical quantities are hypothetical, but you can see the logic behind the counterbalancing procedure. Now both conditions contain some trials in which progressive error is relatively high and others in which it is relatively low, but the total units of error are the same for both conditions.

Using reverse counterbalancing, each subject gets the *ABBA* sequence. This ensures that progressive error affects conditions *A* and *B* about equally for each subject, assuming progressive error follows the pattern shown in Figure 11.5. If there are more than two treatment conditions, we can counterbalance for each subject by continuing the pattern. With three conditions, the sequence for each subject would be *ABCCBA*; with four, the sequence would be *ABCDDCBA*; and so on.

Progressive error, however, is not necessarily this easy to control completely. Figure 11.5 illustrates error that is *linear*; that is, described by one straight line. But suppose true error has a more complex distribution across trials. Perhaps subjects get a little better with practice, and they also fatigue to some extent. On a long series of trials, they might catch their second wind and do a bit better as the experiment draws to a close. The effects of progressive error may be *curvilinear* (like an inverted U) or *nonmonotonic* (changing direction), as in Figure 11.6. Suppose the impact of progressive error looks more like that represented in Figure 11.6. If we use the *ABBA* procedure, progressive error for condition *A* will equal 3 units (1 + 2), and progressive error for condition *B* will equal 5 units (2 + 3). This is no better than simply testing everyone on *A* first, then *B*.

### Block Randomization

When progressive error is nonlinear, researchers often prefer to use block randomization. (This technique was discussed in Chapter 9 as a method of assigning subjects to treatment conditions in between-subjects designs.) Each set of treatments (e.g., *ABCD*) is considered as a single block, and treatments

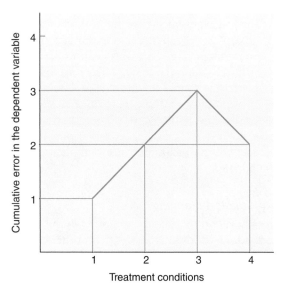

FIGURE **11.6** Nonlinear impact of progressive error in an experiment.
© Cengage Learning

within each block are given in random order. For block randomization to be successful in controlling nonlinear progressive error, it is usually necessary to present each treatment several times, resulting in a sequence containing a number of randomized blocks. For example, if you decided to give each treatment (*ABCD*) 5 times, block randomization could produce the following sequence of five treatment blocks:

BDCA • DBAC • ACDB • CABD • BADC

The experiment would consist of 20 trials (five repeats of each condition). Clearly, block randomization in which subjects are presented with many blocks is not ideal for all types of experiments. However, it is commonly used in cognition, perception, and psychophysics experiments in which treatment conditions are relatively short.

In reality, we rarely know precisely what progressive error will look like. Therefore, it is especially important to be cautious when planning a design involving repeated measures for each subject. The available control procedures might not be adequate to distribute the effects of progressive error equally across all conditions. We rely on prior research to guide our decisions. Occasionally, progressive error itself must become a variable for study. When we clarify its impact beforehand, we can set up the most effective controls.

## Across-Subjects Counterbalancing

One drawback of counterbalancing within each subject is that we have to present each condition to each subject more than once. As the number of conditions increases, the length of the sequence of treatments also increases.

Depending on the experiment, the procedures can become time-consuming, expensive, or just plain boring for the subjects as well as for the experimenter. As an alternative, we can often use the second general approach, across-subjects counterbalancing. These procedures serve the same basic purpose as subject-by-subject counterbalancing: They are used to distribute the effects of progressive error so that if we average across subjects, the effects will be the same for all conditions of the experiment. We are not always concerned about the individual subject's responses, but we still want to be sure that progressive error affects each of the various treatment conditions equally. These across-subjects techniques are complete counterbalancing and partial counterbalancing.

### Complete Counterbalancing

If we always present treatment conditions in the same order, progressive error will affect some conditions more than others. Complete counterbalancing controls for this effect by using all possible sequences of the conditions and using every sequence the same number of times. If we had only two treatments (*AB*), as we did in the cola experiment, we would give half the subjects *A* first and then *B*. We would give the other subjects *B* first and then *A*. You can see that this is very similar to what we did to control order effects within each subject by giving each subject both sequences, *AB* and *BA*. But when we counterbalance across subjects, we need to give each subject only one sequence. Different subjects are assigned to the sequences at random, and we give each sequence to an equal number of subjects. Some subjects go through condition *A* without any practice; others go through *B* without any practice. The effects of progressive error should turn out to be about the same for each condition if we pool the data from all subjects.

It is easy to counterbalance completely when there are only two conditions, but suppose there are more. Let's say that we are testing memory for faces displaying different emotions. In our experiment, we have three sets of target photographs. One set (*A*) shows people who are smiling. The second set (*B*) shows people who are frowning. The third set (*C*) is used as a control; it shows people whose faces appear to be neutral. Later, we will ask subjects to go through another much larger set and pick out the people they have seen before. In this experiment, we do not want to show all subjects the happy target faces first because people tend to have better recall for the first (and last) things they see; things in the middle are less well recalled. We can control for this kind of error by using complete counterbalancing. We use all possible sequences of the *ABC* treatment conditions; we also use each sequence the same number of times.

Table 11.1 shows complete counterbalancing for an experiment with three treatment conditions. There are six possible order sequences for the three conditions. For our face recognition experiment, we would need order sequences like happy, neutral, sad (*ACB*) and sad, happy, neutral (*BAC*). To counterbalance completely, we must use all the sequences and use each one the same number of times. Thus, for six sequences, we would need at least six subjects. Ideally, we should have more than one subject for each sequence,

TABLE **11.1**

The six sequences of three treatment conditions

| A B C | B A C |
|-------|-------|
| B C A | C B A |
| C A B | A C B |

© Cengage Learning

so we need a number of subjects that is a multiple of 6. Remember that we have to use all the sequences an equal number of times. We can use 6, or 12, or 18 subjects but not 9, 11, or 17 because these are not multiples of 6.

Can we tell in advance how many sequences and how many subjects we will need? How can we be sure we did not miss a sequence? You can find the number of possible sequences by computing $N$ factorial, represented by $N!$. We get $N!$ by computing the product of $N$ and all integers smaller than $N$ until we reach 1. In an experiment with four treatment conditions, $4!$ is

$$4 \times 3 \times 2 \times 1 = 24$$

$4!$ is equal to 24. This tells us that when we have four treatment conditions, there are 24 possible orders in which to present them. Earlier we saw that there are six possible sequences if we have three conditions. You can verify that by computing $3!$:

$$3 \times 2 \times 1 = 6$$

The number of possible order sequences clearly expands very quickly as the number of treatment conditions increases. To counterbalance an experiment completely, we need at least one subject for each possible sequence. That means we need at least 4 times as many subjects for a four-condition experiment as we do for a three-condition experiment (24 versus 6 possible sequences). We also need to present each sequence an equal number of times. If we want more than one subject per sequence, we will need multiples of 24 for a four-condition experiment—a minimum of 48 subjects.

### Partial Counterbalancing

You can see that it is economical to keep the number of treatments to a minimum. If we double the number of conditions from three to six, we increase the minimum number of subjects needed to counterbalance completely from 6 to 720. Of course, it makes sense to omit any condition that is not necessary for a good test of the hypothesis. Still, sometimes six or even more conditions are essential. In those cases, we may use partial counterbalancing procedures. The basic idea is the same. We use these procedures when we cannot do complete counterbalancing but still want to have some control over progressive error across subjects. Partial counterbalancing controls progressive error by using some subset of the available order sequences; these sequences are chosen through special procedures.

The simplest partial counterbalancing procedure is randomized partial counterbalancing. When there are many possible order sequences, we randomly select out as many sequences as we have subjects for the experiment. Suppose we have 120 possible sequences (five treatment conditions) and only 30 subjects. We would randomly select 30 sequences, and each subject would get one of those sequences. You can see that this procedure may not control for order effects quite as effectively as complete counterbalancing, but it is better than simply using the same order for all subjects. If possible, use complete counterbalancing because it is safer. If you must use partial counterbalancing, be realistic about it. If there are 720 possible order sequences in the experiment, running three subjects just does not make sense. You will not be able to get good control over order effects. *As a general rule, use at least as many randomly selected sequences as there are experimental conditions.*

Another procedure commonly used to select a subset of order sequences is called Latin square counterbalancing. A matrix, or square, of sequences is constructed that satisfies the following condition: Each treatment appears only once in any order position in the sequences. Table 11.2 shows a basic Latin square for an experiment with four treatment conditions (a 4 × 4 matrix). Each row represents a different order sequence. Notice that each of the four treatment conditions appears in the first, second, third, and fourth position only once. This method controls adequately for progressive error caused by order effects because each treatment condition occurs equally often in each position.

Once you have selected your sequences, you would assign subjects at random to receive the different orders. Remember that each sequence is used equally often. With four sequences, you would need to run at least four subjects. If you have more subjects available, it is always better to run more than one subject in each order condition. For the four-condition experiment, any multiple of 4 subjects could be used: 8, 12, 16, and so on.

Using a Latin square to determine treatment sequences will provide protection against order effects, but it cannot control for other kinds of systematic interference between two treatment conditions. Notice in Table 11.2 that some parts of the sequences tend to repeat themselves. For instance, condition *A* comes right before *B* in two out of four of the sequences. If exposure to condition *A* affects how subjects will respond to condition *B*, the Latin square will not provide enough control. The experiment can still be confounded. This kind of systematic interference is called a *carryover effect*.

TABLE **11.2**

Latin square counterbalancing
for four treatment conditions

| | | | |
|---|---|---|---|
| *A* | *B* | *C* | *D* |
| *B* | *A* | *D* | *C* |
| *C* | *D* | *A* | *B* |
| *D* | *C* | *B* | *A* |

© Cengage Learning

## Carryover Effects

Perry Mason, the great fictional defense attorney, always wins his cases (except once, when the client really was guilty). He always finds a way to get to the truth before the end of the trial. Imagine Mason in court, cross-examining a witness. His large, imposing frame commands respect. A witness has just identified the defendant as the woman who passed close by him in the hallway outside the murder victim's apartment. The witness vividly recalls the defendant's rare and expensive perfume. No, he could not be mistaken about it. Mason wants to test the man's ability to identify other scents. He presents the witness with a small vial. "It is essence of lilac," says the witness confidently. The witness sniffs a second vial and correctly states, "This smells like gasoline!" Now Mason presents the critical test—a vial containing the defendant's perfume. A dismayed and confused witness is unable to identify it. His testimony crumbles. He breaks down and confesses to the crime.

A dramatic and fanciful story indeed, but it illustrates another key problem in the within-subjects design. Mason was using a within-subjects approach when he presented the witness with the vials. What the witness did not know was that Mason was playing with carryover effects: The effects of some treatments will persist, or carry over, after the treatments are removed. A few whiffs of gasoline spoiled the witness's ability to identify any other scents for a time. The guilty witness panicked and confessed.

On a smaller scale, imagine how carryover effects could sabotage experiments. Earlier in the chapter, we saw how some combinations of treatments are impossible to administer to the same subjects because one treatment precludes another. For instance, we cannot both do and not do surgery on the same animal. Similarly, we do not want to allow one experimental condition to interfere with a subsequent condition. For example, we do not want to give subjects treatments that will give them clues to what they should do in later conditions. We do not want one experimental treatment to make a later treatment easier (or harder). We do not want the effects of early conditions to contaminate later conditions.

Researchers studying emotions are forced to work around this problem all the time. Suppose we are interested in studying facial muscle movements during different emotional states. Smiling, for example, is accompanied by movement of the *zygomaticus major,* the muscle that lifts up the corners of the mouth; frowning comes about when the *corrugator supercilii* pulls the brows together and down. In this area of research, within-subjects designs are preferred because there are large individual differences in people's facial muscle activity. A researcher might use a series of film clips to induce different emotions in an experiment while several pairs of electrodes are connected to the subject's face.

Ordinarily, a very funny film sketch brings on a wide smile in viewers, and a lot of electrical activity is recorded from the pair of electrodes placed above the *zygomaticus.* Conversely, the *corrugator* typically shows a lot of activity during a very sad scene. However, we cannot apply one of these treatment conditions right after another because of carryover effects. A funny scene does not seem nearly as funny as it should if a subject has just watched a tragic death scene. If we were recording the facial muscles, we would find that the activity of the *zygomaticus* was dampened by the previous emotion. When inducing different emotions within subjects, researchers have to take precautions to ensure that one emotion has completely passed before they begin each new treatment.

Notice that carryover effects differ from order effects in an important way. Order effects emerge as a result of the position of a treatment in a sequence (first, second, third, etc.). It does not matter what the specific treatment is; if it occurs first in a sequence, subjects will handle it differently than if it occurs last. Carryover, however, is a function of the treatment itself. Gasoline will produce changes in the ability to detect subsequent odors no matter whether the subject smells it first, second, or tenth. Feeling sadness will carry over to the next emotion regardless of whether sadness is the first, second, or fourth condition in the experiment.

We can control for carryover effects to some extent by using some of the same counterbalancing procedures that control for order effects. Subject-by-subject counterbalancing and complete counterbalancing will usually control carryover effects adequately by balancing them out the entire experiment. Control is less certain with randomized counterbalancing, and it might not be controlled at all if Latin square counterbalancing is used. Using mathematical techniques, however, it is possible to construct special Latin squares, called balanced Latin squares, that can control for both order and carryover effects. In balanced Latin squares, each treatment condition (1) appears only once in each position in the order sequences and (2) precedes and follows every other condition an equal number of times. Table 11.3 represents a balanced Latin square for four treatment conditions (*ABCD*).

Compare the balanced Latin square with the Latin square depicted in Table 11.2. Can you see the important differences that allow the balanced square to control for carryover as well as order effects? In both tables, each treatment appears only once in each position in the sequence as a control for order effects, but the sequences in Table 11.3 also control for carryover effects. Here, every treatment precedes and follows every other treatment an equal number of times. Parts of the sequences, such as *A* preceding *B*, do not repeat themselves, so potential carryover effects are distributed equally over the entire experiment. Box 11.2 shows you how to construct a balanced Latin square.

TABLE **11.3**

Balanced Latin square counterbalancing for four treatment conditions

| | | | |
|---|---|---|---|
| *A* | *B* | *D* | *C* |
| *B* | *C* | *A* | *D* |
| *C* | *D* | *B* | *A* |
| *D* | *A* | *C* | *B* |

© Cengage Learning

## BOX 11.2  Constructing a Balanced Latin Square

To construct a balanced Latin square, you simply follow a set of rules for each row. For experiments with an even number of conditions, each treatment will appear once in each row (like the sequences in the *ABCD* square in Table 11.3). For experiments with uneven numbers of conditions, each treatment will need to appear twice in each sequence to balance out carryover effects, doubling the length of the rows.

Let's construct a balanced Latin square for six conditions (*ABCDEF*).

For the first row of the square, use the following formula:

*A, B, N, C, N–1, D, N–2, E, N–3, F,* and so on.

(The letter *N–5* is the last treatment.)

The first row of our balanced Latin square would look like this:

A  B  F  C  E  D

To construct the second row, use the treatment that immediately follows each of those in the first row. (When you get to the last treatment, *F*, go back to *A*.) *A* is in the first position in row 1, so *B* will be in the first position in row 2; treatment *B* in row 1 becomes *C* in row 2, and so on.

A  B  F  C  E  D
B  C  A  D  F  E

Construct the remaining rows in the same manner:

| | | | | | |
|---|---|---|---|---|---|
| Row three: | C | D | B | E | A | F |
| Row four: | D | E | C | F | B | A |
| Row five: | E | F | D | A | C | B |
| Row six: | F | A | E | B | D | C |

Here's the complete 6 × 6 balanced Latin square:

A  B  F  C  E  D
B  C  A  D  F  E
C  D  B  E  A  F
D  E  C  F  B  A
E  F  D  A  C  B
F  A  E  B  D  C

To construct a balanced Latin square for an uneven number of treatments, simply construct the first square using the rules above. Then reverse the sequence to complete the other half of each row. Here's a balanced Latin square for three conditions (*ABC*):

A  B  C  •  C  B  A
B  C  A  •  A  C  B
C  A  B  •  B  A  C

## Choosing Among Counterbalancing Procedures

Every experiment with a within-subjects condition will need some form of counterbalancing. In a within-subjects design with one independent variable or a within-subjects factorial design, you must counterbalance all conditions. If the design is a within-subjects factorial, remember to multiply the levels of each factor together to get the total number of conditions. For instance, our earlier factorial example of comparing slides of men and women displaying four different expressions (a 4 × 2 within-subjects design) has eight conditions that need to be counterbalanced. In a mixed design, only within-subjects factors need to be counterbalanced.

Deciding whether to use subject-by-subject or across-subjects counterbalancing can be a problem in itself. We need to counterbalance for each subject when we expect large differences in the pattern of progressive error from subject to subject. In a weightlifting experiment, we might expect subjects to fatigue at different rates. In that sort of experiment, it makes sense to counterbalance conditions for each person in the study because that would give the most control over order and carryover effects. In some experiments, we do not expect large differences in the way progressive error influences each subject. When we know the effects will be about the same for everyone, we do not need to worry about progressive error within each subject—we can counterbalance across subjects instead.

There are practical things to consider, too. You might not have the time to run through all the conditions more than once for each subject. Or you might not have enough subjects to make complete counterbalancing feasible. The same considerations that come into play as you select a within- or between-subjects design can also limit your choice of controls in the within-subjects experiment. For guidance, you should look at the procedures that have been used in similar experiments.

If prior researchers have had success with across-subjects counterbalancing, it is probably all right to use it. Try to avoid randomized and Latin square counterbalancing if you expect carryover effects. When in doubt, counterbalance subject by subject if you can. The worst that can happen is that you might overcontrol the experiment. It is always a good idea to use the procedures that give the most control, simply because you might not know what the extraneous variables are or whether progressive error really will be the same for all subjects.

Although we have talked about counterbalancing mainly in the context of within-subjects designs, counterbalancing procedures can be useful in between-subjects experiments, too. For example, in a between-subjects experiment on list learning, a researcher might compare two different study conditions on people's ability to memorize a list of 10 words. The researcher would want both groups to memorize the same 10 words to make sure that the lists were equally difficult in both study conditions. In addition, it might be desirable to use several different random orders of the items on each list and randomly assign some number of subjects in each group to each different list. If just one order were used, the possibility exists that the list contained some logical sequence that was easier to learn under one set of conditions than another. Whenever subjects are presented with an experimental stimulus that is really a group of items (words, pictures, stories, and the like), the order of the items should be counterbalanced to avoid confounding. You may find other opportunities to apply the counterbalancing procedures you have learned as you design your own experiments.

## Order as a Design Factor

If you are concerned that a partial counterbalancing technique might not be controlling adequately for progressive error or carryover effects, there is a way to test whether treatments are producing similar effects in all order sequences. Researchers do this fairly routinely if they use a Latin square and have four or less order sequences. You can simply include treatment order as an additional factor in the design. Suppose you wanted to conduct the happy (*H*) versus sad (*S*) film clip experiment described earlier. You might be concerned that one type of film produces more carryover than another. It would be a good idea to include order as a factor in your design. With only two treatment conditions, it should be fairly easy to use both possible order sequences: Half the subjects receive the sequence *HS,* and the others receive *SH.* Your experiment would be statistically analyzed as a 2 × 2 (Order × Film) mixed-factorial design. (Treatment order is always a between-subjects factor.) If the order factor produced no significant effects, you can feel more confident that your counterbalancing procedure worked. However, if the order of treatments produced significant effects, you will know your experiment is confounded by order. Effects on the dependent variable could have been produced by the order of treatments, rather than by the treatments themselves.

Sometimes, as we saw with Perry Mason and the gasoline, you will find that the effect of one condition is much greater than that of others. Gasoline altered the witness's performance more than the smell of lilacs did. When one condition has more impact than others, we say that the carryover effects are asymmetrical—or, more simply, lopsided. When one condition carries over more than others, control is extremely difficult, if not impossible. In such situations, an experimenter should reconsider the design of the experiment and switch to a between-subjects design if possible.

## HOW CAN YOU CHOOSE A DESIGN?

How do you decide whether to use a within-subjects or a between-subjects design? First, as always, think about the hypothesis of the experiment. How many treatment conditions do you need to test the hypothesis? Would it be possible to have each subject in more than one of these conditions? If so, you might be able to use a within-subjects design. Do your treatment conditions interfere with one another? Yes? Then you might want to use a between-subjects design.

Consider the practical advantages of each approach. Is it simpler to run the experiment one way or the other? Which will be more time-consuming? If you can get only a few subjects, the within-subjects design might be better. Remember that there is a trade-off: The longer the experiment takes, the harder it might be to find willing subjects (and the more likely it is that they will become fatigued). You can control subject variables best in a within-subjects design. If there are likely to be large individual differences in the way subjects respond to the experiment, the within-subjects approach is usually better.

Remember to review the research literature. If other experimenters have used within-subjects designs for similar research problems, it is probably because that approach works best. If all other things seem equal, use the within-subjects design. It is better from a statistical standpoint, because you maximize your chances of detecting the effect of the independent variable.

## SUMMARY

*Within-subjects designs* are designs in which each subject takes part in more than one condition of the experiment. These designs are advantageous because they enable us to compare the behavior of the same subjects under different treatment conditions. We can often get a more precise picture of the effects of the independent variable from a within-subjects design. Subject variables are better controlled in the within-subjects experiment. We eliminate the error produced by differences between subjects and thus make a more precise assessment of the effect of the independent variable; therefore, a within-subjects design has more *power*. *Within-subjects factorial designs* and *mixed designs* can also be used.

Complicated control problems occur in experiments using within-subjects designs, however, because each subject takes part in more than one condition of the experiment. In these experiments, we have to control for two kinds of extraneous variables, order effects and carryover effects.

*Order effects* are the positive and negative changes in performance that occur when a treatment condition falls in different places in a series of treatments. Changes in performance over the course of an experiment sometimes occur from *fatigue effects* or *practice effects*. All these changes, both positive and negative, are called *progressive error*: Results are distorted as the experiment progresses. We looked at a number of *counterbalancing* procedures for controlling order effects. All have the same basic function, to distribute progressive error more equally across the different treatment conditions of the experiment.

*Subject-by-subject counterbalancing* controls for progressive error for each individual subject; it consists of presenting all treatment conditions more than once. One type, *reverse counterbalancing,* presents treatments first in one order, then in reverse order. For example, with two treatment conditions, *A* and *B*, each subject will get the sequence *ABBA*. The second form of counterbalancing for each subject uses *block randomization*. Here, each set of treatments is considered as a block, and treatments within each block are given in random order. Subjects typically receive a number of blocks.

*Across-subjects counterbalancing* can accomplish some of the same goals by pooling all subjects' data together to equalize the effects of progressive error for each condition. One type, *complete counterbalancing,* requires using all the possible sequences that can be formed from the treatment conditions and using each sequence the same number of times. The number of subjects needed for complete counterbalancing increases very rapidly as the number of treatment conditions increases. With three conditions, there must be at least 6 subjects (3 factorial, or 3!); with six conditions, there must be at least 720 subjects (6!). When complete counterbalancing is not feasible, we may use a *partial counterbalancing* procedure in which a subset of all possible sequences is selected. *Randomized partial counterbalancing* involves selecting a subset at random. A second partial counterbalancing technique, *Latin square counterbalancing,* is a particularly effective procedure for controlling order effects.

In addition to order effects, a within-subjects experiment can also have *carryover effects*. These occur when the treatment conditions affect each other. Most carryover effects can be controlled adequately by using within-subjects counterbalancing or complete counterbalancing, but constructing a *balanced Latin square* is another option. One technique to consider for assessing order or carryover effects is taking treatment order as a factor in the design.

Deciding on the particular form of counterbalancing to use can be difficult. Subject-by-subject counterbalancing offers the most control and should be used whenever possible. If this cannot be used, across-subjects counterbalancing has many practical advantages. Counterbalancing of some form must be used in every experiment that has a within-subjects design. The procedures can also be useful in between-subjects experiments containing series of stimuli. It is always better to err on the side of controlling too much; there is more danger in failing to control an element of the experiment that could confound the results.

## KEY TERMS

**Across-subjects counterbalancing** A technique for controlling progressive error that pools all subjects' data together to equalize the effects of progressive error for each condition.

**Balanced Latin square** A partial counterbalancing technique for constructing a matrix, or square, of sequences in which each treatment condition (1) appears only once in each position in a sequence and (2) precedes and follows every other condition an equal number of times.

**Block randomization** A process of randomization that first creates treatment blocks containing one random order of the conditions in the experiment; subjects are then assigned to fill each successive treatment block.

**Carryover effect** The persistence of the effect of a treatment condition after the condition ends.

**Complete counterbalancing** A technique for controlling progressive error using all possible sequences that can be formed out of the treatment conditions and using each sequence the same number of times.

**Counterbalancing** A technique for controlling order effects by distributing progressive error across the different treatment conditions of the experiment; may also control carryover effects.

**Fatigue effects** Changes in performance caused by fatigue, boredom, or irritation.

**Latin square counterbalancing** A partial counterbalancing technique in which a matrix, or square, of sequences is constructed so that each treatment appears only once in any order position.

**Mixed design** A factorial design that combines within-subjects and between-subjects factors.

**Order effects** Change in subjects' performance that occurs when a condition falls in different positions in a sequence of treatments.

**Partial counterbalancing** A technique for controlling progressive error by using some subset of the available sequences of treatment conditions.

**Power** The chance of detecting a genuine effect of the independent variable.

**Practice effect** Change in subjects' performance resulting from practice.

**Progressive error** Changes in subjects' responses that are caused by testing in multiple treatment conditions; includes order effects, such as the effects of practice or fatigue.

**Randomized partial counterbalancing** The simplest partial counterbalancing procedure in which the experimenter randomly selects as many sequences of treatment conditions as there are subjects for the experiment.

Reverse counterbalancing A technique for controlling progressive error for each individual subject by presenting all treatment conditions twice, first in one order, then in the reverse order.

Subject-by-subject counterbalancing A technique for controlling progressive error for each

individual subject by presenting all treatment conditions more than once.

Within-subjects design A design in which each subject takes part in more than one condition of the experiment; also called a repeated-measures design.

Within-subjects factorial design A factorial design in which subjects receive all conditions in the experiment.

## REVIEW AND STUDY QUESTIONS

1. How does a within-subjects experiment differ from a between-subjects experiment?

2. Discuss three advantages and three disadvantages of using a within-subjects design.

3. Outline a within-subjects experiment to test this hypothesis: Children who play with weaponlike toys (for example, toy guns and knives) become more aggressive.

4. Mary is very excited about the within-subjects approach. "Now I'll never need to run large numbers of subjects again," she says. What has she forgotten?

5. For each of the following dependent measures, evaluate the pros and cons of using a within-subjects approach:
   a. The taste of a new toothpaste
   b. The cavity-preventing properties of a new toothpaste
   c. The readability of a new typeface
   d. The impact of good and bad news

6. What requirements must be met to make the within-subjects approach feasible?

7. You are planning an experiment on anagrams (scrambled words). You want to test whether different scramble patterns lead to different solution rates. For instance, the letter order 54321 might be easier to solve than 41352 (12345 represents the actual word). You want to use the same words in all conditions so that the type of word will not be a confounding variable. People solve anagrams at different rates, so you are thinking about using a within-subjects design.

   a. If you use a within-subjects design for this experiment, will you have to worry about order effects? Why or why not?
   b. Review the four counterbalancing techniques (reverse counterbalancing, block randomization, complete, and partial) for handling order effects discussed in this chapter. Which would help you most in this experiment? Why?
   c. What are carryover effects? Would they be a problem in this experiment? How would you handle them?

8. Lawson, Downing, and Cetola (1998) tested the effects of audience laughter on the perceived funniness of recorded jokes. After receiving one of four possible manipulations (Laughter strength: strong vs. weak × Constraint: constrained vs. unconstrained), subjects judged how funny they believed the audience found the comedy routine. This question was either first or fourth in a questionnaire. As expected, strong laugher did lead to higher ratings of funniness than weak laughter, but the order of the questions also produced a main effect. Subjects rated the comedy routine significantly less funny when they were asked this question first than when it came fourth. As the authors noted, "This was an unexpected, and puzzling, result" (p. 247).

   a. Is this experiment confounded by order?
   b. Explain why or why not?

9. A television commercial showed people tasting and choosing between two colas. The first cola was labeled R; the second was labeled Q. The majority of people said they liked cola R better than cola Q. Given what you know about experimental design, would you accept the ad's claim that cola R tastes better than cola Q? Why or why not? How might you change the procedures to get more acceptable data?

10. Explain why (when it is used as a factor in a design) order is always a between-subjects factor.

11. Figure 11.7 illustrates progressive error measured in an experiment on breathing rate during weightlifting. Because of warm-up and fatigue effects across subjects, progressive error was curvilinear. Based on the figure, what strategy would you recommend for handling progressive error in this experiment and why?

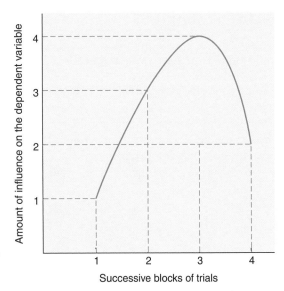

FIGURE **11.7** Progressive error in an experiment on breathing rate during weightlifting.
© Cengage Learning

## CRITICAL THINKING EXERCISE

*The candy company's research:* A candy company conducted taste tests of its new candy-coated chocolates (a direct competitor with M&Ms). Subjects in the experiment were asked to taste both candies; half the subjects tasted the new candy first, and half tasted the M&Ms first. Subjects rated each candy on a scale from −5 (extremely bad) to +5 (extremely good). Results of the taste test are depicted in the graph in Figure 11.8.

*The problem:* The statistical analysis of the 2 (Order) × 2 (Type of Candy) mixed design showed that there were no significant main effects for type of candy or order; overall, the two candies were rated equivalently, and the average ratings in both orders were about the same. The Candy × Order interaction, however, was highly significant. Explain what happened in the taste test experiment in terms of carryover effects.

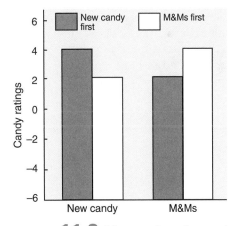

FIGURE **11.8** Mean ratings for each condition.
© Cengage Learning

## ONLINE RESOURCES

You can find a workshop to review concepts for within-subjects designs at the following site: http://www.wadsworth.com/psychology_d/templates/student_resources/workshops/workshops.html

For interesting research findings on carryover effects from our emotions to our economic decisions, go to the following site: www.psychologicalscience.org/pdf/ps/lerner.pdf

Learn more about Huntsman spiders at: www.austmus.gov.au/factsheets/huntsman_spiders.htm

## CHAPTER 12

# Within-Subjects Designs: Small *N*

**Small *N* Designs**
A Small *N* Design: Talking to Plants

***ABA* Designs**
Variations of the *ABA* Format

**Multiple Baseline Design**

**Statistics and Variability in Small *N* Designs**

**Changing Criterion Designs**

**Discrete Trials Designs**

**When to Use Large *N* and Small *N* Designs**

SUMMARY
KEY TERMS
REVIEW AND STUDY QUESTIONS
CRITICAL THINKING EXERCISE
ONLINE RESOURCES

## CHAPTER OBJECTIVES

● Understand the rationale for conducting small *N* experiments

● Learn the ABA family of reversal designs

● Learn other methods used in small *N* research

All the experimental designs we have discussed thus far have required manipulating or selecting independent variables and testing a number of subjects. These are called large *N* designs (*N* stands for the number of subjects needed in the experiment). The large *N* approach is by far the most common technique used in research design, but it is not the only approach used by contemporary researchers.

-----

## SMALL *N* DESIGNS

Some researchers prefer to use small *N* designs, which test only one or a very few subjects. These researchers argue that large *N* designs lack precision because they pool, or combine, the data from many different subjects to reach conclusions about the effects of independent variables. The conclusions of large *N* experiments can sometimes be misleading because they obscure the results of individual subjects, who can vary widely in their responses to treatment conditions. Small *N* researchers argue that aggregate effects are artificial because they often do not represent what really occurs with any individual subject—instead, large *N* experiments can reveal only general trends, which might produce dubious conclusions. For example, it is possible to miss the effect of an independent variable in a large *N* experiment. Responses of different subjects to the same independent variable can vary greatly; sometimes they even cancel each other out, giving the appearance that no effects at all were produced. The following example will demonstrate how that might happen.

Suppose you used an experimental group–control group design to test the hypothesis that children pay more attention to violent cartoons than they pay to control cartoons. You measure attention by tracking the children's eye movements. At the end of the experiment, your statistics show no differences between the two groups. You conclude that children do not pay more attention to violent cartoons—but your conclusion might be erroneous. Your conclusion could be wrong if there are large individual differences in the way children respond to violence. For instance, when cartoons are violent, fearful children might spend less time watching the screen, but nonfearful children might spend more. In this case, the experimental group's pooled data might look quite similar to data from the control group. Your large *N* design is simply not sensitive enough to detect two competing kinds of effects.

A related disadvantage of large *N* designs is that the results of data aggregated over groups of subjects might not really be a good reflection of the reactions of individual subjects. Studies of learning can provide a good example. Learning a new concept, such as how to pronounce the vowel "u" correctly in French, is often a case of trial and error. The French "u" sound is notoriously difficult for English speakers to learn. It can take many, many trials (and lots of errors) before we can pronounce it well enough not to be ignored in a French restaurant. But, once we master the concept, we are unlikely to make future errors. If we mapped the process in a single individual, learning might resemble Figure 12.1a. Here, it took nine trials to get the correct sound. A second individual might look very different, as in Figure 12.1b. This person got it right on the seventh trial. A third individual might perform like Figure 12.1c. This person did not make the correct sound until trial number 18. Once they had learned the correct sound, though, each person was able to reproduce it correctly on all subsequent trials. If a researcher pooled the data from 20 different subjects trying to learn how to pronounce "u," it might look like the graph in Figure 12.1d. Figure 12.1d suggests that people get closer and closer to the correct sound with every trial, but was that really the case with any single individual? No. Some trials resulted in a closer approximation of the correct sound; other trials produced poorer pronunciation. When we averaged the data for an entire group, we lost the real pattern. The pooled data, in fact, would have given a highly erroneous picture of how the concept was learned.

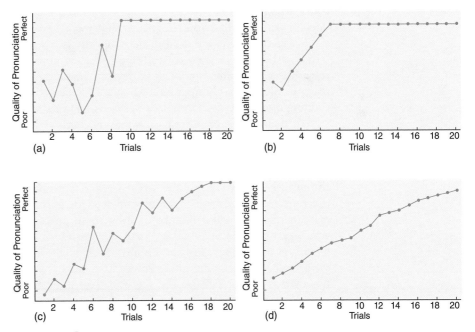

FIGURE **12.1** (a) One individual learning to pronounce the French "u" sound. (b) Second individual learning to pronounce the French "u" sound. (c) Third individual learning to pronounce the French "u" sound. (d) Pooled data from 20 individuals learning to pronounce the French "u" sound.
© Cengage Learning

Small *N* designs take a very different approach to studying effects of independent variables. Here the behavior of one or a few subjects is studied much more intensely. Typically, the researcher measures the subject's behavior many times. A subject can be studied in one intensive session or over a period of weeks, months, or even years. When group or large *N* designs are used, subjects are generally measured at only one point in time—right after the experimental manipulation—and that measurement might or might not be a good representation of the subject's response to the treatment. In addition, Morgan and Morgan (2001) make the following argument for using a small *N* design:

> For parents, teachers, therapists, and others charged with changing behavior, the individual ordinarily constitutes the unit of analysis, and change makes itself known only through multiple measures taken over prolonged observational periods. The single-participant design evolved because it allowed for a sensitive assessment of developing behavioral repertoires, which remains its primary advantage, whether realized in the basic laboratory or in clinical settings. (p. 122)

Sometimes small *N* designs are used for practical reasons. In clinical psychopathology research, for example, a psychologist might want to conduct an experiment to test a new therapy treatment for depressed individuals. The researcher might not be able to find enough depressed individuals to form experimental and control groups for a large *N* study; however, a small *N* experiment could be conducted in which the progress of one or a few patients could be studied intensively. (This is one approach to solving the ethical dilemma of untreated control groups that we talked about in Chapter 9.)

Small *N* designs are used in the laboratory and in clinical and other field settings; they can be used to study both human and animal behavior. Animal researchers very often use small *N* designs for practical reasons. Research animals, from mice to chimpanzees, are costly to acquire and maintain, and their training often involves months or years. Sometimes animals must be sacrificed so that their brains or other tissues may be studied. In these cases, researchers try to use as few animals as possible; here small *N* designs make a great deal of sense.

Another area of psychology in which small *N* designs are common is psychophysics (the study of how we sense and perceive physical stimuli). Basic psychophysical processes operate similarly for most individuals, so researchers can obtain a good picture of how these processes operate by testing a very small number of subjects. Small *N* research of this kind has a venerable history in psychology. In fact, a major component of early experimentation in the United States in the late 19th century was the study of psychophysical processes, which relied on the single-subject approach almost exclusively. If additional subjects were tested at all, they were used to replicate effects produced on a single subject. It wasn't until Sir Ronald Fisher invented the statistical technique called analysis of variance in the 1930s (Fisher, 1935) that large *N* or group designs requiring inferential statistics began to gain in popularity.

Small *N* designs are used in many areas of psychology, but they are used most extensively in experimentation using principles of operant conditioning.

The well-known behaviorist B. F. Skinner (discussed in Chapter 6) studied changes in the rate of behavior based on the introduction of positive or negative consequences (reinforcement) using the small *N* design. His techniques have become known as "the experimental analysis of behavior." Skinner strongly believed that there was more to gain by careful, continuous measurement of the behavior of a single subject than by using statistical tests to compare data obtained from different groups of subjects. Skinner's approach uses just one or two subjects and requires special measurement procedures. Let us look at these procedures in a simple hypothetical experiment.

## A Small *N* Design: Talking to Plants

We want to test the notion that talking to a plant makes it grow better. Of course, we want to approach this hypothesis in a rigorous, scientific way. On the one hand, we could use a large *N* design, such as a two-group experiment. We could compare different groups of plants by talking to one group but not to the other. Then we would measure their growth and see how the groups compare. Or we might plan a multiple-groups experiment and use varying amounts of talking as our treatment conditions. We might even choose (as we did in our plant example in Chapter 10) to look at a second variable, such as music, and set up a factorial design.

On the other hand, instead of sacrificing our entertainment budget for a whole year to purchase enough plant subjects to conduct a large *N* study, we could use a small *N* design to do our experiment. First, we carefully choose our subject. Cactus grows too slowly to be of much use; bamboo grows very quickly but needs a temperate climate. After some library research, we settle on the hardy *Ficus elastica,* better known as the rubber plant. We begin with the control condition of the experiment (condition *A*): For a time, we do not talk to the plant at all. During this period—say, 3 months—we simply chart its growth by measuring it each Monday. This establishes a baseline of behavior, a measure of behavior as it normally occurs without the experimental manipulation. In the second phase of the experiment, we introduce the experimental manipulation (condition *B*): For another 3 months, we talk to the plant for 2 hours each day. "Talking" is operationally defined as reading aloud from Larry Hodgson's *Houseplants for Dummies* (1998). We continue to chart the plant's growth each Monday throughout this phase of the experiment. If talking aids growth, the plant should grow more during the second part of the experiment. If talking has no effect on growth, the plant should continue to grow about as much as it did in the baseline condition.

So far, this procedure looks very much like what we do when we carry out a two-group design: We use a control group to establish a baseline of behavior, and we compare behavior in the experimental condition with what we see in the control condition. In those respects, the procedures are similar, but there is also an important difference. Because we are using only one subject, we are looking at that subject at different points in time. Our rubber plant is 3 months older by the time we finish the first set of observations. The season has changed. The plant now gets a different amount of light each day. The humidity has probably changed, too. Of course, some of these

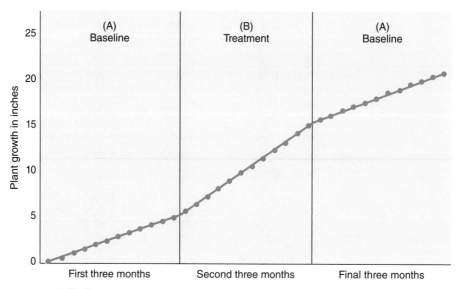

FIGURE **12.2** Hypothetical growth of a single *Ficus elastica* in an *ABA* experiment.
© Cengage Learning

extraneous variables can be controlled. We can raise our plant in a laboratory in which light, temperature, and moisture are always the same. But we cannot discount the fact that the plant has aged. Any differences in the amount of growth we see during the experimental manipulation might be caused by natural changes in the growth cycle of this plant (the classic threat called *maturation*). In other words, we might have confounding. For this reason, the small N experiment includes one additional, crucial step. After completing the experimental manipulation, we remove the independent variable and return to the original control condition (*A*). We do not talk to the subject at all during the last 3 months of the experiment; we simply continue to monitor its growth (see Figure 12.2).

We can verify the effect of our independent variable in the small N experiment by returning to the original baseline condition. Our hypothesis is that talking to a plant makes it grow faster. Suppose, as Figure 12.2 shows, that our plant did grow faster in the second phase of the experiment; compared with the baseline condition, the plant grew faster when we talked to it. If the change in growth rate was produced by some extraneous variable such as maturation, the growth rate will probably not change much after we stop talking to the plant. On the other hand, if talking caused the plant to grow faster, we would expect a decline in the growth rate after we stop. But under some circumstances, the change in behavior caused by an experimental manipulation can persist even after the experimental manipulation has been discontinued. If the target behavior does not return to the baseline level, we cannot automatically rule out the effect of the independent variable. One problem is that no matter how hard we try, we might not be able to re-create the original baseline conditions perfectly. This is especially true in experiments outside the laboratory. In these cases, we may want to repeat the procedures more than once. We can return to the baseline condition and reapply the experimental manipulation many times if we wish. Often we need to do that several times to make sure our findings were not produced by some chance variation in the testing situation.

## *ABA* DESIGNS

The small *N* experiment on the rubber plant used an *ABA* design. *ABA* refers to the order of the conditions of the experiment: *A* (the baseline condition) comes first, followed by *B* (the experimental condition). Finally, we return to the baseline condition (*A*) to verify that the change in behavior is linked to the independent variable. *ABA* designs may only be used if the treatment conditions are reversible; for that reason, they are also called *reversal designs*. Many small *N* experiments use the *ABA* design. The *ABA* design is sometimes used for large *N* experiments, too. An interesting example can be found in Box 12.1.

### Variations of the *ABA* Format

Frequently, researchers use other variations of the *ABA* format. In one amusing experiment, Hall, Alley, and Cox report on the case of a new bride who was having a problem with her husband: "According to the wife, Jim's jacket was a permanent fixture on the back of the couch and his shoes could usually be found close by. Occasionally he would decorate the back of the chair with a sweater" (1971, p. 43). The bride did not want to pick up after Jim or continue nagging him to put his clothes away. The solution was found through a simple behavior modification experiment. In these kinds of experiments, researchers try to change behaviors by applying various rewards and punishments as the independent variable. Rewards and punishments are presented as a consequence of the target behaviors to be modified. Researchers often use small *N* designs to do this. Let us look further at Hall et al.'s experiment, which used an *ABABA* design.

First, of course, the experimenters needed a baseline of behavior. We need to know how often the husband left his clothes in the living room under the usual circumstances. Each day for a week, records were made of how many items of clothing remained in the living room for more than 15 minutes; the average was two per day. During the experimental phase of the study, husband and wife agreed that whoever left more clothing in the living room during the week would have to do the dishes the following week. Leaving clothing in the living room then had a specific consequence. The husband could avoid that consequence by putting his clothes away. During the 2-week experimental period, the husband left no clothing in the living room. (Presumably, the tidy wife did the same, so it is not clear who actually did the dishes during that time.) The results are shown in days 8 through 21 of Figure 12.4.

Did the threat of doing the dishes (the independent variable) really produce the change in behavior? Perhaps the husband just became more aware of his wife's concern for the appearance of the house. The wife thought the

## BOX **12.1**    An Example of an *ABA* Design Using a Large *N*

Correia and Benson (2006) conducted an interesting large *N ABA* experiment using contingency management to reduce smoking in college students. In essence, they paid subjects for not smoking. This technique had already been shown by other researchers to be effective in reducing other unhealthy behaviors and has worked to reduce smoking in high school students and in pregnant women. To test its effect on college students, Correia and Benson set up a strict schedule of contingencies: College student smokers had to show up at the university clinic twice a day (between 8:00 and 10:00 AM and between 4:00 and 6:00 PM), Monday through Friday, to have their breath analyzed for levels of carbon monoxide (CO), an indicator of cigarette smoking. A payment schedule was set up to reward them for not smoking. Two levels of payments were explored in different groups of smokers (low-reinforcer or high-reinforcer conditions).

During the first week (*A*), there was no contingency: Subjects' baseline CO levels were measured twice a day, and they filled out questionnaires about their recent smoking activity. All subjects were paid $4 for each session they attended and could earn $40 if they attended all 10 sessions. During the second week (*B*), subjects continued to be paid $4 for each measurement session they attended, but they could also earn additional payments if their CO levels were below 8 ppm (considered the level for a nonsmoker). In the low-reinforcer condition, payments started at $1.00 for the first time their CO level was below 8 ppm; then, payments were increased by an additional $.50 each time their CO measured less than 8 ppm. So, the second time they received $1.50, the third time they received $2.00, and so on. They also got a bonus of $3.75 if CO levels were less than 8 ppm for 5 consecutive sessions. If their CO levels were too high or they failed to show up for a session, the payment schedule dropped back to $1.00. Procedures were identical for

the high-reinforcer group except that payments contingent on not smoking were doubled. The third week (*A*) was identical to week one—the payment contingencies for not smoking were removed, but subjects could earn money for attending sessions, plus an extra bonus for the total number of sessions they attended.

How well did the interventions work? You can see from Figure 12.3 that both contingencies reduced smoking during the intervention week, but the high-reinforcer condition worked much better. In this *ABA* design, the researchers showed that the reduction in smoking was most likely caused by the intervention because when the intervention was removed, CO levels rose, indicating that subjects were smoking again. This reversal provided good evidence that the contingency management interventions had indeed decreased smoking, if only temporarily.

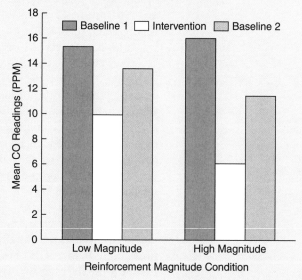

FIGURE **12.3** Mean carbon monoxide readings.
© Cengage Learning

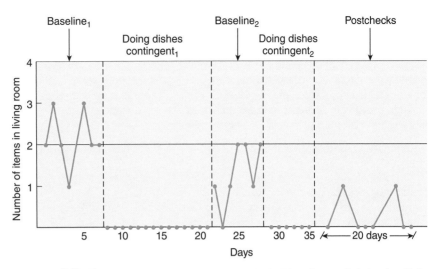

FIGURE **12.4** A record of the number of clothing items left in the living room by a newlywed husband.

From *Managing Behavior, 3, Applications in School and Home,* by R. V. Hall, S. J. Alley, and L. Cox.

problem was solved, so she let her husband know that the threat of dishwashing was lifted; nothing more would happen if he left his clothes in the living room. The outcome is illustrated in days 22 through 28 in Figure 12.4. You can see that the husband went back to leaving his clothes in the room when the threat of doing the dishes was withdrawn.[1] It seemed that the threat really did affect his behavior. Still, you can also see from the figure that he did not leave quite as many clothes around as before. It may be that the second baseline period was not exactly identical to the first. For instance, if the weather had warmed up, Jim's jacket may have stayed in the closet during that time. This story had a happy ending. As you can see from the figure, after additional training (doing dishes, contingent₂), Jim was much more consistent in putting his clothes away.

It is also possible to use several different experimental conditions in a small *N* experiment by extending the *ABA* format. We can proceed using different treatment conditions as follows: *ABACADA,* and so on, where *B, C,* and *D* represent three different treatments. What is important is that we collect baseline data before any experimental intervention and that we return to the baseline condition after each experimental treatment.

The small *N* design is frequently used to test the effects of positive or negative reinforcement on individuals with behavioral problems. The small *N* approach can be applied to many behavior modification problems (see Box 12.2).

---

[1] *ABA* reversal designs are sometimes referred to as *withdrawal designs* because treatment or contingencies are withdrawn as we return to baseline to evaluate their influence.

## BOX 12.2    An *ABAB* Design to Improve Children's Homework Performance

Miller and Kelley (1994) designed behavioral interventions to improve children's homework performance. Two boys and two girls (ages 9–11) participated along with a parent who would actually implement the treatment program. The researchers combined two behavioral techniques usually employed alone: goal setting and contingencies. Each parent and child signed a contract similar to the following:

> The following materials need to be brought home every day: **homework pad, workbooks, textbooks, pencils.**
>
> If (child's name) remembers to bring home all of these materials, then he/she may choose one of the following rewards: **gumballs, 10¢.**
>
> However, if (child's name) forgets to bring home some homework materials, then he/she: **does not get a snack before bed.**
>
> (child's name) may choose one of the following rewards if he/she meets 90% to 100% of his/her goals: **late bedtime (by 20 minutes), 2 stickers;** or one of these if he/she meets 75% to 89% of his/her goals: **soda, 1 sticker.**
>
> If (child's name) meets **80%** or more of the goals on at least **3** days this week, he/she may choose one of the following BONUS rewards: **renting a videotape, having a friend from school over to play.**

_____
Child's signature

_____
Parent's signature

The researchers tailored each child's program and contract to include appropriate goals and contingencies, including rewards that ranged from gumballs to trips to the mall. Homework accuracy was one of the dependent measures. An *ABAB* design was used. Baseline levels of homework accuracy were measured first (baseline$_1$). Then, accuracy was measured during a period of treatment (the goals and contracted contingencies were in place). Next, to ascertain whether the intervention was responsible for improvement, the treatment was removed and accuracy was again measured (baseline$_2$). Finally, the intervention was reinstituted, and accuracy was measured again.

Each child's homework performance was better during the treatment periods than during the baseline periods, suggesting that the interventions were successful. Some children, however, improved more

Sometimes, clinical experience leads researchers to decide to implement some, but not all, baseline levels, using variations of the *ABA* format. Jones and Friman (1999), for example, reported some intriguing results from a small *N* study of a 14-year-old boy with insect phobia (entomophobia). The boy was terrified of crickets and other bugs, and his phobia interfered with his performance in the classroom. Whenever an insect was present in the classroom, Mike would ignore his work and yell or pull the hood of his jacket over his head. Unfortunately, some of his classmates enjoyed taunting him by saying "Mike, there is a bug under your chair!" (p. 96). The teasing produced the same reaction as seeing a real bug. The researchers tested the effect of a graduated exposure hierarchy on Mike's reactions toward the primary phobic stimulus (crickets). There were nine steps in the hierarchy; each one was progressively more difficult. The first level was holding a jar of

than others. Children who showed the fewest behavioral problems, in general, improved the most. The actual performance of one of the children (Richard) is graphed in Figure 12.5. (The data points vary across the four conditions because homework was not assigned every night.)

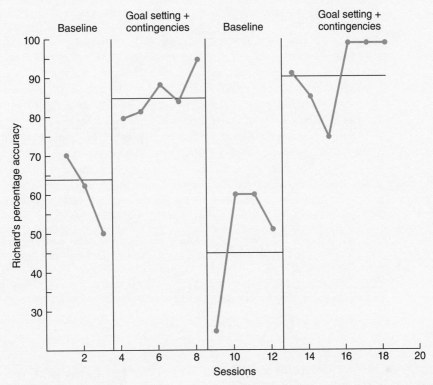

FIGURE **12.5** Results based on an *ABAB* experiment conducted by Miller and Kelley (1994).
© Cengage Learning

crickets. The fifth level was picking up a cricket with gloves on. The ninth and most difficult level was holding a cricket in each bare hand for 20 seconds. Instead of measuring fear levels, as is typically done, however, the researchers used Mike's performance on math problems as the dependent measure.

The researchers first took baseline measures of Mike's math performance with and without actual crickets on the floor. Not surprisingly, it was poor when crickets were present and substantially better without them! Then Jones and Friman implemented the first treatment condition—the hierarchy—*B*. Mike's math performance began to improve a little after three sessions but then dropped sharply to the previous poor performance level (with crickets present). Because Mike's performance was already so low, it would not have made sense to remove the hierarchy just to see what happened. Clearly, the hierarchy alone did not seem to be working. Instead, the researchers added reinforcement to the hierarchy (*BC*). Mike was exposed to the hierarchy, but now he was awarded points for correct math solutions, and these points could be redeemed for prizes, such as videos and candy. His performance improved dramatically.

Once they had established that the hierarchy plus reinforcement appeared to be working, the researchers returned to the original baseline condition (crickets present). In the first two sessions, Mike performed fairly well, but soon his performance dropped sharply. Rather than allow Mike's performance to continue to drop, Jones and Friman went back to the hierarchy plus reinforcement treatment condition (*BC*). When this treatment was reinstituted, Mike's performance quickly improved until it was at the same level as his first baseline measurement without any bugs present. No more reversals were instituted. This was an *A-B-BC-A-BC* design with convincing results.

Until now, we have focused on the importance of returning to the baseline conditions to verify the impact of our independent variable. However, in many clinical and behavior modification studies, researchers choose not to return to the baseline condition, even temporarily. Kazdin explains why:

> If behavior did revert to baseline levels when treatment was suspended temporarily, such a change would be clinically undesirable. Essentially, returning the client to baseline levels of performance amounts to making behavior worse .... In most circumstances, the idea of making a client worse just when treatment may be having an effect is ethically unacceptable. (2003, p. 283)

This is clearly true in experiments done to modify self-injurious behaviors. Suppose you were working with a disturbed boy who hit his head against the wall, kicked himself, and punched himself with his fists. If you concluded that the child performed these behaviors as a way of getting attention from caregivers, then one possible treatment would be to withhold paying any attention to the child until the self-injurious behaviors stopped. Whenever the boy begins to harm himself, you stop talking to him and turn away. Suppose your treatment worked, and the self-destructive behaviors decreased.

How do we know that withdrawing attention actually caused the change in the boy's behavior? Perhaps the change was just a coincidence. Would we want to find out? Would we want to return to an original set of conditions that might make the boy hurt himself again? No. Even though the experimental procedures require a return to the baseline conditions, psychologists sacrifice some scientific precision for ethical reasons. When we make an intervention that we hope will be therapeutic, our primary goal is helping the patient. If we succeed in changing a patient's behavior to something more adaptive using only an *AB* design, we have accomplished that goal.

## MULTIPLE BASELINE DESIGN

At times, a researcher might want to assess the effects of a treatment on two or more different behaviors in the same person. Or a researcher might be interested in testing the effects of an intervention on a behavior that occurs in multiple settings or situations. Alternatively, a researcher might want to evaluate a particular kind of treatment on more than one individual. In all three instances, the researcher has the option of using a multiple baseline design, in which a series of baselines and treatments are compared, but once a treatment is established, it is not withdrawn.

Let us look briefly at a hypothetical example of one of these designs (shown in Figure 12.6). Imagine that a parent wants to institute a program to decrease the amount of time a 6-year-old boy spends watching television cartoons. The most cartoon viewing occurs in two settings: before school and after school. The parent decides to reward the child when he does something else at these times by awarding him points, which can be accumulated and traded in at the end of each week for toys. To use a multiple baseline design, the parent would collect baseline data for each setting and institute the reinforcement program at staggered intervals. Suppose the parent begins with the early morning setting first (Treatment$_1$). After behavior change is established here, the parent can add treatment for the second setting (Treatment$_2$). Now the boy would receive reinforcement for both the early morning and after school sessions. Each setting is continuously monitored during the entire period so that the parent can see that cartoon viewing in each of the two settings drops after it is reinforced, but not before, suggesting that the reward program has been successful. If other settings, such as weekend mornings, were also a problem, the parent could have included them in the design as well.

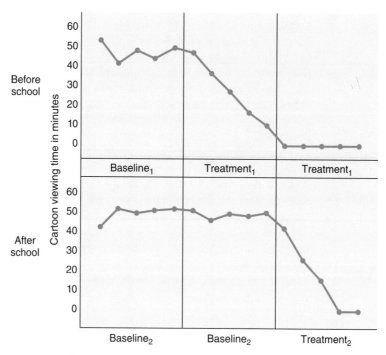

FIGURE **12.6** Hypothetical results of multiple baseline design to reduce cartoon viewing time of a 6-year-old boy.
© Cengage Learning

Sometimes, a multiple baseline design can be used to solve the ethical problem posed by withdrawing effective treatment. Let's go back to the example of the disturbed boy with self-injurious behaviors. We could increase the certainty that our treatment, rather than something else, produced the boy's behavior change by using a multiple baseline design. If the self-injurious behavior occurs in more than one setting, a multiple baseline design is possible. Suppose the boy engaged in self-injurious behaviors at home, at school, and during therapy sessions. Baseline behavior in all three settings could be recorded concurrently, and then the treatment could be applied in the first setting. Once behavior change was established in the first setting, the treatment could be applied in the second setting. If self-injurious behaviors declined in the first two settings but not the third, a good case can be made that the treatment was indeed efficacious.

A multiple baseline design can be a very effective way of demonstrating the efficacy of an intervention technique without reversal to the baseline condition. Instead of testing the same intervention across different settings in the same individual, researchers also can test the intervention on two or more individuals using a multiple baseline design. If the intervention produces an effect on several individuals, our confidence that the effect was actually produced by the treatment is increased and the study has greater internal validity. In addition, each subject added to the experiment serves to replicate the effect produced on a single subject.

An example of this procedure can be found in a multiple baseline experiment conducted by Danforth (1998), which tested an intervention to reduce noncompliance in young children diagnosed with Oppositional Defiant Disorder (ODD) along with Attention Deficit Hyperactivity Disorder (ADHD). A significant number of children with ADHD also have ODD. ODD is characterized by a cluster of extremely disruptive childhood behaviors, including defiance, anger, temper tantrums, and hostility toward parents and authority figures. Danforth's intervention consisted of a program to train the mothers of eight ADHD-ODD children in specific techniques to control and remediate noncompliant behaviors. The mothers were taught special techniques for using commands, reasoning, praise, reprimands, and timeouts in once-a-week sessions over a period of 4 weeks. The experimental timeline and results for three of the children (Child 1, Child 4, and Child 6) are shown in Figure 12.7.

Notice how the baseline and training sessions are once again staggered in the multiple baseline design. All the participants began at the same time, but introduction of the intervention occurred at different times. During

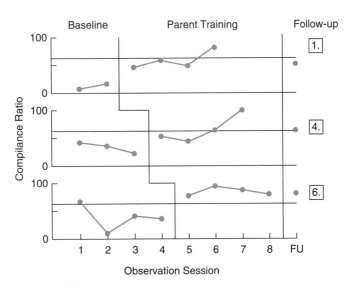

FIGURE **12.7** The percentage of parent commands to which each child complied.

Note: The dashed horizontal line indicates a compliance ratio below 60%, in the clinically deviant range.

From J. S. Danforth (1998). The outcome of parent training using the behavior management flow chart with mothers and their children with Oppositional Defiant Disorder and Attention-Deficit Hyperactivity Disorder. *Behavior Modification*, (4), 443–473.

© Cengage Learning

weeks one and two, baseline measurements of compliance were taken for all three children. During week three, training began for Child 1's mother, while baseline measurements continued for Child 4 and Child 6. During week four, training continued for Child 1's mother and was started for Child 4's mother, while baseline measurements continued for Child 6. During week five, training was started for Child 6's mother and continued for the others. Training sessions continued until each mother had received four training sessions, at which time the measurements stopped. A follow-up measurement was taken a year later to evaluate the longer-term success of the intervention.

## STATISTICS AND VARIABILITY IN SMALL *N* DESIGNS

Have you noticed something unusual about the small $N$ experiments you have learned about so far? We have not mentioned statistics at all. That is because most small $N$ experiments in the past have not used them. Often it is possible to determine whether the independent variable had an effect simply by looking at a graph of the data. For example, in the hypothetical multiple baseline study to reduce cartoon viewing, statistics would not be necessary to judge whether the boy's cartoon viewing had dropped. It is easy to see just by looking at Figure 12.6 that a meaningful drop occurred. The data presented in Figure 12.7 also illustrate a clearly observable effect (although Danforth *did* present statistics to support his conclusions).

The use of statistics in small $N$ designs remains controversial among small $N$ researchers (Morgan & Morgan, 2001), but the use of statistics appears to be increasing as new statistical approaches become available (Ator, 1999).[2] Statistics can be especially helpful when the pattern of data is too ambiguous to interpret just by looking—for instance, when there are frequent ups and downs (i.e., variability) in the behavior of interest. Unlike the straightforward and unambiguous examples that are generally used to teach experimental designs, there is frequently a great deal of variability in subjects' responses both within a single subject and between different subjects. For example, how would we best interpret the results of Figure 12.8, which depicts a single-subject *AB* experiment in which there is a lot of variability in the subject's behavior? It looks like the intervention did something because the average scores in the intervention phase seem higher than those in the baseline phase, but is behavior during the intervention *really* different from what it was at the end of the baseline? Without statistics, it is impossible to tell.

---

[2] One role of statistics is to allow us to make inferences about the population from our sample data; therefore, it may not be reasonable to make generalizations about whole populations from data on one or a very few subjects. Many traditional statistical tests used for large group designs (such as those described in Chapter 14) may not be appropriate for small $N$ studies unless 50 or more measurements are taken during each baseline and treatment phase. In recent years, however, a number of new statistical approaches have become available that can be used with these designs, but these are beyond the scope of this textbook. For an excellent overview, see Barlow, Nock, and Hersen (1999).

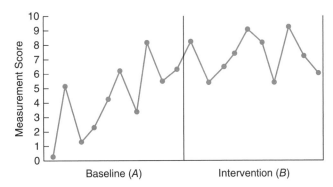

FIGURE **12.8** A single subject *AB* design with variability.
© Cengage Learning

In multiple baseline designs, we frequently encounter an additional problem. In addition to variability within a single subject, an intervention can produce highly variable results in different individuals. A study by Friman and his colleagues (1997) provides an excellent example of this kind of variability. When the researchers implemented a treatment program to decrease disruptive behavior in adolescent boys living in a residential treatment setting, they found that the treatment appeared to work very well on half of the six boys tested—but did not work on the other three. Across-subject variability is likely in both small *N* and large *N* designs

## CHANGING CRITERION DESIGNS

In some types of small *N* research using operant conditioning techniques, the behavior being modified cannot be changed all at once. Instead, in a changing criterion design, the behavior will be modified in increments, and the criterion for success will intentionally be changed as the behavior is modified. Beginning a program of weight training is a good example of an instance in which a personal trainer could use a changing criterion design. In the initial stages of lifting free weights, the trainer would verbally reinforce the client for lifting fairly light weights. As the client gets stronger, however, the criterion weight that the client is expected to lift for the same praise from the trainer gets heavier!

The same scheme is useful in behavior therapy settings. For example, after baseline performance has been established, a therapist might contract with a parent and child to begin a program to increase the time the child spends doing homework (recall a similar contract in Box 12.2). A changing criterion design might be used. Here, the amount of homework time that is required to earn prizes and rewards changes during the therapy. For the first couple of weeks, rewards might be earned for one-half hour of homework a day. Once the half-hour criterion is well established, it might be increased to 45 minutes a day. Now it will take 45 minutes of homework a day to earn the rewards. The criterion can be shifted upward incrementally until it reaches a suitable amount of time. This design is particularly useful when the eventual, desired behavior must be shaped. First, simple behaviors and then closer-and-closer approximations of the final, desired behavior are reinforced until the complete behavior is performed.

## DISCRETE TRIALS DESIGNS

The designs we have looked at so far have all used baselines to control for behavior as it normally occurs without the experimental manipulation. However, another type of small N design frequently used in psychophysical research is the discrete trials design, which does not rely on baselines. Instead, it relies on presenting and averaging across many, many applications of different treatment conditions and comparing performance on the dependent variable across treatment conditions. Repeated presentation over many trials can provide a reliable picture of the effects of the independent variable. And because individuals' sensory systems are similar, the results from a small number of subjects are likely to be generalizable to others. An experiment testing auditory perception will demonstrate how the design works.

Ivry and Lebby (1993) wanted to know whether auditory perception of high- and low-frequency tones would evidence right versus left hemisphere asymmetry. Stated simply, the researchers investigated whether different sides of the brain processed the two kinds of tones more efficiently. To find out, they tested four subjects using a discrete trials design. The subjects' task was to judge whether a set of three different tones was higher or lower than a target tone (Ivry & Lebby, 1993, experiment 4). The target tones were either high (ranging around 1,900 Hz) or low (ranging around 200 Hz) frequency. Each subject participated in four different sessions; two tested high-frequency tones, and two tested low-frequency tones. The tones were presented to either the right or left ear. Discrimination of high-frequency tones was faster and more accurate when the tones were presented to the right ear (the right ear is controlled by the left hemisphere of the brain). In contrast, discrimination of low-frequency tones was faster and more accurate when they were presented to the left ear (controlled by the right hemisphere).

Hemispheric differences were quite small. For example, it took subjects slightly more than 500 msec (half a second) to make each judgment, and the difference between tones presented to the right or left ear averaged only about 20 msec. In this experiment, statistics were used to compare tones presented to different ears, showing that the hemispheric asymmetry was significant. Each subject participated in 2,688 trials during the four experimental sessions, providing a clear picture of the small, but stable, asymmetry. See Box 12.3 for an interesting discrete trials experiment that used dogs as subjects.

BOX **12.3**  **Comparing Dogs Catching Frisbees with Baseball Players Catching Fly Balls**

Several studies have been conducted in recent years to investigate how baseball fielders intercept and catch fly balls. When baseball outfielders run to catch a fly ball, they appear to use a strategy that selects a running path to intercept the ball that maintains a linear optical trajectory (LOT) for the ball. Successful interception and catch occurs when the fielder's running speed and direction are equivalent to the ball's rate of change in both the horizontal and vertical optical angles of the ball's trajectory. The fielders' running paths can be analyzed rather simply by considering the optical information provided by the (two) horizontal and vertical dimensions. Typically, fielders run fastest laterally just after the ball is hit, ending up a little ahead of the ball. Then, they slow down somewhat to wait for the ball.

Shaffer, Krauchunas, Eddy, and McBeath (2004) wondered if dogs trained to catch Frisbees used the same LOT strategy. To find out, the researchers tested two experienced Frisbee dogs by mounting

small battery-operated cameras on their heads and recording the trajectory of thrown Frisbees from the perspective of the dog. Lilly, a border collie, is shown in Figure 12.9 in one of her 63 discrete trials. Interestingly, the dogs showed a two-dimensional LOT strategy to catch the Frisbees that was very similar to the strategy used by the outfielders to catch fly balls. But the physics of fly balls is usually much simpler than the physics of Frisbees. Sometimes, a Frisbee will be moving in one direction, and then suddenly it will dramatically shift direction—when this occurs, however, the dogs have a strategy for it. They are able to recalculate the Frisbee's LOT as the Frisbee changes direction, and then the dogs simply alter their running speed and direction to match the new LOT so that they can successfully intercept the Frisbee. (Future research will need to investigate whether or not human beings use the same strategy to catch objects that change direction ... )

Courtesy of Dennis Shaffer

FIGURE **12.9** Lilly.

## WHEN TO USE LARGE *N* AND SMALL *N* DESIGNS

The small *N* design is appropriate when you are studying a particular subject, such as a disturbed child. It is also useful when very few subjects are available. You can actually carry out an entire experiment with just one subject, although this is not always ideal. Without replication, a small *N* study might have little external validity. When we do experiments, we usually want to be able to generalize from our results—we want to be able to make statements about people or pigeons (see Box 12.4) that were not actually subjects in an experiment. Many researchers prefer to do large *N* studies because they believe that they can generalize from their results more successfully. All other things being equal, an experiment with more subjects has greater generalizability.

In a large *N* study, we may form separate groups of subjects for each treatment condition. The subjects run through their assigned conditions, and we then measure them on the dependent variable. We pool data from each group and evaluate them statistically to see if the groups behaved differently. In a small *N* experiment, we watch one or a few subjects over an extended period. We record baseline data. We introduce the experimental intervention and monitor the changes in the dependent variable throughout the experimental condition. Typically, we take several measurements. We can see whether the effect of the experimental intervention is instant or whether it builds over time. Unless it would be unwise, therapeutically, to remove a treatment that seems to be working, we continue to measure after the intervention is removed. We can verify that the independent variable causes changes in behavior because we can see what happens when that variable is removed. In short, we can often get a more complete and accurate picture of the effects of independent variables from a small *N* study than from a large *N* study that tests the same hypothesis.

Then why not use a small *N* design for every experiment? We would certainly save a lot of time recruiting subjects. But is it safe to generalize from a small *N* study? Small *N* researchers say yes, as long as we can evaluate how "typical" our small sample is. One *Ficus elastica* may be much like another; one pigeon may or may not be. We could compare the behavior of our pigeon during the baseline condition with the records of other pigeons in the research literature. If our pigeon seems to behave about the same as other pigeons do, we would probably assume it is a typical subject. However, even if the subject behaves typically in our baseline conditions, we still cannot be sure this particular subject is not unusually sensitive to the independent variable.

Generalizing from the results of one or a few subjects is particularly risky when the subjects are people. No two people would be expected to react in exactly the same way. Pooling the responses of many individual subjects makes it more likely that the effects are generalizable to people outside the experiment. Generalizing also depends on the type of process that is being measured. Some psychophysical processes are quite similar in most people. We all react in much the same way to a loud, unexpected sound, such as a gunshot, by displaying a startle reaction. Other psychological processes—such as whether we will laugh in relief or get angry at an experimenter who

BOX **12.4**   **Teaching Pigeons to Discriminate Paintings by Monet and Picasso**

Watanabe, Sakamoto, and Wakita (1995) conducted a small *N* experiment using pigeons as subjects, which produced surprising results—pigeons could be trained to discriminate the painting style of Monet from that of Picasso—and even to recognize the painter's style in paintings not seen before. This experiment featured a special form of changing criterion design.

The researchers first selected a set of 20 slides of paintings (10 by Monet and 10 by Picasso). Monet and Picasso were chosen because the styles differed dramatically: Most of the paintings of Monet, an Impressionist, have round contours (as in Figure 12.10); typical paintings by Picasso, considered a Cubist, have sharp contours (as in Figure 12.11). To make sure that the pigeons were not influenced by the different colors favored by the two artists, all slides were black and white. Each day the full set was shown to four separate pigeons in specially constructed cages. Each cage was set up with a special food dispenser, which the pigeon could operate by pecking at a food key. The experimenters set up the food keys

to dispense the reward of hemp seeds only in instances when the pigeons correctly performed a discrimination task. In the first part of the experiment, the pigeons were trained to discriminate between the Monets and the Picassos in the slide set.

Two pigeons received a reward if they correctly pecked the food key when a Monet was displayed; two were rewarded for pecking at a Picasso. Each slide set was shown to each pigeon once a day until a criterion of 90% correct responses in two successive sessions was achieved. The number of training sessions needed ranged from 6 to 24. After each pigeon was trained, it was tested to see if it had learned the artist's style. During the test, each bird was shown a new set of 20 slides: four new paintings by Monet and four by Picasso, along with four each by Renoir, Matisse, and Delacroix. Each of the birds achieved test scores averaging around 90% correct for the new set! It appears they had learned the artist's style. Learning to discriminate a Monet from a Picasso generalized to a completely new set of stimuli.

FIGURE **12.10** Round contours.

FIGURE **12.11** Sharp contours.

fired off a gun close to our head—show large individual differences. If we are measuring a process that is relatively invariant, the results from a small $N$ experiment would have greater generalizability than if we were measuring a behavior for which we expected large differences among people.

In a small $N$ study, we also cannot be sure that the results are not caused by some unseen accident (a *history* threat). For instance, a well-meaning cleaning person who gives fertilizer to our subject just at the time we begin talking to it could contaminate our plant study. For these reasons, it is important to replicate the findings of a small $N$ experiment before generalizations are made. An experiment with multiple applications of a treatment and multiple returns to baseline is more convincing than a single application.

It is impossible to say whether small or large $N$ studies always have greater generality. All things rarely are equal. A large $N$ study with a badly biased sample might tell us little about behavior in the population, whereas the findings of a well-controlled experiment with a single subject might be successfully replicated again and again on different subjects. By gathering baseline data, applying the experimental manipulation, and then returning to the baseline condition, we can get a very clear idea of the impact of the independent variable.

## SUMMARY

The *small N design* is used to study the behavior of only one or a few subjects. This approach requires very careful control over the conditions of the experiment. A typical small $N$ experiment begins with observing and recording the subject's behavior under the control condition (before the independent variable is introduced). This is called the *baseline*. The experimental intervention is then introduced, and the subject's behavior is monitored throughout the experimental period. This behavior is then compared with the baseline records. To rule out the possibility of confounding by extraneous variables, we return to the original control condition. Multiple applications of the treatment and multiple returns to baseline are most convincing. To increase external validity, small $N$ experiments should be replicated.

Most small $N$ studies use some form of reversal, or *ABA design*. ABA refers to the order of the treatment conditions. Sometimes, for ethical reasons, the researcher would not want to remove treatment; in this case, an *AB design* is used, even though without reversal it cannot be shown that the treatment caused the change in behavior. An *ABAB design* is fairly common in behavior therapy research; it can be more convincing than an *AB* or *ABA* design and has the benefit of leaving an efficacious treatment in place. We can also use the *ABA* approach or some variation, such as *ABABA*, in experiments with groups of subjects as well as with individuals. The main limitation on this approach is that we can use it only with experimental treatments that are reversible.

When it is not desirable to reverse a treatment, researchers can sometimes use a *multiple baseline design*. This design is very useful for testing a treatment on several behaviors or in different settings and for testing the same treatment on a few different individuals. In the past, researchers relied on visual inspection of graphs of the data to interpret effects; however, when responses show a lot of variability, interpretation can be difficult. A number of special statistical techniques have been developed for small *N* designs, and the use of statistics appears to be increasing.

At times, the behavior being modified cannot be changed all at once. Instead, in a *changing criterion design,* behavior will be modified in increments, and the criterion for success will change as the behavior is modified. Another small *N* approach, called a *discrete trials design,* is particularly popular with researchers testing psychophysical processes. This design does not use baselines, but instead relies on averaging responses across many, many trials to obtain a stable picture of effects of the experimental manipulation.

Whether to choose a small or *large N design* depends on several factors. Both practical and methodological considerations come into play. A small *N* design can be used to study the behavior of a single individual in depth, or it can be used when subjects are scarce. For example, psychologists who want to study the effects of a therapeutic intervention on a single client with a rare psychopathology could use a small *N* design. A small *N* design requires fewer subjects, and it is less time-consuming when each human or animal subject requires extensive training. Discrete trials designs using more than one subject typically include statistics to evaluate treatment effects.

## KEY TERMS

AB design A design in which a baseline condition (*A*) is measured first, followed by measurements during the experimental intervention (*B*); there is no return to the baseline condition.

ABA design A design in which a baseline condition (*A*) is measured first, followed by measurements during the experimental condition (*B*), followed by a return to the baseline condition (*A*) to verify that the change in behavior is linked to the experimental condition; also called a *reversal design.*

ABAB design A design in which a baseline condition (*A*) is measured first, followed by measurements during a treatment condition (*B*), followed by a return to the baseline condition (*A*) to verify that the change in behavior is linked to the experimental condition, followed by a return to the treatment condition (*B*).

ABABA design A design in which a baseline condition (*A*) is measured first, followed by measurements during a treatment condition (*B*), followed by a return to the baseline measurement condition (*A*), followed by a return to the treatment

condition (*B*) and a final baseline measurement condition (*A*) to verify that the change in behavior is linked to the experimental condition.

Baseline A measure of behavior as it normally occurs without the experimental manipulation; a control condition used to assess the impact of the experimental condition.

Changing criterion design A design used to modify behavior when the behavior cannot be changed all at once; instead, the behavior is modified in increments, and the criterion for success changes as the behavior is modified.

Discrete trials design A design that relies on presenting and averaging across many, many experimental trials; repeated applications result in a reliable picture of the effects of the independent variable.

Large *N* design A design in which the behavior of groups of subjects is compared.

Multiple baseline design A small $N$ design in which a series of baselines and treatments are compared; once established, however, a treatment is not withdrawn.

Small $N$ design A design in which just one or a few subjects are used; typically, the experimenter collects baseline data during an initial control condition, applies the experimental treatment, then reinstates the original control condition to verify that changes observed in behavior were caused by the experimental intervention.

## REVIEW AND STUDY QUESTIONS

1. Discuss the relative advantages and disadvantages of small $N$ versus large $N$ designs.

2. What is an *ABA* design? Why is it really a family of designs?

3. What do we mean by a reversal (or withdrawal) design?

4. Explain how a baseline condition in a small $N$ experiment is similar to a control group in a large $N$ experiment.

5. Outline a small $N$ experiment to test this hypothesis: Children who are given weapon-like toys (for example, toy guns and knives) become more aggressive.
   a. What are the independent and dependent variables?
   b. How would you operationally define aggression?
   c. What procedures would you use to test the hypothesis?
   d. What are the disadvantages of using a small $N$ design for this experiment?

6. One student is still looking for shortcuts. He says, "Running through the baseline condition of an experiment twice is silly. I'll just run through $A$ and $B$ and draw my conclusions from that." What would you say to him to convince him that carrying out the entire *ABA* design would be a better idea?

7. Give an example of a clinical study in which the student from question 6 would be justified in using an *AB* design.

8. Describe how you would conduct an *ABAB* experiment in which punishment (a squirt bottle containing 9 parts water to 1 part vinegar) was used to control barking in a dog.

9. Why was an *ABAB* design used in question 8 rather than an *ABA* design?

10. Draw a graph to illustrate a *successful* multiple baseline experiment to control two problem behaviors (barking and chasing the cat) exhibited by the dog from question 8. Assume the squirt bottle is your intervention.

11. Explain the two types of variability that can be expected in small $N$ designs.

12. Using a changing criterion design, create a study to get one of your "couch potato" friends to exercise more. Graph your successful results.

13. Discuss the benefits of a discrete trials design.

## CRITICAL THINKING EXERCISE

An interesting *ABA* design was conducted in a natural setting—the Olympic Games in Spain (Fernandez-Dols & Ruiz-Belda, 1995). The researchers were interested in the relationship between facial expressions and happiness. They predicted that happiness would only produce smiling when subjects were interacting with others. They measured smiling in individual gold medalists at three different points in time: waiting behind the podium for the officials to get into position (*A*), standing on the podium interacting with the officials and the audience (*B*), and standing on the podium watching the flag while their national anthem played (*A*). A pilot study had shown that gold medalists felt only intense happiness at all three of these points in time. As the researchers predicted, the gold medalists produced beaming smiles when interacting with others (*B*) but not during the other two points in time.

*The problem*: Are you convinced that this study demonstrated that happy people only smile when they are interacting with others? Explain.

## ONLINE RESOURCES

Try the Research Methods Workshop on Small *N* Designs at the following site:

http://www.wadsworth.com/psychology_d/templates/student_resources/workshops/workshops.html

# PART 3

# Results: Coping with Data

**13** Why We Need Statistics

**14** Analyzing Results

## CHAPTER 13

# Why We Need Statistics

**The Argument for Using Statistics**

**Weighing the Evidence**

**Statistical Inference: An Overview**
Defining Variability
Testing the Null Hypothesis
The Process of Statistical Inference

**Applying Statistical Inference: An Example**
Choosing a Significance Level
Type 1 and Type 2 Errors

**Going Beyond Testing the Null Hypothesis**

**The Odds of Finding Significance**
The Importance of Variability
One-Tailed and Two-Tailed Tests

**Test Statistics**

**Organizing and Summarizing Data**
Organizing Data
Summarizing Data: Using Descriptive
    Statistics
Measures of Central Tendency
Measures of Variability

SUMMARY
KEY TERMS
REVIEW AND STUDY QUESTIONS
CRITICAL THINKING EXERCISE
ONLINE RESOURCES

### CHAPTER OBJECTIVES

* Learn how hypotheses are tested in experiments

* Understand the meaning of significance levels

* Learn how to summarize data with descriptive statistics

Somehow, the word *statistics* brings terror to the eyes of even the most dedicated student—and, if you have not yet taken a statistics course, you may be feeling the same emotion. If you glance through this chapter, however, you will find that only a few basic computations are presented. Instead, the chapter is intended to give you a general review (or preview) of the foundations underlying the use of statistics in research. For those of you who have already completed a course in statistics, a review of statistical principles at this point will enable you to better integrate statistics into the research designs covered so far in the text. For those of you who have not yet had a statistics course, we will introduce the basic terms you need to understand how statistics are applied and how the results of statistical tests are presented and interpreted in psychological research reports. We will talk about the principles of statistical inference and the logic behind statistical tests as they are employed in the lion's share of contemporary research in psychology. We will also explore the current debate about testing for statistical significance in psychology research, and we will discuss some new approaches.

## THE ARGUMENT FOR USING STATISTICS

Statistics are quantitative measurements of samples. Through statistics, we can quantify the phenomena we observe. Statistics provide researchers with objective and consensual techniques for describing their results. A statistic may be thought of as a numerical index of some characteristic of the data, and many different kinds of statistics can be computed on any given sample. Each statistic describes something different about the data, much as miles per gallon and compression ratios each tell us something different about our cars. Selecting appropriate statistical tests is central to hypothesis testing, and, as Keren and Lewis have explained, "The choice of which method is the appropriate one under given circumstances is part of what constitutes the art of scientific inquiry" (1993, p. xii). We work with statistics because they allow us to evaluate *objectively* the data we worked so hard to collect. Let us look at a hypothetical murder mystery to demonstrate the kind of evaluation that takes place.

## WEIGHING THE EVIDENCE

Ms. Adams has just been arrested for murder. Detective Katz has found the victim's car keys, footprints, and bifocals in Ms. Adams's apartment. Witnesses say the victim and Ms. Adams were having dinner together at the local coffee shop a short time before the crime was committed. Yes, there is evidence against her. But did she actually commit the crime? Detective Katz knows he must establish her guilt beyond a reasonable doubt. Can he do that? Yes, he has the keys, the footprints, and even the bifocals that were found in Ms. Adams' apartment. He has witnesses who will swear they saw the suspect and victim dining calmly on hot pastrami sandwiches a short time before the murder. But, is this proof? What Detective Katz has put together is a case based on circumstantial evidence. The evidence suggests that Ms. Adams knew the victim well enough to share pastrami sandwiches and that the victim visited her apartment sometime before the murder. The evidence implicates Ms. Adams in the crime, but it does not prove that she did it. Other people might have known the victim well enough to share sandwiches, too. And other people could have committed the murder. Given the evidence, the best Detective Katz can do is attempt to establish Ms. Adams' guilt beyond a reasonable doubt. He can show that Ms. Adams, more than anyone else, is likely to be the murderer.

When we carry out a psychological experiment, we find ourselves in a plight similar to the one Detective Katz is in. Katz has investigated a case; we have run an experiment. Katz has collected evidence; we have gathered data. Katz would like to prove his suspect committed the crime; we would like to prove our independent variable caused the changes we see in our dependent variable.

Given all you have learned about experimentation, you will not be too surprised to learn that we can never actually prove that an independent variable caused the changes we see in a dependent variable. Proving something means establishing the truth of it by presenting evidence and logical arguments. Do you remember doing proofs in geometry? You began with a premise such as this: *In every right triangle, the square of the hypotenuse is equal to the sum of the squares of the legs ($A^2 + B^2 = C^2$).* You would then use all the facts you knew about geometry to construct a logical argument that would prove the premise true. Your proof would show that the premise is true because there would be no logical alternative. You would come down to a final step that would look something like this: $AB = AB$.

Unfortunately, outside of mathematics, proving things is not always so straightforward. Detective Katz would like to prove Ms. Adams guilty. He strongly believes she is. But can he develop a proof as airtight as $AB = AB$? No. His evidence is circumstantial, so the best he can do is show that she is probably guilty. When we evaluate the data from a psychological experiment, we do a very similar thing. We carry out statistical tests to determine whether the independent variable *probably* caused changes in the dependent variable from one treatment condition to another. Other factors such as coincidence or chance can also lead to differences. Nevertheless, we can make some statements about how likely it is that the independent variable had an effect. We base those statements on the statistical tests that we do.

"HOW DO YOU WANT IT — THE CRYSTAL MUMBO-JUMBO OR STATISTICAL PROBABILITY?"

Used by permission of Sidney Harris/ScienceCartoonsPlus.com

## STATISTICAL INFERENCE: AN OVERVIEW

As we evaluate the results of an experiment, we naturally want to be able to come to conclusions about the impact of the independent variable. When we run an experiment, we typically start with a sample of subjects drawn from a population. The population consists of all people, animals, or objects that have at least one characteristic in common, and the sample is a group that *represents* the larger population. Remember that we typically test samples, but we want to be able to make inferences about the entire population we have sampled. Fortunately, the way statistics work allows us to do exactly that.

When the samples are randomly selected, statistics allow us to infer that the effect obtained from samples in an experiment would generalize to others from the same population. When our samples are not randomly selected (for example, when convenience samples are used), we are able to generalize our findings only to the extent that our samples truly represent the larger population. If your sample contains unique or special characteristics that set it apart from the larger population, then inferences might be limited to the type of subjects in your experiment.

Within any population, the scores on a dependent variable will differ somewhat. Because the members of a population are different individuals, we do not expect everyone to score exactly the same. The scores of the subjects we sample will also differ. The question we ask with statistics is this: Are the differences we see between treatment groups significantly greater than what we would expect to see between any samples of scores drawn from this population? Answering this question involves a statistical inference, making a statement about the population and all its samples based on what we see in the samples we have.

Suppose two groups of students in a class are asked to report their weights. To make a statistical inference about the two groups (samples), we must first calculate the average (or *mean)* weight of each group by adding up the students' weights and then dividing the sum by the total number of weights. The mean weight of the 12 students on the window side of the room is 152 pounds. The mean weight of the 12 students on the opposite side of the room is 147 pounds, a difference of 5 pounds. Would you conclude from these measurements that individuals on the two sides of the room belong to different populations of students? Of course not. Perhaps, on the window side there is one particularly big individual whose weight varies a great deal from the weights of the other students (an unusual score like this is called an *outlier).* More likely, you are thinking that it is silly to make anything of a difference of 5 pounds. After all, not everybody has the same weight; the average weight of any two groups is bound to differ somewhat. You have made a statistical inference based on your knowledge of the weight of these groups. You conclude they probably belong to the same population—even though you have not measured everyone in that population.

## Defining Variability

When we measure subjects on any variable, we do not expect everyone to come out with exactly the same score. If we measure two or more groups on almost any dimension, we can expect some variability, or fluctuation, in their scores, just as we would expect that the weights of the 12 individuals in each of the two groups in our example would vary. Variability is one of the most important concepts you need to understand to analyze the results of experiments. In a commonsense way, variability is the amount of change or fluctuation we see in something. The altitude of California varies from its highest point, Mt. Whitney, which is 4,418 meters (14,494 feet) high to its lowest point in Death Valley, which is 86 meters (282 feet) below sea level.[1] In between are areas at sea level, inland valleys, and foothills. We could say there is a lot of variability in the altitude of places in California. In contrast, there is relatively little variability in the altitude of Florida; most of Florida lies very close to sea level. The highest point in Florida is an unnamed place 105 meters (345 feet) high.

---

[1] *National Geographic Atlas of the World* (6th ed.) (1990), pp. 22, 26.

When we do a statistical test, we are asking whether our pattern of results is significantly different from what we would expect to see given the usual variability among different people in the population. We are using the scientific method, so we want to answer this question in an objective way. A researcher might argue that his or her results are obviously significant. You might disagree. Instead of leaving the choice up to the individual, statistical tests have been set up so that we have standards—conventions or guidelines about what is significant—so that everyone can agree about whether results are significant or not. In law, we accept the verdict of the jury as our standard of guilt or innocence. In psychology, we accept the outcome of statistical tests to establish whether an independent variable had an effect in a particular experiment.

## Testing the Null Hypothesis

In our legal system, a person is presumed innocent until proven guilty. We assume that the person did not do anything wrong until convincing evidence shows otherwise. We make a similar assumption about the independent variable as we set up statistical tests. Until we can determine otherwise, we assume an independent variable has no effect.

We do not actually test the research hypothesis of an experiment directly. Instead, we formulate and test the null hypothesis ($H_0$), which states that the performance of the treatment groups is so similar that the scores could have been sampled from the same population. In effect, the null hypothesis says that any differences we see between treatments amount to nothing. We assume that a suspect is innocent until the evidence leads us to conclude that he or she is guilty. Similarly, we assume that the data from different treatment groups came from the same population, and any differences between them amount to nothing more than the ordinary variability in scores we would expect in any population. We hold to the assumption that the null hypothesis is correct until the evidence shows the assumption can be rejected.

At this point, you may be feeling a bit confused. "Don't we get our samples from the same population to begin with? Why do we have to assume that the data came from the same population?" Actually, the null hypothesis is not as strange as it seems. We do take our sample of subjects from the same population, at least as far as we know. Ideally, we take random samples of subjects from the same population and use random assignment to avoid creating treatment groups that differ from each other before the experiment even begins. In the experiment, however, we manipulate the independent variable so that the treatment groups are exposed to different conditions. When the experiment is over, we would like to be able to *reject the null hypothesis* by showing that the effect produced by the independent variable led to real differences in the responses of the groups. We reject the null hypothesis by showing that our treatments produced differences sufficiently large that they are unlikely to be encountered within the same population even if we take normal variability into account. And in a sense, even though we test only a sample, the experiment is testing whether the population of treated subjects' scores now differs from the population of untreated subjects' scores.

We use statistical tests to tell us if we can reject the null hypothesis or not. If we reject the null hypothesis, we are confirming a change between the groups that occurred as a result of the experiment: We say that our results are statistically significant. If we can reject the null hypothesis, we are saying that the data from the treatment groups are now so different that they look as if they came from different populations; the normal variability of scores on the dependent measure is not enough to account for our results. When we fail to reject the null hypothesis, however, we are saying that the scores from the treatment groups are still so similar that the experimental manipulation must have had little impact; the pattern could be explained simply by normal variability in a single population.

There is no way to directly test the alternative hypothesis ($H_1$) —the research hypothesis—which states that the data came from different populations. Therefore, we can never really *prove* that our research hypothesis is correct. There is no way to prove that the data came from different populations or that the independent variable caused the pattern of results. The best we can do is show that it is unlikely that the pattern occurred from chance variation within the population we sampled: We can only show that the null hypothesis is *probably* wrong.

Let us suppose our experiment deals with the effects of background music on job performance. We form two random groups of subjects and place them in identical testing rooms. We give them sets of purchase invoices and instruct them to write a seven-digit account number on each one, separate out the carbon copies, and order them alphabetically. The task is routine and similar to some office jobs. We want to test the research hypothesis that background music enhances job performance. We can only test this alternative hypothesis indirectly by attempting to show that the null hypothesis is probably false. We predict that the experimental group that hears background music will process more invoices in a set amount of time than will a control group that does not hear background music. So that we will not create experimenter effects during the testing, we operate all our equipment controls from outside the testing rooms. After playing taped instructions over an intercom, we turn on the music for the experimental group by flipping a switch on a control panel. The control group performs in an identical but quiet room.

When the testing hour is over, we return to collect our materials. We debrief the subjects, explaining the purpose of the experiment and what we expected to find. To our dismay, subjects in the experimental group become uneasy. They are concerned about their hearing because it seems they did not hear any music at all. With a little checking, we discover that the control switch is not working. When we thought we turned on the music, nothing happened. The music affected our experimental group as much as it did the control group—not at all.

What do you think would happen if we went ahead and counted up the number of invoices each group processed anyway? Our treatment groups were randomly selected from the same population and randomly assigned to the two conditions. Thus, we would expect both groups to have processed about the same average number of invoices. Our independent variable had no effect on the experimental group, so there is no reason to expect the performance of the two groups to be very different. We expect their performance will continue to look like the performance of two groups drawn from the same population.

When we do a statistical test, we begin by doing essentially the same thing: We formulate the null hypothesis by stating that the performance of the treatment groups is so similar that the groups must belong to the same population. We reject the null hypothesis when the difference between treatments is so large that chance variations cannot explain it. A series of *frequency distributions* in Figure 13.1 illustrates the general way this process works in an experiment in which the independent variable has a large effect. You will be seeing other frequency distributions on the pages to come; they are explained in Box 13.1.

## The Process of Statistical Inference

Researchers use the following process to apply statistical inference:

1. Consider the population to be sampled: Because of variability, individual scores on the dependent variable will differ.
2. Consider different random samples within the population: Their scores on the dependent variable will also differ because of normal variability. Assume the null hypothesis is correct.
3. Apply the treatment conditions to randomly selected, randomly assigned samples.
4. After the treatment, the samples now appear to belong to different populations: Reject the null hypothesis.

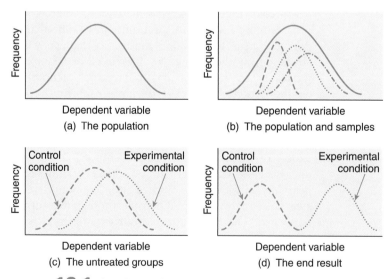

FIGURE **13.1** A schematic representation of statistical inference in an experiment in which the independent variable had a large effect.
© Cengage Learning

BOX **13.1**  **Frequency Distributions of Scores**

We often represent a group of scores by graphing them as a frequency distribution. In graphing a frequency distribution, you should mark off possible values of the dependent variable along the *abscissa,* the *X* or horizontal axis at the bottom. Frequencies (numbers of individuals) are marked off on the *ordinate,* the *Y* or vertical axis.

Suppose you have a data set consisting of scores from 38 subjects on a 7-point rating scale—a scale with numbers from 0 to 6 used as the dependent measure. The possible values of the scale would be listed at equidistant points along the abscissa. The leftmost mark along the abscissa would be the smallest possible value—0. This would be followed by a mark for 1, 2, 3, and so on, up to 6.

Frequency would be marked off on the *ordinate,* beginning with a frequency of 0 near the bottom of the ordinate, then 1, 2, and so on, until you get to the number representing the maximum frequency for any score. Let's say that the number 3 on the scale was chosen by more people than any other number and that it was chosen by 10 subjects. The maximum frequency for any score, then, will be 10. So the last value you would mark off near the top of the ordinate

is a 10. Now that you have labeled the graph, you simply plot the frequency for each value of the dependent variable as we have done in Figure 13.2.

Because the dependent variable has seven values, you would end up with seven points on the graph. Each point represents the number of individuals (frequencies) that chose each of the seven values: One person chose 0; four people chose 1, and so on. (You can tell the number of individuals by adding up the individual frequencies: $1 + 4 + 7 + 10 + 8 + 6 + 2 = 38$.) Finally, you simply connect the dots. The distribution of your sample data is now represented by a curve, sometimes called a frequency polygon. You will notice that the frequency distributions illustrating general concepts rather than actual sets of data look more symmetrical and do not have the abscissa or ordinate completely labeled. Of course, graphs do need to be completely labeled if an actual data set is used. Although we will not cover the procedure in this book, statistics courses teach ways that you can transform a data set so that it more closely approximates a normal curve. This sometimes makes it easier to reject the null hypothesis.

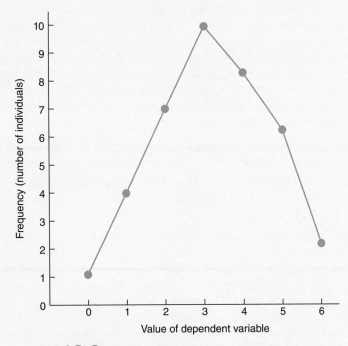

FIGURE **13.2** Hypothetical frequency distribution for a data set from a sample of 38 participants.
© Cengage Learning

Whether or not we will reject the null hypothesis depends largely on variability. When there is a great deal of variability in the population, large differences between samples will be common. The more variability there is on the dependent measure, the greater the difference between treatment groups has to be before we can say that the data look like they belong to different populations. *The more variability, the harder it will be to reject the null hypothesis.* The reasoning is the same when we evaluate the data from a within-subjects experiment. If the difference in the data from various treatment conditions is large in relation to variability, then we might be able to reject the null hypothesis. Let us turn to a research example so we can look at these principles in a more concrete way.

## APPLYING STATISTICAL INFERENCE: AN EXAMPLE

Imagine we are running another experiment. This is our hypothesis: Time passes quickly when you are having fun (this was actually tested by Sackett, Meyvis, Nelson, Converse, & Sackett, 2010). This is a directional hypothesis; it predicts the way the difference between groups will go. We are saying that time will go faster, not slower, for people who are having fun than for people who are not having fun. We have decided to use a two-group, between-subjects design. We operationally define "having fun" as looking at a collection of cartoons. Our experimental group will be given the cartoons and instructed to examine them to see how funny they are. We will not tell subjects that they will be given exactly 10 minutes for the task. The control group will also be given exactly 10 minutes to examine the same cartoons, minus the captions. Control subjects will see the drawings, but they will miss the punch lines and will not have much fun. The independent variable is fun. After subjects examine the cartoons for 10 minutes, we ask them to estimate the amount of time that has passed since they started. The dependent variable is subjects' estimates of the amount of time that elapses during the experiment. For our experiment:

$H_0$ = The time estimates of the two groups will look similar; in statistical terms, the scores look like they came from the same population.

$H_1$ = The fun group will make shorter time estimates than the control group will; in statistical terms, the scores look like they came from different populations.

Suppose we have actually run the experiment and computed the means. The mean estimated elapsed time for the control group is 14.2 minutes. The mean estimated elapsed time for the experimental group is 9.6 minutes. On the face of it, the experimental group really did seem to experience the time as going more quickly than the control group. To the experimental group it seemed they had been at their task for less time than the actual clock time. In contrast, the control group estimated the elapsed time to be longer than it really was. Can we conclude that having fun makes the time pass more quickly?

Not yet. First, we have to consider the variability in the data. We need to evaluate our data with statistical tests. Our first step was to state a null hypothesis: The time estimates came from the same population. Now if we could measure the population from which our samples were drawn—say, all college sophomores—we would find that ability to estimate elapsed time varies. Some people are very accurate; others are inaccurate. Some overestimate time; others underestimate. If we could somehow test all college sophomores and ask them to estimate the length of a 10-minute interval, we might get a frequency distribution that looks something like the one shown in Figure 13.3. This distribution forms a normal curve—a symmetrical, bell-shaped curve. Many of the scores represented by this distribution fall close to the center. Most students' estimates will be fairly accurate and close to the mean. The further away the scores get from the mean in either direction—larger or smaller—the lower the frequency with which they appear. As estimates become more inaccurate, the frequency gets lower, and there are fewer and fewer of them. Many of the statistical tests used by psychologists include the assumption that the population you have sampled is normally distributed on the dependent variable. This means that if you could somehow measure everyone in the population on that variable (like time estimation), the frequency distribution of all those measurements would be a normal curve.

Test statistics have *known distributions* that we can use to make inferences about our data. The statistical inference process requires some knowledge of probability theory. We make our decisions about the null hypothesis based on probabilities. How likely is it that a difference so large occurred just by chance? What are the odds that the usual variability in the population led to treatment groups that differ so much on the dependent variable?

We test the null hypothesis ($H_0$) for two reasons. First, it is the most likely explanation of what has occurred. When we measure different samples, or even the same sample at different times, we expect some variation between them. It would actually be very unusual to get exactly the same data from different groups. So when groups differ, we are most likely observing variations that would occur even if there had been no experimental intervention. Second, there is no way we can directly verify the alternative to the null

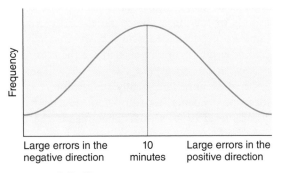

FIGURE **13.3** A normal curve: Hypothetical distribution of time estimates of all college sophomores estimating the length of a 10-minute time interval.
© Cengage Learning

hypothesis. The alternative hypothesis ($H_1$) states that the treatment means are so different that they come from distinct populations. $H_1$ is actually what we would like to show. We would like to be able to say that the treatment groups differ because of our experimental manipulation. Unfortunately, no matter how different the groups are, there is always some chance that the results were caused by sampling error. Like Detective Katz, the best we can do is show that our explanation for what happened is probably true.

## Choosing a Significance Level

To decide whether the differences between our treatment conditions are significant, we need a significance level, a criterion for deciding whether to reject the null hypothesis or not. When we reject the null hypothesis, we would like to know that our decision is probably correct. How sure we need to be can vary depending on the circumstances. Suppose you are at a sidewalk sale and you find a good-looking, cheap shirt. But because it is a sidewalk sale, you cannot try on the shirt, and if you buy it, you cannot return it. You guess there is a 1 in 10 chance that the shirt will not fit. Will you buy it anyway? Your decision will be based on what you stand to lose. If the shirt costs $5, you might risk it. But you might not risk $20. If you are short of cash, you might not be willing to risk anything.

Similarly, when we evaluate the results of an experiment, we evaluate the risks involved in making the wrong decision. If we are dealing with life-and-death research on new drug therapies or suicide prevention, we will be much less willing to risk being wrong. We might be somewhat more relaxed in an experiment on time estimation. What an experimenter does in a particular experiment depends on what he or she is testing. However, there are conventions for deciding whether to accept or reject the null hypothesis. In psychology, by convention, we generally reject the null hypothesis if the probability of obtaining this pattern of data by chance alone is less than 5%.[2] Then we say the significance level is $p < .05$ (read "$p$ less than .05"). A significance level of $p < .05$ would be appropriate for our time-estimation experiment.

When we choose a significance level of .05, we are saying that we will reject the null hypothesis if we get a pattern of data so unlikely that it could have occurred by chance less than 5 times out of 100. That is actually less than the odds of tossing a coin 4 times and getting four consecutive heads.[3] It is possible to get four heads in a row—but it is not very likely. If we saw it happen, we would probably ask to see the coin. If we see such unlikely differences between our treatment groups, we will reject the null hypothesis and say that our results are statistically significant.

In some experiments, we may want a stricter criterion. We could choose a significance level of $p < .01$. That means the odds of getting such large

---

[2] In some statistics textbooks, the conventional level of significance is shown as $p \leq .05$ ($p$ less than *or equal to* .05) rather than $p < .05$. We have chosen to use $p < .05$, because it is more commonly used by psychological researchers.

[3] For the curious reader, the actual probability of four heads in a row is $p = .0625$ (.5 × .5 × .5 × .5).

treatment effects by chance are less than 1 in 100—that is, a little less than the odds of tossing a coin 6 times and getting six consecutive heads. Pharmaceutical research, for example, generally adopts this criterion. An even stricter criterion, such as $p < .001$ (less than 1 in 1,000), might be chosen for some medical research or other projects in which being wrong about a treatment effect could have disastrous human consequences.

To make a valid test of a hypothesis, we must think ahead and decide what the significance level will be before running the experiment. The level we select will be stated in our research report. It is not legitimate to collect all the data and then pick the significance level depending on how the results turned out. The experiment would yield significant results—but only because we stacked the deck in our favor. For instance, we might find that the difference between the performance of two treatment groups is significant at the .20 level. That would mean a difference this large could have occurred just by chance about 20 times out of 100. We might accept this as a meaningful difference, but we would not be making a very rigorous test of the hypothesis. A $p$ value this large would not be considered statistically significant by most other researchers. Now that precise probability levels are easily obtained using computer data analysis programs, researchers report the exact significance levels of the results they obtained and let readers evaluate them on their own.

In the time-estimation experiment, we are testing the notion that time passes quickly when a person is having fun. Assume we had chosen $p < .05$ as the significance level for this experiment. We would evaluate the results against this criterion. If the results could have occurred by chance 5% of the time or more, we would not reject the null hypothesis: The data are too similar to say that they probably came from different populations, and the results are not statistically significant. If the results could have occurred by chance less than 5% of the time, however, we are able to reject the null hypothesis: The data are statistically significant—they look as if they came from different populations. This is just another way of saying that the independent variable apparently had an effect: It altered the behavior of the treatment groups. Our groups started out the same, but after the experiment their scores on time estimation now look as if they came from two different populations.

Figure 13.4 illustrates the way the distributions of sample means from those two populations might look. The figure represents what we would find if we were able to test all possible samples from both populations—people who are having fun and people who are not. Of course, there is variability among the samples drawn from both populations; some samples give more accurate estimates than others. In this idealized situation, however, you can see that the populations do not overlap. On time estimation, people who are having fun are distinctly different from people who are not. On the average, people who are having fun consistently say that time passes more quickly than it does for the control subjects who are not having fun. If that were really so, we would expect to obtain large differences between treatment groups exposed to different levels of the independent variable (fun). We would expect a significant difference between treatment groups if the independent variable had such a large effect on subjects' behaviors.

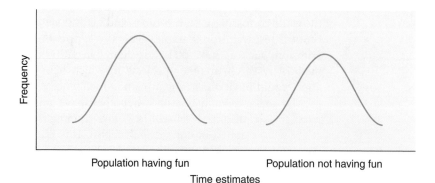

FIGURE **13.4** Hypothetical distributions of populations having fun and not having fun. The independent variable had a large effect on subjects' time estimates.
© Cengage Learning

In reality, the picture is rarely so perfect. Many extraneous variables can affect the outcome of an experiment, and the data might not be a true reflection of the independent variable's impact. Recall from Chapter 8 that variability also can be produced by the many forms of experimental errors. Experimental errors are variations in subjects' scores produced by uncontrolled extraneous variables in the experimental procedure, experimenter bias, or other influences on subjects not related to effects of the independent variable.[4] Also, although the experimental manipulation is effective, its impact might not be as powerful as the one we have drawn in Figure 13.4. More typically, we expect some overlap between treatment populations. But we cannot be sure exactly how much overlap there is because we usually cannot measure every possible sample. And because of this overlap, our conclusions about the results could be wrong.

## Type 1 and Type 2 Errors

Even though our results were statistically significant, there is always some probability that the null hypothesis could still be true. It could be that we have somehow obtained treatment means that really do belong to the same population. These means can appear to be significantly different even though the independent variable really had no effect. What are the odds of making

---

[4] Increased variability in scores from sample data can be caused by any number of uncontrolled factors in an experiment. Some "errors" can be caused by the behavior of the experimenter or deficiencies in the manipulation or measurement procedures; others could be the result of chance differences in subjects at the time of the experiment. For example, suppose the experimenter is having a bad morning and inadvertently treats one subject in a less friendly manner than usual, making the subject somewhat anxious. This subject's anxiety can alter scores on the dependent variable from what they would have been otherwise, contributing variability to the group's scores. Similarly, subjects could have a bad day or be overtired or sick, affecting their scores and thereby adding variability to the data.

that mistake? After all, we reject the null hypothesis only if the treatment groups are very different. Is this really a problem? How serious the error is depends on the actual experiment. If the decision involves a life-and-death issue, the consequences could be very serious.[5] From a practical standpoint, however, making the wrong decision about the null hypothesis is always serious. Why bother to run a carefully controlled experiment only to draw the wrong conclusions at the end?

If we reject the null hypothesis when it really is true, we have made a Type 1 error: A Type 1 error occurs when we say that significant differences between treatments were produced by the independent variable even though it really had little or no effect at all. In the time-estimation experiment, we would make a Type 1 error if we said that our treatment produced effects when it really made little or no difference in time estimates. *The odds of making a Type 1 error are equal to the value we choose as the significance level for rejecting the null hypothesis.* If we are using a .05 significance level, the probability of a Type 1 error is .05. If our significance level is .05, then 5 times out of 100 (or 5% of the time), we will reject the null hypothesis when we should not. If we choose a more extreme .01 significance level, the probability of a Type 1 error is .01, or 1 chance in 100.

Could we minimize the odds of a Type 1 error simply by choosing a more extreme significance level? Yes, but there is a trade-off in doing that. We can make a second kind of error, a Type 2 error: We can fail to reject the null hypothesis even though it is really false. When we conclude that the pattern of results was caused by chance variations when it was really caused by the independent variable, we have made a Type 2 error. We have missed a treatment effect that was really present.

The more extreme the significance level, the more likely we are to make a Type 2 error. There is a greater chance of a Type 2 error at $p < .01$ than there is at $p < .05$. But how does a Type 2 error happen? Won't the differences between treatments be so large that we will surely find them? Not necessarily. Treatment effects are easier to find when the independent variable has a very dramatic effect and there is not much variability on the dependent variable. Then, we might wind up sampling from two completely distinct populations, such as people having fun and people not having fun (as in Figure 13.4), which show no similarity at all. More typically, however, the responses of the populations will overlap. Figure 13.5 illustrates that possibility for the experiment on time estimation.

The probability of making a Type 2 error is affected by the amount of overlap between the populations being sampled. If the responses of people having fun are very similar to those of people not having fun, the populations will overlap, and it will be hard to show that fun altered the responses in any way. The more overlap there is, the harder it is to detect the effect of the independent variable.

---

[5] Rejecting the null hypothesis when it is really true is analogous to getting a *false positive* result for a medical diagnostic test. Imagine the consequences of receiving a false positive diagnosis on a test for HIV! It could have life-altering consequences.

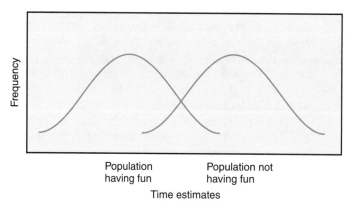

FIGURE **13.5** Hypothetical distribution of populations having fun and not having fun. The independent variable had a moderate effect on subjects' time estimates.

© Cengage Learning

The probability of making a Type 2 error is represented by the Greek letter β (beta). We would be able to find the exact value of β only if we could measure all possible samples of both populations. But say we knew that the odds of making a Type 2 error were equal to exactly .75 in our experiment. Then the odds of making a correct decision would be equal to 1 − .75, or .25. If we are likely to be wrong 3 out of 4 times (.75), then we should be right 1 out of 4 times (.25). The odds of correctly rejecting the null hypothesis when it is false are always equal to 1 − β.

This last quantity (1 − β) is also referred to as the *power* of the statistical test. In Chapter 9, we touched on the concept of power in connection with sample size. Even though we cannot measure the precise value of β, we can reduce it by increasing our sample size. We stand a better chance of correctly rejecting $H_0$ with a sample of 50 than with a sample of 20. As you know, the ability to detect a treatment effect is also related to how much variability there is in the population; therefore, we can also reduce β by reducing the variability in our sample data (for instance, by controlling extraneous variables or using a within-subjects or matched-groups design). We can also reduce β by using more powerful statistical tests, called *parametric tests*. They make certain assumptions about the parameters of the population represented by our samples (e.g., normally distributed data, comparable variability across groups, interval or ratio scale data). Tests known as nonparametric tests are used when these assumptions cannot be met. They are somewhat less powerful. (We will come back to these types of tests in Chapter 14.)

We can also reduce β if we accept a less extreme significance level. We are more likely to detect a difference using a significance level of $p < .05$ than one of $p < .01$. Remember, however, that adopting a less extreme significance level also increases the chance of a Type 1 error. The probability of making a Type 1 error is represented by the Greek letter α (alpha). There is some chance (α) that we will reject the null hypothesis when we should have

TABLE **13.1**

Evaluating results: The four possible outcomes and the odds that they will occur

| | Your Decision | |
| --- | --- | --- |
| | Not to reject the null hypothesis | Reject the null hypothesis |
| Null hypothesis is true. (The data came from the same population.) | You are correct: $p = 1 - \alpha$ | You have made a Type 1 error: $p = \alpha$ |
| *The Real Story* | | |
| Null hypothesis is false. (The data belong to different populations.) | You have made a Type 2 error: $p = \beta$ | You are correct: $p = 1 - \beta$ |

© Cengage Learning

conditionally retained it. There is a $1 - \alpha$ chance that we will fail to reject the null hypothesis when that is the correct decision. Altogether, there are four possible decisions we can make when we evaluate the data from an experiment. These are summarized in Table 13.1.

When we make a Type 2 error, the independent variable has produced an effect, but we are unable to detect it. Making a Type 2 error is generally considered to be less serious than making a Type 1 error. When we make a Type 1 error, we explain an effect that does not really exist, and this can often be a more serious error than failing to detect an effect.[6] For example, a Type 1 error has greater implications for the suspect in Detective Katz's murder case. Making a Type 1 error is like putting an innocent person in jail. We attribute a crime to someone who did nothing at all. The two types of errors for the time-estimation experiment are illustrated in Table 13.2. The possibility of making Type 1 or Type 2 errors makes it especially important that we replicate the findings of experiments.

## GOING BEYOND TESTING THE NULL HYPOTHESIS

Historically, the use of statistics and significance levels to test the null hypothesis has been the standard approach among psychological researchers for demonstrating treatment effects. This approach, however, has its critics (Masson & Loftus, 2003), and null hypothesis significance testing is currently an area of strong controversy among statistically oriented psychologists. Critics of null hypothesis testing point out that in the history of psychology,

---

[6] Once in a while, the consequences of missing a treatment effect, a Type 2 error, might be just as disastrous as making a Type 1 error. A Type 2 error is analogous to a *false negative* result on a medical test—the test says you do not have the disease, but you really do—the test simply failed to detect it.

TABLE **13.2**

Possible errors in the time estimation experiment

| | |
|---|---|
| **Type 1** | We conclude that there was a difference in the time estimates made by the "fun" and "no-fun" groups even though the treatments produced little or no effect at all. *(Reporting an effect that doesn't really exist)* |
| **Type 2** | We conclude that there was no difference in the time estimates made by the "fun" and "no-fun" groups even though the treatments did produce an effect. *(Missing an effect that does really exist)* |

© Cengage Learning

many of the most lasting theoretical contributions have been made without the benefit of statistics or $p$ values. For example, Piaget's theory of cognitive development, Freud's psychodynamic theory, and Skinner's theory of operant conditioning did not rely on statistical hypothesis testing at all. Yet, they remain among the most cited works by contemporary psychologists (Smith, Best, Cylke, & Stubbs, 2000). Critics also note that there is nothing magic about the .05 criterion, pointing out that psychologists have made an arbitrary decision to consider only experiments in which $p < .05$ to represent statistically significant results. Why not .06? or .04?

In 1994, Cohen argued persuasively that estimates of the effect size of an experimental treatment provided more compelling evidence that a treatment worked than did simply reporting $p$ values for rejecting the null hypothesis. Effect size, you will recall from Chapter 9, is a statistical estimate of the size or magnitude of a treatment effect. Cohen also argued for the use of confidence intervals: a range of values that we feel confident will include the population mean (the true mean). Following Cohen's lead, the American Psychological Association convened a task force to "elucidate some of the controversial issues surrounding applications of statistics including significance testing and its alternatives" (Wilkinson & Task Force on Statistical Inference, 1999).

The task force reached the conclusion that null hypothesis significance testing should not be abandoned. Instead, they recommended that statistical hypothesis testing should be supported by other techniques—namely, effect size estimates and confidence intervals. As a result, the most recent edition of the *Publication Manual of the American Psychological Association* (2010) strongly recommends reporting both along with $p$ values. Because both effect sizes and confidence intervals are most easily calculated after test statistics have been completed, we will return to them in the next chapter.

Some critics of null hypothesis significance testing have argued that psychologists should eliminate entirely the reporting of $p$ values in research reports, and many other statistical approaches that do not involve null hypothesis testing are currently being debated in the literature. *Psychological Science*, the flagship journal of the American Psychological Society, has taken a bold step by formally eschewing $p$ values in favor of a statistic called $p_{rep}$

(Killeen, 2005), the average probability of replication.[7] For now, however, null hypothesis significance testing, reporting $p$ values, and including effect sizes and confidence intervals are the most common interpretive strategies.

# THE ODDS OF FINDING SIGNIFICANCE

Together with choosing and applying a significance level, it is important to understand how the odds of finding significance are affected by two factors: the amount of variability in the data and whether we have a directional or a nondirectional hypothesis. Let us take a closer look at how these factors influence the outcome of an experiment.

## The Importance of Variability

Suppose we could somehow measure all possible samples of college sophomores on time estimation. We would see that the distribution of means of those samples is a normal distribution—a symmetrical, bell-shaped curve. Like individual subjects, some samples perform better than others do. Most are about average, but some do well and some do poorly.

Now, suppose we could take all possible pairs of samples and find the *differences between their means*. We would get another distribution. The outcome would resemble Figure 13.6. You can see that many of the differences between pairs of sample means fall right around zero. Because time estimation is normally distributed, the means of most samples will be close to the mean of the population. Thus, the differences between pairs of those sample means will tend to be very small.

Some differences, however, will be very large; they occur at the extremes of the distribution. They represent differences between means of groups that are far apart on time estimation. As you can see, extreme differences are infrequent. We find fewer and fewer instances as we move away from zero. There is variability in the differences between means just as there is variability between samples.

Some differences between means are more likely than others. For normal distributions, it is possible to calculate the odds that each difference will occur (and statisticians have spent a lot of time calculating these odds for us). The odds of getting very small differences—close to zero—between the means of any two samples are high. Most sample means fall close to the mean of the population, so if you subtract one sample mean from another, the difference will be close to zero. We should not be too surprised if the groups in our experiment turn out to be very close together on the dependent variable. But the odds of seeing much larger differences are less. The exact odds depend on the amount of variability in the population.

---

[7] The $p_{rep}$ statistic is not the probability of replicating the original experiment; instead, it estimates the probability that "averaged over all populations likely to have given the original mean," a same-sign (+ or −) result will be obtained (Cumming, 2005, p. 1002). Assume that the $p_{rep}$ obtained in the time-estimation experiment is .88. In that experiment, the mean time estimation of the fun group was 4.6 minutes *less* than the estimation of the no-fun group. The obtained $p_{rep}$ calculates that the probability that subsequent replications would also show the fun group as having a lower time estimate than the no-fun group is .88 (or 88%).

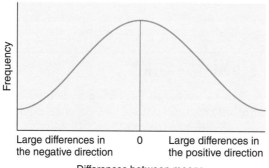

Frequency

Large differences in     0     Large differences in
the negative direction          the positive direction

Differences between means

FIGURE **13.6** Hypothetical distribution of the differences between all possible pairs of means drawn from a population.
© Cengage Learning

Large differences are more likely in populations that have high variability on the dependent measure. Figure 13.7 shows you three distributions of differences between sample means. The distributions are similar except for the amount of variability in the populations sampled. The first distribution shows differences between the means of samples from a population in which the variable that was measured showed little variability. Because the sample means are all relatively close to each other (that is, they showed little variability), the differences between them also tend to be small. The second distribution is based on a population in which the variable measured showed a moderate amount of variability. You can see that the differences between means of samples from this population tend to be larger than the differences in the first distribution. The third distribution is based on a population in which the variable measured showed a great deal of variability. You can see that this distribution is the widest. The differences between the means of the samples from this population tend to be very large because there is a great deal of variability in the population.

The shaded areas of the curves in Figure 13.7 are the critical regions ($p <$ .05), the parts of each distribution that make up the most extreme 5% of the differences between means. Differences large enough to fall within these areas will occur by chance less than 5% of the time. If our significance level is $p <$ .05, we will reject the null hypothesis if the treatment groups differ by amounts that fall within these critical regions. Do you notice anything special about where the cutoffs for the 5% levels are? You will find that they fall in a different place for each distribution. Actually, as the amount of variability in the distribution goes up, the critical regions fall farther from the center of the distribution. When there is more variability, larger differences between means of samples are required to reject the null hypothesis.[8]

---

[8] When there is very little variability, however, statistically significant results can sometimes be obtained from very small differences between treatment groups—so small that they can seem trivial. We will return to this idea in Chapter 15.

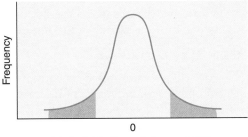

(a) A distribution with low variability

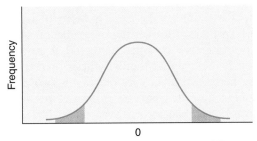

(b) A distribution with moderate variability

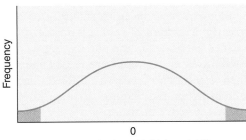

(c) A distribution with high variability

FIGURE **13.7** Three hypothetical distributions of differences between sample means. Shaded areas represent the most extreme 5% of each distribution.
© Cengage Learning

Ideally, we want our treatment conditions to be the only source of variability in an experiment. We reduce experimental error by controlling variables such as testing conditions and practice time that might create differences between subjects' scores and therefore introduce unwanted variability. For instance, in the time-estimation experiment, we must be careful to give everyone exactly 10 minutes to look at the cartoons. Remember, we will be making inferences about the population based on the samples we observe. If our samples produce highly variable data, we must assume that the population is also highly variable on the dependent measure. If the population has high variability, finding a statistically significant effect requires very large differences between the mean scores from different treatment groups in the experiment. Therefore, any unnecessary sources of variation in an experiment will not only reduce the chances of rejecting the null hypothesis, they will also increase the chances of a Type 2 error. It will be difficult to get significant results if extraneous variables are not carefully controlled.

## One-Tailed and Two-Tailed Tests

In Figure 13.7, you will also notice that the critical regions of the distributions have been divided up between both ends of the curves. For each curve, the 5% critical region includes 2.5% on the low end and an additional 2.5% on the high end. These curves have been marked to illustrate a two-tailed test of a hypothesis: The critical region of the distribution is divided between its two tails.

We use a two-tailed test whenever we have a nondirectional hypothesis, one that does not predict the exact pattern of results—the direction of the effect we will produce through the experimental manipulation. For example, we might propose that cars driven on oil A perform differently from cars driven on oil B. Notice that the hypothesis predicts there will be a difference between the performance of cars driven on two different brands of oil, but there is no indication of what the pattern of results will be. Will cars driven on A perform better than those driven on B? Or, will cars on B perform better than A? The researcher has not made a prediction on that. The hypothesis is nondirectional.

You can understand why we use a two-tailed test with such a hypothesis if you think about what we mean by significance level and critical region. We want to know if our pattern of results is so unlikely that it was probably not caused by chance variations in the population; we want to know whether differences between treatment groups are large enough to fall within the critical regions. When a researcher states a nondirectional hypothesis, he or she is willing to accept extreme differences that go in either direction. It does not matter whether A is better than B or vice versa; the researcher has only postulated that the independent variable produces a difference. Because differences in either direction are acceptable, the critical region, the most extreme 5% of the distribution, has to be split between both tails of the curve. Suppose we did not split it, but instead included 5% on each end of the distribution. If we did that, we would be changing the significance level—in fact, we would have doubled it. We would be saying that we would reject the null hypothesis if the difference falls within the most extreme 10% of the distribution.

Often we are able to make a more precise prediction about the effects of the independent variable. These may be based on our own pilot studies or on our review of prior research. A nondirectional hypothesis can often be transformed into one that is directional: for example, we could hypothesize that cars driven on oil A perform better than cars driven on oil B. Now we are predicting exactly what we will see when we evaluate the performance of cars driven on oils A and B; we predict that A will fare better than B.

When we have a directional hypothesis, we make a one-tailed test: The 5% critical region is located in just one tail of the distribution. The hypothesis that time passes quickly when you are having fun is a directional hypothesis, and it requires a one-tailed test. Figure 13.8 shows the relative locations of the critical regions of the same distribution using a one-tailed and a

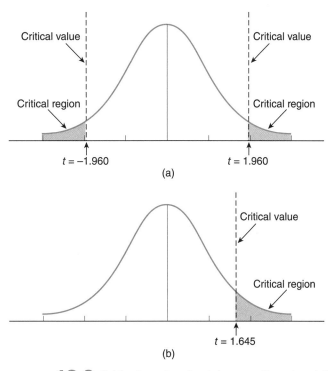

FIGURE **13.8** Critical region for (a) a nondirectional (two-tailed) test and (b) a directional (one-tailed) test.
© Cengage Learning

two-tailed test.[9] The advantage of using a one-tailed test is obvious. The size of the critical region is larger and closer to the center of the distribution, making it easier for differences between means to be large enough to fall there. You can see from the figure that the critical value, the statistical value we need to achieve $p < .05$, will be smaller when we do a one-tailed test. Treatment effects do not need to be as dramatic when we have a directional hypothesis; we can get significant results more easily when we use a directional hypothesis and a one-tailed test.

You may be thinking that it will be easy to get significance now if we just state our hypothesis in a directional way. Then, if the data go in the other direction, we will change the hypothesis and still have significant results. It may be a reasonable idea, but unfortunately, we cannot handle things that way. Just as you need to choose a significance level in advance, you need to decide on the hypothesis in advance and stick to it. Otherwise, you have not conducted a fair test. If you write a hypothesis to fit results you already have, you are actually describing a set of data after the fact. Of course, there is

---

[9] The distribution shown depicts locations of critical regions for the $t$ statistic, which will be reviewed in the next chapter.

PROBABILITY

IF YOU HAVE 5 DOGS, 3 WILL BE ASLEEP

nothing inherently wrong with offering explanations for observations. That is how we generate new hypotheses. However, we cannot call that experimentation. By definition, when we experiment we make a controlled test of a hypothesis that has already been stated.

So far, we have looked at hypothetical distributions based on the means of all the samples that could be drawn from a population. These make wonderful illustrations of the concepts we are discussing. To draw these figures, however, we had to assume we were somehow able to take huge numbers of samples. In the real world, that is nearly always impossible. We do not have the actual distributions of all sample means when we run an experiment; we rarely even know the average score for the whole population. Instead, we have to draw conclusions from the few samples of subjects that we do have. To do that, we compute inferential statistics.

## TEST STATISTICS

Inferential statistics are statistics that can be used as indicators of what is going on in the population. They are also called test statistics because they can be used to evaluate results. A test statistic is a numerical summary of what is going on in our data. When we compute a test statistic, we transform the relationship between treatment differences and variability into a simple quantitative measure. Generally speaking, the larger the value of the test statistic, the more likely it is that the independent variable produced a change in subjects' responses. A large test statistic indicates that the differences we see across treatments are large relative to the amount of variability in the data.[10] We are more likely to be able to reject the null hypothesis if we obtain a large value of a test statistic.

You know there is always some chance that the null hypothesis really is true. It is always possible that even a large test statistic is within the range of events that could occur by chance. But think about a throw of the dice. You know that the odds of rolling 7 are greater than the odds of rolling snake eyes. How do you know? You can calculate the odds of each event. There are many more ways to make 7 than there are to make 2. Similarly, statisticians have worked hard to calculate just how likely every value of a test statistic would be. Each test statistic has its own distribution of values. For each value, statisticians have calculated the probability that the value could occur just by chance due to random sampling. Those values and probability levels are summarized in tables like the ones you will find at the back of this book.

## ORGANIZING AND SUMMARIZING DATA

Suppose we have actually run an experiment, and we have the data. What do we do with them? Where do we begin? There are three basic steps in analyzing any set of data: First, we organize it. Second, we summarize it. Third, we apply a statistical test to interpret our results.

### Organizing Data

We start by organizing the data we have collected. Hypothetical data from our time-estimation experiment have been organized in Table 13.3. You can see that these data have been laid out in columns. Subjects' responses are divided into two columns, one for each of the two treatment groups; each subject in each group is listed by number next to his or her datum. Statistical work will go more quickly and be more accurate if you begin by organizing the data and labeling them in a clear and orderly way. Especially with more complex designs, you will avoid a great deal of confusion if you take the time to prepare data tables. Many students prepare their data tables using computer spreadsheets such as Excel; others find it easiest to use columnar paper, such as bookkeeping paper. At the very least, do your work on lined paper so you will be sure which datum belongs to which subject. You can simplify the task by preparing an orderly data sheet that you can use to record subjects' responses throughout the experiment. Organizing the data in this way will also facilitate data entry for computer statistical programs and make data entry errors less likely.

---

[10] Distributions for some test statistics, such as the chi-square test covered in the next chapter, are not based on population means and variability; they have a different basis for rejecting the null hypothesis.

TABLE **13.3**

Laying out organized data

| Group 1 (Incomplete Cartoons) | | Group 2 (Complete Cartoons) | |
|---|---|---|---|
| Subject | Time Estimate (min) | Subject | Time Estimate (min) |
| $S_1$ | 11.2 | $S_6$ | 13.6 |
| $S_2$ | 16.2 | $S_7$ | 10.9 |
| $S_3$ | 13.3 | $S_8$ | 5.5 |
| $S_4$ | 12.1 | $S_9$ | 8.8 |
| $S_5$ | 18.2 | $S_{10}$ | 9.2 |

© Cengage Learning

## Summarizing Data: Using Descriptive Statistics

Published articles rarely contain all of the data obtained from every subject in the experiment. The data we record as we run an experiment are called raw data. Whenever we report the results of an experiment, we report summary data rather than raw data. Unless we are running a small $N$ experiment, readers are not interested in the scores of individual subjects, and neither are we. Rather, we want to compare treatment effects, and we do that by comparing group data. When we have group data, we summarize them with descriptive statistics, shorthand ways of describing data. For example, when we want to order a window shade, we do not carry the window frame to the hardware store. Instead, we summarize its characteristics using the standard dimensions of length and width. Similarly, we summarize and describe data by using some of the standard descriptive statistics: measures of central tendency (mean, median, and mode) and measures of variability (range, variance, and standard deviation).

## Measures of Central Tendency

As you know, statistics are quantitative indexes of the characteristics of our samples. Some of the most commonly computed and reported statistics are measures of central tendency, summary statistics that describe what is typical of a distribution of scores. The mode is the score that occurs most often. The median is the score that divides the distribution in half so that half the scores in the distribution fall above the median, half below (see Box 13.2). The mean is the arithmetic average: Add all the scores together and divide by the total number of scores, and you have the mean. The mean is by far the most commonly reported measure of central tendency, and you will need to include it in your research report. Only the mean can be manipulated algebraically (an important feature in statistical analysis).

Together, the mean, median, and mode are useful indicators of the shape of the distribution of values in the data. If the distribution is symmetrical and has only one mode (no scores tied for most frequent), the mean, median, and mode will coincide. Distributions of sample data are rarely perfectly

## BOX **13.2**   Computing the Median Score

The median is the value that falls in the middle of a set of scores. It is the score that divides the data so that half the scores fall above and half below the median. Computing the median score is simple, but first you must order all of your scores from the smallest to the largest. Following is a set of eight raw scores:

8  6  7  4  6  9  5  3

After you have put them in order from smallest to largest, they look like this:

3  4  5  6  6  7  8  9

Next, count how many numbers are in your set and add 1. Here, there are eight numbers, so your total is 9.

Divide by 2    $9/2 = 4.5$

Beginning with the lowest number, count up to that value in your ordered set of scores. If you end up on one of the numbers, that is your median. When you fall between two numbers, you must add them up and divide by 2. In this case, counting up 4.5 numbers would place you between the two sixes, so add them up and divide by 2:

$$(6 + 6)/2 = 6$$

The median score is 6.0.

symmetrical. More often, they are asymmetrical, or skewed—one tail of the distribution will be longer than the other, representing more extreme low or high scores. In a skewed distribution, the mean, median, and mode will be different, and each can lead to different impressions about the data. The mean is particularly sensitive to skew; it is pulled in the direction of extreme scores. Consider this set of scores:

3 4 5 6 6 6 7 8 9

These data form a symmetrical distribution. The mean is 6, the mode is 6, and the median is also 6. Suppose we substitute a higher score (18) into the set:

3 4 5 6 6 6 7 8 18

The distribution of scores is no longer symmetrical. Substituting the single extreme score has altered the shape of the distribution; to accommodate the extreme score, one tail is now longer than the other, so the curve has become skewed. The mode and median are still 6. However, the mean is now 7. The mean has increased because of one exceptionally large score. Alternatively, if our distribution had been skewed in the direction of an extreme low score rather than an extreme high score, the mean would have been less than the mode and median.

Even when the means of two distributions are the same, the distributions might be quite different. Consider these examples:

a. 5 5 6 6 6 6 7 7
b. 1 2 5 8 10 10

In (a) the mean is 6 and is truly typical of the data because the distribution is symmetrical. In (b) the mean is also 6, but clearly 6 is not a usual score. Note that the mode can be useful to describe distributions that contain many identical scores. The mode of (a) is 6 and the mode of (b) is 10, but the mode would be more representative of (a) than (b).

The summary statistic we choose to report can make a difference in the impression we create through our data. Income is often cited as one category of data that is subject to distortion. The distribution of income in the United States is not symmetrical but is positively skewed (there is a much longer tail on the positive side of the distribution); lots of people earn relatively small amounts of money, whereas a few earn a great deal. Thus, the mean income is always higher than the median or the mode because millionaires pull the mean up. Corporate management would prefer to use means in salary negotiations; labor would prefer to talk in terms of median or modal salaries. When evaluating any descriptive data, it is important to ask who is reporting what statistic and for what purpose.

Figure 13.9 depicts the mean, median, and mode of various distributions. Panel (a) illustrates a symmetrical distribution (the mean, median, and mode are the same). Panel (b) illustrates a bimodal distribution (two scores are tied for most frequent). Panel (c) represents a positively skewed distribution, and (d) represents one that is negatively skewed (in the latter two, the mean, median, and mode are three different values).

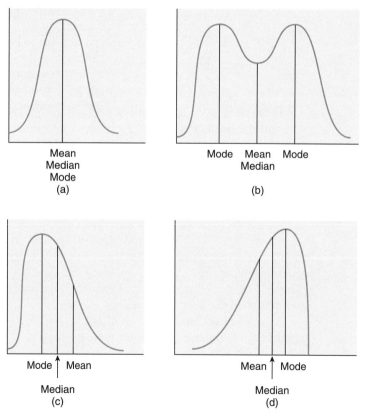

FIGURE **13.9** Mean, median, and mode in different distributions.
© Cengage Learning

## Measures of Variability

We also use descriptive statistics to measure the amount of variability in data. You will need to include a measure of variability in your research report. So far, we have talked about variability in a commonsense way: We say that anything that fluctuates has variability. When we do statistical tests, variability has more specific meanings. It is defined numerically by one of several descriptive statistics: the range, the variance, and the standard deviation. By using these statistics, we can compare the variability of one sample with that of another. The simplest measure of variability is the range, the difference between the largest and smallest scores in a set of data. If the scores on an exam varied from a high of 100 points to a low of 74, we would say that the range is 26. (Just subtract 74 from 100.) The range is often a useful measure; it can be computed quickly, and it gives a straightforward indication of the spread between the high and low scores in a distribution.

The problem with using the range is that it does not reflect the precise amount of variability in all the scores. Figure 13.10 shows you two distributions of test scores with the same range. You can see that the distributions are quite different from each other. The distribution for class 1 indicates that the test scores varied a great deal from student to student. In class 2, however, most students got similar scores; one extreme score accounts for the relatively large size of the range in this case. Knowing that these distributions have the same range tells us very little about them.

When we measure variability, we would like to be able to compare different samples in a more precise way. Computing the statistic we call *variance* enables us to do that. Computing the variance is a way of transforming variability into a standard form that provides a good but simple description of how much individual scores differ from one another. By using the variance, we can talk about the variability of all our scores without having to present

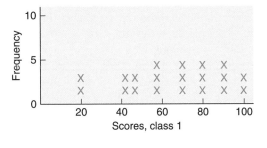

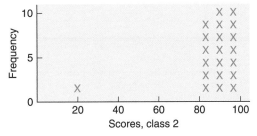

FIGURE **13.10** Two distributions with the same range (80 points).
© Cengage Learning

an entire set of data each time, just as we can order a window shade without carrying the window frame to the store.

The variance is the average squared deviation of scores from their mean. The variance tells us something about how much scores are spread out, or dispersed, around the mean of the data. Are they spread out a great deal around some central value, or are they tightly clustered around the mean? This can be useful information. Merchants sometimes use the concept of variance when they select stock for their stores. Let's take the example of figuring out how many pairs of women's shoes to order in a particular style. We know that the average shoe size of American women is 8. Clearly, an individual woman's shoe size can vary considerably from this mean. But how much do sizes typically vary? Are most women going to wear a size close to an 8, or will many women wear sizes far away from this average? Knowing how much variability to expect would help a store owner know how many pairs of each size to keep on hand. If shoe size varies only a little, most customers will wear a size close to 8, and the owner could safely stock only sizes that are close to the average without missing too many sales. But if there is a lot of variance in shoe size, the owner would want to stock some number of all the smaller and larger sizes, too, because the next customer who walks through the door could have either very small or very large feet!

One way or another, you will be computing the variance in just about every statistical test that you do, so it is important to master this concept. The steps for computing the variance for the time-estimation experiment are shown in Appendix A (Table A.2). The variance ($s^2$) for the subjects who were shown the incomplete cartoons is 8.6 minutes. This tells us that, on average, the *square* of each subject's deviation from the group mean is 8.6 minutes. If we take the square root of the variance, we have another useful measure of variability, the standard deviation, or *s*. It reflects the average deviation of scores about the mean.[11] We cannot compute that average directly by adding the deviations; the total of the deviations from the mean is always zero. So we use the square root of the variance to return to the original unsquared units of measurement. The standard deviation of our "no-fun" group is 2.9 minutes. This means that, on average, we can expect each individual subject to deviate from the group mean by 2.9 minutes. We use the same procedures for each treatment group. To save time, we will tell you that those computations yield a group mean of 9.6 minutes and a variance of 8.8 minutes for the "fun" group, subjects who saw cartoons complete with caption. You may want to verify those figures by working through the formulas on your own.[12]

---

[11] The standard deviation for American women's shoe sizes is about 1.5, and about two-thirds of women wear between size 6 ½ and size 9 ½.

[12] To make the discussion simpler, we have rounded off the variance and the standard deviation to tenths. However, when you include summary statistics in a research report, the *Publication Manual of the American Psychological Association* (2010) recommends that the values should be rounded off to two digits more than are presented in the raw data. For example, because our raw data were expressed as whole numbers and tenths, the value of $s^2$ we would include in our report is 8.555 (whole number plus thousandths). You can use the following conventions for rounding off: Round up if the digit to be rounded off is an odd number; simply drop the 5 if the digit to be rounded is an even number. Thus 8.55 (or 8.555) becomes 8.6, and 4.65 becomes 4.6.

When we report the results of our experiments, we usually report summary statistics in place of raw data. Typically, we report the mean and the standard deviation of each treatment group. We have now completed the first two stages of analyzing our results: We have organized and summarized the data. The third step is to apply a statistical test to interpret our results. We will use the summary data from the time-estimation experiment again when we discuss test statistics in the next chapter.

## SUMMARY

In principle, experimenters would like to prove that the independent variable caused the changes observed in the behavior of subjects under different conditions. In practice, however, the best they can do is show that the differences observed were probably caused by the experiment. Experimenters use *statistics* to determine whether the independent variable probably caused the changes in the dependent variable. They really cannot prove that it did, but they can make statements about how likely it is that the independent variable had an effect.

In a statistical analysis of data, we test the *null hypothesis* ($H_0$), which states that the differences between treatments amount to nothing more than expected variability in the data. Variability is the amount of fluctuation observed in scores on a dependent variable. We assume the null hypothesis is true until the evidence shows it can be rejected. To know whether or not to reject the null hypothesis, an experimenter needs to know how much variability is present on the dependent measure. The more variability there is, the greater the difference between groups has to be before we can say that the data probably came from different populations. We cannot actually measure the populations, so we make *statistical inferences* from the samples we do measure.

Some differences between treatments are more likely than others, and it is possible to calculate the odds that each difference will occur. The *means* (averages) of most samples are close to the mean of the population. Thus, the odds of getting treatment means that are fairly similar are high. The odds of seeing much larger differences are less. The exact odds depend on the amount of variability in the population. We decide whether the differences between treatments are *statistically significant* on the basis of probabilities. In psychology, we usually reject the null hypothesis if the difference between treatments is so extreme that it would have occurred by chance less than 5 times out of 100. This is called a .05 *significance level*. In effect, it says that the probability of getting so large a difference just by chance is less than .05 ($p < .05$).

When we reject the null hypothesis, the *alternative hypothesis* ($H_1$), which states that the treatment data are sampled from different populations, is supported. When we reject the null hypothesis, we are saying that the experiment is the most likely explanation for the differences we have observed. Null hypothesis significance testing and use of the .05 criterion is not without its critics. As a result, the APA guidelines now recommend reporting effect size estimates and confidence intervals along with $p$ values.

In hypothesis testing, there are two types of decision errors, Type 1 and Type 2. A *Type 1 error* means the experimenter has incorrectly rejected the null hypothesis: The researcher concluded that the differences between treatment means were probably *not* caused by chance—although, in fact, they were. *Type 2 errors* occur when the null hypothesis is not rejected when the treatment means were actually drawn from different populations. Thus, a Type 2 error means that the independent variable really did have an effect, but the experimenter failed to detect it.

Researchers can use either one-tailed or two-tailed hypothesis tests, depending on whether $H_1$ is directional or nondirectional. A *directional hypothesis* predicts the direction of the expected difference between treatment groups, and a *one-tailed test* may be used. A *nondirectional hypothesis* predicts that treatment groups will differ but does not specify how; a more stringent *two-tailed test* is needed. Statistical significance can be obtained with smaller statistical values using a one-tailed test because the *critical region* of the test distribution (representing $p < .05$) is located in a single tail, rather than being split over both tails.

It is possible to make inferences about populations from results of samples using *inferential statistics,* also called test statistics. *Test statistics* are numerical summaries of effects produced by sample data. For each test statistic, statisticians have calculated the probability of each possible value. Those probabilities are used to judge the significance of the results.

Three basic steps for analyzing results are (1) organize the data; (2) summarize them; (3) apply the appropriate statistical test to interpret the results. We organize data by making sure that all subjects' responses are labeled clearly and separated by treatment condition. We summarize data by computing *descriptive statistics,* shorthand representations of data. Some commonly used descriptive statistics are the *measures of central tendency* (mean, median, and mode) and measures of *variability* (range, variance, and standard deviation).

The *mean* is the arithmetic average of all scores in a group. The *mode* is the most frequent score. The *median* is the score that divides the distribution in half.

We also want to know how much variability exists among subjects' scores. The *range* is the difference between the largest and the smallest scores in a set of data. Two distributions with the same range can look strikingly different; the range shows only how much the highest and lowest scores differ. The *variance* ($s^2$) is a more precise indication of the amount of variability. It reflects the amount of variability among all the scores in a distribution, and so it is a more useful indicator than the range. The larger the variance, the more subjects' scores differ from one another. The *standard deviation* ($s$) is the square root of the variance. It reflects the average deviation of scores about the mean.

# KEY TERMS

**Alternative hypothesis ($H_1$)** A statement that the data came from different populations; the research hypothesis, which cannot be tested directly.

**Critical region** Portion in the tail(s) of the distribution of a test statistic extreme enough to satisfy the researcher's criterion for rejecting the null hypothesis—for instance, the most extreme 5% of a distribution where $p < .05$ is the chosen significance level.

**Descriptive statistics** The standard procedures used to summarize and describe data quickly and clearly; summary statistics reported for an experiment, including mean, range, and standard deviation.

**Directional hypothesis** A statement that predicts the exact pattern of results that will be observed, such as which treatment group will perform best.

**Experimental error** Variation in subjects' scores produced by uncontrolled extraneous variables in the experimental procedure, experimenter bias, or other influences on subjects not related to effects of the independent variable.

**Inferential statistics** Statistics that can be used as indicators of what is going on in a population; also called *test statistics*.

**Mean** An arithmetical average computed by dividing the sum of a group of scores by the total number of scores; a measure of central tendency.

**Measures of central tendency** Summary statistics that describe what is typical of a distribution of scores; include mean, median, and mode.

**Median** The score that divides a distribution in half, so that half the scores in the distribution fall above the median, half below; a measure of central tendency.

**Mode** The most frequently occurring score in a distribution; a measure of central tendency.

**Nondirectional hypothesis** A statement that predicts a difference between treatment groups without predicting the exact pattern of results.

**Normal curve** The distribution of data in a symmetrical, bell-shaped curve.

**Null hypothesis ($H_0$)** A statement that the performance of treatment groups is so similar that the groups must belong to the same population; a way of saying that the experimental manipulation had no important effect.

**One-tailed test** A statistical procedure used when a directional prediction has been made; the critical region of the distribution of the test statistic is measured in just one tail of the distribution.

**Range** The difference between the largest and smallest scores in a set of data; a rough indication of the amount of variability in the data.

**Raw data** Data recorded as an experiment is run; the responses of individual subjects.

**Significance level** The statistical criterion for deciding whether to reject the null hypothesis or not, typically $p < .05$.

**Standard deviation** The square root of the variance; measures the average deviation of scores about the mean, thus reflecting the amount of variability in the data.

**Statistical inference** A statement made about a population and all its samples based on the samples observed.

**Statistical significance** Meeting the set criterion for significance; the data do not support the null hypothesis, confirming a difference between the groups that occurred as a result of the experiment.

**Statistics** Quantitative measurements of samples; quantitative data.

**Summary data** Descriptive statistics computed from the raw data of an experiment, including the measures of central tendency and variability.

**Test statistics** Statistics that can be used as indicators of what is going on in a population and can be used to evaluate results; also called *inferential statistics*.

**Two-tailed test** A statistical procedure used when a nondirectional prediction has been made; the critical region of the distribution of the test statistic is divided over both tails of the distribution.

Type 1 error An error made by rejecting the null hypothesis even though it is really true; stating that an effect exists when it really does not.

Type 2 error An error made by failing to reject the null hypothesis even though it is really false; failing to detect a treatment effect.

Variability Fluctuation in data; can be defined numerically as the range, variance, or standard deviation.

Variance The average squared deviation of scores from their mean; a more precise measure of variability than the range.

## REVIEW AND STUDY QUESTIONS

1. What is variability? Give three examples of dependent measures that you would expect to have high variability.

2. Jack is still looking for a shortcut. After running an experiment, he says, "Oh, wow. The difference between my two treatment means is 60 points. I mean, like, that's such a large difference that I'm sure my independent variable had an effect." What is Jack forgetting? Explain how you could account for his findings without assuming that his independent variable produced the difference between his treatment means.

3. What is a null hypothesis?

4. You have run an experiment to test the effects of noise on motor dexterity. It was a three-group experiment. Your three conditions were a control condition with no noise, a low-noise condition, and a high-noise condition. Your three treatment means are different. State the null hypothesis for your experiment.

5.
   a. Julie is going to run an experiment tomorrow in which her significance level will be $p < .05$. What does that mean?
   b. If she decides instead to use $p < .01$ as her significance level, will it be easier or harder for her to detect the effect of the independent variable? Why?

6. For each of the following examples, explain whether the researcher has committed a Type 1 or Type 2 error and why.
   a. Dr. G. rejects the null hypothesis although the independent variable had no effect.

   b. Dr. R. rejects the null hypothesis when it is false.
   c. Although the independent variable had an effect, Dr. E. does not reject the null hypothesis.

7.
   a. What are the odds that you will make a Type 1 error in an experiment?
   b. How could you reduce those odds?

8. Describe three ways to reduce $\beta$.

9. Explain why each of the following hypotheses is directional or nondirectional and whether it would require a one-tailed or two-tailed statistical test:
   a. Adversity builds character.
   b. Television viewing can affect children's attention spans.
   c. Recall of nonsense syllables improves with repeated presentations.
   d. Newborns behave differently under bright versus dim lights.

10. Jill is a little discouraged. She says, "If we cannot prove that our independent variable had an effect, why bother doing an experiment?" Explain to Jill what we do accomplish when we evaluate the results of an experiment.

11. What are the three basic steps for analyzing the results of an experiment?

12. What are descriptive statistics? Why do we need them in an experiment?

13. Define each of the following and explain what each tells us about a set of data:
   a. The mean, median, and mode

b. The range, variance, and standard deviation

14. Following are two distributions of scores on a memory test. Find the mean, median, range, and variance of each group.

| Group 1 | Group 2 |
|---------|---------|
| 5 | 3 |
| 6 | 1 |
| 8 | 3 |
| 3 | 2 |
| 1 | 5 |

## CRITICAL THINKING EXERCISE

*The myth:* The average IQ is exactly 100.

*The scientific findings:* Standardized intelligence tests have been designed to create a mean of 100 and a standard deviation of 15. The distribution for IQ scores, however, is slightly negatively skewed because there is a larger than expected number of individuals with extreme pathology whose IQ scores fall at the low end.

*The problem:* Draw a graph to illustrate this kind of distribution and draw vertical lines through the graph at the points where you would expect the mean and median to fall.

## ONLINE RESOURCES

To explore the impact of Type 1 and Type 2 errors on global climate change, go to the following site:

http://greennature.com/article284.html

For additional practice with the statistical concepts in this chapter, you will find several workshops available at this site:

http://www.wadsworth.com/psychology_d/templates/student_resources/workshops/workshops.html

## CHAPTER 14

# Analyzing Results

**Which Test Do I Use?**
Levels of Measurement
Selecting a Statistical Test

**Statistics for Two-Group Experiments**

**The Chi-Square Test**
Degrees of Freedom
Interpreting the Chi Square

**The *t* Test**
Effects of Sample Size
The *t* Test for Matched Groups

**Analyzing Multiple Groups and Factorial Experiments**

**Analysis of Variance**

**Sources of Variability**

**A One-Way Between-Subjects Analysis of Variance**
Within- and Between-Groups Variability
Statistical Control for Differences Between
    Groups

**One-Way Repeated Measures Analysis of Variance**

**Analyzing Data from a Between-Subjects Factorial Experiment**

**Two-Way Analysis of Variance**
Evaluating the *F* Ratios

**Repeated Measures and Mixed Factorial Designs**
Interpreting Significant Effects

SUMMARY
KEY TERMS
REVIEW AND STUDY QUESTIONS
CRITICAL THINKING EXERCISE
ONLINE RESOURCES

## CHAPTER OBJECTIVES

- Learn how to select the appropriate statistical tests

- Understand the concepts behind the chi-square test and how to compute it

- Understand the differences between the two types of *t* tests

- Understand the concept of variance in an experiment

- Learn how different components of variance can be compared in analysis of variance to detect significant treatment effects

- Learn how to interpret F ratios for multiple group and factorial experiments

In the last chapter, we discussed the logic behind statistical tests, hypothesis testing, and statistical inference. We covered two of the three basic steps in analyzing results: organizing and summarizing the data. In this chapter, we will review the application of statistical tests to interpret our findings. We will review the most commonly used test statistics: chi square ($\chi^2$), *t* tests, and analysis of variance (ANOVA). The statistical tests covered in this chapter can be used for quasi-experimental and true experimental designs. As previewed in the last chapter, we will also discuss effect size estimates to accompany these test statistics and the computation and reporting of confidence intervals. If you have access to a computer with an up-to-date statistical software package, such as SPSS, you can use this software to carry out the statistical procedures covered in this chapter.

---

## WHICH TEST DO I USE?

When we design experiments, we always select an experimental design before we conduct an experiment. As we design our experiment, we also consider the statistical tests that we will use once the data are collected. When we looked at experimental designs, we developed a set of questions to help us choose the best design for an experiment. We can make decisions about which statistical tests to use in much the same way. The number of independent variables is still important. How many independent variables do you have? How many levels of each? Is the experiment within or between subjects? Did you use matching? As you become more familiar with selecting and using statistics, you will not need to go through all these steps, but you will find it much easier to choose the right test if you begin with these questions while you are designing your experiment. Along with the number of independent variables, we need to consider the type of data we are analyzing. The way we measure the dependent variable makes a difference in how we analyze the results, because there are different statistical tests for different kinds of data.

## Levels of Measurement

Recall from Chapters 4 and 7 that the level of measurement is the kind of scale used to measure a variable. Let's review the four levels of measurement quickly:

A *ratio scale* has equal intervals between all its values and an absolute zero point. These attributes enable us to express relationships between values on these scales as ratios: We can say 2 minutes is twice as long as 1 minute.

An *interval scale* also measures magnitude, or quantitative size, and has equal intervals between values. However, it has no true zero point.

An *ordinal scale* reflects differences only in magnitude, where magnitude is measured in the form of ranks. We cannot be sure that the intervals between values are equal, and the scale has no true zero.

A *nominal scale* classifies items into distinct categories that have no quantitative relationship to one another. Nominal scaling provides the least information. It tells nothing about magnitude, nor does it have equal intervals between values.

Variables may be measured by using one of these four types of scales. Our examples have used mainly ratio and interval scale data because these scales yield the most information, and researchers generally prefer them. But remember that different techniques are needed for different types of data.

## Selecting a Statistical Test

The selection of a test statistic, along with a significance level, should be made as you plan the experimental design and create the measurement scale for the dependent variable. To select the appropriate statistical test, first decide which level of measurement is being used to measure the dependent variable and then answer the other questions summarized in Table 14.1. You now have all the information you need to select a statistical test.

Table 14.2 shows the most common statistical tests, organized by the number of independent variables they can handle, the level of measurement of the dependent variable, and whether the experiment is within- or between-subjects, or mixed. Notice that the same statistics are used for within-subjects designs and matched designs. Other tests not listed are used less often, and you may not

TABLE **14.1**

## The parameters of data analysis

1. How many independent variables are there?
2. How many treatment conditions are there?
3. Is the experiment run between- or within-subjects?
4. Are the subjects matched?
5. What is the level of measurement of the dependent variable?

© Cengage Learning

TABLE **14.2**
Selecting a possible statistical test by number of independent variables and level of measurement

| Level of measurement of dependent variable | One Independent Variable | | | | Two Independent Variables | | | |
|---|---|---|---|---|---|---|---|---|
| | Two Treatments | | More Than Two Treatments | | Factorial Designs | | | |
| | Two independent groups | Two matched groups (or within subjects) | Multiple independent groups | Multiple matched groups (or within subjects) | Independent groups | Matched groups (or within subjects) | Independent groups and matched groups (or between subjects and within subjects) |
| Interval or ratio | *t* test for independent groups | *t* test for matched groups | One-way ANOVA | One-way ANOVA (repeated measures) | Two-way ANOVA | Two-way ANOVA (repeated measures) | Two-way ANOVA (mixed) |
| Ordinal | Mann-Whitney U test | Wilcoxon test | Kruskal-Wallis test | Friedman test | | | |
| Nominal | Chi-square test | | Chi-square test | | Chi-square test | | |

Note: You can find explanations of these tests in most standard or advanced texts on statistics.
© Cengage Learning

need them until you take more advanced courses. We will focus on the tests you are most likely to need for your first experiments. Table 14.2 indicates "possible" tests; it does not tell us what we will definitely need in all cases. That is because we may be able to use more than one test. As you learn about the tests, you will also learn that each test has its own additional requirements.

## STATISTICS FOR TWO-GROUP EXPERIMENTS

First, let us consider a simple two-independent-groups experiment that uses nominal data. Imagine that a researcher wants to test whether subjects can be induced to make errors on a test question by first presenting them with a task designed to prime, or elicit, a certain incorrect response—a homophone (like the "cherry pit"—>"Brad Pitt" experiment by Burke et al., 2004). Subjects in the experimental group are asked the following priming question by the experimenter: "What do the letters T-O-P-S spell?" Subjects will answer, "Tops." Then they are asked the following test question: "What does a car do at a green light?" Of course, the experimenter hopes subjects will give the wrong answer, "Stops," instead of the correct answer, "Goes," because just saying the word *Tops* should make the rhyming word *Stops* more likely to come to mind than the nonrhyming word *Goes*. Here the experimenter would merely record whether the subject made the error or not.

The control group could be asked a different question. One question that would not be expected to produce very much interference with the correct answer to the test question might be this: "What do the letters C-A-R spell?" After the subject responds, the same test question is asked, and the subjects' responses, correct or incorrect, are recorded. The data collected are nominal; each subject's answer falls into either the correct or incorrect category. How would we analyze the data from this experiment?

First, answer the questions from Table 14.1:

1. There is one independent variable (priming).
2. There are two treatment conditions (priming versus no priming).
3. The experiment is run between subjects. (There are different subjects in each treatment condition.)
4. The subjects are not matched.
5. The dependent variable is measured by a nominal scale.

Next, with this information, we can select a possible test to use for the data from the tests suggested in Table 14.2. Table 14.2 suggests a chi-square test for our priming experiment.

## THE CHI-SQUARE TEST

One type of inferential statistic is the chi-square test. Because we make inferences about the population, we can use many of the concepts from Chapter 13: testing the null hypothesis, sampling distributions, significance levels, and Type 1 and Type 2 errors. Using the data we have obtained, we will compute a statistical value and compare it with the appropriate critical value for the chi-

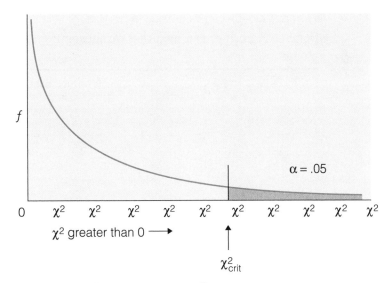

FIGURE **14.1** Distribution of $\chi^2$ statistic.

From *Basic Statistics for the Behavioral Sciences*, 5th edition by G. W. Heiman. Copyright 2005 by Houghton Mifflin Company. Used with permission.

square statistic—the value that must be exceeded to reject the null hypothesis at the chosen significance level. However, the chi-square test is a *nonparametric* test; it does not assume that the population has certain parameters, such as a normal distribution of scores, or that variances in the two groups are approximately equal. Instead of relating differences between treatment means to the amount of variability we would expect to see between any two sets of data drawn from the same population, a chi square compares frequencies (e.g., how many subjects answered correctly; how many incorrectly). A chi-square ($\chi^2$) test determines whether the frequencies of responses in our sample represent frequencies expected in the population.

The chi-square distribution is illustrated in Figure 14.1. It looks different from the normal distributions that were pictured in Chapter 13, but it is used the same way. When $H_0$ is true, $\chi^2 = 0$, because the frequencies of responses in our sample do not differ in a meaningful way from those we would expect in the untreated population. As differences between expected and obtained frequencies become greater, the value of $\chi^2$ increases. When $\chi^2$ is larger than the critical value, we can reject $H_0$ at $p < .05$. The test requires that all responses be sampled independently; this simply means that you cannot test each subject more than once. It is commonly used for nominal data.[1]

---

[1] When sample data are extremely skewed or large differences exist in the variances of data from different groups in the experiment, assumptions from statistical tests designed for interval or ratio data may be violated. In these cases, the researcher might switch to a chi-square test to avoid inflating the Type 1 error rate.

TABLE **14.3**

Number of correct and incorrect responses from experimental and control groups

| | Outcome of Study | | |
| --- | --- | --- | --- |
| | Correct Responses | Incorrect Responses | Row Totals |
| Experimental group | 4 | 16 | 20 |
| | (12) | (8) | |
| Control group | 20 | 0 | 20 |
| | (12) | (8) | |
| Column totals | 24 | 16 | |

Note: Expected frequencies are shown within parentheses.
© Cengage Learning

In Chapter 13, we pointed out that researchers mostly prefer to use parametric tests (requiring interval and ratio scales of measurement) because they are more powerful. Nevertheless, computed chi squares are frequently encountered in the research literature when nominal data are the best or only choice for the dependent measure.

To conduct a chi-square test, data are first organized in the form of a 2 × 2 contingency table.[2] Frequency counts are tabulated and placed in the appropriate cells. The chi square compares the frequencies obtained in the experiment, called *obtained frequencies* (O), with expected population frequencies, called *expected frequencies* (E), to test the null hypothesis. $H_0$, here, is that obtained frequencies are not different from expected frequencies, or O = E. If the chi-square test is significant, we can reject $H_0$. For a two-group experiment like this one, statisticians recommend that the expected frequency in each cell should be at least 10. Hypothetical data from 20 experimental and 20 control subjects from the priming experiment are shown in Table 14.3. The chi-square formula and calculations using these data are shown in Appendix A-3.

We obtained a chi-square value of 26.67 (rounded off) for our priming experiment example. Is that value large enough to reject the null hypothesis? To know, we must compare the value we obtained ($\chi^2_{obt}$) with the critical value needed to reject $H_0$. The value we obtained must exceed the critical value to reject the null hypothesis at our chosen significance level. The critical value can be found in the $\chi^2$ table of critical values (Table B.2 in Appendix B). To select the appropriate $\chi^2$ distribution from the table, however, we need to first understand the concept of degrees of freedom.

---

[2] For reporting, it is very simple to organize and summarize data for a chi square using frequency counts as data: A 2 × 2 table that includes both obtained and expected frequencies (as in Table 14.3) serves both to organize and to summarize the data. There is no need to calculate measures of central tendency or variability.

## Degrees of Freedom

We select the appropriate distribution for test statistics such as $\chi^2$ based on degrees of freedom (*df*). The degrees of freedom tell us how many members of a set of data could vary or change value without changing the value of a statistic we already know for those data. Samples that are the same size can have different degrees of freedom depending on the way the experiment is designed and on the statistic being computed. Let us say we know the mean of the data. Then the degrees of freedom tell us how many members of that set of data could change without altering the value of the mean.

Imagine that a phone number is a set of data with a mean of 5. It has seven digits; therefore, to produce a mean of 5, the total of the seven digits must equal 35. Suppose that the first six digits of the number are 6, 7, 4, 3, 9, and 2. Can you find the last digit? Of course you can. Because you know the total and six of the digits, you can easily compute the value of the last digit, *which is not free to vary*. Different combinations of the first six digits are possible. But once their values have been set, the value of the last digit is also set if the total must equal 35. If we tried to substitute any other value for the seventh digit, the total would no longer equal 35, and the mean, the known statistic, would no longer be correct. The degrees of freedom for this phone number therefore equal 6. If we include an area code in the data—say 2, 1, 2—we would say that the telephone number has 10 digits. It now totals 40, and its degrees of freedom now equal 10 − 1, or 9. Clearly, the degrees of freedom are related to the number of digits, or data, in a sample.

Similarly, the degrees of freedom in the distribution of a statistic vary in a way related to the number of subjects sampled. However, we compute degrees of freedom differently for different test statistics. For analysis of a 2 × 2 contingency table, there is only 1 *df*. The actual formula for computing the degrees of freedom is this: number of rows minus 1 × number of columns minus 1; in this case $(2 - 1) \times (2 - 1) = 1$.

Sometimes all but one value of a set of data can change, sometimes many fewer, as is the case with $\chi^2$. The way we compute the degrees of freedom can also vary with different applications of the same statistic, as we will see later in the chapter. If we are using different statistics or the same statistic applied in different ways, we may have different degrees of freedom even though sample sizes are identical. That is why the critical values of test statistics are always presented and organized by degrees of freedom rather than by number of subjects.

## Interpreting the Chi Square

Now that we know the $\chi^2$ test for our experiment has 1 *df*, we can look up the critical value in Appendix B. For a significance level of .05, the critical value is 3.84. To reject $H_0$ at $p < .05$, the value we obtained must exceed this number. In this case, $\chi^2_{obt}$ is 26.67, which is much larger than the critical value necessary for significance at $p < .05$. Notice that if we had set our significance level at .01, our test would still have been statistically significant. In the priming experiment, it is very likely that the independent variable had an effect. If we were writing up the results of this experiment, we could now say the following:

1.  The research hypothesis was supported. (We never say it was "proven." Why?)
2.  As predicted by the research hypothesis, there was a significant difference between the experimental and the control condition.
3.  Subjects who received the T-O-P-S prime were much more likely to give the incorrect response "Stop," than were subjects who were given the control prime.

If you are using packaged software for your statistical analyses, you will not need to look up any critical values; instead, the program prints out the actual level of statistical significance obtained by the test. If it is less than the level of significance you selected (typically $p < .05$), your results are considered significant. This is one of the many advantages of using computers to analyze data. Once you have a thorough background in statistics, statistical analysis with computers can be a great time-saver and offers tremendous flexibility. But there are disadvantages, too.

The program will accept whatever data you have; for example, it will run programs designed for interval or ratio data even if your data are nominal. And the program will not tell you how your results should be interpreted; only a good grounding in statistics will provide those kinds of answers. (Incidentally, it is usually easy for your instructor to tell when a student uses a statistic that he or she does not fully understand.) Figure 14.2 shows a sample SPSS printout for the $\chi^2$ analysis of the priming data. What was the actual significance level obtained? (Answer: $p = .000$ can be interpreted as $p < .0001$.) What is phi?

Cramer's coefficient phi ($\phi$) is an estimate of the degree of association between the two categorical variables tested by $\chi^2$. Cramer's coefficient phi is similar to $r$, the correlation coefficient you learned about in Chapter 5. Cramer's $\phi$ is simple to calculate once you have computed $\chi^2$:

$$\phi = \sqrt{\frac{\chi^2}{N(S-1)}}$$

$N$ = the number of observations; $S$ = the smaller number of rows or columns; in the priming experiment: $N = 40$; $S = 2$.

Cramer's coefficient $\phi$ for our priming experiment is .816, suggesting a very strong association between the priming manipulation and responses to the test question. Cohen (1988) suggests the following criteria for interpreting the size of $\phi$: $\phi = .10$ = a small degree of association; $\phi = .30$ = medium degree of association; $\phi = .50$ = large degree of association. And, like $r^2$, $\phi^2$ can be interpreted as the proportion of variance shared by the two variables, so it can be reported as an estimate of the effect size in the experiment. An interesting experiment that reported chi-square statistics is described in Box 14.1.

| | | | CORR_INC | | |
|---|---|---|---|---|---|
| | | | correct | incorrect | Total |
| EXP_CNT | exp | Count<br>Expected Count | 4<br>12.0 | 16<br>8.0 | 20<br>20.0 |
| | cnt | Count<br>Expected Count | 20<br>12.0 | 0<br>8.0 | 20<br>20.0 |
| Total | | Count<br>Expected Count | 24<br>24.0 | 16<br>16.0 | 40<br>40.0 |

**Chi-Square Tests**

| | Value | df | Asump. Sig.<br>(2-sided) | Exact Sig.<br>(2-sided) | Exact Sig.<br>(1-sided) |
|---|---|---|---|---|---|
| Pearson Chi-Square<br>Fisher's Exact Test<br>N of Valid Cases | 26.667<br><br>40 | 1 | .000 | <br>.000 | <br>.000 |

**Symmetric Measures**

| | | Value | Approx. Sig. |
|---|---|---|---|
| Nominal by Nominal<br>N of Valid Cases | Phi | −.816<br>40 | .000 |

FIGURE **14.2** SPSS analysis of data from the priming experiment.
© Cengage Learning

## THE *T* TEST

Now, let us return to our hypothetical time-estimation experiment from the previous chapter and answer the questions from Table 14.1 to select a statistical test.

1. There is one independent variable ("fun").
2. There are two treatment conditions ("fun" versus "no fun").
3. The experiment is run between subjects. (Each treatment condition has different subjects.)
4. The subjects are not matched.
5. The dependent variable is measured by a ratio scale (time).

For this hypothetical experiment, Table 14.2 suggests the *t* test for independent groups, a common test statistic. When we want to evaluate interval or ratio data from a two-group experiment, we compute the test statistic *t*, which is a computational way of relating differences between treatment means to the amount of variability we would expect to see between any two sets of data drawn from the same population. Thus, the *t* test is a parametric

## BOX **14.1** Do Dogs Really Resemble Their Owners?

We have all observed people who resemble their pets, but is there really anything more than simple coincidence going on when we make these observations? Roy and Christenfeld (2004) conducted a very interesting study to answer this question. At visits to three California dog parks, the researchers took photographs of 45 dogs and separate photographs of their 45 owners (15 from each park). In all, 25 purebred and 20 mixed breed dogs were used in the study; about half of their owners were female and half were male. The backgrounds of the photos were controlled so that the dogs and owners could not be related to each other by looking at the backgrounds.

To test whether subjects could match up the dogs and the owners by looking at their photos, the researchers made up photo sets that consisted of three photos: one dog, its owner, and another dog. They used complete counterbalancing to ensure that every owner-dog pair was presented with every other dog photographed at the same dog park. Twenty-eight undergraduate students served as judges. A dog was considered to resemble its owner if a majority of the judges (>14) matched the dog with its correct owner.

The findings were interesting—if not easily explained. The judges were unable to correctly match up the mixed breed dogs and their owners: There were 7 matches, 4 ties, and 9 misses, $\chi^2 = .64$, not a significant effect. In contrast, the judges were much better at matching the purebred dogs with their owners, $\chi^2 = 6.75$, $p < .05$, with 16 matches, 0 ties, and 9 misses—an accuracy level significantly greater than chance.

The authors also attempted to explain what features the judges were using to match up dogs and owners; they evaluated characteristics such as

hairiness, size, sharpness of features, attractiveness, perceived friendliness, perceived energy level, owner hairstyle/dog ear type, but they could not find any significant correlations between ratings on these characteristics and owner-dog matches. The only characteristic that showed any kind of trend was for purebred dogs and their owners to receive somewhat similar ratings on perceived friendliness ($r = .31$, $p = .13$). The authors concluded, "When people pick a pet, they seek one that, at some level, resembles them, and when they get a purebred, they get what they want" (p. 361).

FIGURE **14.3** A good match? Andreas Kuehn/Getty Images.

test. When we introduced the concepts of one- and two-tailed tests in the last chapter, we illustrated these concepts with a figure of a $t$ distribution (Figure 13.8) showing critical regions and critical values for statistical significance. When we evaluate the likelihood of obtaining a particular value of $t$, we are performing a $t$ test.

The exact probabilities for each value of $t$ have been calculated for us. However, the distribution of these values changes depending on the number of subjects in the samples. Let us examine the family of $t$ distributions and the effects of sample size.

## Effects of Sample Size

The size of our sample is very important. If we take both small and large samples from the same population, we will generally find that small samples vary more from the mean of the population than large samples do. You already know that parametric test statistics represent a relationship between treatment effects and variability. If sample size affects variability, it also affects the size of the test statistics.

For a test statistic such as *t*, sample size is important because the exact shape of the distribution of *t* changes depending on the size of the samples. The *t* statistic has a whole family of distributions, some of which are shown in Figure 14.4. The *t* distributions resemble the normal curve we looked at in Chapter 13. They are symmetrical, with the greatest concentration of values around the mean. The shape of the *t* distribution becomes more and more like the normal curve as the sample size increases. With small samples, the *t* distribution has a flatter and wider shape.

Sample size is also important because of the assumptions we make whenever we apply *t*. One of the requirements of a *t* test is that the data to be analyzed (interval or ratio) come from populations that are normally distributed. This is because the probabilities of getting each individual *t* value have been worked out for populations that are normally distributed. If the data do not come from such populations, the odds that have been worked out for *t* will be wrong for those data. Of course, we can hardly ever measure all the members of a population. We get around this problem by using large samples so that the correct odds of each *t* value are very close to what they would be if the population was normally distributed.

This is rarely a problem because the *t* test is robust. When a test is robust, it means that the assumptions of the test, such as a normal distribution of population values and comparable variances within treatment groups, can be violated without changing the rate of Type 1 and Type 2 errors.

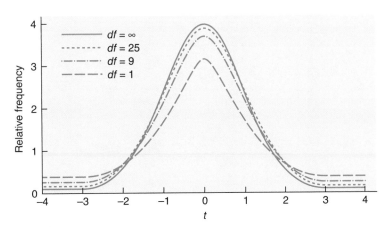

FIGURE **14.4** Some members of the family of *t* distributions.
Adapted from Quantitative methods in psychology, by D. Lewis.

If there are at least 20 subjects in each treatment group, a *t* test is probably safe; with 30 subjects in a group, most researchers would not worry at all.

As we saw earlier with $\chi^2$, we select the appropriate *t* distribution based on degrees of freedom rather than sample size. (Figure 14.4 refers to degrees of freedom [*df*] rather than to number of subjects.) Let us look more closely at two distributions of *t* to get a clearer idea of how degrees of freedom will affect the critical value of *t*. The critical value of *t* is the value we need to exceed to reject the null hypothesis at our chosen significance level. Figure 14.5 shows distributions of *t* for 25 and 9 degrees of freedom. It also shows the critical values of *t* for the $p < .05$ significance level using a two-tailed test. What is the relationship between these levels?

As the *t* distribution changes shape, the critical value of *t* needed to reject the null hypothesis at our chosen significance level also changes. Remember that the significance level refers to probabilities. We are looking to see whether the value of *t* that we compute from our data is more or less likely than our chosen critical value. If the experimental manipulation was effective, the computed value of *t* should be more extreme than the chosen critical value. For probabilities, this means that the computed value of *t* is so extreme that it could have occurred by chance less than 5% of the time.

It is easy to see that the distribution for 9 degrees of freedom is flatter and wider than the other curve shown. Fewer degrees of freedom mean more variability between samples. More variability means that more and more cases will be far from the mean of the population; large differences between samples can be expected to occur relatively often just by chance. With only 9 degrees of freedom, the most extreme 5% of this distribution falls relatively far out on the curve (±2.262). To reject the null hypothesis at $p < .05$, the obtained value of *t* must be greater than this critical value. With 25 degrees of freedom, variability is less, and the most extreme 5% of the distribution falls closer to the mean. With 25 *df*s we only need to exceed a critical value of ±2.060 to reject $H_0$ at $p < .05$. Now you can see why it is easier to get a

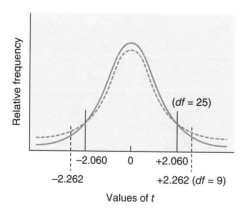

FIGURE **14.5** The *t* distributions for 25 and 9 degrees of freedom and critical values at $p < .05$.
© Cengage Learning

significant effect with larger samples! Larger samples make it easier to reject $H_0$ because the critical value of $t$ gets smaller as sample size (and, thus, degrees of freedom) increases.

As we saw when we compared distributions with 9 and 25 $df$s, the critical value of $t$ is larger when the degrees of freedom are smaller. The fewer the subjects, the higher the critical value of $t$ needed to demonstrate a statistically significant effect from an experimental manipulation. The fewer the subjects, the less likely it is that we will be able to reject the null hypothesis. Therefore, with fewer subjects, we also have a greater chance of making a Type 2 error.

Finally, we need to understand that critical values of $t$ will change depending on the type of hypothesis we are testing—whether it is nondirectional (two-tailed) or directional (one-tailed). You already know from the last chapter that it is easier to get significance with a one-tailed test, because the entire 5% critical region falls in a single tail of the distribution. Let's look at an example of the difference in critical values between one- and two-tailed $t$ tests.

In our time-estimation experiment, we actually have a directional hypothesis. Our directional hypothesis predicts that the average time estimate of the no-fun group will be greater than the average time estimate of the fun group. That means that we may use a one-tailed test. We chose a $p < .05$ significance level. The degrees of freedom ($df$) for this experiment equal the total number of subjects in both groups minus the number of groups. Here, $df = 5 + 5 - 2$, or 8. Now turn to Table B.3 in Appendix B, which shows the critical values of $t$ for both one- and two-tailed tests and numerous degrees of freedom. Find the critical value of $t$ for 8 $df$, a one-tailed test, and $p < .05$.

The critical value of $t$ is 1.86 for this experiment. If the computed value of $t$ is greater than 1.86, we can reject the null hypothesis. If the computed value of $t$ is more extreme than the critical value in the table, it is unlikely that the differences between treatment groups can be explained simply by chance. In a well-controlled experiment, the most likely explanation is that differences were produced by the independent variable. If we had not made a directional prediction, the critical value of $t$ (two-tailed, $p < .05$) would have been 2.306. Clearly, to achieve a statistically significant effect, the obtained value of $t$ needs to be larger when our hypothesis is nondirectional.

Summary data for the hypothetical time-estimation experiment are shown in Table 14.4. The table tells us at a glance that the performance of the groups is different: The mean time estimate of subjects in the "no-fun" group is 14.2 minutes; that of subjects in the "fun" group is 9.6 minutes. Of course, we know that this difference might not be significant. We have to evaluate the difference by the amount of variability we find between any samples drawn from the population, and we have to decide whether to reject the null hypothesis or not. To do that, we must compute the value of $t(t_{obs})$ for these data using the following formula (the actual computations of the $t$ test for independent groups are shown in Appendix A-4):

$$t_{obs} = \frac{\overline{X}_1 - \overline{X}_2}{\sqrt{\left(\frac{(N_1 - 1)s_1^2 + (N_2 - 1)s_2^2}{(N_1 + N_2 - 2)}\right) \cdot \left(\frac{1}{N_1} + \frac{1}{N_2}\right)}}$$

TABLE **14.4**

Summary data for a hypothetical experiment on fun and time estimation.

| No-Fun Group (Group 1) | Fun Group (Group 2) |
|---|---|
| $\overline{X}_1 = 14.2$ min | $\overline{X}_2 = 9.6$ min |
| $s_1^2 = 8.6$ min | $s_2^2 = 8.8$ min |
| $N_1 = 5$ | $N_2 = 5$ |

Note: We predicted that the "no-fun" group would make larger time estimates, so we labeled that group "group 1." Given our prediction, $\overline{X}_1 - \overline{X}_2$ should be a positive number and our computed value of $t$ should be positive. It does not really matter which way the groups are labeled as long as we set up the critical value of $t$ (in a positive or negative direction) consistent with our predictions and our computations of $t$. We are using hypothetical data here to keep things simple. If you were actually running this experiment, you would want to have more than five subjects in each treatment group.
© Cengage Learning

When we first talked about parametric test statistics in a general way, we said that they represent a relationship between treatment effects and variability. If you think about what is shown in the formula for $t$, you will see clearly how that principle is applied. The numerator (top) tells us to find the difference between the means of the two treatment groups. If the independent variable had a large effect, we would expect this difference to be relatively large.[3] Notice that the denominator (bottom) of the formula is a collection of terms that represents the variances of the treatment groups and the number of subjects in each group. The denominator is an estimate of variability. If the ratio between the two components is relatively large, we may be able to reject the null hypothesis. Here we will reject it if the computed value of $t$ is more extreme than 1.86. If the value of $t_{obs}$ is larger than that, the odds are very good that the difference between the groups did not occur by chance.

The computed value of $t$ turns out to be 2.47. A value of 2.47 is more extreme than the critical value, so we can reject the null hypothesis: There is a significant difference between the time estimates of subjects who had fun and subjects who did not. How much importance we attach to these findings depends partly on our assessment of the quality of this experiment. Were control procedures adequate? Were variables defined appropriately? The possibility of a Type 1 error must be considered. Before we can draw any sweeping conclusions from the findings, we should replicate the experiment. However, as long as the experiment was conducted properly using appropriate control procedures, we can now say the following:

1. The research hypothesis was supported.
2. There was a significant difference between the group that was "having fun" and the group that was "not having fun."

---

[3] Computed and critical values of $t$ will be negative numbers in cases where the mean of group 2 is larger than the mean of group 1.

3.  As predicted by the research hypothesis, subjects who were "having fun" gave significantly shorter time estimates than did subjects who were "not having fun."

Next, we should calculate and report the effect size. A simple method for estimating effect size for the differences between means of two groups is to transform $t$ values and $df$s to a correlation coefficient, $r$. Once $t$ has been calculated, it is easy to compute $r$:

$$r = \sqrt{\frac{t^2}{t^2 + df}}$$

$$r = \sqrt{\frac{(2.47)^2}{(2.47)^2 + 8}}$$

$$r = .66$$

According to Cohen (1988), $r \geq .50$ is considered a large effect. If we convert $r = .66$ to $r^2$ (as we learned in Chapter 5), we will see that the independent variable in our experiment accounted for approximately 44% of the variance in time-estimation scores. When we think about all the influences that can produce variability in scores, 44% is a substantial proportion, and it would be considered a large effect size in most experiments.

Finally, as previewed in the last chapter, the APA publication manual recommends that we report confidence intervals for the data we obtain in an experiment. When we use inferential statistics, we are estimating the mean of the subject population (the true mean) based on our sample data. Confidence intervals represent a range of values above and below our sample mean that is likely to contain the population mean with the probability level (usually at 95% or 99%) that the mean of the population (the true mean) would actually fall somewhere in that range.

Suppose we have a sample with a mean of 20 and we calculate a 95% confidence interval equal to ±3.20. The range for our 95% confidence interval would be 20 ±3.20; doing the addition and subtraction yields a confidence interval (CI) ranging from 16.80 to 23.20. This means that we can be 95% confident that the true mean falls somewhere within this range. We can calculate confidence intervals for a single sample using this formula:

$$CI = \overline{X} \pm t_{\text{critical}}\left(\frac{s}{\sqrt{N}}\right)$$

Let's calculate a 95% confidence interval for the "no-fun" group in our time-estimation experiment. Using the mean ($\overline{X} = 14.2$) and standard deviation ($s = 2.9$) from Table 14.4, we can follow these two steps:

*Step 1:* Find $t_{\text{critical}}$ for this sample.

For a 95% confidence interval, we want $t_{critical}$ for $p < .05$ $(1 - .95)$.[4] To obtain $t_{critical}$, we also need to calculate the *df* for our sample $(df = N - 1)$; here, $df = 4$. Using Table B.3 in Appendix B, we find that $t_{critical} = 2.776$. Substituting our "no-fun" values into the formula:

$$CI = 14.2 \pm 2.776 \left(\frac{2.9}{\sqrt{5}}\right)$$

$$CI = 14.2 \pm 2.776 \left(\frac{2.9}{2.4}\right)$$

$$CI = 14.2 \pm 3.35$$

*Step 2:* Find the upper and lower values of the CI.

For the lower value of the CI, subtract 3.35 from 14.2; for the upper value, add 3.35 to 14.2.

$$CI = 10.85-17.55$$

The CI we have calculated tells us that there is a 95% probability that the true population mean for "no fun" would fall somewhere between 10.85 and 17.55. For the "fun group," there is a 95% probability that the true mean would fall between 5.91 and 13.29. When reporting confidence intervals in research reports, adding them to either a bar graph or a line graph can be an effective strategy (see Figure 14.6).

You may be familiar already with a similar technique used by national polling agencies, such as Gallup and Harris. When they report mean scores for responses to poll questions, they often give a "margin of error" along with the

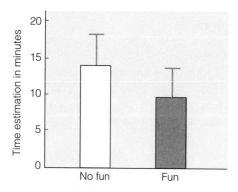
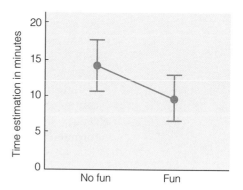

FIGURE **14.6** (a) Bar graph with 95% confidence intervals. (b) Line graph with 95% confidence intervals.
© Cengage Learning

[4] Note: For a 99% CI, we would look up $t_{critical}$ for $<.01$ $(1 -.99)$.

scores. They might say that 67% of the public responded "yes" to a question about taxes, with a margin of error of ±3% at 95% confidence. That's the polling agency's way of reporting a CI for responses from their sample. The agency is really saying that there is a 95% chance that the actual percent of "yes" responses in the population would fall somewhere between 64% and 70%.

### The *t* Test for Matched Groups

In the time-estimation experiment, the two samples of subjects are independent groups. We need different statistical procedures when we look at the data for two matched groups of subjects or a two-group within-subjects experiment. If we did statistical tests for these experiments in the same way as for an independent-groups experiment, we would overestimate the amount of variability in the population sampled.

You know that subjects are apt to differ on a dependent variable simply because subjects are not all the same. Even if we are testing cockroaches, we find that some run faster than others do. One source of variability is individual differences. Subjects' scores vary because subjects differ from one another. Even the scores of the same subjects measured at different times vary, but they usually do not vary quite as much as the responses of different subjects; neither do the scores of subjects who are matched on a relevant variable. For these reasons, the way that we compute variability changes when we use matched-groups or a within-subjects design. You will get a better sense of how these procedures compare by looking at an example of a within-subjects experiment done with two treatment conditions. The research problem is summarized in Box 14.2.

This experiment is similar to the time-estimation example in that we are looking at one independent variable with two treatment conditions ("hot flame" and "cold flame"). Secrecy was measured using an interval scale (0 −5). The secrecy experiment, however, was run with only one group of subjects, making it a within-subjects experiment. The appropriate statistical test is therefore a *t* test for matched groups (also called a *within-subjects t test*). Obviously, the treatment groups in this experiment were not matched in the usual sense of the term; they were the same subjects, and there might be no better match than that!

The *t* test for matched groups uses the same family of *t* distributions you have already seen. It also applies to interval and ratio data and requires the assumption that the population sampled is normally distributed on the dependent variable. But, because this test is used to evaluate data from an experiment in which the treatment groups are not independent, the computations are handled differently. Appendix A-5 shows data and computations based on the secrecy experiment. The data are hypothetical and are presented just to illustrate the procedures simply; Wegner and his colleagues actually used many more subjects. The scores for each subject represent the level of secrecy reported by subjects in each treatment condition (higher scores indicate greater secrecy). The table also illustrates the computation of *t* for matched groups: We use exactly the same procedures for within-subjects and matched-groups experiments with two treatment conditions.

## BOX 14.2  A Two-Group Within-Subjects Example: Secrecy and Allure

Dan Wegner and his colleagues have studied the effects of "thought suppression" for a number of years. They have found that when people try to suppress a thought (i.e., keep it out of consciousness), the thought can take on obsessive qualities: It can be much more likely to pop into our head than thoughts that have not been suppressed. Wegner's classic "White Bear" study (Wegner, 1989) is a good example. When subjects were told that they were *not* to think about a white bear—no matter what—thoughts of a white bear were much more likely to come to consciousness than if subjects were not told to suppress the thought of a white bear. In a subsequent study, Wegner found that trying to keep a thought secret from someone else has the same qualities as trying to suppress it; trying to keep it secret actually makes the thought more likely to automatically pop into our heads!

These findings led to a within-subjects experiment (Wegner, Lane, & Dimitri, 1994) that tested the allure of secret relationships. The researchers predicted that the most alluring old flames would be those that were most secret. The researchers asked people to recall as many as five old flames, and to rank them from the one they still thought about the most to the one they thought about the least. Among other questions, the researchers asked people to rate how secret each relationship had been at the time. The researchers then compared the level of secrecy for each participant's most-thought-about past partner ("hot flame") and their least-thought-about past partner ("cold flame"). The researchers found that relationships with hot flames had been significantly more secret ($p < .02$) than relationships with cold flames!

Yuri Arcurs 2010/Used under license from Shutterstock.Com

From Appendix A-5, you can see that we compute $t$ for these data by looking at differences between each subject's secrecy ratings in the two treatment conditions. This procedure reflects the logic behind the design we are using; we are evaluating the effect of the independent variable within each subject. Similarly, when we have matched pairs of subjects, we want to look at the effects of our independent variable within each matched pair. The computed value of $t$ for the secrecy data is $t_{obs} = 4.81$. How does that compare with the critical value of $t$? Can we reject the null hypothesis? To figure out what the critical value of $t$ would be, we need to look at Table B.3 in Appendix B. Assume that the researchers had decided to use a $p < .05$ significance level. Should we use a one- or a two-tailed test? Although Wegner, Lane, and Dimitri might have made a directional prediction based on prior evidence, they were simply testing the prediction that secrecy would affect how often people thought about their old flames, so a two-tailed test is appropriate.

We computed $t$ for this experiment with different procedures, so we also have to compute $df$ differently. Because we are looking at differences between pairs of scores, our $df$ is based on the number of pairs. The $df$ for two matched groups is $N - 1$, where $N$ is the number of pairs. For this experiment the $df$ is $5 - 1$, or 4. If you look at Table B.3, you will see that the critical value of $t$ for 4 $df$ and a two-tailed test ($p < .05$) is 2.776. The computed value of $t$ (4.81) is more extreme than the critical value, so we can reject the null hypothesis, which says that these data were sampled from the same population. Assuming the experiment was conducted properly, what three things can we now say about the results?

Notice that using the within-subjects procedures affects the critical value of $t$. In the time-estimation example, we had five subjects in each treatment group for a total of 10 scores—just as we have here—but when we use the within-subjects or matched-groups $t$, we end up with many fewer degrees of freedom. Even though we have the same number of actual scores in both examples, we have about half as many degrees of freedom when we use the $t$ test for matched groups. Table B.3 shows that the critical value of $t$ needed to reject the null hypothesis increases as the degrees of freedom get smaller. Generally speaking, the fewer degrees of freedom we have, the more difficult it will be to reject the null hypothesis. It takes a more extreme $t_{obs}$ to reach significance in a matched-groups or within-subjects experiment. Compare the two-tailed critical values of $t$ ($p < .05$) for 4 $df$ and 8 $df$, and you will see that you need a larger $t$ when you have fewer degrees of freedom.

If we need a larger value of $t$ in a within-subjects or matched-groups experiment, why would we bother to match subjects or use a within-subjects design at all? It seems as though an easier task would be to find a significant difference with the independent-groups design. Actually, it would not. We have not yet discussed all the reasons for variability in data, but one thing should be clear: If we measure the responses of different subjects, we are likely to get much more variability than if we measure the same subjects or matched subjects. Using a within-subjects or matched-groups design lowers the amount of variability in the data. Compare the two formulas for $t$ shown in Appendix A-4 and Appendix A-5. The denominator of each formula reflects variability. When we reduce variability among individual subjects, we make the denominator of the $t$ formula smaller. That in turn makes the computed value of $t$ a great deal larger. To put it more simply, when we use a matched-groups or a within-subjects design, we have a trade-off: We lower the degrees of freedom for the experiment, but we also lower the amount of variability produced by factors other than the independent variable. This trade-off almost always works to make the $t$ test for matched groups a more powerful test than the $t$ test for independent groups and decreases the chance of a Type 2 error.[5]

---

[5] Don't forget another benefit of the within-subjects design—you have only used half as many subjects as you did in the matched-groups or independent-groups design.

## ANALYZING MULTIPLE GROUPS AND FACTORIAL EXPERIMENTS

So far, we have covered some of the techniques for data from experiments with two groups. Very often, however, we need to test more than two levels of an independent variable. We might need three or more groups to give an adequate idea of the way that a particular variable operates. We might even want to study more than one independent variable in factorial experiments. For those experiments, we need other kinds of statistical procedures. These procedures fall under the general heading of analysis of variance.

## ANALYSIS OF VARIANCE

The analysis of variance (ANOVA) is a statistical procedure used to evaluate differences among three or more treatment means.[6] The name reflects the basic nature of the test, which divides all the variance in the data into component parts and then compares and evaluates them for statistical significance. Each part represents variability produced by different influences in the experiment.

When we computed *t*, we calculated differences between treatment groups—differences between treatment means for the independent-groups design and differences between pairs of scores in the matched-groups design. We looked at those differences in relation to our estimates of the amount of variability in the populations sampled. An analysis of variance enables us to test the null hypothesis in a slightly different way. It breaks up the variability in the data into component parts. In the simplest analysis of variance, all the variability in the data can be divided into two parts: within-groups variability and between-groups variability. Within-groups variability is the degree to which the scores of subjects in the *same* treatment group differ from one another (that is, how much subjects vary from others in the group). Between-groups variability is the degree to which the scores of *different* treatment groups differ from one another (that is, how much subjects vary across each different level of the independent variable). The proportions of the within-groups and between-groups variability differ from one experiment to another. Sometimes between-groups variability is larger than within-groups variability; sometimes the two parts are about the same. Their relative proportions vary depending on the impact of the independent variable. When we carry out an analysis of variance, we are actually evaluating the likelihood that the proportions we observe could occur by chance. To understand how this process works, we need to look more closely at the sources of variability that produce these components.

---

[6] In a two-group experiment, a researcher could actually use either a *t* test or an analysis of variance; both are found in the research literature. When statistics must be calculated by hand, the *t* test has been preferred because it is easier to calculate. For a two-group experiment, however, *t* values and ANOVA values (called *F*s) are directly related. In fact, $F = t^2$ when only two groups are being tested.

# SOURCES OF VARIABILITY

Ideally, when we run an experiment we would like to be able to show that the pattern of data obtained was caused by the experimental manipulation. However, you already know that if we observe changes in the dependent variable across treatment conditions, those changes might not be entirely caused by the effects of the independent variable. What else accounts for changes in the dependent variable? What else might produce variability in the scores of subjects across treatment conditions?

One common source of variability is individual differences. Within each treatment group, subjects' scores will differ from one another because subjects are different from one another. We use random assignment or matching in each experiment so that these differences do not confound the results of the experiment. We do not want differences between groups to be produced solely by extraneous subject variables. No two groups will be identical in every way, so individual differences can lead to variability between groups as well as within the same group.

There are other sources of variability in data. Some differences between scores will be the result of procedures we did not handle well in the experiment. For instance, we might have made small mistakes in measuring lines that subjects drew or in timing their answers. Extraneous variables of all kinds can produce more variability, causing changes in subjects' behavior that we might not detect; for example, one subject is tested when the room is cool and so does a little better than the others. As with individual differences, these factors can lead to variability within the same group of subjects as well as between different treatment groups. We can lump all these factors together in a single category called error: Individual differences, undetected mistakes in recording data, variations in testing conditions, and a host of extraneous variables are all aspects of error that produce variability in subjects' data both within and between treatment groups.

Another major source of variability in data is the experimental manipulation. We test subjects under different treatment conditions. We predict that these conditions will alter subjects' behavior; we expect subjects under different treatment conditions to behave differently from one another. In other words, we expect our treatment conditions to create variability in the responses of subjects who are tested under different levels of an independent variable.

The experimental manipulation, however, does not operate in the same manner as other sources of variability in the experiment. Error can lead to variability between different treatment groups; it can also produce variability within the same group. Unlike those sources of variability, treatment conditions produce variability only between the responses of different treatment groups. Subjects within the same treatment group are all treated in the same manner. Their scores may differ because of individual differences or error but not because they were exposed to different levels of the independent variable: Subjects in the same treatment group all receive the same level of the independent variable.

When we do an analysis of variance, we break the variability in our data into parts that reflect the sources of variability in the experiment: within-groups variability and between-groups variability. Within-groups variability

TABLE **14.5**

Sources of variability in an experiment with one independent variable

| Variability Within Groups | Variability Between Groups |
| --- | --- |
| A. Error: | A. Error: |
| Individual differences | Individual differences |
| Extraneous variables | Extraneous variables |
| | B. Treatment effects |

© Cengage Learning

is the extent to which subjects' scores differ from one another under the same treatment conditions. The factors that we call error explain the variability that we see within groups. Between-groups variability is the extent to which group performance differs from one treatment condition to another. Between-groups variability is made up of error and the effects of the independent variable. These components are summarized in Table 14.5.

We can evaluate the effect of the independent variable by comparing the relative size of these components of variability. The logic behind this is straightforward. The variability within groups comes from error and nothing else; the variability between groups comes from both error and treatment effects. If the independent variable had an effect, the between-groups variability should be larger than the within-groups variability. We compare the relative sizes of these components by computing a ratio between them called the $F$ ratio. Conceptually, it looks like this:

$$F = \frac{Variability\ from\ treatment\ effects + error}{Variability\ from\ error}$$

or

$$F = \frac{Variability\ between\ groups}{Variability\ within\ groups}$$

Theoretically, if the independent variable had no effect, the $F$ ratio should equal 1. There should be just as much variability within groups as there is between them: The same sources of variability would be operating both within and between treatments. The larger the effect of the independent variable is, however, the larger the $F$ ratio should be. The independent variable will lead to greater differences between the scores of subjects who receive different levels of the independent variable. Figure 14.7 represents both possibilities graphically.

We use the distribution of $F$ to evaluate the significance of the $F$ ratio that we compute. $F$, like $t$, is actually a whole family of distributions. The shape of the distribution changes as the size of the sample changes. Again, we use the degrees of freedom to select the correct distribution and critical value for each experiment. If the $F$ ratio is statistically significant, the amount of between-groups variability is large compared with the amount of

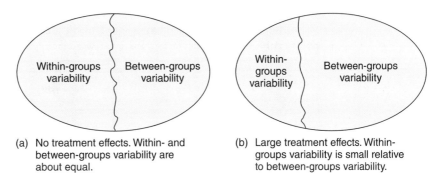

(a) No treatment effects. Within- and between-groups variability are about equal.

(b) Large treatment effects. Within-groups variability is small relative to between-groups variability.

FIGURE **14.7** The components of variability in an experiment with two possible outcomes.
© Cengage Learning

within-groups variability—so large that it is unlikely that all the group means belong to the same population. If *F* is significant, we reject the null hypothesis that all the treatment means were drawn from the same population: We confirm the existence of differences across the groups that were probably produced by the independent variable.

## A ONE-WAY BETWEEN-SUBJECTS ANALYSIS OF VARIANCE

Now that you have a general idea of how ANOVA works, let us turn to an example of a multiple-group experiment. Strahilevitz and Lowenstein (1998) conducted an interesting three-group experiment to look at the effect of "ownership history" on the value we place on objects. They hypothesized that mere ownership of an object increases our perceptions of its value, and the longer we own it, the more we value it. To test their hypothesis, they created an experimental situation in which subjects were required to place a cash value on several items (e.g., a mug, a key chain, a T-shirt, and a box of candy). The experiment was set up to last about 50 minutes. To create a 50-minute experiment, all subjects filled out questionnaires (which were not really part of the experiment) before they were asked to evaluate the set of items. Strahilevitz and Lowenstein's experiment had three conditions: no ownership; brief ownership; and long ownership. In one condition of the experiment, subjects were not given any of the items (no ownership). In a second condition, subjects were given the mug as a gift for participating, but it wasn't given to them until just before they were asked to place a value on all of the items (brief ownership). In the third condition, subjects were given the mug at the beginning of the experiment as a gift for participating (long ownership). The researchers found that their hypothesis was supported: Subjects placed a significantly higher value on the mug if they owned it than if they didn't, and the highest value was placed on the mug when subjects had owned it for a longer time.

We will use their experiment to look at some hypothetical data obtained from three independent groups of subjects who owned an object for 0, 1, or 50 minutes (no ownership, brief ownership, or long ownership). It has one

TABLE **14.6**

Hypothetical data from an experiment on object valuation under different ownership conditions

| | Group 1 (No Ownership) | Group 2 (Brief Ownership) | Group 3 (Long Ownership) |
|---|---|---|---|
| $S_1$ | 2 | 1 | 3 |
| $S_2$ | 2 | 3 | 4 |
| $S_3$ | 1 | 3 | 2 |
| $S_4$ | 0 | 3 | 3 |
| $S_5$ | 1 | 3 | 4 |
| | $\overline{X}_1 = 1.2$ | $\overline{X}_2 = 2.6$ | $\overline{X}_3 = 3.2$ |
| | $s_1^2 = .7$ | $s_2^2 = .8$ | $s_3^2 = .7$ |

Note: Scores represent the dollar values placed on mug.
© Cengage Learning

independent variable—length of time of ownership: 0, 1, or 50 minutes. The dependent variable is the dollar value subjects placed on the mug. Subjects could use any whole-dollar amount from 0 to 5 (a ratio scale measure). This experiment uses a between-subjects design, ratio scale data, and has only one independent variable, so the statistical test we do is called a one-way between-subjects analysis of variance.

As in any experiment, we will test the null hypothesis that the means of the three groups were sampled from the same population. Table 14.6 shows some hypothetical data. As you can see, there are three groups. Their scores represent the dollar value they placed on the mug. We have already begun our analysis of the data by organizing and summarizing it in table form.

Certain assumptions about our data should be met if we are to use analysis of variance procedures appropriately. First, the procedures we will describe here require that treatment groups be independent from each other and that the samples have been selected at random. Our procedures also require that the populations from which the groups are sampled are normally distributed on the dependent variable and that the variances of those populations are roughly equal, or *homogeneous*. However, like the *t* test, ANOVA is a robust test. If we have fairly large groups of subjects, the assumptions can be violated without an increase in Type 1 or 2 errors. To simplify the illustrations, we are presenting data from very few subjects. In practice, of course, it would be better to have larger treatment groups, as Strahilevitz and Lowenstein actually did, because of the assumptions of the ANOVA procedures.

## Within- and Between-Groups Variability

To compute an *F* ratio for these data, we need two pieces of information: the within-groups variance and the between-groups variance. Recall that variance represents the average squared deviation from the mean, and ANOVA uses the term mean square (MS) to denote variability or variance. The mean square is an average squared deviation. To compute $F$, you must calculate both the mean square within groups ($MS_w$) and the mean square between groups ($MS_b$). The $MS_w$ represents the portion of the variability in the data that is produced by the combination of sources that we call error. Computation of $MS_w$ for our three-group example is shown in Appendix A-6. The value of the mean square within groups will constitute the denominator, or bottom, of the $F$ ratio. $MS_b$ represents the amount of variability produced by both error and treatment effects in the experiment. Computations for $MS_b$ are shown in Appendix A-7. The mean square between groups will form the numerator, or top, of the $F$ ratio.

You already know that the $F$ ratio represents this relationship:

$$F = \frac{Variability\ from\ treatment\ effects + error}{Variability\ from\ error}$$

The statistical form of this ratio is

$$F = \frac{MS_b}{MS_w}$$

If we substitute our computed values into this formula, we find that for our three-group example,

$$F = \frac{5.28}{.73}\ or\ 7.23$$

To test our $F$ ratio for significance, we need to find the critical value using Table 14.4 in Appendix B. As you know, $F$ is a whole family of distributions. We use our degrees of freedom to locate the appropriate distribution. When we compute the mean squares needed for the $F$ ratio, we calculate separate degrees of freedom for $MS_b$ and $MS_w$. Degrees of freedom for $MS_b$ (the numerator) are used to locate the column for the critical value by moving along the top of the table. Then, we locate the correct row by using the degrees of freedom for $MS_w$ (the denominator) to move down the side of the table. The place in the table where those two lines meet contains the critical value.

For our example, the $df$s are 2 and 12, and the critical value at the .05 level is 3.88; 6.93, shown in boldface, is the critical value of $F$ at the .01 level. Remember, these values apply only to an $F$ test with 2 and 12 degrees of freedom. We have to look up the critical value for each experiment. Figure 14.8 illustrates the distribution of $F$ with 2 and 12 degrees of freedom. It also shows the distribution of $F$ with 2 and 6 degrees of freedom. As you can see, the critical values change dramatically as the degrees of freedom change.

We chose a significance level of $p < .05$ for our three-group experiment. To be statistically significant, we need a computed value of $F$ that is greater than the table value for our level of significance. Our computed value of $F$ was 7.23. The table value of $F$ is 3.88 at the .05 level; therefore, our computed $F$ is significant. We reject the null hypothesis that the treatment means came from the same population. Our computed $F$ is large enough, in fact, that it is also

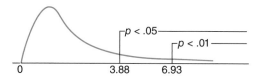

(a) The distribution of *F* with 2 (numerator) and 12 (denominator) degrees of freedom

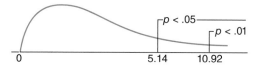

(b) The distribution of *F* with 2 (numerator) and 6 (denominator) degrees of freedom

FIGURE **14.8** The *F* distribution with varying degrees of freedom.
© Cengage Learning

significant at the .01 level: It is greater than 6.93, the critical value of *F* at the .01 level. Computational steps are summarized in Table 14.7.

### Interpreting the Results

We are not finished with this statistical analysis of the data in the group ownership experiment. It is very important to remember that when we compute *F*, *we test only the overall pattern of treatment means.* Our significant *F* in this example tells us that across all the group means (no ownership = 1.2, brief ownership = 2.6, and long ownership = 3.2), there is a significant difference. If we had only two treatment groups, we would know immediately that one group mean was significantly higher than another, and we could interpret the results easily. But when three or more groups are being compared, as they are in our experiment, the ANOVA does not identify specific differences between each pair of means, and we do not know exactly where the difference is.

It seems likely that the no ownership and long ownership groups are significantly different from each other. After all, they differ the most. However, the difference between, say, the no ownership and the brief ownership groups might or might not be significant. After a significant *F* has been obtained,

TABLE **14.7**

Analysis-of-variance summary table

| Source | *df* | SS | MS | F |
|--------|------|------|------|-----|
| Between groups | 2 | 10.55 | 5.28 | $\frac{MS_b}{MS_w} = 7.23^*$ |
| Within groups | 12 | 8.80 | .73 | |
| Total | 14 | 19.35 | | |

$^*p < .01$
© Cengage Learning

further statistics are needed to determine which groups are really different from each other. (If an *F* is nonsignificant, we would not need to go any further.) When we need to pinpoint the exact source of the differences across several treatment groups, we need to conduct follow-up tests. The two basic types of follow-up tests are post hoc tests and a priori comparisons.

There are many different post hoc tests—tests done after the overall analysis indicates a significant difference. We will not go into the details of these tests here, but some of the names you will see are the Tukey and the Scheffé tests. These tests have essentially the same function: They can be used to make pair-by-pair comparisons of the different groups to pinpoint the source of a significant difference across several treatments. For instance, by comparing each treatment group with every other group in our object valuation experiment, post hoc tests can tell us whether the mugs were valued significantly more in the long ownership condition than in the brief ownership condition (or whether they were only valued significantly more in the long ownership condition than in the no ownership condition). Post hoc tests can also tell us whether or not the mugs were valued significantly more in the brief ownership condition than in the no ownership condition.

Couldn't we just use a series of *t* tests to make these pairwise comparisons? No, because, as we mentioned at the beginning of this chapter, we would be increasing our odds of making a Type 1 error. With three treatment groups, our chances of making a Type 1 error could be as high as 3 times our significance level ($3 \times .05 = .15$). Post hoc tests, however, are more conservative statistical tests. They are conservative because they are specifically designed to guard against increasing the chances of Type 1 error.

These kinds of post hoc tests can, however, result in less power to detect treatment effects, and they can increase the chances of making a Type 2 error. One way around this dilemma is to use another statistical procedure—a priori comparisons—for pinpointing significant effects.

A priori comparisons are tests between specific treatment groups that were anticipated, or planned, before the experiment was conducted. For this reason, they are also called *planned comparisons* (or *planned contrasts*). Strahilevitz and Lowenstein (1998) used planned comparisons to test specific predictions from their hypothesis. They predicted that (1) mugs would be valued higher after brief ownership than after no ownership and (2) mugs would be valued higher after long ownership than after brief ownership. If we had planned these comparisons in advance, we would conduct two a priori comparisons after the overall ANOVA was significant. Unlike post hoc tests, a priori comparisons are considered part of the original analysis of variance. Typically, we do not worry about increasing the odds of a Type 1 error as long as the number of planned comparisons is *less than* the number of treatment groups in the experiment.[7] The manner of computing a priori comparisons is less conservative than post hoc tests, making them more powerful.

---

[7] Planned comparisons can also be used to test predictions that one group will be different from all the others in the experiment, but the statistical procedures are more complex. For instance, we might have planned to contrast the no ownership condition with the two ownership conditions.

Wouldn't we always use planned comparisons rather than post hoc tests, then? Not necessarily. Sometimes we have too many predictions, making the chances of a Type 1 error unacceptable. Other times (particularly when things do not turn out exactly the way we expected) we want to explore group differences that we did not predict in advance. Just as we cannot change our hypotheses or our significance levels to suit the way the data come out, it is always inappropriate to use planned comparisons to pinpoint unplanned effects.

Suppose we had made the two a priori comparisons discussed earlier for our experiment. How would we interpret the results of the significant ANOVA along with the two planned comparisons that supported our predictions? If the ANOVA and both a priori comparisons were significant, we could now report the following:

1. The research hypothesis was supported.
2. As predicted, there was a significant difference in object valuation between groups that differed by length of time of ownership.
3. Objects were valued higher after brief ownership than if they had never been owned, and long ownership produced higher object value than brief ownership did. (Notice how specific and detailed we are when we describe the effects of statistical analyses.)

Another statistical test, however, still remains to be done. We need to calculate the effect size for the ownership treatment. One frequently used estimate of effect size, $\eta^2$ (eta$^2$), can be computed easily from information obtained from the ANOVA:

$$\frac{df_1 F}{df_1 F + df_2}$$

Let us calculate an effect size for the object valuation experiment. The obtained value of $F$ was 7.23; the numerator ($df_1$) and denominator ($df_2$) degrees of freedom were 2 and 12.

$$\frac{2(7.23)}{2(7.23) + 12} = .55$$

The estimated effect size is .55. In the case of an analysis of variance, $\eta^2$ represents the proportion of variance in all the scores that can be accounted for, or explained, by the treatment—in this case, 55% of all of the variability in subjects' scores in the experiment can be accounted for by the treatment. Considering the great number of potential influences on subjects' scores in any psychology experiment, this would be considered a substantial effect. According to Cohen (1988), an $\eta^2 \geq .1379$ may be called a large treatment effect. Most computer statistics programs, such as SPSS, allow you to select effect size and follow-up tests as part of the computations of an ANOVA.

### Graphing the Results

Sometimes, a useful way of summarizing the results of a factorial experiment is to construct a line or bar graph. Look closely at Figure 14.9, which presents the results of our experiment as a line graph. The figure illustrates

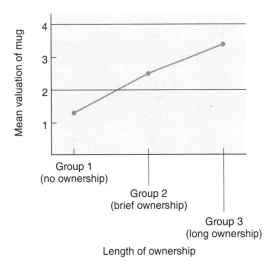

several general points you should keep in mind when constructing graphs. Notice that the figure is well proportioned; the vertical axis is roughly three-fourths the size of the horizontal axis. Notice also that the independent variable is plotted on the horizontal axis; the dependent variable is plotted on the vertical axis. Finally, note that the data points represent group means. We do not graph the data of individual subjects unless we have a small N design. Of course, the axes are labeled clearly so that readers will know exactly what the figure represents. We will have more to say about graphing results in Chapter 16.

## Statistical Control for Differences Between Groups

You are already familiar with the concept of control. You have learned many procedures for controlling extraneous variables that might affect the dependent variable. You have also learned about controlling for potentially important subject variables by matching subjects on characteristics that are expected to influence their responses to experimental manipulations. You also know that subject variables can be used as factors in an experiment.

At some times, however, researchers want to exert control over extraneous variables, particularly demographic variables, that cannot be controlled experimentally. Suppose, for example, a researcher is worried that object valuation in the ownership experiment might be influenced by the amount of money subjects have; subjects with a lot of money might spend more for a mug than subjects with a smaller income might. The researcher considered matching subjects on income but decided against it because she knows that it could work against her if income is not an important *moderating variable* (one that can moderate, or change, the influence of the independent variable). Instead, she used random assignment to conditions.

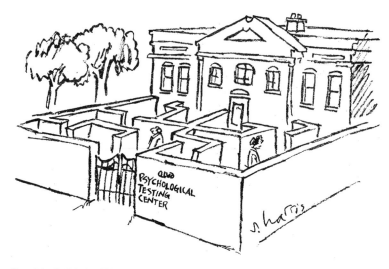

Copyright © 2001 by Sidney Harris/ScienceCartoonsPlus.com

There is a way the researcher can still exert some control over this "uncontrolled" variable. A more complex form of ANOVA, called *analysis of covariance* (ANCOVA), can be used to control statistically for potential moderating variables. ANCOVA works by removing the variance produced by scores on the moderating variable, called the covariate, from the variance in the ANOVA that was produced by error. According to Keppel, ANCOVA can be used to accomplish the following two objectives: "(1) to refine estimates of experimental error and (2) to adjust treatment effects for any differences between the treatment groups that existed before the start of the experiment" (1982, p. 483). ANCOVA is analogous to holding the moderating variable constant or statistically equating subjects before the experiment and can increase the sensitivity of the experiment to detect the independent variable's effects. ANCOVA is very difficult to compute by hand, but including a covariate is a simple option in most computer statistics programs. Part of the analysis also calculates whether the covariate was an important influence or not, adding precision to interpretation of statistical results.

## ONE-WAY REPEATED MEASURES ANALYSIS OF VARIANCE

The basic principles of the analysis of variance apply in many multiple-group experiments. For example, we can use an ANOVA to analyze the effects in a multiple-group experiment testing one independent variable that uses a within-subjects design. This is called a **one-way repeated measures ANOVA**.

Suppose we conducted a simple experiment in which subjects were presented with three different lists of words and were asked to recall as many as they could from each list. One list contained only positively valenced words (e.g., smile, treasure, love). A second contained negatively valenced words (e.g., frown, burglar, hate). The third contained neutral words (e.g., house, car, hat). We predicted that valence would influence the number of words that subjects recalled from each list. If we had completely counterbalanced the order in which subjects received each list, we would not need to use order as a factor in the design, and we would have a three-group within-subjects experiment. In this case, we would analyze the results with a one-way within-subjects (or repeated measures) ANOVA. Conceptually, the within-subjects ANOVA is the same as the ANOVA for independent groups; however, the denominator is calculated somewhat differently. The principles of analysis of variance can also be extended to handle more complex research designs: between-subjects factorials, within-subjects factorials, and mixed factorial designs. We will carry these principles further in our next example, an experiment with a between-subjects factorial design.

# ANALYZING DATA FROM A BETWEEN-SUBJECTS FACTORIAL EXPERIMENT

Factorial experiments are designed to look at the effects of more than one independent variable at a time and at the interaction between variables. In Chapter 10 you learned that the impact of one independent variable may differ depending on the values of the other independent variables in the experiment. When we analyze the data from a factorial experiment, we evaluate both kinds of effects. We look at the impact of each independent variable, the *main effects* produced by each factor. We also evaluate any *interaction* between the factors. Let us look at an example of a simple between-subjects factorial experiment and see which statistical procedures are used to accomplish these goals.

Assume we have set up and run an experiment to explore the relationship between word frequency and recall. Half the subjects saw words that appear often in the English language (high-frequency words), and half saw words that are relatively uncommon (low-frequency words). From searching the literature, we predicted that high-frequency words would be recalled better than low-frequency words. We also tested another factor in the same experiment: cueing. Besides evaluating the effect of frequency, we also manipulated the testing procedures so that half the subjects were asked simply to recall the words they saw on the original list; the other half were given cues to aid them in remembering the words they saw. For instance, suppose subjects saw the word *camel* on the original list. If they were in the "no-cue" condition, they were simply asked to recall the word. If they were in the "cue" condition, we provided the name of the category the word belongs to—animal. Category cues were given for all words on the list. Cueing has also been shown to aid word recall. Our 2 × 2 design is diagrammed in Figure 14.10.

We have two independent variables in this experiment—word frequency and category cues. Our dependent variable is the number of words correctly recalled from each list, a ratio measure. We will use $p < .05$ as our

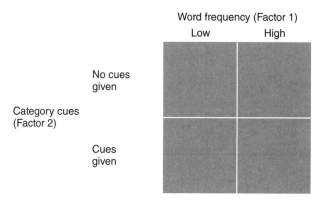

Word frequency (Factor 1)

FIGURE **14.10** Diagram of a 2 × 2 factorial experiment on the effects of word frequency and cueing on recall.
© Cengage Learning

significance level. Referring back to Table 14.2, we find that the statistical test indicated for these data is a two-way between-subjects analysis of variance.

Similar principles apply to all ANOVA procedures, but when we have a factorial design, determining treatment effects is more complex than it is with one independent variable. We want to evaluate the main effect of each factor; we need to know whether word frequency or category cues significantly affect the ability to recall words. Of course, we also want to know whether there was any interaction between the two factors. We want to know whether the effect of word frequency on recall will change depending on whether cues are given—or whether the effect of cues could differ depending on whether the word to be recalled is relatively frequent or infrequent.

To answer all these questions with an analysis of variance, we need to break down the variance in the data into more components than we had before. In the one-way ANOVA, we had one independent variable, and we divided all the variability in the data into just two parts: within-groups and between-groups variability. Within-groups variability is created by all those sources of error in the experiment: individual differences, the experimenter's mistakes, and other extraneous variables. Between-groups variability is created by all those sources of error plus the effect of the independent variable.

The same is true in a factorial experiment. We can separate variability into within-groups and between-groups variance. However, the picture is more complex here. Between-groups variability comes from error and treatment effects, but there are several sources of treatment effects in the factorial experiment. Each independent variable may produce its own unique treatment effects; each can produce a portion of the between-groups variability or a main effect. The interaction of the independent variables can produce another portion. This is represented graphically in Figure 14.11, which compares the components of variability for the one-way analysis of variance against a two-way analysis of variance for a two-factor experiment.

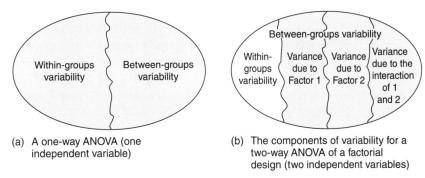

(a) A one-way ANOVA (one independent variable)

(b) The components of variability for a two-way ANOVA of a factorial design (two independent variables)

FIGURE **14.11** The components of variability for (a) a one-way ANOVA (one independent variable) and (b) a two-way ANOVA (two independent variables).

© Cengage Learning

## TWO-WAY ANALYSIS OF VARIANCE

The procedures and formulas for a two-way between-subjects ANOVA are based on the same set of assumptions as the one-way ANOVA procedures we examined earlier (independent treatment groups and so forth). For the sake of illustration, the computations in this textbook use only five subjects per treatment group; however, the assumptions behind the ANOVA procedures are more likely to be met with larger groups of subjects. In addition, in the procedures shown here, we assume an equal number of subjects ($n$) in each group. If you have unequal $n$'s, you will need more complicated procedures if you are doing the computations by hand. The same is true if you have used within-subjects procedures. If you are using a computer statistics program, however, you may not notice any difference. In either case, consult your instructor or statistics textbook if you need the precise formulas.

Finally, these procedures are set for fixed models, experiments in which the values of the independent variables are fixed by the experimenter. In other words, the experimenter chooses to run subjects at certain levels of each independent variable. In our example, the experimenter has chosen to use high and low word frequencies and two levels of the category-cue variable—cues versus no cues. In experiments with random models (randomly selected values of the independent variables), different statistical procedures are required, however; most experiments follow the fixed model, as we do here. Table 14.8 presents some hypothetical data and group means from our experiment to test the effect of word frequency and category cues on recall.

With the increased accessibility of computers for calculating statistics, the use of complicated analyses of variance has greatly expanded. Forty years ago, researchers had to do all their statistics by hand (or they used clunky electric calculators), so the experimental designs they selected tended to be much simpler than they are today. Now it would be difficult indeed to find a researcher who does hand computations. However, even the most

TABLE **14.8**

Hypothetical data from a two-factor experiment: The effects of word frequency and category cues on recall in a list-learning task

| | | Word Frequency (Factor 1) | | | |
|---|---|---|---|---|---|
| | | Low | | High | |
| Category Cues (Factor 2) | No cues given | 2<br>3<br>1<br>4<br>5 | $\overline{X}_1 = 3$ | 4<br>5<br>4<br>6<br>6 | $\overline{X}_2 = 5$ |
| | Cues given | 4<br>6<br>5<br>6<br>9 | $\overline{X}_3 = 6$ | 7<br>6<br>9<br>8<br>10 | $\overline{X}_4 = 8$ |

Note: Scores represent number of words correctly recalled from a list.
© Cengage Learning

sophisticated computer software programs still require the user to select the appropriate ANOVA model to apply to the data, to set up follow-up tests, and, of course, to interpret the results. For these reasons, it is still necessary to understand the logic behind ANOVA and other statistical procedures even if you do not analyze your data by hand. Let us look briefly at how the two-way ANOVA for the data from our factorial experiment is computed.

*Step 1:* We begin by computing the within-groups variability ($MS_w$). Remember that the $MS_w$ represents variability produced by individual differences, extraneous variables, and other sources of error in the experiment. We use $MS_w$ to evaluate the impact of the independent variables and their interaction. The actual computations are shown in Appendix A-8.

*Step 2:* Next, we compute the total sum of squares between groups ($SS_b$), which represents all of the variability we have among the treatment groups. The computation of $SS_b$ is shown in Appendix A-9. To complete the ANOVA, it will be necessary to divide the $SS_b$ into its main components: the parts associated with each factor ($SS_1$ and $SS_2$) and the part associated with the interaction ($SS_{1\times2}$).

*Step 3:* When we evaluate the main effect of one independent variable, we treat the data as if that variable is the only one in the experiment. We simply ignore all the other experimental manipulations that were done: We say we *collapse* the data across the other conditions of the experiment. In effect, we pretend that those conditions did not exist. Computation of $SS_1$ for our first factor, word frequency, is shown in Appendix A-10, and computation of $SS_2$ is shown in Appendix A-11.

TABLE **14.9**
Steps 4 and 5: Summary table; analysis of variance for a 2 × 2 factorial experiment and computed *F* values

| Source | df | SS | MS | F |
|---|---|---|---|---|
| Between groups | | $65^a$ | | |
|    Factor 1 (word frequency) | $q - 1 = 1$ | 20 | 20 | $F_1 = \dfrac{20}{2.38}$ or 8.40* |
|    Factor 2 (category cues) | $p - 1 = 1$ | 45 | 45 | $F_2 = \dfrac{45}{2.38}$ or 18.91** |
|    Interaction 1 × 2 | $(p - 1)(q - 1) = 1$ | $0^b$ | 0 | $F_{1 \times 2} = \dfrac{0}{2.38}$ or 0 |
| Within groups | $N - pq = 16$ | 38 | 2.38 | |
| Total | $N - 1 = 19$ | | | |

*$p < .05$

**$p < .01$

$^a$SS$_b$ is usually not shown in published studies.
$^b$The SS$_{1 \times 2}$ represents all the between-groups variability that is not explained by the main effect of either independent variable. Its degrees of freedom depend on the degrees of freedom for the main effects. Here, there is no interaction.

© Cengage Learning

*Step 4:* The variability associated with the interaction of the two independent variables is simply what remains after the main effects of the independent variables have been taken into account. The variability between groups that is not explained by either independent variable can be explained by their interaction (SS$_{1 \times 2}$). The sum of squares for the interaction is found by simple subtraction:

$$SS_{1 \times 2} = SS_b - SS_1 - SS_2$$

*Step 5:* We can summarize the calculations in a summary table (Table 14.9). The table is similar to the one we prepared for the simple ANOVA except for the way it represents the sources of variability. Because we have two independent variables in this experiment, we have three sources of variability: factor 1, factor 2, and their interaction, and we will compute an *F* value for each one. The within-groups variability (MS$_w$) is used as the denominator of all three *F* ratios. The three *F* values have been computed and are shown in the summary table.

## Evaluating the *F* Ratios

When we compute *F* ratios without the aid of computer programs, we judge whether the computed *F* values are significant by comparing them with the table values of *F*. We can find those values in Table B.4 of Appendix B. The procedures are the same as those used for the simple ANOVA. We locate the critical value of *F* by using the degrees of freedom of the *F* ratio (see Table 14.9). We look across the top of Table B.4 to find the degrees of freedom that belong to the top, or numerator, of the *F* ratio. We look along the side of the table to find the degrees of freedom for the denominator of our $F$ ratio. Each $F$ ratio we compute has its own degrees of freedom. That means that each ratio has its own critical value or table value of $F$.

When we evaluate each $F$ ratio, we must be sure we are using the correct degrees of freedom and the correct critical value. The $F$ ratio for factor 1 (word frequency) has 1 degree of freedom for the numerator ($MS_1$); it has 16 degrees of freedom for the denominator ($MS_w$). The table value of $F(1, 16)$ is 4.49 at $p < .05$ and 8.53 at $p < .01$. Our computed value of $F$ for factor 1 is 8.40. Therefore, the effect of factor 1 is significant at $p < .05$ but not quite large enough for $p < .01$. Because our computed value of $F$ is clearly larger than the table value at $p < .05$, the main effect of word frequency is so large that it is probably not due to chance. Whether the lists contained high- or low-frequency words made a significant difference in subjects' recall. We can reject the null hypothesis that the means of the high- and low-frequency groups were sampled from the same population. But does the significant effect support the alternative hypothesis that high-frequency words are easier to recall than low-frequency words?

Because there are only two levels of factor 1, we do not need to worry about post hoc or a priori tests to pinpoint the significant difference; we can see that the high-frequency group has a higher mean recall score than the low-frequency group does. So, we can now say that the high-frequency group had significantly better recall than the low-frequency group as predicted by the research hypothesis.

When we look up the critical value for factor 2 (cueing), we find that the main effect of factor 2 is significant at $p < .01$; our computed value of $F$ for factor 2 is more extreme than the table value at $p < .01$. Once again, because there are only two groups in this factor, we can interpret the effects simply by comparing the two group means.[8] We can say that subjects who received category cues recalled significantly more items than did subjects who did not receive cues (and we can say that the difference was significant at $p < .01$ because our computed $F$ value was more extreme than the critical value for $p < .01$). We can reject the null hypothesis that the means of the groups under the two levels of factor 2 were sampled from the same population, and we can say that the data analysis supports the research hypothesis.

The computed $F$ for the interaction is 0. This value is not significant.[9] In effect, it tells us that the variability between treatment groups can be explained by the effect of either word frequency or category cues acting separately on subjects' scores. The impact of each independent variable was also

---

[8] If our experiment had included factors with three or more levels, we would have needed post hoc tests to interpret significant main effects, exactly as we did with the three-group experiment that used a one-way ANOVA.

[9] If our experiment had produced a significant interaction, we would have needed post hoc tests to pinpoint the exact sources of group differences. The use of post hoc tests to interpret an interaction is very similar to the steps we took to interpret the significant effect from a three-group experiment that used a one-way ANOVA. In a 2 × 2 factorial, we would need to use post hoc tests to determine how the *four* conditions of the experiment actually differed. We will discuss an example in the next section.

unrelated to the value of the other independent variable; the effect of word frequency was the same whether or not subjects received category cues. Similarly, the effect of giving category cues was the same whether subjects saw high- or low-frequency words.

If the interaction had been significant, we would be limited in what we could conclude about the main effects in this experiment. We learned in Chapter 10 that whenever there is a significant interaction, the discussion of simple main effects needs to be tentative because experimental effects really depend on levels of both factors. If there is a significant interaction, it is more useful to discuss the impact of the independent variables in combination with each other. A significant interaction means that the impact of one independent variable differs depending on the value of the other. We can make accurate predictions about subjects' performance only when we know the subjects' position with respect to both variables. For instance, in this example a significant interaction would mean that we could accurately predict the approximate number of items the average subject would recall—but only if we knew the subject's position on both variables (for example, if we knew that the subject saw high-frequency words and also received cues). Without a significant interaction, however, we can make a reasonably good prediction if we know the subject's position on only one variable. If we know that Carl was given category cues, we automatically also know that he probably did better than the subjects who did not get cues, regardless of whether he saw high- or low-frequency words.

### Calculating Effect Sizes

For factorial designs, we would calculate an effect size for each significant effect (main effects and interactions). If we want to calculate $\eta^2$ for both significant main effects in our experiment, we can use the same formula provided for one-way analysis of variance. We would use the appropriate $F$ value and $df$s for each variable. For example, to calculate $\eta^2$ for category cues, we would use $F_2 = 18.91$, with $df_b = 1$ and $df_w = 16$ from Table 14.9.

$$\eta^2 = \frac{df_b(F_2)}{df_b(F_2) + df_w}$$

$$\eta^2 = \frac{1(18.91)}{1(18.91) + 16} = .54$$

Because the word frequency factor has a smaller $F$ value but uses the same $df$s, $\eta^2$ would be somewhat smaller (.34), but effect sizes for both significant main effects would be considered large (Cohen, 1988).

### Graphing Factorials

When we had only one independent variable in the time estimation and in the mug valuation experiments, we had only one line to graph. In a factorial experiment, however, we need to do more. The results of our experiment are presented as a line graph in Figure 14.12a and as a bar graph in Figure 14.12b.

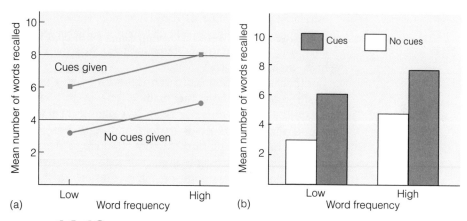

FIGURE **14.12** Recall of word lists as a function of word frequency and category cues.
© Cengage Learning

Notice that the vertical axis still represents the dependent variable, and the horizontal axis represents the different levels of one independent variable.

Within a line graph, each line presents the data from a different level of the other independent variable. In Figure 14.12a, one line represents the recall of subjects who were given category cues; the other stands for recall under the no-cues condition. You can see from the location of the lines that there are differences between the scores of subjects under the various conditions of this experiment. In Figure 14.12b, bars were created to represent each level of both factors. Graphs are useful for summarizing the results of an experiment to give an overall view of the findings, and they are especially useful in constructing summaries of findings for experimental reports. But graphs do not substitute for statistical analysis. Even though the results look impressive, we need to carry out all the statistical procedures before we can make precise statements about whether we will accept them as significant findings.

## REPEATED MEASURES AND MIXED FACTORIAL DESIGNS

There are also ANOVA procedures for within-subjects (repeated measures) factorial designs and mixed factorial designs. The logic behind all the analysis of variance procedures is similar: Total variability is broken down into component parts representing treatment and error, and an F ratio is computed. The obtained F values for main effects and interactions are compared with critical values needed to reject the null hypothesis. ANOVAs for mixed designs and repeated measures, which are extremely time-consuming to calculate by hand, have become much more frequent in the literature as computers have become increasingly available for data analysis. Let us look at a research example of a mixed design.

Siiter and Ellison (1984) were interested in studying stereotypes of a "police personality." As these researchers have reported, there is a commonly held belief that law enforcement officers are a breed apart: "The police, it is

TABLE **14.10**

Summary of analysis of variance from Siiter and Ellison's experiment

| Source | SS | df | MS | F |
|---|---|---|---|---|
| Between groups | 55,063.50 | 123 | — | — |
| Groups (G) | 8,211.00 | 1 | 8,211.00 | 21.38* |
| Error$_b$ | 46,852.50 | 122 | 384.04 | — |
| Within subjects | 72,290.60 | 124 | — | — |
| Target (T) | 9,725.03 | 1 | 9,725.03 | 30.14* |
| T × G | 23,206.45 | 1 | 23,206.45 | 71.93* |
| Error$_w$ | 39,359.12 | 122 | 322.62 | — |
| Total | 127,354.11 | 247 | — | — |

Note: Results from Siiter and Ellison (1984).
*$p < .0001$
© Cengage Learning

said, like the rich, are different from you and me" (p. 334). Many people believe that the police are more suspicious, more cynical, and more *authoritarian* (insisting on strict obedience to rules and authority) than are people in general. Actually, some evidence indicates that police officers might have somewhat different personality traits than the general population, but little or no support exists for the hypothesis that police officers are more authoritarian than anyone else. Siiter and Ellison tested the stereotype in two groups of male subjects: 62 undergraduates and 62 law enforcement officers. Type of group (a subject variable) was the two-level between-subjects factor.

All subjects filled out a standard scale of authoritarianism twice: once for their own beliefs and once as they felt a typical member of the other group might respond. Target of the responses (self or other group) was the two-level within-subjects factor. This clever design allowed the researchers to assess actual levels of authoritarianism in both groups as well as each group's perceptions of how authoritarian the other group was. The authoritarianism scale data were analyzed with a mixed factorial ANOVA. A summary table is shown in Table 14.10. Results from the between-subjects factor are shown first, followed by the results from the within-subjects factor. You can see by looking at the table that both main effects and the interaction were highly significant.

## Interpreting Significant Effects

Interpreting two significant main effects along with a significant interaction can be tricky. Recall that we said earlier in the chapter that whenever a two-way interaction is significant, we are limited in what we can conclude about any significant main effects in the experiment. If there is a significant interaction, it is more appropriate to discuss effects of the independent variables in combination because the impact of one independent variable differs depending on the value of the other. Knowing a subject's position on only one of

TABLE **14.11**
Mean authoritarianism scores from Siiter and Ellison's experiment

| Group | College Males | Police Officers |
|-------|---------------|-----------------|
| Self | $87.13_a$ | $94.97_a$ |
| Others | $119.00_b$ | $88.15_a$ |

Means with different subscripts are significantly different ($p < .05$).
© Cengage Learning

the two factors would not allow us to predict responses. To interpret the set of results from this study, we would want to say that both main effects and the interaction were significant, but we would focus the interpretation on the significant interaction. The group means are shown in Table 14.11.

We cannot interpret the significant interaction, however, until we have conducted post hoc tests to pinpoint differences among the four experimental conditions involved in the interaction. The null hypothesis for this interaction would be that the four groups were sampled from the same population; the significant interaction simply tells us that they probably were not. A significant $F$ value for the interaction does not specify exactly which of the four groups are different from each other. We need post hoc tests to do this.

The results of the post hoc tests can be seen (as subscripts) in Table 14.11. These tests indicated that the college students' ratings of police ($\overline{X} = 119.00$) were significantly higher than scores of the other three groups ($p <. 0001$). The other three groups did not differ from one another; despite small differences among the three means (87.13, 94.97, and 88.15), they were statistically equivalent. Now that we have pinpointed the differences among the four conditions, we can interpret the effects. Let's look at the actual levels of authoritarianism first. Results indicated that the students and the police evidenced similar authoritarianism levels (87.13 and 94.97 were not significantly different mean scores).

Next, we can look at how accurate the judgments of the police and students were: The college men rated police officers significantly higher in authoritarianism than police rated themselves (119.00 vs. 94.97); whereas the police officers' judgments about the students were quite similar to their actual scores (88.15 vs. 87.13). Taken as a whole, the results suggested that only the students held a negative stereotype about police, greatly overestimating how authoritarian they were.

In the next chapter, we will go into detail about interpreting results. We will discuss some problems with interpreting statistical significance, and we will discover a number of other important considerations in interpreting the results of experiments.

## SUMMARY

Five basic questions help us choose an appropriate statistical test: (1) How many independent variables are there? (2) How many treatment conditions are there? (3) Is the experiment run between or within subjects? (4) Are the subjects matched? (5) What is the level of measurement of the dependent variable?

For a two-independent-groups experiment with nominal data, we use a *chi-square* ($\chi^2$) test. Chi square ($\chi^2$) is an inferential statistic that tests whether the frequencies of responses in our sample represent certain frequencies in the population. Unlike the other tests covered in this text, however, the chi square is a nonparametric test because it does not make assumptions about the population (normal distribution, equal variances, etc.). The appropriate $\chi^2$ distribution is selected based on the *degrees of freedom (df)* for the experiment. The degrees of freedom indicate how many members of a set of data could vary or change value without changing the value of a statistic already known for those data.

When a two-group experiment consists of independent groups and the data are interval or ratio, the *t test for independent groups* is used. The *t* statistic is a computational way of relating differences between treatment means to the amount of variability expected between any two samples of data from the same population. One of the assumptions of the test is that the data come from populations that are normally distributed on the dependent variable; therefore, it is a parametric test. A *t* test is done by computing a *t* statistic for the data. The computed value of *t* is compared with the critical value of *t* based on the chosen significance level (generally $p < .05$). If the computed value of *t* is more extreme than the critical value, the null hypothesis is rejected; the difference between treatment means is statistically significant. Computed statistical values, such as *t,* need to be stated in research reports; effect sizes and *confidence intervals* for significant effects should also be included.

The *t* statistic has a whole family of distributions based on the degrees of freedom for the experiment. With two independent groups, the degrees of freedom for *t* are equal to the total number of subjects minus 2. As the degrees of freedom of *t* get larger, the critical value of *t* gets less extreme. Besides the degrees of freedom, the critical value of *t* also depends on whether the hypothesis is directional or nondirectional.

A within-subjects design or matching in a two-group experiment requires a different statistical procedure, the *t test for matched groups*. The same family of *t* distributions that apply to the independent-groups procedures are used for this test. However, *t* for matched or within-subjects data is computed by looking at the differences between each pair of responses. This procedure decreases the degrees of freedom, making it somewhat harder to reject the null hypothesis. However, using the matched-groups procedures to compute *t* greatly reduces the estimate of variability in the data, and this trade-off almost always results in a more powerful test of the effects of the independent variable.

*Analysis of variance (ANOVA)* procedures are used in experiments having more than two treatment conditions and interval or ratio data. An analysis of variance evaluates the effect of treatment conditions by looking at the variability in data. In the *one-way between-subjects ANOVA*, all the variability in the data can be divided into two parts: within-groups variability and between-groups variability. Within-groups variability is the degree to which the scores of subjects in the same treatment group differ from one another; between-groups variability is the degree to which different treatment groups differ from one another.

Variability is caused by all the sources of *error* in the experiment: differences between subjects as well as measurement errors, experimental errors, and other extraneous variables. Error contributes to *within-groups* and *between-groups variability*. Between-groups variability, however, also reflects variability caused by treatment conditions. If the independent variable had an effect, there should be more variability between treatment groups than there is within them: Between-groups variability should be large relative to the amount of variability within each group.

The relationship of within- and between-groups variability is evaluated by computing the statistic called *F*, which represents the ratio between the variability observed between treatment groups and the variability within the groups. The larger the *F ratio*, the more likely it is that the variability between groups was caused by the independent variable. *F* is found by computing these quantities: sum of squares between groups ($SS_b$) and sum of squares within groups ($SS_w$). Each of these quantities is divided by its respective degrees of freedom (*df*) to obtain the *mean square between groups* ($MS_b$) and *mean square within groups* ($MS_w$). The degrees of freedom of the experiment are used to locate the *critical values* of *F* in standardized tables. If the computed value of *F* is greater than the table value at the chosen level of significance, the null hypothesis that treatment means were sampled from the same population is rejected. Both the *t* test and the analysis of variance are *robust*, so they can be used even if assumptions of normality and homogeneity of variance are violated.

The analysis of variance tests the overall pattern of means in the different treatment groups. When more than two treatment groups are tested, the ANOVA does not test for significant differences between each pair of means. To pinpoint the exact location of the differences across several treatment groups, we need to conduct follow-up tests: *post hoc tests* or *a priori comparisons*. A somewhat different formula is used to compute *F* for a *one-way within-subjects (or repeated measures) ANOVA*, but the concept behind the procedures is very similar.

The basic ANOVA procedures may be extended to handle the data from experiments with more than one independent variable. In factorial experiments, the variability in data can be caused by several sources: It can be produced by error; it can also be produced by each independent variable in the experiment. The effects of each independent variable are called main effects. Variability can also be the result of the interaction or combination of variables in the experiment. There is an interaction when the effect of one independent variable changes across different levels of another independent variable in the experiment. In analyzing data from a factorial experiment, an *F* ratio is computed to evaluate each main effect and each possible interaction. Post hoc tests are needed to interpret significant main effects involving three or more groups and significant interactions. Finally, there are ANOVA formulas for within-subjects (repeated measures) and mixed factorial designs. These formulas are conceptually similar, but they can be very time-consuming to calculate by hand.

## KEY TERMS

**Analysis of variance (ANOVA)** The statistical procedure used to evaluate differences among three or more treatment means by breaking the variability in the data into components that reflect the influence of error and error plus treatment effects.

**A priori comparison** Statistical test between specific treatment groups that was anticipated, or planned, before the experiment was conducted; also called *planned comparison.*

**Between-groups variability** The degree to which the scores of different treatment groups differ from one another (that is, how much subjects vary under different levels of the independent variable); a measure of variability produced by treatment effects and error.

**Chi square ($\chi^2$)** A nonparametric, inferential statistic that tests whether the frequencies of responses in our sample represent certain frequencies in the population; used with nominal data.

**Confidence interval** A range of values above and below a sample mean that is likely to contain the population mean with the probability level (usually at 95% or 99%) that the mean of the population (the true mean) would actually fall somewhere in that range.

**Critical value** The value of the test statistic that must be exceeded to reject the null hypothesis at the chosen significance level.

**Degrees of freedom (*df*)** The number of members of a set of data that can vary or change value without changing the value of a known statistic for those data.

**Error** The variability within and between treatment groups that is not produced by changes in the independent variables; variability produced by individual differences, experimental error, and other extraneous variables.

**F ratio** A test statistic used in the analysis of variance; the ratio between the variability observed between treatment groups and the variability observed within treatment groups.

**Mean square (MS)** An average squared deviation; a variance estimate used in analysis-of-variance procedures and found by dividing the sum of squares by the degrees of freedom.

**Mean square between groups ($MS_b$)** The variance (or average squared deviation) across different treatment groups produced by error and treatment effects; found by dividing the sums of squares by the degrees of freedom.

**Mean square within groups ($MS_w$)** The variance (or average squared deviation) within a single treatment group; produced by the combination of sources called *error.*

**One-way between-subjects analysis of variance** Statistical procedure used to evaluate a between-subjects experiment with three or more levels of a single independent variable.

**One-way within-subjects (or repeated measures) ANOVA** Statistical procedure used to evaluate a within-subjects experiment with three or more levels of a single independent variable.

**Post hoc test** Statistical test performed after the overall analysis indicates a significant difference; used to pinpoint which differences are significant.

**Robust** A term describing a statistical test that can be used without increasing the probability of Type 1 or Type 2 errors even though its assumptions (e.g., the population is normally distributed and has equal variances) are violated.

**t test** A statistic that relates differences between treatment means to the amount of variability expected between any two samples of data from the same population; used to analyze the results of a two-group experiment with one independent variable and interval or ratio data.

**t test for independent groups** A statistic that relates differences between treatment means to the amount of variability expected between any two samples of data from the same population; used to analyze the results of a two-group experiment with independent groups of subjects.

**t test for matched groups** A statistic that relates differences between treatment means to the amount of variability expected between any two samples of data from the same population; used to analyze two-group experiments using matched-subjects or within-subjects designs. Also called a within-subjects $t$ test.

Within-groups variability The degree to which the scores of subjects in the *same* treatment group differ from one another (that is, how much subjects vary from others in the group); an index of the degree of fluctuation among scores that is attributable to error.

## REVIEW AND STUDY QUESTIONS

1. What five basic questions must we answer before we can select the appropriate statistical test for an experiment?

2. A two-independent-groups experiment was conducted to study the effects of low versus high anxiety on people's desire to affiliate with others. (Assume the procedures were the same as those used in the two-group experiment by Schachter discussed in Chapter 7.) After the anxiety manipulation, each subject could elect to wait either in an empty room or a room where another person was waiting. The data are shown in the following 2 × 2 contingency table:

|  | Desire to Affiliate | |
|---|---|---|
|  | Yes | No |
| Low anxious subjects | 10 | 20 |
| High anxious subjects | 20 | 10 |

a. What is the $H_0$ in this experiment?
b. What is the researcher's $H_1$?
c. Analyze the data using a $\chi^2$. Can the researcher reject the null hypothesis at $p < .05$?

3. Briefly outline the difference between the $t$ test for independent groups and the $t$ test for matched groups.

4. Our computed value of $t$ is $+3.28$. Our critical value of $t$ is $+2.048$. We have 28 degrees of freedom, and we are using a two-tailed (nondirectional) test. Draw a figure of the $t$ distribution to illustrate the relationship between the critical and the computed values of $t$ for this result.

5. Suppose that we had not made a directional prediction in the time-estimation experiment. Would the results still have been statistically significant if we had used a two-tailed test?

6. A researcher has studied subjects' ability to learn to translate words into Morse code. He has experimented with two treatment conditions. In one condition, the subjects are given massed practice; they spend 8 full hours working on the task. In the other condition, subjects are given distributed practice; they also spend 8 hours practicing, but their practice is spread over 4 days—they practice 2 hours each day. After the subjects have completed their practice, they are given a test message to encode. The dependent variable is the number of errors made in encoding the test message. Intelligence might affect the learning of this new skill, so the researcher has matched the subjects on that variable. The results for errors are given in the following table. Decide which statistical test would be appropriate for these data, carry out the test, and evaluate the outcome. Assume that the researcher has chosen a $p < .05$ level of significance and that the direction of the outcome has not been predicted.

| Massed Practice | | Distributed Practice | |
|---|---|---|---|
| $S_1$ | 6 | $S_1$ | 5 |
| $S_2$ | 4 | $S_2$ | 3 |
| $S_3$ | 3 | $S_3$ | 2 |
| $S_4$ | 5 | $S_4$ | 2 |
| $S_5$ | 2 | $S_5$ | 3 |

8. Assume that the Morse code researcher did not match the subjects.
a. Which statistical test would be appropriate? Carry out that test and evaluate the outcome for $p < .05$ and a nondirectional prediction.

b. Follow the same procedure as in 7a, but assume that the researcher has now predicted that the massed practice group will make more errors.

9. When do we use a one-way analysis of variance?

10. What are the sources of within-groups variability?

11. What are the sources of between-groups variability in an experiment with one independent variable?

12. Explain how the one-way analysis of variance works: How do we use within- and between-groups variability?

13. A researcher computed the F ratio for a four-group experiment. The computed F is 4.86. The degrees of freedom are 3 for the numerator and 16 for the denominator.
    a. Is the computed value of F significant at $p < .05$? Explain.
    b. Is it significant at $p < .01$? Explain.

14. Suppose we have done a one-way analysis of variance for a three-group experiment and our computed value of F is significant.
    a. Without further tests, what can we say about the means of the three treatment groups in our experiment?
    b. Explain why we would need to conduct either post hoc tests or a priori comparisons to interpret these results completely.

15. Practice carrying out the one-way ANOVA procedures by calculating the F ratio for these data. The hypothetical scores below represent the responses of subjects in four treatment groups who were given four different driver education programs. The dependent variable is the subjects' errors on their state examinations for driver's licenses:

| Group 1 | Group 2 | Group 3 | Group 4 |
|---------|---------|---------|---------|
| 3 | 1 | 1 | 2 |
| 3 | 2 | 0 | 3 |
| 4 | 1 | 0 | 2 |
| 3 | 2 | 1 | 2 |
| 2 | 2 | 0 | 1 |

a. What is the computed value of F for these data?
b. Is F significant at $p < .05$?
c. Prepare a summary table for your data.
d. Graph the results.
e. Conduct follow-up tests to pinpoint the location of significant group differences. Explain your results.

16. An experimenter has studied the effects of cigarette smoking on learning. Two levels of the smoking variable were used: All the subjects are smokers, but only half are given cigarettes to smoke during the half-hour before the experiment; the other half are not allowed to smoke after they arrive at the laboratory. There are also two levels of the learning variable: Subjects are all given the same materials to study, but half the subjects are told they will be asked to recall the words they see (intentional learning condition). The remaining subjects are told they will be asked to rate various types of printing for readability. They are not told they will be asked to recall the actual words they see (incidental learning condition). Following are hypothetical data from the learning and smoking experiment.

|  | Factor 1 (Smoking) | |
|---|---|---|
|  | Smoked | Did not smoke |
| Intentional | 4 | 5 |
|  | 3 | 4 |
|  | 5  $\bar{X} = 4$ | 4  $\bar{X} = 4.2$ |
|  | 4 | 3 |
| Factor 2 (Learning) | 4 | 5 |
| Incidental | 3 | 4 |
|  | 2 | 3 |
|  | 2  $\bar{X} = 2.4$ | 4  $\bar{X} = 3.2$ |
|  | 3 | 3 |
|  | 2 | 2 |

a. Practice the two-way between-subjects ANOVA on these data.

b. Graph the means of the four treatment groups.

c. Interpret the effects of the experiment.

17. Following is an SPSS printout of a summary table for a 2 × 2 between-subjects ANOVA on the data from the learning and smoking experiment. How did your calculations fare against the computer's analysis?

| Source | Type II Sum of Squares | df | Mean Square | F | Sig. |
|---|---|---|---|---|---|
| Smoking | 1.250 | 1 | 1.250 | 2.273 | .151 |
| Learning | 8.450 | 1 | 8.450 | 15.364 | .001 |
| Smoking * Learning | .450 | 1 | .450 | .818 | .379 |
| Error | 8.800 | 16 | .550 | | |
| Total | 257.000 | 20 | | | |

## CRITICAL THINKING EXERCISE

*The myth:* "The apple never falls far from the tree" and "Like father, like son" are two familiar bits of folk wisdom. Both argue for expectations of similarity between offspring from different generations.

*The scientific findings:* Psychologists have discovered that there is a strong genetic component to almost every trait and behavioral characteristic that has been studied (Plomin & Neiderhiser, 1992). Even our attitudes, such as those we hold about punishing criminals or premarital sex, show strong heritability (Bouchard, Jr., et al., 2003).

*The problem:* The heritability of IQ has been studied extensively. Heritability estimates, or $H^2$, reflect the amount of variance in a characteristic in a particular population that can be attributed to genetic influence—$H^2$ is conceptually similar to $r^2$. Heritability estimates for IQ range from about $H^2 = .10$ to $H^2 = .65$ across studies of different populations. The average heritability estimate for identical twins raised together is $H^2 = .55$; for identical twins raised apart, $H^2 = .52$. Compare this with the heritability estimate for cousins, $H^2 = .02$, who share fewer genes (Bouchard, Jr., & McGue, 1981). Interpret these heritability estimates in terms of effect sizes.

## ONLINE RESOURCES

For additional practice, try the workshops on *t* tests and ANOVA at the following site:

http://www.wadsworth.com/psychology_d/templates/student_resources/workshops/workshops.html

For a real-world example of reported confidence intervals (i.e., margins of error) used in polls, see

http://www.novinite.com/view_news.php?id=101423

# PART 4

# Discussion

**15** Drawing Conclusions: The Search for the Elusive Bottom Line

**16** Writing the Research Report

# Drawing Conclusions: The Search for the Elusive Bottom Line

**Evaluating the Experiment from the Inside: Internal Validity**
Statistical Conclusion Validity

**Taking a Broader Perspective: The Problem of External Validity**
Generalizing from the Results
Generalizing Across Subjects
Generalizing from Procedures to Concepts:
   Research Significance
Generalizing Beyond the Laboratory
Increasing External Validity

**Handling a Nonsignificant Outcome**
Faulty Procedures
Faulty Hypothesis

SUMMARY
KEY TERMS
REVIEW AND STUDY QUESTIONS
CRITICAL THINKING EXERCISE
ONLINE RESOURCES

## CHAPTER OBJECTIVES

- Learn to make valid conclusions based on an experiment's internal validity
- Understand the limits to generalizing results from a single study
- Learn techniques for increasing external validity
- Understand the causes of nonsignificant findings

We have now discussed all the major steps for setting up a psychological experiment, running it, and evaluating the results with statistics. The goal of an experiment is to establish a cause-and-effect relationship between an independent and a dependent variable, and we have covered a variety of experimental designs and control procedures that enable us to do this in a legitimate way. After the data are analyzed using statistics, two important questions remain: What does it all mean? Have we accomplished our goal? These are the questions we need to answer in the Discussion section of the research report.

Keep in mind that even when a significant treatment effect is present, we have only established a statistical outcome. We have demonstrated that the treatments in our experiment produced differences so large that they could occur by chance only a small percentage of the time—but we have not tested the experimental hypothesis directly. Statistical significance tells us nothing about the quality of the experiment; statistically significant results might or might not have any practical or theoretical implications.

Naturally, we would like to find statistically significant differences that support our research hypothesis, but we would also like our findings to be convincing and to have applications in settings outside the experiment. When we interpret the results of experiments, we look beyond the simple question of whether they are statistically significant; we evaluate the pros and cons of accepting these results at face value. A discussion and evaluation of findings are included in all research reports: Besides telling others what we did, we want to tell them what we think it means. We also want to point out any methodological problems or other potential limitations on the findings.

In this chapter, we will discuss some problems of drawing conclusions from the results of an experiment. We will review some of the criteria—internal and external validity—used to evaluate the worth of an experiment. We will also focus on some aspects of the generality of research findings beyond the context of an experiment. Finally, we will look at the special problems that arise when our predictions are not confirmed.

---

## EVALUATING THE EXPERIMENT FROM THE INSIDE: INTERNAL VALIDITY

When evaluating an experiment, we begin by judging it from the inside: Is the experiment methodologically sound? Is it internally valid? An experiment is internally valid when the effects of an extraneous variable—a variable not the focus of the experiment—have not been mistaken for the effects of the independent variable. An internally valid experiment is free of confounding; effects on the dependent variable can be attributed solely to the experimental treatment.

All the articles published in major journals (for example, those published by the American Psychological Association, the Association for Psychological Science, or other professional organizations) are carefully reviewed before they are accepted; therefore, you will not find many obvious examples of internally invalid experiments in the research literature. In rare instances, an editor may make the decision to publish an article with an obvious confound if the experiment produced results that were deemed important. Here, the rationale is to spur additional research in an area where little is known.

For example, even though rap music with violent lyrics ("gangsta rap") had been around for a number of years and had been strongly criticized in the media, the first two experiments showing its effects were not published until 1995. Interestingly, they came to opposite conclusions. One study suggested that a short exposure to gangsta rap videos produced positive, prosocial changes in attitudes; the other found negative, antisocial changes. However, both studies had confounds (discussed in Hansen, 1995).

In the study that found negative effects, the authors concluded that male African American adolescents were significantly more accepting of violence when they had just watched violent rap videos than when they had just watched nonviolent rap videos. One of the problems with the study, however, was the choice of videos. The violent videos (by artists like Public Enemy) indeed portrayed many acts of violence against both authority figures and street people. In comparison, the nonviolent videos did not contain any acts of violence, but they did contain many other things that the violent videos did not, such as dancing, partying, and overt sexual content (e.g., *Whoomp There It Is*, by Tag Team). To be certain that we are studying effects of the violence in the rap videos, the amount of violent content should be the only systematic difference between the video conditions. Otherwise, the experiment is confounded, and the results can be interpreted in another way: Instead of accepting the conclusion that violent rap videos *increased* acceptance of violence, we have to consider an alternative explanation for the results. Perhaps the difference between the two conditions occurred because the fun and sexy rap videos *decreased* the boys' acceptance of violence instead. We cannot tell from this experiment. Even so, an editorial decision was made to publish the studies because it was hoped that the two experiments would have *heuristic value*—that they would lead other researchers to conduct more experiments on rap music. And it worked!

Experiments that contain an obvious source of confounding rarely make it into print. As you read the literature, however, be on the lookout for subtler problems. Perhaps a researcher overlooked something that could be important. If you can make a good case for your criticism, you may have the beginning of your own study to settle the question. Box 15.1 presents an interesting example of a series of studies undertaken by researchers to explore possible confounding in their own published results.

Abreu and Gabarain (2000) explored potential confounding in several previously published experiments investigating counselor preferences among ethnic minorities. Past research had shown that ethnic minorities preferred counselors with similar ethnic backgrounds to European American counselors. In a meta-analysis (Coleman, Wampold, & Casali, 1995), this preference appeared very strong (with an effect size of .73). Abreu and Gabarain hypothesized that the effects of past research might be confounded by a social desirability bias. To test this, they exposed Mexican American subjects to written introductions and photographs of two female counselors—one Mexican American and one European American—and asked subjects to state which counselor they would prefer for an academic problem and which one they would prefer for a personal problem. The introductions were carefully designed to set up each counselor's ethnicity while describing them to appear very similar in other characteristics. The photographs had been pilot tested on another group of Mexican American subjects to ensure that the photos portrayed the appropriate ethnicity and were equal in attractiveness.

In addition, the researchers measured each subject's tendency toward socially desirable responding using the Marlowe-Crown Social Desirability Scale (Crowne & Marlowe, 1964) that we described in Chapter 8. The first data analysis looked solely at preferences without considering social desirability, and, as past research had found, subjects expressed a preference for an ethnically similar counselor. Then, to test their hypothesis, a second data analysis included subjects' social desirability scores as a covariate in the statistical analysis (ANCOVA, as described in Chapter 14), essentially taking out the variance in subjects' preferences that was the result of social desirability. When the influence of social desirability was removed, preference ratings for Mexican American and European American counselors were no longer different, strongly suggesting that preference ratings had been influenced by a social desirability response set. Perhaps, expressing a preference for an ethnically similar counselor might reflect ethnic pride and may be perceived to be the socially desirable response among ethnic minorities (Coleman et al., 1995).

BOX **15.1** **Isolating Variables in Recall**

In the first of a series of experiments, Ritchey (1982) reported the findings of a study on children's recall. Age was treated as one independent variable: Third-graders, sixth-graders, and adults were the three levels of this variable. The type of stimulus was another independent variable: words, outline drawings, and detailed drawings, as shown in Figure 15.1.

Ritchey found that, contrary to predictions, children remembered outline drawings better in a subsequent recall task. This outcome was unexpected because the detailed drawings included more features that could be encoded in memory. However, even though outline drawings are less elaborate, they are more distinctive (unusual) because they differ from the drawings we usually see.

GIRAFFE                    GIRAFFE

FIGURE **15.1** Stimuli used to test pictorial detail and recall: detailed (left) and outline (right) drawings. The figure on the right is less elaborate but more distinctive than the figure on the left.
Drawings furnished by Gary H. Ritchey. Used with permission.

In later experiments, Ritchey and Armstrong (1982) showed that subjects recalled detailed drawings better than less elaborate drawings— when the degree of distinctiveness was controlled. Distinctiveness, as in the caricature in Figure 15.2, made items easier to recall when the amount of

elaboration (detail) was controlled. Thus, the original confounding between elaboration and distinctiveness led to further research. This research in turn helped clarify the relationship between the two variables as they influence free recall.

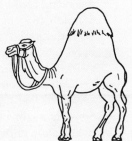

FIGURE **15.2** Stimuli used to separate effects of elaboration and distinctiveness. Left to right: detailed, outline, caricature drawings. The figures on the left and the right are equally elaborate, but the right-hand figure is more distinctive.
Drawings furnished by Gary H. Ritchey. Used with permission.

Of course, the best way to ensure internal validity is to plan ahead. As you design experiments, you must be sure that your procedures incorporate appropriate methodology and control techniques. Be certain that you have included enough levels of the IV to make an adequate test of your hypothesis and try to anticipate any potential confounding variables. Be sure to use standard techniques like random assignment, constancy of conditions, and counterbalancing throughout your research. But, when you are ready to evaluate the outcome of the experiment, do not forget to consider what actually happened. You will need to ask yourself whether the experimental setup actually created the conditions you intended. Did subjects follow instructions properly? Did you manipulate the independent variable successfully? Did the sad film really make the subjects feel sad? Were subjects in the low-anxiety condition really less anxious than subjects in the high-anxiety condition? Some researchers include such an assessment as part of their experimental procedures. This is called a manipulation check because it verifies how successfully the experimenter manipulated the situation he or she intended to produce.

But even the most careful plans can go wrong. You might have designed a tight set of procedures before you began testing subjects, but in practice you might have been forced to deviate from the plan. Did these small changes influence the way subjects responded? You want to be certain that all your procedures accomplished what you intended. Did you find that subjects in your control group did not understand directions? Did they keep asking questions to clarify their task in the experiment? Your instructions might have been confusing in that condition. Can you be sure, then, that those subjects really did what you wanted them to do?

Many researchers incorporate an informal interview (or even a written questionnaire) at the end of the experiment to elicit this kind of information. They ask subjects to talk about their thoughts and feelings during the experiment. They also ask about any questions that subjects might have had during the procedures. If subjects did not follow instructions, the experimental manipulation might not be the best explanation of the findings. In an informal interview, the researcher can also try to get a sense of whether subjects guessed the experimental hypothesis by asking them what they thought the experiment was trying to show. If a group of subjects guessed the hypothesis, their data could be of limited value. You might find it advantageous to spend a little extra time interviewing the first few subjects in depth, so that any potential problems in the procedures can be corrected before you run a large number of subjects through the experiment, wasting your time and theirs.

Some of these validity issues are difficult to resolve because of the demand characteristics of the experiment itself. For instance, Orne (1969) suggested that a *pact of ignorance* forms between subjects and experimenter. Subjects might be aware that if they guess the hypothesis of the experiment, their data will be discarded. If you ask them what they understood about the purpose of the experiment, they might not reveal all they know. To counter this natural hesitancy, subjects need to believe that you really want a truthful answer. Some researchers have gone as far as offering subjects an incentive for guessing the experimental hypothesis during informal interviews. Orne also pointed out that experimenters might not really press subjects for much information because it could mean that some data may not be usable. Most researchers do not want to spend unnecessary time testing additional subjects, thus they might be tempted to accept subjects' reports at face value instead of requesting additional information that could provide a more objective evaluation. Avoid this temptation if you want to be sure your experiment is internally valid. When you interpret the results of your experiment, always be open to other potential explanations for your findings.

On the one hand, beginning researchers often spend *too much time* listing everything imaginable that could have influenced any of the subjects' responses ("Some subjects could have stayed up too late the night before." "Some may have been in a hurry to get to the experiment and did not have time to eat a good breakfast.") As long as these events are infrequent and could occur randomly for subjects in any of the experimental conditions, they are not considered a problem with the experiment—they just add error to the data, making it harder to detect effects. Do not list them.

On the other hand, students often spend *too little time* thinking about other potential explanations for their results. Could anything else have changed along with levels of the independent variable? Were high-frequency words shorter than low-frequency words? Could an authoritarianism scale be less valid for police officers than for college students? Could increasing the negative ions in the air also make it less humid? Think carefully about any other effects that could have been produced when you varied the levels of the independent variable.

If something other than the independent variable can explain the results, the experiment is not internally valid. Before concluding that your experiment is internally valid, review the classic threats to internal validity covered in Chapter 7. Remember that it is better if you are the one to discover any substantial problems in your experiment; an experienced reader is certain to find them and think even less of your abilities as a researcher if you have missed them. Discuss problems openly in the discussion section of your report. And do not forget that even the most well-constructed experiment does not prove your hypothesis is correct; we never confirm our research hypothesis directly, and we certainly never "prove" it. Statistical tests allow us to make probability statements only, and there is always a chance of Type 1 error (concluding that your treatment had an effect when it really did not). Good scientists are always skeptical about their own results.

## Statistical Conclusion Validity

Let's hope that your experiment will be free of such confounding variables. But confounding is not the only threat to an experiment's internal validity; other kinds of problems can lead to false conclusions about cause-and-effect relationships between experimental variables. We also need to evaluate the experiment in light of the results we obtained from statistical tests. We want to be certain that any inferences we make about the relationship between independent and dependent variables have statistical conclusion validity, the validity of drawing conclusions about a treatment effect from the statistical results that were obtained (Cook & Campbell, 1979). Whenever the assumptions of a statistical test are violated, statistical conclusion validity is in doubt. If we used a test statistic inappropriately (an ANOVA for nominal data, for example), there would be some doubt about the validity of conclusions we could draw from a "statistically significant" effect. But less obvious factors can influence statistical conclusion validity, too. The number of statistical tests computed and the power of the statistical test are two common sources of low validity.

You already know the problem created by too many pairwise comparisons—a higher chance of making a Type 1 error. If the chances of making a Type 1 error have been increased, then statistical conclusion validity has been lowered. Inferring a cause-and-effect relationship is much riskier. You also know that it is easier to get statistical significance with a large than with a small sample because small samples reduce the power of statistical tests. If your experimental results were barely significant even though you tested 400 subjects, you probably should be cautious about drawing conclusions. We will return to the notion of statistical power and validity when we discuss null findings later in the chapter. Keep in mind that findings can be statistically significant but not very meaningful. For example, if your calculated effect size is small, you will want to avoid drawing any sweeping conclusions. Or if the confidence intervals you computed for different treatment groups actually have some overlap, be extremely cautious; you may have made a Type 1 error.

# TAKING A BROADER PERSPECTIVE: THE PROBLEM OF EXTERNAL VALIDITY

So far, we have talked about evaluating an experiment from the inside, but we also want to look beyond the experiment to broader questions. We want to know whether the experiment has external validity: Do the findings have implications outside the experiment? Can we make any general statements about the impact of the independent variable? An experiment is externally valid if the results can be extended to other situations accurately. External validity, however, is not an either/or matter. It is a continuum. Some experiments are more externally valid than others.

## Generalizing from the Results

When an experiment has external validity, we can generalize from the results. We make our findings more universal than they actually are by ignoring the specific details of the experiment. Instead of speaking of a particular sample (for example, 30 female undergraduates) and a specific set of operational definitions (for example, scores on the Manifest Anxiety Scale), we draw broader inferences from the findings through inductive thinking. When we think inductively, we reason from specific facts to more general principles. Early in the text, you saw how we can use induction to formulate research hypotheses. We also use induction when we make generalizations based on a specific set of findings. The accuracy of our generalizations depends on a variety of factors that affect the external validity of an experiment.

An externally valid experiment meets two basic requirements. First, the experiment is internally valid; it clearly demonstrates a cause-and-effect relationship. The experiment is free of confounding. Second, findings that are externally valid can be replicated. We (or other researchers) can replicate the original findings in other experiments. If we get statistically significant results again, we can be more certain that the results were not just a fluke of our sampling procedures or a Type 1 error. Valid experimental findings appear again and again. Similar effects should reappear in similar studies. Findings that appear once and cannot be replicated have limited scientific importance, and any general conclusions that we draw from such findings could be inaccurate.

Of course, when you complete a single experiment, you do not know whether the findings can be replicated unless you are actually replicating some earlier findings. Partly for that reason, you will often see single articles that contain reports of several experiments. These series of experiments typically extend the findings of one principal study. They provide data on alternative explanations and applications of those findings; they also provide evidence that the findings can be replicated. If a researcher consistently obtains confirmation of a hypothesis throughout a series of experiments, the findings have some amount of external validity.

Along with the overall requirements of internal validity and replicability, we can also look at external validity as it applies to several important issues: generalizability across subjects, across procedures, and beyond the laboratory.

## Generalizing Across Subjects

How much can we generalize from one group of subjects to another? How much can we generalize from a sample to the population that interests us? These questions have no hard-and-fast answers. Experiments may have different outcomes when they are run on different samples. For that reason, we try to get samples from the population we want to discuss. If we want to make statements about college students, we ought to sample college students. It makes sense to assume that all college students have some characteristics in common that enable us to speak of them as a group. Nevertheless, we need to be cautious in drawing conclusions about all students on the basis of one study. What is true for students in Kansas might not be true for students in New York.

Practical problems also prevent us from obtaining truly random samples. There is typically *bias* in the way human subjects are chosen, if only because they are all volunteers. The student (or parent or salesperson) who volunteers might not be typical. You already know that volunteers can be quite different from nonvolunteers (Rosenthal & Rosnow, 1975).

The problem becomes even more acute when we try to extend our findings to a larger group, such as all people. Other writers have commented that a rather large number of research findings in psychology have come from studies of white rats and college students. Of course, many of these findings have been replicated in studies with different species and with a variety of human subjects, too. But the fact remains that the generality of our research is often constrained by practical problems. College students may be intrinsically interesting, but they are also more available for research than the average adult who spends the better part of the day at a regular job. White rats are relatively easy to keep, and they cost less than monkeys. These mundane factors shape the research that we do. When we have trouble finding subjects, we will also have trouble getting samples that are typical of the population we are trying to study, thereby limiting the external validity of the experiment.

How far can we go in generalizing from a single study? The further from the population actually sampled, the shakier our position becomes, at least until we do more testing. As research findings are replicated in subsequent studies with different types of subjects, their generality is supported. Findings that appeared only with left-handed, 19-year-old Stanford University students might not have much generality.

At times, it makes sense to explore some of the questions of generality across subjects within the same experiment. When an experiment uses both male and female subjects, for example, subject sex is routinely included as a factor in most experiments. If we suspect that age or social class will alter the impact of an independent variable, we may treat those subject variables as additional independent variables. We might, for example, test several different age groups. When that is not feasible, we might be forced to rely on later studies to clarify the role of those additional variables. We might, however, accept the generality of some findings for ethical reasons. Manufacturers use laboratory animals to test the safety of new drugs. A product that proved harmful to nonhuman subjects would not be marketed, even though there was no direct evidence that it was dangerous to humans.

## Generalizing from Procedures to Concepts: Research Significance

Ideally, our research results also illustrate the operation of general principles; they are not unique to the particular procedures used in the experiment. For instance, Hess (1975) showed that pupil size affected the ratings men gave to photographs. A picture of the same woman received more favorable ratings when she was shown with larger pupils. If this finding has generality across procedures, we would expect to get similar results with different sets of photographs (as did Niedenthal & Cantor, 1986, and Tombs & Silverman, 2004); we would not expect the findings to be peculiar to the photos of just one person. If the findings also have generality across subjects, we would expect that different types of men would give similar data. We might also expect to see similar responses from women rating photos of men.

Sometimes attempts to generalize across procedures raise theoretical issues that are hard to resolve. These issues arise when we study variables that can have multiple operational definitions. An operational definition, in principle, defines a variable in terms of observable operations, procedures, and measurements. As we saw in Chapter 7, some variables, such as anxiety, may be defined in various ways. When we generalize from the results of an experiment, we face the problem of going from a specific operational definition of a concept to conclusions about the concept itself. We do not want to talk about the number of errors that subjects made; instead, we want to talk about the concept of learning. We might not be interested in the effects of difficult mazes per se; we want to talk about the concept of frustration. Naturally, it is desirable to view findings from this more abstract perspective; we would like to discover principles that explain behavior in general. Ultimately, we would like to use induction to build new theories and to apply our findings to practical problems.

Typically, however, it is risky to generalize from the findings of a single experiment in this way. The reasons are closely related to some of the issues we discussed earlier. We cannot always be certain of how reliable or valid our procedures are. For example, is your definition of learning tapping into the same phenomenon tested by others in prior research? One experiment may be suggestive, but we go far beyond our data when we expand our findings to explain all possibilities. For these reasons, researchers hedge a bit when they discuss generalizability. The Discussion sections of research reports are dotted with qualifying statements: "These findings suggest ...," "It seems reasonable that ...," "It appears that ...". Such statements often distress new researchers who would prefer to be able to state that something will occur with certainty. But the probabilistic nature of experimentation restricts the kinds of statements we can make about our findings.

Also, as we formulate general conclusions, we move further away from the actual observations that we made. We can make some statements with confidence; we can report exactly what we did and what we observed in the experiment. When we begin to interpret results, we go beyond what we actually did and what we actually observed. As we do so, we are on increasingly shaky ground. Researchers qualify the conclusions they draw because there is no way to be certain their generalizations will always be true. Perhaps the findings describe the effects of the independent variable only under a very specific set of circumstances—namely, those defined in one experiment. Perhaps other operational definitions of the variables would lead to other outcomes. As we know, testing different sorts of subjects might do the same.

Still, if our findings have some degree of generality, we expect them to be consistent with the findings of prior researchers who have studied the same variables. Thus, as we evaluate the generality of our results, we look at them in the context of the work that has already been done in the field.

We have talked about evaluating statistical significance. But findings also have research significance. As we evaluate them, we ask several pertinent questions. First, are our findings consistent with prior studies? If so, how do they clarify or extend our knowledge? Do they have any implications for broader theoretical issues? At this stage, we are coming full circle on the research process. We began our experimental plan by reviewing the research literature. We used findings of prior researchers as a guide to the important issues and the most suitable procedures for the area we studied. Now, with our results in hand, we consider the place of our findings in the context of prior work in that area. Our knowledge of psychological principles proceeds in small steps as new findings are integrated into what is already known.

If our findings are inconsistent with earlier findings, our experiment could be suspect. For instance, we know that newborn babies prefer looking at patterns configured like human faces rather than at other kinds of patterns (Turati, 2004). If we have devised an experiment that leads us to conclude that babies actually prefer nonface patterns, we have a problem. We must be able to reconcile our findings with what has already been shown. Novel findings are suspicious when the prior findings have been replicated; the burden of explanation usually falls on the researcher who claims the novel findings. The possibility of an undetected flaw in the experiment must be evaluated with special caution.

You will occasionally read reports of findings that appear to be conflicting (as occurred with the two early experiments on rap music described at the beginning of the chapter). Most often, the apparent contradictions result from subtle differences in the operational definitions, the procedures, and the subjects used in various experiments. These inconsistencies may lead researchers into new studies to discover more general principles.

This is part of the process of theory building we discussed in Chapter 1 and, again, in Chapter 6 when we described how equity theory was devised. A theory is meant to make sense of many bits of data. The theory can stand as long as it is adequate to explain observed results. New information can produce scientific benefits by correcting existing theories. As conflicting data appear, however, more and more supporting assumptions may be needed to explain new findings. Ultimately, the theory may become so burdened by assumptions and exceptions that it must be discarded and replaced by theories with greater explanatory power.

## Generalizing Beyond the Laboratory

So far, we have talked about using induction to extend the results of specific experiments to other samples, other populations and procedures, and more general concepts. You know by now that we have some difficulty generalizing from one set of experimental procedures to another with accuracy. As you can imagine, we come up against an even greater problem when we extend the results of a laboratory experiment to what we might observe in the real world. Remember that a laboratory experiment is carried out under specific, controlled conditions. Because the laboratory researcher tries to eliminate all the extraneous influences that might affect the outcome of the experiment, the laboratory experiment is the most precise tool we have for measuring the effect of an independent variable as it varies under controlled conditions. The problem in extending laboratory findings is simple in principle: The variables we study usually do not occur under the same controlled conditions in real life. All sorts of extraneous factors can affect the influence of any one variable. An example of difficulties that can arise when laboratory findings are taken to the real world is found in Box 15.2.

## Increasing External Validity

How safe is it to extend the results of a laboratory experiment to everyday life? There is no clear-cut answer to that question. It is often impossible to

BOX **15.2**   **Bringing Lab Results to the Real World: Best Practices for Eyewitness Identification**

Law enforcement has long recognized that convictions based on eyewitness testimony can be error-prone and unreliable. The major cause (over 75%) of wrongful convictions and imprisonment is misidentification of suspects by eyewitnesses. For example, of the 207 cases that have been reversed on the basis of DNA evidence, 154 of the convictions were largely based on eyewitness identification. But, despite its unreliability, eyewitness identification can be very strong and compelling evidence for jury members.

In the laboratory, psychologists have identified a number of problems with the typical lineup procedures used to allow witnesses to identify guilty suspects. The two major problems are:[*]

1.  Law enforcement personnel are not blind to the suspect's identity. Personnel conducting the identification typically know who the suspect is and may transmit their knowledge to the witness through body language or tone of voice.
2.  Witnesses are usually asked to pick out the perpetrator from a lineup that simultaneously

presents the suspect along with other "filler" individuals, or they are asked to identify the perpetrator from a group of photos in which the suspect's photo is shown along with the "fillers."

Many laboratory studies have demonstrated that fewer perpetrators are incorrectly identified when personnel conducting the sessions are blind to the suspect's identity and when individuals in the lineup are presented sequentially (i.e., one at a time) rather than all together (see meta-analysis by Stebley, Dysart, Fulero, & Lindsay, 2001). Because of the research conducted by psychologists and other behavioral scientists, the U.S. Department of Justice has issued a comprehensive manual consisting of voluntary procedural guidelines for law enforcement (www.ojp.usdoj.gov/nij/pubs-sum/188678.htm) recommending blind personnel and sequential presentation in lineups. A number of law enforcement jurisdictions have switched to these procedures (e.g., the State of Wisconsin; Boston, Massachusetts), and more are planning changes.

know whether the findings of a particular experiment are externally valid until we do additional studies. Researchers use at least five general approaches to increase and verify the external validity of laboratory findings: aggregation, multivariate designs, nonreactive measurements, field experiments, and naturalistic observation. Let us look at each in turn.

### Aggregation

If experiments create a limited, artificial context for behavior, we can begin to increase the generality and external validity of our findings by combining the results of experiments done in different ways. This is the logic behind meta-analysis, discussed in Chapter 6. Meta-analysis uses statistics to combine and quantify data obtained from many different experiments testing a similar phenomenon. A meta-analysis describes the consistency with which an effect has been obtained in past research and will provide effect sizes. For example, meta-analyses by Raudenbush (1984) and Harris and Rosenthal (1985) found that the Rosenthal effect discussed in Chapter 8 was indeed strong and consistently obtained in experiments testing teacher expectancy effects.

Epstein (1980) called this approach aggregation, the grouping together and averaging of data gathered in various ways. Epstein described four types

Rich Legg/IStockphoto.com

Recently, researchers have begun studying these procedures in the field, but translating laboratory experiments into field experimentation can be very difficult or, at times, impossible. For example, in the laboratory, conditions can be set up so that subjects view a "crime" taking place and later try to identify the perpetrator from a lineup. Here, researchers know whether the guilty person is in the lineup or not. In the field, the actual guilt or innocence of a suspect cannot be known or controlled, so it is not possible to know how accurate an eyewitness's identification really is.

True field experiments comparing blind vs. nonblind administrators and sequential vs. simultaneous presentation have not been conducted; instead, researchers analyze and compare procedures and identification rates using existing police records as data. These field studies have shown that variables such as eyewitness and suspect race, relationship between the eyewitness and the suspect, and the number and position of "fillers" can all affect identification rates. These variables can be easily controlled in the laboratory but not in the field. In addition, some field study results have failed to support the laboratory findings. For example, when field researchers compared police records from blind-sequential lineups (the new procedure) with nonblind-simultaneous lineups (the old procedure), the blind-sequential presentation reduced the percentage of suspects who were identified as perpetrators, but it also increased the misidentification of innocent "fillers" as guilty (Mecklenburg, 2006). So, the controversy continues (Schachter, et al., 2008).

*Other procedural problems include not telling witnesses that the perpetrator might not be in the lineup, so that they feel forced to choose someone; not asking witnesses how confident they are in their decision; and using "fillers" that are either too different from the suspect, so that the suspect stands out, or using "fillers" that do not fit the description of the perpetrator.

of aggregation that can be used to increase the external validity of our data and broaden the scope of our experimental findings.

**Aggregation Over Subjects** Combining data from several subjects is already typical of large *N* psychology studies. Rather than relying on one or two subjects who could be unusual, we sample greater numbers. Their data are pooled, and our conclusions are based on group averages, as we saw in the last two chapters. Presumably, the larger sample is more representative of the population. In principle, these group data should have greater external validity than smaller samples from the same population.

**Aggregation Over Stimuli or Situations** In addition to generalizing to a population, researchers commonly want to generalize their results across a range of stimuli. For instance, an experiment on color matching that uses only 20 pairs of colors could be used to draw conclusions about the full range of 7500 different colors. In what sense do the 20 selected colors represent the overall range of 7500?

Epstein argued that stimuli must be sampled as effectively as we sample subjects; so must the context of the experiment. A social psychological experiment on helpfulness, for instance, might yield different results during the holiday season, when subjects might feel especially cooperative and helpful, than at other times of the year. We should not assume that such seemingly irrelevant factors do not alter experimental outcomes. Having sampled in a variety of situations, we can have more confidence in our results.

**Aggregation Over Trials or Occasions** By using many trials and combining multiple testing sessions, we minimize the effects associated with specific trials. If an experimenter unwittingly gives a cue to the correct response on a particular trial, combining data from many trials will cancel out the distortion.

Testing on various occasions also minimizes the effects created by the uniqueness of each testing session. A researcher might be more enthusiastic one time than the next; he or she might use slightly different words to introduce the experiment each time. We expect that physical, social, personality, and context variables (from Chapter 8) can exert different effects on different occasions during the experiment. Aggregating across many occasions provides data on the replicability of findings obtained in specific testing sessions.[1]

**Aggregation Over Measures** Finally, Epstein recommended using multiple measuring procedures. When we select a measure, such as one achievement test, we are sampling from all the measures available. But our one selection might not be the best. Measuring in more than one way can offset the errors we may make using one inadequate instrument. The different forms of aggregation provide converging lines of evidence for an explanation of behavior. The relative importance of the various forms of aggregation is still open to empirical verification. We have more confidence in results that can be reproduced using different subjects, in different situations, and on different occasions and that can be measured in more than one way.

### Multivariate Designs

In this text, we have focused on research designs that have one independent and one dependent variable. Because variables do not usually occur separately, however, we also looked at factorial designs in which we explore the effects of more than one independent variable at a time. As complicated as those designs may have seemed at first, other designs are even more elaborate. These are called multivariate designs because they deal with multiple dependent variables. These designs have become increasingly important in psychological research as computer statistics programs become more widely available. Without computers, multivariate statistical analysis would not be practical.

Multivariate designs enable us to look at many dependent variables in combination.[2] Measurements can be made on one or several samples. The

---

[1] This practice is analogous to the use of grade point averages (GPA) to represent academic achievement. Occasionally, you might feel you received too low a grade; another instructor might surprise you with a grade higher than you expect. These differences tend to cancel out. The more courses you take, the better the chances that your GPA reflects your true level of achievement.

[2] A factorial design is also "multivariate" in the sense that it has more than one independent variable; however, the term *multivariate* is customarily restricted to designs with multiple dependent variables.

procedures used to evaluate the results of these studies are extensions of the basic techniques you have already learned. Some of the more common multivariate designs are multiple correlation and factor analysis, which were discussed in Chapter 5, and multivariate analysis of variance. Here we will take a brief look at multivariate analysis of variance so that you will have some idea of why multivariate procedures are desirable.

The multivariate analysis of variance is an extension of the analysis of variance described in Chapter 14. We used the ANOVA to study the effect of more than one independent variable in a factorial design. However, those designs had only one dependent variable. By using a multivariate analysis of variance (MANOVA), the researcher can measure the effects of independent variables as they affect sets of dependent variables. He or she can evaluate whether the independent variables influence subjects' scores on the dependent variables as they occur in combination.

Through this type of design, a researcher interested in improvement after psychotherapy could approach the problem in a more comprehensive way than would be possible through a simpler factorial design. For instance, he or she could explore the effects of several independent variables: type of therapy, type of patient, sex of patient, sex of therapist. The researcher could also measure several aspects of improvement instead of just one, for example, the patients' self-reports, the therapists' reports, and symptoms as rated by objective observers. This combination of measurements could provide a more comprehensive index of "improvement" than any single one.

The MANOVA tests the effects of the independent variables on the whole set of measures at once. As with the simpler ANOVA procedures, the researcher would also be able to test for interactions among the independent variables on this set of improvement measures. Type of therapy and type of patient might interact to affect improvement. Higher-order interactions would be possible, too; several independent variables may operate together to affect improvement. With a MANOVA, the researcher also has the option of analyzing differences in trends among the various dependent measures. Effects produced by independent variables could be stronger on some measures than on others. Perhaps patients' reports show greater improvement than symptom ratings by objective observers. In short, a MANOVA provides much more information than the simpler analysis of variance.

The advantage of this and other multivariate procedures is that they allow us to look at combinations of variables that can be more representative of reality. Instead of focusing on just one aspect of improvement in therapy, such as self-report, the researcher can evaluate a wider spectrum of behavior. This broader focus provides a perspective on behavior that can have greater external validity than the simpler univariate approach. For that reason, there are now special journals devoted primarily to multivariate research, for example, *Multivariate Behavioral Research* and *Journal of Multivariate Experimental Personality and Clinical Psychology*. We may be able to increase the external validity of some studies by using multivariate rather than univariate approaches. We can also extend earlier findings by applying these new techniques to old questions.

### Nonreactive Measurements

We can also increase external validity by working to minimize reactivity in an experiment. Subjects react to being subjects. They react to being observed. Their responses might not be the same as the responses of others who are not observed, and thus, they might not have external validity.

We dealt with the problem of reactivity when we discussed survey techniques in Chapter 4 and demand characteristics of an experiment in Chapter 8. If an experiment has obvious demand characteristics, the results might not have much generalizability. They might not reflect what we would see outside the laboratory. When a subject comes into an experiment, the subject assumes an active role. The subject has certain expectations about what will happen in the experiment. If the researcher inadvertently gives cues that tell the subject what to do, the problem is even more serious. Subjects could actively try to generate data that support the researcher's predictions. The opposite can also happen: A subject might "guess" the hypothesis and then try to produce data to refute it.

We try to control demand characteristics and, thus, reactivity partly by being careful not to give subjects unnecessary cues. As Orne (1969) suggested, however, it can be difficult to get accurate information about our procedures. The pact of ignorance that forms between subjects and experimenters can affect external as well as internal validity. We can make better assessments of the impact of experimental manipulations through single- and double-blind experiments because the results will be less influenced by subjects' reactivity.

Some subjects react differently from others, so we need controls for other social and personality variables as well. We have to be especially wary of variables such as social desirability. We know, for instance, that subjects in interviews are apt to present a more favorable picture of themselves, distorting their responses in order to "look good" in the eyes of the researcher. Results distorted in this way might have little generality; they might not reflect what is true of behavior outside the laboratory.

**Developing Unobtrusive Measures**   As long as subjects know they are being observed and measured, their responses may be distorted in some way. If nothing else, subjects may be a little nervous. For that reason, researchers have also tried to develop procedures to measure subjects' behavior without letting them know they are being measured. These unobtrusive measures, also called *nonreactive measures*, are not influenced by subjects' reactions. They have greater external validity because they yield data more similar to what we expect to see outside an experiment.

Many unobtrusive measures depend on physical aspects of the environment. For example, we could evaluate the popularity of several attractions in a national park by comparing the condition of the trails leading to those sites; the more popular attractions should have well-worn trails. Similarly, we could judge the seating preferences of patrons of a theater by the condition of the seats. Or we could study presidential voter preferences by counting bumper stickers in the months before an election.

Other unobtrusive measures use data collected for other purposes. Reviews of hospital charts, for example, are a common method for comparing the efficacy of different kinds of medical or psychological treatments. School records and standardized test results are frequently used to study the effectiveness of various educational programs. Moss and McDonald (2004), for example, measured changes in children's reading preferences over the course of an entire year by analyzing borrowing records from a school library.

We can also gather data by observing subjects unobtrusively. For example, Marston, London, Cooper, and Cohen (1977) made unobtrusive observations of obese and thin diners in a restaurant. Without diners' knowledge, they recorded behaviors such as toying with food, size of bites, and rate of eating. They identified a "thin eating" pattern among women: smaller bites, a generally slower rate of eating, and more extraneous behaviors, such as putting down the fork now and then. The unobtrusive approach seems to have greater external validity than does bringing subjects into a laboratory to observe their eating behavior.

Sometimes cameras are used to make unobtrusive observations in public spaces or roadways. Cooper and his colleagues (2007), for example, assessed the influence of subjects' expressed safe driving intentions and self-reported adherence to motor vehicle regulations on their actual driving behavior by installing inconspicuous speed cameras on roads with posted speed limits. Whenever unobtrusive measures are used, ethical guidelines need to be carefully considered (as described in Chapter 2). For instance, informed consent is required for observations of any behavior that people generally consider private but may not be required for observations of public behavior such as eating in a restaurant or driving a car.

### Field Experiments

Perhaps the most obvious way of dealing with the whole problem of external validity is simply to take the experiment out of the laboratory, where most unobtrusive measures are used. If we suspect that subjects will behave differently under more realistic conditions, we can try it and see. Some experimental problems do not lend themselves to this approach, but those that do can lead us into fruitful new tests of our hypotheses.

The field experiment meets the basic requirements of an experiment: We manipulate antecedent conditions and observe the outcome on dependent measures of behavior. Instead of studying subjects in the laboratory, however, we observe them in a natural setting. This approach has greater external validity. For instance, Blais and Bacher (2007) used a clever field experiment to study the effects of threats of punishment on economic crimes. They used real claimants from four Canadian insurance companies as subjects. Each claimant was randomly assigned to either an experimental group or a control group. Subjects in the control group were exposed to each company's normal claim procedures; whereas subjects in the experimental group received a deterrent letter in the mail that emphasized the illegality of padding insurance claims (i.e., claiming more than the value actually lost) and the company's intent to prosecute false claims. To ensure that it had actually been read, the deterrent letter required the claimant to sign the form and to mail it back to the company. As the researchers predicted, the written deterrent significantly reduced the monetary amount claimed by subjects, saving the insurance companies an average of $300.00 per claim.

This approach illustrates the advantages of the field experiment. It would be difficult to set up a laboratory situation that would be a credible representation of "an economic crime." However, field experiments also have certain limitations. One potential problem is that the researcher often has little control over choice of participants in the experiment: Whoever submitted a claim to one of the four companies was included. Thus, samples might not be random. We could also have more difficulty specifying the characteristics of these samples than we do in a laboratory experiment, where we are usually able to get more information about subject variables. Assigning subjects in the field to treatment conditions at random provides some control for subject variables, but we are usually less able to control extraneous variables in a field setting.

Field experiments also can be used to validate findings obtained in the laboratory. If results under controlled laboratory conditions have some degree of external validity, we should observe similar outcomes when we study behavior in more realistic settings. Remember the discussion of equity theory in Chapter 6? Greenberg (1988) conducted a field experiment in the workplace to test equity theory in a real-life setting. Employees of a large company were randomly assigned, temporarily, to other offices while their own offices were being renovated. They were assigned to use the offices of coworkers of higher, lower, or equal status. According to equity theory, the reward value of the status of the offices should create increases, decreases, or no change in performance, depending on which type of office was assigned. To maintain equity, those assigned to higher-status offices should increase their performance; those assigned to lower-status offices should decrease their performance; those assigned to equal-status offices should maintain their current performance levels. That is exactly what happened. By conducting a field experiment testing equity theory, Greenberg was able to demonstrate the theory's external validity. He was also able to expand the theory to include outcomes that were not monetary. A further extension of the validation process would be to evaluate findings in the context of ongoing behavior, without experimental intervention. This takes us back to one of the basic methods of gathering psychological data—naturalistic observation.

### *Naturalistic Observation*

Miller (1977) has advocated for the application of naturalistic observation in psychological research. In particular, he suggested, "naturalistic observation can be used to validate or add substance to previously obtained laboratory findings" (p. 214). Miller also suggested that the process of laboratory research and naturalistic observation can be used in a complementary way. We can use naturalistic observation to suggest specific hypotheses about behavior and then test those hypotheses under the controlled conditions of the laboratory. We can return to the naturalistic setting to verify our findings.

The important implication of Miller's statement is this: Although we often think of the experiment as a unique, perhaps isolated method of research, we can use it to best advantage in combination with other modes of research. Psychologists try to discover principles and applications that will ultimately benefit humanity. Most of us do not live in laboratories, so our research must have some link to everyday life. Psychologists can strengthen that link by using a variety of research methods in combination. In this way, they can maintain precision without sacrificing relevance.

# HANDLING A NONSIGNIFICANT OUTCOME

Until now, we have approached the problems of interpreting data from a fairly optimistic perspective. We have more or less assumed that the results we are trying to evaluate were statistically significant and that they supported the predictions. But suppose we have run a well-planned experiment that did not work: Our predictions were not confirmed; our treatment means are embarrassingly similar. Can anything be gained from such an experiment?

Research journals give the impression that all experiments yield significant results. Unfortunately, we do not see all the studies carried out that did not make it into print. The occasional negative outcome reported in the literature is there because that outcome has implications for a theoretical position that predicts there should be significant differences. In reality, many studies do not turn out exactly the way the researcher expected.

If you ran an experiment and your results were not significant, don't be discouraged; even the best researchers have an occasional failure. One of the characteristics of a good researcher is that he or she uses nonsignificant findings in a constructive way. A good researcher asks, "Why didn't things go as expected?" and uses the answers to generate better studies. If your experiment did not support your predictions, you should evaluate it from two perspectives. First, were the procedures right? Second, was the hypothesis reasonable?

## Faulty Procedures

We might not confirm our predictions because our procedures were faulty. Of course, we are always on the lookout for confounding. For instance, we could have inadvertently allowed control subjects a little more practice time, which compensated for the effects of the special training procedures used in the experimental condition. Review everything you did. Did you apply all the appropriate control procedures? Did you use random assignment? Counterbalancing? Are there problems with demand characteristics or experimenter bias?

Another possibility is that although there were no confounding variables in the experiment, numerous uncontrolled variables increased the amount of variability between individual subjects' scores. If there was a lot of uncontrolled variability in scores on the dependent measure, treatment effects might not have been detectable. Perhaps your reading of the instructions varied from time to time. Maybe some of the subjects were recruited in a Laundromat, whereas others came from a nightclub or an office. Perhaps your measuring instrument was unreliable, or perhaps there were scoring errors by experimenters. Even though the effects of these variables tend to "randomize out" across treatment conditions, they still have the net effect of increasing the amount of within-groups or error variance, making it more difficult to find a significant difference between conditions.

If we happen to be studying an independent variable that has a relatively weak effect, we could be in trouble. Our experimental manipulation might not be powerful enough to override the effect of all the other sources of variation in the experiment. We could be attempting to find a needle in a haystack. We might be unable to reject the null hypothesis even though the independent variable had an effect—that is, we might be making a Type 2 error. You can also see that when an experiment produces a large error variance, statistical conclusion validity is lowered. In this case, a decision not to reject the null hypothesis based on the results of the statistical test could be an invalid conclusion.

When you get null findings, always ask yourself whether your sample was large enough. It can be difficult to get statistically significant effects using very small samples unless your treatment effects are very strong. You might simply not have had enough power in your statistical test if only a small number of subjects were used. Low power reduces the statistical conclusion validity and can produce a Type 2 error. The technique for assessing power can be found in Cohen (1988) and many statistics textbooks. Keep in mind that Type 2 errors can occur; failing to reject the null hypothesis does not mean that the null hypothesis is necessarily correct. Even if your experiment failed to support your research hypothesis, a subsequent experiment might.

Another possible cause of null results is that the experimental manipulation was inadequate: The independent variable might have had a powerful effect if we had defined treatment levels in a better way. Our "hungry" rats were deprived of food for only 6 hours; perhaps 24 hours would have been more effective. We instructed our experimental subjects to form mental images of each of the words shown on a computer monitor; perhaps our control subjects did the same even though we didn't tell them to. Better procedures might be needed. Of course, the only way to verify these possibilities is by running new experiments.

We also look for problems in the way we measured the dependent variable. Did we measure what we intended? Was the measure reliable and valid? Suppose we are trying to assess the effect of different camera angles on the sexual appeal of photographs. We ask subjects to rate a series of photographs, some of which are mildly erotic. Subjects' ratings could be contaminated by their need to give socially desirable responses. We could end up measuring social desirability rather than the true appeal of the photos.

Always check to see if subjects used the full range of scores on the dependent variable. If scores on the dependent variable are too restricted, finding significance can be extremely difficult. If most of your subjects use only the top (or bottom) ratings on your scale, there will be little or no variability caused by treatment, so your results are not likely to be significant. Imagine you are an ice cream maker for Ben & Jerry's. You want to compare your new version of chocolate cherry fudge with the old version. You invite people to taste the old or the new version and rate how much they like it on a scale from 0 (not at all) to 10 (very much). The old version gets all 10s (because it is really good). The new version tastes even better, but it gets all 10s, too,

INCONCLUSIVE EXPERIMENT:
PAVLOV'S CAT

because your scale doesn't allow people to discriminate between, say, very good and scrumptious! When subjects tend to "top out" on the scale, it is called a *ceiling effect*. The same thing can occur if people only use the bottom of the range; then it is called a *floor effect*.

If the experimental procedures or measures are faulty, we have not made a valid test of our hypothesis. The best time to deal with faulty procedures is before running the experiment. It seems easy enough to formulate after-the-fact explanations: "I did not get significant results because there were flies in the room when I tested my experimental group." Well, maybe.

No one enjoys coming to the end of a data analysis only to find no significant differences between the treatment groups—all that work and so little to show for it! At best, it is disappointing. Perhaps, to save face, we sometimes get caught up in attempts to explain that what we did was fine; we designed sound procedures that were internally valid. Was it our fault that a fire drill was called in the middle of the experiment? Of course not. But few of us like to consider the possibility that the experiment was doomed from the start.

### Faulty Hypothesis

When we evaluate the outcome of an experiment, we must look at it from the standpoint of all of the internal components we have discussed. Besides procedural aspects, we want to be sure that the experiment represents good thinking. If we have what seems to be a flawless procedure for studying a hypothesis, if we have executed the experiment carefully and the results are not significant, we must at least consider the possibility that the hypothesis was faulty. We will need to go back and rethink the problem. Perhaps we overlooked some key feature of prior studies; perhaps our reasoning was confused. The good researcher uses this evaluation process to decide where to go next.

Be cautious in drawing conclusions from nonsignificant results. Researchers often find themselves in a quandary when their results are *almost* statistically significant, for instance, when $p < .10$. Claiming the experiment "almost worked" or the data were "almost significant" is simply not convincing, even if the probability value is close to being significant. When the obtained $p$ value is higher than the significance level we selected, we should consider that the null hypothesis might actually be correct. Generally speaking, we treat as new knowledge *only* statistically significant disconfirmations of the null hypothesis. Consider the possibility that the hypothesis needs to be reworked. Use what you learned in this experiment to plan a better one the next time.

This chapter has presented the major factors that need to be considered when experimental findings are interpreted and conclusions are drawn. In the final chapter of the text, we will learn how to present these interpretations and conclusions in a research report.

## SUMMARY

Some of the problems we encounter in evaluating and drawing conclusions from the results of an experiment have to do with whether or not an experiment is internally and externally valid. An experiment that is internally valid is free of confounding. In evaluating the internal validity of an experiment, the researcher needs to consider both the plan for running the experiment and what actually happened. A *manipulation check* can determine whether the independent variable was manipulated as intended. If extraneous variables affected the results, however, the findings might not be interpretable. The classic threats to internal validity are always potential confounding variables that should be considered. Researchers always need to be open to the possibility of other explanations for their findings. Inferences about the relationship between independent and dependent variables must have *statistical conclusion validity*, too. Some statistically significant results might not be very meaningful; calculating the effect size of significant statistical values is one way to estimate the usefulness of treatment effects.

An experiment is externally valid if the results can be extended to other situations with accuracy. Inductive thinking can be used to generalize from the results of the particular experiment to broader principles and implications. To be externally valid, an experiment must first be internally valid. External validity is a continuum rather than an either/or situation; some studies have greater external validity than others. Findings that are externally valid can be replicated. They can be extended to different samples of subjects and to the larger population. Externally valid findings can also be extended to different experimental procedures and, perhaps, to different operational definitions of the variables.

A major part of interpreting research involves placing it in the context of prior work. Knowledge advances in small steps. If findings are consistent with prior work, we discuss how they extend our knowledge. Or, if findings are inconsistent with prior studies, the discrepancy must be explained. These inconsistencies may form the basis of new experiments.

Externally valid results can also have implications outside the experimental setting; however, it is usually difficult to make this determination within the context of a single study. Researchers use at least five approaches to increase as well as verify the degree of external validity of their findings: aggregation of data, multivariate designs, nonreactive measures, field experiments, and naturalistic observation. Data can be *aggregated*, or combined, over subjects, stimuli, or situations (as in a meta-analysis). Findings can also be verified through multiple trials or testing occasions and by measuring outcomes through more than one measuring instrument. *Multivariate designs* test multiple dependent variables and can be analyzed using a *MANOVA*. Researchers also try to decrease *reactivity* in their studies; they measure behavior in such a way that the outcome will not be affected by subjects' reactions to the experiment. Reactivity can be reduced by controlling demand characteristics and by using *unobtrusive measures*. Conducting a *field experiment* is another means of increasing external validity. Finally, researchers may confirm the validity of laboratory findings through *naturalistic observation*. Using research methods in combination is another fruitful way to study behavior.

There is also the practical dilemma of dealing with nonsignificant findings. Experimental procedures must always be reviewed for sources of internal invalidity, such as uncontrolled extraneous variables. Low statistical power and weak manipulation of the independent variable need to be considered. Finally, the thinking that led to the hypothesis should be reviewed to be sure the predictions were reasonable.

## KEY TERMS

**Aggregation** The grouping together and averaging of data gathered in various ways, including aggregation over subjects, over stimuli and/or situations, over trials and/or occasions, and over measures.

**Field experiment** An experiment conducted outside the laboratory that is used to increase external validity, verify earlier laboratory findings, and investigate problems that cannot be studied successfully in the laboratory.

Manipulation check An assessment to determine whether the independent variable was manipulated successfully.

Multivariate analysis of variance (MANOVA) The statistical procedure used to study the impact of independent variables on two or more dependent variables; an extension of analysis of variance.

Multivariate design Research design or statistical procedure used to evaluate the effects of many dependent variables in combination, including multiple correlation, factor analysis, and multivariate analysis of variance.

Naturalistic observation A descriptive, nonexperimental method of observing behaviors as they occur spontaneously in natural settings.

Reactivity The tendency of subjects to alter their responses or behaviors when they are aware of the presence of an observer.

Statistical conclusion validity The degree to which conclusions about a treatment effect can be drawn from the statistical results obtained.

Unobtrusive measure A procedure used to assess subjects' behaviors without their knowledge; used to obtain more nonreactive data.

## REVIEW AND STUDY QUESTIONS

1. Discuss three potential sources for decreasing the internal invalidity in an experiment. How would you control each one?

2. How does internal validity affect the conclusions that may be drawn from the results of an experiment?

3. What are the eight classic threats to internal validity presented in Chapter 7? Why are they potential confounds?

4. What factors influence statistical conclusion validity?

5. What do we mean when we say that results can be significant but not meaningful? What is a good approach for judging how meaningful an effect is?

6. What is external validity?

7. An experiment that is not internally valid cannot be externally valid. Why?

8. Why is replicability a requirement for external validity?

9. Explain how we use inductive thinking to extend the findings of an experiment beyond the particular study.

10. What issues affect the decision to generalize the findings of an experiment to other samples of subjects? To other populations?

11. The operational definition of a given variable may be changed from one experiment to another. Explain how and why this change of definition affects the generality of research findings.

12. In writing up a research report, a psychologist concluded by saying, "These results prove my hypothesis. They provide conclusive evidence that working crossword puzzles improves vocabulary." Without knowing the details of the researcher's procedures, what could you say about each of the following:
   a. Assuming that the findings are statistically significant, are the researcher's conclusions justified? Explain.
   b. Assume that several researchers have conducted similar experiments. The previous findings have been inconclusive. What can be said about the conclusion in view of prior research?
   c. Given your answers to (a) and (b), reword the experimenter's conclusions appropriately.
   d. If you chose to conduct a similar study, what extraneous variables might affect the internal validity of the experiment?
   e. Explain how aggregation could be used to broaden the implications of these findings.

13. What are multivariate procedures? How can they be used to increase the external validity of an experiment?

14. How does the reactivity of subjects influence the external validity of an experiment? Discuss three techniques for reducing reactivity.

15. Deanna is not quite sure how to interpret the results of an experiment she did. She found that her data were almost significant ($p < .07$). What advice would you give her about explaining her findings?

## CRITICAL THINKING EXERCISE

*The myth:* Warning labels on food help consumers to make better food choices.

*The scientific findings:* They can backfire. Bushman (1998) found that laboratory subjects more frequently chose to eat full-fat cream cheese (rather than low-fat or no-fat cream cheese) when it was labeled as a high-fat food than when it wasn't. The author believes that warning labels can engender "reactance" (opposition produced by feelings that our behavior is being constrained), causing increased consumption of the very foods about which we are being warned.

*The problem:* If we can generalize this result, it could be an important health finding. Describe several ways you could increase the external validity of the study.

## ONLINE RESOURCES

You can find workshops to review concepts from this chapter at:

http://www.wadsworth.com/psychology_d/templates/student_resources/workshops/workshops.html

For an interesting look at eyewitness identification problems and DNA evidence, try

www.innocenceproject.org/fix/Eyewitness-Identification.php

## CHAPTER 16

# Writing the Research Report

**The Written Report: Purpose and Format**

**Major Sections**
Title
Abstract
Introduction
Method
Results
Discussion
References

**Looking at a Journal Article**
General Orientation
A Sample Journal Article

**Preparing Your Manuscript: Procedural Details**

**Making Revisions**

SUMMARY
KEY TERMS
REVIEW AND STUDY QUESTIONS
CRITICAL THINKING EXERCISE
ONLINE RESOURCES

## CHAPTER OBJECTIVES

- Learn techniques for scientific writing
- Learn the components of each section of an APA style research report
- Learn to write a research report using a sample journal article as a guide
- Learn the differences between published and typed versions of a report

Report writing is a major part of the research process. In this chapter, we will discuss the purpose and structure of psychological research reports. As you know, the overall structure of this textbook parallels the general structure of these reports. In each report, we find an Introduction, a Method section, a Results section, and a Discussion. Each report also has an abstract or summary and a list of references. We will begin by reviewing the basic content of each section. Then we will look at an example of a published research article to see how these ideas are put into practice. We will also focus on specific aspects of preparing the manuscript of a report and on points that frequently cause problems for beginners.

---

## THE WRITTEN REPORT: PURPOSE AND FORMAT

The primary purpose of a written report is communication. Through our report, we tell others what we did and what we found. In addition to reporting findings, we provide enough information to enable other researchers to make a critical evaluation of procedures and a reasonable judgment about the quality of the experiment. In addition, we want to provide enough information to enable others to replicate and extend the findings.

Research reports are written in a scientific writing style. You have probably noticed that the writing style in published articles seems fact-filled, highly structured, and more concise than other kinds of writing. This is deliberate. The goal of an experimental report is to provide objective information—not to entertain the reader, express opinions, or talk about personal life experiences. Even so, the writing should be interesting and lively.

You already know that all facts need to be documented by citing the published sources where you read about them. When you write a research report, you must also avoid seeming opinionated about your topic. Try to keep your personal feelings out of the report; it is a scientific document for public communication, not an essay or personal statement. Most authors will avoid personal pronouns like *I* or *we* whenever possible (their occasional use is acceptable, though, to avoid awkward sentences).

The scientific style is also parsimonious—the author attempts to give complete information in as few words as possible. Because the amount of publication space in journals is limited, authors write as concisely as possible, selecting their words carefully. Each word is chosen for its precision. (Yes, scientific writers use the dictionary and thesaurus a lot.) Do not be surprised if your instructor crosses out many words (particularly adjectives and adverbs) or even whole sentences in your report. Beginning writers typically use many more words than necessary. Most of us need practice to write scientifically because it is very different from more common styles of writing. If you can avoid writing any sentences that seem flowery, you will be on your way to a scientific writing style. Always avoid slang; it lacks exact meaning and might not be universally familiar.

When you write your research report, be careful to use unbiased language. The American Psychological Association (APA), the Association for Psychological Science (APS), and other publishers of psychological research reports are committed to encouraging language free of gender and ethnic bias in their publications. There are several techniques for avoiding bias: When writing about ethnic groups, for example, use the term that is currently preferred by most members of that group. For example, the terms "White," "Black," (or "African American"), "American Indian" (or "Native American"), "Mexican American," (or "Hispanic") and "Asian American" are most often found in contemporary usage to describe common American racial and ethnic groups. If known, you can specify the country of origin, such as "Chinese American" or "Cuban American" or the Native American tribe (e.g., Hopi, Seminole, etc.). Race or ethnicity should only be included if it is relevant to the study.

Always use nonsexist language. Whenever you are writing about individuals (research participants, people in general), select words that are free of gender bias. Because some sexist words are so embedded in our language, this can seem awkward at first.[1] For example, do not talk about the benefits of psychological research for "man" or "mankind" when you really mean "all people"—say "people" instead. Don't refer to a participant as "he" (unless all your participants really were male); use "he or she" or "they" instead. If you use "he or she," however, do so sparingly or the usage becomes distracting to readers. Never alternate between "he or she" and "she or he," because that is especially distracting. Never use contrived contractions, like "s/he," or "he/she," which suggest that the genders are interchangeable. When discussing people of both genders, most experienced researchers try to construct gender-free sentences instead. Often, just pluralizing the sentence can take care of the problem. Instead of saying, "When a subject arrived, *he* was ... ," say, "When subjects arrived, *they* were ... ," and so forth. Never assume that a researcher is male; at least 50% of those currently graduating with PhDs in psychology are women. More hints are given in Table 16.1.

---

[1] McMinn, Williams, and McMinn (1994, experiment 3) found that identification of sexist language was improved after training. Psychologists feel that it is important to make these language changes because a number of experiments have demonstrated that gender-biased language reinforces sexist attitudes and behaviors (e.g., Gastil, 1990; Silveira, 1980).

TABLE **16.1**

Usage of gender-related terms

| Nonpreferred | Preferred |
|---|---|
| 1. … 40 males and 42 females | … 40 men and 42 women |
| *("Male" and "female" are adjectives [e.g., 42 female teachers]; instead, use "men" and "women" for individuals age 18 and over; "boys" and "girls" or "children" can be used for individuals under the age of 12; and "male adolescents," "female adolescents," or "young men" and "young women" can be used for young people through age 17.)* | |
| 2. Some sex differences occurred … | Some gender differences occurred … |
| *(Use "sex" to describe biologically based differences; use "gender" to refer to men and women as cultural or social groups. The term "gender" is most often preferred.)* | |
| 3. … 40 female doctors; 30 male nurses … | … 40 doctors; 30 nurses … |
| *(Do not specify gender unless gender is a variable; e.g., "The experiment compared 40 female doctors and 40 male doctors …")* | |
| 4. chairman | chair or chairperson |
| 5. mothering | parenting, caregiving (or specify the behaviors) |
| 6. manpower | workforce, personnel, staff |

© Cengage Learning

Avoid other kinds of language with negative overtones. Do not call lesbians and gay men "homosexuals." Use nonhandicapping language when referring to people with mental or physical disabilities. Referring to your participants as "20 people diagnosed with obsessive-compulsive disorder" is much better than saying "20 obsessive-compulsives." Describing them as "persons diagnosed with mental illness" is much preferred to "mentally ill people." Similarly, don't use the name of a physical disability to characterize a person. Saying "a person living with paraplegia" is much better than saying "a paraplegic." Also avoid using the terms "elderly" and "senior," which have negative connotations; instead, say "older adults" and give the actual age range (e.g., "between the ages of 71 and 86").

One of the most common pitfalls of a first report is taking too much for granted. After you have worked on a study for some time, what you did might seem completely obvious. The problem is that an element that seems obvious to you might not be obvious to your readers unless you explain it. Remember that the whole point of writing a report is to communicate information. A reader should be able to understand what you did and why simply by reading the report.

Psychological reports are expected to follow the format set by APA. It is presented in detail in the sixth edition of the *Publication Manual of the American Psychological Association* (2010), which was prepared to make the job of reporting easier for researchers as well as readers. As early as 1928, psychologists and other social scientists recognized the need for standards for presenting research data. The first "manual" was a 7-page article that appeared in *Psychological Bulletin* in 1929. The present manual is almost 300 pages long and contains material on all aspects of appropriate content as well as detailed explanations of specific layout and style requirements. Our presentation here will be brief; if you have questions about specific problems, you should refer to the manual.

The need for a standard format for reports becomes clear when you consider the tremendous volume of research going on today. The APA alone publishes nearly 60 journals, which translates to several thousand articles per year. Even more are published in the many non-APA psychology journals. Many thousands more are reviewed and not accepted for publication.[2] If everyone used a different format for writing reports, reviewers would have a much harder time evaluating the work, writers would agonize over its presentation, and readers would have trouble locating the information they need. The place for creativity is the design of your experiment, not the format of your report, which should conform to APA standards. Even though some details of format vary slightly from one journal to another, most follow the overall structure outlined here.

When you prepare the manuscript of your research report, some of the format requirements will seem strange at first. That is because the format has been designed with publishers, as well as readers, in mind. It simply makes the job of translating a written report into a published article easier. In the last section of this chapter, you will learn these procedural details. You will see that the manuscript version of a research report does not look exactly like the published version. But let us first look at what goes into the major sections of the report.

## MAJOR SECTIONS

Every research report must contain these major components: a title, an abstract, an Introduction, a Method section, a Results section, a Discussion section, and a list of references. We will look at each section in turn so that you will have a clear idea of the basic requirements of each. Many reports contain additional features, such as footnotes, tables, figures (graphs, pictures, or drawings), or an appendix. For now, we will focus on the content of the major sections. Try to develop a feel for what each section accomplishes. Later, we will look at layout requirements and additional components.

### Title

Reports need a descriptive Title that gives readers an idea of what the report is about. The simplest way to achieve this goal is by including both the independent and dependent variables of the study in the title, stating the

---

[2] Most high-quality journals reject 70% to 85% of all the articles that are submitted (a few reject even more).

relationship between them. Here are some examples from articles we have discussed in previous chapters:

(1) Negative Ions and Behavior: Impact on Mood, Memory, and Aggression Among Type A and Type B Persons (Baron, Russell, & Arms, 1985).
(2) Anxiety, Fear, and Social Affiliation (Sarnoff & Zimbardo, 1961).
(3) Social Enhancement and Impairment of Performance in the Cockroach (Zajonc, Heingartner, & Herman, 1969).

When testing a theory, you may want to include it as part of the title:

(4) An Attributional Explanation for the Effect of Audience Laughter on Perceived Funniness" (Lawson, Downing, & Cetola, 1998).

Titles like "A Psychological Experiment" or "An Experiment on Music" are far too vague to help a reader who is trying to track down specific information. The recommended title length, however, is 12 words or less, so titles must be concise.

## Abstract

An Abstract is a summary of the report. The length of the summary will vary for different journals, but typically it ranges from 150 to 250 words. Write the abstract in the same general style you use in the report, and write it in the past tense (because the research has already happened). The abstract should be a concise synopsis of the experiment, written so that it makes sense and can stand by itself. It should contain a statement of the problem studied, the method, the results, and the conclusions. Unless you are replicating a specific published experiment, leave out citations. Begin the abstract by describing the problem you are investigating. Include important characteristics of the subjects you used; for example, "Participants were 40 male and 40 female students (mean age = 18.6 years) from a large west-coast university." Summarize the procedures used in the experiment and important features of the methodology (e.g., survey, case study, experiment, etc.), and briefly state the *major* findings. Include significance levels and/or confidence intervals and effect sizes. You should also state the important and interesting conclusions you reached.

At this point you may be thinking, "All that in 150 words? You must be kidding!" Actually, we're quite serious. But it might help you to know that abstracts are notoriously difficult to write—they require a technique few of us practice very often. For that reason, most people find it easiest to write the abstract after they write the report. Keep in mind that the abstract is a very important part of the research report because it will appear in searchable online databases like PsycINFO and in all the other abstract sources that are the guides to the literature in psychology. You will recall that we discussed these sources in Chapter 6 when you learned how to conduct a literature search.

The abstract is probably the most frequently read portion of any article. If the abstract is poor, uninteresting, or uninformative, readers might not go on to read the entire article. That is why it is especially important to include all the pertinent facts of an experiment in the abstract. Good abstracts make our research more accessible to our readers. Good titles do the same because the title determines how an article will be indexed in PsycINFO and other sources. When you are using abstracts in your review of the research literature, you are also preparing for the next major section of your research report, the Introduction.

## Introduction

The Introduction of your research report sets the stage for what follows. A good introduction tells readers what you are doing and why: It introduces your hypothesis and how you will test it. As you write your introduction, think about what readers should get out of it. Your focus should be the experiment's hypothesis. After reading the introduction, readers should have answers to the following questions: What problem are you studying? Why is it important? What does the prior literature in the area say about the problem? What is your hypothesis? What thinking led up to that hypothesis? What is the overall plan for testing the hypothesis?

An introduction usually begins with a description of the general topic area your research falls under (for instance, aggression or anorexia). The description should provide evidence for the importance of studying your topic (APA, 2010; Pyrczak & Bruce, 2000). Some writers use a funnel analogy for writing an introduction: Begin with the broad topic area and gradually narrow the focus of your writing to the specific research question your experiment was designed to answer. The introduction includes a concise review of the research literature that led to your hypothesis or that lends support to it. For instance, you might show how prior findings have been inconsistent or ambiguous; then explain how your experiment might clarify the problem. It is not necessary to cite every bit of research that has ever been done in an area; cite only what is most essential to understanding the nature of the problem you investigated.

Be careful to show how you got to your hypothesis. Readers should be able to follow the thinking that took you there. Do not assume that anything is obvious, but remember that you are writing for an audience that is probably already familiar with your research area, so an exhaustive review of the literature is unnecessary. Be careful about citations. Cite all articles that the background experiments for your hypothesis came from, as well as any source from which you obtained your ideas. APA uses the author-year format for citations. Formats for citations are shown in Table 16.2.

State your hypothesis explicitly in the introduction. Usually it appears toward the end, after you have explained the research and the thinking behind it. Identifying independent and dependent variables is appropriate. You may then want to say something about general procedures if that seems warranted. You might also want to include a sentence or two about operational definitions to prepare readers for what follows in the next section of the report. If you have made predictions about the outcome of the study, state them specifically here. Be sure you explain why you expect these results; do not expect readers to guess what you are thinking. By the time they have finished reading the introduction, readers should be prepared for the Method section.

TABLE **16.2**
Reference citations

1. A single author:
   In her study of consent forms, Mann (1994) compared beliefs of people …
   or
   One recent study of consent forms (Mann, 1994) compared beliefs of people …
2. Two authors:
   In their classic book on quasi-experimental designs, Campbell and Stanley (1966) described several …
   or
   The classic book on quasi-experimental designs (Campbell & Stanley, 1966) contains descriptions of several …
   *(Note that the word "and" is used to link authors within the text of a sentence, whereas an ampersand, &, is used when the entire citation is within parentheses.)*
3. Three, four, or five authors:
   *First time cited—*
   Baron, Russell, and Arms (1985) found an interaction between …
   or
   One negative ion study (Baron, Russell, & Arms, 1985) found an interaction between …
   *Subsequent citations—*
   Baron et al. (1985) found an interaction between …
   or
   One negative ion study (Baron et al., 1985) found an interaction between …
4. Six or more authors:
   According to Aronson et al. (1999), a stereotype for men's mathematics skills …
   or
   In one study of stereotypes of men's mathematics skills (Aronson et al., 1999), the researchers found …
   *(Use the first author et al. form each time the reference is cited, but be sure to list the first six authors in the References section; additional authors are replaced by et al.)*
5. Two or more works in the same citation:
   A smile may have multiple meanings (Fridlund, 1989; Fridlund, Ekman, & Oster, 1987).
   *(List all citations in alphabetical order by first author; separate each citation by a semicolon. If there is more than one citation by the same author(s) in a single year, the citations are designated as a , b,… and separated by a comma (as in Rothbart, 2003a, 2003b).*
6. To cite a quotation or specific aspect of text:
   Baron, Russell, and Arms (1985, p. 748) gave the following explanation: "The interaction …"
   *(Include page number for direct quotations or when referring to specific text, e.g., chapter, figure, table, equation, etc.)*

## Method

The Method section tells readers how you went about doing the experiment. Here, you will describe the materials and procedures used during experimental sessions in enough detail to allow another researcher to replicate the experiment. The Method section is split into a number of separately labeled subsections. You should adjust the format and label the subsections according to the kind of study you are presenting. Some examples of subheadings are shown in Table 16.3. The Method section, however, typically begins with a subsection labeled participants (or subjects).

### Participants

This subsection explains the important characteristics of your sample. It should answer these key questions: How many participants did you have? What are their relevant characteristics (age, sex, species, weight, and so on)? How were participants recruited or selected? Were they paid or given course credit? Give any additional information that might be important to understanding your experiment. Remember that the reader will need to know the characteristics of your sample to assess the external validity of your results. (If you need to, refer back to the detailed section on reporting samples in Chapter 4.) If any participants dropped out of the study, report that, too, and explain the circumstances.

### Measures

The Method section needs to include descriptions of the measures used for data collection (e.g., questionnaires, behavioral observations, interviews). If you created your own measuring instrument, describe the instrument and include sample items in the Method section; lengthy questionnaires are often placed in an appendix at the end of the report. If a standardized questionnaire is used, identify it by name and include a citation—for instance,

TABLE **16.3**

### Some recommended subheadings for the Method section

| | |
|---|---|
| Participants | Treatment(s) |
| Subjects | Independent variable(s) |
| Participants and design | Apparatus |
| Participants and procedure(s) | Stimuli |
| Measures | Design |
| Dependent variable(s) | Procedure(s) |
| Materials and procedure | Procedure and design |
| Materials | Procedure and materials |
| Manipulation(s) | Specific variable name(s)* |

*It is very common to use the name of the independent or dependent variable(s) as a subheading

© Cengage Learning

"Subjects filled out the Social Desirability Scale (Crowne & Marlowe, 1964)." Also include a brief description of what the scale was designed to measure. You will also want to include information about the reliability and validity of your measuring instruments, if available, and describe any methods you used to augment reliability and validity (e.g., training of observers, training in content analysis procedures, or pilot testing of questionnaires). Also describe your computer equipment and software programs if data collection is computerized.

### Manipulations

Describe the content of treatments or interventions utilized in each condition of the experiment (including control conditions). You may want to include the exact instructions you gave to participants, particularly if the instructions constituted your experimental manipulation. Otherwise, simply summarize them. If they are lengthy, use an appendix.

If you built your own equipment or prepared your own stimulus figures, an illustration or sample items will probably need to be included. If your equipment or materials are extremely complex, you can include a complete description in an appendix. You should refer to any ready-made, specialized equipment by name, manufacturer, size, and model number—for example, "The happy, sad, fearful, and angry film clips were presented on a wall-mounted Sony BRAVIA® 40-inch LCD HDTV, model KDL-40Z5100." Be sure to provide all the information essential for replication, including physical dimensions like length, width, and color, if appropriate. Unless another measure is standard (e.g., inches are used for TV screens in the United States), always give measurements in metric units, such as centimeters and meters.

You will also need to provide readers with a clear description of all the procedures followed in your experiment. Include information on how subjects were assigned to the different groups in the experiment (e.g., random assignment, selected by scores on a personality test, etc.). Describe the experimental setting, the number of trials, exposures or treatments, and the duration of the treatments. After reading this section, a person should be able to carry out the experiment just as you did. "Participants were seated in a chair located approximately 3.85 m from the television screen. There was a 1-min rest period between film clips."[3] Any special control procedures you used should be identified here—for instance, "To control for order effects, the film clips were presented in counterbalanced order." By the end of the Procedure section, readers should be able to identify the kind of research design you have.

### Design

If your experimental design is not easily understood by reading the procedures, consider the option of including a subsection called *Design*. If you have chosen a complex factorial design, for instance, it can be very helpful to the reader if you include a design statement with the factor labels (as you

---

[3] Units of measurement and some measures of time, such as "minutes," have standardized abbreviations (see APA guidelines, 2010, Chapter 4); minute (and minutes) is abbreviated as *min*.

learned in Chapter 10). For instance, in a 6 × 4 × 3 factorial design, write out the factor names along with the design. Specify whether the design was between subjects, within subjects, or mixed—for example, "The experiment was a 6 × 4 × 3 (Reinforcement × Food Deprivation × Age) between-subjects factorial design." In mixed designs, you will need to specify the within- and between-subjects factors because they might not be obvious to the reader. For example, if reinforcement had been a within-subjects factor in this experiment, you could say, "Level of reinforcement was a within-subjects factor; food deprivation and age were between-subjects factors." As the design becomes more complicated, readers usually need more explicit help in structuring the plan of the experiment.[4] Do what makes the most sense to clarify your study. Finally, specify the dependent variable: "The dependent variable was the amount of time it took to learn the maze."

## Results

The Results section of a report should tell readers what statistical procedures you used and what you found. Describe the statistical tests you used to evaluate the data, along with the obtained values of test statistics. Indicate degrees of freedom and significance levels. Be sure that you have stated all group means included in important findings (or cell frequencies for nominal variables).[5] Some measure of group variability (typically, the standard deviation, $SD$) is required whenever you are reporting values of $F$ or $t$. You should also state the significance level you selected, typically, $p < .05$. Remember that we usually do not report individual scores unless we have a small $N$ design.

Recall from Chapter 13 that in addition to reporting the results of null hypothesis significance tests, the APA guidelines now require reporting effect sizes and confidence intervals for statistically significant results. Use a single confidence level (either 95% or 99%) throughout.

Here is an example. Suppose a student researcher replicated a prior finding from the literature (Greeson & Williams, 1986) that violent music videos can increase people's acceptance of violent behavior. The student conducted an experiment testing the effects of watching either violent or nonviolent music videos on subjects' attitudes toward violence. She designed a questionnaire to measure attitudes toward violence; the higher the score, the more accepting an individual was of violent behavior. A between-subjects $t$ test showed that the prediction was confirmed by her experiment, and she was able to reject the null hypothesis at $p < .05$. She could report her results like this:

> An alpha level of .05 was selected. A $t$ test for independent groups was used to test the hypothesis that attitudes toward violence would be more positive after viewing

---

[4] If the design is fairly straightforward from a written description of the procedures, some researchers prefer to state the design factors in the first paragraph of the Results section as part of the description of the statistical analysis. For example, you might find a statement like this: "A 6 × 4 × 3 (Reinforcement × Food Deprivation × Age) between-subjects ANOVA was conducted on the maze running data."

[5] When reporting means in journal articles, we use the abbreviation $M$ instead of $\overline{X}$; for example, a group mean would be reported as $M = 7.89$.

violent music videos than after viewing nonviolent ones. Results indicated that attitude scores were significantly different after violent videos than after nonviolent ones, $t(34) = 3.12$, $p < .01$, $r = .51$. Subjects who viewed a violent music video were more accepting of violence ($M = 7.89$, $SD = 2.10$, 95% CI [5.43, 9.86]) than were subjects who watched a nonviolent video ($M = 4.20$, $SD = 1.89$, 95% CI [2.34, 6.21]).

Notice that the effect size is reported right after the obtained statistical value and probability level. The means and standard deviations for each group are provided, followed by confidence intervals. Group means and confidence intervals can be reported either in the text or in a figure. There are no hard-and-fast rules for presenting statistics—as long as the presentation is complete and the results are clear to the reader.

In a simple two-group experiment, the Results section would probably not be very long. But if you have a factorial design, you will have more results to report (main effects, interactions, post hoc tests, and the like). If you have more than one dependent measure, you might want to present the results for each measure separately. You may split the Results section into subsections if you wish. As with the simpler experiment, report all the effects produced by your statistical tests and provide relevant summary data for each kind of effect. Typically, we report main effects first and then go on to the interaction(s). Finally, give the results of post hoc tests or other group comparisons if you used them. If the number of subjects in each group was not equal, report the cell sizes, and if data are missing, explain how cell sizes are affected. Be sure that the reader can understand one effect completely before going on to the next. If you have presented many statistics, it is helpful to the reader if you summarize the effects in words at some point. If you have conducted a manipulation check to verify that your treatment worked as intended, report these analyses also.

Sometimes results can be summarized most easily through figures or tables. A figure or table should enhance what you have to say about the data. Avoid reporting the same statistics or summary data in the text and in a table or graph. If your $F$ values, means, $SD$s, effect sizes, and CIs are presented in a table, simply refer the reader to the table at the appropriate time—for instance, "Results of the statistical tests and summary data are shown in Table 1." Never duplicate the same information in a table *and* a figure. Figures and tables must be referred to within the text and should be an integral part of the presentation. (Later in the chapter, you will learn how to include them in your written report.) The Results section is used only to present the objective data as they appeared in the experiment. Interpretation of the results belongs in the next section.

## Discussion

The overall purpose of the Discussion section is to evaluate your experiment and interpret the results. As you learned in the previous chapter, the discussion should tie things together for readers. In the Introduction, you reviewed the literature and showed readers how you arrived at your hypothesis and predictions. In the Method section, you described the details of what you did. In the Results section, you presented what you found. Now, in the Discussion you need to pull everything together. You need to explain what you have accomplished: Was your hypothesis supported? How do the findings fit in with prior research in the area? Are they consistent? If not, can any discrepancies be reconciled? What do your results add to current knowledge? The Discussion section is also the place to talk about what you think your results mean: What are the implications of the research? Can you generalize from the findings? Does further research suggest itself?

Begin the Discussion section with a clear summary sentence or two restating your results (in words only—no statistics), and explain whether the hypothesis was supported or not. For example,

> The results of the current experiment supported the hypothesis that exposure to violent music videos would produce greater acceptance of violent behavior. Subjects who watched music videos containing violence expressed significantly more positive attitudes toward violence than did subjects who watched music videos without any violence.

Then, go on to explain how your findings fit into what is already known about your topic. Explain how your findings are consistent (or inconsistent) with the most important findings from past studies that you talked about in your Introduction section.

> These results are consistent with the results of a number of other experiments reported in the literature. For example, [citation] also showed that ... In addition, [citation] found similar effects when subjects....

In contrast, if your results are not in agreement with findings reported by other researchers, try to explain why you believe your findings differed from theirs:

> The present findings, however, are inconsistent with those reported by [citation]. The present study demonstrated that...; whereas [citation] found that.... The most likely explanation for the inconsistency is that [citation] used a different procedure for ... Their procedure could have resulted in....

Any sources of confounding or problems with the experiment that might influence the interpretation of the data need to be reported. But be reasonable; it is not necessary to mention things that are probably irrelevant. Whether or not all subjects had breakfast probably is not critical, especially if you assigned them to conditions at random. However, if half the experimental subjects walked out on the experiment before it was over because they were faint from hunger, your readers should know that, as well as how that could have affected the data.

If your hypothesis was not supported, offer a plausible explanation if you can, but do not go overboard in offering excuses. Rethink both your procedures and your hypothesis if necessary. Apologies for small samples often lead to this common error: "If more subjects had been tested, the results probably would have been significant." Avoid being tempted to make something out of nonsignificant findings, even if they go in the direction you predicted. A trend in the right direction does not guarantee a significant outcome with a larger sample. Very small samples are unreliable; the trend could easily reverse itself if you had a larger sample! Running the experiment with more subjects is the only way to validate your hunch.

If you believe your study suggests a new theoretical model or has practical, real-world implications, you may say so here, but be humble about it. The results of a single study are rarely earth-shattering. If another study would clarify the findings, you can propose your idea for future research.

Keep in mind that when readers finish the Discussion section, they should have a sense of closure. They should know where you were going and why. They should know how you got there, what you found, and where it fits in the context of what was already known about the problem.

### References

Any articles or books mentioned in the report should be listed in your References section at the end. This list enables readers to go back and make their own evaluations of the literature. Be sure that the references are accurate and that they follow the most recent APA procedures for listing them (described later in the section on procedural details).

# LOOKING AT A JOURNAL ARTICLE

Now let us take a detailed look at the requirements of a research report by going through an actual journal article. We have selected an article that is relatively short; many journal articles are considerably longer. First, we will examine the basic content of the article; then we will look at the procedures to follow when preparing the manuscript. We will do this in separate steps just as you should when writing your own manuscript. Work on the content first, then put in the procedural details as you create your final draft. Keeping these stages separate will simplify your task. The article will appear on the following right-hand pages with our comments on the left-hand pages so that you can shift back and forth easily between the two.

### General Orientation

Journal articles are usually written for informed audiences. They are also written with strict constraints on the amount of space that can be devoted to any single topic. That is why you could find some articles difficult to follow unless you have already read somewhat extensively in the field. Therefore, before we launch into our examination of the sample article, let us review some general concepts you need to understand it.

The article (Gerend & Cullen, 2008) is a published report of an experiment testing the effects of message framing on the persuasiveness of an alcohol prevention message given to college students. Half the students received the message framed in terms of "gains," and half received the message framed in terms of "loss." The gain-framed message focused on the *advantages of stopping* risky drinking behaviors, whereas the loss-framed message focused on the *disadvantages of continuing* risky drinking behaviors. Based on the results from past research on message framing, the researchers hypothesized that a gain-framed message would be more persuasive than a loss-framed message in reducing problem drinking.

Using a factorial design, the researchers explored a second independent variable, called temporal context, in the same experiment. Temporal context refers to whether the messages focus on short-term or long-term consequences of the risky behavior. Some research suggests that messages focused on short-term consequences may be more persuasive than messages focused on consequences that are expected to occur further out in the future (even if the consequences being described are the same). The relationship between framing and temporal context, however, might be somewhat complex—gain-framed messages focused on long-term consequences of risky behaviors might tend to be discounted more than loss-framed messages, resulting in an interaction between the two factors.

Male and female undergraduates were randomly assigned to one of four experimental conditions (gain-framed messages with either short- or long-term consequences or loss-framed messages with either short- or long-term consequences). In the first session, subjects read one of the messages and then completed a survey asking about their perceptions of the message and how they felt about it. After about a month, they returned to the lab for a second session. This time they filled out a survey asking them to report on their use of alcohol during the past month, including questions about the frequency and quantity of alcohol consumption and binge drinking. As predicted, Gerend and Cullen found that when the messages focused on short-term consequences, gain-framed messages resulted in significantly lower reports of alcohol consumption and problem drinking than did loss-framed messages. But, when the messages focused on long-term consequences, the type of framing (gain vs. loss) did not matter.

## A Sample Journal Article[6]

( 1 ) *Title*

Note that the title, "Effects of Message Framing and Temporal Context on College Student Drinking Behavior," identifies the main focus of the study. Without reading any further, we have a good idea of what the researchers investigated.

( 2 ) *Names and Affiliation*

The authors' names are given as they would ordinarily be written; titles (Dr., Mr., Ms.) are not stated. The university, agency, or business affiliation of the authors is also listed.

( 3 ) *Abstract*

In published journal articles, the Abstract is conspicuously indented and set off by smaller type. Notice that the Abstract summarizes what was done and what was found; all the main points of the article are presented.

( 4 ) *Author Notes*

Author Notes always include contact information for the "corresponding author," the person to contact about the article. Author Notes also provide information about special circumstances—for instance, if the results were presented elsewhere or were part of a dissertation or thesis project. Author Notes also acknowledge special contributions such as support from granting organizations or individuals who facilitated the research.

( 5 ) *Introduction*

In a published article, the Introduction begins immediately after the Abstract. The Introduction is labeled in some psychology journals (as it is in this one), but not in others. In this section, the authors present the logic and background research that suggested this study. The general problem area is mentioned in the opening paragraphs—here, both independent variables are introduced. This is followed by a brief review of relevant published findings for message framing along with the theory that the authors use to explain them. In this case, the authors have chosen "prospect theory," which has been used by other researchers to explain differences in the effects of gain-framed vs. loss-framed health messages.

---

[6]From Gerend, M. A., & Cullen, M. (2008). Effects of message framing and temporal context on college student drinking behavior. *Journal of Experimental Social Psychology*, 44, 1167–1173. Copyright © 2008 Elsevier, Inc. Reprinted by permission.

Journal of Experimental Social Psychology 44 (2008) 1167–1173

Contents lists available at ScienceDirect

# Journal of Experimental Social Psychology

journal homepage: www.elsevier.com/locate/jesp

Reports

# Effects of message framing and temporal context on college student drinking behavior

Mary A. Gerend *, Margaret Cullen

*Department of Medical Humanities and Social Sciences, College of Medicine, Florida State University, 1115 W. Call Street, Tallahassee, FL 32306-4300, USA*

ARTICLE INFO

Article history:
Received 18 May 2007
Revised 22 February 2008
Available online 6 March 2008

Keywords:
Message framing
Temporal context
Alcohol
Risk behavior

ABSTRACT

This study evaluated the interactive effects of message framing and temporal context on college student alcohol use. Participants ($n = 228$) were randomly assigned to read an alcohol prevention message that varied by message frame (gains vs. losses) and temporal context (short- vs. long-term consequences). Participants returned to the lab one month later to report their drinking behavior over the past month. As predicted, students exposed to the gain-framed message reported lower alcohol use (drank less frequently, drank fewer alcoholic beverages per drinking occasion, and engaged in less binge drinking) as compared to students exposed to the loss-framed message, but only if they read about short-term consequences of alcohol use. Message frame had no effect when participants were exposed to long-term consequences. This investigation extends previous research by demonstrating the effectiveness of message framing for reducing health-damaging behaviors and by identifying temporal context as a moderator of framing effects.

© 2008 Elsevier Inc. All rights reserved.

## Introduction

People's choices are shaped by a number of important psychological processes. Many theories of judgment and decision-making suggest that choices are guided by consideration of the potential outcomes associated with one's actions (Edwards, 1962). Theories of message framing indicate that the manner in which these outcomes are framed—in terms of either potential losses or gains—can profoundly affect people's choices and behavior (Rothman, Bartels, Wlaschin, & Salovey, 2006; Rothman & Salovey, 1997). Indeed, numerous studies have demonstrated the effectiveness of framed messages for influencing decisions, particularly in the realm of health behavior (e.g., exercise, mammography, sunscreen use; Rothman et al., 2006).

The current research extends theories of message framing in two ways. First, although many studies have demonstrated the utility of message framing for promoting *positive* health behaviors, very few have examined its effectiveness for reducing unwanted health behaviors (e.g., binge drinking, cigarette smoking). The current study therefore examined whether message framing would provide a useful means of reducing a common and potentially health-damaging behavior—problem drinking among college students. Second, little is known about the ideal content of framed messages (Rothman et al., 2006). We were interested in assessing the possibility that framing effects depend on the temporal context

in which outcomes are considered—that is, whether a message highlights short- or long-term outcomes associated with a given behavior. In the current study, we evaluated the potentially interactive effects of framing and temporal context on college student alcohol use. We propose that messages emphasizing the immediate benefits of reducing risk behavior may prove to be an especially effective strategy for decreasing health-damaging behaviors such as problem drinking.

### Message framing

Message framing—providing equivalent outcome information in terms of either gains or losses—has proven to be an effective strategy for promoting behavior change across a wide range of health-related practices (Rothman & Salovey, 1997; Rothman et al., 2006). Gain-framed messages typically highlight the benefits of engaging in a health protective behavior or avoiding a risky behavior, whereas loss-framed messages highlight the costs of not engaging in a health protective behavior or engaging in a risky behavior. Message framing is theoretically grounded in prospect theory (Tversky & Kahneman, 1981), which suggests that people respond differently to information highlighting gains versus losses. Specifically, prospect theory holds that individuals are generally more willing to pursue a risky course of action when considering losses, but tend to be more risk averse when considering gains.

Drawing on prospect theory, Rothman and Salovey (1997) proposed that whether a gain- or loss-framed appeal will be more effective depends largely upon whether the recommended

* Corresponding author. Fax: +1 850 645 1773.
 *E-mail address:* mary.gerend@med.fsu.edu (M.A. Gerend).

*Introduction* (*continued*)

Notice the format for citing prior research illustrated by this sentence from the last paragraph of the *Message framing* section: "In both of these studies, gain-framed appeals emphasizing the benefits of smoking cessation were found to be more effective than loss-framed appeals emphasizing the costs of smoking in promoting anti-smoking beliefs and attitudes (Schneider, Pizarro, Pallonen, et al., 2001) and in encouraging stronger intentions to quit smoking (Steward, Schneider, Pizarro, & Salovey, 2003)."

When you describe the results of past research, you need to cite the author(s) and year of the study in which the results were published. All factual statements must carry citations of this type. To avoid plagiarism, full credit must be given to the source of ideas, procedures, or phrases. The full references will be listed at the end of the article.

In another section (*Temporal context*), the authors described what is known about short-term vs. long-term consequences and provided evidence from prior research to support the idea that health messages focused on short-term consequences are more persuasive than messages focused on long-term consequences. Next, a brief overview of the present study was provided, and the authors stated their hypotheses explicitly at the end of this section.

In the Introduction, the authors tell us (1) the problem area they are studying, (2) the pertinent facts about the problem area, and (3) how these facts relate to the hypotheses of the experiment. Finally, the hypotheses are given. In a section called *Overview of the present study*, the authors also provided enough information about the rationale and procedures to prepare us for the full description of the experiment in the Method section.

(6) **Running Head**

A running head is an abbreviated title (with a maximum of 50 characters) that is printed above pages of the article to help readers identify it in a journal containing other articles. In their typed manuscript, which can be found in Appendix C, Gerend and Cullen used "Message Framing and Temporal Context" as their running head. Most psychology journals will use your running head, but this journal has a different style—it uses the author names and journal information instead.

behavior is perceived to involve risk. The degree of risk associated with a given behavior is often signaled by its purpose: whether its goal is to detect or to prevent disease. Because the purpose of a detection or screening behavior (e.g., mammography, colonoscopy) is to reveal a potentially life-threatening health problem, engaging in screening behaviors could be viewed as risky (at least in the proximal sense). In contrast, because the purpose of a preventive health behavior (e.g., using sunscreen, eating fruits and vegetables) is to thwart disease, engaging in these behaviors is typically viewed as safe.

Linking this framework to prospect theory, Rothman and Salovey (1997) suggested that because people are relatively open to taking risks when faced with potential losses, loss-framed appeals should be most effective in promoting disease *detection* behaviors—behaviors that signal potential risk. However, because people tend to avoid risks in the face of potential gains, gain-framed appeals should be most effective in promoting *preventive* health behaviors—behaviors that signal low risk. Indeed, this conceptual framework is supported by a large body of empirical research (Apanovitch, McCarthy, & Salovey, 2003; Detweiler, Bedell, Salovey, Pronin, & Rothman, 1999; Kiene, Barta, Zelenski, & Cothran, 2005; Robberson & Rogers, 1988; Schneider et al., 2001).

One goal of the present study was to extend the application of message framing to interventions aimed at reducing unhealthy behaviors. Rothman and Salovey (1997) suggested that people who engage in risk behavior may be more responsive to messages that focus on the *advantages of stopping* the risky behavior (a gain frame) than the *disadvantages of continuing* the risky behavior (a loss frame). The reasoning is that, because initiating a healthy behavior and reducing an unhealthy behavior share the same goal of disease prevention (and because people become more risk averse in the face of certain gains), a gain-framed message is expected to outperform a loss-framed message in motivating people to refrain from risky behaviors. Few studies have tested this hypothesis empirically, however, and thus the extent to which gain frames are effective in motivating individuals to stop unhealthy behaviors is unclear (Rothman et al., 2006).

Two previous studies have examined effects of framed messages on reducing health-damaging behavior. In both of these studies, gain-framed appeals emphasizing the benefits of smoking cessation were found to be more effective than loss-framed appeals emphasizing the costs of smoking in promoting anti-smoking beliefs and attitudes (Schneider, Salovey, Pallonen, et al., 2001) and in encouraging stronger intentions to quit smoking (Steward, Schneider, Pizarro, & Salovey, 2003). Neither study, however, was able to demonstrate significant effects on behavior. Nevertheless, the gain-frame advantage was attributed to the fact that smoking cessation is typically perceived to be a disease prevention behavior that involves relatively certain and safe outcomes. Because gain-framed messages encourage people to pursue courses of action with certain outcomes, gain-framed messages should be more effective than loss-framed messages in motivating risk reduction behaviors such as smoking cessation. Applying this reasoning to the current study, we predicted that a message highlighting the benefits of responsible drinking (a gain-framed message) should be more effective at reducing alcohol abuse than a message highlighting the costs of problem drinking (a loss-framed message).

*Temporal context*

Another goal of the present study was to assess the extent to which the temporal context in which framed outcomes are considered influences the effects of message framing. Most behaviors result in both short-term and long-term consequences. Drinking excessive amounts of alcohol, for example, can damage one's interpersonal relationships in the days and weeks to follow, and can also negatively affect one's relationships over a longer time span into the future. Previous research on temporal discounting implies that framing effects may well depend on whether people are considering the short-term versus long-term consequences of their actions (e.g., Estle, Green, Myerson, & Holt, 2006; Green & Myerson, 2004). In particular, many studies suggest that individuals tend to discount the future (e.g., Green & Myerson, 2004). That is, behavior tends to be more strongly affected by consideration of short-term consequences, as compared to consideration of long-term consequences, even when the outcomes themselves are objectively the same over time (Chapman, 2005; Mischel, Shoda, & Rodriguez, 1989; Rachlin, 1995). Future outcomes tend to be discounted for several reasons: compared to long-term consequences, short-term consequences tend to be more salient, more relevant, and easier for individuals to conceptualize (Petty & Cacioppo, 1984). From this perspective one might expect that messages focusing on the short-term consequences of a behavior would be more impactful than messages focusing on the possible long-term consequences of a behavior.

Evidence for temporal discounting suggests that the extent to which people discount future outcomes depends on whether they are considering potential gains versus potential losses. Although both long-term gains and long-term losses tend to be discounted (relative to short-term gains and losses), the discounting function is somewhat steeper for gains than for losses (Estle et al., 2006). As one considers positive outcomes that are farther off into the future, the less psychologically impactful those positive outcomes tend to be. In the context of the current study, therefore, we expected that the relative advantage of a gain-framed message for reducing a health-damaging behavior (problem drinking) would be strong when people are considering short-term consequences, but might be reduced or eliminated when people are considering long-term consequences.

*Overview of the present study*

The present study integrated theories of message framing and temporal discounting to develop a brief, low-cost intervention for reducing alcohol use among college students. Alcohol abuse continues to be a large problem in the United States, especially on university campuses. About four in five college students drink alcoholic beverages and about 40% engage in binge drinking (Goldman, Boyd, & Faden, 2002). Problem drinking is associated with negative academic, interpersonal, and health consequences (Engs, Diebold, & Hanson, 1996; Goldman et al., 2002; Wechsler, Davenport, Dowdall, Moeykens, & Castillo, 1994; Wechsler, Lee, Kuo, & Lee, 2000). University freshman are at particularly high risk for problematic alcohol use (Larimer & Cronce, 2002).

Interventions aimed at reducing risky behaviors tend to emphasize future health problems that may result from continuing the risk behavior. Many of these interventions attempt to arouse feelings of threat and fear by emphasizing the *long-term costs of engaging in risk behavior* (e.g., smoking greatly increases your chances of developing lung cancer and heart disease) (Mahler, Kulik, Gibbons, Gerrard, & Harrell, 2003). As described above, however, theory and research pertaining to message framing and temporal discounting suggest that emphasizing the immediate benefits of refraining from the risk behavior may be a more effective strategy.

The current study investigated the interactive effects of message framing and temporal context on college student alcohol use. Students were exposed to an alcohol prevention message and asked to return to the lab one month later. When considering short-term consequences, we expected that participants would report lower alcohol use when exposed to the gain-framed message, as compared to the loss-framed message. In contrast, when considering long-term consequences, no difference in alcohol use was ex-

(7) *Method*

The Method section describes in detail how the experiment was carried out. Notice that the authors have adapted the format of the subsections to fit the kind of information they need to present; each subsection is clearly labeled. The *Participants* subsection includes important information about the subjects: Here, their geographic area, their student status, their ages, and their ethnicities are reported. It is also important to describe what compensation subjects received, if any. Relevant information is included to give the reader a clear picture of the sample for purposes of assessing external validity and comparing results across different experiments.

Manipulation of the independent variables was embedded within a written message that subjects were instructed to read. The authors described the procedures of the experiment and the operationalization of the independent variables in a single subsection labeled *Procedure and materials*. This subsection begins with a statement about random assignment of subjects to one of the four experimental conditions, and the design is described in shorthand notation form as a 2 (message frame: gain vs. loss frame) × 2 (temporal context: short-term vs. long-term consequences) between-subjects design, allowing us to visualize the four conditions of the factorial design quite easily. So that the reader can see the messages given to the four groups of subjects, the actual words used in each condition are shown in Table 1 on the next journal article page.

In addition, the procedures they used in the study for both session one and session two were described in detail here. Because not all subjects (< 80%) returned for session two, the authors wisely considered the potential for a subject mortality threat (from Chapter 7). To eliminate this possibility, they reported statistical analyses which showed that (1) dropout rates did not differ across the four experimental conditions and (2) subjects who completed the second session did not differ in age, gender, ethnicity, or year in college from those who failed to complete session two.

Finally, the authors utilized a subsection called *Measures* to describe each of the measuring instruments (surveys) used in the experiment. Two surveys were used in session one—one given before the message requesting demographic information (gender, age, etc.) and one after the message asking about their perceptions of the message and how they felt about it. The final survey was given in session two. This survey asked about their drinking behavior since session one (frequency, quantity, and binge drinking).

(8) *Results*

Before they reported statistical analyses testing their hypotheses, the authors used a section called *Manipulation checks* to verify that the two factors, framing and temporal context, were successfully manipulated in the messages given to subjects.

Notice the way in which the authors used statistics to convey to the reader that the messages successfully expressed the two desired levels of framing and the two desired levels of temporal context. Actual statistical values were provided along with means and standard deviations. Gerend and Cullen also provided statistical evidence showing that the alcohol messages were not different on any of several other important dimensions (e.g., level of

pected among participants exposed to the gain- versus loss-framed message. Overall, we expected individuals exposed to the short-term, gain-framed message to report lower alcohol use over the one-month assessment period than individuals exposed to the other three messages.

## Method

### Participants

A sample of 228 undergraduate students (70 men; 158 women) from a large southeastern university participated in exchange for course credit. The mean age was 18.6 ($SD = 1.2$; range 17–26). Most participants (71%) were in their freshman year of college. The majority of participants were white (79%; 7% black or African American, 3% Asian, 11% mixed or other. Nineteen percent reported that they were of Hispanic or Latino ethnicity.

### Procedure and materials

The experiment took place over two sessions, approximately one month apart. Participants were randomly assigned to one of four conditions in a 2 (message frame: gain vs. loss frame) × 2 (temporal context: short-term vs. long-term consequences) between-subjects design. After completing a pre-test survey, participants were given 5 min to read an information sheet about alcohol use, which included a discussion of binge drinking, warning signs of problem drinking, and a gain- or loss-framed message about either the short-term or long-term consequences of alcohol use. The same outcomes were presented in all conditions; only the frame and timing of those outcomes varied.

Framed messages vary both the action that is taken (whether something is attained or not attained) and the outcome of that action (whether it is desirable or undesirable) (Rothman & Salovey, 1997). Gain-framed appeals thus focus on either "attaining a desirable outcome" or "not attaining an undesirable outcome." In contrast, loss-framed appeals focus on "not attaining a desirable outcome" or "attaining an undesirable outcome." Because previous research suggests that the framing component of a message (whether it is gain or loss) is more important than the specific action or outcome described (e.g., Detweiler et al., 1999), we used a combination of these constructions to create the alcohol prevention messages. Each condition focused on alcohol-related outcomes for health (e.g., liver, weight), social interactions (relationships), psychological functioning (judgment, memory), and performance (college/career). See Table 1 for excerpts from each of the four messages discussing health-related and psychological outcomes associated with alcohol use. After reading the message, participants completed a brief post-test survey that assessed their perceptions of and emotional reactions to the message.

Participants returned to the lab approximately one month later to complete a survey that assessed their alcohol use over the past month. Nearly 80% ($n = 181$) of participants returned for session two. Relative to completers, non-completers were similar in age, gender, ethnicity, race (white vs. non-white), and year in college (all $ps > .20$). Dropout rates were the same across the four experimental conditions ($p > .30$).

### Measures

The pre-test survey assessed demographic and background variables (e.g., age, ethnicity). The post-test survey assessed overall impressions of the message (e.g., the extent to which the information was interesting, easy to understand, and informative;

1 = disagree strongly to 6 = agree strongly), affective reactions to the information (e.g., the extent to which they felt anxious, afraid, hopeful, and relieved; 1 = not at all to 6 = extremely), and manipulation checks (whether the message focused on the benefits of not drinking vs. the costs of drinking; whether the message focused on short-term vs. long-term consequences). Ratings for each manipulation check were made on a 6-point scale.

The one-month follow-up survey assessed alcohol use since the first session of the experiment. Self-reported alcohol use measures were adapted from previous research (Collins & Marlatt, 1981; D'Amico & Fromme, 2002). We assessed the (a) frequency of alcohol use since session one (never, once, 2–4 times during the month, 2–3 times a week, 4 or more times a week; coded 0 though 4, respectively), (b) quantity of alcohol use since session one (number of alcoholic drinks consumed on a typical day when drinking: none, 1 or 2, 3 or 4, 5 or 6, 7–9, 10 or more; coded 0–5, respectively), and (c) frequency of binge drinking (having 5 or more drinks on any one occasion) since session one (0 = never to 5 = very often).

## Results

### Manipulation checks

We conducted a series of factorial analyses of variance (ANOVAs) to confirm the effectiveness of the framing and temporal context manipulations. Relative to participants in the loss-framed condition ($M = 1.81$, $SD = 1.24$), those in the gain-framed condition reported that the information focused more on the benefits of not drinking than on the costs of drinking ($M = 4.07$, $SD = 1.75$), $F(1,224) = 126.13$, $p < .001$. Further, participants in the short-term condition ($M = 3.12$, $SD = 1.45$) reported that the message focused more on short-term consequences than did participants in the long-term condition ($M = 5.03$, $SD = 0.91$), $F(1,224) = 142.51$, $p < .001$. There were no interactions between the framing and temporal context manipulations on either manipulation check. Across the four conditions, participants rated the information equally interesting, easy to understand, and informative. No significant effects of message frame, temporal context, or their interaction were found on the degree to which participants felt anxious, hopeful, or relieved after reading the message. However, participants who read the loss-framed message reported feeling more afraid ($M = 1.58$, $SD = 0.94$) than those who read the gain-framed message ($M = 1.32$, $SD = 0.64$), $F(1,224) = 6.169$, $p < .05$.

### Effects of message framing and temporal context on drinking behavior

Factorial ANOVAs were used to test for effects of message frame and temporal context on drinking-related measures assessed one-month after exposure to the manipulation. Dependent variables included quantity of alcohol use since session one, frequency of binge drinking since session one, and frequency of alcohol use since session one. We conducted a 2 (message frame: gain or loss) by 2 (temporal context: short-term or long-term consequences) ANOVA for each dependent variable. Moreover, we conducted planned contrasts to test the hypothesis that the gain-framed short-term consequences message would be more effective than the other three messages combined.

For quantity of alcohol use (number of alcoholic drinks per drinking occasion), we observed a main effect of temporal context, $F(1,177) = 3.858$, $p = .05$, such that participants exposed to the short-term consequences message reported having fewer drinks per drinking occasion than participants exposed to the long-term consequences message. There was no main effect of frame. The main effect of temporal context was qualified by a significant

*Results* (*continued*)

difficulty, affective responses, etc.) that might have confounded the experiment if they had not been evaluated.

Next, the authors reported the statistical results of their hypothesis tests in the subsection titled *Effects of message framing and temporal context on drinking behavior*. (To see this subsection, you will need to return to the previous journal article page.) They first described the dependent variables, the hypotheses, and the statistical analyses used to test the hypotheses. Next, they analyzed the effects of message framing and temporal context on quantity of drinking, number of drinking occasions, and frequency of binge drinking since the first session. For these analyses, they used a 2 (message framing) × 2 (temporal context) ANOVA. They also used a planned contrast (from Chapter 14) to evaluate their hypothesis that the most effective message would be the gain-framed, short-term consequences message.

**Table 1**
Excerpts from the four alcohol prevention messages discussing health and psychological consequences

| Message frame | Temporal context | |
|---|---|---|
| | Short-term consequences | Long-term consequences |
| Gain | What are the *immediate* consequences of alcohol use? If you decide to drink or are drinking already, it is important for you to know about the negative consequences of alcohol use *you can avoid within days and even hours after use.* *Health:* If you are going to drink, responsible alcohol use can help you *avoid immediate negative health consequences.* You will increase the likelihood of driving safely, having a healthy liver, and maintaining a healthy weight. Moreover, people who drink responsibly are less likely to engage in risky sexual behavior placing them at risk for sexually transmitted diseases. (STDs), unintended pregnancy, and regretted sexual experiences *Psychological:* Limiting your alcohol use now can help you *avoid psychological problems that can occur soon after drinking.* Alcohol use may result in impaired judgment, poorer memory, and difficulty concentrating. Limiting alcohol use may lead to better mood and higher self-esteem in the near future. | What are the *long-term* consequences of alcohol use? If you decide to drink or are drinking already, it is important for you to know about the negative consequences of alcohol use *you can avoid for years into the future.* *Health:* If you are going to drink, responsible alcohol use can help you *avoid long-term negative health consequences.* You will increase the likelihood of driving safely, having a healthy liver, and maintaining a healthy weight. Moreover, people who drink responsibly are less likely to engage in risky sexual behavior placing them at risk for sexually transmitted diseases (STDs), unintended pregnancy, and regretted sexual experiences. *Psychological:* Limiting your alcohol use now can help you *avoid psychological problems that can occur long after drinking.* Alcohol use may result in impaired judgment, poorer memory, and difficulty concentrating. Limiting alcohol use may lead to better mood and higher self-esteem in the distant future. |
| Loss | What are the *immediate* consequences of alcohol use? If you decide to drink or are drinking already, it is important for you to know about the negative consequences of alcohol use that *you can experience within days and even hours after use.* *Health:* If you are going to drink, irresponsible alcohol use can lead you to *experience immediate negative health consequences.* You will increase the likelihood of driving accidents, having an unhealthy liver, and gaining weight. Moreover, people who drink irresponsibly are more likely to engage in risky sexual behavior placing them at risk for sexually transmitted diseases (STDs), unintended pregnancy, and regretted sexual experiences. *Psychological:* Not limiting your alcohol use now can lead you to *experience psychological problems that can occur soon after drinking.* Alcohol use may result in impaired judgment, poorer memory, and difficulty concentrating. Not limiting alcohol use may lead to depressed mood and lower self-esteem in the near future. | What are the *long-term* consequences of alcohol use? If you decide to drink or are drinking already, it is important for you to know about the negative consequences of alcohol use *you can experience for years into the future.* *Health:* If you are going to drink, irresponsible alcohol use can lead you to *experience long-term negative health consequences.* You will increase the likelihood of driving accidents, having an unhealthy liver, and gaining weight. Moreover, people who drink irresponsibly are more likely to engage in risky sexual behavior placing them at risk for sexually transmitted diseases (STDs), unintended pregnancy, and regretted sexual experiences. *Psychological:* Not limiting your alcohol use now can lead you to *experience psychological problems that can occur long after drinking.* Alcohol use may result in impaired judgment, poorer memory, and difficulty concentrating. Not limiting alcohol use may lead to depressed mood and lower self-esteem in the distant future. |

frame by temporal context interaction, $F(1,176) = 4.794$, $p < .05$ (see Fig. 1). To interpret the interaction we tested the simple effect of message frame within the short-term and long-term consequences conditions. Among participants in the short-term condi-

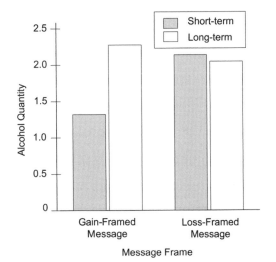

**Fig. 1.** Alcohol quantity over the past month as a function of message frame and temporal context. In the short-term condition, exposure to the gain-framed message led to fewer drinks per drinking occasion than did exposure to the loss-framed message. In the long-term condition, no such difference was observed. Response scale: none = 0; 1 or 2 drinks = 1; 3 or 4 drinks = 2; 5 or 6 drinks = 3; 7–9 drinks = 4; 10 or more drinks = 5.

tion, exposure to the gain-framed message ($M = 1.36$; $SD = 1.35$) led to a significantly lower number of drinks per occasion than did exposure to the loss-framed message ($M = 2.10$; $SD = 1.37$), $F(1,92) = 7.04$, $p < .01$, partial $\eta^2 = .07$. However, no differential effects of the gain- ($M = 2.24$; $SD = 1.39$) versus loss-framed message ($M = 2.02$; $SD = 1.37$) were observed among participants in the long-term condition, $F < 1$. Furthermore, results from the planned contrast revealed that, compared with the other three conditions, participants in the gain-framed, short-term consequences condition consumed significantly fewer drinks per occasion over the past month, $F(1,179) = 10.511$, $p < .001$, partial $\eta^2 = .06$.

Similar analyses were conducted for frequency of binge drinking. We again observed the predicted message frame by temporal context interaction effect, $F(1,173) = 3.77$, $p = .05$ (see Fig. 2). No main effects were observed. Simple effect tests revealed that, among participants in the short-term consequences condition, exposure to the gain-framed message ($M = 1.21$; $SD = 1.70$) led to a significantly lower rate of binge drinking than did exposure to the loss-framed message ($M = 2.02$; $SD = 1.90$), $F(1,89) = 4.48$, $p < .05$, partial $\eta^2 = .05$. However, no differential effect of the gain- ($M = 1.88$; $SD = 1.74$) versus loss-framed message ($M = 1.66$; $SD = 1.66$) was observed among participants in the long-term consequences condition, $F < 1$. This pattern is consistent with the pattern found for overall quantity of alcohol use. Compared with the other three conditions, participants in the gain-framed, short-term consequences condition were less likely to engage in binge drinking in the past month, $F(1,175) = 4.339$, $p < .05$, partial $\eta^2 = .02$.

For frequency of alcohol use (number of drinking occasions per month), we observed only a main effect of message frame, such that exposure to the gain-framed message resulted in lower alcohol use frequency ($M = 1.67$; $SD = 1.20$) than did exposure to the loss-framed message, ($M = 2.03$; $SD = 1.08$), $F(1,177) = 4.448$, $p < .05$, partial $\eta^2 = .03$. Although the interaction between message frame and temporal context was not statistically significant

*Results* (*continued*)

The authors tested the hypotheses that (1) gain messages would be more effective than loss messages and (2) short-term consequences messages would be more effective than long-term consequences messages. They first tested these hypotheses on the quantity of drinking since the first session. The analysis produced a significant main effect for temporal context, but not for framing. As expected, messages with short-term consequences resulted in reports of less drinking since session one than messages with long-term consequences. The temporal context effect, however, was qualified by a significant Context × Frame interaction. The statistical results for the significant interaction were reported: $F(1,176) = 4.794$, $p < .05$, and the pattern of effects for the quantity of alcohol consumed since the last session is depicted visually in the bar graph labeled Figure 1. This bar graph makes it very easy to see the effects of the interaction; here, one condition (the gain-framed message with short-term consequences) seems to result in a much lower quantity of alcohol consumption than any of the other three conditions, as predicted. Post hoc tests used to explain the significant interaction are also reported. As recommended by the APA publication guidelines, the authors included the relevant message condition means, standard deviations, and effect size estimates (although they did not include CIs, which were optional before the most recent APA publication guidelines.)

Next, using the same analytic strategy, Gerend and Cullen reported the statistics for the frequency of binge drinking and the frequency of drinking occasions since the last session. The results were very similar to those for the quantity of alcohol consumed, and the effects can be easily seen in Figures 2 and 3.

Note the format used to report test statistics. The test statistic (for example, *F*) is indicated first, in italics. (All test statistics, such as *F*, *t*, *r*, *M*, *SD*, or $\eta^2$, and the letter *p* to represent significance levels, should be italicized.) Degrees of freedom are shown in parentheses. Then the computed value, the obtained significance level, and the effect size estimate are given:

$$F(1, 89) = 4.48, \text{p} < 05, \text{ partial } \eta^2 = .05$$

We never include the critical values from the statistical tables—the reader can look them up if necessary. However, any time you have used a one-tailed test, you should indicate that.

⑨ *Discussion*

Gerend and Cullen begin the Discussion section by summarizing their major findings: Considering the benefits of avoiding a risky behavior, like drinking, produces greater avoidance than consideration of the costs of the risky behavior, but only when the benefits occur in the near future (rather than in the distant future). If replicated, these effects could have important consequences for the design of intervention strategies for reducing many kinds of risky health behaviors.

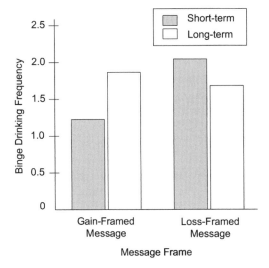

**Fig. 2.** Frequency of binge drinking over the past month as a function of message frame and temporal context. In the short-term condition, exposure to the gain-framed message led to significantly less binge drinking than did exposure to the loss-framed message. In the long-term condition, no such difference was observed. Response scale: never = 0 to very often = 5.

($p$ = .12), the overall pattern of findings was similar to that for the other two dependent measures (see Fig. 3). Simple effect tests revealed that among participants in the short-term consequences condition, exposure to the gain-framed message ($M$ = 1.44; $SD$ = 1.29) led to significantly lower rates of alcohol use than did exposure to the loss-framed message ($M$ = 2.06; $SD$ = 1.05), $F(1,92)$ = 6.519, $p$ < .05, partial $\eta^2$ = .07. No differential effect of the gain- ($M$ = 1.90; $SD$ = 1.06) versus loss-framed message

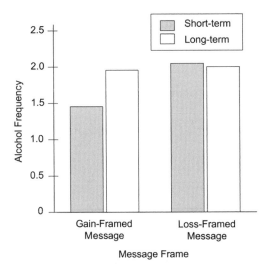

**Fig. 3.** Frequency of alcohol use (number of drinking occasions) over the past month as a function of message frame and temporal context. In the short-term condition, exposure to the gain-framed message led to significantly lower rates of alcohol use than did exposure to the loss-framed message. In the long-term condition, no such difference was observed. Response scale: never = 0, once = 1, 2–4 times during the month = 2, 2–3 times a week = 3, 4 or more times a week = 4.

($M$ = 2.00; $SD$ = 1.13) was observed among participants in the long-term consequences condition, $F$ < 1. Compared with the other three conditions, participants in the gain-framed, short-term consequences condition consumed alcohol less frequently during the assessment period, $F(1,179)$ = 7.974, $p$ < .01, partial $\eta^2$ = .04. This pattern was consistent with those observed for alcohol quantity and binge drinking.

## 9 Discussion

The current study demonstrates the benefits of framed messages for reducing potentially health-damaging behaviors. This study also extends psychological theories of message framing by identifying temporal context as an important moderator of framing effects. We found that the effects of gain- and loss-framed messages on drinking behavior were moderated by whether alcohol-related outcomes were said to occur immediately versus in the future. As predicted, when faced with the short-term consequences of alcohol use, participants exposed to a gain-framed message reported lower alcohol use than participants exposed to a loss-framed message. In contrast, when faced with the long-term consequences, no differences in alcohol use were observed among participants exposed to a gain- or loss-framed message. Indeed, relative to students in the other three conditions, those exposed to the immediate benefits of limited alcohol use reported drinking fewer alcoholic beverages per drinking occasion, drinking less frequently, and engaging in less binge drinking over the one-month follow-up period. Overall, findings suggest that asking people to consider the benefits associated with avoiding a risky health behavior is more effective than asking them consider the costs of engaging in the risky behavior, but only when those outcomes occur in the short-term.

The present study advances research and theory on message framing in two important ways. First, this work extends the application of framing interventions to risky behaviors. Most previous studies have demonstrated the effectiveness of message framing for motivating engagement in health-promoting behaviors (e.g., using sunscreen (Detweiler et al., 1999; Rothman, Salovey, Antone, Keough, & Martin, 1993); flossing (Mann, Sherman, & Updegraff, 2004); using condoms (Kiene et al., 2005); getting vaccinated (Gerend & Shepherd, 2007). To the best of our knowledge only two previous studies have examined effects of message framing for motivating cessation or reduction of potentially health-damaging behaviors (e.g., smoking; Schneider, Salovey, Pallonen, et al., 2001; Steward et al., 2003). Moreover, neither study showed effects on behavior. Findings from the current study suggest that, like initiation of a health protective behavior, reduction of a risk behavior is most likely to occur when individuals are exposed to short-term potential gains associated with changing their behavior. Findings may shed light on why, in the context of alcohol prevention research, interventions emphasizing the negative consequences of drinking (e.g., Drug Abuse Resistance Education, also known as DARE) tend to be relatively ineffective at reducing alcohol use (D'Amico & Fromme, 2002).

The second major advance of the present findings is the identification of an important boundary condition on framing effects. We observed the advantage of a gain-framed message only when the message emphasized the short-term (as opposed to the long-term) benefits of responsible alcohol use. The extent to which messages framed in terms of gains or losses affect behavior appears to depend on whether those outcomes are expected to occur in the present or future. Findings are consistent with previous research suggesting that individuals tend to discount future outcomes (Estle et al., 2006; Green & Myerson, 2004). Findings are also consistent with the smoking literature, which has shown that campaigns

*Discussion* (*continued*)

Next, the authors discuss how the results of their study fit into the context of what is already known about framing persuasive messages with a goal of producing healthier behaviors. They first explain how the results of the current study are consistent with previous framing research on the promotion of healthy behaviors and the reduction of unhealthy behaviors. Then they explain how their study advances our knowledge by demonstrating that interventions focusing on near-term gains are likely to be the most effective. They also explain an important boundary condition on framing effects. Considerable past research has shown that, in general, gain messages are more effective than loss messages, but the current study has shown that this may only be true when the consequences are near-term rather than in the distant future—an important limitation to the benefits of positively framed interventions.

Next, the authors discuss the practical implications of their research as it applies to the problem of excessive drinking among college students. The authors argue that many existing intervention programs on college campuses stress the negative consequences of problem drinking and focus on long-term costs, neither of which might be the best tactic. They also suggest that messages stressing short-term benefits from reducing problem drinking behaviors could easily be incorporated into existing intervention programs.

The authors include a subsection called *Study limitations and directions for future research*. Here, they discuss limitations of the study, such as the self-reports of drinking behaviors, which constituted the dependent measures. They also discuss the possibility that framing effects might be influenced by individual difference variables, such as differences in the way individuals perceive near-term vs. future consequences. They conclude this section by advocating future research to investigate the generalizability of the current findings to different areas of risky health behaviors and also to behaviors completely outside of the health arena. Finally, the authors opted for a *Conclusion* subsection at the end, which restates the major results of the experiment and the important implications of their findings.

(10) **References**

Here the authors cite all the sources mentioned in the article following a set format. Here are examples of how your references need to be typed. Notice that references are typed in the "hanging indent" style. The first line begins at the left margin and the remaining lines are indented 5–7 spaces. The general format is provided first, followed by examples.

**Printed Sources**
**For journal articles**

Author(s) surname(s), and initial(s). The year of publication (in parentheses). Title of the article with only the first word (or first word following a colon, if present) capitalized. *The Name of the Journal, Volume number*, page numbers.

Gerend, M. A., & Cullen M. (2008). Effects of message framing and temporal context on college student drinking behavior. *Journal of Experimental Social Psychology, 44*, 1167–1173.

focusing on the immediate consequences of smoking (e.g., stained teeth and hands, bad breath, expensive habit), compared to its long-term consequences (e.g., lung cancer; heart disease), have been relatively more successful in reducing smoking behavior (Evans, Dratt, Raines, & Rosenberg, 1988; Pechmann, Zhao, Goldberg, & Reibling, 2003).

In addition to its theoretical implications, the current research has potentially important implications for programs aimed at curbing problem drinking, particularly on college campuses. Previous interventions aimed at reducing risk behavior typically emphasize the health-related problems or negative consequences of engaging in risky behaviors, as opposed to the potential benefits of reducing or eliminating the unhealthy behaviors (Mahler et al., 2003). Moreover, most interventions tend to focus on long-term health problems associated with the behavior—consequences that typically will not emerge until the distant future, if they emerge at all (Mahler et al., 2003; Pechmann et al., 2003). Findings from the present study suggest that when attempting to reduce risky behavior, focusing on short-term benefits, rather than long-term costs, is likely to be more effective.

Reducing excessive alcohol use among college students has proven to be a challenging problem for prevention researchers (Goldman et al., 2002; Larimer & Cronce, 2002). The current study demonstrates the effectiveness of a brief, low-cost, and easy-to-implement health communication strategy for reducing alcohol use in a high-risk population. Messages with similar content could easily be incorporated into existing interventions aimed at reducing problem drinking. Integrating these findings into programs that include other strategies found to reduce problem drinking such as self-monitoring, alcohol skills training, and motivational feedback, may be particularly effective (D'Amico & Fromme, 2002; Larimer & Cronce, 2002).

*Study limitations and directions for future research*

The present study should be considered in light of its methodological limitations, which provide important opportunities for future research. The present findings are based on self-reported alcohol use that reflects alcohol quantity and frequency. Although these measures provide a reliable estimate of drinking behavior, they are limited in that they may not fully assess sporadic heavy drinking episodes, episodes that may be particularly common in a student population. Future studies might benefit from using additional measures (e.g., daily drinking estimation methods such as alcohol timeline follow back) that capture more detailed information about drinking behavior (Sobell & Sobell, 2001).

In addition, research has suggested that the effectiveness of persuasive communications may depend on individual differences in the extent to which people consider short- versus long-term outcomes. Orbell, Perugini, and Rakow (2004) demonstrated that present-oriented individuals expressed the most interest in a cancer screening program when the health communication emphasized its short-term benefits and long-term costs. The reverse was true for future-oriented individuals. Including individual difference measures of time perspective such as the Consideration of Future Consequences scale (Strathman, Gleicher, Boninger, & Edwards, 1994) or the Zimbardo Time Perspective Inventory (Zimbardo & Boyd, 1999) may have shed further light on the present findings.

Although the current study provides novel evidence bearing on the effectiveness of message framing for reducing alcohol use, this is but one health-damaging behavior to which theories of message framing and temporal context might apply. Combining message framing with temporal context could prove to be an effective health communication strategy for reducing a range of risky health behaviors (e.g., smoking, tanning bed use; eating a high fat diet). Future studies should evaluate the extent to which the current

findings generalize to other risky behaviors. Moreover, the current findings may have implications for behaviors beyond the domain of health. Many behaviors are shaped by consideration of the possible outcomes (e.g., in deciding whether or not to pursue a particular career, one is likely to consider the potential costs and benefits, both in the short- and long-term). The current research therefore may shed light on factors guiding behavioral decision making across a variety of domains.

Findings from the present study highlight a potentially important issue to be explored in future message framing research: the content of the framed message. While empirical studies have demonstrated important effects associated with the frame of a message (gain vs. loss) (Rothman & Salovey, 1997; Rothman et al., 2006), less attention has focused on the nature of the outcomes highlighted within the message (for exceptions, see Detweiler et al., 1999; Kiene et al., 2005). The current study suggests that the specific outcomes communicated in a message may play a key role in shaping how framed messages are processed. Future studies may benefit from examining additional content areas beyond temporal context (e.g., appearance vs. health outcomes; Jones & Leary, 1994; Mahler et al., 2003).

## Conclusion

Message framing has proven to be a very effective and easy-to-implement persuasive communication strategy for motivating health behavior (Rothman et al., 2006). The current study extends the framing literature by demonstrating the use of framing manipulations for the reduction of health-damaging behaviors and by identifying temporal context as an important moderator of framed messages. These findings suggest a powerful communication strategy for reducing a wide variety of problematic behaviors.

## References

Apanovitch, A. M., McCarthy, D., & Salovey, P. (2003). Using message framing to motivate HIV testing among low-income, ethnic minority women. *Health Psychology, 22*, 60–67.

Chapman, G. B. (2005). Short-term cost for long-term benefit: Time preference and cancer control. *Health Psychology, 24*, S41–S48.

Collins, R. L., & Marlatt, G. A. (1981). Social modeling as a determinant of drinking behavior: Implications for prevention and treatment. *Addictive Behavior, 6*, 233–239.

D'Amico, E. J., & Fromme, K. (2002). Brief prevention for adolescent risk-taking behavior. *Addiction, 97*, 563–574.

Detweiler, J. B., Bedell, B. T., Salovey, P., Pronin, E., & Rothman, A. J. (1999). Message framing and sunscreen use: Gain-framed messages motivate beach-goers. *Health Psychology, 18*, 189–196.

Edwards, W. (1962). Subjective probabilities inferred from decisions. *Psychological Review, 69*, 109–135.

Engs, R. C., Diebold, B. A., & Hanson, D. J. (1996). The drinking patterns and problems of a national sample of college students. *Journal of Alcohol and Drug Education, 41*, 13–33.

Estle, S. J., Green, L., Myerson, J., & Holt, D. D. (2006). Differential effects of amount on temporal and probability discounting of gains and losses. *Memory & Cognition, 34*, 914–928.

Evans, R. I., Dratt, L. M., Raines, B. E., & Rosenberg, S. S. (1988). Social influences on smoking initiation: Importance of distinguishing descriptive versus mediating process variables. *Journal of Applied Social Psychology, 16*, 220–227.

Gerend, M. A., & Shepherd, J. E. (2007). Using message framing to promote acceptance of the human papillomavirus vaccine. *Health Psychology, 26*, 745–752.

Goldman, M. S., Boyd, G. M., & Faden, V. (2002). College drinking, what it is, and what to do about it: A review of the state of the science. *Journal of Studies on Alcohol, Supplement, 14*, 1–250.

Green, L., & Myerson, J. (2004). A discounting framework for choice with delayed and probabilistic rewards. *Psychological Bulletin, 130*, 769–792.

Jones, J. L., & Leary, M. R. (1994). Effects of appearance-based admonitions against sun exposure on tanning intentions in young adults. *Health Psychology, 13*, 86–90.

Kiene, S. M., Barta, W. D., Zelenski, J. M., & Cothran, D. L. (2005). Why are you bringing up condoms now? The effect of message content on framing effects of condom use messages. *Health Psychology, 24*, 321–326.

Larimer, M. E., & Cronce, J. M. (2002). Identification, prevention and treatment: A review of individual-focused strategies to reduce problematic alcohol

Zimbardo, P. G., & Boyd, J. N. (1999). Putting time in perspective: A valid, reliable individual-difference metric. *Journal of Personality and Social Psychology, 77,* 1271–1288.

**For books**

Author(s) surname(s), and initial(s). The year of publication (in parentheses). *Title of the book with only the first word (and first word following a colon, if present) capitalized* (edition number, if any, in parentheses). City of publication[7]: Publisher's name.

Myers, A., & Hansen, C. (2012). *Experimental psychology* (7th ed.). Belmont, CA: Cengage Learning.

**For chapters from edited books**

Chapter author(s) surname(s), and initial(s). The year of publication (in parentheses). Title of the chapter with only the first word (and the first word following a colon, if present) capitalized. In book author(s) initial(s), and surname(s) (Ed[s].), *Title of the book with only the first word and word following a colon capitalized* (edition number [if any], chapter pages in parentheses). City of publication: Publisher's name.

Sobell, L. C., & Sobell, M. B.. (2001). Alcohol consumption measures. In J. P. Allen & V. B. Wilson (Eds.), *Assessing alcohol problems: A guide for clinicians and researchers* (2nd ed., pp. 75–99). Bethesda, MD: National Institute on Alcohol Abuse & Alcoholism.

## References retrieved from the Internet

Finding reference sources online, rather than obtaining the printed sources, has become the most common method. There are so many different types of potential Internet sources (e.g., journals and books available online, e-journals, blogs, wikis, etc.) that describing how to reference all of them would take many, many pages. Formats for the most common sources are given here. For information on formatting less common sources, consult the APA publication manual (2010; Chapters 6–7). A general rule for Internet sources is to include information about retrieval. The best information is the recently developed *digital object identifier* (DOI), an alphanumeric string indicating a location that does not change or disappear like URLs frequently do. The DOI, if available, is located on the first page of the online source without underlining.

### For Internet articles based on a printed source

Author(s) surname(s), and initial(s). The year of publication (in parentheses). Title of the article with only the first word (or first word following a colon, if present) capitalized. *The Name of the Journal, Volume number,* page numbers. DOI, if available (or home page URL if no DOI is present).

Gerend, M. A., & Cullen, M. (2008). Effects of message framing and temporal context on college student drinking behavior. *Journal of Experimental Social Psychology, 44,* 1167–1173. DOI:10.1016/j.jesp.2008.02.007

---

[7]If the city is well known (e.g., New York), just name the city; if it is not, include both the name of the city and the postal code abbreviation for the state (e.g., Belmont, CA).

consumption by college students. *Journal of Studies on Alcohol, Supplement, 14*, 148–163.

Mahler, H. I., Kulik, J. A., Gibbons, F. X., Gerrard, M., & Harrell, J. (2003). Effects of appearance-based interventions on sun protection intentions and self-reported behaviors. *Health Psychology, 22*, 199–209.

Mann, T., Sherman, D., & Updegraff, J. (2004). Dispositional motivations and message framing: A test of the congruency hypothesis in college students. *Health Psychology, 23*, 330–334.

Mischel, W., Shoda, Y., & Rodriguez, M. I. (1989). Delay of gratification in children. *Science, 244*, 933–938.

Orbell, S., Perugini, M., & Rakow, T. (2004). Individual differences in sensitivity to health communications: Consideration of future consequences. *Health Psychology, 23*, 388–396.

Pechmann, C., Zhao, G., Goldberg, M. E., & Reibling, E. T. (2003). What to convey in antismoking advertisements for adolescents: The use of protection motivation theory to identify effective message themes. *Journal of Marketing, 67*, 1–18.

Petty, R. E., & Cacioppo, J. T. (1984). The effects of involvement on responses to argument quality and quantity: Central and peripheral routes to persuasion. *Journal of Personality and Social Psychology, 46*, 69–81.

Rachlin, H. (1995). The value of temporal patterns in behavior. *Current Directions in Psychological Science, 4*, 188–192.

Robberson, M. R., & Rogers, R. W. (1988). Beyond fear appeals: Negative and positive persuasive appeals to health and self-esteem. *Journal of Applied Social Psychology, 13*, 277–287.

Rothman, A. J., Bartels, R. D., Wlaschin, J., & Salovey, P. (2006). The strategic use of gain- and loss-framed messages to promote health behavior: How theory can inform practice. *Journal of Communication, 56*, S202–S220.

Rothman, A. J., & Salovey, P. (1997). Shaping perceptions to motivate healthy behavior: The role of message framing. *Psychological Bulletin, 121*, 3–19.

Rothman, A. J., Salovey, P., Antone, C., Keough, K., & Martin, C. D. (1993). The influence of message framing on intentions to perform health behaviors. *Journal of Experimental Social Psychology, 29*, 408–433.

Schneider, T. R., Salovey, P., Apanovitch, A. M., Pizarro, J., McCarthy, D., Zullo, J., et al. (2001). The effects of message framing and ethnic targeting on mammography use among low-income women. *Health Psychology, 20*, 256–266.

Schneider, T. R., Salovey, P., Pallonen, U., Mundorf, N., Smith, N. F., & Steward, W. T. (2001). Visual and auditory message framing effects on tobacco smoking. *Journal of Applied Social Psychology, 31*, 667–682.

Sobell, L. C., & Sobell, M. B. (2001). Alcohol consumption measures. In J. P. Allen & V. B. Wilson (Eds.), *Assessing alcohol problems: A guide for clinicians and researchers* (2nd ed., pp. 75–99). Bethesda, MD: National Institute on Alcohol Abuse & Alcoholism.

Steward, W. T., Schneider, T. R., Pizarro, J., & Salovey, P. (2003). Need for cognition moderates responses to framed smoking-cessation messages. *Journal of Applied Social Psychology, 33*, 2439–2464.

Strathman, A., Gleicher, F., Boninger, D. S., & Edwards, S. (1994). The consideration of future consequences: Weighing immediate and distant outcomes of behavior. *Journal of Personality and Social Psychology, 66*, 742–752.

Tversky, A., & Kahneman, D. (1981). The framing of decisions and the psychology of choice. *Science, 211*, 453–458.

Wechsler, H., Davenport, A., Dowdall, G., Moeykens, B., & Castillo, S. (1994). Health and behavioral consequences of binge drinking in college. A national survey of students at 140 campuses. *Journal of the American Medical Association, 272*, 1672–1677.

Wechsler, H., Lee, J. E., Kuo, M., & Lee, H. (2000). College binge drinking in the 1990s: A continuing problem. Results of the Harvard School of Public Health 1999 College Alcohol Study. *Journal of American College Health, 48*, 199–210.

Zimbardo, P. G., & Boyd, J. N. (1999). Putting time in perspective: A valid, reliable individual-differences metric. *Journal of Personality and Social Psychology, 77*, 1271–1288.

### For e-journals

Author(s) surname(s), and initial(s). The year of publication, month, and date (in parentheses). Title of the article with only the first word (or first word following a colon, if present) capitalized. *The Name of the Journal, Volume number*, issue number (in parentheses, not italicized, only used when each issue begins with page 1). Retrieved from (the home page URL)

Sillick, T. J., & Schutte, N. S. (2006). Emotional intelligence and self-esteem mediate between perceived early parental love and adult happiness. *E-Journal of Applied Psychology, 2*(2), 38–48. Retrieved from http://ojs.lib.swin.edu.au/index.php/ejap

### For message boards, blogs, and other online communities

For these kinds of sources, we need to provide enough information that someone else can retrieve and read our source material. If the source material changes (e.g., wikis), include the retrieval date along with the URL.

Author(s) surname(s), and initial(s) or source if no author is listed. The year created, and month with day (in parentheses; if no date is given, use the abbreviation n.d.). Re: Title of post or thread [description of form in brackets]. Retrieved from (provide URL; no underlining and no final period)

American Psychological Association. (2009, October 13). People who work after retiring enjoy better health, according to national study [Press release]. Retrieved from http://www.apa.org/releases/working-retirees.html

## PREPARING YOUR MANUSCRIPT: PROCEDURAL DETAILS

By now you have a good idea of what we want to accomplish through a research paper. You have also seen some of the specific techniques used to achieve these goals. Now let's look at the details of setting up the typed copy. Written reports do not look exactly like published articles. There are specific guidelines to follow that make the task of reviewing submitted manuscripts easier for journal editors and reviewers and facilitate the publication process. Nowadays, most journal submissions are online. Your job is to put together a draft that could easily be turned into the published form. A typed version of the Gerend and Cullen (2008) article is reproduced for you in Appendix C so that you can refer to it as you prepare your own report.

Be careful to follow the format for spacing precisely. Double-space everything in the manuscript. Leave margins of at least 1 inch all the way around. Let the right margin "float"; do not use the word-processing function that alters word spacing to create a uniform right margin (called *justification*). The recommended typeface is Times New Roman with a 12-point font size. Here we will look at the layout of sections and headings as shown in Figure 16.1. Your manuscript should be laid out exactly like the sample pages shown.

The first page of every manuscript is the title page; here you will type your title, your name, and your affiliation, all centered in the top half of the page. You will also need to create a page header that includes the running head (flush left) and the page number (flush right). The title page will be page 1. As we saw earlier, the *running head* is a brief version of your title, typed in capital letters. It should be 50 characters or less, including spaces between words. If the full title is short, your running head may be the same

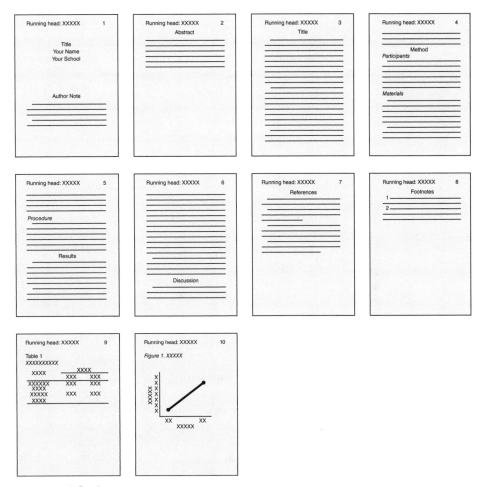

FIGURE **16.1** The general layout of a research report. Use uniform margins of at least 1 inch (2.54 cm) on all sides. Double-space throughout.
© Cengage Learning

as your full title. As shown in Figure 16.1, the running head and page number appear at the top of every manuscript page.

Author notes are also included on the title page. The first paragraph of the author notes includes each author's name, departmental affiliation, and university. Acknowledgments of financial support (grants or other support) come next. If you wish to acknowledge personal assistance, such as students running experimental sessions or help preparing your manuscript, you can include a thank you here. End this section with the name and correspondence address (mailing and e-mail address) of the author to contact about the article.

The second page of your manuscript contains the abstract. Type the word *Abstract* as a centered heading in boldface type on page 2. Type the abstract in block form (no paragraph indent) and use double spacing.

Type the complete title in uppercase and lowercase letters, centered, at the top of page 3. Then begin typing the body of the Introduction in paragraph form, using 5- to 7-space paragraph indents. Do not label the Introduction section. Continue to use double spacing throughout the report. Do not leave any extra line spaces between the title and the beginning of the paper or between different paragraphs or between different sections of the report.

You do not need a new page to start the Method section; begin it wherever the introduction ends. Type the word *Method* as a boldfaced, centered heading. Label each subsection of the method section with the appropriate subheading. Type each subheading (such as *Participants* in boldface, flush with the left margin of the page. Type the information in paragraph form using indents. There are five levels of headings that can be used, but you probably will not need more than two or three. The Gerend and Cullen article used only level 1 and level 2 headings. The first three levels are shown in Table 16.4. If you need more than three levels, consult the APA manual.

Your Results section is also started within a page. Start it where the Method section ends, and simply type the word *Results* as a boldfaced, centered heading. Be sure to follow the correct format for reporting statistical data.

Graphs, drawings, charts, or photographs are called figures. Rows and columns of numbers or text are called tables. If you want to use a table or figure, be sure to refer to it in words in the text—for instance: "See Table 1"; or "The group means are shown in Table 1"; or "Figure 1 illustrates the significant interaction." Tables are numbered consecutively: Your first table is called "Table 1"; your second table is called "Table 2," and so on. Figures are numbered the same way: Your first figure is always called "Figure 1," your second is "Figure 2," and so forth.

Prepare each table and each figure on a separate page. Tables and figures may be created using computer word-processing or graphing programs as long as the tables and figures are high quality and easy to read. Stay with black and white for your tables and figures unless color is important for

TABLE **16.4**

## Format for three levels of headings

Level 1: Centered, boldface type; use uppercase and lowercase letters.

**Method**

Level 2: Flush with left margin, boldface type, use uppercase and lowercase letters.

**Participants and Design**

**Materials and Procedure**

Level 3: Indented 5–7 spaces, boldface type, capitalize only the first letter of the first word.

    **Personality measures**

    **Interview questions**

*Note.* When using level 2 or level 3 headings within a section, you must have at least two of them; similar to levels of an outline, you cannot use only a single level 2 or level 3 heading.

© Cengage Learning

TABLE **16.5**

Example of a table in APA style

Table 1

*Gender differences in attitudes toward violence after viewing violent or nonviolent music videos*

|  |  | 95% CI | |
| --- | --- | --- | --- |
| Gender | *M (SD)* | LL | UL |
| Men | 6.3 (3.5) | 4.1 | 8.6 |
| Women | 3.7 (2.8) | 1.6 | 5.9 |

*Note.* CI = Confidence Interval; LL = lower limit; UL = upper limit.

© Cengage Learning

comprehension. Notice that APA-style tables do not have any vertical lines. Even though they generally appear in either the Method or Results section of a published article, tables and figures are not typed within the body of these text sections. Instead, they follow the References and Footnotes pages in your typed manuscript. The double-space rule may be ignored for tables and figures; you may use either single or double spacing as long as your table or figure is easily readable. Table formats will vary depending on the information you wish to present. An example of a simple table of summary data for one independent variable (gender) can be found in Table 16.5. The APA publication manual (2010) provides many examples for more complicated tables.

Bar and line graphs are the most common types of figures. In general, we use line graphs to present data (usually group means) from the effects of independent variables whose levels represent successive *quantities* of the IV, such as 1, 2, or 3 cups of coffee or 2, 4, 6, or 8 minutes of practice. When we want to show effects from independent variables whose levels represent different *qualities* of the IV, such as high protein versus high carbohydrate food, introverts versus extroverts, or the gain-framed versus loss-framed messages used in Gerend and Cullen's experiment, bar graphs are generally used. Gerend and Cullen used three bar graphs in their article. Confidence intervals are often included in bar and line graphs. An example of a line graph with CIs is shown in Figure 16.2.

After you complete the Results section, continue on to the Discussion. Type the word *Discussion* as a bold, centered heading after the Results section ends, and then type your discussion in paragraph form.

Begin your reference list on a new page. Type the centered heading *References* in bold at the top of the page. List all your references in alphabetical order by the last name of the first author. Use the hanging indent style described earlier in the chapter, and start each reference on a new line. If your article contains footnotes, begin a new page by typing the centered heading *Footnotes* in bold at the top. Designate footnotes within the text by using superscripts (as we have done in this book), and use the corresponding

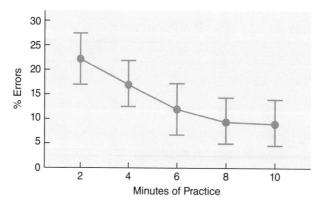

FIGURE **16.2** Example of an APA-style line graph with confidence intervals.
© Cengage Learning

superscripts on your footnotes page. Each footnote is numbered with its superscript, and the first line is indented.

If you need to present material that would be very distracting if presented in the body of the manuscript (e.g., the 20-item Scale of Irrational Beliefs that you constructed for your study), you might consider an appendix. An appendix is infrequently used in psychological reports and is not shown in Figure 16.1. The appendix (or Appendix A, Appendix B, etc., if you have more than one) is typed on a separate page. Center the word *Appendix* (add *A, B*, etc. if you have more than one) at the top of the page; below that, center the title of the appendix. Then type the information you want to append. Appendices go at the very end of the typed report.[8] Table 16.6 summarizes the order of pages in a typed manuscript. Refer to Appendix C to see how all these details come together in an actual manuscript.

## MAKING REVISIONS

Now that we have covered most of the major reporting principles, let's spend a bit more time looking at the overall picture. Remember that your task in writing a report is to communicate exactly what you did in the experiment. You need to do that as clearly and concisely as possible. Often authors are asked to cut articles down to save expensive journal space.

At first, you may feel overwhelmed by the many procedural details of report writing, but, with practice, you will find that they actually make the task of communicating a complicated experiment easier by providing you with a ready-made structure for presenting your work. In your first report, strive to present your ideas clearly and in a logical sequence. You can use

---

[8] If you need to present a great deal of material, consider an online supplemental archive. See the APA guidelines (2010) for more information.

TABLE **16.6**
Order of pages in typed manuscript

---

Title page (start on page 1)
Abstract (start on page 2)
Introduction through Discussion (start Introduction on p. 3; paginate text consecutively until Discussion is complete)
References (start on new page)
Footnotes (start on new page)
Tables (start on new page; one per page)
Figures (start on new page; one per page; include figure caption at the top of each figure)
Appendices (start each on new page)

---

© Cengage Learning

well-written journal articles, such as the one in this chapter, as a guide. Scientific writing is economical, clear, and precise—you will need to choose your words carefully—but it does not have to be dull.

Your report will be more interesting to read if you use the active voice whenever possible. For example, say "Smith and Jones found that ..." rather than "It was found by Smith and Jones that ...". When discussing or describing research that has already taken place (even your own study), use the past tense in your descriptions. Also use the past tense to describe your results (e.g., "binge drinking *decreased* significantly"). The present tense, however, is usually preferred for defining terms, making general claims, discussing implications of your results, or stating conclusions (e.g., "the current study *extends* the message-framing literature").

The job of presenting a great many facts and details can be accomplished smoothly with the careful use of transitional words (such as *then, next, furthermore, therefore,* or *besides*). Try not to pack too much information into a single sentence. When possible, keep your sentences short. Avoid unusual syntax and technical jargon—it is distracting and makes your report more difficult to read. Never use euphemisms for everyday words: Don't say "financially challenged" when you really mean "poor." Check your spelling and punctuation carefully. Any grammatical or typographical errors that are present will detract greatly from your research report.

Try to model your writing style after the precise language of a journal article. Try to say exactly what you mean. That is not as simple as it sounds. One technique some students use is reading aloud. How does it sound? Your own ear can be a guide. Would you be able to understand it if you had not written it? Try to put yourself in your reader's place. Better yet, try to get the opinion of a reader who is not already familiar with your experiment. Can your reader follow what you did? Can you make it clearer? Then revise your report.

Many people are surprised to learn that when researchers sit down to write reports, they do not usually stop at a first draft. They may continue to revise and rework the same paper several times before they feel it is acceptable. Though the thought of rewriting may seem unnerving, even the best writers make revisions. Good writing takes work. The first draft of your report should be just that—a first draft. Work on improving it, polishing it, refining it. Put as much care into writing your report as you put into doing the study itself. A good study merits a good presentation. Evaluate your draft to make sure you have accomplished the goals of each section of the report. Make the necessary changes or additions.

As you work on revisions, be aware of some common errors that can detract from your report. First, be sure you understand the difference between *affect* and *effect*. Both of these words can be either a noun or a verb. *Affect* can be a verb ("The powerful heat *affected* their thinking"). *Affect* can be a noun meaning emotion ("The participants demonstrated gender differences in masking negative *affect*"). *Effect* can be a noun ("The *effect* of food deprivation was transient—but food deprivation *affects* learning"). Finally, *effect* can be a verb meaning to bring about or cause to happen ("The goal of therapy is to *effect* a positive behavior change").

Other errors that we commonly encounter include not knowing whether to use *than* or *then* and difficulties deciding among *there, their,* and *they're*. Novice writers sometimes substitute *then* for *than*. *Than* is a comparative word: X is better *than* Y, or bigger *than*, or quicker *than*.... *Then* refers to a point in time: "We were less studious *then*." Or, "First we studied, *then* we went out." The following sentence can help with *there, their,* and *they're*: "*They're* putting *their* coats over *there*." *They're* (a contraction of *they are*) putting *their* (denotes possession) coats over *there* (denotes a place). Be

"OH, HOW I HATE THE RE-WRITING!"

Sidney Harris/ScienceCartoonsPlus.com

careful of other spelling errors, too. If your word-processing program has a spelling and grammar checker, be sure to use it. Note that the word *data* is a plural noun ("The data *are* convincing"). Double-check for biased or sexist language. As with any writing, try to form each paragraph around a single main idea, but avoid paragraphs that are composed of only one or two sentences. If an idea is important enough for a report, it probably deserves at least three sentences. You can often combine several points in the same paragraph (as we did in this one).

When you are describing numbers in a sentence, know when to use numerals (10, 20, etc.) and when to use words to express them. The APA rule is to use numerals to express numbers 10 and above and words to express numbers below 10. But there are a few exceptions. Never begin a sentence with a numeral—instead use the word(s): "Eighty-five participants ...". Use numerals whenever the number directly precedes a unit of measurement; for example, 5 meters or 2.45 inches. Use numerals rather than words for percentages, ages, and dollar amounts. Also use numerals for all numbers when at least one of them in the sentence is 10 or above: "Word lists containing 5, 10, or 15 adjectives ...". (See the APA *Publication Manual* for a number of other guidelines for using numbers.)

It is inaccurate as well as disappointing to say, "There were no results in this experiment." You always get results, even though they might not be what you predicted. Conversely, do not make grand statements based on the data from one experiment. Your results may enable you to reject the null hypothesis; however, you have not "proven" anything; you simply confirmed your predictions. Don't forget that you could be making a Type 1 error. Remember that your statistics are only making probability statements, so use words like *probably, likely,* and *might*; avoid words like *proven, true,* and *absolutely.*

Finally, keep in mind that this process is part of a scientific venture. We are looking for observable data that can be evaluated on the basis of objective criteria. This is not the place to talk about personal experiences, popular knowledge, or common sense. All your statements need to be documented. Stick to the literature and facts that can be documented. Present and discuss data. Pay particular attention to your Discussion section. Remember that your discussion should wrap things up. Readers should finish your report with an understanding of what the study was about and where it fits within the body of knowledge in your topic area. You may offer suggestions for future research, but try to view each report as a document that has a beginning, a middle, and an end.

## SUMMARY

The purpose of a *research report* is communication. A *scientific writing style* is used in research reports. Through a report, we tell others what we did and what we found. A report should contain enough information to permit other researchers to evaluate the findings and replicate them if they choose. The language used is objective, unbiased, and nonsexist.

The *Publication Manual of the American Psychological Association*, 6th edition, includes detailed information regarding the format, content, and layout of reports. We follow these standards by convention so that writers as well as readers will have a consistent model for dealing with psychological research.

The psychological research report has these main components: a *Title*, an *Abstract*, an *Introduction*, a *Method section*, a *Results section*, a *Discussion*, and a list of *References*. Additional components include author notes, footnotes, appendices, and tables or figures. The first page of the report includes the title and the author's name and affiliation as well as a *running head* and *author notes*.

There are many specific procedural details for carrying out the goals of each section of the report. Each section must contain certain kinds of information. There is a set format for typed manuscripts, which must be followed exactly. The published and typed versions of the report contain the same information, but they look quite different.

Reports are written in stages; the first stage is a draft, which is then revised and polished to give the experiment the best possible presentation. Grammatical, spelling, or typographical errors will greatly detract from the credibility of your research report, so proofread your manuscript carefully and learn to use the spelling and grammar checkers available in most word-processing programs.

## KEY TERMS

**Abstract** A brief summary of the report (approximately 150–250 words), which precedes the four major sections.

**Discussion** The fourth major section of the research report, used to draw conclusions and to integrate the experimental findings into the existing body of knowledge.

**Introduction** Beginning section of a research report that guides the reader toward your research hypothesis; includes a selective review of relevant, recent research.

**Method** The section of a research report in which the subjects and experiment are described in enough detail that the experiment may be replicated by others; it is typically divided into subsections, such as Participants, Stimuli or Materials, and Procedures.

**References** A list of books and articles cited in the research report; placed at the end of the report.

**Research report** Written report of psychological research, which contains four major sections: Introduction, Method, Results, and Discussion.

**Results** The section of a research report in which the findings are described and the results of statistical tests and summary data are presented.

**Running head** A short version of the title, which will appear as a header at the top of pages of the published report.

**Scientific writing style** A concise, impersonal, and unbiased form of writing used in research reports.

**Title** The name of the report, which describes what the report is about; typically includes the variables tested and the relationship between them.

## REVIEW AND STUDY QUESTIONS

1. What is the purpose of a research report?

2. What is a scientific writing style? How is it different from writing a letter to a friend?

3. What are the major sections that should be included in each report?

4. Think of three terms that are ethnically biased, three that are sexist, and three that "handicap" people mentally or physically. Think of some alternative, unbiased terms and practice them in everyday conversation.

5. What should be described in a good title?

6. Practice writing report titles by suggesting a good title for reports on each of the following sets of independent and dependent variables:
   a. Food deprivation; the speed of maze running
   b. Practice; time required to solve a word problem
   c. Maturation; fear of strangers
   d. Font style and size; reading rate

7. What is the function of the abstract of a research report? What basic information should it contain?

8. What is the *Publication Manual of the American Psychological Association?*

9. What is the function of the Introduction of a report? What basic information should you include in an introduction?

10. What is the function of the Method section of a report? What basic information should you include in the Method section?

11. You want to divide a Method section into subsections. What subsections are commonly used? What information would you include in each?

12. What information should you include in the Results section?

13. The Discussion section of a report serves several functions. What are they?

14. Why do we need to include a References section at the end of a report?

15. Jack is not pleased with this chapter. He says, "If I have to follow all these silly rules for writing a report, I won't have any chance to be creative." Tell him why a standard format for writing reports is important.

16. Explain how you would show each of the following in a report:
   a. The results of a *t* test with 38 degrees of freedom, where the obtained value of *t* was 1.38 and the significance level was .20.
   b. The results of an ANOVA with 1 and 12 degrees of freedom, where the computed value of *F* was 6.26, the significance level was .001, and the $\eta^2$ equaled .18.
   c. Means for the two conditions of the previous ANOVA were 7.32 (for women) and 8.44 (for men). When confidence intervals were computed, for women the LL was 5.99 and the UL was 9.76; for men the LL was 6.83 and the UL was 10.28.

## CRITICAL THINKING EXERCISE

*The controversy:* The APA journal, *Psychological Bulletin*, published an article entitled, "A Meta-Analytical Examination of Assumed Properties of Child Sexual Abuse Using College Students" (July, 1998) by Rind, Tromovitch, and Bauserman. Among its many reported findings of deleterious effects of childhood sexual abuse, the article included a statement that experiences of adolescents who had been involved in consensual sexual relations with adults did not always produce negative long-term effects, and in some cases, the "victims" had even regarded the experiences as positive. Among a number of other critics, the radio personality Dr. Laura lambasted APA for allowing publication of a study containing this conclusion, and months of controversy followed.

*The problem:* Retrieve (1) the journal article by Rind et al. (1998) and (2) the APA policy statement on child sexual abuse, which is located at: www.apa.org/about/governance/council/policy/child-sexual-abuse.aspx

Use the information to explain the ethical issues involved in APA's stance on publication of controversial research findings.

## ONLINE RESOURCES

A number of excellent free resources for learning to write in APA style can be found at the following website:

http://apastyle.apa.org/

For more information about DOIs, see

http://www.doi.org

If you enjoyed the Sidney Harris' cartoons, you can find many more at:

http://www.sciencecartoonsplus.com

# Computational Formulas

TABLE **A.1**

A simple correlation: Computational formulas

| Step 1. Square X and Y scores. | Score X | $X^2$ | Score Y | $Y^2$ | XY |
|---|---|---|---|---|---|
| | 2 | 4 | 4 | 16 | 8 |
| | 3 | 9 | 5 | 25 | 15 |
| Step 2. Multiply X scores by Y scores. | 3 | 9 | 6 | 36 | 18 |
| | 4 | 16 | 7 | 49 | 28 |
| | 4 | 16 | 7 | 48 | 28 |

Step 3. Total all columns.

$\Sigma X = 16 \qquad \Sigma X^2 = 54 \qquad \Sigma Y = 29 \qquad \Sigma Y^2 = 175 \qquad \Sigma XY = 97$

Step 4. Square total X and total Y scores.

$(\Sigma X)^2 = 256 \qquad\qquad\qquad (\Sigma Y)^2 = 841$

Step 5. Multiply total X by total Y. Divide by N. (N = number of pairs of scores.) Subtract this value from the total of XY scores.

$$\Sigma XY - \frac{(\Sigma X)(\Sigma Y)}{N}$$

$$= 97 - \frac{464}{5}$$
$$= 97 - 92.8$$
$$= 4.2$$

Step 6. Find sums of squares of X and Y.

$$SS_X = \Sigma X^2 - \frac{(\Sigma X)^2}{N} \qquad\qquad SS_Y = \Sigma Y^2 - \frac{(\Sigma Y)^2}{N}$$

$$SS_X = 54 - \frac{256}{5} \qquad\qquad SS_Y = 175 - \frac{841}{5}$$

$$SS_X = 54 - 51.2 \qquad\qquad SS_Y = 175 - 168.2$$

$$SS_X = 2.8 \qquad\qquad SS_Y = 6.8$$

TABLE **A.1**
A simple correlation: Computational formulas (continued)

| | $X - \overline{X}$ | $Y - \overline{Y}$ | $(X - \overline{X})(Y - \overline{Y})$ |
|---|---|---|---|
| Step 7. Calculate the mean deviations for each pair of X and Y scores. (Subtract the mean of X from each X score and subtract the mean of Y from each Y score.) Find the product of each mean deviation $(X - \overline{X})(Y - \overline{Y})$. Sum the products. | $-1.2$ | $-1.8$ | 2.16 |
| | $-0.2$ | $-0.8$ | 0.16 |
| | $-0.2$ | 0.2 | $-.04$ |
| | 0.8 | 0.96 | 0.96 |
| | 0.8 | 0.96 | 0.96 |

$$\Sigma(X - \overline{X})(Y - \overline{Y}) = 4.2$$

Step 8. Compute $r$ using this formula.

$$r = \frac{\Sigma(X - \overline{X})(Y - \overline{Y})}{\sqrt{SS_X \cdot SS_Y}}$$

$$r = .96$$

TABLE **A.2**
## Computing the variance: Time estimates of subjects who saw incomplete cartoons (in minutes)

*Step 1.* List each subject's score $(X_i)$:

| Subject | $X_i$ |
|---------|-------|
| $S_1$ | 11.2 |
| $S_2$ | 16.2 |
| $S_3$ | 13.3 |
| $S_4$ | 12.1 |
| $S_5$ | 18.2 |

*Step 2.* Add the scores together:
$\Sigma X_i = 71.0$

*Step 3.* Compute the mean:
$$\overline{X} = \frac{\Sigma X_i}{N}$$
$$\overline{X} = \frac{71.0}{5}$$
$$\overline{X} = 14.2 \text{ min}$$

*Step 4.* Compute the deviation from the mean for each subject $(X_i - \overline{X})$:

$11.2 - 14.2 = -3.0$
$16.2 - 14.2 = 2.0$
$13.3 - 14.2 = -0.9$
$12.1 - 14.2 = -2.1$
$18.2 - 14.2 = 4.0$

*Step 5.* Square the deviation from the mean for each subject $(X_i - \overline{X})^2$:

$(-3.0)(-3.0) = 9.00$
$(2.0)(2.0) = 4.00$
$(-0.9)(-0.9) = 0.81$
$(-2.1)(-2.1) = 4.41$
$(4.0)(4.0) = 16.00$

*Step 6.* Add the squared deviations together:
$\Sigma(X_i - \overline{X})^2 = 34.22$

*Step 7.* Compute the variance:
$$s^2 = \frac{\Sigma(X_i - \overline{X})^2}{N-1}$$
$$s^2 = \frac{34.22}{5-1} \quad \text{or } 8.6 \text{ min}$$

TABLE **A.3**
Computation of $\chi^2$ using data from Table 14-3

Computing $\chi^2$ is very easy with a hand calculator. First, obtain the expected frequency ($E$) for each of the four cells in the table using the following formula:

$$E = \frac{(\text{Row Total}) \times (\text{Column Total})}{N}$$

$N =$ the total number of responses (in this case, 40). Each of the expected frequencies is shown in Table 14-3, but let us compute $E$ for the top left cell:

$$E = \frac{(20) \times (24)}{40}$$

$$E = \frac{480}{40}$$

$$E = 12$$

Once you have the expected frequencies, you can calculate $\chi^2$ using this formula:

$$\chi^2 = \Sigma \frac{(O - E)^2}{E}$$

Substituting our data, we would have the following:

$$\chi^2 = \frac{(4 - 12)^2}{12} + \frac{(16 - 8)^2}{8} + \frac{(20 - 12)^2}{12} + \frac{(0 - 8)^2}{8}$$

$$\chi^2 = \frac{(-8)^2}{12} + \frac{8^2}{8} + \frac{8^2}{12} + \frac{(-8)^2}{8}$$

$$\chi^2 = 5.333 + 8 + 5.333 + 8 = 26.667$$

TABLE **A.4**
Computation of $t$ using data from Table 14-4

Step 1. Lay out the formula.

$$t_{obs} = \frac{\overline{X}_1 - \overline{X}_2}{\sqrt{\left(\frac{(N_1 - 1)s_1^2 + (N_2 - 1)s_2^2}{(N_1 + N_2 - 2)}\right)\cdot\left(\frac{1}{N_1} + \frac{1}{N_2}\right)}}$$

Step 2. Put in all the quantities needed.

$$t_{obs} = \frac{14.2 - 9.6}{\sqrt{\left(\frac{(5 - 1)8.6 + (5 - 1)8.8}{(5 + 5 - 2)}\right)\cdot\left(\frac{1}{5} + \frac{1}{5}\right)}}$$

Step 3. Calculate the difference between treatment means; begin simplifying the denominator.

$$t_{obs} = \frac{4.6}{\sqrt{\left(\frac{(4)8.6 + (4)8.8}{(8)}\right)\cdot\left(\frac{1}{5} + \frac{1}{5}\right)}}$$

Step 4. Continue simplifying the denominator.

$$t_{obs} = \frac{4.6}{\sqrt{\left(\frac{34.4 + 35.2}{(8)}\right)\cdot\left(\frac{1}{5} + \frac{1}{5}\right)}}$$

Step 5. Remember to complete all operations inside the parentheses first.

$$t_{obs} = \frac{4.6}{\sqrt{\left(\frac{69.6}{8}\right)\cdot\left(\frac{2}{5}\right)}}$$

Step 6. Convert all fractions in the denominator to decimals.

$$t_{obs} = \frac{4.6}{\sqrt{(8.7)\cdot(.40)}}$$

Step 7. Complete the multiplication.

$$t_{obs} = \frac{4.6}{\sqrt{(3.48)}}$$

Step 8. Remember to take the square root of the denominator.

$$t_{obs} = \frac{4.6}{1.86}$$

Step 9. Divide the numerator by the denominator and you have the computed value of $t$. Compare it with the critical value.

$$t_{obs} = 2.47$$

Note: $df = N_1 + N_2 - 2$; $df = 5 + 5 - 2$, or 8.

TABLE **A.5**

Computation of $t$ test for matched groups using data from secrecy experiment (Box 14-2)

| Subject (or Pair) | Hot Flames $(X_1)$ | Cold Flames $(X_2)$ | Difference Scores $(X_1 - X_2) = D_i$ | $D_i^2$ |
|---|---|---|---|---|
| $S_1$ | 5 | 3 | $(5 - 3) = 2$ | 4 |
| $S_2$ | 3 | 2 | $(3 - 2) = 1$ | 1 |
| $S_3$ | 4 | 3 | $(4 - 3) = 1$ | 1 |
| $S_4$ | 5 | 3 | $(5 - 3) = 2$ | 4 |
| $S_5$ | 3 | 0 | $(3 - 0) = 3$ | 9 |
| | | | $\Sigma D_i = 9$ | $\Sigma D_i^2 = 19$ |

*Computing t*

*Step 1.* This formula for $t$ requires difference scores $(D_i)$. The computation of $t$ is based on differences between pairs of scores rather than group means. (Note how difference scores were computed above.)

$$t_{obs} = \frac{\Sigma D_i}{\sqrt{\dfrac{N\Sigma D_i^2 - (\Sigma D_i)^2}{N - 1}}}$$

*Step 2.* Put in all the required values. Note that $N$ stands for the number of pairs of data.

$$t_{obs} = \frac{9}{\sqrt{\dfrac{5(19) - (9)^2}{5 - 1}}}$$

*Step 3.* Simplify the denominator. Remember to take the square root.

$$t_{obs} = \frac{9}{\sqrt{\dfrac{(95) - (81)}{4}}} \text{ or } \frac{9}{\sqrt{\dfrac{14}{4}}}$$

*Step 4.* Our computed $t$. We are now ready to make a decision on the null hypothesis. $df = N - 1$, where $N$ is the number of pairs of scores.

$$t_{obs} = 4.81$$

Note: Scores represent level of secrecy, $0 - 5$. A $t$ test for matched groups is used for two matched groups or a two-group within-subjects experiment using interval or ratio data.

TABLE **A.6**
Computing the within-groups variance for the three-groups example. Data represent valuation of objects in dollars

| Step 1. Compute the deviation of each score from its group mean. | Group 1 (No Ownership) | $(X_1 - \overline{X}_1)$ | $(X_1 - \overline{X}_1)^2$ |
|---|---|---|---|
| | $S_1 2$ | .8 | .64 |
| | $S_2 2$ | .8 | .64 |
| | $S_3 1$ | $-.2$ | .04 |
| | $S_4 0$ | $-1.2$ | 1.44 |
| | $S_5 1$ | $-.2$ | .04 |
| | $\overline{X}_1 = 1.2$ | | $\Sigma(X_1 - \overline{X}_1)^2 = 2.80$ |
| Step 2. Square the deviation of each score from its group mean. | Group 2 (Brief Ownership) | $(X_2 - \overline{X}_2)$ | $(X_2 - \overline{X}_2)^2$ |
| | $S_1 1$ | $-1.6$ | 2.56 |
| | $S_2 3$ | .4 | .16 |
| | $S_3 3$ | .4 | .16 |
| | $S_4 3$ | .4 | .16 |
| | $S_5 3$ | .4 | .16 |
| | $\overline{X}_2 = 2.6$ | | $\Sigma(X_2 - \overline{X}_2)^2 = 3.20$ |
| Step 3. Total the square deviation scores for each group. | Group 3 (Long Ownership) | $(X_3 - \overline{X}_3)$ | $(X_3 - \overline{X}_3)^2$ |
| | $S_1 3$ | $-2$ | .04 |
| | $S_2 4$ | .8 | .64 |
| | $S_3 2$ | $-1.2$ | 1.44 |
| | $S_4 3$ | $-.2$ | .04 |
| | $S_5 4$ | .8 | .64 |
| | $\overline{X}_3 = 3.2$ | | $\Sigma(X_3 - \overline{X}_3)^2 = 2.80$ |

Step 4. Add all the group totals together to find $SS_w$

$$\boxed{SS_w = \Sigma(X_1 - \overline{X}_1)^2 + \Sigma(X_2 - \overline{X}_2)^2 + \Sigma(X_3 - \overline{X}_3)^2 = 8.80}$$

Step 5. Find $df_w$

$$\boxed{df_w = N - p}$$ 

$N$ = Number of scores
$p$ = Number of groups

$df_w = 15 - 3$
$df_w = 12$

Step 6. Find $MS_w$

$$\boxed{MS_w = \frac{SS_w}{df_w}}$$

$$MS_w = \frac{8.80}{12}$$
$$MS_w = .73$$

Note: The same procedures apply when the groups are unequal in size.

TABLE **A.7**
**Computing the between-groups variance for the three groups example. Data represent valuation of objects in dollars**

| Step 1. Compute the grand mean, the mean of all the group means. | Group 1 (No Ownership) $\overline{X}_1 = 1.2$ | Group 2 (Brief Ownership) $\overline{X}_2 = 2.6$ | Group 3 (Long Ownership) $\overline{X}_3 = 3.2$ |
|---|---|---|---|

Grand mean
$(\overline{X}_G)$

$$\boxed{\overline{X}_G = \frac{\Sigma \overline{X}}{p}}$$

$$\overline{X}_G = \frac{1.2 + 2.6 + 3.2}{3}$$

$$\overline{X}_G = \frac{7}{3}$$

$$\overline{X}_G = 2.3$$

**Step 2.** Compute the differences between each group and the grand mean.

| | | |
|---|---|---|
| $\overline{X}_1 - \overline{X}_G =$ $1.2 - 2.3 = -1.1$ | $\overline{X}_2 - \overline{X}_G =$ $2.6 - 2.3 = .3$ | $\overline{X}_3 - \overline{X}_G =$ $3.2 - 2.3 = .9$ |

**Step 3.** Put those differences in the $SS_b$ formula; $n$ is the number of subjects in each group; $p$ is the number of groups—this general formula can handle any number of groups.

$$\boxed{SS_b = n_1(\overline{X}_1 - \overline{X}_G)^2 + n_2(\overline{X}_2 - \overline{X}_G)^2 + n_3(\overline{X}_3 - \overline{X}_G)^2 ... n_p(\overline{X}_p - \overline{X}_G)^2}$$

$$SS_b = 5(-1.1)^2 + 5(.3)^2 + 5(.9)^2$$

**Step 4.** Square all deviations from the grand mean.

$$SS_b = 5(1.21) + 5(.09) + 5(.81)$$

**Step 5.** Carry out all multiplications.

$$SS_b = 6.05 + .45 + 4.05$$

**Step 6.** Obtain the total $SS_b$.

$$SS_b = 10.55$$

**Step 7.** Calculate the degrees of freedom; $p$ is the number of groups.

$$\boxed{df_b = p - 1}$$

$$df_b = 3 - 1, \text{ or } 2$$

TABLE **A.7**
Computing the between-groups variance for the three groups example. Data represent valuation of objects in dollars (continued)

| | |
|---|---|
| *Step 8*. Divide $SS_b$ by $df_b$ to find the mean square between groups, the second estimate of population variance. | $$\boxed{MS_b = \frac{SS_b}{df_b}}$$ $$MS_b = \frac{10.55}{2}$$ $$MS_b = 5.28$$ |

Note: At this point you can check your work by computing $SS_T$, which represents the total sum of squares for the data. Because we are simply dividing the variability into two components, $SS_b + SS_w$ should equal $SS_T$. You can compute $SS_T$ with this formula:

$SS_T = \Sigma(X^2) - \frac{(\Sigma X)^2}{N}$. N is the number of scores. For this example,

$SS_T = 101 - \frac{(35)^2}{15}$

$SS_T = 101 - \frac{1225}{15}$

$SS_T = 101 - 81.67$

$SS_T = 19.33$

Check:
$SS_T = SS_b + SS_w$
$19.33 = 10.55 + 8.80$
(The small discrepancy is due to rounding error.)

TABLE **A.8**

Computing the within-groups variability $(SS_w)$ for a $2\times2$ factorial experiment using data from Table 14-8

| | | Word Frequency (Factor 1) | | | | | |
|---|---|---|---|---|---|---|---|
| | | Low | | | High | | |
| | | $X_1$ | $(X_1 - \overline{X}_1)$ | $(X_1 - \overline{X}_1)^2$ | $X_2$ | $(X_2 - \overline{X}_2)$ | $(X_2 - \overline{X}_2)^2$ |
| No cues given | | 2 | −1 | 1 | 4 | −1 | 1 |
| | | 3 | 0 | 0 | 5 | 0 | 0 |
| | | 1 | −2 | 4 | 4 | −1 | 1 |
| | | 4 | 1 | 1 | 6 | 1 | 1 |
| | | 5 | 2 | 4 | 6 | 1 | 1 |
| | | $\overline{X}_1 = 3$ | | $\Sigma(X_1 - \overline{X}_1)^2 = 10$ | $\overline{X}_2 = 5$ | | $\Sigma(X_2 - \overline{X}_2)^2 = 4$ |
| Cues given | | $X_3$ | $(X_3 - \overline{X}_3)$ | $(X_3 - \overline{X}_3)^2$ | $X_4$ | $(X_4 - \overline{X}_4)$ | $(X_4 - \overline{X}_4)^2$ |
| | | 4 | −2 | 4 | 7 | −1 | 1 |
| | | 6 | 0 | 0 | 6 | −2 | 4 |
| | | 5 | −1 | 1 | 9 | 1 | 1 |
| | | 6 | 0 | 0 | 8 | 0 | 0 |
| | | 9 | 3 | 9 | 10 | 2 | 4 |
| | | $\overline{X}_3 = 6$ | | $\Sigma(X_3 - \overline{X}_3)^2 = 14$ | $\overline{X}_4 = 8$ | | $\Sigma(X_4 - \overline{X}_4)^2 = 10$ |

(Row labels at left: Category (Factor 2))

$$\boxed{SS_w = \Sigma(X_1 - \overline{X}_1)^2 + \Sigma(X_2 - \overline{X}_2)^2 + \Sigma(X_3 - \overline{X}_3)^3 + \Sigma(X_4 - \overline{X}_4)^2 + \cdots + \Sigma(X_{pq} - \overline{X}_{pq})^2}$$

$SS_w = 10 + 4 + 14 + 10$

$SS_w = 38$

$\boxed{df_w = N - pq}$  $N$ = Number of scores; $pq$ = Number of rows × number of columns

$df_w = 20 - 4$, or 16

$$\boxed{MS_w = \frac{SS_w}{df_w}}$$

$MS_w = \dfrac{38}{16}$

$MS_w = 2.38$

TABLE **A.9**

Computing the between-groups variability $(SS_w)$ for a $2 \times 2$ factorial experiment using data from Table 14-8

| | Group 1 | Group 2 | Group 3 | Group 4 | Grand Mean $(\overline{X}_G)$ |
|---|---|---|---|---|---|
| *Step 1.* Compute the grand mean, the mean of all the group means. | $\overline{X}_1 = 3$ $n_1 = 5$ | $\overline{X}_2 = 5$ $n_2 = 5$ | $\overline{X}_3 = 6$ $n_3 = 5$ | $\overline{X}_4 = 8$ $n_4 = 5$ | $\boxed{\overline{X}_G = \dfrac{\text{Total of all group means}}{\text{Number of groups}}}$ $\overline{X}_G = \dfrac{3+5+6+8}{4}$ $\overline{X}_G = \dfrac{22}{4}$ |
| *Step 2.* Compute the deviation of each group mean from the grand mean. | $\overline{X}_1 - \overline{X}_G =$ $3 - 5.5$ or $-2.5$ | $\overline{X}_2 - \overline{X}_G =$ $5 - 5.5$ or $-.5$ | $\overline{X}_3 - \overline{X}_G =$ $6 - 5.5$ or $.5$ | $\overline{X}_4 - \overline{X}_G$ $8 - 5.5$ or $2.5$ | $\overline{X}_G = 5.5$ |

*Step 3.* Put the deviations in the $SS_b$ formula; $n$ is the number of subjects in each group.

$$\boxed{SS_b = n_1(\overline{X}_1 - \overline{X}_G)^2 + n_2(\overline{X}_2 - \overline{X}_G)^2 + n3(\overline{X}_3 - \overline{X}_G)^2 + \cdots + n_{pq}(\overline{X}_{pq} - \overline{X}_G)^2}$$

$$SS_b = 5(-2.5)^2 + 5(-.5)^2 + 5(.5)^2 + 5(2.5)^2$$

*Step 4.* Square all deviations from the grand mean.

$$SS_b = 5(6.25) + 5(.25) + 5(.25) + 5(6.25)$$

*Step 5.* Complete all multiplications.

$$SS_b = 31.25 + 1.25 + 1.25 + 31.25$$
$$SS_b = 65$$

TABLE **A.10**
Computing the main effect for Factor 1 (word frequency) for a $2\times2$ factorial experiment using data from Table 14-8

| | | | Word Frequency (Factor 1) | |
|---|---|---|---|---|
| | | | Low | High |
| *Step 1.* Find the mean at each level of Factor 1: Ignore Factor 2 (rows) and find the mean of each column. N is the number of scores. | Category Cues (Factor 2) | No cues given | $\overline{X}_1 = 3$ $(N = 5)$ | $\overline{X}_2 = 5$ $(N = 5)$ |
| | | Cues given | $\overline{X}_3 = 6$ $(N = 5)$ | $\overline{X}_4 = 8$ $(N = 5)$ |
| | | Column means | $\overline{X}_{col1} = 4.5$ | $\overline{X}_{col2} = 6.5$ |
| *Step 2.* Find the difference between each column mean and the grand mean. | | Column mean– Grand mean $\overline{X}_G = 5.5$ | $\overline{X}_{col1} - \overline{X}_G =$ $4.5 - 5.5 = -1.0$ | $\overline{X}_{col2} - \overline{X}_G =$ $6.5 - 5.5 = -1.0$ |

*Step 3.* Put those differences in the $SS_1$ formula; $n$ is the number of subjects in each group; $p$ is the number of rows; $q$ is the number of columns. This general formula will handle any number of columns.

$$SS_1 = np\Sigma[(\overline{X}_{col1} - \overline{X}_G)^2 + (\overline{X}_{col2} - \overline{X}_G)^2 + \cdots + (\overline{X}_{colq} - \overline{X}_G)^2]$$

$SS_1 = 5(2)\Sigma[(-1.0)^2 + (1.0)^2]$
$SS_1 = 10[(1) + (1)]$
$SS_1 = 10(2)$
$SS_1 = 20$

*Step 4.* To get $MS_1$, divide $SS_1$ by $df_1$.

$$MS_1 = \frac{SS_1}{df_1} \qquad df_1 = q - 1$$
$$df_1 = 2 - 1, \text{ or } 1$$

$$MS_1 = \frac{20}{1}$$
$$MS_1 = 20$$

TABLE **A.11**

Computing the main effect for Factor 2 (category cue) in a $2 \times 2$ factorial experiment using data from Table 14-8

*Step 1.* Find the mean at each level of Factor 2: Ignore Factor 1 (columns) and find the mean of each row.

*Step 2.* Find the difference between each row mean and the grand mean.

|  | | Word Frequency (Factor 1) | | | |
|---|---|---|---|---|---|
|  | | Low | High | Row means | Row Mean–Grand Mean |
| Category Cues (Factor 2) | No cues given | $\overline{X}_1 = 3$ | $\overline{X}_2 = 5$ | $\overline{X}_{row1} = 4$ | $\overline{X}_{row1} - \overline{X}_G =$ 4 – 5.5 or – 1.5 |
|  | Cues given | $\overline{X}_3 = 6$ | $\overline{X}_4 = 8$ | $\overline{X}_{row2} = 7$ | $\overline{X}_{row2} - \overline{X}_G =$ 7 – 5.5 or 1.5 |

$$(\overline{X}_G = 5.5)$$

*Step 3.* Put those differences in the $SS_2$ formula; $n$ is the number of subjects in each group; $q$ is the number of columns; $p$ is the number of rows. This general formula will handle any number of rows.

$$SS_2 = nq\Sigma[(\overline{X}_{row1} - \overline{X}_G)^2 + (\overline{X}_{row2} - \overline{X}_G)^2 + \cdots + (\overline{X}_{row\,p} - \overline{X}_G)^2]$$

$$SS_2 = 5(2)[(-1.5)^2 + (1.5)^2]$$
$$SS_2 = 10[2.25 + 2.25]$$
$$SS_2 = 10(4.50) \text{ or } 45$$

*Step 4.* To get $MS_2$, divide $SS_2$ by $df_2$.

$$MS_2 = \frac{SS_2}{df_2} \quad \begin{array}{l} df_2 = p - 1 \\ df_2 = 2 - 1 \text{ or } 1 \end{array}$$

$$MS_2 = \frac{45}{1}$$
$$MS_2 = 45$$

# APPENDIX B

# Statistical Tables

# TABLE B.1
## Random numbers

| | | | | | | | | | | | | | | | | | | | | | | | | |
|---|---|---|---|---|---|---|---|---|---|---|---|---|---|---|---|---|---|---|---|---|---|---|---|---|
| 03 | 47 | 43 | 73 | 86 | 36 | 96 | 47 | 36 | 61 | 46 | 98 | 63 | 71 | 62 | 33 | 26 | 16 | 80 | 45 | 60 | 11 | 14 | 10 | 95 |
| 97 | 74 | 24 | 67 | 62 | 42 | 81 | 14 | 57 | 20 | 42 | 53 | 32 | 37 | 32 | 27 | 07 | 36 | 07 | 51 | 24 | 51 | 79 | 89 | 73 |
| 16 | 76 | 62 | 27 | 66 | 56 | 50 | 26 | 71 | 07 | 32 | 90 | 79 | 78 | 53 | 13 | 55 | 38 | 58 | 59 | 88 | 97 | 54 | 14 | 10 |
| 12 | 56 | 85 | 99 | 26 | 96 | 96 | 68 | 27 | 31 | 05 | 03 | 72 | 93 | 15 | 57 | 12 | 10 | 14 | 21 | 88 | 26 | 49 | 81 | 76 |
| 55 | 59 | 56 | 35 | 64 | 38 | 54 | 82 | 46 | 22 | 31 | 62 | 43 | 09 | 90 | 06 | 18 | 44 | 32 | 53 | 23 | 83 | 01 | 30 | 30 |
| | | | | | | | | | | | | | | | | | | | | | | | | |
| 16 | 22 | 77 | 94 | 39 | 49 | 54 | 43 | 54 | 82 | 17 | 37 | 93 | 23 | 78 | 87 | 35 | 20 | 96 | 43 | 84 | 26 | 34 | 91 | 64 |
| 84 | 42 | 17 | 53 | 31 | 57 | 24 | 55 | 06 | 88 | 77 | 04 | 74 | 47 | 67 | 21 | 76 | 33 | 50 | 25 | 83 | 92 | 12 | 06 | 76 |
| 63 | 01 | 63 | 78 | 59 | 16 | 95 | 55 | 67 | 19 | 98 | 10 | 50 | 71 | 75 | 12 | 86 | 73 | 58 | 07 | 44 | 39 | 52 | 38 | 79 |
| 33 | 21 | 12 | 34 | 29 | 78 | 64 | 56 | 07 | 82 | 52 | 42 | 07 | 44 | 38 | 15 | 51 | 00 | 13 | 42 | 99 | 66 | 02 | 79 | 54 |
| 57 | 60 | 86 | 32 | 44 | 09 | 47 | 27 | 96 | 54 | 49 | 17 | 46 | 09 | 62 | 90 | 52 | 84 | 77 | 27 | 08 | 02 | 73 | 43 | 28 |
| | | | | | | | | | | | | | | | | | | | | | | | | |
| 18 | 18 | 07 | 92 | 46 | 44 | 17 | 16 | 58 | 09 | 79 | 83 | 86 | 19 | 62 | 06 | 76 | 50 | 03 | 10 | 55 | 23 | 64 | 05 | 05 |
| 26 | 62 | 38 | 97 | 75 | 84 | 16 | 07 | 44 | 99 | 83 | 11 | 46 | 32 | 24 | 20 | 14 | 85 | 88 | 45 | 10 | 93 | 72 | 88 | 71 |
| 23 | 42 | 40 | 64 | 74 | 82 | 97 | 77 | 77 | 81 | 07 | 45 | 32 | 14 | 08 | 32 | 98 | 94 | 07 | 72 | 93 | 85 | 79 | 10 | 75 |
| 52 | 30 | 28 | 19 | 95 | 50 | 92 | 26 | 11 | 97 | 00 | 56 | 76 | 31 | 38 | 80 | 22 | 02 | 53 | 53 | 86 | 60 | 42 | 04 | 53 |
| 37 | 45 | 94 | 35 | 12 | 83 | 39 | 50 | 08 | 30 | 42 | 34 | 07 | 96 | 88 | 54 | 42 | 06 | 87 | 98 | 35 | 85 | 29 | 48 | 39 |
| | | | | | | | | | | | | | | | | | | | | | | | | |
| 70 | 29 | 17 | 12 | 13 | 40 | 33 | 20 | 38 | 26 | 13 | 89 | 51 | 03 | 74 | 17 | 76 | 37 | 13 | 04 | 07 | 74 | 21 | 19 | 30 |
| 56 | 62 | 18 | 37 | 35 | 96 | 83 | 50 | 87 | 75 | 97 | 12 | 25 | 93 | 47 | 70 | 33 | 24 | 03 | 54 | 97 | 77 | 46 | 44 | 80 |
| 99 | 49 | 57 | 22 | 77 | 88 | 42 | 95 | 45 | 72 | 16 | 64 | 36 | 16 | 00 | 04 | 43 | 18 | 66 | 79 | 94 | 77 | 24 | 21 | 90 |
| 16 | 08 | 15 | 04 | 72 | 33 | 27 | 14 | 34 | 09 | 45 | 59 | 34 | 68 | 49 | 12 | 72 | 07 | 34 | 45 | 99 | 27 | 72 | 95 | 14 |
| 31 | 16 | 93 | 32 | 43 | 50 | 27 | 89 | 87 | 19 | 20 | 15 | 37 | 00 | 49 | 52 | 85 | 66 | 60 | 44 | 38 | 68 | 88 | 11 | 80 |
| | | | | | | | | | | | | | | | | | | | | | | | | |
| 68 | 34 | 30 | 13 | 70 | 55 | 74 | 30 | 77 | 40 | 44 | 22 | 78 | 84 | 26 | 04 | 33 | 46 | 09 | 52 | 68 | 07 | 97 | 06 | 57 |
| 74 | 57 | 25 | 65 | 76 | 59 | 29 | 97 | 68 | 60 | 71 | 91 | 38 | 67 | 54 | 13 | 58 | 18 | 24 | 76 | 15 | 54 | 55 | 95 | 52 |
| 27 | 42 | 37 | 86 | 53 | 48 | 55 | 90 | 65 | 72 | 96 | 57 | 69 | 36 | 10 | 96 | 46 | 92 | 42 | 45 | 97 | 60 | 49 | 04 | 91 |
| 00 | 39 | 68 | 29 | 61 | 66 | 37 | 32 | 20 | 30 | 77 | 84 | 57 | 03 | 29 | 10 | 45 | 65 | 04 | 26 | 11 | 04 | 96 | 67 | 24 |
| 29 | 94 | 98 | 94 | 24 | 68 | 49 | 69 | 10 | 82 | 53 | 75 | 91 | 93 | 30 | 34 | 25 | 20 | 57 | 27 | 40 | 48 | 73 | 51 | 92 |
| | | | | | | | | | | | | | | | | | | | | | | | | |
| 16 | 90 | 82 | 66 | 59 | 83 | 62 | 64 | 11 | 12 | 67 | 19 | 00 | 71 | 74 | 60 | 47 | 21 | 29 | 68 | 02 | 02 | 37 | 03 | 31 |
| 11 | 27 | 94 | 75 | 06 | 06 | 09 | 19 | 74 | 66 | 02 | 94 | 37 | 34 | 02 | 76 | 70 | 90 | 30 | 66 | 38 | 45 | 94 | 30 | 38 |
| 35 | 25 | 20 | 16 | 20 | 33 | 32 | 51 | 26 | 38 | 79 | 78 | 45 | 04 | 91 | 16 | 92 | 53 | 56 | 16 | 02 | 76 | 59 | 95 | 98 |
| 38 | 23 | 16 | 86 | 38 | 42 | 38 | 97 | 01 | 50 | 87 | 75 | 66 | 81 | 41 | 40 | 01 | 74 | 91 | 62 | 48 | 51 | 84 | 08 | 32 |
| 31 | 96 | 25 | 91 | 47 | 96 | 44 | 33 | 49 | 13 | 34 | 86 | 82 | 53 | 91 | 00 | 52 | 43 | 48 | 85 | 27 | 55 | 26 | 89 | 62 |
| | | | | | | | | | | | | | | | | | | | | | | | | |
| 66 | 67 | 40 | 67 | 14 | 64 | 05 | 71 | 95 | 86 | 11 | 05 | 65 | 09 | 68 | 76 | 83 | 20 | 37 | 90 | 57 | 16 | 00 | 11 | 66 |
| 14 | 90 | 84 | 45 | 11 | 75 | 73 | 88 | 05 | 90 | 52 | 27 | 41 | 14 | 86 | 22 | 98 | 12 | 22 | 08 | 07 | 52 | 74 | 95 | 80 |
| 68 | 05 | 51 | 18 | 00 | 33 | 96 | 02 | 75 | 19 | 07 | 60 | 62 | 93 | 55 | 59 | 33 | 82 | 43 | 90 | 49 | 37 | 38 | 44 | 59 |
| 20 | 46 | 78 | 73 | 90 | 97 | 51 | 40 | 14 | 02 | 04 | 02 | 33 | 31 | 08 | 39 | 54 | 16 | 49 | 36 | 47 | 95 | 93 | 13 | 30 |
| 64 | 19 | 58 | 97 | 79 | 15 | 06 | 15 | 93 | 20 | 01 | 90 | 10 | 75 | 06 | 40 | 78 | 78 | 89 | 62 | 02 | 67 | 74 | 17 | 33 |
| | | | | | | | | | | | | | | | | | | | | | | | | |
| 05 | 26 | 93 | 70 | 60 | 22 | 35 | 85 | 15 | 13 | 92 | 03 | 51 | 59 | 77 | 59 | 56 | 78 | 06 | 83 | 52 | 91 | 05 | 70 | 74 |
| 07 | 97 | 10 | 88 | 23 | 09 | 98 | 42 | 99 | 64 | 61 | 71 | 62 | 99 | 15 | 06 | 51 | 29 | 16 | 93 | 58 | 05 | 77 | 09 | 51 |
| 68 | 71 | 86 | 85 | 85 | 54 | 87 | 66 | 47 | 54 | 73 | 32 | 08 | 11 | 12 | 44 | 95 | 92 | 63 | 16 | 29 | 56 | 24 | 29 | 48 |
| 26 | 99 | 61 | 65 | 53 | 58 | 37 | 78 | 80 | 70 | 42 | 10 | 50 | 67 | 42 | 32 | 17 | 55 | 85 | 74 | 94 | 44 | 67 | 16 | 94 |
| 14 | 65 | 52 | 68 | 75 | 87 | 59 | 36 | 22 | 41 | 26 | 78 | 63 | 06 | 55 | 13 | 08 | 27 | 01 | 50 | 15 | 29 | 39 | 39 | 43 |

(continued)

| | | | | | | | | | | | | | | | | | | | | | | | | |
|---|---|---|---|---|---|---|---|---|---|---|---|---|---|---|---|---|---|---|---|---|---|---|---|---|
| 17 | 53 | 77 | 58 | 71 | 71 | 41 | 61 | 50 | 72 | 12 | 41 | 94 | 96 | 26 | 44 | 95 | 27 | 36 | 99 | 02 | 96 | 74 | 30 | 83 |
| 90 | 26 | 59 | 21 | 19 | 23 | 52 | 23 | 33 | 12 | 96 | 93 | 02 | 18 | 39 | 07 | 02 | 18 | 36 | 07 | 25 | 99 | 32 | 70 | 23 |
| 41 | 23 | 52 | 55 | 99 | 31 | 04 | 49 | 69 | 96 | 10 | 47 | 48 | 45 | 88 | 13 | 41 | 43 | 89 | 20 | 97 | 17 | 14 | 49 | 17 |
| 60 | 20 | 50 | 81 | 69 | 31 | 99 | 73 | 68 | 68 | 35 | 81 | 33 | 03 | 76 | 24 | 30 | 12 | 48 | 60 | 18 | 99 | 10 | 72 | 34 |
| 91 | 25 | 38 | 05 | 90 | 94 | 58 | 28 | 41 | 36 | 45 | 37 | 59 | 03 | 09 | 90 | 35 | 57 | 29 | 12 | 82 | 62 | 54 | 65 | 60 |
| 34 | 50 | 57 | 74 | 37 | 98 | 80 | 33 | 00 | 91 | 09 | 77 | 93 | 19 | 82 | 74 | 94 | 80 | 04 | 04 | 45 | 07 | 31 | 66 | 49 |
| 85 | 22 | 04 | 39 | 43 | 73 | 81 | 53 | 94 | 79 | 33 | 62 | 46 | 86 | 28 | 08 | 31 | 54 | 46 | 31 | 53 | 94 | 13 | 38 | 47 |
| 09 | 79 | 13 | 77 | 48 | 73 | 82 | 97 | 22 | 21 | 05 | 03 | 27 | 24 | 83 | 72 | 89 | 44 | 05 | 60 | 35 | 80 | 39 | 94 | 88 |
| 88 | 75 | 80 | 18 | 14 | 22 | 95 | 75 | 42 | 49 | 39 | 32 | 82 | 22 | 49 | 02 | 48 | 07 | 70 | 37 | 16 | 04 | 61 | 67 | 87 |
| 90 | 96 | 23 | 70 | 00 | 39 | 00 | 03 | 06 | 90 | 55 | 85 | 78 | 38 | 36 | 94 | 37 | 30 | 69 | 32 | 90 | 89 | 00 | 76 | 33 |
| 53 | 74 | 23 | 99 | 67 | 61 | 32 | 28 | 69 | 84 | 94 | 62 | 67 | 86 | 24 | 98 | 33 | 41 | 19 | 95 | 47 | 53 | 53 | 38 | 09 |
| 63 | 38 | 06 | 86 | 54 | 99 | 00 | 65 | 26 | 94 | 02 | 82 | 90 | 23 | 07 | 79 | 62 | 67 | 80 | 60 | 75 | 91 | 12 | 81 | 19 |
| 35 | 30 | 58 | 21 | 46 | 06 | 72 | 17 | 10 | 94 | 25 | 21 | 31 | 75 | 96 | 49 | 28 | 24 | 00 | 49 | 55 | 65 | 79 | 78 | 07 |
| 63 | 43 | 36 | 82 | 69 | 65 | 51 | 18 | 37 | 88 | 61 | 38 | 44 | 12 | 45 | 32 | 92 | 85 | 88 | 65 | 54 | 34 | 81 | 85 | 35 |
| 98 | 25 | 37 | 55 | 26 | 01 | 91 | 82 | 81 | 46 | 74 | 71 | 12 | 94 | 97 | 24 | 02 | 71 | 37 | 07 | 03 | 92 | 18 | 66 | 75 |
| 02 | 63 | 21 | 17 | 69 | 71 | 50 | 80 | 89 | 56 | 38 | 15 | 70 | 11 | 48 | 43 | 40 | 45 | 86 | 98 | 00 | 83 | 26 | 91 | 03 |
| 64 | 55 | 22 | 21 | 82 | 48 | 22 | 28 | 06 | 00 | 61 | 54 | 13 | 43 | 91 | 82 | 78 | 12 | 23 | 29 | 06 | 66 | 24 | 12 | 27 |
| 85 | 07 | 26 | 13 | 89 | 01 | 10 | 07 | 82 | 04 | 59 | 63 | 69 | 36 | 03 | 69 | 11 | 15 | 83 | 80 | 13 | 29 | 54 | 19 | 28 |
| 58 | 54 | 16 | 24 | 15 | 51 | 54 | 44 | 82 | 00 | 62 | 61 | 65 | 04 | 69 | 38 | 18 | 65 | 18 | 97 | 85 | 72 | 13 | 49 | 21 |
| 34 | 85 | 27 | 84 | 87 | 61 | 48 | 64 | 56 | 26 | 90 | 18 | 48 | 13 | 26 | 37 | 70 | 15 | 42 | 57 | 65 | 65 | 80 | 39 | 07 |
| 03 | 92 | 18 | 27 | 46 | 57 | 99 | 16 | 96 | 56 | 30 | 33 | 72 | 85 | 22 | 84 | 64 | 38 | 56 | 98 | 99 | 01 | 30 | 98 | 64 |
| 62 | 95 | 30 | 27 | 59 | 37 | 75 | 41 | 66 | 48 | 86 | 97 | 80 | 61 | 45 | 23 | 53 | 04 | 01 | 63 | 45 | 76 | 08 | 64 | 27 |
| 08 | 45 | 93 | 15 | 22 | 60 | 21 | 75 | 46 | 91 | 98 | 77 | 27 | 85 | 42 | 28 | 88 | 61 | 08 | 84 | 69 | 62 | 03 | 42 | 73 |
| 07 | 08 | 55 | 18 | 40 | 45 | 44 | 75 | 13 | 90 | 24 | 94 | 96 | 61 | 02 | 57 | 55 | 66 | 83 | 15 | 73 | 42 | 37 | 11 | 61 |
| 01 | 85 | 89 | 95 | 66 | 51 | 10 | 19 | 34 | 88 | 15 | 84 | 97 | 19 | 75 | 12 | 76 | 39 | 43 | 78 | 64 | 63 | 91 | 08 | 25 |
| 72 | 84 | 71 | 14 | 35 | 19 | 11 | 58 | 49 | 26 | 50 | 11 | 17 | 17 | 76 | 86 | 31 | 57 | 20 | 18 | 95 | 60 | 78 | 46 | 75 |
| 88 | 78 | 28 | 16 | 84 | 13 | 52 | 53 | 94 | 53 | 75 | 45 | 69 | 30 | 96 | 73 | 89 | 65 | 70 | 31 | 99 | 17 | 43 | 48 | 76 |
| 45 | 17 | 75 | 65 | 57 | 28 | 40 | 19 | 72 | 12 | 25 | 12 | 74 | 75 | 67 | 60 | 40 | 60 | 81 | 19 | 24 | 62 | 01 | 61 | 16 |
| 96 | 76 | 28 | 12 | 54 | 22 | 01 | 11 | 94 | 25 | 71 | 96 | 16 | 16 | 88 | 68 | 64 | 36 | 74 | 45 | 19 | 59 | 50 | 88 | 92 |
| 43 | 31 | 67 | 72 | 30 | 24 | 02 | 94 | 08 | 63 | 38 | 32 | 36 | 66 | 02 | 69 | 36 | 38 | 25 | 39 | 48 | 03 | 45 | 15 | 22 |
| 50 | 44 | 66 | 44 | 21 | 66 | 06 | 58 | 05 | 62 | 58 | 15 | 54 | 35 | 02 | 42 | 35 | 48 | 96 | 32 | 14 | 52 | 41 | 52 | 48 |
| 22 | 66 | 22 | 15 | 86 | 26 | 63 | 75 | 41 | 99 | 58 | 42 | 36 | 72 | 24 | 58 | 37 | 52 | 18 | 51 | 03 | 37 | 18 | 39 | 11 |
| 96 | 24 | 40 | 14 | 51 | 23 | 22 | 30 | 88 | 57 | 95 | 67 | 47 | 29 | 83 | 94 | 69 | 40 | 06 | 07 | 18 | 16 | 36 | 78 | 86 |
| 31 | 73 | 91 | 61 | 19 | 60 | 20 | 72 | 93 | 48 | 98 | 57 | 07 | 23 | 69 | 65 | 95 | 39 | 69 | 58 | 56 | 80 | 30 | 19 | 44 |
| 78 | 60 | 73 | 99 | 84 | 43 | 89 | 94 | 36 | 45 | 56 | 69 | 47 | 07 | 41 | 90 | 22 | 91 | 07 | 12 | 78 | 35 | 34 | 08 | 72 |
| 84 | 37 | 90 | 61 | 56 | 70 | 10 | 23 | 98 | 05 | 85 | 11 | 34 | 76 | 60 | 76 | 48 | 45 | 34 | 60 | 01 | 64 | 18 | 39 | 96 |
| 36 | 67 | 10 | 08 | 23 | 98 | 93 | 35 | 08 | 86 | 99 | 29 | 76 | 29 | 81 | 33 | 34 | 91 | 58 | 93 | 63 | 14 | 52 | 32 | 52 |
| 07 | 28 | 59 | 07 | 48 | 89 | 64 | 58 | 89 | 75 | 83 | 85 | 62 | 27 | 89 | 30 | 14 | 78 | 56 | 27 | 86 | 63 | 59 | 80 | 02 |
| 10 | 15 | 83 | 87 | 60 | 79 | 24 | 31 | 66 | 56 | 21 | 48 | 24 | 06 | 93 | 91 | 98 | 94 | 05 | 49 | 01 | 47 | 59 | 38 | 00 |
| 55 | 19 | 68 | 97 | 65 | 03 | 73 | 52 | 16 | 56 | 00 | 53 | 55 | 90 | 27 | 33 | 42 | 29 | 38 | 87 | 22 | 13 | 88 | 83 | 34 |

Source: From *Statistical Tables for Biological, Agricultural and Medical Research*, Sixth Edition, by Fisher and Yates (1963), Addison Wesley Longman. Reprinted by permission of Pearson Education.

TABLE **B.2**
Critical Values for the $\chi^2$ Distribution

| df | .10 | .05 | .025 | .01 | .005 |
|---|---|---|---|---|---|
| 1 | 2.706 | 3.841 | 5.024 | 6.635 | 7.879 |
| 2 | 4.605 | 5.992 | 7.378 | 9.210 | 10.597 |
| 3 | 6.251 | 7.815 | 9.348 | 11.345 | 12.838 |
| 4 | 7.779 | 9.488 | 11.143 | 13.277 | 14.860 |
| 5 | 9.236 | 11.071 | 12.833 | 15.086 | 16.750 |
| 6 | 10.645 | 12.592 | 14.449 | 16.812 | 18.548 |
| 7 | 12.017 | 14.067 | 16.013 | 18.475 | 20.278 |
| 8 | 13.362 | 15.507 | 17.535 | 20.090 | 21.955 |
| 9 | 14.684 | 16.919 | 19.023 | 21.666 | 23.589 |
| 10 | 15.987 | 18.307 | 20.483 | 23.209 | 25.188 |
| 11 | 17.275 | 19.675 | 21.920 | 24.725 | 26.757 |
| 12 | 18.549 | 21.026 | 23.337 | 26.217 | 28.300 |
| 13 | 19.812 | 22.362 | 24.736 | 27.688 | 29.819 |
| 14 | 21.064 | 23.685 | 26.119 | 29.141 | 31.319 |
| 15 | 22.307 | 24.996 | 27.488 | 30.578 | 32.801 |
| 16 | 23.542 | 26.296 | 28.845 | 32.000 | 34.267 |
| 17 | 24.769 | 27.587 | 30.191 | 33.409 | 35.718 |
| 18 | 25.989 | 28.869 | 31.526 | 34.805 | 37.156 |
| 19 | 27.204 | 30.144 | 32.852 | 36.191 | 38.582 |
| 20 | 28.412 | 31.410 | 34.170 | 37.566 | 39.997 |
| 21 | 29.615 | 32.671 | 35.479 | 38.932 | 41.401 |
| 22 | 30.813 | 33.925 | 36.781 | 40.290 | 42.796 |
| 23 | 32.007 | 35.172 | 38.076 | 41.638 | 44.181 |
| 24 | 33.196 | 36.415 | 39.364 | 42.980 | 45.559 |
| 25 | 34.382 | 37.653 | 40.647 | 44.314 | 46.929 |
| 26 | 35.563 | 38.885 | 41.923 | 45.642 | 48.290 |
| 27 | 36.741 | 40.113 | 43.195 | 46.963 | 49.645 |
| 28 | 37.916 | 41.337 | 44.461 | 48.278 | 50.994 |
| 29 | 39.087 | 42.557 | 45.722 | 49.588 | 52.336 |
| 30 | 40.256 | 43.773 | 46.979 | 50.892 | 53.672 |
| 40 | 51.805 | 55.759 | 59.342 | 63.691 | 66.767 |
| 50 | 63.167 | 67.505 | 71.420 | 76.154 | 79.490 |
| 60 | 74.397 | 79.082 | 83.298 | 88.381 | 91.955 |
| 70 | 85.527 | 90.531 | 95.023 | 100.424 | 104.213 |

Source: From Lehman, R. S. (1995). *Statistics in the Behavioral Sciences: A Conceptual Introduction.* Pacific Grove, CA: Brooks/Cole Publishing.

TABLE **B.3**
Critical Values of *t*

| | Level of Significance for One-tailed Test | | | |
| --- | --- | --- | --- | --- |
| | .05 | .025 | .01 | .005 |
| | Level of Significance for Two-tailed Test | | | |
| df | .10 | .05 | .02 | .01 |
| 1 | 6.314 | 12.706 | 31.821 | 63.657 |
| 2 | 2.920 | 4.303 | 6.965 | 9.925 |
| 3 | 2.353 | 3.182 | 4.541 | 5.841 |
| 4 | 2.132 | 2.776 | 3.747 | 4.604 |
| 5 | 2.015 | 2.571 | 3.365 | 4.032 |
| 6 | 1.943 | 2.447 | 3.143 | 3.707 |
| 7 | 1.895 | 2.365 | 2.998 | 3.499 |
| 8 | 1.860 | 2.306 | 2.896 | 3.355 |
| 9 | 1.833 | 2.262 | 2.821 | 3.250 |
| 10 | 1.812 | 2.228 | 2.764 | 3.169 |
| 11 | 1.796 | 2.201 | 2.718 | 3.106 |
| 12 | 1.782 | 2.179 | 2.681 | 3.055 |
| 13 | 1.771 | 2.160 | 2.650 | 3.012 |
| 14 | 1.761 | 2.145 | 2.624 | 2.977 |
| 15 | 1.753 | 2.131 | 2.602 | 2.947 |
| 16 | 1.746 | 2.120 | 2.583 | 2.921 |
| 17 | 1.740 | 2.110 | 2.567 | 2.898 |
| 18 | 1.734 | 2.101 | 2.552 | 2.878 |
| 19 | 1.729 | 2.093 | 2.539 | 2.861 |
| 20 | 1.725 | 2.086 | 2.528 | 2.845 |
| 21 | 1.721 | 2.080 | 2.518 | 2.831 |
| 22 | 1.717 | 2.074 | 2.508 | 2.819 |
| 23 | 1.714 | 2.069 | 2.500 | 2.807 |
| 24 | 1.711 | 2.064 | 2.492 | 2.797 |
| 25 | 1.708 | 2.060 | 2.485 | 2.787 |
| 26 | 1.706 | 2.056 | 2.479 | 2.779 |
| 27 | 1.703 | 2.052 | 2.473 | 2.771 |
| 28 | 1.701 | 2.048 | 2.467 | 2.763 |
| 29 | 1.699 | 2.045 | 2.462 | 2.756 |
| 30 | 1.697 | 2.042 | 2.457 | 2.750 |
| 40 | 1.684 | 2.021 | 2.423 | 2.704 |
| 60 | 1.671 | 2.000 | 2.390 | 2.660 |
| 120 | 1.658 | 1.980 | 2.358 | 2.617 |
| ∞ | 1.645 | 1.960 | 2.326 | 2.576 |

Source: From *Statistical Tables for Biological, Agricultural and Medical Research*, Sixth Edition, by Fisher and Yates (1963), Addison Wesley Longman. Reprinted by permission of Pearson Education.

## TABLE B.4
### Critical values of F (.05 level in roman type, .01 level in **bold**)

Degrees of Freedom for Greater Mean Square (numerator)

| Denominator df | 1 | 2 | 3 | 4 | 5 | 6 | 7 | 8 | 9 | 10 | 11 | 12 | 14 | 16 | 20 | 24 | 30 | 40 | 50 | 75 | 100 | 200 | 500 | ∞ |
|---|---|---|---|---|---|---|---|---|---|---|---|---|---|---|---|---|---|---|---|---|---|---|---|---|
| 1 | 161 | 200 | 216 | 225 | 230 | 234 | 237 | 239 | 241 | 242 | 243 | 244 | 245 | 246 | 248 | 249 | 250 | 251 | 252 | 253 | 253 | 254 | 254 | 254 |
|  | **4,052** | **4,999** | **5,403** | **5,625** | **5,764** | **5,859** | **5,928** | **5,981** | **6,022** | **6,056** | **6,082** | **6,106** | **6,142** | **6,169** | **6,208** | **6,234** | **6,261** | **6,286** | **6,302** | **6,323** | **6,334** | **6,352** | **6,361** | **6,366** |
| 2 | 18.51 | 19.00 | 19.16 | 19.25 | 19.30 | 19.33 | 19.36 | 19.37 | 19.38 | 19.39 | 19.40 | 19.41 | 19.42 | 19.43 | 19.44 | 19.45 | 19.46 | 19.47 | 19.47 | 19.48 | 19.49 | 19.49 | 19.50 | 19.50 |
|  | **98.49** | **99.00** | **99.17** | **99.25** | **99.30** | **99.33** | **99.36** | **99.37** | **99.39** | **99.40** | **99.41** | **99.42** | **99.43** | **99.44** | **99.45** | **99.46** | **99.47** | **99.48** | **99.48** | **99.49** | **99.49** | **99.49** | **99.50** | **99.50** |
| 3 | 10.13 | 9.55 | 9.28 | 9.12 | 9.01 | 8.94 | 8.88 | 8.84 | 8.81 | 8.78 | 8.76 | 8.74 | 8.71 | 8.69 | 8.66 | 8.64 | 8.62 | 8.60 | 8.58 | 8.57 | 8.56 | 8.54 | 8.54 | 8.53 |
|  | **34.12** | **30.82** | **29.46** | **28.71** | **28.24** | **27.91** | **27.67** | **27.49** | **27.34** | **27.23** | **27.13** | **27.05** | **26.92** | **26.83** | **26.69** | **26.60** | **26.50** | **26.41** | **26.35** | **26.27** | **26.23** | **26.18** | **26.14** | **26.12** |
| 4 | 7.71 | 6.94 | 6.59 | 6.39 | 6.26 | 6.16 | 6.09 | 6.04 | 6.00 | 5.96 | 5.93 | 5.91 | 5.87 | 5.84 | 5.80 | 5.77 | 5.74 | 5.71 | 5.70 | 5.68 | 5.66 | 5.65 | 5.64 | 5.63 |
|  | **21.20** | **18.00** | **16.69** | **15.98** | **15.52** | **15.21** | **14.98** | **14.80** | **14.66** | **14.54** | **14.45** | **14.37** | **14.24** | **14.15** | **14.02** | **13.93** | **13.83** | **13.74** | **13.69** | **13.61** | **13.57** | **13.52** | **13.48** | **13.46** |
| 5 | 6.61 | 5.79 | 5.41 | 5.19 | 5.05 | 4.95 | 4.88 | 4.82 | 4.78 | 4.74 | 4.70 | 4.68 | 4.64 | 4.60 | 4.56 | 4.53 | 4.50 | 4.46 | 4.44 | 4.42 | 4.40 | 4.38 | 4.37 | 4.36 |
|  | **16.26** | **13.27** | **12.06** | **11.39** | **10.97** | **10.67** | **10.45** | **10.29** | **10.15** | **10.05** | **9.96** | **9.89** | **9.77** | **9.68** | **9.55** | **9.47** | **9.38** | **9.29** | **9.24** | **9.17** | **9.13** | **9.07** | **9.04** | **9.02** |
| 6 | 5.99 | 5.14 | 4.76 | 4.53 | 4.39 | 4.28 | 4.21 | 4.15 | 4.10 | 4.06 | 4.03 | 4.00 | 3.96 | 3.92 | 3.87 | 3.84 | 3.81 | 3.77 | 3.75 | 3.72 | 3.71 | 3.69 | 3.68 | 3.67 |
|  | **13.74** | **10.92** | **9.78** | **9.15** | **8.75** | **8.47** | **8.26** | **8.10** | **7.98** | **7.87** | **7.79** | **7.72** | **7.60** | **7.52** | **7.39** | **7.31** | **7.23** | **7.14** | **7.09** | **7.02** | **6.99** | **6.94** | **6.90** | **6.88** |
| 7 | 5.59 | 4.74 | 4.35 | 4.12 | 3.97 | 3.87 | 3.79 | 3.73 | 3.68 | 3.63 | 3.60 | 3.57 | 3.52 | 3.49 | 3.44 | 3.41 | 3.38 | 3.34 | 3.32 | 3.29 | 3.28 | 3.25 | 3.24 | 3.23 |
|  | **12.25** | **9.55** | **8.45** | **7.85** | **7.46** | **7.19** | **7.00** | **6.84** | **6.71** | **6.62** | **6.54** | **6.47** | **6.35** | **6.27** | **6.15** | **6.07** | **5.98** | **5.90** | **5.85** | **5.78** | **5.75** | **5.70** | **5.67** | **5.65** |
| 8 | 5.32 | 4.46 | 4.07 | 3.84 | 3.69 | 3.58 | 3.50 | 3.44 | 3.39 | 3.34 | 3.31 | 3.28 | 3.23 | 3.20 | 3.15 | 3.12 | 3.08 | 3.05 | 3.03 | 3.00 | 2.98 | 2.96 | 2.94 | 2.93 |
|  | **11.26** | **8.65** | **7.59** | **7.01** | **6.63** | **6.37** | **6.19** | **6.03** | **5.91** | **5.82** | **5.74** | **5.67** | **5.56** | **5.48** | **5.36** | **5.28** | **5.20** | **5.11** | **5.06** | **5.00** | **4.96** | **4.91** | **4.88** | **4.86** |
| 9 | 5.12 | 4.26 | 3.86 | 3.63 | 3.48 | 3.37 | 3.29 | 3.23 | 3.18 | 3.13 | 3.10 | 3.07 | 3.02 | 2.98 | 2.93 | 2.90 | 2.86 | 2.82 | 2.80 | 2.77 | 2.76 | 2.73 | 2.72 | 2.71 |
|  | **10.56** | **8.02** | **6.99** | **6.42** | **6.06** | **5.80** | **5.62** | **5.47** | **5.35** | **5.26** | **5.18** | **5.11** | **5.00** | **4.92** | **4.80** | **4.73** | **4.64** | **4.56** | **4.51** | **4.45** | **4.41** | **4.36** | **4.33** | **4.31** |
| 10 | 4.96 | 4.10 | 3.71 | 3.48 | 3.33 | 3.22 | 3.14 | 3.07 | 3.02 | 2.97 | 2.94 | 2.91 | 2.86 | 2.82 | 2.77 | 2.74 | 2.70 | 2.67 | 2.64 | 2.61 | 2.59 | 2.56 | 2.55 | 2.54 |
|  | **10.04** | **7.56** | **6.55** | **5.99** | **5.64** | **5.39** | **5.21** | **5.06** | **4.95** | **4.85** | **4.78** | **4.71** | **4.60** | **4.52** | **4.41** | **4.33** | **4.25** | **4.17** | **4.12** | **4.05** | **4.01** | **3.96** | **3.93** | **3.91** |
| 11 | 4.84 | 3.98 | 3.59 | 3.36 | 3.20 | 3.09 | 3.01 | 2.95 | 2.90 | 2.86 | 2.82 | 2.79 | 2.74 | 2.70 | 2.65 | 2.61 | 2.57 | 2.53 | 2.50 | 2.47 | 2.45 | 2.42 | 2.41 | 2.40 |
|  | **9.65** | **7.20** | **6.22** | **5.67** | **5.32** | **5.07** | **4.88** | **4.74** | **4.63** | **4.54** | **4.46** | **4.40** | **4.29** | **4.21** | **4.10** | **4.02** | **3.94** | **3.86** | **3.80** | **3.74** | **3.70** | **3.66** | **3.62** | **3.60** |
| 12 | 4.75 | 3.88 | 3.49 | 3.26 | 3.11 | 3.00 | 2.92 | 2.85 | 2.80 | 2.76 | 2.72 | 2.69 | 2.64 | 2.60 | 2.54 | 2.50 | 2.46 | 2.42 | 2.40 | 2.36 | 2.35 | 2.32 | 2.31 | 2.30 |
|  | **9.33** | **6.93** | **5.95** | **5.41** | **5.06** | **4.82** | **4.65** | **4.50** | **4.39** | **4.30** | **4.22** | **4.16** | **4.05** | **3.98** | **3.86** | **3.78** | **3.70** | **3.61** | **3.56** | **3.49** | **3.46** | **3.41** | **3.38** | **3.36** |
| 13 | 4.67 | 3.80 | 3.41 | 3.18 | 3.02 | 2.92 | 2.84 | 2.77 | 2.72 | 2.67 | 2.63 | 2.60 | 2.55 | 2.51 | 2.46 | 2.42 | 2.38 | 2.34 | 2.32 | 2.28 | 2.26 | 2.24 | 2.22 | 2.21 |
|  | **9.07** | **6.70** | **5.74** | **5.20** | **4.86** | **4.62** | **4.44** | **4.30** | **4.19** | **4.10** | **4.02** | **3.96** | **3.85** | **3.78** | **3.67** | **3.59** | **3.51** | **3.42** | **3.37** | **3.30** | **3.27** | **3.21** | **3.18** | **3.16** |

Degrees of Freedom for Lesser Mean Square (denominator)

Note: Find the critical value of F for each of your F ratios. Locate the degrees of freedom associated with the numerator of your F ratio along the top of the table. Locate the degrees of freedom associated with the denominator of your F ratio along the side of the table. The place where the correct row and column meet indicates the appropriate critical values. The numbers in light type give you the values at the .05 level; the numbers in dark type give you the values at the .01 level. Reject the null hypothesis when the computed value of F is greater than the table value.

TABLE **B.4**
Critical values of F (.05 level in roman type, .01 level in **bold**) (continued)

| Degrees of Freedom for Greater Mean Square (numerator) | | | | | | | | | | | | | | | | | | | | | | | | |
| | 1 | 2 | 3 | 4 | 5 | 6 | 7 | 8 | 9 | 10 | 11 | 12 | 14 | 16 | 20 | 24 | 30 | 40 | 50 | 75 | 100 | 200 | 500 | ∞ |
|---|---|---|---|---|---|---|---|---|---|---|---|---|---|---|---|---|---|---|---|---|---|---|---|---|
| 14 | 4.60 | 3.74 | 3.34 | 3.11 | 2.96 | 2.85 | 2.77 | 2.70 | 2.65 | 2.60 | 2.56 | 2.53 | 2.48 | 2.44 | 2.39 | 2.35 | 2.31 | 2.27 | 2.24 | 2.21 | 2.19 | 2.16 | 2.14 | 2.13 |
| | **8.86** | **6.51** | **5.56** | **5.03** | **4.69** | **4.46** | **4.28** | **4.14** | **4.03** | **3.94** | **3.86** | **3.80** | **3.70** | **3.62** | **3.51** | **3.43** | **3.34** | **3.26** | **3.21** | **3.14** | **3.11** | **3.06** | **3.02** | **3.00** |
| 15 | 4.54 | 3.68 | 3.29 | 3.06 | 2.90 | 2.79 | 2.70 | 2.64 | 2.59 | 2.55 | 2.51 | 2.48 | 2.43 | 2.39 | 2.33 | 2.29 | 2.25 | 2.21 | 2.18 | 2.15 | 2.12 | 2.10 | 2.08 | 2.07 |
| | **8.68** | **6.36** | **5.42** | **4.89** | **4.56** | **4.32** | **4.14** | **4.00** | **3.89** | **3.80** | **3.73** | **3.67** | **3.56** | **3.48** | **3.36** | **3.29** | **3.20** | **3.12** | **3.07** | **3.00** | **2.97** | **2.92** | **2.89** | **2.87** |
| 16 | 4.49 | 3.63 | 3.24 | 3.01 | 2.85 | 2.74 | 2.66 | 2.59 | 2.54 | 2.49 | 2.45 | 2.42 | 2.37 | 2.33 | 2.28 | 2.24 | 2.20 | 2.16 | 2.13 | 2.09 | 2.07 | 2.04 | 2.02 | 2.01 |
| | **8.53** | **6.23** | **5.29** | **4.77** | **4.44** | **4.20** | **4.03** | **3.89** | **3.78** | **3.69** | **3.61** | **3.55** | **3.45** | **3.37** | **3.25** | **3.18** | **3.10** | **3.01** | **2.96** | **2.98** | **2.86** | **2.80** | **2.77** | **2.75** |
| 17 | 4.45 | 3.59 | 3.20 | 2.96 | 2.81 | 2.70 | 2.62 | 2.55 | 2.50 | 2.45 | 2.41 | 2.38 | 2.33 | 2.29 | 2.23 | 2.19 | 2.15 | 2.11 | 2.08 | 2.04 | 2.02 | 1.99 | 1.97 | 1.96 |
| | **8.40** | **6.11** | **5.18** | **4.67** | **4.34** | **4.10** | **3.93** | **3.79** | **3.68** | **3.59** | **3.52** | **3.45** | **3.35** | **3.27** | **3.16** | **3.08** | **3.00** | **2.92** | **2.86** | **2.79** | **2.76** | **2.70** | **2.67** | **2.65** |
| 18 | 4.41 | 3.55 | 3.16 | 2.93 | 2.77 | 2.66 | 2.58 | 2.51 | 2.46 | 2.41 | 2.37 | 2.34 | 2.29 | 2.25 | 2.19 | 2.15 | 2.11 | 2.07 | 2.04 | 2.00 | 1.98 | 1.95 | 1.93 | 1.92 |
| | **8.28** | **6.01** | **5.09** | **4.58** | **4.25** | **4.01** | **3.85** | **3.71** | **3.60** | **3.51** | **3.44** | **3.37** | **3.27** | **3.19** | **3.07** | **3.00** | **2.91** | **2.83** | **2.78** | **2.71** | **2.68** | **2.62** | **2.59** | **2.57** |
| 19 | 4.38 | 3.52 | 3.13 | 2.90 | 2.74 | 2.63 | 2.55 | 2.48 | 2.43 | 2.38 | 2.34 | 2.31 | 2.26 | 2.21 | 2.15 | 2.11 | 2.07 | 2.02 | 2.00 | 1.96 | 1.94 | 1.91 | 1.90 | 1.88 |
| | **8.18** | **5.93** | **5.01** | **4.50** | **4.17** | **3.94** | **3.77** | **3.63** | **3.52** | **3.43** | **3.36** | **3.30** | **3.19** | **3.12** | **3.00** | **2.92** | **2.84** | **2.76** | **2.70** | **2.63** | **2.60** | **2.54** | **2.51** | **2.49** |
| 20 | 4.35 | 3.49 | 3.10 | 2.87 | 2.71 | 2.60 | 2.52 | 2.45 | 2.40 | 2.35 | 2.31 | 2.28 | 2.23 | 2.18 | 2.12 | 2.08 | 2.04 | 1.99 | 1.96 | 1.92 | 1.90 | 1.87 | 1.85 | 1.84 |
| | **8.10** | **5.85** | **4.94** | **4.42** | **4.10** | **3.87** | **3.71** | **3.56** | **3.45** | **3.37** | **3.30** | **3.23** | **3.13** | **3.05** | **2.94** | **2.86** | **2.77** | **2.69** | **2.63** | **2.56** | **2.53** | **2.47** | **2.44** | **2.42** |
| 21 | 4.32 | 3.47 | 3.07 | 2.84 | 2.68 | 2.57 | 2.49 | 2.42 | 2.37 | 2.32 | 2.28 | 2.25 | 2.20 | 2.15 | 2.09 | 2.05 | 2.00 | 1.96 | 1.93 | 1.89 | 1.87 | 1.84 | 1.82 | 1.81 |
| | **8.02** | **5.78** | **4.87** | **4.37** | **4.04** | **3.81** | **3.65** | **3.51** | **3.40** | **3.31** | **3.24** | **3.17** | **3.07** | **2.99** | **2.88** | **2.80** | **2.72** | **2.63** | **2.58** | **2.51** | **2.47** | **2.42** | **2.38** | **2.36** |
| 22 | 4.30 | 3.44 | 3.05 | 2.82 | 2.66 | 2.55 | 2.47 | 2.40 | 2.35 | 2.30 | 2.26 | 2.23 | 2.18 | 2.13 | 2.07 | 2.03 | 1.98 | 1.93 | 1.91 | 1.87 | 1.84 | 1.81 | 1.80 | 1.78 |
| | **7.94** | **5.72** | **4.82** | **4.31** | **3.99** | **3.76** | **3.59** | **3.45** | **3.35** | **3.26** | **3.18** | **3.12** | **3.02** | **2.94** | **2.83** | **2.75** | **2.67** | **2.58** | **2.53** | **2.46** | **2.42** | **2.37** | **2.33** | **2.31** |
| 23 | 4.28 | 3.42 | 3.03 | 2.80 | 2.64 | 2.53 | 2.45 | 2.38 | 2.32 | 2.28 | 2.24 | 2.20 | 2.14 | 2.10 | 2.04 | 2.00 | 1.96 | 1.91 | 1.88 | 1.84 | 1.82 | 1.79 | 1.77 | 1.76 |
| | **7.88** | **5.66** | **4.76** | **4.26** | **3.94** | **3.71** | **3.54** | **3.41** | **3.30** | **3.21** | **3.14** | **3.07** | **2.97** | **2.89** | **2.78** | **2.70** | **2.62** | **2.53** | **2.48** | **2.41** | **2.37** | **2.32** | **2.28** | **2.26** |
| 24 | 4.26 | 3.40 | 3.01 | 2.78 | 2.62 | 2.51 | 2.43 | 2.36 | 2.30 | 2.26 | 2.22 | 2.18 | 2.13 | 2.09 | 2.02 | 1.98 | 1.94 | 1.89 | 1.86 | 1.82 | 1.80 | 1.76 | 1.74 | 1.73 |
| | **7.82** | **5.61** | **4.72** | **4.22** | **3.90** | **3.67** | **3.50** | **3.36** | **3.25** | **3.17** | **3.09** | **3.03** | **2.93** | **2.85** | **2.74** | **2.66** | **2.58** | **2.49** | **2.44** | **2.36** | **2.33** | **2.27** | **2.23** | **2.21** |
| 25 | 4.24 | 3.38 | 2.99 | 2.76 | 2.60 | 2.49 | 2.41 | 2.34 | 2.28 | 2.24 | 2.20 | 2.16 | 2.11 | 2.06 | 2.00 | 1.96 | 1.92 | 1.87 | 1.84 | 1.80 | 1.77 | 1.74 | 1.72 | 1.71 |
| | **7.77** | **5.57** | **4.68** | **4.18** | **3.86** | **3.63** | **3.46** | **3.32** | **3.21** | **3.13** | **3.05** | **2.99** | **2.89** | **2.81** | **2.70** | **2.62** | **2.54** | **2.45** | **2.40** | **2.32** | **2.29** | **2.23** | **2.19** | **2.17** |
| 26 | 4.22 | 3.37 | 2.98 | 2.74 | 2.59 | 2.47 | 2.39 | 2.32 | 2.27 | 2.22 | 2.18 | 2.15 | 2.10 | 2.05 | 1.99 | 1.95 | 1.90 | 1.85 | 1.82 | 1.78 | 1.76 | 1.72 | 1.70 | 1.69 |
| | **7.72** | **5.53** | **4.64** | **4.14** | **3.82** | **3.59** | **3.42** | **3.29** | **3.17** | **3.09** | **3.02** | **2.96** | **2.86** | **2.77** | **2.66** | **2.58** | **2.50** | **2.41** | **2.36** | **2.28** | **2.25** | **2.19** | **2.15** | **2.13** |

Degrees of Freedom for Lesser Mean Square (denominator)

## TABLE B.4
Critical values of F (.05 level in roman type, .01 level in **bold**) (continued)

Degrees of Freedom for Greater Mean Square (numerator)

| Degrees of Freedom for Lesser Mean Square (denominator) | 1 | 2 | 3 | 4 | 5 | 6 | 7 | 8 | 9 | 10 | 11 | 12 | 14 | 16 | 20 | 24 | 30 | 40 | 50 | 75 | 100 | 200 | 500 | ∞ |
|---|---|---|---|---|---|---|---|---|---|---|---|---|---|---|---|---|---|---|---|---|---|---|---|---|
| 27 | 4.21 | 3.35 | 2.96 | 2.73 | 2.57 | 2.46 | 2.37 | 2.30 | 2.25 | 2.20 | 2.16 | 2.13 | 2.08 | 2.03 | 1.97 | 1.93 | 1.88 | 1.84 | 1.80 | 1.76 | 1.74 | 1.71 | 1.68 | 1.67 |
| | **7.68** | **5.49** | **4.60** | **4.11** | **3.79** | **3.56** | **3.39** | **3.26** | **3.14** | **3.06** | **2.98** | **2.93** | **2.83** | **2.74** | **2.63** | **2.55** | **2.47** | **2.38** | **2.33** | **2.25** | **2.21** | **2.16** | **2.12** | **2.10** |
| 28 | 4.20 | 3.34 | 2.95 | 2.71 | 2.56 | 2.44 | 2.36 | 2.29 | 2.24 | 2.19 | 2.15 | 2.12 | 2.06 | 2.02 | 1.96 | 1.91 | 1.87 | 1.81 | 1.78 | 1.75 | 1.72 | 1.69 | 1.67 | 1.65 |
| | **7.64** | **5.45** | **4.57** | **4.07** | **3.76** | **3.53** | **3.36** | **3.23** | **3.11** | **3.03** | **2.95** | **2.90** | **2.80** | **2.71** | **2.60** | **2.52** | **2.44** | **2.35** | **2.30** | **2.22** | **2.18** | **2.13** | **2.09** | **2.06** |
| 29 | 4.18 | 3.33 | 2.93 | 2.70 | 2.54 | 2.43 | 2.35 | 2.28 | 2.22 | 2.18 | 2.14 | 2.10 | 2.05 | 2.00 | 1.94 | 1.90 | 1.85 | 1.80 | 1.77 | 1.73 | 1.71 | 1.68 | 1.65 | 1.64 |
| | **7.60** | **5.42** | **4.54** | **4.04** | **3.73** | **3.50** | **3.33** | **3.20** | **3.08** | **3.00** | **2.92** | **2.87** | **2.77** | **2.68** | **2.57** | **2.49** | **2.41** | **2.32** | **2.27** | **2.19** | **2.15** | **2.10** | **2.06** | **2.03** |
| 30 | 4.17 | 3.32 | 2.92 | 2.69 | 2.53 | 2.42 | 2.34 | 2.27 | 2.21 | 2.16 | 2.12 | 2.09 | 2.04 | 1.99 | 1.93 | 1.89 | 1.84 | 1.79 | 1.76 | 1.72 | 1.69 | 1.66 | 1.64 | 1.62 |
| | **7.56** | **5.39** | **4.51** | **4.02** | **3.70** | **3.47** | **3.30** | **3.17** | **3.06** | **2.98** | **2.90** | **2.84** | **2.74** | **2.66** | **2.55** | **2.47** | **2.38** | **2.29** | **2.24** | **2.16** | **2.13** | **2.07** | **2.03** | **2.01** |
| 32 | 4.15 | 3.30 | 2.90 | 2.67 | 2.51 | 2.40 | 2.32 | 2.25 | 2.19 | 2.14 | 2.10 | 2.07 | 2.02 | 1.97 | 1.91 | 1.86 | 1.82 | 1.76 | 1.74 | 1.69 | 1.67 | 1.64 | 1.61 | 1.59 |
| | **7.50** | **5.34** | **4.46** | **3.97** | **3.66** | **3.42** | **3.25** | **3.12** | **3.01** | **2.94** | **2.86** | **2.80** | **2.70** | **2.62** | **2.51** | **2.42** | **2.34** | **2.25** | **2.20** | **2.12** | **2.08** | **2.02** | **1.98** | **1.96** |
| 34 | 4.13 | 3.28 | 2.88 | 2.65 | 2.49 | 2.38 | 2.30 | 2.23 | 2.17 | 2.12 | 2.08 | 2.05 | 2.00 | 1.95 | 1.89 | 1.84 | 1.80 | 1.74 | 1.71 | 1.67 | 1.64 | 1.61 | 1.59 | 1.57 |
| | **7.44** | **5.29** | **4.42** | **3.93** | **3.61** | **3.38** | **3.21** | **3.08** | **2.97** | **2.89** | **2.82** | **2.76** | **2.66** | **2.58** | **2.47** | **2.38** | **2.30** | **2.21** | **2.15** | **2.08** | **2.04** | **1.98** | **1.94** | **1.91** |
| 36 | 4.11 | 3.26 | 2.86 | 2.63 | 2.48 | 2.36 | 2.28 | 2.21 | 2.15 | 2.10 | 2.06 | 2.03 | 1.98 | 1.93 | 1.87 | 1.82 | 1.78 | 1.72 | 1.69 | 1.65 | 1.62 | 1.59 | 1.56 | 1.55 |
| | **7.39** | **5.25** | **4.38** | **3.89** | **3.58** | **3.35** | **3.18** | **3.04** | **2.94** | **2.86** | **2.78** | **2.72** | **2.62** | **2.54** | **2.43** | **2.35** | **2.26** | **2.17** | **2.12** | **2.04** | **2.00** | **1.94** | **1.90** | **1.87** |
| 38 | 4.10 | 3.25 | 2.85 | 2.62 | 2.46 | 2.35 | 2.26 | 2.19 | 2.14 | 2.09 | 2.05 | 2.02 | 1.96 | 1.92 | 1.85 | 1.80 | 1.76 | 1.71 | 1.67 | 1.63 | 1.60 | 1.57 | 1.54 | 1.53 |
| | **7.35** | **5.21** | **4.34** | **3.86** | **3.54** | **3.32** | **3.15** | **3.02** | **2.91** | **2.82** | **2.75** | **2.69** | **2.59** | **2.51** | **2.40** | **2.32** | **2.22** | **2.14** | **2.08** | **2.00** | **1.97** | **1.90** | **1.86** | **1.84** |
| 40 | 4.08 | 3.23 | 2.84 | 2.61 | 2.45 | 2.34 | 2.25 | 2.18 | 2.12 | 2.07 | 2.04 | 2.00 | 1.95 | 1.90 | 1.84 | 1.79 | 1.74 | 1.69 | 1.66 | 1.61 | 1.59 | 1.55 | 1.53 | 1.51 |
| | **7.31** | **5.18** | **4.31** | **3.83** | **3.51** | **3.29** | **3.12** | **2.99** | **2.88** | **2.80** | **2.73** | **2.66** | **2.56** | **2.49** | **2.37** | **2.29** | **2.20** | **2.11** | **2.05** | **1.97** | **1.94** | **1.88** | **1.84** | **1.81** |
| 42 | 4.07 | 3.22 | 2.83 | 2.59 | 2.44 | 2.32 | 2.24 | 2.17 | 2.11 | 2.06 | 2.02 | 1.99 | 1.94 | 1.89 | 1.82 | 1.78 | 1.73 | 1.68 | 1.64 | 1.60 | 1.57 | 1.54 | 1.51 | 1.49 |
| | **7.27** | **5.15** | **4.29** | **3.80** | **3.49** | **3.26** | **3.10** | **2.96** | **2.86** | **2.77** | **2.70** | **2.64** | **2.54** | **2.46** | **2.35** | **2.26** | **2.17** | **2.08** | **2.02** | **1.94** | **1.91** | **1.85** | **1.80** | **1.78** |
| 44 | 4.06 | 3.21 | 2.82 | 2.58 | 2.43 | 2.31 | 2.23 | 2.16 | 2.10 | 2.05 | 2.01 | 1.98 | 1.92 | 1.88 | 1.81 | 1.76 | 1.72 | 1.66 | 1.63 | 1.58 | 1.56 | 1.52 | 1.50 | 1.48 |
| | **7.24** | **5.12** | **4.26** | **3.78** | **3.46** | **3.24** | **3.07** | **2.94** | **2.84** | **2.75** | **2.68** | **2.62** | **2.52** | **2.44** | **2.32** | **2.24** | **2.15** | **2.06** | **2.00** | **1.92** | **1.88** | **1.82** | **1.78** | **1.75** |
| 46 | 4.05 | 3.20 | 2.81 | 2.57 | 2.42 | 2.30 | 2.22 | 2.14 | 2.09 | 2.04 | 2.00 | 1.97 | 1.91 | 1.87 | 1.80 | 1.75 | 1.71 | 1.65 | 1.62 | 1.57 | 1.54 | 1.51 | 1.48 | 1.46 |
| | **7.21** | **5.10** | **4.24** | **3.76** | **3.44** | **3.22** | **3.05** | **2.92** | **2.82** | **2.73** | **2.66** | **2.60** | **2.50** | **2.42** | **2.30** | **2.22** | **2.13** | **2.04** | **1.98** | **1.90** | **1.86** | **1.80** | **1.76** | **1.72** |
| 48 | 4.04 | 3.19 | 2.80 | 2.56 | 2.41 | 2.30 | 2.21 | 2.14 | 2.08 | 2.03 | 1.99 | 1.96 | 1.90 | 1.86 | 1.79 | 1.74 | 1.70 | 1.64 | 1.61 | 1.56 | 1.53 | 1.50 | 1.47 | 1.45 |
| | **7.19** | **5.08** | **4.22** | **3.74** | **3.42** | **3.20** | **3.04** | **2.90** | **2.80** | **2.71** | **2.64** | **2.58** | **2.48** | **2.40** | **2.28** | **2.20** | **2.11** | **2.02** | **1.96** | **1.88** | **1.84** | **1.78** | **1.73** | **1.70** |

## TABLE B.4
### Critical values of F (.05 level in roman type, .01 level in **bold**) (continued)

Degrees of Freedom for Greater Mean Square (numerator)

Degrees of Freedom for Lesser Mean Square (denominator)

| | 1 | 2 | 3 | 4 | 5 | 6 | 7 | 8 | 9 | 10 | 11 | 12 | 14 | 16 | 20 | 24 | 30 | 40 | 50 | 75 | 100 | 200 | 500 | ∞ |
|---|---|---|---|---|---|---|---|---|---|---|---|---|---|---|---|---|---|---|---|---|---|---|---|---|
| 50 | 4.03 | 3.18 | 2.79 | 2.56 | 2.40 | 2.29 | 2.20 | 2.13 | 2.07 | 2.02 | 1.98 | 1.95 | 1.90 | 1.85 | 1.78 | 1.74 | 1.69 | 1.63 | 1.60 | 1.55 | 1.52 | 1.48 | 1.46 | 1.44 |
| | **7.17** | **5.06** | **4.20** | **3.72** | **3.41** | **3.18** | **3.02** | **2.88** | **2.78** | **2.70** | **2.62** | **2.56** | **2.46** | **2.39** | **2.26** | **2.18** | **2.10** | **2.00** | **1.94** | **1.86** | **1.82** | **1.76** | **1.71** | **1.68** |
| 55 | 4.02 | 3.17 | 2.78 | 2.54 | 2.38 | 2.27 | 2.18 | 2.11 | 2.05 | 2.00 | 1.97 | 1.93 | 1.88 | 1.83 | 1.76 | 1.72 | 1.67 | 1.61 | 1.58 | 1.52 | 1.50 | 1.46 | 1.43 | 1.41 |
| | **7.12** | **5.01** | **4.16** | **3.68** | **3.37** | **3.15** | **2.98** | **2.85** | **2.75** | **2.66** | **2.59** | **2.53** | **2.43** | **2.35** | **2.23** | **2.15** | **2.06** | **1.96** | **1.90** | **1.82** | **1.78** | **1.71** | **1.66** | **1.64** |
| 60 | 4.00 | 3.15 | 2.76 | 2.52 | 2.37 | 2.25 | 2.17 | 2.10 | 2.04 | 1.99 | 1.95 | 1.92 | 1.86 | 1.81 | 1.75 | 1.70 | 1.65 | 1.59 | 1.56 | 1.50 | 1.48 | 1.44 | 1.41 | 1.39 |
| | **7.08** | **4.98** | **4.13** | **3.65** | **3.34** | **3.12** | **2.95** | **2.82** | **2.72** | **2.63** | **2.56** | **2.50** | **2.40** | **2.32** | **2.20** | **2.12** | **2.03** | **1.93** | **1.87** | **1.79** | **1.74** | **1.68** | **1.63** | **1.60** |
| 65 | 3.99 | 3.14 | 2.75 | 2.51 | 2.36 | 2.24 | 2.15 | 2.08 | 2.02 | 1.98 | 1.94 | 1.90 | 1.85 | 1.80 | 1.73 | 1.68 | 1.63 | 1.57 | 1.54 | 1.49 | 1.46 | 1.42 | 1.39 | 1.37 |
| | **7.04** | **4.95** | **4.10** | **3.62** | **3.31** | **3.09** | **2.93** | **2.79** | **2.70** | **2.61** | **2.54** | **2.47** | **2.37** | **2.30** | **2.18** | **2.09** | **2.00** | **1.90** | **1.84** | **1.76** | **1.71** | **1.64** | **1.60** | **1.56** |
| 70 | 3.98 | 3.13 | 2.74 | 2.50 | 2.35 | 2.23 | 2.14 | 2.07 | 2.01 | 1.97 | 1.93 | 1.89 | 1.84 | 1.79 | 1.72 | 1.67 | 1.62 | 1.56 | 1.53 | 1.47 | 1.45 | 1.40 | 1.37 | 1.35 |
| | **7.01** | **4.92** | **4.08** | **3.60** | **3.29** | **3.07** | **2.91** | **2.77** | **2.67** | **2.59** | **2.51** | **2.45** | **2.35** | **2.28** | **2.15** | **2.07** | **1.98** | **1.88** | **1.82** | **1.74** | **1.69** | **1.62** | **1.56** | **1.53** |
| 80 | 3.96 | 3.11 | 2.72 | 2.48 | 2.33 | 2.21 | 2.12 | 2.05 | 1.99 | 1.95 | 1.91 | 1.88 | 1.82 | 1.77 | 1.70 | 1.65 | 1.60 | 1.54 | 1.51 | 1.45 | 1.42 | 1.38 | 1.35 | 1.32 |
| | **6.96** | **4.88** | **4.04** | **3.56** | **3.25** | **3.04** | **2.87** | **2.74** | **2.64** | **2.55** | **2.48** | **2.41** | **2.32** | **2.24** | **2.11** | **2.03** | **1.94** | **1.84** | **1.78** | **1.70** | **1.65** | **1.57** | **1.52** | **1.49** |
| 100 | 3.94 | 3.09 | 2.70 | 2.46 | 2.30 | 2.19 | 2.10 | 2.03 | 1.97 | 1.92 | 1.88 | 1.85 | 1.79 | 1.75 | 1.68 | 1.63 | 1.57 | 1.51 | 1.48 | 1.42 | 1.39 | 1.34 | 1.30 | 1.28 |
| | **6.90** | **4.82** | **3.98** | **3.51** | **3.20** | **2.99** | **2.82** | **2.69** | **2.59** | **2.51** | **2.43** | **2.36** | **2.26** | **2.19** | **2.06** | **1.98** | **1.89** | **1.79** | **1.73** | **1.64** | **1.59** | **1.51** | **1.46** | **1.43** |
| 125 | 3.92 | 3.07 | 2.68 | 2.44 | 2.29 | 2.17 | 2.08 | 2.01 | 1.95 | 1.90 | 1.86 | 1.83 | 1.77 | 1.72 | 1.65 | 1.60 | 1.55 | 1.49 | 1.45 | 1.39 | 1.36 | 1.31 | 1.27 | 1.25 |
| | **6.84** | **4.78** | **3.94** | **3.47** | **3.17** | **2.95** | **2.79** | **2.65** | **2.56** | **2.47** | **2.40** | **2.33** | **2.23** | **2.15** | **2.03** | **1.94** | **1.85** | **1.75** | **1.68** | **1.59** | **1.54** | **1.46** | **1.40** | **1.37** |
| 150 | 3.91 | 3.06 | 2.67 | 2.43 | 2.27 | 2.16 | 2.07 | 2.00 | 1.94 | 1.89 | 1.85 | 1.82 | 1.76 | 1.71 | 1.64 | 1.59 | 1.54 | 1.47 | 1.44 | 1.37 | 1.34 | 1.29 | 1.25 | 1.22 |
| | **6.81** | **4.75** | **3.91** | **3.44** | **3.14** | **2.92** | **2.76** | **2.62** | **2.53** | **2.44** | **2.37** | **2.30** | **2.20** | **2.12** | **2.00** | **1.91** | **1.83** | **1.72** | **1.66** | **1.56** | **1.51** | **1.43** | **1.37** | **1.33** |
| 200 | 3.89 | 3.04 | 2.65 | 2.41 | 2.26 | 2.14 | 2.05 | 1.98 | 1.92 | 1.87 | 1.83 | 1.80 | 1.74 | 1.69 | 1.62 | 1.57 | 1.52 | 1.45 | 1.42 | 1.35 | 1.32 | 1.26 | 1.22 | 1.19 |
| | **6.76** | **4.71** | **3.88** | **3.41** | **3.11** | **2.90** | **2.73** | **2.60** | **2.50** | **2.41** | **2.34** | **2.28** | **2.17** | **2.09** | **1.97** | **1.88** | **1.79** | **1.69** | **1.62** | **1.53** | **1.48** | **1.39** | **1.33** | **1.28** |
| 400 | 3.86 | 3.02 | 2.62 | 2.39 | 2.23 | 2.12 | 2.03 | 1.96 | 1.90 | 1.85 | 1.81 | 1.78 | 1.72 | 1.67 | 1.60 | 1.54 | 1.49 | 1.42 | 1.38 | 1.32 | 1.28 | 1.22 | 1.16 | 1.13 |
| | **6.70** | **4.66** | **3.83** | **3.36** | **3.06** | **2.85** | **2.69** | **2.55** | **2.46** | **2.37** | **2.29** | **2.23** | **2.12** | **2.04** | **1.92** | **1.84** | **1.74** | **1.64** | **1.57** | **1.47** | **1.42** | **1.32** | **1.24** | **1.19** |
| 1000 | 3.85 | 3.00 | 2.61 | 2.38 | 2.22 | 2.10 | 2.02 | 1.95 | 1.89 | 1.84 | 1.80 | 1.76 | 1.70 | 1.65 | 1.58 | 1.53 | 1.47 | 1.41 | 1.36 | 1.30 | 1.26 | 1.19 | 1.13 | 1.08 |
| | **6.66** | **4.62** | **3.80** | **3.34** | **3.04** | **2.82** | **2.66** | **2.53** | **2.43** | **2.34** | **2.26** | **2.20** | **2.09** | **2.01** | **1.89** | **1.81** | **1.71** | **1.61** | **1.54** | **1.44** | **1.38** | **1.28** | **1.19** | **1.11** |
| ∞ | 3.84 | 2.99 | 2.60 | 2.37 | 2.21 | 2.09 | 2.01 | 1.94 | 1.88 | 1.83 | 1.79 | 1.75 | 1.69 | 1.64 | 1.57 | 1.52 | 1.46 | 1.40 | 1.35 | 1.28 | 1.24 | 1.17 | 1.11 | 1.00 |
| | **6.64** | **4.60** | **3.78** | **3.32** | **3.02** | **2.80** | **2.64** | **2.51** | **2.41** | **2.32** | **2.24** | **2.18** | **2.07** | **1.99** | **1.87** | **1.79** | **1.69** | **1.59** | **1.52** | **1.41** | **1.36** | **1.25** | **1.15** | **1.00** |

Source: From *Statistical Methods*, Sixth Edition, by G. W. Snedecor and W. G. Cochran, Iowa State University Press (1967) Reprinted by permission.

# A Journal Article in Manuscript Form

Note:

Some procedures for preparing and submitting a manuscript vary from journal to journal. Consult the correct APA publication manual and the specific journal before submitting any manuscript for publication.

Running head: MESSAGE FRAMING AND TEMPORAL CONTEXT        1

Effects of Message Framing and Temporal Context

on College Student Drinking Behavior

Mary A. Gerend and Margaret Cullen

Florida State University

Author Note

Mary A. Gerend and Margaret Cullen are affiliated with the Department of Medical Humanities and Social Sciences, College of Medicine, Florida State University.

Correspondence concerning this article should be addressed to Mary A. Gerend, Department of Medical Humanities and Social Sciences, College of Medicine, Florida State University, 1115 W. Call Street, Tallahassee, Florida 32306-4300. E-mail: mary.gerend@med.fsu.edu

## Abstract

This study evaluated the interactive effects of message framing and temporal context on college student alcohol use. Participants ($n = 228$) were randomly assigned to read an alcohol prevention message that varied by message frame (gains versus losses) and temporal context (short- versus long-term consequences). Participants returned to the lab one month later to report their drinking behavior over the past month. As predicted, students exposed to the gain-framed message reported lower alcohol use (drank less frequently, drank fewer alcoholic beverages per drinking occasion, and engaged in less binge drinking) as compared to students exposed to the loss-framed message, but only if they read about short-term consequences of alcohol use. Message frame had no effect when participants were exposed to long-term consequences. This investigation extends previous research by demonstrating the effectiveness of message framing for reducing health-damaging behaviors and by identifying temporal context as a moderator of framing effects.

*Key words:* message framing; temporal context; alcohol; risk behavior

Effects of Message Framing and Temporal Context on

College Student Drinking Behavior

People's choices are shaped by a number of important psychological processes. Many theories of judgment and decision-making suggest that choices are guided by consideration of the potential outcomes associated with one's actions (Edwards, 1962). Theories of message framing indicate that the manner in which these outcomes are framed—in terms of either potential losses or gains— can profoundly affect people's choices and behavior (Rothman, Bartels, Wlaschin, & Salovey, 2006; Rothman & Salovey, 1997). Indeed, numerous studies have demonstrated the effectiveness of framed messages for influencing decisions, particularly in the realm of health behavior (e.g., exercise, mammography, sunscreen use; Rothman et al., 2006).

The current research extends theories of message framing in two ways. First, although many studies have demonstrated the utility of message framing for promoting *positive* health behaviors, very few have examined its effectiveness for reducing unwanted health behaviors (e.g., binge drinking, cigarette smoking). The current study therefore examined whether message framing would provide a useful means of reducing a common and potentially health-damaging behavior— problem drinking among college students. Second, little is known about the ideal content of framed messages (Rothman et al., 2006). We were interested in assessing the possibility that framing effects depend on the temporal context in which outcomes are considered—that is, whether a message highlights short- or long-term outcomes associated with a given behavior. In the current study, we evaluated the potentially interactive effects of framing and temporal context on college student alcohol use. We propose that messages emphasizing the immediate benefits of reducing risk behavior may prove to be an especially effective strategy for decreasing health-damaging behaviors such as problem drinking.

## Message Framing

Message framing—providing equivalent outcome information in terms of either gains or losses—has proven to be an effective strategy for promoting behavior change across a wide range of health-related practices (Rothman et al., 2006; Rothman & Salovey, 1997). Gain-framed messages typically highlight the benefits of engaging in a health-protective behavior or avoiding a risky behavior, whereas loss-framed messages highlight the costs of not engaging in a health-protective behavior or engaging in a risky behavior. Message framing is theoretically grounded in prospect theory (Tversky & Kahneman, 1981), which suggests that people respond differently to information highlighting gains versus losses. Specifically, prospect theory holds that individuals are generally more willing to pursue a risky course of action when considering losses, but tend to be more risk-averse when considering gains.

Drawing on prospect theory, Rothman and Salovey (1997) proposed that whether a gain- or loss-framed appeal will be more effective depends largely upon whether the recommended behavior is perceived to involve risk. The degree of risk associated with a given behavior is often signaled by its purpose: whether its goal is to detect or to prevent disease. Because the purpose of a detection or screening behavior (e.g., mammography, colonoscopy) is to reveal a potentially life-threatening health problem, engaging in screening behaviors could be viewed as risky (at least in the proximal sense). In contrast, because the purpose of a preventive health behavior (e.g., using sunscreen, eating fruits and vegetables) is to thwart disease, engaging in these behaviors is typically viewed as safe.

Linking this framework to prospect theory, Rothman and Salovey (1997) suggested that because people are relatively open to taking risks when faced with potential losses, loss-framed appeals should be most effective in promoting disease *detection* behaviors—behaviors that signal potential risk. However, because people tend to avoid risks in the face of potential gains, gain-framed appeals should be most effective in promoting *preventive* health behaviors— behaviors that signal low risk. Indeed, this conceptual framework is supported by a large body of empirical research (Apanovitch, McCarthy, & Salovey, 2003; Detweiler, Bedell, Salovey, Pronin, & Rothman, 1999; Kiene, Barta, Zelenski, & Cothran, 2005; Robberson & Rogers, 1988; Schneider et al., 2001).

One goal of the present study was to extend the application of message framing to interventions aimed at reducing unhealthy behaviors. Rothman and Salovey (1997) suggested that people who engage in risk behavior may be more responsive to messages that focus on the *advantages of stopping* the risky behavior (a gain frame) than the *disadvantages of continuing* the risky behavior (a loss frame). The reasoning is that, because initiating a healthy behavior and reducing an unhealthy behavior share the same goal of disease prevention (and because people become more risk averse in the face of certain gains), a gain-framed message is expected to outperform a loss-framed message in motivating people to refrain from risky behaviors. Few studies have tested this hypothesis empirically, however, and thus the extent to which gain-frames are effective in motivating individuals to stop unhealthy behaviors is unclear (Rothman et al., 2006).

Two previous studies have examined effects of framed messages on reducing health-damaging behavior. In both of these studies, gain-framed appeals emphasizing the benefits of smoking cessation were found to be more effective than loss-framed appeals emphasizing the costs of smoking in promoting anti-smoking beliefs and attitudes (Schneider, Salovey, Pallonen, Mundorf, Smith, & Steward, 2001) and in encouraging stronger intentions to quit smoking (Steward, Schneider, Pizarro, & Salovey, 2003). Neither study, however, was able to demonstrate significant effects on behavior. Nevertheless, the gain-frame advantage was attributed to the fact that smoking cessation is typically perceived to be a disease prevention behavior that involves relatively certain and safe outcomes. Because gain-framed messages encourage people to pursue courses of action with certain outcomes, gain-framed messages should be more effective than loss-framed messages in motivating risk-reduction behaviors such as smoking cessation. Applying this reasoning to the current study, we predicted that a message highlighting the benefits of responsible drinking (a gain-framed message) should be more effective at reducing alcohol abuse than a message highlighting the costs of problem drinking (a loss-framed message).

**Temporal Context**

Another goal of the present study was to assess the extent to which the temporal context in which framed outcomes are considered influences the effects of message framing. Most behaviors result in both short-term and long-term consequences. Drinking excessive amounts of alcohol, for example, can damage one's interpersonal relationships in the days and weeks to follow and can also negatively affect one's relationships over a longer time span into the future. Previous research on temporal discounting implies that framing effects may well depend on whether people are considering the short-term versus long-term consequences of their actions (e.g., Estle, Green, Myerson, & Holt, 2006; Green & Myerson, 2004). In particular, many studies suggest that individuals tend to discount the future (e.g., Green & Myerson, 2004). That is, behavior tends to be more strongly affected by consideration of short-term consequences, as compared to consideration of long-term consequences, even when the outcomes themselves are objectively the same over time (Chapman, 2005; Mischel, Shoda, & Rodriguez, 1989; Rachlin, 1995). Future outcomes tend to be discounted for several reasons: compared to long-term consequences, short-term consequences tend to be more salient, more relevant, and easier for individuals to conceptualize (Petty & Cacioppo, 1984). From this perspective one might expect that messages focusing on the short-term consequences of a behavior would be more impactful than messages focusing on the possible long-term consequences of a behavior.

Evidence for temporal discounting suggests that the extent to which people discount future outcomes depends on whether they are considering potential gains versus potential losses. Although both long-term gains and long-term losses tend to be discounted (relative to short-term gains and losses), the discounting function is somewhat steeper for gains than for losses (Estle et al., 2006). As one considers positive outcomes that are farther off into the future, the less psychologically impactful those positive outcomes tend to be. In the context of the current study, therefore, we expected that the relative advantage of a gain-framed message for reducing a health-damaging behavior (problem drinking) would be strong when people are considering short-term consequences, but might be reduced or eliminated when people are considering long-term consequences.

**Overview of the Present Study**

The present study integrated theories of message framing and temporal discounting to develop a brief, low-cost intervention for reducing alcohol use among college students. Alcohol abuse continues to be a large problem in the United States, especially on university campuses. About four in five college students drink alcoholic beverages and about 40% engage in binge drinking (Goldman, Boyd, & Faden, 2002). Problem drinking is associated with negative academic, interpersonal, and health consequences (Engs, Diebold, & Hanson, 1996; Goldman et al., 2002; Wechsler, Davenport, Dowdall, Moeykens, &

Castillo, 1994; Wechsler, Lee, Kuo, & Lee, 2000). University freshmen are at particularly high risk for problematic alcohol use (Larimer & Cronce, 2002).

Interventions aimed at reducing risky behaviors tend to emphasize future health problems that may result from continuing the risk behavior. Many of these interventions attempt to arouse feelings of threat and fear by emphasizing the *long-term costs of engaging in risk behavior* (e.g., smoking greatly increases your chances of developing lung cancer and heart disease) (Mahler, Kulik, Gibbons, Gerrard, & Harrell, 2003). As described above, however, theory and research pertaining to message framing and temporal discounting suggest that emphasizing the immediate benefits of refraining from the risk behavior may be a more effective strategy.

The current study investigated the interactive effects of message framing and temporal context on college student alcohol use. Students were exposed to an alcohol prevention message and asked to return to the lab one month later. When considering short-term consequences, we expected that participants would report lower alcohol use when exposed to the gain-framed message, as compared to the loss-framed message. In contrast, when considering long-term consequences, no difference in alcohol use was expected among participants exposed to the gain- versus loss-framed message. Overall, we expected individuals exposed to the short-term, gain-framed message to report lower alcohol use over the one-month assessment period than individuals exposed to the other three messages.

## Method

### Participants

A sample of 228 undergraduate students (70 men; 158 women) from a large southeastern university participated in exchange for course credit. The mean age was 18.6 ($SD = 1.2$; range 17–26). Most participants (71%) were in their freshman year of college. The majority of participants were white (79%;

7% black or African American, 3% Asian, 11% mixed or other). Nineteen

percent reported that they were of Hispanic or Latino ethnicity.

**Procedure and Materials**

The experiment took place over two sessions, approximately one month

apart. Participants were randomly assigned to one of four conditions in a 2

(message frame: gain vs. loss frame) × 2 (temporal context: short-term vs.

long-term consequences) between-subjects design. After completing a pretest

survey, participants were given 5 minutes to read an information sheet about

alcohol use, which included a discussion of binge drinking, warning signs of

problem drinking, and a gain- or loss-framed message about either the

short-term or long-term consequences of alcohol use. The same outcomes were

presented in all conditions; only the frame and timing of those outcomes varied.

Framed messages vary both the action that is taken (whether something

is attained or not attained) and the outcome of that action (whether it is desirable

or undesirable) (Rothman & Salovey, 1997). Gain-framed appeals thus focus on

either "attaining a desirable outcome" or "not attaining an undesirable

outcome." In contrast, loss-framed appeals focus on "not attaining a desirable

outcome" or "attaining an undesirable outcome." Because previous research

suggests that the framing component of a message (whether it is gain or loss) is

more important than the specific action or outcome described (e.g., Detweiler

et al., 1999), we used a combination of these constructions to create the alcohol

prevention messages. Each condition focused on alcohol-related outcomes for

health (e.g., liver, weight), social interactions (relationships), psychological

functioning (judgment, memory), and performance (college/career). See Table 1

for excerpts from each of the four messages discussing health-related and

psychological outcomes associated with alcohol use. After reading the message, participants completed a brief posttest survey that assessed their perceptions of and emotional reactions to the message.

Participants returned to the lab approximately one month later to complete a survey that assessed their alcohol use over the past month. Nearly 80% ($n = 181$) of participants returned for session two. Relative to completers, noncompleters were similar in age, gender, ethnicity, race (white vs. non-white), and year in college (all $ps > .20$). Dropout rates were the same across the four experimental conditions ($p > .30$).

**Measures**

The pretest survey assessed demographic and background variables (e.g., age, ethnicity). The posttest survey assessed overall impressions of the message (e.g., the extent to which the information was interesting, easy to understand, and informative; $1 =$ disagree strongly to $6 =$ agree strongly), affective reactions to the information (e.g., the extent to which they felt anxious, afraid, hopeful, and relieved; $1 =$ not at all to $6 =$ extremely), and manipulation checks (whether the message focused on the benefits of not drinking vs. the costs of drinking; whether the message focused on short-term vs. long-term consequences). Ratings for each manipulation check were made on a 6-point scale.

The one-month follow-up survey assessed alcohol use since the first session of the experiment. Self-reported alcohol use measures were adapted from previous research (Collins & Marlatt, 1981; D'Amico & Fromme, 2002). We assessed the (a) frequency of alcohol use since session one (never, once, 2–4 times during the month, 2–3 times a week, 4 or more times a week; coded 0 though 4, respectively), (b) quantity of alcohol use since session one (number of alcoholic drinks consumed on a typical day when drinking: none, 1 or 2, 3 or 4, 5 or 6, 7 to 9, 10 or more; coded 0 through 5, respectively), and (c) frequency of binge drinking (having 5 or more drinks on any one occasion) since session one (0 = never to 5 = very often).

## Results

### Manipulation Checks

We conducted a series of factorial analyses of variance (ANOVAs) to confirm the effectiveness of the framing and temporal context manipulations. Relative to participants in the loss-framed condition ($M = 1.81$, $SD = 1.24$), those in the gain-framed condition reported that the information focused more on the benefits of not drinking than on the costs of drinking ($M = 4.07$, $SD = 1.75$), $F (1, 224) = 126.13$, $p < .001$. Further, participants in the short-term condition ($M = 3.12$, $SD = 1.45$) reported that the message focused more on short-term consequences than did participants in the long-term condition ($M = 5.03$, $SD = 0.91$), $F (1, 224) = 142.51$, $p < .001$. There were no interactions between the framing and temporal context manipulations on either manipulation check. Across the four conditions, participants rated the information equally interesting, easy to understand, and informative. No significant effects of message frame, temporal context, or their interaction were found on the degree to which participants felt anxious, hopeful, or relieved after reading the message. However, participants who read the loss-framed message reported feeling more afraid ($M = 1.58$, $SD = 0.94$) than those who read the gain-framed message ($M = 1.32$, $SD = 0.64$), $F (1, 224) = 6.169$, $p < .05$.

### Effects of Message Framing and Temporal Context on Drinking Behavior

Factorial ANOVAs were used to test for effects of message frame and temporal context on drinking-related measures assessed one month after exposure to the manipulation. Dependent variables included quantity of alcohol use since session one, frequency of binge drinking since session one, and frequency of alcohol use since session one. We conducted a 2 (message frame: gain or loss) by 2 (temporal context: short-term or long-term consequences) ANOVA for each dependent variable. Moreover, we conducted planned contrasts to test the hypothesis that the gain-framed short-term consequences message would be more effective than the other three messages combined.

For quantity of alcohol use (number of alcoholic drinks per drinking occasion), we observed a main effect of temporal context, $F (1, 177) = 3.858$, $p = .05$, such that participants exposed to the short-term consequences message reported having fewer drinks per drinking occasion than participants exposed to the long-term consequences message. There was no main effect of frame. The main effect of temporal context was qualified by a significant frame by temporal context interaction, $F (1, 176) = 4.794$, $p < .05$ (see Figure 1). To interpret the interaction we tested the simple effect of message frame within the short-term and long-term consequences conditions. Among participants in the short-term condition, exposure to the gain-framed message ($M = 1.36$; $SD = 1.35$) led to a significantly lower number of drinks per occasion than did exposure to the loss-framed message ($M = 2.10$; $SD = 1.37$), $F (1, 92) = 7.04$, $p < .01$, partial $\eta^2 = .07$. However, no differential effects of the gain- ($M = 2.24$; $SD = 1.39$) versus loss-framed message ($M = 2.02$; $SD = 1.37$) were observed among participants in the long-term condition, $F < 1$. Furthermore, results from the planned contrast revealed that, compared with the other three conditions, participants in the gain-framed, short-term consequences condition consumed significantly fewer drinks per occasion over the past month, $F (1, 179) = 10.511$, $p < .001$, partial $\eta^2 = .06$.

Similar analyses were conducted for frequency of binge drinking. We again observed the predicted message frame by temporal context interaction effect, $F (1, 173) = 3.77$, $p = .05$ (see Figure 2). No main effects were observed. Simple effect tests revealed that, among participants in the short-term consequences condition, exposure to the gain-framed message ($M = 1.21$; $SD = 1.70$) led to a significantly lower rate of binge drinking than did exposure to the loss-framed message ($M = 2.02$; $SD = 1.90$), $F (1, 89) = 4.48$, $p < .05$, partial $\eta^2 = .05$. However, no differential effect of the gain- ($M = 1.88$; $SD = 1.74$) versus loss-framed message ($M = 1.66$; $SD = 1.66$) was observed among participants in the long-term consequences condition, $F < 1$. This pattern is consistent with the pattern found for overall quantity of alcohol use. Compared with the other three conditions, participants in the gain-framed, short-term consequences condition were less likely to engage in binge drinking in the past month, $F (1, 175) = 4.339$, $p < .05$, partial $\eta^2 = .02$.

For frequency of alcohol use (number of drinking occasions per month), we observed only a main effect of message frame, such that exposure to the gain-framed message resulted in lower alcohol use frequency ($M = 1.67$; $SD = 1.20$) than did exposure to the loss-framed message ($M = 2.03$; $SD = 1.08$), $F (1, 177) = 4.448$, $p < .05$, partial $\eta^2 = .03$. Although the interaction between message frame and temporal context was not statistically significant ($p = .12$), the overall pattern of findings was similar to that for the other two dependent measures (see Figure 3). Simple effect tests revealed that among participants in the short-term consequences condition, exposure to the gain-framed message ($M = 1.44$; $SD = 1.29$) led to significantly lower rates of alcohol use than did exposure to the loss-framed message ($M = 2.06$; $SD = 1.05$), $F (1, 92) = 6.519$, $p < .05$, partial $\eta^2 = .07$. No differential effect of the gain- ($M = 1.90$; $SD = 1.06$) versus loss-framed message ($M = 2.00$; $SD = 1.13$) was observed among participants in the long-term consequences condition, $F < 1$. Compared with the other three conditions, participants in the gain-framed, short-term consequences condition consumed alcohol less frequently during the assessment period, $F (1, 179) = 7.974$, $p < .01$, partial $\eta^2 = .04$. This pattern was consistent with those observed for alcohol quantity and binge drinking.

## Discussion

The current study demonstrates the benefits of framed messages for reducing potentially health-damaging behaviors. This study also extends psychological theories of message framing by identifying temporal context as an important moderator of framing effects. We found that the effects of gain- and loss-framed messages on drinking behavior were moderated by whether alcohol-related outcomes were said to occur immediately versus in the future. As predicted, when faced with the short-term consequences of alcohol use, participants exposed to a gain-framed message reported lower alcohol use than participants exposed to a loss-framed message. In contrast, when faced with the long-term consequences, no differences in alcohol use were observed among participants exposed to a gain- or loss-framed message. Indeed, relative to students in the other three conditions, those exposed to the immediate benefits of limited alcohol use reported drinking fewer alcoholic beverages per drinking occasion, drinking less frequently, and engaging in less binge drinking over the one-month follow-up period. Overall, findings suggest that asking people to consider the benefits associated with avoiding a risky health behavior is more effective than asking them to consider the costs of engaging in the risky behavior, but only when those outcomes occur in the short term.

The present study advances research and theory on message framing in two important ways. First, this work extends the application of framing interventions to risky behaviors. Most previous studies have demonstrated the effectiveness of message framing for motivating engagement in health-promoting behaviors (e.g., using sunscreen; Detweiler et al., 1999; Rothman, Salovey, Antone, Keough, & Martin, 1993); flossing (Mann, Sherman, &

Updegraff, 2004); using condoms (Kiene et al., 2005); getting vaccinated (Gerend & Shepherd, 2007). To the best of our knowledge only two previous studies have examined effects of message framing for motivating cessation or reduction of potentially health-damaging behaviors (e.g., smoking; Schneider, Salovey, Pallonen, et al., 2001; Steward et al., 2003). Moreover, neither study showed effects on behavior. Findings from the current study suggest that, like initiation of a health-protective behavior, reduction of a risk behavior is most likely to occur when individuals are exposed to short-term potential gains associated with changing their behavior. Findings may shed light on why, in the context of alcohol prevention research, interventions emphasizing the negative consequences of drinking (e.g., Drug Abuse Resistance Education, also known as DARE) tend to be relatively ineffective at reducing alcohol use (D'Amico & Fromme, 2002).

The second major advance of the present findings is the identification of an important boundary condition on framing effects. We observed the advantage of a gain-framed message only when the message emphasized the short-term (as opposed to the long-term) benefits of responsible alcohol use. The extent to which messages framed in terms of gains or losses affect behavior appears to depend on whether those outcomes are expected to occur in the present or future. Findings are consistent with previous research suggesting that individuals tend to discount future outcomes (Estle et al., 2006; Green & Myerson, 2004). Findings are also consistent with the smoking literature, which has shown that campaigns focusing on the immediate consequences of smoking (e.g., stained teeth and hands, bad breath, expensive habit), compared to its long-term consequences (e.g., lung cancer, heart disease), have been relatively more successful in reducing smoking behavior (Evans, Dratt, Raines, & Rosenberg, 1988; Pechmann, Zhao, Goldberg, & Reibling, 2003).

In addition to its theoretical implications, the current research has potentially important implications for programs aimed at curbing problem drinking, particularly on college campuses. Previous interventions aimed at reducing risk behavior typically emphasize the health-related problems or negative consequences of engaging in risky behaviors, as opposed to the potential benefits of reducing or eliminating the unhealthy behaviors (Mahler et al., 2003). Moreover, most interventions tend to focus on long-term health problems associated with the behavior–consequences that typically will not emerge until the distant future, if they emerge at all (Mahler et al., 2003; Pechmann et al., 2003). Findings from the present study suggest that when attempting to reduce risky behavior, focusing on short-term benefits, rather than long-term costs, is likely to be more effective.

Reducing excessive alcohol use among college students has proven to be a challenging problem for prevention researchers (Goldman et al., 2002; Larimer & Cronce, 2002). The current study demonstrates the effectiveness of a brief, low-cost, and easy-to-implement health communication strategy for reducing alcohol use in a high-risk population. Messages with similar content could easily be incorporated into existing interventions aimed at reducing problem drinking. Integrating these findings into programs that include other strategies found to reduce problem drinking, such as self-monitoring, alcohol skills training, and motivational feedback, may be particularly effective (D'Amico & Fromme, 2002; Larimer & Cronce, 2002).

**Study Limitations and Directions for Future Research**

The present study should be considered in light of its methodological limitations, which provide important opportunities for future research. The present findings are based on self-reported alcohol use that reflects alcohol quantity and frequency. Although these measures provide a reliable estimate of drinking behavior, they are limited in that they may not fully assess sporadic heavy drinking episodes, episodes that may be particularly common in a student population. Future studies might benefit from using additional measures (e.g., daily drinking estimation methods such as alcohol timeline followback) that capture more detailed information about drinking behavior (Sobell & Sobell, 2001).

In addition, research has suggested that the effectiveness of persuasive communications may depend on individual differences in the extent to which people consider short- versus long-term outcomes. Orbell, Perugini, and Rakow (2004) demonstrated that present-oriented individuals expressed the most interest in a cancer screening program when the health communication emphasized its short-term benefits and long-term costs. The reverse was true for future-oriented individuals. Including individual difference measures of time perspective such as the Consideration of Future Consequences scale (Strathman, Gleicher, Boninger, & Edwards, 1994) or the Zimbardo Time Perspective Inventory (Zimbardo & Boyd, 1999) may have shed further light on the present findings.

Although the current study provides novel evidence bearing on the effectiveness of message framing for reducing alcohol use, this is but one health-damaging behavior to which theories of message framing and temporal context might apply. Combining message framing with temporal context could prove to be an effective health communication strategy for reducing a range of risky health behaviors (e.g., smoking, tanning bed use, eating a high-fat diet). Future studies should evaluate the extent to which the current findings generalize to other risky behaviors. Moreover, the current findings may have implications for behaviors beyond the domain of health. Many behaviors are shaped by consideration of the possible outcomes (e.g., in deciding whether or not to pursue a particular career, one is likely to consider the potential costs and benefits, both in the short and long term). The current research therefore may shed light on factors guiding behavioral decision making across a variety of domains.

Findings from the present study highlight a potentially important issue to be explored in future message-framing research: the content of the framed message. While empirical studies have demonstrated important effects associated with the frame of a message (gain versus loss) (Rothman et al., 2006; Rothman & Salovey, 1997), less attention has focused on the nature of the outcomes highlighted within the message (for exceptions, see Detweiler et al., 1999; Kiene et al., 2005). The current study suggests that the specific outcomes communicated in a message may play a key role in shaping how framed messages are processed. Future studies may benefit from examining additional content areas beyond temporal context (e.g., appearance vs. health outcomes; Jones & Leary, 1994; Mahler et al., 2003).

**Conclusion**

Message framing has proven to be a very effective and easy-to-implement persuasive communication strategy for motivating health behavior (Rothman et al., 2006). The current study extends the framing literature by demonstrating the use of framing manipulations for the reduction of health-damaging behaviors and by identifying temporal context as an important moderator of framed messages. These findings suggest a powerful communication strategy for reducing a wide variety of problematic behaviors.

# References

Apanovitch, A. M., McCarthy, D., & Salovey, P. (2003). Using message framing to motivate HIV testing among low-income, ethnic minority women. *Health Psychology, 22,* 60–67.

Chapman, G. B. (2005). Short-term cost for long-term benefit: Time preference and cancer control. *Health Psychology, 24,* S41–48.

Collins, R. L., & Marlatt, G. A. (1981). Social modeling as a determinant of drinking behavior: Implications for prevention and treatment. *Addictive Behavior, 6,* 233–239.

D'Amico, E. J., & Fromme, K. (2002). Brief prevention for adolescent risk-taking behavior. *Addiction, 97,* 563–574.

Detweiler, J. B., Bedell, B. T., Salovey, P., Pronin, E., & Rothman, A. J. (1999). Message framing and sunscreen use: Gain-framed messages motivate beach-goers. *Health Psychology, 18,* 189–196.

Edwards, W. (1962). Subjective probabilities inferred from decisions. *Psychological Review, 69,* 109–135.

Engs, R. C., Diebold, B. A., & Hanson, D. J. (1996). The drinking patterns and problems of a national sample of college students. *Journal of Alcohol and Drug Education, 41,* 13–33.

Estle, S. J., Green, L., Myerson, J., & Holt, D. D. (2006). Differential effects of amount on temporal and probability discounting of gains and losses. *Memory & Cognition, 34,* 914–928.

Evans, R. I., Dratt, L. M., Raines, B. E., & Rosenberg, S. S. (1988). Social influences on smoking initiation: Importance of distinguishing descriptive versus mediating process variables. *Journal of Applied Social Psychology, 16,* 220–227.

Gerend, M. A., & Shepherd, J. E. (2007). Using message framing to promote acceptance of the human papillomavirus vaccine. *Health Psychology, 26*, 745–752.

Goldman, M. S., Boyd, G. M., & Faden, V. (2002). College drinking, what it is, and what to do about it: A review of the state of the science. *Journal of Studies on Alcohol, Supplement 14*, 1–250.

Green, L., & Myerson, J. (2004). A discounting framework for choice with delayed and probabilistic rewards. *Psychological Bulletin, 130*, 769–792.

Jones, J. L., & Leary, M. R. (1994). Effects of appearance-based admonitions against sun exposure on tanning intentions in young adults. *Health Psychology, 13*, 86–90.

Kiene, S. M., Barta, W. D., Zelenski, J. M., & Cothran, D. L. (2005). Why are you bringing up condoms now? The effect of message content on framing effects of condom use messages. *Health Psychology, 24*, 321–326.

Larimer, M. E., & Cronce, J. M. (2002). Identification, prevention and treatment: A review of individual-focused strategies to reduce problematic alcohol consumption by college students. *Journal of Studies on Alcohol, Supplement 14*, 148–163.

Mahler, H. I., Kulik, J. A., Gibbons, F. X., Gerrard, M., & Harrell, J. (2003). Effects of appearance-based interventions on sun protection intentions and self-reported behaviors. *Health Psychology, 22*, 199–209.

Mann, T., Sherman, D., & Updegraff, J. (2004). Dispositional motivations and message framing: A test of the congruency hypothesis in college students. *Health Psychology, 23*, 330–334.

Mischel, W., Shoda, Y., & Rodriguez, M. I. (1989). Delay of gratification in children. *Science, 244*, 933–938.

Orbell, S., Perugini, M., & Rakow, T. (2004). Individual differences in sensitivity to health communications: Consideration of future consequences. *Health Psychology, 23*, 388–396.

Pechmann, C., Zhao, G., Goldberg, M. E., & Reibling, E. T. (2003). What to convey in antismoking advertisements for adolescents: The use of protection motivation theory to identify effective message themes. *Journal of Marketing, 67*, 1–18.

Petty, R. E., & Cacioppo, J. T. (1984). The effects of involvement on responses to argument quality and quantity: Central and peripheral routes to persuasion. *Journal of Personality and Social Psychology, 46*, 69–81.

Rachlin, H. (1995). The value of temporal patterns in behavior. *Current Directions in Psychological Science, 4*, 188–192.

Robberson, M. R., & Rogers, R. W. (1988). Beyond fear appeals: Negative and positive persuasive appeals to health and self-esteem. *Journal of Applied Social Psychology, 13*, 277–287.

Rothman, A. J., Bartels, R. D., Wlaschin, J., & Salovey, P. (2006). The strategic use of gain- and loss-framed messages to promote health behavior: How theory can inform practice. *Journal of Communication, 56*, S202–220.

Rothman, A. J., & Salovey, P. (1997). Shaping perceptions to motivate healthy behavior: The role of message framing. *Psychological Bulletin, 121*, 3–19.

Rothman, A. J., Salovey, P., Antone, C., Keough, K., & Martin, C. D. (1993). The influence of message framing on intentions to perform health behaviors. *Journal of Experimental Social Psychology, 29*, 408–433.

Schneider, T. R., Salovey, P., Apanovitch, A. M., Pizarro, J., McCarthy, D., Zullo, J., et al. (2001). The effects of message framing and ethnic targeting on mammography use among low-income women. *Health Psychology, 20*, 256–266.

Schneider, T. R., Salovey, P., Pallonen, U., Mundorf, N., Smith, N. F., & Steward, W. T. (2001). Visual and auditory message framing effects on tobacco smoking. *Journal of Applied Social Psychology, 31,* 667–682.

Sobell, L. C., & Sobell, M. B. (2001). Alcohol consumption measures. In J. P. Allen & V. B. Wilson (Eds.), *Assessing alcohol problems: A guide for clinicians and researchers* (2nd ed., pp. 75–99). Bethesda, MD: National Institute on Alcohol Abuse & Alcoholism.

Steward, W. T., Schneider, T. R., Pizarro, J., & Salovey, P. (2003). Need for cognition moderates responses to framed smoking-cessation messages. *Journal of Applied Social Psychology, 33,* 2439–2464.

Strathman, A., Gleicher, F., Boninger, D. S., & Edwards, S. (1994). The consideration of future consequences: Weighing immediate and distant outcomes of behavior. *Journal of Personality and Social Psychology, 66,* 742–752.

Tversky, A., & Kahneman, D. (1981). The framing of decisions and the psychology of choice. *Science, 211,* 453–458.

Wechsler, H., Davenport, A., Dowdall, G., Moeykens, B., & Castillo, S. (1994). Health and behavioral consequences of binge drinking in college. A national survey of students at 140 campuses. *Journal of the American Medical Association, 272,* 1672–1677.

Wechsler, H., Lee, J. E., Kuo, M., & Lee, H. (2000). College binge drinking in the 1990s: A continuing problem. Results of the Harvard School of Public Health 1999 College Alcohol Study. *Journal of American College Health, 48,* 199–210.

Zimbardo, P. G. & Boyd, J. N. (1999) Putting time in perspective: A valid, reliable individual-differences metric. *Journal of Personality and Social Psychology, 77,* 1271–1288.

Table 1

*Excerpts from the Four Alcohol Prevention Messages Discussing Health and Psychological Consequences*

| | Temporal Context | |
|---|---|---|
| Message Frame | Short-term Consequences | Long-term Consequences |
| Gain | **What Are the <u>Immediate</u> Consequences of Alcohol Use?** | **What Are the <u>Long-term</u> Consequences of Alcohol Use?** |
| | If you decide to drink or are drinking already, it is important for you to know about the negative consequences of alcohol use <u>you can avoid within days and even hours after use.</u> | If you decide to drink or are drinking already, it is important for you to know about the negative consequences of alcohol use <u>you can avoid for years into the future.</u> |
| | **Health**: If you're going to drink, responsible alcohol use can help you <u>avoid immediate negative health consequences.</u> You will increase the likelihood of driving safely, having a healthy liver, and maintaining a healthy weight. Moreover, people who drink responsibly are less likely to engage in risky sexual behavior placing them at risk for sexually transmitted diseases (STDs), unintended pregnancy, and regretted sexual experiences. | **Health:** If you're going to drink, responsible alcohol use can help you <u>avoid long-term negative health consequences.</u> You will increase the likelihood of driving safely, having a healthy liver, and maintaining a healthy weight. Moreover, people who drink responsibly are less likely to engage in risky sexual behavior placing them at risk for sexually transmitted diseases (STDs), unintended pregnancy, and regretted sexual experiences. |
| | **Psychological**: Limiting your alcohol use now can help you <u>avoid psychological problems that can occur soon after drinking.</u> Alcohol use may result in impaired judgment, poorer memory, and difficulty concentrating. Limiting alcohol use may lead to better mood and higher self-esteem in the near future. | **Psychological**: Limiting your alcohol use now can help you <u>avoid psychological problems that can occur long after drinking.</u> Alcohol use may result in impaired judgment, poorer memory, and difficulty concentrating. Limiting alcohol use may lead to better mood and higher self-esteem in the distant future. |

| Loss | What Are the <u>Immediate</u> Consequences of <u>Alcohol Use?</u> | What Are the <u>Long-term</u> Consequences of <u>Alcohol Use?</u> |
|---|---|---|
| | If you decide to drink or are drinking already, it is important for you to know about the negative consequences of alcohol use that <u>you can experience within days and even hours after use.</u> | If you decide to drink or are drinking already, it is important for you to know about the negative consequences of alcohol use <u>you can experience for years into the future.</u> |
| | **Health**: If you're going to drink, irresponsible alcohol use can lead you to <u>experience immediate negative health consequences.</u> You will increase the likelihood of driving accidents, having an unhealthy liver, and gaining weight. Moreover, people who drink irresponsibly are more likely to engage in risky sexual behavior placing them at risk for sexually transmitted diseases (STDs), unintended pregnancy, and regretted sexual experiences. | **Health**: If you're going to drink, irresponsible alcohol use can lead you to <u>experience long-term negative health consequences.</u> You will increase the likelihood of driving accidents, having an unhealthy liver, and gaining weight. Moreover, people who drink irresponsibly are more likely to engage in risky sexual behavior placing them at risk for sexually transmitted diseases (STDs), unintended pregnancy, and regretted sexual experiences. |
| | **Psychological**: Not limiting your alcohol use now can lead you to <u>experience psychological problems that can occur soon after drinking.</u> Alcohol use may result in impaired judgment, poorer memory, and difficulty concentrating. Not limiting alcohol use may lead to depressed mood and lower self-esteem in the near future. | **Psychological**: Not limiting your alcohol use now can lead you to <u>experience psychological problems that can occur long after drinking.</u> Alcohol use may result in impaired judgment, poorer memory, and difficulty concentrating. Not limiting alcohol use may lead to depressed mood and lower self-esteem in the distant future. |

Source: Mary A. Gerend and Margaret Cullen, Effects of Message Framing and Temporal Context on College Student Drinking Behavior, *Journal of Experimental Social Psychology*, 44(4), July 2008, 1167-1173. Printed with permission from Elsevier.

*Figure 1.* Alcohol quantity over the past month as a function of message frame and temporal context. In the short-term condition, exposure to the gain-framed message led to fewer drinks per drinking occasion than did exposure to the loss-framed message. In the long-term condition, no such difference was observed. Response scale: none = 0; 1 or 2 drinks = 1; 3 or 4 drinks = 2; 5 or 6 drinks = 3; 7 to 9 drinks = 4; 10 or more drinks = 5.

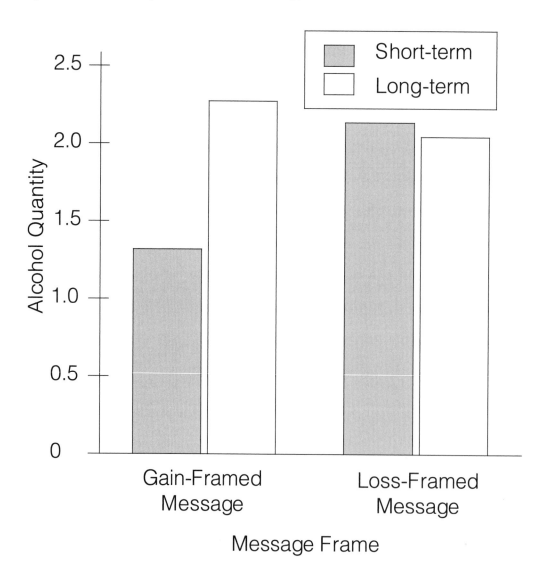

*Figure 2.* Frequency of binge drinking over the past month as a function of message frame and temporal context. In the short-term condition, exposure to the gain-framed message led to significantly less binge drinking than did exposure to the loss-framed message. In the long-term condition, no such difference was observed. Response scale: never = 0 to very often = 5.

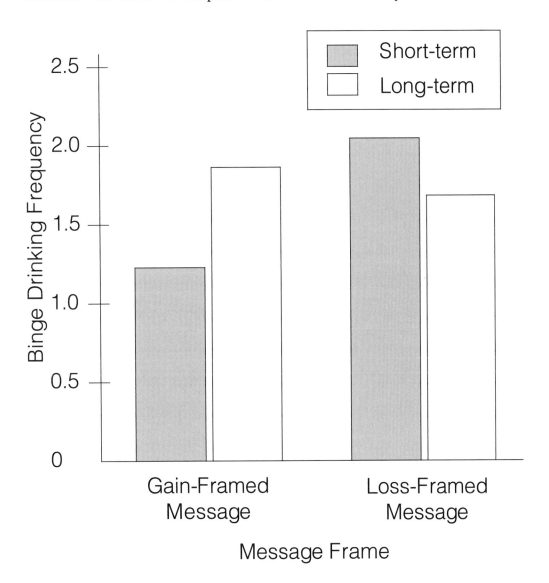

*Figure 3.* Frequency of alcohol use (number of drinking occasions) over the past month as a function of message frame and temporal context. In the short-term condition, exposure to the gain-framed message led to significantly lower rates of alcohol use than did exposure to the loss-framed message. In the long-term condition, no such difference was observed. Response scale: never $= 0$, once $= 1$, 2–4 times during the month $= 2$, 2–3 times a week $= 3$, 4 or more times a week $= 4$.

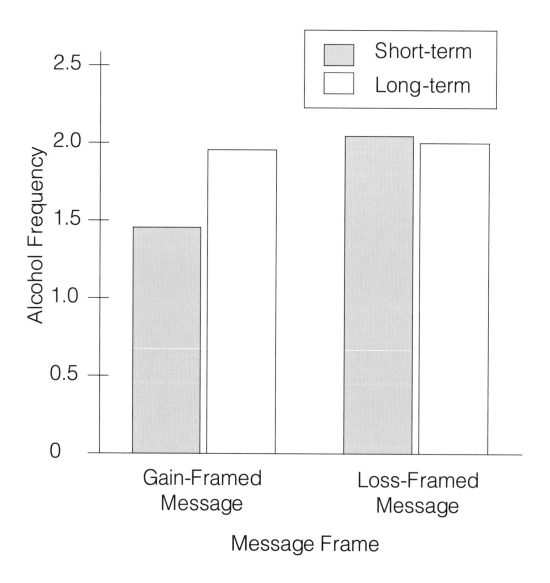

# Answers to Selected Review and Study Questions and Critical Thinking Exercises

## CHAPTER 1

### Answers to Selected Review and Study Questions

1. Scientific methods are very important because without them, our ideas of how things work are not very objective and are subject to many biases (covered in the chapter).

5. Objectivity is important for all three tools of the scientific method. (Observation) Objectivity is necessary to avoid distorting our data because of our expectations. (Measurement) To measure objectively, we need to use standardized units to measure our results, and we apply the same instruments and procedures each time. (Experimentation) When we experiment, we do not use procedures that are bound to give us the results we are looking for and we do not give subjects subtle cues to respond in a certain way.

6. There is no way to test the age of an ovum that has produced a child, so the hypothesis is not currently testable. Even if we could measure the age of an ovum, it would be difficult or impossible to construct an ethical test of the hypothesis.

9. Some of the scenarios may have more than one correct answer. (a) She did not use correct measurement procedures, so it is possible that she drove a different number of miles each week. (b) Mike's findings could not be replicated, so his finding is questionable. (c) The author did not use experimentation correctly, so it is impossible to know the effects of

the vitamin. (d) The researcher did not use the tool of observation correctly; she did not develop a suitable observable sign for people's moods.

10. Astrology gives the appearance of being scientific because it is purported to be based on the precise movement of the stars and planets. It is a pseudoscience because the influence of celestial bodies on human behavior has not been confirmed using the tools of the scientific method: observation, measurement, and experimentation.

### Answers to Critical Thinking Exercise

Problem 1. This myth could have become a part of our culture because it has been espoused many times by pop psychologists as the notion of "catharsis."

Problem 2. Violent and angry behavior by guests on the show makes it more likely that they will be violent and angry again the next time they are in a similar situation.

## CHAPTER 2

### Answers to Selected Review and Study Questions

1. IRBs are required by federal law in institutions that receive federal research dollars. Their major functions are to safeguard research participants by conducting a risk/benefit analysis and making sure that subjects are giving informed consent.

4. It violates part of the principle of informed consent. Consent must be given freely, without force, duress, or coercion.

6. The principle of confidentiality has been violated. The situation could have been avoided by ensuring that all subjects' answers were recorded anonymously or by allowing subjects to put their completed questionnaires in a location that was inaccessible to the experimenter (such as a locked drop box).

9. Conduct a risk/benefit analysis. Discuss how the potential benefits of the study need to be weighed against the sacrifice of the animals. You might also discuss the relevance of higher versus lower animal species.

### Answer to Critical Thinking Exercise

The ethical argument for the deception is that the hypothesis could not feasibly be tested unless deception was used. (Subjects would not respond normally if they knew they were being deceived.)

## CHAPTER 3

### Answers to Selected Review and Study Questions

2. External validity is the ability to generalize the research findings to other subjects and settings. Nonexperimental studies can be higher in external validity because they do not manipulate or control subjects' behavior in the ways that experiments do. Laboratory experiments are sometimes criticized for their artificiality, which can reduce external validity.

3. Internal validity is our confidence that effects produced in the research were caused by the antecedent conditions that have been specified. Non-experimental research cannot be used to test hypotheses about cause and effect because antecedent conditions are not manipulated or controlled in any way, so there is no way to know which antecedents may have caused a behavior.

6. a. You could measure class sizes, percentage of students attending each class, or obtain the data from course evaluations that are routinely collected at the end of the course.

   b. You could measure wear and tear on the books or obtain data from the library on the frequency with which books are checked out.

   c. You could measure wear and tear on the seats and/or the left versus right aisles.

   d. You could try the lost letter technique.

7. a. You would probably use naturalistic observation because people might not want to tell you about engaging in this (socially undesirable) behavior.

   b. You would need to use a qualitative design (e.g., empirical phenomenology) because you can't really measure daydreaming directly.

   c. You could conduct a field study using unobtrusive methods or conduct qualitative research (perhaps focus groups).

   d. You might do a naturalistic observation study in the library and other places where students tend to study or conduct a qualitative study. You could also consider a case study of one or a few persons.

   e. You could do a case study of your one patient.

## Answer to Critical Thinking Exercise

The internal validity of your study would depend on how carefully you controlled for other things in addition to the different types of clothing. [Did you look and act in exactly the same manner in jeans and in a business suit? Did you wear both sets of clothes at the same time of day? On the same day of the week? Did you count the reactions of people who had seen you before wearing other clothes (they might be more likely to smile at you the second time)?] The more carefully you controlled for any other factors that might influence smiling, the more internal validity your study has. Unfortunately, this study hasn't much external validity because only one researcher was used. Responses to someone else who looks and acts differently or to a person of the other gender might be quite different.

# CHAPTER 4

## Answers to Selected Review and Study Questions

2. Open-ended questions can often generate more information in the response, but they are difficult to quantify because they must be content analyzed. Closed questions provide less specific and more specific responses, but they are easy to quantify for statistical analysis.

4. Suppose you are surveying attitudes toward animal research in psychology, and one survey objective is to look for potential differences in attitudes about animals of different species.

  a. (nominal scale) Which of the following types of animal subjects would probably generate the most useful data for learning about human psychology (circle one)?
     Primates Dogs Cats Pigeons

  b. (ordinal scale) Rank the following animals from 1 to 4 in terms of their potential usefulness in learning about human psychology.
     ___ pigeons
     ___ primates
     ___ cats
     ___ dogs

  c. (interval scale) On the following scale, rate the usefulness of each type of animal subject for learning about human psychology:

| Not useful at all | Somewhat useful | Moderately useful | Extremely useful |
|:---:|:---:|:---:|:---:|
| 1 | 2 | 3 | 4 |

  d. (ratio scale) To what extent do you feel that information from studies using primate subjects can generalize to human beings (circle one)?

     0% 10% 20% 30% 40% 50% 60% 70% 80% 90% 100%

7. a. nominal (car brand category)
   b. nominal (each couple either divorced or did not)
   c. ratio (number of yards)
   d. nominal (3 size categories)
   e. interval

10. Reliability refers to the consistency of the survey itself; validity refers to how well it measures what it is supposed to be measuring.

13. a. Asking every third driver is okay, but the people who stop at that particular corner may not be representative of the general population.
    b. Not everyone reads the local paper, so...
    c. This technique only samples people with land lines who are listed in the phone book, so...
    d. Those who volunteer because they are getting paid may differ from the general population, so...

## Answer to Critical Thinking Exercise

First, you need to consider the kind of website it is and what kind of people would go there. Next, you need to consider what type of person would be more likely to take the survey once they saw the website. Finally, you need to consider that there is no way to verify the age or gender (or other demographics) of people answering the survey. Compare these with expectations if the same survey were given in-person or through the mail.

# CHAPTER 5

### Answers to Selected Review and Study Questions

2. Leilani should check her math; $r$ can only range from $-1.00$ to $+1.00$.

5. Beta weights are used to represent the degree of correlation between elements in a path analysis.

6. A cross-lagged panel design attempts to find the most likely causal direction between two correlated variables. The third variable problem can never be ruled out.

9. Claire cannot say that rap music makes people more sexist (or that classical music makes them less sexist) because it is possible that other unmeasured differences between fans of the two kinds of music (such as their genders, ages, or how they were raised) might actually be responsible for the differences in sexism observed in the study. Claire may say that the two types of fans differ in their levels of sexism, but she may not say that the music is the known cause.

11. a. A researcher could measure the temperature with the amount of violence in the streets over a period of time and correlate the two sets of scores (a correlational study).

   b. A researcher could take measurements of the amount of exposure to rap music and sexism at two different points in time and use a cross-lagged panel design.

   c. A researcher could measure the severity of schizophrenia symptoms, cognitive deficits, genetic predisposition, and autonomic arousal in a large sample of children and conduct a multiple linear regression analysis of the last three variables on the first variable to see how well they predict it.

   d. The researcher could select a group of older people and a group of middle-aged people and measure the amount of exercise they engage in (an ex post facto study).

### Answer to Critical Thinking Exercise

Hypothesis 1: More left-handed individuals are being born now than there used to be: You'd simply track the figures over time to look for increases (but it would take many, many years to support your hypothesis).

Hypothesis 2: Left-handed people die earlier, so fewer older left-handers are around to contribute to the averages: A longitudinal study is needed to follow samples of right- and left-handed males and females until they die; then you could evaluate whether left-handers die earlier.

# CHAPTER 6

### Answers to Selected Review and Study Questions

1. a. Synthetic because it is testable in the "If…, then…" form (but it is not a very good hypothesis, is it?).

   b. Synthetic because it can be translated into a testable hypothesis: "If individuals are out of sight, then they are out of mind (i.e., not thought about)."

    c.   Analytic because it is always true

    d.   Contradictory because it is always false

6. a.   Sometimes we have a hunch about the cause of behavior that seems to come from intuition.

    b.   Intuition is not scientific in itself, but our hunch can become scientific if it results in a testable hypothesis.

    c.   Herb Simon has argued that intuitions (hunches) are better if we are very familiar or expert in an area (and someone who knows a lot about a topic would be expected to have "better" hunches).

8. Hypothesis: Children who watch a lot of television will have shorter attention spans than children who watch less television. Randomly assign children from volunteering families into one of two groups: more TV or less TV. Arrange a month-long experiment so that children in the "more" group watch 10 hours of TV a week and children in the "less" group watch only 2 hours a week. At the end of the month, give all of the children a task that requires attention, such as finding missing parts of objects in a drawing. Compare the average performance of the two groups to see if the "more" group finds fewer missing parts than the "less" group.

### Answer to Critical Thinking Exercise

The hypothesis can be found in the abstract and in the last paragraph of the article's Introduction section. The simple physiological effect that is hypothesized is more parsimonious than proposing that rats feel an emotion that results in vocalization because "feeling an emotion" adds an additional (and unnecessary) step to the vocalization process.

## CHAPTER 7

### Answers to Selected Review and Study Questions

2. a.   IV = absence (absence or presence)

    c.   IV = room color (pink or blue)

3. a.   DV = amount of fondness

    c.   DV = amount of sadness

4. a.   For a week, subjects may not see or talk to their significant other for a week (absence) or subjects may see and talk to their significant others as usual (presence).

    c.   Room colors are Benjamin Moore's "Ribbon Pink" or "Blue Hydrangea".

5. a.   Fondness is measured by observing body language in each pair using a coding system.

    c.   Sadness is measured using a standard scale of emotions.

8. Internal validity represents our confidence that results were produced by our IV and not by anything else and is important because the goal of experimentation is being able to explain the cause of behavior by showing that changes in the IV (and not anything else) produce changes in the DV.

10. a.   Ex post facto = Selection threat

### Answer to Critical Thinking Exercise

Because this study could not be conducted as a true experiment, it does not have high internal validity. Measurements of blood pressure, immune function, and stress are compared in two preexisting groups of subjects: a group of people who tend to laugh a lot and another group of people who do not laugh very much (an ex post facto design). This design has a selection threat, so it is possible that one or more extraneous variables (e.g., eating habits, amount of exercise, or genetic factors) also might differ systematically across the two groups, confounding the results.

## CHAPTER 8

### Answers to Selected Review and Study Questions

1. Physical variables are elements of the testing conditions that need to be controlled (the room, the noise, etc.).
3. Balancing is the control procedure of distributing the impact of extraneous variables (such as testing time or different testing rooms) equally across all treatment conditions.
5. You can use balancing to control for effects of the two different rooms and times of day. Randomly assign half the subjects to the small room (the other half will go to the larger room). Randomly assign half the small-room subjects to A and half to B; do the same for the larger room.
8. Dr. L's idea is a poor one because each treatment condition would be run by a different experimenter, confounding the experiment. It would not be possible to tell if effects were produced by the two different treatments or by the two different experimenters. Instead, randomly assign half the rats in each condition to Dr. L and the other half to the additional experimenter.
10. Experimenter behavior can influence how subjects respond in an experiment. If experimenters behave differently toward subjects, they will produce variability in subjects' responses, making it more difficult to detect treatment effects. (If their behavior is systematically different across treatment conditions, they become a confound.)

### Answer to Critical Thinking Exercise

A simple test could be made by constructing a questionnaire (or using one that has already been standardized) to measure conscientiousness or other traits/behaviors of interest. The questionnaire could be given out to subjects and experimenters who had been randomly assigned to similar experimental sessions at the same time and place on a Friday and on another weekday. The hypothesis that Fridays are different would be supported if researchers and subjects tested on Friday were significantly less conscientious than those tested on other weekdays. If you merely tested people who scheduled themselves for a Friday rather than another weekday, you would be measuring differences in the people rather than differences caused by the day of the week.

# CHAPTER 9

## Answers to Selected Review and Study Questions

2. Deciding on the number of subjects is not a simple matter. If the behavior of interest is expected to be very similar across individuals, a smaller number is OK. If the behavior is expected to have variability across individuals, a larger number will be required. Also, the larger the effect size, the fewer subjects will be needed to detect it. Use the past literature as a guide. You could use 15–20 subjects per condition as a minimum, although most researchers would prefer 30 in each condition.

4. You cannot accept this conclusion because it is possible that jogging *improves* mental health (instead of subway riding *damaging* it). You cannot tell without a control group.

6. The simplest way to test this hypothesis would be to use two experimental groups: one in which subjects stand close to another person (say 18") and one in which they stand farther away (perhaps 36"). But it would be better to use a multiple-groups design (perhaps 18", 36", 72") because the effect may not be linear. It may be that 18" is too close for comfort; whereas 36" is about right, but 72" is too far apart.

9. You could test this using a two-experimental-groups design: one condition in which subjects watch a pot of boiling water until it boils; another in which the pot is left to boil without observation (but you would need to figure out a way to know when it is boiling!).

## Answer to Critical Thinking Exercise

One variable that might have confounded the results was the type of news given to the experimental group (interesting news story). If they had read a sad or violent story, the results might have been different. A second variable that might have produced a confound was a product of the "no-treatment" (no-news) condition. Nothing was done to control for what subjects in the experimental group were doing while they were waiting. Waiting without anything to do might have made subjects in the no-treatment group very bored, and perhaps boredom caused them to make more negative judgments rather than the absence of any type of news.

# CHAPTER 10

## Answers to Selected Review and Study Questions

2. A main effect is the effect of one IV or factor by itself; an interaction is the effect of two or more factors in combination.

4. We need a 2 × 2 (Gender of Subject: male, female × Type of Toy: for building, not for building) factorial design.
9.
   a. The experiment is a 2 × 2 (Gender: male, female × Prime: independence, interdependence) factorial design.
   b. Two main effects were reported: independent > interdependent; male > female.

c.

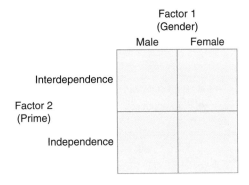

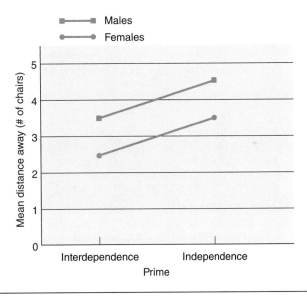

## Answer to Critical Thinking Exercise

The everyday meaning of the aphorism is that people are never satisfied with their own situation—they tend to think that other people have it better than they do. So one factor in the experiment might be type of situation (the same situation could be described as the subject's or as someone else's); the other factor will be a subject variable (high vs. low optimism). Subjects could rate the positivity of the situation on a scale from 0 (not at all positive) to 10 (extremely positive). Here is a graph of results indicating that "the grass is always greener on the other side of the fence" and especially so for highly optimistic people.

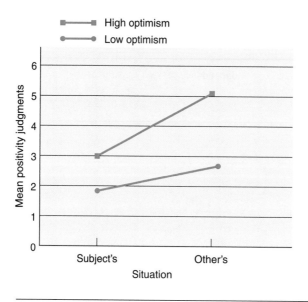

# CHAPTER 11

## Answers to Selected Review and Study Questions

3. Preschool children could participate in two play sessions on different days. In one session, the playroom would contain weaponlike toys, and in the other session it would not. Researchers could measure the number of aggressive behaviors (carefully operationally defined) in each condition and compare them statistically. But the order of the two conditions must be counterbalanced: half the kids get the weapon toy session first; half get the nonweapon toy session first. If you only have one preschool class to use as subjects, and they must all be tested together, it would be better to use *ABBA* counterbalancing to control for progressive error and give the kids four sessions instead of two.

5. a. The within-subjects approach is more powerful, but you would need to worry about carryover effects—chemical residue from the first toothpaste might make the second toothpaste taste worse.

   c. A within-subjects design would be more powerful, and as long as the amount of reading was relatively small in the different typeface conditions, this experiment is a good candidate for the within-subjects approach as long as the order of the conditions is counterbalanced.

8. Technically, yes. But, because there was a significant main effect for strength but not a strength × order interaction, their conclusion that strong laughter increases funniness is probably valid. (Even so, when the funniness question was fourth, something about questions 1–3 did seem to make subjects judge the jokes as particularly funny. They may want to drop this condition because it is unexplainable.)

11. The nonlinear pattern of progressive error suggests that block randomization might work, but with this technique it is better to present each treatment several times. In this experiment, this might be too fatiguing. So, researchers should probably use a balanced Latin square design.

### Answer to Critical Thinking Exercise

It looks like what happened in this taste test is that people always liked the first candy they tasted better than the second. This looks like a carryover effect! There may have been some chemical incompatibilities in the two candies, so that residue from the first candy interacted with chemicals in the second candy, making it taste worse than it should. The researchers should have waited longer between giving the two candies or they should have asked subjects to rinse out their mouth thoroughly before tasting each candy.

## CHAPTER 12

### Answers to Selected Review and Study Questions

2. *ABA* designs are really a family of designs that can be modified in many ways, such as dropping the final *A*, repeating the *AB* sequences, or adding more treatment conditions (*C*, *D*, etc.).

4. Both control for the behavior of individuals in the absence of the IV.

6. Without withdrawing the treatment in the last *A* condition, you cannot be certain that the treatment produced the results. You need to see two things: that the treatment produces an effect over baseline; and that the effect disappears when the treatment is withdrawn.

9. The initial *ABA* showed that the treatment worked, but now the dog is barking again! You would want to return to the treatment condition (the last *B*) to stop the barking.

10. Your graph should look very much like the one in Figure 12-6 in the text. The top row would represent barking behavior, and the bottom row would represent chasing the cat.

### Answer to Critical Thinking Exercise

I'm not *completely* convinced. There might have been another reason that the medalists did not smile in the final *A* condition: They may have felt it would be inappropriate to smile while their national anthem was playing even though they were feeling intensely happy.

# CHAPTER 13

## Answers to Selected Review and Study Questions

2. It is easy to account for the 60-point difference in scores if there is a lot of variability in the dependent variable. For example, if the DV measured the distance people could jump in millimeters, 60 mm (about 2.36 inches) would not be a large difference, especially if the treatment groups were small.

4. The null hypothesis *always* states that the means came from the same population (i.e., that there is no difference between the groups).

5. b. It will be harder because it takes a larger critical value to reject the null hypothesis at $p < .01$ than it does at $p < .05$.

6. a. Type 1
   b. Dr. R's decision is correct.
   c. Type 2

8. Increase the number of subjects; increase the size of the treatment effect; increase $\alpha$.

14. Group 1: mean = 4.60; median = 5; range = 7; $s^2 = 7.30$

## Answer to Critical Thinking Exercise

The distribution would have a small bump at the negative end, so the median would fall slightly to the right of the mean as it does in Figure 13-9(d). IQ tests are renormed periodically, however, so that the mean score remains 100.

# CHAPTER 14

## Answers to Selected Review and Study Questions

2. a. People with low and high anxiety will not differ in their desire to affiliate with others.
   b. Could be either: Low- and high-anxious people will differ in their desire to affiliate with others (nondirectional) or high-anxious people will have a greater desire to affiliate with others than low-anxious people (directional).
   c. Computed value is $\chi^2 (1) = 6.67$. The null hypothesis can be rejected at $p < .01$ (even better than $p < .05$).

6. Using a t test for matched subjects (within-subjects t test), the results were $t(4) = 1.58$—not large enough to reject the null hypothesis at $p < .05$.

7. a. Using an independent groups t test, the results were $t(8) = 1.12$—not large enough to reject $H_0$ (needed 2.31).
   b. Value of t still not large enough (needed 1.86).

14. a. $F (3,16) = 14.46$
    b. Yes, in fact it is large enough to be significant at $p < .001$.
    e. A Tukey test resulted in the group differences tabled below. You can see that subjects in group 4 had significantly fewer errors than any other treatment group. Groups 4 and 2 were equal, and both had significantly fewer errors than treatment group 1.

## Mean number of errors in each treatment group

| Treatment 1 | Treatment 4 | Treatment 2 | Treatment 3 |
|:---:|:---:|:---:|:---:|
| $3.00_a$ | $2.00_b$ | $1.60_b$ | $.40_c$ |

Note: Means with different subscripts are significantly different from each other.

### Answer to Critical Thinking Exercise

Both heritability estimates for identical twins would be considered strong effect sizes; the estimate for cousins represents a very weak effect.

# CHAPTER 15

### Answers to Selected Review and Study Questions

2. If an experiment does not have internal validity, no conclusions can be drawn.
4. Statistical conclusion validity is influenced by: violating the assumptions of a statistical test, computing too many tests, and the power of the test.
7. No conclusions at all can be drawn from an experiment that is not internally valid, so it would not make sense to talk about external validity!
9. Through induction, we draw conclusions that are broader than the specific details of the experiment. For example, if an IV produced a significant difference in TMAS scores across two groups totaling 60 student subjects, we would speak of the IV producing effects on "anxiety" in people in general rather than on TMAS scores in 60 subjects.
12. a. The researcher's claims are not justified; we never "prove" our hypothesis (statistical significance is probabilistic—never certain), and the results from a single experiment are never "conclusive" (could be Type 1 error).
    b. The researcher needs to say that the findings support some previous research studies but are inconsistent with others.
    c. The research findings *suggest* that working crossword puzzles can improve vocabulary.
15. Deanna's findings were not significant; she cannot reject the null hypothesis. Now that she can calculate the strength of the effect of her IV, she should check the power of her experiment to see if she had sufficient power to detect a significant effect with the number of subjects she used.

### Answer to Critical Thinking Exercise

Describe procedures you could use for aggregation of data, a multivariate design, nonreactive measures, a field experiment, and naturalistic observation. For example, you could test subjects' behavior toward more than one product (cream cheese, cottage cheese, and ice cream) using a multivariate design. Or you could conduct the study in a grocery store as a field experiment.

# CHAPTER 16

## Answers to Selected Review and Study Questions

3. The four major sections are the introduction, method, results, and discussion.

6. a. The Effect of Food Deprivation on Maze Running Speed in Canus Familiaris

   b. The Influence of Infants' Maturation Levels on Fear of Strangers

15. A standard format makes it much easier to organize the paper when you are writing a research report. You don't have to think about how to organize it; the structure is already provided. It also makes it easier for journal editors and reviewers to read and evaluate manuscripts submitted for publication.

16. a. No significant difference was found between $X$ and $Y$, $t(38) = 1.38$, $p = .20$.

   b. There was a significant difference between $X$ and $Y$, $F(1, 12) = 6.26$, $p = .001$, $\eta^2 = .18$.

   c. Female subjects who viewed a violent music video were less accepting of violence ($M = 7.32$, $SD = 2.10$, 95% CI [5.99, 9.76]) than were male subjects ($M = 8.44$, $SD = 1.89$, 95% CI [6.83, 10.28]).

## Answer to Critical Thinking Exercise

APA has stated unequivocally that it is the society's opinion that child sexual abuse is very damaging to individuals who have been exposed to it, but that does not mean APA will not publish an author's conclusions if they differ from the position of APA.

**AB design** A design in which a baseline condition (*A*) is measured first, followed by measurements during the experimental intervention (*B*); there is no return to the baseline condition.

**ABA design** A design in which a baseline condition (*A*) is measured first, followed by measurements during the experimental condition (*B*), followed by a return to the baseline condition (*A*) to verify that the change in behavior is linked to the experimental condition; also called a *reversal design*.

**ABAB design** A design in which a baseline condition (*A*) is measured first, followed by measurements during a treatment condition (*B*), followed by a return to the baseline condition (*A*) to verify that the change in behavior is linked to the experimental condition, followed by a return to the treatment condition (*B*).

**ABABA design** A design in which a baseline condition (*A*) is measured first, followed by measurements during a treatment condition (*B*), followed by a return to the baseline measurement condition (*A*), followed by a return to the treatment condition (*B*) and a final baseline measurement condition (*A*) to verify that the change in behavior is linked to the experimental condition.

**Abstract** A brief summary (approximately 120 words or 960 characters) of the report, which precedes the four major sections.

**Across-subjects counterbalancing** A technique for controlling progressive error that pools all subjects' data together to equalize the effects of progressive error for each condition.

**Aggregation** The grouping together and averaging of data gathered in various ways, including aggregation over subjects, over stimuli and/or situations, over trials and/or occasions, and over measures.

**Alternative hypothesis ($H_1$)** A statement that the data came from different populations; the research hypothesis, which cannot be tested directly.

**Analysis of variance (ANOVA)** The statistical procedure used to evaluate differences among two or more treatment means by breaking the variability in the data into components that reflect the influence of error and error plus treatment effects.

**Analytic statement** A statement that is always true.

**Animal rights** The concept that all sensate species who feel pain are of equal value and have rights.

**Animal welfare** The humane care and treatment of animals.

**Antecedent conditions** All circumstances that occur or exist before the event or behavior to be explained; also called *antecedents*.

**Applied research** Research that is designed to solve real-world problems.

**A priori comparison** Statistical test between specific treatment groups that was anticipated, or planned, before the experiment was conducted; also called *planned comparison*.

**Archival study** A descriptive method in which already existing records are re-examined for a new purpose.

**At minimal risk** The subject's odds of being harmed are not increased by the research.

**At risk** The likelihood of a subject being harmed in some way because of the nature of the research.

**Balanced Latin square** A partial counterbalancing technique for constructing a matrix, or square, of sequences in which each treatment condition (1) appears only once in each position in a sequence and (2) precedes and follows every other condition an equal number of times.

**Balancing** A technique used to control the impact of extraneous variables by distributing their effects equally across treatment conditions.

**Baseline** A measure of behavior as it normally occurs without the experimental manipulation; a control condition used to assess the impact of the experimental condition.

**Basic research** Research designed to test theories or to explain psychological phenomena.

**Between-groups variability** The degree to which the scores of different treatment groups differ from one another (that is, how much subjects vary under different levels of the independent variable); a measure of variability produced by treatment effects and error.

**Between-subjects design** A design in which different subjects take part in each condition of the experiment.

**Block randomization** A process of randomization that first creates treatment blocks containing one random order of the conditions in the experiment; subjects are then assigned to fill each successive treatment block.

**Carryover effect** The persistence of the effect of a treatment condition after the condition ends.

**Case study** The descriptive record of an individual's experiences, behaviors, or both kept by an outside observer.

**Causal modeling** Creating and testing models that may suggest cause-and-effect relationships among behaviors.

**Cause-and-effect relationship** The relation between a particular behavior and a set of antecedents that always precedes it—whereas other antecedents do not—so that the set is inferred to *cause* the behavior.

**Changing criterion design** A design used to modify behavior when the behavior cannot be changed all at once; instead, the behavior is modified in increments, and the criterion for success (i.e., reinforcement) changes as the behavior is modified.

**Chi square** ($\chi^2$) A nonparametric, inferential statistic that tests whether the frequencies of responses in our sample represent certain frequencies in the population; used with nominal data.

**Cluster sampling** A form of probability sampling in which a researcher samples entire clusters, or naturally occurring groups, that exist within the population.

**Coefficient of determination** ($r^2$) In a correlational study, an estimate of the amount of variability in scores on one variable that can be explained by the other variable.

**Commonsense psychology** Everyday, nonscientific collection of psychological

data used to understand the social world and guide our behavior.

**Complete counterbalancing** A technique for controlling progressive error that uses all possible sequences that can be formed out of the treatment conditions and uses each sequence the same number of times.

**Concurrent validity** The degree to which scores on the measuring instrument correlate with another known standard for measuring the variable being studied.

**Confidence interval** A range of values above and below a sample mean that is likely to contain the population mean with the probability level (usually at 95% or 99%) that the mean of the population (the true mean) would actually fall somewhere in that range.

**Confounding** An error that occurs when the value of an extraneous variable changes systematically along with the independent variable in an experiment; an alternative explanation for the findings that threatens internal validity.

**Constancy of conditions** A control procedure used to avoid confounding; keeping all aspects of the treatment conditions identical except for the independent variable that is being manipulated.

**Construct validity** The degree to which an operational definition accurately represents the construct it is intended to manipulate or measure.

**Content analysis** A system for quantifying responses to open-ended questions by categorizing them according to objective rules or guidelines.

**Content validity** The degree to which the content of a measure reflects the content of what is being measured.

**Context effects** Effects produced by the position of a question; where it falls within the question order can influence how the question is interpreted.

**Context variable** Extraneous variable stemming from procedures created by the environment, or context, of the research setting.

**Continuous dimension** The concept that traits, attitudes, and preferences can be viewed as continuous dimensions and each individual can fall at any point along each dimension; for example, sociability can be viewed as a continuous dimension ranging from very unsociable to very sociable.

**Contradictory statement** A statement that is always false.

**Control condition** A condition in which subjects receive a zero value of the independent variable.

**Control group** The subjects in a control condition.

**Convenience sampling** A convenience sample is obtained by using any groups who happen to be convenient; considered a weak form of sampling because the researcher exercises no control over the representativeness of the sample (also called *accidental sampling*).

**Correlation** The degree of relationship between two traits, behaviors, or events, represented by *r*.

**Correlational study** A study designed to determine the correlation between two traits, behaviors, or events.

**Counterbalancing** A technique for controlling order effects by distributing progressive error across the different treatment conditions of the experiment; may also control carryover effects.

**Cover story** A plausible but false explanation of the procedures in an experiment told to disguise the actual research hypothesis so that subjects will not guess what it is.

**Critical region** Portion in the tail(s) of the distribution of a test statistic extreme enough to satisfy the researcher's criterion for rejecting the null hypothesis—for instance, the most extreme 5% of a distribution where $p < .05$ is the chosen significance level.

**Critical value** The value of the test statistic that must be exceeded to reject the null hypothesis at the chosen significance level.

**Cross-lagged panel design** A method in which the same set of behaviors or characteristics are measured at two separate points in time (often years apart); six different correlations are computed, and the pattern of correlations is used to infer the causal direction.

**Cross-sectional study** A method in which different groups of subjects who are at different stages are measured at a single point in time; a method that looks for time-related changes.

**Data** Facts and figures gathered from observations in research. (*Data* is the plural form of the Latin word *datum*).

**Debriefing** The principle of full disclosure at the end of an experiment; that is, explaining to the subject the nature and purpose of the study.

**Deductive model** The process of reasoning from general principles to specific instances; most useful for testing the principles of a theory.

**Degrees of freedom** (*df*) The number of members of a set of data that can vary or change value without changing the value of a known statistic for those data.

**Demand characteristics** The aspects of the experimental situation itself that demand or elicit particular behaviors; can lead to distorted data by compelling subjects to produce responses that conform to what subjects believe is expected of them in the experiment.

**Dependent variable (DV)** The specific behavior that a researcher tries to explain in an experiment; the variable that is measured.

**Descriptive statistics** The standard procedures used to summarize and describe data quickly and clearly; summary statistics reported for an experiment, including mean, range, and standard deviation.

**Deviant case analysis** A form of case study in which deviant individuals are compared with those who are not to isolate the significant variations between them.

**Directional hypothesis** A statement that predicts the exact pattern of results that will be observed, such as which treatment group will perform best.

**Discrete trials design** A design that relies on presenting and averaging across many, many experimental trials; repeated applications result in a reliable picture of the effects of the independent variable.

**Discussion** Concluding section of the research report, used to integrate the experimental findings into the existing body of knowledge, showing how the current research advances knowledge, increases generalizability of known effects, or contradicts past findings.

**Double-blind experiment** An experiment in which neither the subjects nor the experimenter know which treatment the subjects are in; used to control experimenter bias.

**Effect size** A statistical estimate of the size or magnitude of the treatment effect(s).

**Elimination** A technique to control extraneous variables by removing them from an experiment.

**Empirical phenomenology** Contemporary phenomenology that relies on the researcher's own experiences, experiential data provided by study participants, or other available sources such as literature or popular media; a qualitative approach.

**Error** The variability within and between treatment groups that is not produced by changes in the independent variables; variability produced by individual differences, experimental error, and other extraneous variables.

**Experimental condition** A treatment condition in which the researcher applies a particular value of an independent variable to subjects and then measures the dependent variable; in an experimental group–control group design, the group that receives some value of the independent variable.

**Experimental design** The general structure of an experiment (but not its specific content).

**Experimental error** Variation in subjects' scores produced by uncontrolled extraneous variables in the experimental procedure, experimenter bias, or other influences on subjects not related to effects of the independent variable.

**Experimental group** The subjects in an experimental condition.

**Experimental hypothesis** A statement that is a tentative explanation of an event or behavior; it predicts the effects of specified antecedent conditions on a measured behavior.

**Experimental operational definition** The explanation of the meaning of independent variables; defines *exactly* what was done to create the various treatment conditions of the experiment.

**Experimentation** The process undertaken to demonstrate that particular behavioral events will occur reliably in certain specifiable conditions; a principal tool of the scientific method.

**Experimenter bias** Any behavior of the experimenter that can create confounding in an experiment.

**Ex post facto study** A study in which a researcher systematically examines the effects of preexisting subject characteristics (often called subject variables) by forming treatment groups based on these naturally occurring differences between subjects.

**External validity** How well the findings of an experiment generalize or apply to people and settings that were not tested directly.

**Extraneous variable** A variable other than an independent or dependent variable; a variable that is not the focus of an experiment and that can confound the results if not controlled.

**F ratio** A test statistic used in the analysis of variance; the ratio between the variability observed between treatment groups and the variability observed within treatment groups.

**Face validity** The degree to which a manipulation or measurement technique is self-evident.

**Factor** An independent variable in a factorial design.

**Factorial design** An experimental design in which more than one independent variable is manipulated.

**Falsifiable statement** A statement that is worded so that it is falsifiable, or disprovable, by experimental results.

**Falsification** To challenge an existing explanation or theory by testing a hypothesis that follows logically from it and demonstrating that this hypothesis is false.

**Fatigue effects** Changes in performance caused by fatigue, boredom, or irritation.

**Field experiment** An experiment conducted outside the laboratory that is used to increase external validity, verify earlier laboratory findings, and investigate problems that cannot be studied successfully in the laboratory.

**Field study** A nonexperimental research method used in the field or in a real-life setting, typically employing a variety of techniques, including naturalistic observation and unobtrusive measures or survey tools, such as questionnaires and interviews.

**Focus group** A type of group interview; it is an organized discussion session with a small group of people, usually led by a trained facilitator.

**Fraud** The unethical practice of falsifying or fabricating data; plagiarism is also a form of fraud.

**Fruitful statement** A statement that leads to new studies.

**Good thinking** Organized and rational-thought, characterized by open-mindedness, objectivity, and parsimony; a principal tool of the scientific method.

**Grand mean** An average of all the treatment group means.

**Higher-order interaction** An interaction effect involving more than two independent variables.

**History threat** A threat to internal validity in which an outside event or occurrence might have produced effects on the dependent variable.

**Hypothesis** The thesis, or main idea, of an experiment or study consisting of a statement that predicts the relationship between at least two variables.

**Hypothetical construct** Concepts used to explain unseen processes, such as hunger or learning; postulated to explain observable behavior.

**Independent variable (IV)** The variable (antecedent condition) that the experimenter intentionally manipulates.

**Inductive model** The process of reasoning from specific cases to more general principles to form a hypothesis.

**Inferential statistics** Statistics that can be used as indicators of what is going on in a population; also called *test statistics*.

**Informed consent** A subject's voluntary agreement to participate in a research project after the nature and purpose of the study have been explained.

**Institutional animal care and use committee (IACUC)** An institutional committee that reviews proposed research to safeguard the welfare of animal subjects.

**Institutional review board (IRB)** An institutional committee that reviews proposed research to safeguard the safety and rights of human participants.

**Instrumentation threat** A threat to internal validity produced by changes in the measuring instrument itself.

**Interaction** The effect of one independent variable changes across the levels of another independent variable; can only be detected in factorial designs.

**Interitem reliability** The degree to which different items measuring the same variable attain consistent results.

**Internal validity** The certainty that the changes in behavior observed across treatment conditions in the experiment were actually caused by the independent variable.

**Interrater reliability** The degree of agreement among different observers or raters.

**Interval scale** The measurement of magnitude, or quantitative size, having equal intervals between values but no true zero point.

**Introduction** Beginning section of a research report that guides the reader toward the research hypothesis; includes a selective review of relevant, recent research.

**Intuition** The development of ideas from hunches; knowing directly without reasoning from objective data.

**Large *N* design** A design in which the behavior of groups of subjects is compared.

**Latent content** The "hidden meaning" behind a question.

**Latin square counterbalancing** A partial counterbalancing technique in which a matrix, or square, of sequences is constructed so that each treatment appears only once in any order position.

**Laws** General scientific principles that explain our universe and predict events.

**Level of measurement** The type of scale of measurement—either ratio, interval, ordinal, or nominal—used to measure a variable.

**Levels of the independent variable** The two or more values of the independent variable manipulated by the experimenter.

**Linear regression analysis** A correlation-based method for estimating a score on one measured behavior from a score on the other when two behaviors are strongly related.

**Longitudinal design** A method in which the same group of subjects is followed and measured at different points in time; a method that looks for changes across time.

**Main effect** The action of a single independent variable in an experiment; the change in the dependent variable produced by the various levels of a single factor.

**Manifest content** The plain meaning of the words or questions that actually appear on the page.

**Manipulation check** An assessment to determine whether the independent variable was manipulated successfully.

**Maturation threat** A threat to internal validity produced by internal (physical or psychological) changes in subjects.

**Mean** An arithmetical average computed by dividing the sum of a group of scores by the total number of scores; a measure of central tendency.

**Mean square (MS)** An average squared deviation; a variance estimate used in analysis-of-variance procedures and found by dividing the sum of squares by the degrees of freedom.

**Mean square between groups ($MS_b$)** The variance (or average squared deviation) across different treatment groups produced by error and treatment effects; also the variance about the grand mean.

**Mean square within groups ($MS_w$)** The variance (or average squared deviation) within a single treatment group; produced by the combination of sources called *error*.

**Measured operational definition** The description of *exactly* how a variable in an experiment is measured.

**Measurement** The systematic estimation of the quantity, size, or quality of an observable event; a principal tool of the scientific method.

**Measures of central tendency** Summary statistics that describe what is typical of a distribution of scores; includes mean, median, and mode.

**Median** The score that divides a distribution in half, so that half the scores in the distribution fall above the median, half below; a measure of central tendency.

**Meta-analysis** A statistical reviewing procedure that uses data from many similar studies to summarize and quantify research findings about individual topics.

**Method** The section of a research report in which the subjects and experiment are described in enough detail that the experiment may be replicated by others; it is typically divided into subsections, such as Participants, Apparatus or Materials, and Procedures.

**Methodology** The scientific techniques used to collect and evaluate psychological data.

**Minimal risk** The subject's odds of being harmed are not increased by the research.

**Mixed design** A factorial design that combines within-subjects and between-subjects factors.

**Mode** The most frequently occurring score in a distribution; a measure of central tendency.

**Multiple baseline design** A small *N* design in which a series of baselines and treatments are compared within the same person; once established, however, a treatment is not withdrawn.

**Multiple correlation** Statistical intercorrelations among three or more behaviors, represented by $R$.

**Multiple-groups design** A between-subjects design with one independent variable, in which there are more than two treatment conditions.

**Multiple-independent-groups design** The most commonly used multiple-groups design in which the subjects are assigned to the different treatment conditions at random.

**Multiple regression analysis** A correlation-based technique (from multiple correlation) that uses a regression equation to predict the score on one behavior from scores on the other related behaviors.

**Multivariate analysis of variance (MANOVA)** The statistical procedure used to study the impact of independent variables on two or more dependent variables; an extension of analysis of variance.

**Multivariate design** Research design or statistical procedure used to evaluate the effects of many dependent variables in combination, including multiple correlation, factor analysis, and multivariate analysis of variance.

**Naturalistic observation** A descriptive, nonexperimental method of observing behaviors as they occur spontaneously in natural settings.

**Nay-sayers** People who are apt to disagree with a question regardless of its manifest content.

**Negative correlation** The relationship existing between two variables such that an increase in one is associated with a decrease in the other; also called an *inverse relationship*.

**Nominal scale** The simplest level of measurement; classifies items into two or more distinct categories on the basis of some common feature.

**Nondirectional hypothesis** A statement that predicts a difference between treatment groups without predicting the exact pattern of results.

**Nonequivalent-groups design** A design in which the researcher compares the effects of different treatment conditions on preexisting groups of participants.

**Nonexperimental hypothesis** A statement of predictions of how events, traits, or behaviors might be related, but not a statement about cause and effect.

**Nonprobability sampling** Sampling procedures in which subjects are not chosen at random; two common examples are quota and convenience samples.

**Normal curve** The distribution of data in a symmetrical, bell-shaped curve.

**Null hypothesis** ($H_0$) A statement that the performance of treatment groups is so similar that the groups must belong to the same population; a way of saying that the experimental manipulation had no important effect.

**Observation** The systematic noting and recording of events; a principal tool of the scientific method.

**One-tailed test** A statistical procedure used when a directional prediction has been made; the critical region of the distribution of the test statistic ($t$, for instance) is measured in just one tail of the distribution.

**One-way between-subjects analysis of variance** Statistical procedure used to evaluate a between-subjects experiment with three or more levels of a single independent variable.

**One-way within-subjects (repeated measures) ANOVA** Statistical procedure used to evaluate a within-subjects experiment with three or more levels of a single independent variable.

**Operational definition** The specification of the precise meaning of a variable within an experiment; defines a variable in terms of observable operations, procedures, and measurements.

**Order effects** Change in subjects' performance that occurs when a condition falls in different positions in a series of treatments.

**Ordinal scale** A measure of magnitude in which each value is measured in the form of ranks.

**Page header** A header made up of the first few words of a title; used to identify manuscript pages during the editorial process in case the pages get separated.

**Paradigm** The set of attitudes, values, beliefs, methods, and procedures that are generally accepted within a particular discipline at a certain point in time.

**Parsimonious statement** A statement that is simple and does not require many supporting assumptions.

**Parsimony** An aspect of good thinking, stating that the simplest explanation is preferred until ruled out by conflicting evidence; also known as *Occam's razor*.

**Partial correlation** An analysis that allows the statistical influence of one measured variable to be held constant while computing the correlation between the other two measured variables.

**Partial counterbalancing** A technique for controlling progressive error by using some subset of the available sequences of treatment conditions.

**Participant-observer study** A special kind of field observation in which the researcher actually becomes part of the group being studied.

**Path analysis** An important correlation-based method in which subjects are measured on several related behaviors; the researcher creates (and tests) models of possible causal sequences using sophisticated correlational techniques.

**Personality variables** The personal characteristics that an experimenter or volunteer subject brings to the experimental setting.

**Phenomenology** A nonexperimental method of gathering data by attending to and describing one's own immediate experience.

**Physical variables** Aspects of the testing conditions that need to be controlled.

**Pilot study** A mini-experiment using only a few subjects to pretest selected levels of an independent variable before conducting the actual experiment.

**Placebo effect** The result of giving subjects a pill, injection, or other treatment that actually contains none of the independent variable; the treatment elicits a change in subjects' behavior simply because subjects expect an effect to occur.

**Placebo group** In drug testing, a control condition in which subjects are treated exactly the same as subjects who are in the experimental group, except for the presence of the actual drug; the prototype of a good control group.

**Plagiarism** The representation of someone else's ideas, words, or written work as one's own; a serious breach of ethics that can result in legal action.

**Population** All people, animals, or objects that have at least one characteristic in common.

**Position preference** When in doubt about answers to multiple-choice questions, some people always select a response in a certain position, such as answer $b$.

**Positive correlation** The relationship between two measures such that an increase in the value of one is associated with an increase in the value of the other; also called a *direct relationship*.

**Post hoc test** Statistical test performed after the overall analysis indicates a significant difference; used to pinpoint which differences are significant.

**Power** The chance of detecting a genuine effect of the independent variable.

**Practice effect** Change in subjects' performance resulting from practice.

**Precision matching** Creating pairs whose subjects have identical scores on the matching variable.

**Predictive validity** The degree to which a measuring instrument yields information allowing prediction of actual behavior or performance.

**Pretest/posttest design** A research design used to assess whether the occurrence of an event alters behavior; scores from measurements made before and after the event (called the *pretest* and *posttest*) are compared.

**Probability sampling** Selecting samples in such a way that the odds of any subject being selected for the study are known or can be calculated.

**Progressive error** Changes in subjects' responses that are caused by testing in multiple treatment conditions; includes order effects, such as the effects of practice or fatigue.

**Psychological journal** A periodical that publishes individual research reports and integrative research reviews, which are up-to-date summaries of what is known about a specific topic.

**Psychology experiment** A controlled procedure in which at least two different treatment conditions are applied to subjects whose behaviors are then measured and compared to test a hypothesis about the effects of the treatments on behavior.

**Purposive sampling** The selection of nonrandom samples that reflect a specific purpose of the study.

**Qualitative research** Research that relies on words rather than numbers for the data being collected; it focuses on self-reports, personal narratives, and expression of ideas, memories, feelings, and thoughts.

**Quasi-experimental designs** Often seem like (as the prefix *quasi-* implies) real experiments, but they lack one or more of its essential elements, such as manipulation of antecedents and random assignment to treatment conditions.

**Quota sampling** Selecting samples through predetermined quotas that are intended to reflect the makeup of the population; they can reflect the proportions of important population subgroups, but the particular individuals are not selected at random.

**Random assignment** The technique of assigning subjects to treatments so that each subject has an equal chance of being assigned to each treatment condition.

**Random number table** A table of numbers generated by a computer so that every number has an equal chance of being selected for each position in the table.

**Random selection** An unbiased method for selecting subjects in such a way that each member of the population has an equal opportunity to be selected, and the outcome cannot be predicted ahead of time by any known law.

**Randomized counterbalancing** The simplest partial counterbalancing procedure in which the experimenter randomly selects as many sequences of treatment conditions as there are subjects for the experiment.

**Range** The difference between the largest and smallest scores in a set of data; a rough indication of the amount of variability in the data.

**Range matching** Creating pairs of subjects whose scores on the matching variable fall within a previously specified range of scores.

**Rank-ordered matching** Creating matched pairs by placing subjects in order of their scores on the matching variable; subjects with adjacent scores become pairs.

**Ratio scale** A measure of magnitude having equal intervals between values and having an absolute zero point.

**Raw data** Data recorded as an experiment is run; the responses of individual subjects.

**Reactivity** The tendency of subjects to alter their behavior or responses when they are aware of the presence of an observer.

**References** A list of books and articles cited in the research report; placed at the end of the report.

**Regression line** The line of best fit; represents the equation that best describes the mathematical relationship between two variables measured in a correlational study.

**Reliability** The consistency and dependability of experimental procedures and measurements; also, the extent to which a survey is consistent and repeatable.

**Repeated-measures design** A design in which subjects are measured more than once on the dependent variable; same as a within-subjects design.

**Replication** The process of repeating research procedures to verify that the outcome will be the same as before; a principal tool of the scientific method.

**Representativeness** The extent to which the sample responses we observe and measure reflect those we would obtain if we could sample the entire population.

**Research report** Written report of psychological research, which contains four major sections: Introduction, Method, Results, and Discussion.

**Response set** A tendency to answer questions based on their latent content with the goal of creating a certain impression of ourselves.

**Response style** Tendency for subjects to respond to questionnaire items in a specific way, regardless of the content.

**Results** The section of a research report in which the findings are described and the results of statistical tests and summary data are presented.

**Retrospective data** Data collected in the present based on recollections of past events; apt to be inaccurate because of faulty memory, bias, mood, and situation.

**Reverse counterbalancing** A technique for controlling progressive error for each individual subject by presenting all treatment conditions twice, first in one order, then in reverse order.

**Risk/benefit analysis** A determination, made by an institutional review board, that any risks to the individual are outweighed by potential benefits or the importance of the knowledge to be gained.

**Robust** A term describing a statistical test that can be used without increasing the probability of Type 1 or Type 2 errors even though its assumptions (e.g., the population is normally distributed and has equal variances) are violated.

**Rosenthal effect** The phenomenon of experimenters treating subjects differently depending on what they expect from the subjects; also called the *Pygmalion effect.*

**Running head** A short version of the title, which will appear at the top of pages of the published report.

**Sample of subjects** A selected subset of the population of interest.

**Sampling** Deciding who or what the subjects will be and selecting them.

**Scatterplot** A graph of data from a correlational study, created by plotting pairs of scores from each subject; the value of one variable is plotted on the $X$ (horizontal) axis and the other variable on the $Y$ (vertical) axis.

**Science** The systematic gathering of data to provide descriptions of events taking place under specific conditions, enabling researchers to explain, predict, and control events.

**Scientific method** Steps scientists take to gather and verify information, answer questions, explain relationships, and communicate findings.

**Scientific writing style** A concise, impersonal, and unbiased form of writing used in research reports.

**Selection interactions** A family of threats to internal validity produced when a selection threat combines with one or more of the other threats to internal validity; when a selection threat is already present, other threats can affect some experimental groups but not others.

**Selection threat** A threat to internal validity that can occur when nonrandom procedures are used to assign subjects to conditions or when random assignment fails to balance out differences among subjects across the different conditions of the experiment.

**Serendipity** The knack of finding things that are not being sought.

**Shorthand notation** A system that uses numbers to describe the design of a factorial experiment.

**Significance level** The statistical criterion for deciding whether to reject the null hypothesis or not.

**Simple correlations** Relationships between pairs of scores from each subject.

**Simple random sampling** The most basic form of probability sampling whereby a portion of the whole population is selected in an unbiased way.

**Single-blind experiment** An experiment in which subjects are not told which of the treatment conditions they are in; a procedure used to control demand characteristics.

**Small N design** A design in which just one or a few subjects are used; typically, the experimenter collects baseline data

during an initial control condition, applies the experimental treatment, then reinstates the original control condition to verify that changes observed in behavior were caused by the experimental intervention.

**Snowball sampling** A form of nonprobability sampling in which a researcher locates one or a few people who fit the sample criterion and asks these people to locate or lead the researcher to additional individuals who fit the criterion.

**Social variables** The qualities of the relationships between subjects and experimenters that can influence the results of an experiment.

**Standard deviation** The square root of the variance; measures the average deviation of scores about the mean, thus reflecting the amount of variability in the data.

**Statistical conclusion validity** The degree to which conclusions about a treatment effect can be drawn from the statistical results obtained.

**Statistical inference** A statement made about a population and all its samples based on the samples observed.

**Statistical regression threat** A threat to internal validity that can occur when subjects are assigned to conditions on the basis of extreme scores on a test; upon retest, the scores of extreme scorers tend to regress toward the mean even without any treatment.

**Statistical significance** Meeting the set criterion for significance; the data do not support the null hypothesis, confirming a difference between the groups that occurred as a result of the experiment.

**Statistics** Quantitative measurements of samples; quantitative data.

**Stratified random sampling** A form of probability sample obtained by randomly sampling from people in each important population subgroup in the same proportions as they exist in the population.

**Subject** The scientific term for an individual who participates in research.

**Subject-by-subject counterbalancing** A technique for controlling progressive error for each individual subject by presenting all treatment conditions more than once.

**Subject mortality threat** A threat to internal validity produced by differences in dropout rates across the conditions of the experiment.

**Subject variable** The characteristics of the subjects in an experiment or quasi-experiment that cannot be manipulated by the researcher; sometimes used to select subjects into groups.

**Sum of squares (SS)** The sum of the squared deviations from the group mean; an index of variability used in the analysis-of-variance procedures.

**Sum of squares between groups ($SS_b$)** The sum of the squared deviations of the group means from the grand mean.

**Sum of squares within groups ($SS_w$)** The sum of the squared deviations of subjects' scores from the group mean.

**Summary data** Descriptive statistics computed from the raw data of an experiment, including the measures of central tendency and variability.

**Survey research** A useful way of obtaining data about people's opinions, attitudes, preferences, and experiences that are hard to observe directly; data may be obtained using questionnaires or interviews.

**Synthetic statement** A statement that can be either true or false, a condition necessary to form an experimental hypothesis.

**Systematic observation** A system for recording observations; each observation is recorded using specific rules or guidelines, so observations are more objective.

**Systematic random sampling** A variation of random sampling in which a researcher selects every $n$th person from the population.

**$t$ test** A statistic that relates differences between treatment means to the amount of variability expected between any two samples of data from the same population; used to analyze the results of a two-group experiment with one independent variable and interval or ratio data.

**$t$ test for independent groups** A statistic that relates differences between treatment means to the amount of variability expected between any two samples of data from the same population; used to analyze the results of a two-group experiment with independent groups of subjects.

**$t$ test for matched groups** A statistic that relates differences between treatment means to the amount of variability expected between any two samples of data from the same population; used to analyze two-group experiments using matched-subjects or within-subjects designs. Also called a within-subjects *t* test.

**Test statistics** Statistics that can be used as indicators of what is going on in a population and can be used to evaluate results; also called *inferential statistics*.

**Testable** Capable of being tested; typically used in reference to a hypothesis. Two requirements must be met to have a testable hypothesis: Procedures for manipulating the setting must exist, and the predicted outcome must be observable.

**Testable statement** A statement that can be tested because the means exist for manipulating antecedent conditions and for measuring the resulting behavior.

**Testing threat** A threat to internal validity produced by a previous administration of the same test or other measure.

**Test-retest reliability** Consistency between an individual's scores on the same test taken at two or more different times.

**Theory** A set of general principles that attempts to explain and predict behavior or other phenomena.

**Title** The name of the report, which describes what the report is about; typically includes the variables tested and the relationship between them.

**Treatment** A specific set of antecedent conditions created by the experimenter and presented to subjects to test its effect on behavior.

**Two-experimental-groups design** A design in which two groups of subjects are exposed to different levels of the independent variable.

**Two-factor experiment** The simplest factorial design, having two independent variables.

**Two-group design** The simplest experimental design, used when only two treatment conditions are needed.

**Two-independent-groups design** An experimental design in which subjects are placed in each of two treatment conditions through random assignment.

**Two-matched-groups design** An experimental design with two treatment conditions and with subjects who are matched on a subject variable thought to be highly related to the dependent variable.

**Two-tailed test** A statistical procedure used when a nondirectional prediction has been made; the critical region of the distribution of the test statistic (*t*, for instance) is divided over both tails of the distribution.

**Type 1 error** An error made by rejecting the null hypothesis even though it is really true; stating that an effect exists when it really does not.

**Type 2 error** An error made by retaining the null hypothesis even though it is really false; failing to detect a treatment effect.

**Unobtrusive measure** A procedure used to assess subjects' behaviors without their knowledge; used to obtain more nonreactive data.

**Validity** The soundness of an operational definition; in experiments, the principle of actually studying the variables intended to be manipulated or measured; also, the extent to which a survey actually measures the intended topic.

**Variability** Fluctuation in data; can be defined numerically as the range, variance, or standard deviation.

**Variance** The average squared deviation of scores from their mean; a more precise measure of variability than the range.

**Willingness to answer** The differences among people in their style of responding to questions they are unsure about; some people will leave these questions blank, whereas others will take a guess.

**Within-groups variability** The degree to which the scores of subjects in the *same* treatment group differ from one another (that is, how much subjects vary from others in the group); an index of the degree of fluctuation among scores that is attributable to error.

**Within-subjects design** A design in which each subject takes part in more than one condition of the experiment.

**Within-subjects factorial design** A factorial design in which subjects receive all conditions in the experiment.

**Yea-sayers** People who are apt to agree with a question regardless of its manifest content.

# REFERENCES

Abreu, J. M., & Gabarain, G. (2000). Social desirability and Mexican American counselor preferences: Statistical control for a potential confound. *Journal of Counseling Psychology, 47*(2), 165–176.

Ainsworth, M. D. S., Blehar, M., Waters, E., & Wall, S. (1978). *Patterns of attachment*. Hillsdale, NJ: Erlbaum.

Allinson, C. W., & Hayes, J. (1996). The Cognitive Style Index: A measure of intuition—analysis for organizational research. *Journal of Management Studies, 33*(1), 119–135.

Ambady, N., & Rosenthal, R. (1993). Half a minute: Predicting teacher evaluations from thin slices of nonverbal behavior and physical attractiveness. *Journal of Personality and Social Psychology, 64*(3), 431–441.

American Association for Laboratory Animal Science (AALAS). (1984). *Policy statement on biomedical research* (news release, October 26).

American Psychiatric Association. (1994). *Diagnostic and statistical manual of mental disorders* (4th ed.). Washington, DC: Author.

American Psychological Association (2010). *Publication manual of the American Psychological Association* (7th ed.). Washington, DC: Author.

American Psychological Association (2002). Ethical principles of psychologists and code of conduct. *American Psychologist, 57*(12), 1060–1073.

Anastasi, A. (1958). *Differential psychology* (3rd ed.). New York: Macmillan.

Anderson, C. A., Berkowitz, L., Donnerstein, E., Huesmann, L. R., Johnson, J. D., Linz, D., Malamuth, N. M., & Wartella, E. (2003). The influence of media violence on youth. *Psychological Science in the Public Interest, 4*(3), 81–110.

Anderson, C. A., & Dill, K. E. (2000). Video games and aggressive thoughts, feelings, and behavior in the laboratory and in life. *Journal of Personality and Social Psychology, 78*(4), 772–790.

Anderson, K. J. (1990). Arousal and the inverted-U hypothesis: A critique of Neiss's "Reconceptualizing arousal." *Psychological Bulletin, 107*(1), 96–100.

APA Board of Scientific Affairs (CARE). Research with animals in psychology. Retrieved on November 1, 2009 from www.apa.org/SCIENCE/animal2.html

Aronson, J., Lustina, M. J., Good, C., Keough, K., Steele, C. M., & Brown, J. (1999). When white men can't do math: Necessary and sufficient factors in stereotype threat. *Journal of Experimental Social Psychology, 35*, 29–46.

Ator, N. A. (1999). Statistical inference in behavior analysis: Environmental determinants. *Behavior Analyst, 22*, 93–97.

Augé, W. K., & Augé, S. M. (1999). Naturalistic observation of athletic drug-use patterns and behavior in professional-caliber bodybuilders. *Substance Use & Misuse, 34*(2), 217–249.

Azar, B. (1999, July/August). Destructive lab attack sends a wake-up call. *APA Monitor Online, 30*(7) (online). Available: http:www.apa.org

Barber, T. X. (1976). *Pitfalls in human research*. New York: Pergamon.

Barlow, D. H., Nock, M. K., & Hersen, M. (2009). *Single case experimental designs: Strategies for studying behavior change*. Boston: Pearson Education, Inc.

Baron, R. A., Russell, G. W., & Arms, R. L. (1985). Negative ions and behavior: Impact on mood, memory, and aggression among Type A and Type B persons. *Journal of Personality and Social Psychology, 48*, 746–754.

Bassett, E. H., & O'Riordan, K. (2002). Ethics of Internet research: Contesting the human subjects research model. *Ethics and Information Technology, 4*(3), 233–247.

Batson, D. C., Chang, J., Orr, R., & Rowland, J. (2002). Empathy, attitudes, and action: Can feelings for a member of a stigmatized group motivate one to help the group? *Personality and Social Psychology Bulletin, 28*, 1656–1666.

Beckenbach, A. (1995). Computer-assisted questioning: The new survey methods in the perception of the respondents. *Bulletin de Methodologie Sociologique (BMS), 48*, 82–100.

Benjamin, L. T., Jr. (2007). *A brief history of modern psychology.* Malden, MA: Blackwell Publishing.

Berkowitz, L., & Rogers, K. H. (1986). A priming effect analysis of media influences. In J. Bryant & D. Zillmann (Eds.), *Perspectives on media effects* (pp. 57–81). Hillsdale, NJ: Erlbaum.

Berman, M. E., & Taylor, S. (1995). The effects of triazolam on aggression in men. *Experimental and Clinical Psychopharmacology, 3*(4), 411–416.

Bingman, V. P., & Able, K. P. (2002). Maps in birds: Representational mechanisms and neural bases. *Current Opinion in Neurobiology, 12*(6), 745–750.

Blais, E., & Bacher, J-L. (2007). Situational deterrence and claim padding: Results from a randomized field experiment. *Journal of Experimental Criminology, 3*, 337–352.

Blumberg, M. S., Sokoloff, G., Kirby, R. F., & Kent, K. J. (2000). Distress vocalizations in infant rats: What's all the fuss about? *Psychological Science, 11*(1), 78–81.

Boring, E. G. (1950). *A history of experimental psychology* (2nd ed.). New York: Appleton-Century-Crofts.

Borsari, B., & Carey, K. B. (2000). Effects of a brief motivational intervention with college student drinkers. *Journal of Consulting and Clinical Psychology, 68*(4), 728–733.

Bouchard, T. J., Jr., & McGue, M. (1981). Familial studies of intelligence: A review. *Science, 212*, 1055–1059.

Bouchard, Jr., et al. (2003). Evidence for the construct validity and heritability of the Wilson-Patterson Conservatism Scale: A reared-apart twins study of social attitudes. *Personality and Individual Differences, 34*, 959–969.

Bowman, P. J. (1992). Coping with provider role strain: Adaptive cultural resources among Black husband-fathers. In A. Burlew, W. Banks, H. McAdoo, & D. Azibo (Eds.), *African American psychology: Theory, research, and practice* (pp. 135–154). Newbury Park, CA: Sage.

Brady, J. V. (1958). Ulcers in "executive" monkeys. *Scientific American, 199*(4), 95–100.

Bramel, D. (1963). Selection of a target for defensive projection. *Journal of Abnormal and Social Psychology, 66*, 318–324.

Breuer, J., & Freud, S. (1957). *Studies in hysteria.* New York: Basic Books.

Bridges, F. S., Keeton, K. B., & Clark, L. N. (2002). Responses to lost letters about a 2000 general election amendment to abolish prohibition of interracial marriages in Alabama. *Psychological Reports, 91*, 1148–1150.

Bryan, A. D., Aiken, L. S., & West, S. G. (1996). Increasing condom use: Evaluation of a theory-based intervention to prevent sexually transmitted diseases in young women. *Health Psychology, 15*(5), 371–382.

Buchbinder, E., & Eisikovits, Z. (2002). Battered women's entrapment in shame: A phenomenological study. *American Journal of Orthopsychiatry, 73*(4), 355–366.

Burke, D. M., Locantore, J. K., Austin, A. A., & Chae, B. (2004). Cherry pit primes Brad Pitt: Homophone priming effects on young and older adults' production of proper names. *Psychological Science, 15*(3), 164–170.

Burt, C. (1966). The genetic determination of differences in intelligence: A study of monozygotic twins reared together and apart. *British Journal of Psychology, 57*, 137–153.

Burt, C. (1972). Inheritance of general intelligence. *American Psychologist, 27*, 174–190.

Bushman, B. J. (1998). Effects of warning and information labels on consumption of full-fat, reduced-fat, and no-fat products. *Journal of Applied Psychology, 83*, 97–101.

Bushman, B. J., Baumeister, R., & Stack, A. (1999). Catharsis, aggression and persuasive influence: Self-fulfilling or self-defeating prophecies? *Journal of Personality and Social Psychology, 76*(3), 367–376.

Bushman, B. J., & Cantor, J. (2003). Media ratings for violence and sex: Implications for policymakers and parents. *American Psychologist, 58*(2), 130–141.

Butler, S., & Roesel, K. (1991). Students' perceptions of male teachers: Effects of teachers' dress and students' characteristics. *Perceptual and Motor Skills, 73*(3), 943–951.

Byrne, G. (1988). Breuning pleads guilty. *Science, 242*, 27–28.

Campbell, D., Sanderson, R. E., & Laverty, S. C. (1964). Characteristics of a conditioned response in human subjects during extinction trials following a single traumatic conditioning trial. *Journal of Abnormal and Social Psychology, 68*, 627–639.

Campbell, D. T. (1957). Factors relevant to the validity of experiments in social settings. *Psychological Bulletin, 54*, 297–312.

Campbell, D. T., & Stanley, J. T. (1966). *Experimental and quasi-experimental designs for research.* Chicago: Rand McNally.

Cattell, R. B. (1946). *Description and measurement of personality.* New York: World Book.

Chaplin, W. F., Phillips, J. B., Brown, J. D., Clanton, N. R., & Stein, J. L. (2000). Handshaking, gender, personality, and first impressions. *Journal of Personality and Social Psychology, 79*(1), 110–117.

Christensen, L. (1988). Deception in psychological research: When is its use justified? *Personality and Social Psychology Bulletin, 14*, 664–675.

Churchill, W. (1930). *My early life.* New York: Scribners.

Cleckley, J. (1976). *The mask of sanity* (5th ed.). St. Louis: Mosby.

Cohen, J. (1988). *Statistical power analysis for the behavioral sciences.* Hillsdale, NJ: Erlbaum.

Cohen, J. (1992). A power primer. *Psychological Bulletin, 112*(1), 155–159.

Cohen, J. (1994). The earth is round ($p < .05$). *American Psychologist, 49*(12), 997–1003.

Coile, D. C., & Miller, N. E. (1984). How radical animal activists try to mislead humane people. *American Psychologist, 39*, 700–701.

Coleman, L. K., Wampold, B. E., & Casali, S. L. (1995). Ethnic minorities' ratings of ethnically similar and European American counselors: A meta-analysis. *Journal of Counseling Psychology, 42*, 55–64.

Colvin, C. R., & Funder, D. C. (1991). Predicting personality and behavior: A boundary on the acquaintanceship effect. *Journal of Personality and Social Psychology, 60*(6), 884–894.

Conner, M., Lawton, R., Parker, D., Chorlton, K., Manstead, A. S. R., & Stradling, S. (2007). Application of the theory of planned behaviour to the prediction of objectively assessed breaking of posted speed limits. *British Journal of Psychology, 98*(3), 429–453.

Contrada, R. J., Goyal, T. M., Cather, C., Rafalson, L., Idler, E. L., & Krause, T. J. (2004). Psychosocial factors in outcomes of heart surgery: The impact of religious involvement and depressive symptoms. *Health Psychology, 23*(3), 227–238.

Conway, J. C., & Rubin, A. M. (1991). Psychological predictors of television viewing motivation. *Communication Research, 18*(4), 443–463.

Cook, T. D., & Campbell, D. T. (1979). *Quasi-experimentation: Design and analysis issues for field settings.* Boston: Houghton Mifflin.

Cousins, N. (1989). *Head first: The biology of hope.* New York: Dutton.

Crandall, C. S. (1988). Social contagion of binge eating. *Journal of Personality and Social Psychology, 55*, 588–598.

Crano, W. D., & Brewer, M. B. (2002). *Principles and methods of social research.* Mahwah, NJ: Erlbaum.

Cronbach, L. J. (1950). Further evidence on response sets and test design. *Educational and Psychological Measurement, 10*, 3–31.

Crowne, D. P., & Marlowe, D. (1964). *The approval motive.* New York: Wiley.

Crum, A. J., & Langer, E. J. (2007). Mind-set matters: Exercise and the placebo effect. *Psychological Science, 18*(2), 165–171.

Cumming, G. (2005). Commentary: Understanding the average probability of replication: Comment on Killeen (2005). *Psychological Science, 16*(2), 1002–1004.

Cunningham, M. R. (1989). Reactions to heterosexual opening gambits: Female selectivity and male responsiveness. *Personality and Social Psychology Bulletin, 15*(1), 27–41.

Curtin, R., Presser, S., & Singer, E. (2005). Changes in telephone survey nonresponse over the past quarter century. *Public Opinion Quarterly, 69*(1), 87–98.

Czaja, R., & Blair, J. (1996). *Designing surveys: A guide to decisions and procedures.* Thousand Oaks, CA: Pine Forge Press.

Danforth, J. S. (1998). The outcome of parent training using the behavior management flow chart with mothers and their children with Oppositional Defiant Disorder and Attention-Deficit Hyperactivity Disorder. *Behavior Modification, 22*(4), 443–473.

Davison, G. C., & Neale, J. M. (1986). *Abnormal psychology: An experimental clinical approach.* New York: Wiley.

Der, G., Batty, G. D., & Deary, I. D. (2006). Effect of breast feeding on intelligence in children: Prospective study, sibling pairs analysis, and meta-analysis. *British Medical Journal, 333*, 945.

Devlin, P. (2005). Effects of continuous improvement training on student interaction and engagement. *Research & Practice for Persons with Severe Disabilities, 30*(2), 42–59.

Dittmann, M. (2004). What makes good people do bad things? Retrieved on November 2, 2009 from www.apa. org/monitor/oct04/goodbad.html

Domjan, M., & Purdy, J. E. (1995). Animal research in psychology: More than meets the eye of the general psychology student. *American Psychologist, 50*, 496–503.

Donnerstein, E., Linz, D., & Penrod, S. (1987). *The question of pornography: Research findings and policy implications.* New York: Free Press.

Dugas, M. J., Ladouceur, R., Leger, E., Freeston, M. H., Langlois, F., Provencher, M. D., & Boisvert, J-M. (2003). Group cognitive-behavioral therapy for generalized anxiety disorder: Treatment outcome and long-term follow-up. *Journal of Consulting and Clinical Psychology, 71*(4). 821–625.

Dunning, D., Griffin, D. W., Milojkovic, J., & Ross, L. (1990). The overconfidence effect in social prediction. *Journal of Personality and Social Psychology, 58*, 568–581.

Ennemoser, M., & Schneider, W. (2007). Relations of television viewing and reading. *Journal of Educational Psychology, 99*(2), 349–368.

Epstein, S. (1980). The stability of behavior. II. Implications for psychological research. *American Psychologist, 35*(9), 790–806.

Eron, L. D., Huesmann, L. R., Lefkowitz, M. M., & Walder, L. O. (1972). Does television violence cause aggression? *American Psychologist, 27*, 253–263.

Estes, R. J., & Wilensky, H. L. (1978). Life cycles squeeze and the morale curve. *Social Problems, 25*(3), 277–292.

Fazio, R. H. (1990). Multiple processes by which attitudes guide behavior: The mode model as an integrative framework. In M. P. Zanna (Ed.), *Advances in experimental social psychology* (Vol. 23, pp. 75–109). New York: Academic Press.

Fernandez-Dols, J-M., & Ruiz-Belda, M-A. (1995). Are smiles signs of happiness? Gold medal winners at Olympic games. *Journal of Personality and Social Psychology, 69*(6), 1113–1119.

Ferster, C. B., & Skinner, B. F. (1957). *Schedules of reinforcement.* New York: Appleton-Century-Crofts.

Fisher, R. A. (1935). *The design of experiments.* London: Oliver & Boyd.

Fleeson, W. (2004). Moving personality beyond the person-situation debate: The challenge and the opportunity of within-person variability. *Current Directions in Psychological Science, 13*(2), 83–87.

Fournier, A. K., Geller, E. S., & Fortney, E. V. (2007). Human-animal interaction in a prison setting: Impact on criminal behavior, treatment progress, and social skills. *Behavior and Social Issues, 16*, 89–105.

Fowler, F. J., Jr. (1993). *Survey research methods* (2nd ed.). Newbury Park, CA: Sage.

Franklin, K. M., Janoff-Bulman, R., & Roberts, J. E. (1990). Long-term impact of parental divorce on optimism and trust: Changes in general assumptions or narrow beliefs? *Journal of Personality and Social Psychology, 59*(4), 743–755.

Freud, S. (1933). Analysis of a phobia in a five-year-old boy. In *Collected papers* (Vol. 3). London: Hogarth.

Fridlund, A. J. (1989). *The sociality of solitary smiling: Potentiation by an implicit audience.* Paper presented at the 29th Annual Meeting of the

Society for Psychophysiological Research, New Orleans.

Fridlund, A. J., Ekman, P., & Oster, H. (1987). Facial expressions of emotion. In A. W. Siegman & S. Feldstein (Eds.), *Nonverbal behavior and communication* (2nd ed., pp. 143–224). Hillsdale, NJ: Erlbaum.

Friman, P. C., Jones, M., Smith, G., Daly, D. L., & Larzelere, R. (1997). Decreasing disruptive behavior by adolescent boys in residential care by increasing their positive to negative interactional ratios. *Behavior Modification, 21*(4), 470–486.

Galea, S., Nandi, A., Stuber, J., Gold, J., Acierno, R., Best, C. L., Bucuvalas, M., Rudenstine, S., Boscrino, J. A., & Resnick, H. (2005). Participant reactions to survey research in the general population after terrorist attacks. *Journal of Traumatic Stress, 18*(5), 461–465.

Ganzel, B., Casey, B. J., Glover, G., Voss, H. U., & Temple, E. (2007). The aftermath of 9/11: Effect of intensity and recency of trauma on outcome. *Emotion, 7*(2), 227–238.

Gastil, J. (1990). Generic pronouns and sexist language: The oxymoronic character of masculine generics. *Sex Roles, 23*(11/12), 629–643.

Gilbert, A. N., & Wysocki, C. J. (1992). Hand preference and age in the United States. *Neuropsychologia, 30*(7), 601–608.

Gilbert, D. T. (1995). The correspondence bias. *Psychological Bulletin, 117*(1), 21–38.

Grant, R. (2009). Retrieved on April 21, 2009 from www.the-scientist.com/blog/display/55504 and www.the-scientist.com/blog/display/55651

Green, B. F. (1992). Exposé or smear? The Burt affair. *Psychological Science, 3,* 328–331.

Green, C. S., & Bavelier, D. (2007). Action-video-game experience alters the spatial resolution of vision. *Psychological Science, 18*(1), 88–94.

Greenberg, J. (1988). Equity and workplace status: A field experiment. *Journal of Applied Psychology, 73*(4), 606–613.

Greenwald, A., Spangenbert, E., Pratkanis, A., & Eskenazi, J. (1991). Double-blind tests of subliminal self-help audiotapes. *Psychological Science, 2*(2), 119–122.

Greeson, L. E., & Williams, R. A. (1986). Social implications of music videos for youth. *Youth and Society, 18,* 177–189.

Hall, E. T. (1966). *Hidden dimensions.* Garden City, NY: Doubleday.

Hall, R. V., Alley, S. J., & Cox, L. (1971). *Managing behavior. 3: Applications in school and home.* Austin, TX: PRO-ED.

Halpern, D. F. (1989). *Thought and knowledge: An introduction to critical thinking.* Hillsdale, NJ: Erlbaum.

Hamilton, D. L., & Rose, T. L. (1980). Illusory correlations and the maintenance of stereotypic beliefs. *Journal of Personality and Social Psychology, 39*(5), 832–845.

Hannover, B., & Kuhnen, U. (2002). "The clothing makes the self" via knowledge activation. *Journal of Applied Social Psychology, 32*(12), 2513–2525.

Hansen, C. H. (1995). Predicting cognitive and behavioral effects of gangsta rap. *Basic and Applied Social Psychology, 16*(1/2), 43–52.

Hansen, K. M. (2007). The effects of incentives, interview length, and interviewer characteristics on response rates in a CATI study. *International Journal of Public Opinion Research, 19*(1), 112–121.

Harris, I. M., Harris, J. A., & Caine, D. (2002). Mental-rotation deficits following damage to the right basal ganglia. *Neuropsychology, 16*(4), 524–537.

Harris, M. J., & Rosenthal, R. (1985). Mediation of interpersonal expectancy effects: 31 meta-analyses. *Psychological Bulletin, 97,* 363–386.

Harrison, L. J., & Ungerer, J. A. (2002). Child care predictors of infant-mother attachment security at age 12 months postpartum. *Developmental Psychology, 38,* 758–773.

Harzing, A-W. (2006). Response styles in cross-national survey research. *International Journal of Cross Cultural Management, 6*(2), 243–266.

Haven, J. (1862). *Mental philosophy: including the intellect, sensibilities, and will.* Boston, New York: Gould and Lincoln, Sheldon and Company.

Heider, F. (1958). *The psychology of interpersonal relations.* New York: Wiley.

Hein, S., & Austin, W. J. (2001). Empirical and hermeneutic approaches to phenomenological research in psychology: A comparison. *Psychological Methods, 6*(1), 3–17.

Hembroff, L. A., Rusz, D., Rafferty, A., Mcgee, H., & Ehrlich, N. (2005) The cost-effectiveness of alternative advance mailings in a telephone survey. *Public Opinion Quarterly, 69*(2), 232–245.

Herz, R. (1999). Caffeine effects on mood and memory. *Behaviour Research and Therapy, 37,* 869–879.

Herzog, H. A. (1991). Conflicts of interests: Kittens and boa constrictors, pets and research. *American Psychologist, 46,* 246–248.

Hess, E. (1975). Role of pupil size in communication. *Scientific American, 233*(5), 110ff.

Hodgson, L. (1998). *Houseplants for dummies.* New York: IDG Books Worldwide.

Holland, R. W., Roeder, U-R., van Baaren, R. B., Brandt, A. C., & Hannover, B. (2004). Don't stand so close to me. *Psychological Science, 15*(4), 237–242.

Honos-Webb, L., Stiles, W. B., & Greenberg, L. S. (2003). A method of rating assimilation in psychotherapy based on markers of change. *Journal of Counseling Psychology, 50*(2), 189–198.

House, J. D., & Johnson, J. J. (1998). Predictive validity of the Graduate Record Examination for grade performance in graduate psychology courses. *Psychological Reports, 82,* 1235–1238.

Huesmann, L. R., Moise-Titus, J., Podolski, C., & Eron, L. (2003). Longitudinal relations between children's exposure to TV violence and aggressive and violent behavior in young adulthood: 1977–1992. *Developmental Psychology, 39*(2), 201–221.

Huff, D. (1954). *How to lie with statistics.* New York: Norton.

Hurlburt, R. T. (1994). *Comprehending behavioral statistics.* Pacific Grove, CA: Brooks/Cole.

Ingersoll-Dayton, B., Neal, M. B., Ha, J-H., & Hammer, L. B. Redressing inequity in parent care among siblings. *Journal of Marriage and Family, 65,* 201–212.

Institute for Laboratory Animal Research. (1996). *Guide for the care and use of laboratory animals.* Washington, DC: National Academy Press.

Irwin, O. C., & Weiss, L. A. (1934). Differential variations in the activity and crying of newborn infants under different intensities of light: A comparison of observational with polygraph findings. *University of Iowa Studies in Child Welfare, 9,* 139–147.

Isen, A. (1987). Positive affect, cognitive processes, and social behavior. In L. Berkowitz (Ed.), *Advances in experimental social psychology* (Vol. 20, pp. 203–253). New York: Academic Press.

Ivry, R. B., & Lebby, P. C. (1993). Hemispheric differences in auditory perception are similar to those found in visual perception. *Psychological Science, 4*(1), 41–45.

Jacobson, E. (1971). *Depression.* New York: International Universities Press.

James, W. (1950). *Principles of psychology.* New York: Dover. (Original work published 1890.)

Jenkins, C. D., Zyzanski, S. J., & Rosenman, R. H. (1979). *Jenkins Activity Survey.* New York: Psychological Corporation.

Johnson, R. B. (1997). Examining the validity structure of qualitative research. *Education, 118*(3), 282–292.

Jones, E. E., Ghannam, J., Nigg, J. T., & Dyer, J. (1993). A paradigm for single-case research: The time series study of a long-term psychotherapy for depression. *Journal of Consulting and Clinical Psychology, 61*(3), 381–394.

Jones, K. M., & Friman, P. C. (1999). A case study of behavioral assessment and treatment of insect phobia. *Journal of Applied Behavior Analysis, 32*(1), 95–98.

Jones, M. C. (1924). A laboratory study of fear: The case of Peter. *Pedagogical Seminary, 31,* 308–315.

Jones, M. K., & Menzies, R. G. (2000). Danger expectancies, self-efficacy, and insight in spider phobia. *Behaviour Research and Therapy, 38,* 585–600.

Jones, S. S., Collins, K., & Hong, H-W. (1991). An audience effect on smile production in 10-month-old infants. *Psychological Science, 2*(1), 45–49.

Jones, S. S., & Raag, R. (1989). Smile production in older infants: The importance of a social recipient for the facial signal. *Child Development, 60,* 811–818.

Judd, D. B., & Kelly, K. L. (1965). The ISCC-NBS method of designating colors and a dictionary of color names. *U.S. National Bureau of Standards Circular, 553* (2nd ed.). Washington, DC: National Bureau of Standards.

Kahneman, D., & Tversky, A. (Eds.). (2000). *Choices, values and frames.* New York: Cambridge University Press and the Russell Sage Foundation.

Kaplan, R. M., & Saccuzzo, D. P. (2005). *Psychological testing: Principles, applications, and issues* (6th ed.). Belmont, CA: Wadsworth.

Kazdin, A. E. (2003). *Research design in clinical psychology* (4th ed.). Needham Heights, MA: Allyn & Bacon.

Keehn, J. D. (1977). In defence of experiments with animals. *Bulletin of the British Psychological Society, 30,* 404–405.

Kelley, H. H. (1950). The warm-cold variable in the first impressions of persons. *Journal of Personality, 18,* 431–439.

Kelley, H. H. (1971). *Attribution in social interaction.* Morristown, NJ: General Learning Press.

Kendall, P. L., & Wolf, K. M. (1949). The analysis of deviant cases in communications research. In P. F. Lazarfeld (Ed.), *Communications research: 1948–1949* (pp. 152–179). Oxford, England: Harper.

Keppel, G. (1982). *Design and analysis: A researcher's handbook* (2nd ed.). Englewood Cliffs, NJ: Prentice-Hall.

Keren, G., & Lewis, C. (1993). *A handbook for data analysis in the behavioral sciences.* Hillsdale, NJ: Erlbaum.

Kerlinger, F. N., & Lee, H. B. (2000). *Foundations of behavioral research* (4th ed.). Belmont, CA: Wadsworth.

Killeen, P. R. (2005). An alternative to null hypothesis significance tests. *Psychological Science, 16,* 345–353.

Killeen, P. R. (2006). Beyond statistical inference: A decision theory for science. *Psychonomic Bulletin & Review, 13*(4), 549–562.

Kimble, G. A. (1989). Psychology from the standpoint of a generalist. *American Psychologist, 44*(3), 491–499.

Kirsch, I., & Sapirstein, G. (1998). Listening to Prozac but hearing placebo: A meta-analysis of antidepressant medication. *Prevention & Treatment, 1*(2), np.

Konstan, J. A., Rosser, B. R. S., Ross, M. W., Stanton, J., & Edwards, W. M. (2005). The story of subject naught: A cautionary but optimistic tale of internet survey research. *Journal of Computer-Mediated Communication, 10*(2), article 11. http://jcmc.indiana.edu/vol10/issue2/konstan.html

Kraut, R., Olson, J., Banaji, M., Bruckman, A., Cohen, J., & Couper, M. (2004). Psychological research online: Report of board of scientific affairs' advisory group on the conduct of research on the Internet. *American Psychologist, 59*(2), 105–117.

Krawczel, P. D., Friend, T. H., & Windom, A. (2005). Stereotypic behavior of circus tigers: Effects of performance. *Applied Animal Behaviour Science, 95*(3), 189–198.

Kuhn, T. (1970). *The structure of scientific revolutions* (2nd ed.). Chicago: University of Chicago Press.

Kunda, Z., & Nisbett, R. E. (1986). The psychometrics of everyday life. *Cognitive Psychology, 18,* 195–224.

Larzelere, R. E., Kuhn, B. R., & Johnson, B. (2004). The intervention selection bias: An underrecognized confound in intervention research. *Psychological Bulletin, 130*(2), 289–303.

Lassen, C. L. (1973). Effect of proximity on anxiety and communication in the initial psychiatric interview. *Journal of Abnormal Psychology, 81,* 226–232.

Latané, B., & Darley, J. M. (1970). *The unresponsive bystander: Why doesn't he help?* New York: Appleton-Century-Crofts.

Lawson, T. J., Downing, B., & Cetola, H. (1998). An attributional explanation for the effect of audience laughter on perceived funniness. *Basic and Applied Social Psychology, 20*(4), 243–249.

Leavitt, P. (1974). *Drugs and behavior.* Philadelphia: Saunders. Guilford, CT: Dushkin. (Original work published 1977.)

Lewin, T. (2002, October 3). Hamilton College president resigns over speech. *The New York Times,* p. B10.

Likert, R. (1932). A technique for the measurement of attitudes. *Archives of Psychology,* No. 140.

Lonner, W. J. (1990). An overview of cross-cultural testing and assessment. In R. W. Brislin (Ed.), *Applied cross-cultural psychology* (pp. 56–76). Newbury Park, CA: Sage.

Louie, T. A., & Obermiller, C. (2000). Gender stereotypes and social desirability effects on charity donation. *Psychology & Marketing*, 17(2), 121–136.

Mann, T. (1994). Informed consent for psychological research: Do subjects comprehend consent forms and understand their legal rights? *Psychological Science*, 5(3), 140–143.

Marston, A. R., London, P., Cooper, L., & Cohen, N. (1977). In vivo observation of the eating behavior of obese and nonobese subjects. *Journal of Consulting and Clinical Psychology*, 45, 335–336.

Masson, M. E. J., & Loftus, G. R. (2003). Using confidence intervals for graphically based data interpretation. *Canadian Journal of Experimental Psychology*, 57(3), 203–220.

Matsumoto, D. (2000). *Culture and psychology: People around the world* (2nd ed.). Pacific Grove, CA: Brooks/Cole.

Maylor, E. (1990). Recognizing and naming faces: Aging, memory retrieval, and the tip of the tongue state. *Journal of Gerontology: Psychological Sciences*, 45, 215–225.

McGuigan, F. J. (1971). The experimenter: A neglected stimulus object. In J. Jung (Ed.), *The experimenter's dilemma* (pp. 182–195). New York: Harper & Row.

McGuire, W. J. (1997). Creative hypothesis generating in psychology: Some useful heuristics. *Annual Review of Psychology*, 48, 1–30.

McMinn, M. R., Williams, P. E., & McMinn, L. C. (1994). Assessing recognition of sexist language: Development and use of the Gender-Specific Language Scale. *Sex Roles*, 31(11/12), 741–755.

McNemar, Q. (1946). Opinion-attitude methodology. *Psychological Bulletin*, 43, 289–374.

Mecklenburg, S. H. (2006). Report to the legislature of the state of Illinois: The Illinois pilot program on double-blind, sequential lineup procedures. Retrieved July 12, 2008 from http://www.chicagopolice.org/IL%20Pilot%20on%20Eyewitness%20.pdf

Mednick, S. A. (1969). A longitudinal study of children with a high risk for schizophrenia. In M. Zax &

G. Stricker (Eds.), *The study of abnormal behavior*. London: Macmillan.

Mednick, S. A., Schulsinger, F., & Venables, P. H. (1981). The Mauritius project. In S. A. Mednick, A. Baert, & B. P. Bachmann (Eds.), *Prospective longitudinal research* (pp. 314–316). Oxford, England: Oxford University Press.

Mehrabian, A., & Piercy, M. (1993a). Differences in positive-negative connotations of nicknames and given names. *Journal of Social Psychology*, 133(5), 501–508.

Mehrabian, A., & Piercy, M. (1993b). Affective and personality characteristics inferred from length of first names. *Personality and Social Psychology Bulletin*, 19(6), 755–758.

Mellman, T. A., David, D., Kulick-Bell, R., Hebding, J., & Nolan, B. (1995). Sleep disturbance and its relationship to psychiatric morbidity after Hurricane Andrew. *American Journal of Psychiatry*, 152(11), 1659–1663.

Milgram, S. (1963). Behavioral study of obedience. *Journal of Abnormal and Social Psychology*, 67, 371–378.

Milgram, S. (1974). *Obedience to authority*. New York: Harper & Row.

Milgram, S., Mann, L., & Harter, S. (1965). The lost letter technique. *Public Opinion Quarterly*, 34, 437–438.

Miller, D. (1977). Roles of naturalistic observation in comparative psychology. *American Psychologist*, 32(3), 211–219.

Miller, D. L., & Kelley, M. L. (1994). The use of goal setting and contingency contracting for improving children's homework performance. *Journal of Applied Behavior Analysis*, 27, 73–84.

Miller, H. B., & Williams, W. H. (1983). *Ethics and animals*. Clifton, NJ: Humana Press.

Miller, N. (1984). Values and ethics of research on animals. *Laboratory Primate Newsletter*, 23(3), 1–10.

Miller, N. E. (1985). The value of behavioral research on animals. *American Psychologist*, 40, 423–440.

Misra, S. (1992). Is conventional debriefing adequate? An ethical issue in consumer research. *Journal of the Academy of Marketing Science*, 20(3), 269–273.

Morgan, D. L., & Morgan, R. K. (2001). Single-participant research designs: Bringing science to managed care. *American Psychologist*, 56(2), 119–127.

Mori, D., Chaiken, S., & Pliner, P. (1987). "Eating lightly" and the self-presentation of femininity. *Journal of Personality and Social Psychology*, 53, 693–702.

Moss, G., & McDonald, J. W. (2004). The borrowers: Library records as unobtrusive measures of children's reading preferences. *Journal of Research in Reading*, 27(4), 401–412.

Myer, J. L., & Well, A. D. (1991). *Research design and statistical analyses*. New York: HarperCollins.

*National Geographic Atlas of the World* (6th ed). (1990). Washington, DC: National Geographic Society.

Nicoll, C. S., & Russell, S. M. (1990). Analysis of animal rights literature reveals the underlying motives of the movement: Ammunition for counter offensive by scientists. *Endocrinology*, 127, 985–989.

Niedenthal, P. M., & Cantor, N. (1986). Affective responses as guides to category-based inferences. *Motivation and Emotion*, 10, 217–232.

Nisbett, R. E., & Wilson, T. E. (1977). Telling more than we can know: Verbal reports on mental processes. *Psychological Review*, 84, 231–259.

North, A. C., Hargreaves, D. J., & McKendrick, J. (1999). The influence of in-store music on wine selections. *Journal of Applied Psychology*, 84(2), 271–276.

Nosek, B. A., Banaji, M. R., & Greenwald, A. G. (2002). eResearch: Ethics, security, design, and control in psychological research on the Internet. *Journal of Social Issues*, 58(1), 161–176.

O'Neill, P. (2002). Tectonic change: The qualitative paradigm in psychology. *Canadian Psychology*, 43, 190–194.

Orne, M. T. (1969). Demand characteristics and the concept of quasicontrols. In R. Rosenthal & R. L. Rosnow (Eds.), *Artifact in behavioral research*. New York: Academic Press.

Orne, M. T. (1972). On the social psychology of the psychological experiment: With particular reference to demand characteristics and their implications. In A. G. Miller (Ed.), *The* social psychology of psychological research (pp. 233–246). New York: Free Press.

Orne, M. T., & Scheibe, K. E. (1964). The contribution of nondeprivation factors in the production of sensory deprivation effects: The psychology of the "panic button." Journal of Abnormal and Social Psychology, 68, 3–12.

Osgood, C. E., Suci, D. J., & Tannenbaum, P. H. (1957). The measurement of meaning. Urbana: University of Illinois Press.

Patten, M. L. (1998). Questionnaire research. Los Angeles: Pyrczak Publishing.

Pavlov, I. (1927). Conditioned reflexes (G. V. Anrep, Trans.). London: Oxford University Press.

Pedersen, N. L., Plomin, R., Nesselroade, J. R., & McClearn, G. E. (1992). A quantitative genetic analysis of cognitive abilities during the second half of the life span. Psychological Science, 3(6), 346–353.

Pennebaker, J. W., Groom, C. J., Loew, D., & Dabbs, J. M. (2004). Testosterone as a social inhibitor: Two case studies of the effect of testosterone treatment on language. Journal of Abnormal Psychology, 113(1), 172–175.

Petersen, L-E., Dietz, J., & Frey, D. (2004). The effects of Intragroup interaction and cohesion on intergroup bias. Group Processes & Intergroup Relations, 7(2), 107–118.

Pettit, G. S., & Dodge, K. A. (2003). Violent children: Bridging development, intervention, and public policy. Developmental Psychology, 39(2), 187–188.

Piaget, J. (1954). The construction of reality in the child. New York: Basic Books.

Pickery, J., & Loosveldt, G. (2002). A multilevel multinomial analysis of interviewer effects on various components of unit nonresponse. Quality and Quantity, 36, 427–437.

Pliner, P., & Chaiken, S. (1990). Eating, social motives, and self-presentation in women and men. Journal of Experimental Social Psychology, 26(3), 240–254.

Plomin, R., & Neiderhiser, J. M. (1992). Genetics and experience. Current Directions in Psychological Science, 1, 160–163.

Plous, S. (1991). An attitude survey of animal rights activists. Psychological Science, 2(3), 194–196.

Plous, S. (1996a). Attitudes toward the use of animals in psychological research and education: Results from a national survey of psychologists. American Psychologist, 51(11), 1167–1180.

Plous, S. (1996b). Attitudes toward the use of animals in psychological research and education: Results from a national survey of psychology majors. Psychological Science, 7, 352–358.

Plous, S. (1998). Signs of change within the animal rights movement: Results from a follow-up survey of activists. Journal of Comparative Psychology, 112(1), 48–54.

Pomerantz, E. M., & Eaton, M. M. (2001). Maternal intrusive support in the academic context: Transactional socialization processes. Developmental Psychology, 37, 174–186.

Pomerantz, J. R. (1983). The grass is always greener: An ecological analysis of an old aphorism. Perception, 12, 501–502.

Popper, K. R. (1963). Science: Conjectures and refutations. In G. Radnitzky & W. W. Bartley, III (Eds.), Evolutionary epistemology, rationality, and the sociology of knowledge (pp. 139–157). La Salle, IL: Open Court.

Pyrczak, F., & Bruce, R. R. (2000). Writing empirical research reports. Los Angeles: Pyrczak Publishing.

Raudenbush, S. W. (1984). Magnitude of teacher expectancy effects on pupil IQ as a function of the credibility of expectancy induction: A synthesis of findings from 18 experiments. Journal of Educational Psychology, 76(1), 85–97.

Regan, T. (1983). The case for animal rights. Berkeley: University of California Press.

Rennie, D. L., Watson, K. D., & Monteiro, A. M. (2002). The rise of qualitative research in psychology. Canadian Psychology, 43(3), 179–189.

Rind, B., Tromovitch, P., & Bauserman, R. (1998). A meta-analytic examination of assumed properties of child sexual abuse using college samples. Psychological Bulletin, 124, 22–53.

Ritchey, G. H. (1982). Pictorial detail and recall in adults and children. Journal of Experimental Psychology: Learning, Memory, and Cognition, 8(2), 139–141.

Ritchey, G. H., & Armstrong, E. L. (1982). Elaboration, distinctiveness, and recognition time in free recall. Paper presented at the meeting of the Psychonomic Society, Minneapolis, MN.

Rorer, L. G. (1965). The great response-style myth. Psychological Bulletin, 63, 129–156.

Rosenthal, R. (1969). Interpersonal expectations: Effects of the experimenter's hypothesis. In R. Rosenthal & R. L. Rosnow (Eds.), Artifact in behavioral research (pp. 182–277). New York: Academic Press.

Rosenthal, R. (1973). The Pygmalion effect lives. Psychology Today, 7, 56–63.

Rosenthal, R. (1976). Experimenter effects in behavioral research (2nd ed.). New York: Halsted.

Rosenthal, R. (1978). How often are our numbers wrong? American Psychologist, 33(11), 1005–1008.

Rosenthal, R. (1994). Science and ethics in conducting, analyzing, and reporting psychological research. Psychological Science, 5(3), 127–134.

Rosenthal, R., & Fode, K. L. (1963). The effect of experimenter bias on the performance of the albino rat. Behavioral Science, 8, 183–189.

Rosenthal, R., & Jacobson, L. (1966). Teachers' expectancies: Determinants of pupils' IQ gains. Psychological Reports, 19, 115–118.

Rosenthal, R., & Rosnow, R. L. (1969). Artifact in behavioral research. New York: Academic Press.

Rosenthal, R., & Rosnow, R. L. (1975). The volunteer subject. New York: Wiley.

Rosenzweig, M., & Spruill, J. (1986). Twenty years after Twiggy: A retrospective investigation of bulimic-like behaviors. International Journal of Eating Disorders, 6, 24–31.

Rosnow, R., & Rosenthal, R. (1976). The volunteer subject revisited. Australian Journal of Psychology, 28, 97–108.

Ross, L., & Nisbett, R. E. (1991). The person and the situation: Perspectives of social psychology. New York: McGraw-Hill.

Rowan, A. N., & Andrutis, K. A. (1990). Animal numbers: Up, down and swing them all around. Psychologists for the Ethical Treatment of Animals Bulletin, 9(2), 3–5.

Roy, M. M., & Christenfeld, N. J. S. (2004). Do dogs resemble their owners? *Psychological Science,* 15(5), 361–363.

Russell, B. (1945). *A history of western philosophy.* New York: Simon & Schuster.

Ryu, E., Couper, M. P., & Marans, R. W. (2005). Survey incentives: Cash vs. in-kind; face-to-face vs. mail; response rate vs. nonresponse error. *International Journal of Public Opinion Research, 18*(1), 89–106.

Sackett, A. M., Meyvis, T., Nelson, L. D., Converse, B. A., & Sackett, A. L. (2010). You're having fun when time flies: The hedonic consequences of subjective time progression. *Psychological Science, 21*(1), 111–117.

Sadeh, A., Raviv, A., & Gruber, R. (2000). Sleep patterns and sleep disruptions in school-age children. *Developmental Psychology, 36*(3), 291–301.

Sadker, M., & Sadker, D. (1982). *Gender equity handbook for schools.* New York: Longman.

Salomon, M. (2007). Western black widow spiders express state-dependent web-building strategies tailored to the presence of neighbours. *Animal Behaviour, 73*(5), 865–875.

Sarnoff, I., & Zimbardo, P. G. (1961). Anxiety, fear, and social affiliation. *Journal of Abnormal and Social Psychology, 62,* 356–363.

Saucier, D. A., & Cain, M. E. (2006). The foundations of attitudes about animal research. *Ethics & Behavior, 16*(2), 117–133.

Scanlon, T. J., Luben, R. N., Scanlon, F. L., & Singleton, N. (1993, 18–25 December). Is Friday the 13th bad for your health? *British Medical Journal, 307,* 1584–1586.

Schachter, S. (1959). *The psychology of affiliation.* Stanford, CA: Stanford University Press.

Schachter, D., Dawes, R., Jacoby, L. L., Rahneman, D., Lempert, R., Roediger, H. L., & Rosenthal, R. (2008). Policy forum: Studying eyewitness investigations in the field. *Law and Human Behavior, 32,* 3–5.

Schlegel, R. (1972). *Inquiry into science: Its domain and limits.* New York: Anchor.

Serbin, L. A., Zelkowitz, P., Doyle, A., Gold, D., & Wheaton, B. (1990). The socialization of sex-differentiated skills and academic performance: A mediational model. *Sex Roles, 23*(11/12), 613–628.

Shadish, W. R., Cook, T. D., & Campbell, D. T. (2001). *Experimental and quasi-experimental designs for generalized causal inference.* Boston: Houghton Mifflin.

Shaffer, D. M., Krauchunas, S. M., Eddy, M., & McBeath, M. K. (2004). How dogs navigate to catch Frisbees. *Psychological Science, 15*(7), 437–441.

Shaffer, D. R. (2002). *Developmental Psychology.* Belmont, CA: Wadsworth.

Shapiro, K. J. (1997). The separate world of animal research. *American Psychologist, 52*(11), 1250.

Sieber, J. E., Iannuzzo, R., & Rodriguez, B. (1995). Deception methods in psychology: Have they changed in 23 years? *Ethics & Behavior, 5*(1), 67–85.

Siiter, R., & Ellison, K. W. (1984). Perceived authoritarianism in self and others by male college students and police officers. *Journal of Applied Social Psychology, 14,* 334–340.

Silveira, J. (1980). Generic masculine words and thinking. In C. Kramarae (Ed.), *The voice of women and men.* New York: Pergamon.

Simon, H. A. (1967). Motivational and emotional controls of cognition. *Psychological Review, 74,* 29–39.

Singer, P. (1975). *Animal liberation.* New York: New York Review, Random House.

Smith, L. D., Best, L. A., Cylke, V. A., & Stubbs, D. A. (2000). Psychology without *p* values: Data analysis at the turn of the 19th century. *American Psychologist, 55*(2), 260–263.

Soliday, E., & Stanton, A. L. (1995). Deceived versus nondeceived participants' perceptions of scientific and applied psychology. *Ethics & Behavior, 5*(1), 87–104.

Spencer, S. J., Steele, C. M., & Quinn, D. M. (1999). Stereotype threat and women's math performance. *Journal of Experimental Social Psychology, 35,* 4–28.

Sprecher, S., & Duck, S. (1994). The importance of perceived communication for romantic and friendship attraction experienced during a get-acquainted date. *Personality and Social Psychology Bulletin, 20,* 391–400.

Steblay, N. M., Dysart, J., Fulero, S., & Lindsay, R. C. L. (2001). Eyewitness accuracy rates in sequential and simultaneous lineup presentations. *Law and Human Behavior, 25,* 459–474.

Steele, C. M., & Aronson, J. (1995). Contending with a stereotype: African-American intellectual test performance and stereotype threat. *Journal of Personality and Social Psychology, 69,* 797–811.

Stewart, R. B., Mobley, L. A., Van Tuyl, S. S., & Salvador, L. A. (1987). The firstborn's adjustment to the birth of a sibling: A longitudinal assessment. *Child Development, 58,* 341–355.

Story, L. B., Lawrence, E., Karney, B. R., & Bradbury, T. N. (2004). Interpersonal mediators in the intergenerational transmission of marital dysfunction. *Journal of Family Psychology, 18*(3), 519–529.

Strahilevitz, M. A., & Lowenstein, G. (1998). The effect of ownership history on the valuation of objects. *Journal of Consumer Research, 25,* 276–289.

Strange, D., Hayne, H., & Garry, M. (2007). A photo, a suggestion, a false memory. *Applied Cognitive Psychology.* Retrieved online June 1, 2008 from www.interscience.wiley.com, doi:10.1002/acp.1390

Suls, J., & Rosnow, R. (1988). Concerns about artifacts in behavioral research. In M. Morawski (Ed.), *The rise of experimentation in American psychology* (pp. 163–187). New Haven, CT: Yale University Press.

Suskie, L. A. (1992). *Questionnaire survey research: What works.* Tallahassee, FL: Association for Institutional Research.

Taub, E. (1977). Movement in nonhuman primates deprived of somatosensory feedback. *Exercise and sports science reviews* (Vol. 4, pp. 335–374). Santa Barbara, CA: Journal Publishing Affiliates.

Taub, E., & Morris, D. M. (2001). Constraint-induced movement therapy to enhance recovery after stroke. *Current Artherosclerosis Reports, 3,* 279–286.

Taylor, J. A. (1953). A personality scale of manifest anxiety. *Journal of Abnormal and Social Psychology, 48,* 285–290.

Thompson, C. C. (2006). Unintended lessons: Plagiarism and the university. *Teachers College Record, 108* (12), 2439–2449.

Tombs, S., & Silverman, I. Pupillometry: A sexual selection approach.

*Evolution and Human Behavior,* 25(4), 221–228.

Trull, F. L. (2006). The Animal Liberation Front's campaign of terror. Retrieved on November 4, 2009 from www.frontpagemag.com/Articles/ReadArticle.asp?ID=23752

Turati, C. (2004). Why faces are not special to newborns: An alternative account of the face preference. *Current Directions in Psychological Research,* 13(1), 5–8.

U.S. Department of Health, Education, and Welfare (1975, March 13). Protection of human subjects. *Federal Register,* 40(50), Part II. Washington, DC: U.S. Government Printing Office.

U.S. Department of Health, Education, and Welfare (1978). *Guide for the use and care of laboratory animals.* Washington, DC: U.S. Government Printing Office.

Velten, H. V. (1943). The growth of phonemic and lexical patterns in infant language. *Language, 19,* 281–292.

Vineberg, R., & Joyner, J. N. (1983). Performance measurement in the military services. In F. Landy, S. Zedeck, & J. Cleveland (Eds.), *Performance measurement and theory* (pp. 233–250). Hillsdale, NJ: Erlbaum.

Vos, K. D., & Schooler, J. W. (2008). The value of believing in free will: Encouraging a belief in determinism increases cheating. *Psychological Science, 19*(1), 49–54.

Wallerstein, J. S., & Lewis, J. M. (2004). The unexpected legacy of divorce. *Psychoanalytic Psychology, 21*(3), 353–370.

Walster (Hatfield), E., Walster, G., & Berscheid, E. (1978). *Equity: Theory and research.* Boston: Allyn & Bacon.

Wanke, M., & Schwarz, N. (1997). Reducing question order effects: The operation of buffer items. In L. Lyberg et al. (Eds.), *Survey*

*measurement and process quality.* New York: Wiley.

Ward, S. E., Leventhal, H., & Love, R. (1988). Repression revisited: Tactics used in coping with a severe health threat. *Personality and Social Psychology Bulletin, 14*(4), 735–746.

Warwick, D. P., & Lininger, C. A. (1975). *The sample survey: Theory and practice.* New York: McGraw-Hill.

Wasson, J. H., Sauvigne, A. E., Mogielnicki, R. P., et al. (1984). Continuity of outpatient medical care in elderly men: A randomized trial. *Journal of the American Medical Association, 252,* 2413–2417.

Watanabe, S., Sakamoto, J., & Wakita, M. (1995). Pigeons' discrimination of paintings by Monet and Picasso. *Journal of the Experimental Analysis of Behavior, 63,* 165–174.

Watson, J. B., & Rayner, R. (1920). Conditioned emotional reactions. *Journal of Experimental Psychology, 3,* 1–14.

Wegner, D. M. (1989). *White bears and other unwanted thoughts.* New York: Viking.

Wegner, D. M., Lane, J. D., & Dimitri, S. (1994). The allure of secret relationships. *Journal of Personality and Social Psychology, 66*(2), 287–300.

Weiss, J. M. (1972). Psychological factors in stress and disease. *Scientific American, 226*(6), 104–113.

Wheeler, L. (1988). My year in Hong Kong: Some observations about social behavior. *Personality and Social Psychology Bulletin, 14*(2), 410–420.

Which are the safest vehicles? (1994, November 17). *Parade Magazine,* p. 16 (Sunday supplement magazine of the Oakland Press). New York: Parade Publications.

Whitehead, A. N. (1925). *Science and the modern world.* New York: Free Press.

Wilkinson, L., & the Task Force on Statistical Inference. (1999). Statistical methods in psychology journals: Guidelines and explanations. *American Psychologist, 54*(8), 594–604.

Willems, E. P. (1969). Planning a rationale for naturalistic research. In E. P. Willems & H. L. Raush (Eds.), *Naturalistic viewpoints in psychological research.* New York: Holt, Rinehart, & Winston.

Windle, C. (1954). Test-retest effect on personality questionnaires. *Educational Psychology Measurement, 14,* 617–633.

Yepez, M. E. (1994). An observation of gender-specific teacher behavior in the ESL classroom. *Sex Roles, 30*(1/2), 121–133.

Young, A. W., Hay, D. C., & Ellis, A. W. (1985). The face that launched a thousand slips: Everyday difficulties and errors in recognizing people. *British Journal of Psychology, 76,* 495–523.

Zajonc, R. B. (1966). Attitudinal effects of mere exposure. *Journal of Personality and Social Psychology, 9,* 1–27.

Zajonc, R. B. (1968). Cognitive theories in social psychology. In G. Lindzey & E. Aronson (Eds.), *The handbook of social psychology* (2nd ed., *Vol. 1,* pp. 320–411). Reading, MA: Addison-Wesley.

Zajonc, R. B., Heingartner, A., & Herman, E. M. (1969). Social enhancement and impairment of performance in the cockroach. *Journal of Personality and Social Psychology, 13,* 83–92.

Zimbardo, P. G. (2004). A situationist perspective on the psychology of evil: Understanding how good people are transformed into perpetrators. In A. Miller (Ed.), *The social psychology of good and evil: Understanding our capacity for kindness and cruelty.* New York: Guilford.

# INDEX

*ABABA* designs, 351, 353

*ABA* designs, 351–357, 366

*AB* designs, 357

abstract concepts, 75

abstracts, 181–182, 185, 488–489, 498, 513

abuse of animals study, 53–54

accidental sampling, 122

across-subjects counterbalancing, 331–334, 340

Affiliations/Names section of reports, 498

African American men study, 86–87

aggregation, 469–471, 480

air experiment, 19

alternative hypothesis, 379, 403

American Association for Accreditation of Laboratory Animal Care (AAALAC), 50

American Association for Laboratory Animal Science (AALAS), 50, 57

American Psychological Association (APA), 14
   Committee on Animal Research and Ethics (CARE), 50, 56
   *Ethical Principles of Psychologist and Code of Conduct*, 63
   Psychological Abstracts, 181
   PsycINFO, 181–182
   *Publication Manual of the American Psychological Association*, 390, 402, 486–487
   research guidelines, 42–48
   standard for animal use, 51
   task force on significance testing, 390

analysis of covariance (ANCOVA), 438

analysis of variance (ANOVA), 292, 428
   multivariate analysis of variance, 472, 480
   one-way, 431–438, 449
   two-way, 441–446

analytic statements, 167, 184

analyzing results, 428–431. *See also* analysis of variance (ANOVA); measures/measurements; results
   between-subject factorial designs, 431–434
   content analysis, 99–100, 222
   factor analysis, 140–141
   linear regression analysis, 139–140, 147, 160
   meta-analyses, 179–180
   multiple groups and factorial experiments, 428–431
   multiple regression analysis, 142, 147, 161
   multivariate analysis of variance (MANOVA), 472
   path analysis, 143–145, 147, 161

animal behavior research, 48–58, 64

Animal Liberation Front, 56

*Animal Liberation* (Singer), 51

animal subjects, 48–58, 64, 249, 348

anonymity, 48, 49, 64

antecedent conditions, 22, 69–70, 129–131, 148

antisocial personality disorder, 76

anxiety and affiliation experiments, 197–198

Apparatus/Materials section of reports, 226–227, 502

applied research, 18

a priori comparisons, 435

archival studies, 85–87

Aristotle, 11, 172

articles, finding, 181–184

assent/agreement for participation in studies, 38–39

assigning subjects, 282–285

attitudes toward animal research study, 57–58

attractiveness study, 198–199

author notes, 498, 513

authorship credit, 63, 64

balanced Latin squares, 334, 337, 341

balancing of variables, 235–237

Baron, Robert A., 19, 20–21, 22, 73

baseline designs, 357–360

baselines, 349, 356, 366

basic research, 18

behavior
   causes of, 24–25
   eating behavior study, 300–307, 312
   explaining, 6–7, 17
   *Multivariate Behavioral Research*, 472
   negative ions / Type A behavior study, 154, 309
   nonverbal, 9
   observing, 18–20, 30
   predicting, 8–11
   regression (behavior) study, 155

beliefs, 48

beneficence, 40, 41–42

Bernoulli's law of large numbers, 277

beta weights, 142, 143

between-groups variance, 428, 450

between-subjects designs, 23, 218, 286, 297–300, 308–312, 339, 431–434
bias
  avoiding, in reports, 485
  confirmation, 6
  in choosing human subjects, 465
  experimenter, 247–252, 261, 465
  overconfidence, 11
  overestimating cross-situational behavior, 8–11
bidirectional causation, 138
block randomization, 283, 287, 330–331, 340
body-builder study, 84
Breuning, Stephen, 60
buffer items (questionnaires), 109–110
Burt, Sir Cyril, 59

calculations. *See* formulas
cancer coping styles study, 151, 194
car-buying preferences study, 325–326
carryover effects, 335–336, 341
car size study, 152–153
case studies. *See also* examples; studies
  about, 73–78, 91
  Little Hans, 74
  testosterone, 75
catching balls experiment, 363
cat cloning, 55
category errors, 429
causal attributions, 178
causal directions, 138
causality approach, 26
causal modeling, 143–147
causal relationships, 216
causation, 137–138
cause and effect relationships, 24–25, 76, 185, 463–464
ceiling effect, 478
central tendency, 398, 414
changing criterion designs, 361–362, 367
characteristics of modern science
  empirical data, gathering, 11–12, 92
  general principles, seeking, 12–13
  good thinking, 13–14
  publicizing results, 14–15
  replication, 15–16, 59
  scientific mentality, 11
  self-correction, 14
Chicago bars experiment, 86
chi square (x) critical values, 413
chi square test, 412–417, 449
choosing design/test methods. *See also* tests/testing
  chi square, 412–414
  experimental designs, 262, 308–312, 339
  large or small *N*, 364, 366
  questions for statistical test choice, 410, 448
  significance levels, 384–386, 387
  treatments, 285
  *t* test, 417–427

which test to use, 409–412
classical conditioning, 38, 175
cloning, 55
closed (structured) questions, 97, 99
cluster sampling, 120–121
cockroach race study, 274, 275, 276, 277, 278
coding systems, 80–81
coefficient of determination, 139
cognitive priming theory, 14
Cognitive Style Index (CSI), 215
coin-flipping (Bernouli law), 277
cola experiment, 326–327, 328
commonsense psychology, 5–6, 30
companion animals study, 159
comparison groups, 158
comparisons, types of, 435
complete counterbalancing, 332–333, 340
compound (double-barreled) questions, 100–101
computational formulas. *See* formulas
computer surveys, 112
concurrent validity, 213, 228
conditioned stimulus (CS), 38
conditions
  antecedent, 22, 31, 69–70, 129–131, 148
  changing independent variables across, 319–320
  comparing treatment, 22
  constancy of, 234
  control procedures, 234–237, 269
  experimental, 269
  interference between, 325–326
  manipulation of, 69–70, 129–131, 429
  necessary versus sufficient, 25–26
  proportional, 285
  random assignment of, 267–269
  testing, 233–237
conduct disorders, 76
confederates, 45, 300
confidence intervals, 423
confidentiality, 38, 48, 49, 64
confirmation bias, 6
confounding of variables, 194–195, 217–218, 219, 228, 235, 235, 268, 270, 459–460, 462
consent, informed, 38–40, 44–45
constancy of conditions (variables), 234
constructing surveys, 97–101
constructs, 204–207, 228
content analysis, 99–100, 124, 222
content validity, 212
context effects, 109–110
context variables, 254–256, 261
continuous dimensions, 103–104
contradictory statements, 167, 184
control group designs, 157, 269, 271–272, 286
control objective of research, 17–18
control procedures, 23

conditions, 233–237, 269
counterbalancing, 326–329
order effects, 326
for response styles (questionnaires), 109
smiling experiment, 316–318
statistical control, 437–438
variables, 254–256, 340
within-subjects designs, 23, 316–341
convenience sampling, 122, 124
coping styles study, 151
correlational designs, 17, 131–132
  causal modeling, 143–147
  hypotheses, 165
  multiple correlations, 140, 142, 147
  negative correlations, 134–135
  partial correlations, 142
  positive correlations, 134
  simple correlations, 132–133
correlational studies, 17, 129–142
counterbalancing
  across-subjects, 331–334
  carryover effects, 335–336
  choosing among procedures, 337–339
  complete, 332–333
  controlling for order effects, 326–329, 340
  partial, 333–334, 340
  subject-by-subject, 329–331
counterstereotypic performance, 177
covariate statistical analysis, 154
cover stories, 244–247
Cramer's coefficient Phi, 416
critical regions, 392
Cronbach's α, 209
cross-lagged panel designs, 145–146, 147
crossover interactions, 307, 308
cross-sectional studies, 156, 160, 161
cultural issues, 120
curve distributions, 381, 383
curvilinear effects of, 330

data. *See also* reports
  analyzing between-subject factorial designs, 439–440
  anonymous collection of, 48, 49
  collecting, 4, 5, 8–10, 110–116, 124
  empirical, 11–12, 92
  evaluating, 4, 116–117
  fabrication of, 59–61, 64
  organizing/summarizing, 397–403
  previously published, 63, 85–86
  raw, 398
  reduction, 140
  retrospective, 77–78
  sources, 6–7
  summary, 398
  variability sources in, 429–431
data analysis. *See* analysis of variance (ANOVA)
debriefing subjects, 46–47, 48, 49, 63
deception/full disclosure, 45–48, 246–247, 273

deductive model for forming hypotheses, 172, 185
degrees of freedom, 415, 449, 450
demand characteristics, 237–247, 261
dependent variables (DVs), 196, 204, 227–228
describing design variables, 297–298
description objective of research, 16–17
descriptive statistics, 398
design matrixes, 297
designs. *See* experimental designs
design variables, describing, 297–298
determinism, 11
*Developmental Psychology* (APA), 18
deviant case analysis, 75–77
differences between means, 391–392
directional hypotheses, 382, 394–395, 404
disadvantages/advantages, within-subject designs, 323–326
discrete trials designs, 362–363, 367
Discussion section of reports, 181, 494–496, 506, 508, 515
distributions, 380, 381, 382–384, 399
divorce effects study, 150–151, 156
dogs resembling owners experiment, 418
domestic violence victims study, 88, 90
double-barreled (compound) questions, 100–101
double-blind experiments, 248, 250–252, 261
dropout rates of subjects, 223
DSM-IV (*Diagnostic and Statistical Manual of Mental Disorders*, 4th ed.), 71, 75

eating behavior study, 300–307, 312
effect(s)
　calculating effect size, 266–267, 286, 390, 445
　carryover, 335–336, 341
　cause and effect relationships, 24–25, 76, 185
　ceiling, 478
　changes to, 293
　context, 109–110
　curvilinear effects of, 330
　fatigue, 327, 340
　floor, 478
　interpreting significant, 447–448
　linear effects of, 330
　main, 292, 312, 439, 450
　nonlinear effects of, 330–331
　order, 326–329, 336, 340
　placebo effect, 242, 244–245, 250–251, 261, 272, 273, 286
　practice, 327, 340
　Pygmalion effect, 248
　size, 266–267, 286, 390, 445
　understanding, from factorial designs, 303–307
efficient approaches, 291, 292

elimination of variables, 234
empirical data, gathering, 11–12, 92
empirical phenomenology, 88, 90
English as a Second Language study, 80
equations. *See* formulas
equipment, describing, 226–227
equity theory, 172
equivalent treatment, 23
ERIC, 182
error(s). *See also* counterbalancing
　category, 429
　experimental, 386
　experimenters', 386, 462–463
　faulty procedures, 476–479
　linear, 330
　progressive, 327, 329, 340
　sources of, 429, 450
　Type 1 and 2, 386–389, 390, 404, 412–413, 463, 464
ethical issues
　animal subjects, 48–58
　APA guidelines, 42–48
　conducting unethical experiments, 21–22
　ethical reports, 63
　federal guidelines, 37
　human research using control groups, 269, 271–272
　placebo groups, 273
　removing treatment, 366
　research ethics, 36–42
*Ethical Principles of Psychologist and Code of Conduct* (APA), 63
ethnic preferences study, 460
ethology, 78
evaluating experiments, 374, 459–476. *See also* analyzing results; results
events, significant life, 74
evolution of ethics, 40, 42
examples
　ABA design using large N, 352
　applying statistical inference, 382–389
　consent form, 38–39
　homework performance experiment, 354–355
　interval scaling, 102–103
　journal article sample, 499–512
　2 × 2 factorial experiment, 297–300, 300–307
　two group within-subjects, 412
　variables, 197–199
expectancies, theory-based, 12–13
expected frequencies, 414
experimental condition, 269
experimental designs. *See also specific designs, e.g.* within-subjects factorial designs
　about, 262
　choosing, 308–312, 337–339, 341
　describing, in reports, 297–298, 492–493
　unethical, 21–22, 37–38

experimental errors, 386
experimental group, 269
experimental hypotheses. *See* hypotheses
experimental operational definitions, 202–204, 228
experimentation, 21–22, 31
experimenters
　bias, 247–252, 261
　errors caused by, 386, 462–463
　personality of, 252–253
　selection of subjects, 255–256
experiments. *See also* experimental designs; studies
　air experiment, 19
　anxiety and affiliation experiment, 197–198, 201, 203, 204–205
　catching balls experiment, 363
　Chicago bars experiment, 86
　cola experiment, 326–328, 329
　conducting unethical, 21–22
　dogs catching Frisbees, 363
　dogs resembling owners experiment, 418
　double-blind, 248, 250–252, 261
　evaluating, 215–216, 374, 459–476
　eye pupils experiment, 198–199
　field, 85, 474–475, 480
　homework performance experiment, 354–355
　homophone priming of proper names experiment, 319–321
　increased power of, 318
　isolating in recall experiment, 461
　matching before and after, 278–280
　name/personality experiment, 296
　natural, 147
　parenting experiment, 224
　pigeons experiment, 365
　pornography experiments, 47–48
　psychological, 21–22, 31
　secrecy and allure experiment, 426
　sensory-deprivation experiments, 240–241
　single-blind, 242–244, 261
　smiling experiment, 316–318
　talking to plants experiment, 349–351
　unethical, 21
　variables experiment, 197–199
explanation objective of research, 17
ex post facto studies, 148–152, 166, 194
external validity, 69, 90, 91, 131, 464–476, 479–480
extraneous variables, 216–218, 235–237, 256–261
eye pupils experiment, 198–199

fabrication of data, 59–61, 64
face-to-face interviews, 114–115
face validity, 210, 228
facilitators, 115
factor analysis, 140–141
factor and levels methods, 299

factorial designs, 292, 308–312
  analyzing, 428–431
  between-subjects, 431–434
  example, 296
  graphing, 445–446
  laying out, 297–300
  mixed, 324, 446–448
  2 × 2, 297–300, 300–307
  within-subjects, 320–321, 340
factor-labeling methods, 298–300
factors, 292
false positive results, 387
falsifiable statements, 168–169, 184
falsification, 58–60
fatigue effects, 327, 340
faulty hypotheses, 479
faulty procedures, 476–479. *See also*
  error(s)
field experiments, 85, 474–475, 480
field studies, 78–85, 92
figures, in research reports, 514–515
floor effect, 478
focus groups, 89, 115–116
folklore about subjects, 256
format of reports, 484–487
forming independent groups, 274–276
formulas
  calculating effect size, 445
  Cramer's coefficient Phi, 416
  evaluating *F* ratios, 443–445
  regression equation, 139–140
  sum of squares for interactions,
    442, 443
  for testing F ratio, 430–431
*F* ratios, 430–431, 443–445, 450
fraud in science, 58–61, 64
frequency distributions, 380, 381
Freud, Sigmund, 74, 77, 390
fruitful statements, 169–170, 184
full disclosure/deception, 45–48

Galileo, 12, 23
"gambler's fallacy," 10–11
gender-related terms, 486
generalizing, 131, 464–468
good subject phenomenon, 239
good thinking, 13–14, 30
graphing results, 436–437, 445–446
group designs, 269, 271–272, 286
*Guide for the Care and Use of
  Laboratory Animals* (National
  Academy of Sciences), 50

Hall, Stanley G., 26
handshake firmness study, 137
Hess, E., 198–199
heuristic value, 132
higher-order interactions, 295, 312
history threat to validity, 220, 228, 366
homework performance experiment,
  354–355
homophone priming of proper names
  experiment, 319–321

Hong Kong residents study, 80
human research using control groups,
  269, 271–272
Hume, David, 25
hypotheses
  alternative, 379, 403
  building on prior research, 173–174
  characteristics of experimental, 166–170
  combining inductive and deductive,
    172–173
  coming up with, 177–179
  deductive model, 172
  definition, 165
  describing, 489
  directional, 382, 404
  faulty, 479
  inductive, 170–172
  intuition, 171, 175–177
  nondirectional, 394
  nonexperimental, 165
  null, 378–380, 389–391, 403
  searching the literature, 178, 179–184
  serendipity and windfall, 174–175
hypothetical constructs, 204–207, 228

identical twins study, 59
identifying variables, 199–201
If . . . then statements, 167–168, 184
imposition of units, degree of, 70–71
impressions of others study, 269
independent group designs, 274–277,
  286, 449
independent variables (IVs), 193–201,
  202–204, 227, 319–320
inductive model for forming hypotheses,
  170–172, 185
inference(s), 8–11. *See also* statistical
  inference
inferential biases, 11
informed consent, 38–40, 44–45, 49, 63
insignificant results, 476–479
institutional animal care and use
  committee (IACUC), 49–50, 64
institutional review boards (IRBs), 37, 85
instrumentation threat to validity,
  221–222, 228
interactions, 292–296, 306–307, 312, 439
interference between conditions, 325–326
interitem reliability, 209
internal consistency of test items, 209
internal validity, 69, 90, 91, 131,
  215–216, 228, 237, 459–464
interpreting results, 403, 415–417,
  434–436
interpreting significant effects, 447–448
interrater reliability, 208, 228
INTERSECT coding system, 80
interval scaling, 102–103, 104–105,
  124, 207, 410
interviews, 96, 114–115, 124. *See also*
  survey research
introduction section of reports, 181,
  489, 498, 500

intuition, 171, 175–177, 185
isolating variables, 461

James, William, 71, 72
Jones, Mary Cover, 74
journal articles, 185
  general orientation, 496–497
  peer review, 58
  sample, 499–512
  searching, 179–184
  sources for finding, 181–184
journal article
  sample, 499-512. *See also* reports
*Journal of Multivariate Experimental
  Personality and Clinical
  Psychology*, 472
justice, 40, 42

Kahneman, Daniel, 11
known distributions, 383

large *N* designs, 346–348, 352,
  364–366, 367
latent content of survey items, 111
Latin square counterbalancing, 334, 341
laws, 12
laying out factorial designs, 297–300
legal issues
  Health Insurance Portability and
    Accountability Act, 44
  minimal risk, definition of, 43–44
  scientific misconduct, 59–60
level of measurement, 101, 103–105,
  228, 410
levels of the independent variable (IV),
  194
Likert scale, 104–105
limitations, 263–265, 325
linear effects, 330
linear errors, 330
linear regression analysis, 139–140,
  147
lines of best fit (regression lines), 134
literature searches, 179–184
Little Hans case study, 74
logical relationships, 25
longitudinal designs, 155–156, 160, 161
long-term studies, 155–156
lost letter technique, 83

mail surveys, 112
main effects, 292, 312, 439, 450
manifest content of questions, 108, 124
manipulation, 69–73
  of antecedent conditions,
    69–71, 91, 129–131
  checks, 210, 211, 462, 502
  of conditions, 429
  deciding on variable, 199–201
  degree of, 69–70
  description of, in reports, 492
manuscripts, preparing, 512–516. *See
  also* reports

Marlowe-Crown Social Desirability Scale, 111, 252, 460
matched group designs, 277–282, 286, 449
matching, 278–282, 287
Materials/Apparatus section of reports, 226–227, 502
Materials section of reports, 502
math identification study, 308
maturation threat to validity, 220–221, 228, 271, 350
mean score, 139, 398, 400, 404
mean square, 432–433
measured operational definitions, 204, 228
measures/measurements, 20–21. *See also* analyzing results
  aggregation over, 471
  of central tendency, 398, 404
  description of, in reports, 491–492
  level of, 101, 103–105, 228, 410
  measuring survey responses, 101–105
  multivariate analysis of variance (MANOVA), 472
  nonreactive measurements, 473
  one-way repeated measures ANOVA, 438–439
  repeated-measures designs, 318, 446–448
  scales of measurement, 101–103, 206–207
  selecting levels of, 103–105
  tools of, 20–21
  unobtrusive measures, 82, 473–474
  variability, 401–403, 404
median score, 398, 399, 400, 404
media violence study, 137–138, 145–146, 180
MEDLINE, 182
memory, 77
Mensa, 214
meta-analyses, 179–180
methodology, 4, 5–6, 30. *See also* choosing design/test methods
Method section of reports, 225–227, 228, 491–493, 502, 514
Milgram, Stanley, 45
misconduct, scientific, 59–60
mixed designs, 321–323, 324
modern science, characteristics of, 11–16
mode score, 398, 400, 404
more than one independent variable designs, 291–296
motivation for watching TV study, 140–141
multiple baseline designs, 357–360, 366
multiple correlation, 140, 142, 147
multiple groups designs, 282–286, 287
multiple independent groups designs, 282, 287
multiple regression, 140, 142, 147
multivariate analysis of variance (MANOVA), 472, 480
*Multivariate Behavioral Research*, 472

multivariate designs, 471–472
Munsell color chart, 201

name/personality experiment, 296
name retrieval failure study, 319–320
Names/Affiliations section of reports, 498
National Academy of Sciences, 50
National Science Foundation (NSF), 60
natural experiments, 147
naturalistic observation studies, 78–82, 91, 475–476, 480
nay-sayers, 108, 124
negative correlations, 134–135, 161
negative ions studies, 19, 22, 45, 154, 309
negative thinking, 7
nominal scaling, 101–102, 124, 207, 410
nonbiased language, using, 485–486
nonconstruct variables, 206
nondirectional hypotheses, 394
nonequivalent control groups, 158, 160
nonequivalent group designs, 152–155
nonexperimental designs, 129–130
  evaluating surveys/survey data, 116–117
  measuring responses, 101–105
  nonprobability sampling, 121–124
  phenomenology, 71–73
  probability sampling, 118–121
  survey research, 96–117, 124
nonexperimental hypotheses, 165
nonlinear effects of, 330–331
nonlinear trends, 135
nonmonotonic effects of, 330
nonparametric tests, 388, 413
nonprobability samples, 121
nonreactive measurements, 473–474
nonreturn rates of mail surveys, 112
nonscientific inference, 8–11
nonsignificant outcomes, 476–479, 480
nonsynthetic statements, 167–168
nonverbal behavior, 9
normal curves, 383
note-keeping, 227, 228
null hypothesis, 378–380, 389–391, 403
null results, 477–479

objectives of research, 16–18, 97, 30
objectivity, 31
observation, 178–179
  of behavior, 18–20, 30
  naturalistic, 78–82, 475–476, 480
  predicting behavior using, 8–11
  systematic, 80
Obsessive-Compulsive Disorder (OCD), 74
obtained frequencies, 414
obtrusive measures, 82, 83
Occam's razor, 13
occasions, aggregation over, 471
one independent variable designs, 269
one-tailed tests, 394–396
one-way between-subjects ANOVA, 431–438
one-way repeated measures ANOVA, 438–439

online research, 49, 112–113
open-ended questions, 98, 99
operational definitions, 201–207, 208–215, 228
order as design factor, 338–339
order effects, 326–329, 340
ordinal scaling, 102, 124, 207, 410
organizing data, 397–403, 404
outcomes, nonsignificant, 476–479, 480
outliers (extreme scores), 136
overconfidence bias, 11

pacts of ignorance, 462
page headers of reports, 512
paradigms, 87
parametric tests, 388
parenting experiment, 224
parsimonious statements, 169, 184, 485
parsimony, 13, 30
partial correlation, 142, 154, 160
partial counterbalancing, 333–334, 340
participant-observer studies, 82, 84–85
participants. *See* subjects/participants
Participants section of reports, 491, 514
path analysis, 143–145, 147, 161
Pavlov, Ivan, 174–175
Pearson Product Moment Correlation Coefficient, 132–133
peer review, 58
personality variables, 252–254, 261
phenomenology, 71–73, 88, 90, 91
physical variables, 233–237, 256–261
pigeons experiment, 365
pilot studies, 252, 286, 287
placebo effect/placebo groups, 242, 244–245, 250–251, 259, 272, 273, 286
plagiarism, 61–62, 64
planned comparisons, 435
Popper, Karl, 12
population, 117, 124
population frequencies, 414
pornography experiments, 47–48
position preference, 107, 124
positive correlations, 134, 160
post hoc tests, 435, 450
post traumatic stress disorder (PTSD), 74
power charts, 266
power of an experiment, increased, 318
practical limits, 265, 285, 325
practice effects, 157, 327, 340
precision matching, 279, 287
prediction objective of research, 17
predictions, 10–11, 12. *See also* hypotheses
predictive validity, 213, 228
pretest/posttest designs, 156–160, 161
priming, 412
principles
  beneficence, 40, 41–42
  general, 12–13
  justice, 40, 42
  parsimony, 13
  respect for persons, 40

*Principles of Psychology* (James), 71
prior research, building on, 173–174
privacy, 85
probability sampling, 118–121, 124
Procedure section of reports, 502
professional organizations, 14
progressive errors, 327, 329, 340
projection study, 47
proportional conditions, 285
pseudoscience, 27–29
Psychological Abstracts (APA), 181–182
psychological journals. *See* journal articles
psychological science
  establishing cause and effect, 24–25
  experimentation, 21–22
  history of, 26–29
  identifying antecedent conditions, 22
  measurement, 20–21
  necessary versus sufficient conditions, 25–26
  objectives of, 16–18, 30–31, 97
  observation, 18–20
  psychological experiments, 22–24
psychology experiments, 22–24, 31
PsycARTICLES, 181
PsycINFO, 181–182, 183, 184
*Publication Manual of the American Psychological Association*, 390, 402, 486–487
Purkinje, Johannes, 71, 72
purpose of reports, 484
purposive sampling, 122
Pygmalion effect, 248

qualitative research, 20, 87–88, 90
quantitative research, 20
quasi-experimental designs, 17, 129–131, 147–160, 161, 194, 228
quasi-treatment groups, 148
questionnaires, 96, 124. *See also* survey research
  buffer items, 109–110
  Cognitive Style Index (CSI), 215
  content validity, 212
  self-administered, 110, 112
questions
  closed (structured), 97, 99
  compound (double-barreled), 100–101
  exhaustive response choices, 101
  important considerations for, 105–110
  manifest content of, 108
  measuring responses, 101–105
  open-ended, 98, 99
  for statistical test choice, 410, 444
  value laden, 106–107
quota sampling, 121–122

random assignment of subjects, 23, 150, 223, 267–269, 276, 277, 282–283, 286
random digit dialing (RDD), 113
randomization, block, 283, 287, 330–331, 340

randomized partial counterbalancing, 334
random number tables, 119
random sampling, 119, 124
random selection, 118, 119, 124
range, 401, 404
range matching, 279, 287
range truncation, 135–136
rank-ordered matching, 280, 287
rapport, 115
ratio scaling, 103, 124, 207, 410
Raven Progressive Matrices Test, 214
raw data, 398
reactivity, 81–82, 91
record-keeping, 227
recruiting/selecting subjects, 254–256, 263–267
reference citations, 489, 490
References section of reports, 496, 508, 511–512, 515–516
regression (behavior) study, 155
regression lines, 134
regression toward the mean, 222
rejecting the null hypothesis, 379–380
relationships, 24–25, 30, 185, 214–215, 463–464. *See also* correlational designs
reliability
  evaluating, 208–209
  interitem, 209
  interrater, 208, 228
  split-half, 209
  of surveys, 116–117, 124
  test-retest, 209, 228
religiousness study, 88
removing treatment, 364, 266
repeated-measures designs, 318, 331, 446–448
replication of procedures/results, 15–16, 59
reporting samples, 123–124
reports
  Abstract, 488–489, 498, 513
  appendix, 5616
  Author notes, 498, 513
  Discussion, 181, 494–496, 506, 508, 515
  ethical, 63
  gender-related terms, 486
  Introduction, 181, 489, 498, 500
  journal articles, 496–512
  main components, 520
  making revisions, 516–519
  Materials/Apparatus, 226–227, 502
  Method, 225–227, 491–493, 502, 514
  Names/Affiliations, 498
  non-responses to surveys, 112
  page headers, 512
  participants, 491, 514
  preparing your manuscript, 512–516
  Procedure, 502
  purpose and format, 484–487, 519
  References, 496, 508, 511–512, 515–516
  Results, 493–494, 502, 504, 506, 514
  running head, 500, 512–513
  stages of writing, 520

tables and figures, 514–515
  Title, 487–488, 498, 514
representativeness of samples, 117, 124
research
  building on prior, 173–174
  describing activities, 69–71
  objectives of, 16–18, 97
  qualitative, 20, 87–88, 90, 92
respect for persons, 40
response acquiescence, 108
response deviation, 108
response sets, 111, 124, 460
response styles, 108–110, 124
response styles of subjects, 107–110
results. *See also* reports
  analyzing, 428–431
  graphing, 436–437, 445–446
  interpreting, 415–417, 434–436
  publicizing, 14–15
  reporting, 181
  section of reports, 493–494, 502, 504, 506
retrospective data, 77–78
reversal designs, 351
reverse counterbalancing, 330, 340
revising reports, 516–519
risk factors, 37
robust tests, 419
Rosenthal, Robert, 37, 248, 249
Rosenthal effect, 248, 249
running heads (reports), 500, 512–513

samples
  nonprobability, 121
  representativeness of, 117, 124
  size, 265–267, 419–425
sampling
  accidental, 122
  cluster, 120–121, 124
  convenience, 122, 124
  nonprobability, 121–124
  population, 117
  probability, 118–121, 124
  procedures, 117–121, 124
  purposive, 122, 124
  quota, 121–122, 124
  random, 118–120, 124
  snowball, 123, 124
scales of measurement, 101–103, 206–207
scaling techniques, 104–105, 124
scatterplots (scattergraphs), 134, 135, 160
Schacter, Stanley, 197–198, 201, 202, 203, 204, 205, 207, 209, 210, 213
science, 4, 30
*Science and the Modern World* (Whitehead), 11
scientific explanation
  establishing cause and effect, 24–25, 76
  identifying antecedent conditions, 22
  necessary versus sufficient conditions, 25–26
  psychological experiments, 21–22

scientific mentality, 11, 30
scientific method, good thinking, 13–14
scientific misconduct, 59–60
scientific writing style, 484–487, 519–520
searching the literature, 179–184
secrecy and allure experiment, 426
selecting a test. *See* choosing design/test methods
selecting/recruiting subjects, 254–256, 263–267
selection interactions threat to validity, 223, 225, 228
selection threat to validity, 223, 224
self-administered questionnaires, 110, 112
self-correction, 14
semantic differential technique, 104
sensory-deprivation experiments, 240–241
sequences of treatment conditions, 332–334, 336
serendipity and windfall hypotheses, 174–175, 185
sexist language, avoiding, 485, 486
shorthand notation, 297–298, 312
significance. *See also* null hypothesis
  levels, 384–386, 387
  nonsignificant outcomes, 476–479, 480
  odds of finding, 391–396
  statistical, 379, 403
significant effects, 447–448
Simon, Herbert, 176
simple correlations, 132–133, 160
simple random sampling, 118, 124
Singer, Peter, 52, 53
single-blind experiments, 242–244, 250, 261
situations, aggregation over, 469–471
size of samples, 265–267, 419–425
Skinner, B. F., 170–171, 349, 390
sleep study, 148
small *N* designs, 346–351, 353–357, 360–361
smiling experiment, 316–318
snowball sampling, 123, 124
social contagion study, 13–14
social learning theory, 14
social variables, 237–252, 261
Solomon 4-group design, 158
sources of errors. *See* error(s)
sources of variability, 429–431
spatial relationships, 25
spider phobia study, 321–323
split-half reliability, 209
spousal abuse study, 22, 24
stages of writing reports, 520
standard deviation, 402–403, 404
standardized tests, 136, 215
standards/standardization, 20–21
statistical conclusion validity, 463–464, 479

statistical control, differences between groups, 437–438
statistical inference, 376–382, 380, 382–389, 403, 404
statistical procedures, 409–412
statistical regression, 222, 228
statistical significance, 379, 403
statistics
  argument for using, 374
  inappropriate use of, 464
  inferential, 396–397
  odds of finding significance, 391–396
  organizing/summarizing data, 397–403
  presenting, in reports, 493–494
  small *N* designs and, 360–361
  test, 396–397
  for two group experiments, 412
  use of, 312
stereotyping, 10, 177
stimuli, aggregation over, 470–471
strange situation studies, 81
stratified random sampling, 120, 124
structured (closed) questions, 97, 99
structured interviews, 115
studies. *See also* experiments
  abuse of animals study, 53–54
  African American men study, 86–87
  archival, 85–87
  assent/agreement for participation in studies, 38–39
  attitudes toward animal research study, 57–58
  attractiveness study, 198–199
  body-builder study, 84
  cancer coping styles study, 151, 194
  car-buying preferences study, 325–326
  car size study, 152–153
  classical conditioning, 175
  cockroach race study, 274, 275, 276, 277, 278
  companion animals study, 159
  confounding of variables, 194–195, 217–218, 219, 268, 459–460, 462
  coping styles study, 151
  correlational, 17, 129–142
  cross-sectional, 156, 160, 161
  divorce effects study, 150–151, 156
  domestic violence victims study, 88, 90
  eating behavior study, 300–307, 312
  English as a Second Language study, 80
  ethnic preferences study, 460
  ex post facto, 148–152, 160, 161, 194
  field, 78–85, 91
  handshake firmness study, 137
  Hong Kong residents study, 80
  identical twins study, 59
  impressions of others study, 269
  Little Hans case study, 74
  long-term, 155–156
  math identification study, 308

media violence study, 137–138, 145–146
motivation for watching TV study, 140–141
name retrieval failure study, 319–320
naturalistic observation studies, 78–82, 91, 475–476, 480
negative ions studies, 19, 22, 45, 154, 309
participant-observer, 83, 84–85
pilot, 252, 286, 287
projection study, 47
regression (behavior) study, 155
religiousness study, 88
sleep study, 148
social contagion study, 13–14
spider phobia study, 321–323
strange situation, 81
suspended licenses study, 89
testosterone case study, 75
triazolam (Halcion) study, 250–251
TV violence study, 137–138, 145–146, 180
subject-by-subject counterbalancing, 329–331, 340
subject mortality threat to validity, 223, 228
subjects/participants. *See also* ethical issues
  about, 21
  aggregation over, 470
  assigning, 282–285
  bias in choosing, 465
  debriefing, 46–47
  experimenter interactions with, 252–253
  folklore about, 256
  generalizing across, 465–466
  number of, 265–267
  participants section of reports, 491, 514
  random assignment, 23, 150, 267–269, 276, 277, 282–283
  response styles, 107–110, 265
  risk factors for, 37–38
  selecting/recruiting, 254–256, 263–267
  selection of experiment by, 254–255
  volunteer, 253–254, 263–264
subject variables, 148, 161, 265
summarizing data, 397–403, 404
summary tables, 138, 443
survey research, 96–97, 124
  considerations for survey items, 105–110
  constructing surveys, 97–101
  cultural issues, 120
  measurement of responses, 101–105
suspended licenses study, 89
synthetic statements, 167–168, 184
systematic observation, 80, 91
systematic random sampling, 118–119

tables, in research reports, 514–515
talking to plants experiment, 349–351

Taub, Edward, 56–57
Taylor Manifest Anxiety Scale (TMAS), 205, 209
telephone surveys, 113–114
temporal relationships, 24, 25
testability, 21, 184
testable statements, 168
testing the null hypothesis, 378–380
testosterone case study, 75
test-retest reliability, 209, 221, 228
test statistics, 396–397
tests/testing. *See also* choosing design/test methods; statistics; threats to internal validity
    chi square test, 412–417, 449
    choosing appropriate tests, 409–412
    distributions of test statistics, 399
    internal consistency of test items, 209
    nonparametric tests, 388, 413
    the null hypothesis, 378–380
    one-tailed tests, 394–396
    parametric tests, 388
    post hoc tests, 435, 450
    questions for statistical test choice, 410, 448
    Raven Progressive Matrices Test, 214
    reliability, 116, 208, 228
    robust tests, 419
    standardized tests, 136, 215
    task force on significance testing, 390
theories, 12–13, 171–172, 390
third variable problem, 138, 219
threats to internal validity, 218–225, 228, 350
Title section of reports, 487–488, 498, 514
tools of psychological science, 18–22
traits, predicting behavior by observing, 8–11
treatment (medical), removing, 366
treatments/treatment conditions, 22, 31, 129–131
    choosing, 285
    comparing, 22
    random assignment of, 267–269
trials, aggregation over, 471
triazolam (Halcion) study, 250–251
true/false statements, 167–168
*t* statistic, 419, 449
*t* test, 417–427
    for independent groups, 417, 450
Tversky, Amos, 11
TV violence study, 137–138, 145–146, 180
two-dimensional designs, 131
two experimental groups designs, 272, 274–277, 287
two factor experiments, 292
two group design (one independent variable) designs, 267–272
two group designs, 267–282, 286, 412

two group within-subjects experiment, 426
two independent groups designs, 274–277, 286
two matched groups designs, 277–282, 286
two-tailed tests, 394–396
two-way ANOVA, 441–446
2 × 2 factorial experiment, 297–300, 300–307
Type 1 and 2 errors, 386–389, 404, 412–413, 463, 464
Type A/negative ions behavior study, 19, 22, 24, 45, 154, 309

unbiased language, 485
unconditioned response (UCR), 38
unconditioned stimulus (UCS), 38
unethical designs, 37–38
unobtrusive measures, 82, 473–474, 480
unobtrusive observation, 91
unstructured interviews, 115

validity
    concurrent, 213, 228
    construct, 213–215, 228
    content, 212
    convergent, 214
    discriminant, 215
    external, 69, 79, 90, 91, 131, 464–476, 479–480
    face, 210, 228
    history threat to, 220
    of inferences, 90
    instrumentation threat to, 221–222
    internal, 69, 90, 91, 131, 215–216, 228, 459–464
    maturation threat to, 220–221, 271
    predictive, 213, 228
    selection threats to, 223, 224
    statistical conclusion, 463–464, 479
    subject mortality threat to, 223
    in surveys, 116–117, 124
    testing threat to, 221
    threats to, 218
    trading off between internal and external, 237
value laden questions, 106–107
variability, 401
    between-groups, 428
    defining, 377–378
    measures of, 401–403
    small *N* designs and, 360–361
    sources of, 429–431
variables. *See also* dependent variables (DVs); independent variables (IVs)
    balancing of, 235–237
    confounding, 194–195, 217–218, 219, 268
    constancy of, 234
    context, 254–256, 261

control procedures, 256–261
dependent variables (DVs), 196, 204, 228
    describing design, 297–298
    elimination of, 234
    examples, 197–199
    extraneous, 216–218, 228, 256–261
    identifying, 199–201
    independent variable (IV), 193–195
    interactions of, 292–296
    isolating in recall experiment, 461
    level of measurement of each, 206–207
    manipulation, 199–201
    more than one independent variable designs, 291–296
    nonconstruct, 206
    operational definitions, 201–207
    personality, 252–254, 261
    physical, 233–237, 256
    research examples, 197–199
    social, 237–252, 261
    subject, 148–149, 161, 265
    third variable problem, 138, 219
    two group design (one independent variable), 269, 271–272
    to use for matching, 278–280
variables experiment, 197–199
variance, 401–402, 404. *See also* analysis of variance (ANOVA)
volunteer subjects, 253–254, 263–264, 465

Web sites, 181–182
    PsycINFO, 181–182
Wechsler Adult Intelligence Scale (WAIS-III), 209, 221
weight-of-evidence approach, 14, 375
Whitehead, Alfred North, 11
willingness to answer, 107, 124
windfall hypotheses, 174–175
within-groups variability, 428, 432–437
within-subjects designs, 23, 316–318, 325–326
    advantages of, 323–324
    choosing, 339
    controlling, 326–339
    disadvantages of, 325–326
    factorial, 320–321, 340
    homophone priming experiment, 319–321
    mixed designs, 321–323, 324
    reasons for choosing, 323–324
    smiling experiment, 316–318
within-subjects factorial designs, 319–321
writing reports. *See* reports
Wundt, Wilhem, 26

yea-sayers, 108, 124

Zajonc, Robert, 274, 275
Zilstein, Gregor, 197, 202

# PHOTO CREDITS

This page constitutes an extension of the copyright page. We have made every effort to trace the ownership of all copyrighted material and to secure permission from copyright holders. In the event of any question arising as to the use of any material, we will be pleased to make the necessary corrections in future printings. Thanks are due to the following authors, publishers, and agents for permission to use the material indicated.

Page 174    National Library of Medicine

Page 176    Copyright © 2001 by Sidney Harris

Page 180    Jochen Tack/Alamy

Page 183    Courtesy of the American Psychological Association. This material is reprinted with permission of the American Psychological Association publisher of the PsycINFO Database and may not be reproduced without prior permission

Page 184    Courtesy of the American Psychological Association. This material is reprinted with permission of the American Psychological Association publisher of the PsycINFO Database and may not be reproduced without prior permission

## Chapter 7

Page 195    Copyright © 1996 by Sidney Harris

Page 197    Courtesy of Stanley Schachter/Columbia University

Page 199    Stanley Schachter/Columbia University

Page 203    Copyright © 2001 by Sidney Harris.

Page 211    top © Burstein Collection/CORBIS; bottom © Philadelphia Museum of Art/CORBIS

Page 219    Karuka/www.Shutterstock.com

Page 224    © JLP/Deimos/CORBIS

Page 227    © Richard T. Nowitz/CORBIS

## Chapter 8

Page 238    Copyright © 1996 by Sidney Harris

Page 244    Andersen Ross/Getty Images

Page 249    Courtesy of Robert Rosenthal

## Chapter 9

Page 264    Copyright © by Sidney Harris

Page 270    Science Source/Photo Researchers

Page 273    Jeanell Norvell/istockphoto.com

Page 275    Courtesy of Robert Zajonc

## Chapter 11

Page 320    center Bureau L.A. Collection/Sygma/CORBIS; top Galen Rowell/CORBIS

Page 322    Tim Laman/National Geographic/Getty Images

Page 324    Charles Stirling/Alamy

Page 328    Copyright © 2010 by Sidney Harris/ScienceCartoonsPlus.com

## Chapter 12

Page 356    Copyright © 2001 by Sidney Harris

Page 363    Courtesy of Dennis Shaffer

Page 365    bottom left © Peter Willi/SuperStock; bottom right © 2001 Estate of Pablo Picasso/Artists Rights Society (ARS) New York

## Chapter 13

Page 376    Used by permission of Sidney Harris/ScienceCartoonsPlus.com

Page 396    Copyright © 2010 by Sidney Harris/ScienceCartoonsPlus.com

## Chapter 14

Page 418    Andreas Kuehn/Taxi/Getty Images

Page 426    Yuri Arcurs 2010/Used under license from Shutterstock.com

Page 438    Copyright © 2001 by Sidney Harris/ScienceCartoonsPlus.com

## Chapter 15

Page 470    Rich Legg/iStockphoto.com

Page 478    Copyright © 2001 by Sidney Harris/ScienceCartoonsPlus.com

## Chapter 16

Page 518    Copyright © 1996 by Sidney Harris